The Journal of
The Earl of Egmont

THE EARL OF EGMONT

The Journal of
The Earl of Egmont

Abstract of the Trustees Proceedings
for Establishing the Colony of Georgia

1732-1738

Edited with an Introduction by
ROBERT G. McPHERSON

**WORMSLOE FOUNDATION PUBLICATIONS
NUMBER FIVE**

UNIVERSITY OF GEORGIA PRESS
ATHENS

Copyright © 1962
UNIVERSITY OF GEORGIA PRESS

Library of Congress Catalog Card Number: 62-14240

Reissue published in 2021

Most University Press titles are available
from popular e-book vendors.

Printed digitally

ISBN 9780820359847 (Hardcover)
ISBN 9780820359854 (Paperback)
ISBN 9780820359830 (Ebook)

PRINTED IN THE UNITED STATES OF AMERICA

Contents

FOREWORD TO THE REISSUE	vii
FOREWORD	xi
INTRODUCTION	xiii
JOURNAL OF THE EARL OF EGMONT	
1732–1733	3
1733–1734	27
1734–1735	56
1735–1736	93
1736–1737	167
1737–1738	283
INDEX	380

Foreword to the Reissue

In 1962 the University of Georgia Press published the first journal of John Viscount Percival, the Earl of Egmont, long recognized as one of the important founding Trustees of Georgia. The original publication was edited by Robert G. McPherson, a University of Georgia faculty member and scholar of British history. He edited lightly, making changes only for clarity. His introduction, however, is an enlightening summary of Egmont's life, including his family background and education, his rise to an Irish earldom, and some of the personal political issues that existed between Egmont and Sir Robert Walpole. McPherson also provides a helpful provenance of the journal.

Covering the years 1732 to 1738—the beginning of the Georgia project, when the foundling colony's success and even survival were often in doubt—this is the first of three journals kept by Egmont during his tenure as a Trustee. The other two had been more widely available after former Georgia governor Allen Candler's effort to compile and publish many of Georgia's records in the early twentieth century; volumes of the Candler records can now be accessed online through the HathiTrust Digital Library. Egmont's second and third journals comprise volume 5 of the Candler's *Colonial Records of Georgia*, while volume 1 includes the charter, laws and by-laws, and the minutes of the Georgia Trust, and volume 2 contains the minutes of the Common Council. Egmont was a committed record keeper; in addition to these journals, he also authored three volumes of a personal diary, also now accessible online. While the diary touches on his work with the Georgia project, it focuses on his personal life and gives an engaging picture of early eighteenth-century Britain.

Much of the scholarship on colonial Georgia focuses on the story in the colony itself, and many Georgia leaders in the Trustee period have received biographical treatments. James Oglethorpe, the only Trustee who actually came to Georgia, has long fascinated scholars. More recently colonial secretary William Stephens, teacher and later entrepreneur James Habersham, and interpreter Mary Musgrove have been the subject of scholarly monographs. Groups including Native peoples, women colonists, Salzburgers, Scots Highlanders, and others have also been analyzed. While this journal provides some information on all of them, it also illuminates the operations in England as the Trust sought to manage the colony, secure its funding and protection, and ensure that the Trustees' charitable vision survived. It is an important source for any study of these early years.

The journal is an interesting read. While McPherson did not annotate it, Egmont added his own annotations and helpfully his own index. In the originals the notations are to the left side of the journal, but McPherson added them as "N.B" at the end of a day's entry. In these notes, Egmont often identified people whose letters, requests, or business came before the Common Council or the Trustees. Especially interesting are Egmont's candid opinions, such as referring to colonist Robert Parker as the "Sauceyest fool and errant knave I have met with" (211).

Egmont's journal also added facts and opinions about the issues and business before the Trust and the Common Council. While the minutes of these two bodies covered the same ground Egmont did, the focus of the journal was often different. Egmont gave details about decisions or discussions, especially on controversial matters, that were either not mentioned or were succinctly dealt with in the minutes. Two of the most controversial issues in these early years revolved around religion and gender. On several occasions the question of Jews settling in Georgia arose. On December 29, 1733, the council minutes listed one piece of business but made no mention of what Egmont noted in his journal: "The affair of the Jews debated, whose going Surreptitiously over offended every member present" (38). Among Trustees themselves in this early period, one of the most contentious issues to emerge was how to support the minister—glebe land or salary. The debate in February 1736 was so heated that Egmont believed resignations would result. He was right. When one Anglican priest did not preach for the Trustees' anniversary service, Egmont wrote that the minister had the fact that they had not granted the Savannah minister glebe land "Stuck in his gizard" (246).

While the prohibition on using enslaved labor would become a major issue in later years, it only appeared briefly in the journal. But the issue of women's inheritance of land was a recurring theme from the beginning. On several occasions Egmont noted potential settlers deciding not to colonize because of the requirement of Tail Male (male only) inheritance, from the forty Vaudois who knew the silk trade to a group of Swiss Grisons. Various Trustees made proposals over the years to change the official policy to allow for some inheritance by daughters, but none were accepted. While Egmont was in favor of some change, James Oglethorpe remained opposed throughout these years, and the majority deferred to him. Many of these attempts and the resulting discussions did not appear in official minutes, so Egmont is the sole source, and his explanations of the rationales on both sides are enlightening.

Another Egmont addition are the summaries at the end of each Trust year. His statistics give a helpful glimpse into the colony: the number of persons, helpfully divided into gender, sent on Trust charity, and the acreage granted to others who paid their own way. In 1735 he began adding financial income and disbursements to this annual report. Also included are the number of total meetings in a year, then a tally of the attendance of every member at meetings of the Trust and the Common Council. It is immediately revealing. From the beginning Egmont stands out as the most conscientious attendee, followed by James Vernon, whose attentiveness also ranks highly. Oglethorpe was a regular when he was in-country. As initial zeal among the Trustees waned, attendance became an increasing problem. Egmont regularly vented his frustration that the Council could not take any action because as he wrote on many dates, "We were not a board." He saw his colleagues as being petty, as not living up to their responsibilities; his disbelief at their reasons for absences is often clear. In April 1736 he feared that it would be difficult to continue without a working council. He appealed to "consciences, honour, & humanity" for members "not to be careless in their duty of attendance" (149).

In the last two years of the journal, the fate of Georgia was intertwined with the larger geopolitics of relations between Great Britain and Spain. As the buffer colony, Georgia's defense was crucial; both Egmont and Oglethorpe knew that Parliamentary assistance was a necessity. Egmont candidly wrote the inside story of Oglethorpe's dealings with Robert Walpole, including one confrontation when Oglethorpe asked Walpole point-blank if the British planned to give up Georgia. If that was indeed the case, Oglethorpe said, he would instruct the Trust to write the inhabitants so that they could save themselves—he would not simply abandon "over 3000 souls ... to be destroyed by the Spaniards" (296–97). At Oglethorpe's request, Egmont sent a letter attesting to the necessity of support. This journal also demonstrates how the complicated internal politics of Britain at this time could have consequences on the enterprise—who supported whom could affect how Parliament voted on Georgia needs.

One theme that clearly comes through in the journal is the precariousness of the Georgia project, not just on the Georgia side, but across the Atlantic. The Trust dealt with many challenges—the yearly need for but uncertainty of Parliamentary support, the problem of garnering enthusiasm among members of the Common Council, threats of Spanish invasion, crop failures. On the front line was Egmont, who persevered in his role as a public servant. While he did not always agree with Oglethorpe, like Oglethorpe, he believed in the vision of the Georgia venture and he felt responsibility for those they sent across the Atlantic. He was the leader in England that Oglethorpe was in Georgia.

In February 1738 Egmont wrote that many on the Common Council were resolved to quit what they thought was "a falling house" (333). He scathingly noted that they were glad to be involved when things were going well and found it an honor to serve, but when the situation became difficult, "they meanly deserted their Office, and the Service of the Publick" (333). When resignations did come, he characterized those Trustees as "Seeds Sown on Stony ground" (334). But through all the successes and challenges of those early years, the Earl of Egmont persevered. In his last summary in this volume on June 7, 1738, the meetings for that year totaled fifty-four; Egmont had attended fifty. While James Oglethorpe rightly deserves the scholarly interest he has received for his role, John Viscount Percival, Earl of Egmont's persistent work in the mother country also merits additional scrutiny from historians.

LEE ANN CALDWELL

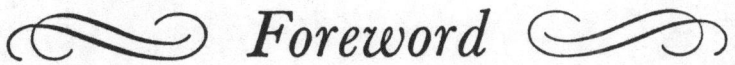
Foreword

THE Wormsloe Foundation is a non-profit organization chartered on December 18, 1951 by the Superior Court of Chatham County, Georgia. In the words of its charter, "The objects and purposes of this Foundation are the promotion of historical research and the publication of the results thereof; the restoration, preservation and maintenance of historical sites and documents and the conduct of an educational program in the study of history of the State of Georgia, and in states adjacent thereto."

As its first important activity, the Foundation has begun the publication of a series of historical works under the title of "Wormsloe Foundation Publications." They will consist of important manuscripts, reprints of rare publications, and historical narratives relating to Georgia and the South. The first volume appeared in 1955, written by E. Merton Coulter and entitled *Wormsloe: Two Centuries of a Georgia Family*. This volume gave the historical background of the Wormsloe estate and a history of the family which has owned it for more than two and a quarter centuries.

The second publication of the Foundation was *The Journal of William Stephens, 1741–1743* and the third volume was *The Journal of William Stephens, 1743–1745*, which is a continuation of the journal as far as any known copy of it is still extant; though it is known that Stephens kept up his journal for some years after 1745. Both of these volumes were edited by E. Merton Coulter and were published in 1958 and 1959, respectively. The fourth publication of the Foundation was the republication of the unique copy of Pat. Tailfer et al., *A True and Historical Narrative of the Colony of Georgia in America . . .* with comments by the First Earl of Egmont, in the John Carter Brown Library at Brown University and published by its permission. It was edited by Clarence L. Ver Steeg.

The present volume, the fifth in the series, is the long-missing first part of Egmont's three manuscript volumes of his journal. It extends from 1732 to 1738 and is edited by Robert G. McPherson.

E. Merton Coulter
General Editor

Introduction

THE Charter of the Colony of Georgia established a corporate body under the name, "The Trustees for establishing the Colony of Georgia in America," naming certain members, and providing for its enlargement without limit. It further designated a Common Council to discharge the more important duties of the corporation. This body was to consist of fifteen members, named in the Charter, and after the enlargement of the Trustees, it was to consist of twenty-four. The smaller body was established in order to avoid the difficulty of assembling the larger one as frequently as the business of the colony would require.[1]

The Common Council thus undertook the more responsible work, and that of the Trustees was of a residual nature. Actually, the attendance of Trustee meetings by Trustees who were not also Common Council members was rare. Therefore almost all work, whether accomplished by the Common Council or the Trustees, was done largely by the same group of men acting in different capacities. A quorum of eight was required for Common Council meetings, and frequently when this number were not present, those attending would hold a Trustee meeting instead.[2]

Each of the two bodies appointed a secretary who kept minutes of their meetings. Besides these two official journals, there was a third and private record kept by John Percival, who became the first Earl of Egmont in 1733. He was an original member of both bodies, and rarely missed their meetings. Because of its private nature, his journal is less restrained, and frequently is of more interest than the official record.

Egmont's account of the Common Council meetings, from 1733 to 1744, was originally set down in three folio volumes, closely written in the Earl's careful hand. All three volumes in time became separated from the Percival family papers, and vanished from sight. In 1881 volumes two and three of the Egmont journal

[1]. "Charter of the Colony of Georgia," in Allen D. Candler, ed., *Colonial Records of the State of Georgia* (Atlanta, 1904), I, 12–14.
[2]. *Ibid.*, 23–24.

were discovered in London and were purchased by an American dealer, Henry Stevens of Vermont. They were presented to the state of Georgia soon after by J. S. Morgan, an American banker in England, and are now housed in the vault of the Secretary of State in Atlanta.

The first publication of the latter two-thirds of the Egmont journal came in 1886 with the appearance of a limited edition of forty-nine copies, privately published by Mrs. Mary De Renne, widow of George Wymberley-Jones De Renne. This part of the journal became generally available to the public, however, only in 1908. In that year, Allen D. Candler, in his compilation of the *Colonial Records of the State of Georgia*, published these latter two volumes of the Egmont journal, as well as the official journals of the Trustees and the Common Council.

Egmont's first manuscript volume, from 1732 to 1738, remained missing. Until the present publication, it was known to scholars only by implication, and through its index. For want of room, Egmont happened to place this index at the beginning of his second manuscript volume, and therefore it was published by Candler. The possibility of the existence of the missing volume long tantalized historians.

The lost journal at length reappeared in England in the collection of Sir Thomas Phillipps (Phillipps MS. 13081), and was offered for sale by the firm of Lionel & Philip Robinson, Ltd., of London, in 1946. It was purchased by the Thomas Gilcrease Institute of American History and Art, of Tulsa, Oklahoma, and is published here with the kind permission and cooperation of the Institute's Board of Directors.

Egmont was a friend and close associate of James Edward Oglethorpe. He had worked with him on the select committee to inquire into the condition of the gaols, which was appointed, at Oglethorpe's instigation, by the House of Commons on February 25, 1728.[3] It was in working together on the committee that they discovered their mutual interest in philanthropic endeavor.

Percival was among the first to whom Oglethorpe revealed his plan for a new Carolina plantation. Because of Percival's connections at court, he was instrumental in securing the charter and in obtaining money for the project. From the time of its inception Egmont was among its most enthusiastic supporters. He faithfully attended meetings of the Trustees, of which the Charter named

---

3. *Journal of the House of Commons* (London, 1728), XXI, 237-38.

him first president, and of the Common Council, of which he often served as chairman. Because of his rank and political associations, Egmont was very useful in retaining the aid of the Ministry, without which the colony could not have survived. He was consistent in his attendance at the meetings between 1732 and 1742, in which latter year he resigned from the Common Council, largely because of ill-health. Although Egmont never visited Georgia, no man other than Oglethorpe himself had greater interest in the colony, or worked harder for its establishment and promotion.

Among historians, the most immediate association with the name Egmont is undoubtedly the first Earl's famous diary, which was published between 1920 and 1923 in three volumes by the British Historical Manuscripts Commission. It covers the years 1730–1747, and is justly considered a mine of social and political information. It throws much light upon the Georgia movement, which dominated Egmont's life for many years.

Egmont was a careful record keeper and a copious writer. He left an extensive collection of papers concerning his private and public affairs, which reveal an admirable character and an active life. Although his lands lay largely in Ireland, and his titles in the Irish peerage, Egmont was a Protestant and an Englishman. The frequency of his visits to Ireland decreased as time went by, though he always maintained a full correspondence with his estate agents and took an active part in the management of his Irish interests. Nevertheless, he came to settle into a routine of life in England which can only be described as that of an absentee landlord, though he strove mightily to avoid the pitfalls customarily associated with absentee landlordism in Ireland.

His ancestry, of which he was inordinately proud, was Norman French, of the Conqueror's time. The Irish association began early in the seventeenth century, though the English roots never became dislodged. The genesis of the family's fortunes, aside from certain medieval antecedents, lay in the Percivals' service of the early Stuarts and of Cromwell in Ireland, and particularly in the career of Sir Philip Percival, Egmont's great-grandfather. In those days of the seventeenth century an acquisitive Englishman could amass great wealth in Ireland. The Percival lands at the height of their Irish fortunes, before the rising of 1641, reached an aggregate of well over 100,000 acres. This had been greatly depleted by Egmont's time—his rent roll in 1704 lists some 22,000 acres in County Cork and County Tipperary, where most of his lands lay—but it was sufficient to provide him an income in 1747–1748 well in excess of £6,000.[4]

At the time of the Restoration, Sir Philip's son John was made a Privy Counsellor and a baronet, his welcome at court having been assured by his persuasion of Henry Cromwell, Lord Deputy of Ireland, to agree to a royal restoration.[5] But the family now became plagued by a series of premature deaths. The first baronet enjoyed his new distinction only four years, at his death the title passing to his eldest son Philip in 1665. Sir Philip held the title for fifteen years, and upon his death in 1680 it passed to Egmont's father, who lived only six years more. Then it went to Egmont's elder brother Edward, at whose death in 1691 at the age of nine the future Earl received the title himself. Longevity reappeared with him, for he lived until 1748, and his son, the second Earl of Egmont, until 1770.

John Percival, the future first Earl, was born at the family seat in County Cork, a manor called Burton, on July 12, 1683. His father died three years later at the age of twenty-nine, entrusting his widow and children to the hands of his uncle, Sir Robert Southwell, of Kings Weston, in England. Here the family took refuge, while their estates in Ireland were plundered by the Irish in the rebellion of 1690, and Burton House was burned.[6] The mother remarried in 1690, and died in childbirth within two years. The youthful Sir Edward Percival had died the year before, two sisters were dead, and so of the family of seven, only Sir John and his younger brother Philip survived by 1692.

The two brothers were reared in the care of their great-uncle, who took his duties seriously. Upon Southwell's death in 1702, his son, Sir Edward Southwell, assumed the boys' wardship. John was tutored by his own father's chaplain, Dr. Henry Roby, until in 1696 he was sent to Mr. Demoeure's Academy, located in Greek Street, Westminster, in the district now known as Soho. He was joined in time by his brother Philip, and the two duly reported their progress to their uncle. The Academy was described in 1702 as "a Place famous for Education at that Time, where *French, Latin,* Geography, Musick, Dancing, Fencing, Vaulting, Quarter-Staff, and other hardy Exercises, were regularly taught. . . ."[7]

---

4. British Museum, Additional Manuscripts 47043, 47013.
5. Historical Manuscripts Commission, *Report on the Manuscripts of the Earl of Egmont* (Dublin, 1909), Part II, v.
6. *Rpt. on MSS. of Earl of Egmont*, Pt. II, 185, 187–88.
7. *A Genealogical History of the House of Yvery in its Different Branches of Yvery, Luvel, Perceval, and Gournay* (London, 1742), II, 404.

INTRODUCTION   xvii

Percival's French became fluent, and many of his letters were later written in that language.

In 1698 he entered Westminster School, which was associated with the Abbey, and there he studied under one of the prebends, Dr. Breval. The next year, at the age of sixteen, he entered Magdalen College, Oxford. Here he was tutored by Richard Smallbrook, who later became successively Bishop of Hereford, of Litchfield, and of Coventry. The classical curriculum of the college held Percival's attention, and his correspondence with his uncle, and also Smallbrook's letters, indicate that he was less addicted to the idleness usual in that day than most of his fellows. After a year and a half, when he was eighteen, he left the university without taking a degree. This omission, however, did not stand in his way when in 1702 he was elected a Fellow of the Royal Society of London for Improving Natural Knowledge, which had been founded some forty years previously. His great-uncle, Sir Robert Southwell, happened to be President of the Society.[8]

Before settling down to the task of administering his estates, Percival undertook a tour of England. In preparation for this he received extensive letters of instruction from acquaintances, pointing out to him the places of interest, particularly in southern and eastern England, which he must visit.[9] The trip was extensive, and Percival's careful journal of his travels indicates his propensity for record-keeping, which became a lifelong habit.

Sir Robert Southwell prepared Percival well for the assumption of his inheritance, carefully instructing him in the processes of good management and in points to be observed in dealing with the Irish. In 1704 Percival went to Ireland, in company with a family friend, the Duke of Ormond, Lord Lieutenant of Ireland. In the general election for a new Irish Parliament, necessitated by the accession of Queen Anne, Percival was elected to the Commons for County Cork, even though he was not yet quite of age. In October he was appointed to the Privy Council, and he remained a member for the next forty-four years, "notwithstanding the frequent Changes and Virulence of Parties." [10] His appointment to the Privy Council was largely an honorary distinction arising from his position as a large Irish landholder. Anne's Council came to number some eighty persons, though only twenty-odd attended its meetings even on important occasions. Membership

8. *Rpt. on MSS. of Earl of Egmont*, Pt. II, xi.
9. *Ibid.*, xii.
10. *House of Yvery*, II, 405.

in the Council had become by now something of a formality rather than a working office in the constitutional framework. The Council was involved in certain official business, but there were no longer serious debates in it, and policy was no longer made there. The Cabinet was coming into being to take its place. Nevertheless, membership in the Privy Council gave Percival a further degree of prestige.

In August of 1705, Percival set out on the grand tour of Europe, which was usual for persons of his station. The tour lasted two years, and his letters indicate that, as intended, it broadened his intellectual horizons. He visited "most of the Courts of *Italy* and *Germany*, and Republicks of *Genoa, Venice,* and *Holland,*" and returned to England in October, 1707.[11] He lost a large collection of objects of art, which fell into the hands of the French, his tour being made during the time of the War of the Spanish Succession.

On his return to England, Percival took up residence at Charlton, his country seat a few miles southeast of London. This, with his town house in Pall Mall, remained his principal residence for the remainder of his life. On his next visit to Ireland, in 1708, he met George Berkeley, then a fellow of Trinity College, Dublin. Their friendship proved to be lifelong, involving the exchange of many letters.[12] Percival was interested in Berkeley's project to create a college in Bermuda for the purpose of training ministers for the Anglican church in America. Percival was instrumental in obtaining the charter for the college, and became a trustee for raising and expending subscriptions for the enterprise. When it was deemed impractical to establish the college in Bermuda, Percival urged the transfer of the undertaking to the mainland, and developed an interest in American affairs which carried over into the Georgia project in the 1730's.

At the age of twenty-seven Percival married Katherine Parker, eldest daughter of Sir Philip Parker à Morley, baronet, of Ewarton, Suffolk. The marriage was eminently happy, as attested by recurrent references in Percival's correspondence. Of the seven children Katherine Percival bore her husband, only three survived to maturity. These were John, who became the second Earl of Egmont, and his two sisters, Katherine and Helena.

Most of Percival's time was spent in England, though he sat in

---

11. *House of Yvery,* II, 405.
12. Benjamin Rand, *Berkeley and Percival; the Correspondence of George Berkeley, afterwards Bishop of Cloyne, and Sir John Percival, afterwards Earl of Egmont* (Cambridge, 1914).

INTRODUCTION

the Irish Parliament in 1711 and 1713, keeping a careful journal of proceedings there and participating actively in the transaction of business. He was all his life closely concerned with Irish economic interests, since they were his own interests too. He was also closely interested in Court life, although his Whig inclinations so alienated him from the Tory regime of the latter portion of Queen Anne's reign that he refused the Tory offer of an English barony.[13]

From August, 1711, until March, 1714, he and his family lived in Ireland, returning to England during the last months of Anne's reign. He followed closely the dramatic events of the change of dynasties, keeping a journal, according to his habit, of the tense developments.[14] King George I landed in England in September, and Percival, as a Privy Counsellor, attended him in the procession from Greenwich to St. James's Palace. The King retained Percival as Privy Counsellor in the new commission issued on October 9. Percival's political leanings and those of the new regime were sufficiently compatible to assure his close connection with the court thereafter for many years.

Evidence of this understanding was soon forthcoming. In 1715 Percival was offered an Irish barony. He refused it on this occasion, saying that it was inferior to the English barony offered him in Anne's reign. He suggested that either an English barony or an Irish earldom would be more acceptable. The government's spokesman in the affair was Joseph Addison, who later became Secretary of State for the Southern Department. He assured Percival of the King's interest, and indicated the impropriety of spurning the Royal will, which was that Percival should accept the Irish barony as it was then offered. Addison gave him the King's assurance that within a few months he would be advanced further in the Irish peerage, and that "he might certainly depend upon that *English* Honour he desired, as soon as the Convenience of his [the King's] Affairs should admit, which would not be very long." [15]

Accordingly Percival accepted and became Baron Percival of Burton. He formally took his seat in the Irish House of Lords on November 12, 1715. The preamble of his patent included, after a eulogy of his and his family's service to the Crown, the statement, "We find ourselves obliged to bestow, *even greater Honours* upon

13. *House of Yvery*, II, 407.
14. Br. Mus., Add. MS. 47087.
15. *House of Yvery*, II, 410.

him than those, which by these Presents, we now confer." [16] This promise was never strictly fulfilled because of the breach which occurred between King George and his son, George, Prince of Wales, late in 1717. At that time, all peers and Privy Counsellors were ordered to choose between the two courts, and in future they were not to attend both. Faced by the dilemma of choosing between the King who had made him a peer, and had promised him further advancement, and the Prince who would likely soon succeed his father, and who might then prove to have a long memory, Percival temporized. For the moment he evaded the order and attended both courts. But soon the King observed his presence, and wrote to him inviting his continued presence, but indicating that he could make no exceptions from his rule that those who attended the princely court must not come to his own. Percival then decided to cast his lot with the Prince of Wales, "conscientiously thinking, that the Justice of the Dispute was on that Side, where he continued ever after." [17] It no doubt also occurred to him that the King's age was fifty-seven, and that of the Prince, thirty-four.

Percival now abandoned hope that the King would ever fulfill his promise, but in 1722 he was elevated again in the Irish peerage to become Viscount Percival of Kanturk. Thus his Majesty, "to his great Honour, kept his Word inviolate, tho' the Title conferred was not of that Degree which answered the Condition of his Lordship, in his first Demand." [18] As for the *"English* Honour," Percival continued to reflect upon it, but as a member of the Prince of Wales' court he could scarcely remind the King of his promise. This state of affairs continued until King George's death in 1727. Percival's connections with the Prince are amply evidenced in his correspondence. His Highness even stood as godfather to Percival's son, who was tactfully named George. In the course of time, in 1733, his support was rewarded with the Irish Earldom of Egmont.

Percival's intellectual interests and pursuits were catholic. He managed his estates with close attention to detail and was very sensitive to any waste of his resources. He was not, however, immune to the financial hysteria arising from the South Sea Company's promotion, and he lost heavily in the ensuing crash.[19] He avidly followed Irish and English politics, leaving copious politi-

16. *Ibid.*
17. *House of Yvery*, II, 410.
18. *Ibid.*
19. *House of Yvery*, II, 430–31.

INTRODUCTION   xxi

cal memoranda among his papers. He composed a number of religious treatises, which reveal his religious devotion. Allusions in his diary show that he enjoyed literature, art, and music. Neither he nor his wife was particularly robust, and the pursuit of good health seems to have preoccupied his mind much of the time.

Percival's adherence to the Prince insured his continuance in the Privy Council when the latter succeeded his father as King George II. Percival then secured his election, in August, 1727, to the English House of Commons for the borough of Harwich, in Essex. This was a rotten borough, and his seat cost him "near £1000." [20] He became a close associate of Sir Robert Walpole and his brother Horace, who was a member of Parliament and an active figure in the Whig party. Although his views were largely Whig, Percival considered himself an independent. Nevertheless his support was consistently thrown behind the Ministry. He developed many friendships which were later of service to him in relation to the Georgia project. His brother-in-law, Sir Philip Parker, was also a member of the Commons, as were many of the promoters of the colony. Percival's notes of Parliamentary proceedings are particularly valuable, since public reporting of Parliamentary debates was as yet illegal.

Percival was very sensitive to real or suspected injury or slight, and in 1733 became the willing spokesman of Irish peers who sought to secure their precedence by gaining the King's assent for their integration next after English peers of the same rank. After much negotiation the Irish peers were successful.

Percival had free access to the court, and frequently mentions special attention paid to himself by the royal family. Queen Caroline frequently conversed with him, and shared his literary interests. She worked with him to induce a French protégé, Dr. Peter Francis Couraye, to translate into French the Latin *Historia sui Temporis* (1620) of Jacques Auguste de Thou (Thuanus). In 1733, Prince Frederick and his wife visited Percival at Charleton. His position at court in this year seemed so secure that he advanced the proposal that he be made an earl—in order, he said, that his children might marry better. He enlisted the aid of Lord Grantham and Sir Robert Walpole, and on August 5, 1733, received his wish, becoming Earl of Egmont, another Irish designation.[21]

20. Historical Manuscripts Commission, *Diary of John Percival, First Earl of Egmont*, I, 293.
21. *Ibid.*, 399.

By this time Percival had for some years been interested in the Georgia undertaking, and his promotion increased his value to the project. Among his personal papers is a description of the origin of the Georgia venture. Here he recounts Oglethorpe's presentation of the undertaking to him, on February 13, 1730:

> That worthy Gentleman Mr. Oglethorpe . . . open'd to me a scheme he had form'd, to which I was before a perfect Stranger, but which I very much approved, . . . to settle a hundred miserable wretches, lately relieved out of jayl, on the Continent of America, and for that end to petition his Majesty for a grant of a suitable quantity of acres, whereon to place these persons, who now they are at liberty starve about the streets, or lye an incumbrance on their friends.[22]

These initial settlers, Oglethorpe continued, would in time increase in number and become a security to their neighbors against bordering Indians and the encroachments of the French. He proposed that they should be employed in raising hemp, "and flax, which being permitted to make up into Yarn, might be returned to England and Ireland, and so promote our manufactures at the same time as be a subsistence to themselves."[23]

Percival was immediately interested in the plan, and thereafter devoted much of his energies to the undertaking. Most of the negotiations between the promoters and the Board of Trade were carried on through Percival or under his name, although Oglethorpe remained the principal guiding force.[24] Percival and Oglethorpe soon interested many of their friends in the House of Commons, many of whom had also served on the gaols commission, and thereby the nucleus of the Board of Trustees was formed. Because of his prominence in the enterprise, Percival was named in the charter, issued on June 9, 1732, as the first president of the Georgia Corporation, an office which was rotated among the members attending each meeting. He took the oath of office on July 7, 1732, and subsequently swore in the other Trustees.

The solicitation of gifts of money from private sources to finance the enterprise was the first concern of the Trustees, and here again the association with a figure of Percival's standing was a great asset. He was personally responsible for many bequests. When the charitable purposes of the plantation were explained

---

22. Br. Mus., Add. MS. 47097.
23. *Ibid.*
24. Ruth and Albert Saye, "John Percival, First Earl of Egmont," in Horace Montgomery, ed., *Georgians in Profile, Historical Essays in Honor of Ellis Merton Coulter* (Athens, Ga., 1958), 10.

to prospective benefactors, the Trustees were rarely refused. Often clergymen volunteered to collect monies for them in their parishes. Sometimes collections were made even without the Trustees' knowledge or consent. Sometimes fraudulent collections were made in their name. Besides the financial cares of the Trustees, there was the duty of screening prospective settlers in order to assure the selection of persons likely to succeed as colonists. Oglethorpe at length departed aboard the *Anne* with over a hundred selected settlers on December 16, 1732.

Work went on as usual for the Trustees in London, for without their constant efforts the colony could not have been sustained. Frequent board meetings were held, generally one each week, the proceedings of which Egmont carefully recorded in his journal. New settlers were examined from time to time, and the constant search for money continued. It was obvious that Parliamentary assistance would be essential for the support of the colony, and to this end the Trustees sought and received a grant of £10,000 in 1733. This source of supply proved much more lucrative than private benefactions, and by far the greater part of Georgia's support was official rather than charitable. Besides funds for general maintenance, there was the cost of the military aspect of the colony, which the Trustees insisted the government bear. They repeatedly stated the impossibility of their undertaking financial responsibility for the protection of the colony.

In the years that followed, the tasks of the Trustees multiplied, and each succeeding yearly section of Egmont's journal becomes longer. As the business of corresponding with settlers, prospective colonists, government officials, and others increased, a Committee of Correspondence was established, with the power to open letters and prepare drafts of answers to be laid before the next meeting of the Trustees. Egmont faithfully indicated the nature of these incoming and outgoing letters, and sometimes reproduced their text as well.

Routine business such as the approval of correspondence and the issuance of grants of land to settlers took up much of the Trustees' time. The encouragement of German religious emigrants was one of their interests, and the regulation of trade with the Indians was a necessity. Arrangements were made with Piedmontese silk producers to go over to stimulate the silk industry in which such great hopes were planted. One of their frequent worries was the over-expenditure of funds on the part of Oglethorpe and other officials in Georgia, concerning which the Trustees could rarely get a satisfactory accounting. They always suffered from a dearth of news from Georgia, and they constantly remonstrated with their agents over the lack of information. Not until William Stephens became their secretary in Savannah did they receive regular reports.

Several men approached the Trustees with financial promotional schemes, which, if accepted, would guarantee a certain percentage of the proceeds to the plan's originator. Others proposed to establish sawmills in Georgia to provide oak timber for the Royal Navy. But most of the plans were visionary, and the Trustees were justly skeptical.

The problem of keeping Georgia "dry" was constantly before the Trustees, and together with trade disputes involved them in bitter quarrels with the South Carolinians, who used the Savannah River to transport rum into their own back country.

The expansion of the original settlement and the establishment of new towns, and their defense, were also concerns of the Trustees, and ones which constituted a heavy financial drain. As they began to press the government for the inclusion of money for the maintenance of the colony in the Annual Estimates, they ran afoul of substantial ill-will in Parliament and in court circles. This hostility had the effect of disenchanting some of the Trustees and Common Councilors, who began to resign their offices under pleas of ill health, protracted absences from town, and the like. Egmont was unsparing in his criticism of individuals who resigned.

He himself threatened to resign on occasion, but refrained from doing so. Only when his health began to fail, especially in the spring and summer of 1742, did he at last resign from the Common Council, rarely being sufficiently well to attend the meetings. His diary reveals his struggle for health. He did remain a Trustee after 1742, and attended in this capacity a score of meetings, as his health permitted, until the last months of his life. The last meeting he attended was on February 13, 1748. He died on May 1 of the same year.

The year following the establishment of the colony, Percival became involved in a difficult situation with the ministry, which ended in his withdrawal from the House of Commons under circumstances that he had not anticipated. Percival's borough of Harwich was one in which the influence of the government was particularly strong, and in which any candidate for office not supported by the government could scarcely be elected. Percival's

INTRODUCTION

first indication of the deterioration of his power in the borough occurred in 1733, when his candidate for the office of mayor of Harwich was defeated.

He had already indicated his intention to Walpole of substituting his son for himself in the next Parliamentary election. It was opposition to the son rather than to Percival himself which appears to have activated the ministry, for Walpole repeatedly assured Percival of his high regard. The ministry did not actively oppose the son, but its endorsement of him came too late, and was in insufficient strength to secure the election for him. The younger Percival was defeated by a vote of 19 to 13, and his father considered himself a much wronged man. Now neither father nor son sat in Parliament, and Egmont never forgave Walpole.

In 1740 the son again sounded out the borough of Harwich, but found it still too hostile to consider standing for election without the strong support of the ministry, which he did not have. Instead, he stood for a seat from the Borough of Haslemere, in Surrey. Here he had the backing of the electorate, having been invited by a majority of the sixty electors to stand. He was opposed by General Oglethorpe, who had represented Haslemere in the last two parliaments, and by Peter Burrell, an official of the reorganized South Sea Company. His success seemed assured until a representative of the government bluntly warned Egmont that all the resources of the Exchequer would be opened against his son unless he withdrew, and that the government would go to any length necessary to prevent his taking his seat even if he should be elected.

Undeterred, Percival continued his campaign. But before the election, circumstances combined against him, and he decided to withdraw. He fell ill, and then observed his supporters giving way to the opposition's solicitations; the government's resources appearing inexhaustible, even his colleague in the campaign confessed himself unwilling to lose more money in an apparently fruitless venture.[25]

The next year Percival became involved in a complicated political intrigue in which the independent voters of the large and important borough of Westminster sought to defy the traditional control to which Westminster had hitherto been subjected. After a tumultuous campaign and election, Percival at last won his seat, and from a borough which in the past had been considered so secure for the government that it was referred to as the "King's

25. *House of Yvery*, II, 458.

borough." These events gave great satisfaction to Egmont, who bore to his grave his grudge against Walpole, justified or not.[26]

After his withdrawal from Parliament, until his death on May 1, 1748, Egmont devoted more attention than ever to the administration of the colony, and to his literary activities. His personal records, in particular his diary and his personal journal of the Trustees' meetings, show the effects of much careful work. It was during this period, in the early 1740's, that Egmont composed his replies to the calumnies against Oglethorpe and the Trustees published by Patrick Tailfer. The latter's pamphlet, interspersed with Egmont's rejoinders, is now to be seen as the fourth publication of the Wormsloe Foundation.[27]

The information provided in the first volume of the Egmont journal is generally more informally presented than that in the official journals, and often it is more instructive. The range of its coverage is as wide as the duties of the Trustees. The earlier part of the record tells of the transportation of the colonists to America, the founding of Savannah, and the progress made in creating a permanent settlement in the wilderness. It speaks of the financial help and encouragement received from Carolina, and the signing of a treaty with the Lower Creek Indians.

The problem of Indian relations occupies a large place in the journal, both with respect to the maintenance of peace and with respect to trade. In the latter connection, grave difficulties soon developed with South Carolina, as Georgia claimed the right to control trade with all Indians within her borders, though Carolina had been accustomed to trading with them in the past. Georgia also petitioned the King not to allow South Carolina grants of land south of the Altamaha River. These and other matters gave rise to bitter quarrels between the partisans of the two colonies in London as well as in America.

Early in 1736 the Trustees began to have trouble with Sir Robert Walpole. The difficulty assumed greater proportions in Egmont's eyes than it would have otherwise, owing to his controversy with Walpole concerning the borough of Harwich, and the elections at Haslemere and Westminster. The proposal to obtain regular funds for the colony through the Annual Estimates created schism, as other factions showed jealousy of the Trustees' plan.

26. *Ibid.*, 459–64.
27. Clarence L. Ver Steeg, ed., *A True and Historical Narrative of the Colony of Georgia by Pat. Tailfer and Others, with Comments by the Earl of Egmont* (Athens, Ga., 1960).

Walpole, accordingly, ever alert to the temper of the Commons, became reluctant to proceed with the plan. The Trustee Board itself was affected deeply by disagreement arising from the proposed plan. In June, 1736, Egmont reported that T. Frederick, a Trustee, intended to resign because he was a friend of Walpole's wife, "who is a great Enemy to our Colony."

Upon his return to England in 1737 Oglethorpe had many interviews with Walpole. Egmont, as a close friend of Oglethorpe, records much of this behind-the-scenes negotiation. Oglethorpe was chiefly concerned at this time with the threat provided by French and Spanish forces in America, and the constant warnings from various quarters that an attack upon Georgia and Carolina was imminent. Walpole agreed at length to send Oglethorpe to America as chief of the military forces of Georgia and Carolina. Later, however, he became frightened at Spanish threats and proposed to drop the scheme. The Trustees then pressed their point with the government, that they were simply unable to defend Georgia with the resources at their disposal, and asked for a protective force. In September, 1737, Walpole at last agreed to allow Oglethorpe to go over with a force of 600 men.

The Trustees had to deal with much discontent in the colony itself. In April, 1735, Egmont notes that the Trustees had received news of an intended insurrection involving wholesale murder and plunder. In July the minister Quincy is said to be in league with the malcontents. William Stephens, in a letter to the Trustees on December 20, 1737, attributed the discontent to the enforcement of land tenure in tail male, and to the prohibition of slavery, two points concerning which the colonists continually complained.

The military danger from the French and Spaniards was constantly a threat. In 1736 Egmont gives an account of an attack by the French Governor Bienville of Louisiana upon the Chickasaw Indians, who were friendly to England. After its repulse, the Chickasaws requested aid from Oglethorpe, who gave them arms and ammunition. Oglethorpe made an inspection of the southernmost reaches of the English dominions in America, the northern side of the St. Johns River, at its mouth. On the basis of the information he acquired, he ordered the construction of several forts. Meantime the Trustees continued to receive report after report of military and naval preparations in Havana and "Moville."

The Trustees did not remain the harmonious body they were at the outset. They often complained at the independent actions of Oglethorpe, particularly at his alleged excessive expenditure of funds, his secretiveness concerning special instructions he received from the King, and his failure to share information with the rest of the Trustees. In March, 1738, Egmont reported that no less than five Trustees had resigned, because of the Carolina dispute and such factors as "the bad state of the Colony . . . as represented by Mr. John Wesley, the low condition of our Cash . . . the great debts contracted by [Mr. Causton] . . . the unreasoning pique . . . of divers of our Members against Col. Oglethorpe, for having accepted a Regiment . . . and Sr. Robert Walpole breaking his word" to include grants in the Annual Estimates. Egmont further records at about this time that Oglethorpe absented himself from meetings "as often as he can without a downright quarrel with us." He gives what he believes are Oglethorpe's reasons for acting as he did, one reason being that "he found the Gentlemen resolved to reduce the Colony's expenses, especially with respect to the military articles."

The journal notes as a stroke of great good fortune the engagement of William Stephens as Secretary in 1737, and records many letters from Stephens regarding progress in the colony with the Trustees' replies and directions.

Normally Egmont wrote only on the right-hand page of his journal, but frequently, apparently at a later time, he inserted on the left-hand page additional or explanatory notes, and sometimes inserted the contents of letters which are only mentioned in the regular text. Usually these entries refer by number to a specific entry on the right-hand page. In the present text, these insertions of Egmont's are interjected immediately after the regular entry to which they refer. If there is no indication of relevance to such an entry, the notation is placed in its proper chronological position. In either case, the entry is preceded by the prefix "[N.B.]"

On occasion Egmont inserted a notation in the text itself, with the prefix "N.B.," in which case it has been reproduced as it appears in the original form, without brackets.

Egmont methodically prepared careful indices for each year's entries, with cross references and often informative comment. These have been integrated and collected at the end of the volume, with references to the pages of the printed text. Care has been exercised in this matter, and in the text itself, to preserve the original usage wherever practicable. Changes have been introduced sparingly, and only for the sake of clarity. In keeping with the usage established in the previous volumes of the Wormsloe

Foundation Publications, no attempt has been made to identify names and places to which the author refers. It has been deemed sufficient to present the journal as Egmont wrote it, including inconsistencies in spelling and arithmetical errors.

It is with pleasure that acknowledgment is made of the public service rendered by the Directors of the Thomas Gilcrease Institute of American History and Art in releasing a prized possession, this volume of the Egmont journal, for publication. Appreciation is also expressed to Mr. James T. Forrest, Executive Director of the Institute, for his efforts in this connection. Publication of the manuscript is made possible by the Wormsloe Foundation, of whose volumes of Georgia history the present work forms the fifth.

Especial gratitude is expressed to Professor E. Merton Coulter, for innumerable kindnesses over many years, and for the writer's introduction to the fascinating subject of the Earl of Egmont.

Robert G. McPherson

Department of History
University of Georgia

Abstract
of the Trustees Proceedings
for establishing the Colony of Georgia
From the date of their
Charter past 9 June 1732

Volume 1.

From 9 June 1732 to 9 June 1738

1732-1733

ABSTRACT OF THE TRUSTEES PROCEEDINGS FOR ESTABLISHING THE COLONY OF GEORGIA

With the name of every Member present each day.

N.B. In the columns
C. Stands for Common Counsellors, who are likewise all Trustees
T. for Trustees not Common Counsellors
Ch. for Chairmen of the Common Council Meetings
P. for Presidents of the Trustee Meetings

Members of the Common Council, in the Order they Stand in his Majesties Charter past 9 June 1732

John Ld. Visct. Percival, afterwds. E. of Egmont	Robert Hucks Esq
Honbl. Edward Digby Esq	Rogers Holland Esq
Honbl. George Carpenter Esq, afterwds. Ld. Carpenter	Willm. Sloper Esq
	Francis Eyles Esq
	John LaRoch Esq
James Oglethorp Esq	James Vernon Esq
George Heathcote Esq.	Willm. Belitha Esq
Thomas Towers Esq	Revd. Stephens Hales A.M. 15
Robert Moore Esq	

These had power to encrease their number to 24, To fill up vacancies, and elect Trustees without limitation.

Trustees not Common Counsellors, in the order they Stand in his Majesties Charter

Revd. John Burton B.D.	Adam Anderson, Gent.
Revd. Richard Bundy A.M.	Capt. Tho. Coram
Revd. Samuel Smith A.M.	Revd. Arthur Bedford A.M. 6

Present at the 1. Meeting, after passing the charter

20 *July* [1732]. 1.

Belitha, Will.	C	Moore, Robt.	C	
Heathcote, Geo.	C	Oglethorp, Ja.	C	
Hucks, Robt.	C	Ld. Percival	C	P

Towers, Tho.	C	Bedford, Arthr.	T
Vernon, Ja.	C	Coram, Tho.	T
Anderson, Adam	T	Smith, Saml.	T

1. Ld. Percival administered the Oath of Office to the 7 Common Council men.

2. A form of a printed letter was agreed to for gathering subscriptions toward planting the colony.

26 July. 2.

Belitha, Will.	C	Towers, Tho.	C
Heathcote, Geo.	C	Vernon, Ja.	C
Hucks, Robt.	C	Anderson, Adam	T
Moore, Robt.	C	Bedford, Arthr.	T
Oglethorp, Ja.	C P	Coram, Tho.	T
Ld. Percival	C	Smith, Saml.	T

1. Order made for Summoning a Common Council to meet the 3d of next month; and Mr. Digby wrote to come from the Country, he being appointed the 1. Chairman of the Common Council, and his presence therefore necessary for effectual entering upon business.

2. Agreed that a proposal be made to the Collectors of charity for the persecuted Saltsburgers, that we would Settle a number of them in Georgia, with promise of lands in Freehold, & maintenance for one year, pay their passage from Frankfort to Rotterdam, & from thence to Georgia: conditionally that the Trustees were allow'd for every couple Man & wife the Infants under 4 years old 20£. For every single man 10£. For the ages from 4 to 12, 5£. And for the ages from 12 to 19, 7.10.0. Which proposal was accepted.

3 Augst. 3.

Belitha, Will.	C	Ld. Percival	C
Digby, Edwd.	C Ch. & P	Towers, Tho.	C
Heathcote, Geo.	C	Vernon, Ja.	C
LaRoch, Jo.	C	Coram, Tho.	T
Oglethorp, Ja.	C	Smith, Saml.	T

1. Mr. Digby & Mr. LaRoch Sworn.

2. Resolv'd that all Officers created, & Commissions given, Shall be by Ballot.

3. Commissioners agreed on for gathering Subscriptions, viz. Ld. Visct. Tirconnel, Ld. Baltimore, Sr. Abrm. Elton Bt., Sr. Roger Meredith Bart., and Mr. Johnson, Govr. of South Carolina.
4. Benjamin Martin appointed Secy.
5. Resolved that his Acct. of Georgia be printed.

10 Aug. 4.

Hales, Steven	C		Ld. Percival	C
Heathcote, Geo.	C	P	Towers, Tho.	C
Hucks, Robt.	C		Vernon, Ja.	C
LaRoch, Jo.	C		Coram, Tho.	T
Oglethorp, Ja.	C		Smith, Saml.	T

1. More deputations Sign'd for collecting money.
2. Minuit taken for appointing a Committee to consider & prepare laws for the good Govermt. of the Colony.

[N.B.] 11 Augst. I went to Bath, and return'd not till 27 October.

23 Augst. 5.

Belitha, Will.	C		LaRoch, Jo.	C
Hales, Steven	C		Oglethorp, Ja.	C Ch.
Heathcote, Geo.	C		Towers, Tho.	C
Hucks, Robt.	C		Vernon, Ja.	C

1. Mr. Harmon Verelts appointed Accomptant.
2. Order'd that the Bank of England be desired to keep the Trustees Cash, and pay it out to the order of _____ 5 of the Common Council.

3 Octobr. 6.

Belitha, Will.	[C]		Hucks, Robt.	[C]
Ld. Carpenter	[C]		Moore, Robt.	[C]
Hales, Steven	[C]	Ch.	Oglethorp, Ja.	[C]
Heathcote, Geo.	[C]		Towers, Tho.	[C]

1. Ld. Carpenter Sworn.
2. Agreement made with Mr. Will. Houston to go Botanist to America, and from the Islands & continent collect valuable roots and plants that may Suit the Soil of Georgia. And 75£ orderd. him.

[N.B.] Mr. Willm. Houston died in Jamaica 14 Aug. 1733, and

left a considerable collection of plants and roots for the Colonys use, which were order'd to be Secured, but the Colony Saw none of them.

3. An Embarkation order'd not exceeding 35 Men and their families.

4. Committee appointed to treat with proper persons concerning the Said embarkation.

5. Order'd a draft of 300£ to be lodged in Mr. Heathcotes hands and draft Sign'd on the bank accordingly.

6. Order'd also a draft on the Bank & Sign'd accordingly to Mr. Hucks for the expence of the Office.

24 Oct. 7.

Belitha, Will.	C	Hucks, Robt.	C
Ld. Carpenter	C	Oglethorp, Ja.	C
Eyles, Fra.	C	Towers, Tho.	C Ch.
Hales, Steven	C	Vernon, Ja.	C
Heathcote, Geo.	C		

1. Mr. Eyles Sworn.

2. The persons appointed for the Embarkation attended: and the Articles of Agreement being read to them, and they being asked if they had any objection to them, Some of them made the following requests: 1. That the Sending Such goods after them as they would not be allow'd to carry with them might be considered. 2. That their daughters might be allow'd to inherit as well as Sons. 3. that the Widows Dower might be consider'd. 4. That they might go on board themselves when their goods went, and that provision might be allow'd them. Then the Common Counsil resolv'd, That the persons who went over, & desired it, Should have the privilege of naming a Successor to their lands, who in case they died without Issue, Should enjoy the Same to them and their Heirs forever, and that the Widows Should have their Thirds as in England. Order'd that each Comradeship Should be lodg'd on board according to Lot. Order'd 300£ into Mr. Heathcotes hands to defray the charges of the Embarkation, and a Draft was Sign'd by Mr. Towers & Mr. Belitha, Mr. Hucks, Mr. Hales & Mr. Vernon for that purpose.

26 Octbr. 8.

Belitha, Will.	C	Eyles, Fra.	C
Ld. Carpenter	C	Hales, Steven	C

[1732]   JOURNAL OF THE EARL OF EGMONT   7

Heathcote, Geo.	C	Towers, Tho.	C
Hucks, Robt.	C Ch.	Vernon, Ja.	C

1. Seal'd a lease & Release of 5000 acres of land, in Trust, to Tho. Christie, Joseph Hughes, & Will. Calvert, for the use of the persons going on this first Embarkation, and of others to be hereafter Sent.

2. It appear'd that the mony collected for that purpose did amount on the 15 Septbr. to 1568.18.10. and I Shall here add by way of anticipation, that by the 9 June 1733, no less than 3723.17.7. was collected.

3. Order'd 2.2.0. to the clerk for transcribing the Lease and Release above mention'd.

4. Refer'd to Mr. Hucks & Mr. Towers the preparing of a chest of medicines for this embarkation.

1 Novbr. 9.

Belitha, Will.	C	Ld. Percival	C
Ld. Carpenter	C	Towers, Ja.	C
Hales, Steven	C	Vernon, Ja.	C
Hucks, Robt.	C P	Coram, Tho.	T
LaRoch, Jo.	C Ch.	Smith, Saml.	T
Oglethorp, Ja.	C		

1. Resolv'd to establish a Civil Govermt. in Georgia, and a Town on the River Savannah to be call'd by that name. That the Township consist of 5000 Acres, and that the Govermt. thereof be by Bailifs, Constables, & Tything Men. That a Court of Oyer & Terminer be created with a judge, justices of Peace &c.

2. Then the Common Council nominated the Magistrates and Officers and added 3 persons to the Embarkation.

3. Mr. Oglethorp offering himself to go in person and conduct the people, Powers under the Corporation Seal were given him, 1. To Set out limit and devide the 500 acres. 2. To give lycence to persons to go out of Georgia as occasion Should require. 3. To direct the Trustees of those 5000 acres in the division of them. 4. To make Grants to the persons going over, not exceeding 50 acres besides their houses and gardens. 5. To remove officers on failure of duty, and to Supply their places in case of death.

4. Then the Passengers being call'd in, they Sign'd Seal'd a deed to Submit to the Laws We Should make, be dutyfull to the Magistratee, Stay 3 years in the Colony, and mutually assist each other in clearing their Lots.

5. A Skilfull Surgeon was appointed to go with them.

6. And the Revd. Mr. Herbert bastard Son to the E. of Torrington, having offer'd his Service to attend them and officiate in Savannah till another Minister Should be found to Succeed him, his offer was accepted. But falling ill of a flux, he return'd for England Some months after, and died in the passage.

8 Novbr. 10.

Belitha, Will.	C	Ld. Percival	C Ch.
Hales, Steven	C	Towers, Tho.	C
Heathcote, Geo.	C	Vernon, Ja.	C
Hucks, Robt.	C	Coram, Tho.	T
LaRoch, Jo.	C	Smith, Saml.	T
Oglethorp, Ja.	C P		

1. Peter Gordon appointed 1. Bailif of Savannah
Willm. Waterland 2d. NB. He was turn'd out 2 Aug. 1733.
Thomas Causton 3d.
Thomas Christie Recorder
Joseph Fitzwalter 1. Constable
Saml. Parker 2d.
John West 1. Tything Man
John Penrose 2d. All of them not worth 20£.
The Store keepers place left to Mr. Oglethorp to fill up.

2. Seal put to a Deed for displacing any of them & naming others in case of death or failure of duty or misbehaviour.

3. Commission granted to Mr. Oglethorp to administer the Oathes of Allegiance, Supreamacy, Abjuration, & Oathes of Office.

4. Power given him to set out 300 acres for the use of the Church at Savannah, a Site for the Same, a Ministers house and a burial place.

5. Agreement made with 6 pot Ash people (4 of whom to go over with Six Servants at Christmas next) & they to have 1200 acres.

6. Agreed also wth. a Carpenter to go over wth. 4 Servants and to have a grant of 500 Acres.

7. Seald Mr. Herberts Commission to perform all Religious and Ecclesiastical Duties in Savannah.

(N.B.) On the 15 of this month November, Mr. Oglethorp and Mr. Herbert fell down the River to Graves End with the new design'd Inhabitants, in number 44 Men, 20 Women, 25 boys and 17 girls, making in all 114 persons, and 91 heads; all on the poor account, who were follow'd before they Sayled by 4 Others. The Expence of their Embarkation was 1414.5.9, besides Some military Equipments presented to the Trustees for the Same use, Church furniture, books &c.

23 Novbr. 11.

Hales, Steven	C	Towers, Tho.	C
Heathcote, Geo.	C P	Vernon, Ja.	C
Holland, Rogers	C	Bundy, Ri.	T
Hucks, Robt.	C	Coram, Tho.	T
Ld. Percival	C	Smith, Saml.	T

1. Mr. Holland Sworn.
2. Order'd a memorial to the Incorporated Society for propagating Christiany. in foreign parts, to obtain a Missionary with Sallary, and to acquaint them that we have order'd 300 Acres of Glebe to be Set out.
3. Some reputable persons were agreed with to go over at their own charge and follow the making of Silk.
4. Some persons were noted down to be Sent next Embarkation.
5. Seal put to Mr. Oglethorps Militia powers.
6. The whole of our Collections was this day Something above 2500£.

30 Novbr. 12.

Ld. Carpenter	C	Ld. Percival	C
Hales, Steven	C	Towers, Tho.	C P
Heathcote, Geo.	C	Vernon, Ja.	C
Holland, Rogers	C	Coram, Tho.	T

1. Some more people noted down for next Embarkation.
2. Agreed that for the future, the names of Such persons as are Sent on the poor Acct. be publickly advertised, that their Creditors be not defrauded.

7 Decbr. 13.

Ld. Carpenter	C	Hucks, Robt.	C
Digby, Edwd.	C	Ld. Percival	C Ch.
Heathcote, Geo.	C	Towers, Tho.	C
Holland, Rogers	C P	Vernon, Ja.	C

Bundy, Ri.   T   Smith, Saml.   T
Coram, Tho.   T

1. The Trustees resolv'd to apply for a Sloop of 8 guns to protect their Settlement, and Mr. Hucks undertook to Speak to the Ld. Torrington.
2. Information given that one Bacon als. Hog was turned Papist, and resolved to offer his Service to the Spaniards at Augustine, the nearest Spanish town to our Settlement, and that he was well acquainted with the Coast of Georgia.
3. A Debate arose whether Jews Should be admitted to Settle in Georgia, but Sentiments differing, nothing was this day determined therein.
4. The Common Council Orders 25£ to the Accomptant for his Services.
5. The Pot Ash people agreed & Settled with.
6. 30 poor persons examin'd, & 4 noted down to be Sent next Embarkation: the rest rejected, because able to earn their bread in England, tho poorly.

21 Decbr. 14.

Ld. Carpenter	C		LaRoch, Jo.	C
Digby, Edwd.	C	Ch.	Ld. Percival	C
Hales, Steven	C	P	Towers, Tho.	C
Heathcote, Geo.	C		Vernon, Ja.	C
Holland, Rogers	C		Coram, Tho.	T
Hucks, Robt.	C		Smith, Saml.	T

1. Benefactions reported to the Trustees.
2. Mr. Quincy a clergyman recommended by the Revd. Mr. Page for Minister in Georgia. The Trustees agreed to Send him for examination to the Incorporate Society, from whom a Sallary was expected.
[N.B.] Mr. Quincy was So often and So long at a time absent from his duty, and So great an encourager of malecontents in the Colony, that complaints came over against him: whereupon the Trustees resolv'd to recall him, which he being apprised of, desired leave to be dismist, and it was very readily granted.
3. Order given for preparing Proposals for Settling Saltsburgers in Georgia.
4. The Common Council put the Seal to the Silk mens grants.
5. Agreed with Ensign Penkerton to make him a grant of 300

[1733] JOURNAL OF THE EARL OF EGMONT 11

acres. But he afterwards changed his mind, and declined going over.

28 Decbr. 15.

Ld. Percival	C P		Bundy, Ri.	T
Towers, Tho.	C		Coram, Tho.	T
Vernon, Ja.	C		Smith, Saml.	T

   1. A Letter was read from Govr. Johnson of South Carolina, advising not to make an Embarkation these 12 months, or until houses were built to receive the people. It was dated 28 Septbr. but came too late.
   2. Letter order'd to Mr. Oglethorp to build as Soon as possible, a Church, and Ministers house, and lay out 300 acres of glebe.
   3. Order'd that advice Should be Sent into Germany, that we would engage to convey 50 Saltsburg Families to our Colony.
   4. The Grants to the Silk men, Bishop & Hetherington, and ye 2 Lacy's deliver'd to them. Each grant 500 Acres.
   5. More people noted down for next Embarkation.

1732–3

10 Jany. [1733] 16.

Ld. Carpenter	C		Ld. Percival	C
Digby, Edwd.	C		Sloper, Will.	C
Hales, Steven	C		Vernon, Ja.	C
Heathcote, Geo.	C Ch.		Burton, Jo.	T
Hucks, Robt.	C		Coram, Tho.	T
LaRoch, Jo.	C			

   1. Mr. Sloper Sworn.
   2. Pinkertons Grant past the Seal.
   3. A Grant past the Seal 8 good Sawyers to embark this day fortnight, miserable objects most of them: One had by Sickness been obliged to Sell his bed, and another was to Sell his tools to pay his Creditors.

17 Jany. 17.

Heathcote, Geo.		Vernon, Ja.	
Ld. Percival		Bundy, Ri.	
Towers, Tho.	P	Coram, Tho.	

1. Ensign Penkerton demurr'd on going to Georgia because of the Tenure in Tail Male only.
2. Several apply'd to go over on the poor Account, others on their own.
3. A Memorial agreed on to the Incorporate Society, recommending Mr. Quincy for the Sallary formerly apply'd for.
4. Agreed to Send over divers Sorts of Seeds, particularly the Italian white mulbery.
5. Thanks ordered to the D. of Montague for a present of Several Tun of Iron.
6. The Same to Mr. Leak of Bath for a present of books for our intended School.
7. Resolv'd to admit no Jews to go over to Settle in the Colony, and to recall the Deputations made to Some principal Jews in London to collect mony.

[N.B.] There was Some disposition to allow the Jews to Settle in Georgia, but the Majority were not for it, because they generally are not cultivators of land, but Small hedge Shopkeepers, and might keep private correspondence with the Spaniards. However a considerable number went over, without the Trustees knowledge, to whom Mr. Oglethorpe gave Lots. A few of them proved industrious, but the greater number not. They were in all 43. Mr. Oglethorp was much displeas'd at their arrival, and took advice of Lawyers in Carolina whether he could not Send them away, but they gave their opinion he could not. Besides eating Capt. Hansons provisions who carry'd them over, they cheated him of their passage money, So that he lost by them about 3 or 400£. Many ran away from their Christian Creditors.

24 Jany. 18.

Ld. Carpenter	C	Anderson, Adam	T
Moore, Robt.	C P	Coram, Tho.	T
Ld. Percival	C	Smith, Saml.	T
Vernon, Ja.	C		

1. A letter order'd to Mr. Oglethorp giving acct. of our proceedings to go to morrow by Capt. Yoakly.
2. The 8 Lawyers formerly mention'd and two others on the poor Acct. Ship'd on board that Capt.
3. Botham Squire also Ship'd himself paying his own passage, but it was granted to him to be one of the Hundred who were to

[1733] JOURNAL OF THE EARL OF EGMONT 13

have the right of Township, and be maintain'd for one year at the Trustees expence.

4. Cash now remaining reduced to 700£.

31 Jany. 19.

Digby, Edwd.	C		Ld. Percival	C
Heathcote, Geo.	C		Towers, Tho.	C Ch.
Holland, Rogers	C P		Vernon, Ja.	C
Hucks, Robt.	C		Coram, Tho.	T
LaRoch, Jo.	C		Smith, Saml.	T
Moore, Robt.	C			

1. Capt. Pennyfeather of Ireld. apply'd for a Grant of land to go over on his own Acct.

2. Resolv'd to apply to Sr. Robt. Walpole for a Parliamentary Supply to Support the Colony.

3. The Resolution for recalling the Deputations made to Jews to collect for us confirm'd.

4. The Grant of Ld. Carterets Share in Georgia, having been approved by the Attorney Genl. and brought to us fairly engrossed, the Same was Sent to his Lordship for his perusal.

[N.B.] The King could grant but 7 eights of Georgia to the Trustees, because the Ld. Carteret refused to Sell to the Crown his property, as the other Proprietors had done. But he made us a grant of his Share in the Same manner the King had done, reserving to himself the Quitrents in the Same proportion his Majy. had fixt them.

5. The Common Council appointed a Committee of Accts. 3 to make a Quorum.

7 Feby. 20.

Digby, Edwd.	C		Moore, Robt.	C
Eyles, Fra.	C		Ld. Percival	C
Heathcote, Geo.	C		Vernon, Ja.	C P
Holland, Rogers	C		Bedford, Arthr.	T
Hucks, Robt.	C		Coram, Tho.	T
LaRoch, Jo.	C		Smith, Saml.	T

The Common Council did not Sit, and the Trustees business was of Small consequence.

14 Feby. 21.

Hales, Steven	C P	Towers, Tho.	C
Holland, Rogers	C	Vernon, Ja.	C
Hucks, Robt.	C	Bundy, Ri.	T
Moore, Robt.	C	Coram, Tho.	T
Ld. Percival	C	Smith, Saml.	T

1. Thanks order'd to the Lady Osborn for 50£ given towards building a church.
2. Read a letter from Sr. Tho. Lomb, commending the Trustees views and the goodness of Carolina Silk above that of all other nations.
3. Nicolas Amatis, brother to Paul Amatis who went over with Mr. Oglethorp to manage the Silk, being just arrived from Piedmont, attended with 7 other Skilfull persons one of whom is expert in making looms.

21 Feby. 22.

Ld. Carpenter	C	Moore, Robt.	C Ch.
Digby, Edwd.	C	Ld. Percival	C
Eyles, Fra.	C	Sloper, Will.	C
Hales, Steven	C	Towers, Tho.	C P
Heathcote, Geo.	C	Vernon, Ja.	C
Holland, Rogers	C	Bundy, Ri.	T
Hucks, Robt.	C	Coram, Tho.	T
LaRoch, Jo.	C	Smith, Saml.	T

1. Order for a Servant to Mr. Quincy, at the Trustees Expence.
2. Ld. Carteret Sent word, that he agreed to the Attorney Genls. draft of his Grant to the Trustees, and desired a Counterpart thereof under the Corporation Seal, as also a Copy of the Kings Grant upon parchment, which was Order'd.
3. Grants Seal'd to Capt. Pennyfeather of 300 acres
    To Will. Gough Senr. 80 acres
    To Will. Gough junr. 80 acres
4. Nicolas Amatis required to Set down his proposal in writing on what terms he will be willing to go to Georgia, & assist his brother in the Silk affair, taking with him the 7 people who came at the Same time. Sr. Tho. Lomb was desired to attend when the Same Should be consider'd next board day.

[1733] JOURNAL OF THE EARL OF EGMONT

28 Feby. 23.

Digby, Edwd.	C		Ld. Percival	C
Hales, Steven	C		Sloper, Will.	C
Heathcote, Geo.	C		Vernon, Ja.	C
Holland, Rogers	C	P & Ch.	Coram, Tho.	T
Moore, Robt.	C		Smith, Saml.	T

1. Letter read from an Alderman of Liverpool, that the Chamber of that town had given 50£ to forward our designs, and that the Ministers of the two Parishes design'd to preach and make Collections for us.

2. Mr. Amatis deliver'd his proposal for going over.

3. Letter read from Mr. Oglethorp that he arrived after 7 weeks passage at Charlestown 13 Jany., and had been well receiv'd by Govr. Johnson, and the Speaker of the Assembly, who promis'd to assist the Colony what lay in their power; and that only 2 children had died in the passage.

4. The Seal was put to the Counterpart of Ld. Carterets Grant of his Interest in the lands of Georgia.

7 March 24.

Digby, Edwd.	C		Towers, Tho.	C
Eyles, Fra.	C		Vernon, Ja.	C
Hales, Steven	C		Bundy, Ri.	T
Hucks, Robt.	C		Coram, Tho.	T
LaRoch, Jo.	C	P	Smith, Saml.	T
Ld. Percival	C			

1. Deputation Sent to Mr. Leak Bookseller at Bath to make Collections, and a letter wrote to the E. of Derby to desire he will accept of one: he being a great encourager of our designs.

2. Order for printing 600 copies of our Secy. Mr. Martins book entitled *Reasons for establishing the Colony of Georgia.*

3. Sr. Thomas Lomb assisted us in our debates concerning the proposal of Nics. Amatis. But we defer'd any resolution thereon till next meeting.

15 March 25.

Digby, Edwd.	C	Heathcote, Geo.	C
Eyles, Fra.	C	Holland, Rogers	C
Hales, Steven	C	Hucks, Robt.	C

Laroch, John	C	Ch.	Anderson, Adam	T	
Moore, Robt.	C		Bedford, Arthr.	T	
Ld. Percival	C		Bundy, Ri.	T	
Sloper, Will.	C		Burton, Jo.	T	
Towers, Tho.	C		Smith, Saml.	T	
Vernon, Ja.	C	P	Coram, Tho.	T	

1. This being the day appointed by Our charter for filling up the number of Common Council Men to 24, & for electing Trustees, We accepted the resignation of Mr. Belitha, who by reason of his constant residence in the Country desired to be exhonorated, and elected Dr. Bundy to be Trustee in his room, together with 9 others, which compleated our number. We also elected 8 new Trustees, our Charter not limitting us as to them. Their names are on the other Side.

[N.B.] Names of the 10 Common Counsellors elected by Ballot 15 March 1732–3

Richd. Bundy D.D. In the room of Mr. Belitha who resign'd, but continued a Trustee
Richd. Chandler Esq. Son to the Bishop of Durham
Thomas Frederick Esq
Willm. Heathcote Esq. afterwds. created Bart.
Willm. Kendal Esq. Aldn. of London. He afterwds. changed his name to Cater & was knighted.
Henry Lapotre [L'Apostre] Esq
James Ld. Visct. Limerick
Ld. Visct. Tirconnel
E. of Shaftsbury
John White Esq.

The 8 Trustees elected at the Same time were

E. of Derby
Ld. Darcy. He died 17 July following.
Sr. John Gonston Kt.
Will Hanbury Esq
John Page Esq
Erasmus Philips Esq. Since Bart. by Sr. John his fathers death
Christopher Towers Esq. Brother to Thomas
Tyrer (George) Esq. Alderman of Liverpool

2. It was resolved that Nicolas Amatis with Jaques Camuche, his wife and 3 children should be sent to Georgia at the Trustees

expence, that the 2 other Italians who came with Amatis Should be Sent back. That the above mention'd Should have leave to quit the Colony if they desired it.

3. Mr. Burton preach'd a Sermon to us in St. Brides Church Suitable to the occasion, which practice has ever Since been follow'd, and the 15 day of March kept as the Anniversary day.

4. After this, the Trustees dined together at the Castle Tavern, and our number with the Strangers invited was about 30.

21 March. 26.

Bundy, Ri.	C	Ld. Percival	C P
Chandler, Ri.	C	Ld. Tirconnel	C
Frederick, Tho.	C	Towers, Tho.	C
Heathcote, Geo.	C	Vernon, Ja.	C Ch.
Hucks, Robt.	C	White, Jo.	C
Kendal, Robt.	C	Bedford, Arthr.	T
Lepotre, Hen.	C	Coram, Tho.	T
Ld. Limerick	C	Smith, Saml.	T
Moore, Robt.	C		

1. Dr. Bundy, Mr. Chandler, Mr. Frederick, Sr. Will. Heathcote, Aldn. Kendal, Mr. Lapotre, Ld. Limerick, Ld. Tirconnel, and Mr. White Sworn.

2. Benefactions reported.

3. The Common Council agreed in part with Nicolas Amatis and his people to go over.

4. Order given for printing Mr. Burtons Sermon, and that preach'd by Mr. Smith the year before.

5. Order that the Members who were in the Trust before the 15 March prepare an account of their proceedings to that day.

6. Resolv'd that if any person will carry over 6 Servants without any charge to the Trust, 500 Acres Shall be granted him on the Same terms with others Settled there, and his Servants Shall have when their Service expires 20 acres each man.

7. Resolv'd that for the future, no Servant Shall have more than 20 Acres granted him.

28 March. 27

Bundy, Ri.	C	Moore, Robt.	C Ch.
Frederick, Tho.	C	Ld. Percival	C
Hales, Steven	C P	E. Shaftsbury	C

Ld. Tirconnel	C	Ld. Darcy	[T]
White, Jo.	C	Smith, Saml.	[T]
Coram, Tho.	[T]		

1. E. of Shaftsbury Sworn.
2. The Silk Undertakers complain'd the Potash people refused to agree with them in admitting them into Partnership for making potash. We told them the Potash people had an exclusive Grant for 10 years, and therefore we could not oblige them thereto, but they might make pot ash each for himself, if they would be at the charge.
3. A Subscription was moved of money to be raised among the Trustees themselves for maintenance of a Saltsburg Minister until other Supplyes came in.
4. Resolv'd that a Grant of 50 acres be made to every Saltsburg family that goes over.
5. Grant Seald to Hen. Fletcher of 200 Acres.

3 April. 28.

Heathcote, Geo.	C	Ld. Percival	C	
Heathcote, Sr. Will.	C	Sloper, Will.	C	P
Hucks, Robt.	C	Ld. Tirconnel	C	Ch.
LaRoch, Jo.	C	Towers, Tho.	C	
Ld. Limerick	C	Vernon, Ja.	C	
Moore, Robt.	C			

1. Final Agreement made with Nicolas Amatis. A house to be alotted him and his Servants, a Grant of 100 Acres to himself, and 50 to his Servt. Jaques Camuche when his Service expires. Provisions to be allow'd him and his Servants; proper materials furnish'd him for making raw Silk; the profits of his labour to be for his own use; a Sallary allow'd him for 4 years of 25£ p ann, on condition he delivers as many machines and Coppers as the Trustees or their Agents Shall require, on paying him 3£ Sterl. for each Machine and Copper, and Shews how to use them, and discovers the Secret of making raw Silk to Such persons as Shall be appointed for that purpose. That the Charge of his and his Servants passage from Georgia to any part of England or Italy Shall be defray'd if required, the quitting all right and claim to the Grant and lands (except Such part as Shall be cultivated) at the end of 5 years, which is to be at his own disposal, with the consent however of the Trustees, & under the usual limitations, and

[1733] JOURNAL OF THE EARL OF EGMONT 19

leaving all the machines & Coppers and materials, which are or Shall be furnish'd him by the Trustees.

2. A Benefaction reported of 100£ from the Bishop of Woster Dr. Hough, and thanks order'd.

18 April. 29.

Digby, Edwd.	C		Ld. Tirconnel	C	
Frederick, Tho.	C	Ch.	Vernon, Ja.	C	
Hales, Steven	C	P	White, Jo.	C	
Heathcote, Geo.	C		Bedford, Arthr.	T	
Hucks, Robt.	C		Coram, Tho.	T	
Lapotre, Hen.	C		Ld. Darcy	T	
Moore, Robt.	C		Smith, Saml.	T	
Ld. Percival	C				

1. Letters lately received from Mr. Oglethorp, Mr. Herbert, Govr. Johnson &c, and the resolution of the Assembly of South Carolina towards Supporting our Colony, were read. Mr. Oglethorp inform'd us that a Town was begun on the Savannah River about 10 miles distant from the Mouth, that half the land of the town was already clear'd, and fortification begun. That an Indian nation 50 miles distant desired our protection, and offer'd to Send their children for instruction. That the Country is fine, and Ships drawing 12 feet water can come up to the town.

2. A fellow Stiling himself Prime Agent to the merchants, publishing bills to invite persons to go & Settle in Georgia without our Orders, it was resolved he Should be prosecuted unless he in print recanted.

3. Order past for applying to Sr. Robert Walpole to know when we may have leave to move the House of Commons for an address to his Majesty for money to carry on our designs.

4. Money imprest to answer a bill drawn by Mr. Oglethorp.

5. Grant of 200 acres past to Samuel Holmes.

25 April. 30.

Frederick, Tho.	C		Ld. Limerick	C
Heathcote, Sr. Will.	C	Ch.	Moore, Robt.	C
Heathcote, Geo.	C		Ld. Percival	C
Holland, Rogers	C		E. of Shaftsbury	C
Hucks, Robt.	C		Sloper, William	C
LaRoch, Jo.	C		Ld. Tirconnel	C

Towers, Tho.	C	White, Jo.	C
Vernon, Ja.	C	Towers, Christn.	T

1. Petition to the Parliamt. prepared, for obtaining money to carry on our designs.

2. Report that the Collection for the Persecuted Saltsburgers amounted to between 3 & 4000£.

3. Order'd that 600 copies of Mr. Martins Reasons for establishing the Colony of Georgia be printed to present the Lords & Commons.

30 April. 31

Digby, Edwd.	C	Ld. Percival	C	Ch.
Eyles, Fra.	C	E. of Shaftsbury	C	P
Frederick, Tho.	C	Sloper, Will.	C	
Heathcote, Geo.	C	Ld. Tirconnel	C	
Heathcote, Sr. Will.	C	Towers, Tho.	C	
Holland, Rogers	C	Vernon, Ja.	C	
LaRoch, Jo.	C	Ld. Darcy	T	
Lapotre, Hen.	C	Philips, Erasmus	T	

1. Order'd that Application be made to the Bishop of London to encourage Collections in his Diocese for the Saltsburgers to be sent to Georgia.

2. Seal put to our petition to the Parliament for money.

3. Sr. Robt. Clifton brought 2 persons of his name to be Sent to Georgia, which we allow'd of, but afterwards declined on Suspicion they were Papists.

4. Mr. Hollingbore a Prussian formerly Secy. to the E. of Chesterfeild in Holland appear'd, and desired a Countryman and Relation of his might go over on his own charge, which was allow'd. But I think he never went.

5. Sr. Abraham Elton appear'd, and desired 3 persons might go on their own charges, have 500 acres each, & their 18 Servants 25 acres each. On this occasion we Suspended our former order of granting but 20 acres to a Servant, they being Bristol men, and that City deserving a particular respect.

9 May. 32.

Ld. Carpenter	C	Ch.	Ld. Tirconnel	C	P
Hales, Steven	C		Towers, Tho.	C	
Moore, Robt.	C		Vernon, Ja.	C	
Ld. Percival	C		White, Jo.	C	

1. Letters read from Govr. Pen of Pensilvanea promising 100£ Sterl. towards advancing our designs. And from Mr. Herbert that he was fallen Sick, and obliged to go to Charlestown. Also that Mr. Oglethorp was ill, and worse than he would own.

2. Report made of 100£ benefaction from the E. of Abercorn for which thanks was order'd. This was the 2d time he gave 100£.

3. Seal put to Several Commissions to collect for us.

10 May. 33.

Hales, Steven	C	Sloper, Will.	C
Heathcote, Sr. Will.	C	Vernon, Ja.	C
Ld. Limerick	C	Coram, Tho.	T
Moore, Robt.	C	Gonston, Sr. Jo.	T
Ld. Percival	C	Smith, Saml.	T

1. Several letters from persons desirous to go to Georgia were read.

2. Commission granted to the Minister & church warden to collect.

[N.B.] 10 May. This day our petition to Parliament for money was presented by Sr. Joseph Jekyl Master of the Rolls. Sr. Robt. Walpole declared his Majesties consent, and Sr. John Barnard a City Member Seconded the bringing it up. Mr. Horace Walpole, Coll. Bladen & I Supported it, and none opposed it but Mr. Winnington & Mr. Fra. Whitworth.

11 May 34

Frederick, Tho.	C		Ld. Limerick	C
Hales, Steven	C		Moore, Robt.	C
Heathcote, Geo.	C	Ch.	Sloper, Will.	C
Heathcote, Sr. Will.	C		Towers, Tho.	C
Holland, Rogers	C		Vernon, Ja.	C
Hucks, Robt.	C		White, Jo.	C
LaRoch, Jo.	C			

1. Order'd that Jacomo Ottone make another Machine for winding Silk to be kept for the use of the Trustees.

2. Grants past to Sr. Abraham Eltons Bristol Men viz.
    to John Williams 500 Acres.
    to Robert Williams 500.
    to Cornelius Sandford 500.

[N.B.] John and Robert Williams went before their Grants could be past

3. Order'd payment of 200£ to Mr. Simonds Mercht. being a bill drawn by Mr. Oglethorp.

[N.B.] 16 May. This day Col. Bladen moved that 10,000£ lying in the Exchequer being part of the money arrising out of the Sale of the St. Christophers lands, might be granted us to carry on the Settlement of the Province, which no body opposed: Only there were one or two to prevent its passing nem. con.

17 May 35.

Ld. Carpenter	C	Ld. Percival	C
Hales, Steven	C	Ld. Tirconnel	C
Heathcote, Sr. Will.	C	Vernon, Ja.	C P
Hucks, Robt.	C	Coram, Tho.	T
Lapotre, Hen.	C	Ld. Darcy	T

1. Memorials of persons desiring to go over were read, but nothing determin'd.
2. Letter order'd to Mr. Oglethorp concerning the Saltsburgers.
3. The Accomptant order'd to State the expence of the persons hitherto Sent over.
4. Grant past to Edward Jenkins of 100 acres.

23 May 36.

Hucks, Robt.	C	Anderson, Adam	T
Kendal, Robt.	C	Bedford, Arthr.	T
LaRoch, Jo.	C	Coram, Tho.	T
Moore, Robt.	C	Ld. Darcy	T
Ld. Percival	C	Gonson, Sr. Jo.	T
Vernon, Ja.	C P	Hanbury, Will.	T
White, Jo.	C	Smith, Saml.	T

1. A letter approved of to be wrote by Mr. Vernon into Germany for bringing over Saltsburgers.
2. The Common Council book was look'd over, and Some Entrys in it of Small consequence were noted with intention to enter them in the Trustees book to wch. they belong'd.
3. Commissions Sign'd to Several Vicars & Rectors of Parishes to Collect mony for our designs.
4. Jacomo Ottone brought the machine we order'd him to make for winding Silk after the Italian manner.

[1733] JOURNAL OF THE EARL OF EGMONT 23

24 May 37.

Frederick, Tho.	C	Ld. Percival	C
Heathcote, Sr. Will.	C	Sloper, Will.	C
Hucks, Robt.	C	Ld. Tirconnel	C
Kendal, Robt.	C	Towers, Tho.	C
Lapotre, Hen.	C	Vernon, Ja.	C
Holland, Rogers	C Ch.	White, Jo.	C P
Moore, Robt.	C		

1. A proposal for Lacy's taking over 20 charity children to be employ'd in the Silk was approved: but was not pursued, their Parents not consenting.

2. Extracts of letters from Georgia order'd to be printed for the Satisfaction of the Publick.

3. A letter order'd to Mr. Oglethorp to acquaint him with our proceedings, and to desire his information what the Subsistance of every family may amount to yearly, that we may calculate our expences. Also to know what tools or amunition is wanting, & whether there is a good Situation for a Saw mill.

4. Resolv'd that if the Collectors for the Saltsburgers will deposite in our hands 1250£ We will engage the payment of the 50£ p ann to their Minister, till lands Shall be cultivated for that End.

5. A Weekly payment of 5 Shill. order'd to our messenger, & of 2/6 a week to his wife our Housekeeper.

6. Resolv'd to Send forthwith 50 able bodied men to cultivate the Saltsburg land till their arrival.

29 May 38.

Frederick, Tho.	C	Moore, Robt.	C
Heathcote, Geo.	C	E. of Shaftsbury	C
Heathcote, Sr. Will.	C	Sloper, Will. C.	C Ch.
Holland, Rogers	C	Towers, Tho.	C P
Hucks, Robt.	C	White, Jo.	C
Kendal, Robt.	C		

1. Order past 23 Oct. 1732 that 5 of the Common Council might Sign drafts on the Bank repeal'd, and a new one made that any 5 of the Common Council may Sign.

2. Order past for Separating the Trusteeship of Mr. Dalones legacy from the care of the Trustees of our charter for Settling the Colony of Georgia, which hitherto had been blended with it,

but is of a distinct nature. 109.8.6 was therefore order'd to be taken out of the Cash belonging to the Trustees of Georgia and restored to the Trustees of Dalones legacy.

[N.B.] The reason why these 2 Trusts were both under the management of the Trustees of the Colony of Georgia, was that a person had given hopes of 5000£ towards furthering the Settlement thereof conditionally that the gentlemen who conducted it were united to Some known Trust, for this was before the passing his Majesties charter. Whereupon a new Commission of Trustees of Mr. Dalones legacy for conversion of Negroes to Christianity past, and the Trustees of Georgia were incorporated into them. But afterwards that person changed his mind, and would give nothing to Georgia, whereupon Some gentlemen desired the Two Trusts might be Separated, the One having no relation to the other.

5 June 39.

Ld. Carpenter	C	Kendal, Robt.	C
Eyles, Fra.	C	LaRoch, Jo.	C
Frederick, Tho.	C Ch.	Moore, Robt.	C
Heathcote, Geo.	C	Ld. Percival	C
Heathcote, Sr. Will.	C	Towers, Tho.	C
Holland, Rogers	C	White, Jo.	C
Hucks, Robt.	C	Coram, Tho.	T

1. The following numbers were noted down to embark on board the Georgia Pink, Daubur commander who proposes to sail the 15 inst. viz 43 Men, 17 women, 18 boys and 10 girls, in all 88 persons.

2. The quantities of the Sevl. necessaries to be Sent this Embarkation were adjusted, as Canon, muskets, Swords, powder and ball, Vinegar, beer, water, Oatmeal, tarpauling for tents, Nails, Engines for pulling up roots of trees, knives, hatchets, Saws, Presents to the Indians, druggs &c.

6 June 40

Ld. Percival	C P	Coram, Tho.	T
Towers, Tho.	C	Smith, Saml.	T
Bedford, Arthr.	T		

1. Directions given for buying Some few more necessarys for the embarkation.

2. Agreed that Mr. Towers and I wait on Sr. Joseph Jekyl to return him the thanks of the Trustees for his considerable benefaction, being 500£, besides 100£ given by his Lady.

[N.B.] The Number of days the Trustees met this year were 40. On which were held 33 Trustee and 25 Common Council Boards. And the days each Gentleman attended were as follows

Belitha, Will.	9	Kendal, Robt.	5
Bundy, Ri.	9	Lapotre, Hen.	5
Ld. Carpenter	13	LaRoch, Jo.	18
Chandler, Ri.	1	Moore, Robt.	14
Digby, Edwd.	12	Oglethorp, Ja.	8
Eyles, Fra.	8	Ld. Percival	34
Frederick, Tho.	9	E. of Shaftsbury	4
Hales, Steven	13	Sloper, Will.	10
Heathcote, Geo.	28	Ld. Tirconnel	6
Heathcote, Sr. Will.	10	Towers, Tho.	30
Holland, Rogers	16	Vernon, Ja.	32
Hucks, Robt.	29	White, Jo.	10

Trustees Only

Anderson, Adam	5	Hanbury, Will.	1
Bedford, Arthr.	4	Page, John	0
Burton, Jo.	2	Philips, Erasmus	1
Coram, Tho.	29	Smith, Saml.	22
Ld. Darcy	4	Towers, Christn.	1
E. of Derby	0	Tyrer, Geo.	0
Gonson, Sr. John	2		

The Persons Sent within this year at the Trustees charge were Men 93, Women 59. In all 152.

The Country Lots granted this year were

To Philip Bishop	acr.	500	⎫
To Joseph Hethrington		500	⎬ 21 Dec 1732
To Roger Lacy		500	
To James Lacy		500	⎭
To John Pennyfeather		300	21 Feby. 1732–3
		2300	
To Willm. Gough Sen		80	⎫ 21 Feb. 1732–3
To Will. Gough junr.		80	⎭
To Hen. Fletcher		200	28 March 1733
To Saml. Holmes		200	18 April 1733

To Jo. Williams	500
To Robt. Williams	500
To Cornelius Sandford	500
To Edwd. Jenkins	100 17 May 1733
	5460
Add the 5000 acs. for Savannah Township	5000
Acres granted 1st year	10460

Here end the Transactions of One year, being the first from the passing the Charter

1733-1734

Transactions of the 2d year
from 9 June 1733 to 9 June 1734

11 June [1733] 1.

Frederick, Tho.	C	Moore, Robt.	C	
Eyles, Fra.	C	Towers, Tho.	C	
Hucks, Robt.	C	Vernon, Ja.	C	
LaRoch, Jo.	C	White, Jo.	C	Ch.
Ld. Limerick	C			

Seal put to a Grant of 2800 acres in Trust to Jo. Barnes, Henry Parker and Joseph Sacheveril.

13 June 2.

Heathcote, Sr. Will.	C	Towers, Tho.	C	
Holland, Rogers	C	Vernon, Ja.	C	
Hucks, Robt.	C	Bedford, Arthr.	T	
Kendal, Robt.	C	Coram, Tho.	T	
LaRoch, Jo.	C	Smith, Saml.	T	
Ld. Percival	C	P.Ch.		

1. Thanks orderd to the Speaker for his handsom expressions of Georgia in his Speech to his Majesty on the Throne.
2. Commission given to Dr. Warren to collect for us in his Parish, and thanks orderd him for his offer to give us a Sermon on the Anniversary day.
3. Review of the persons who are to go over at the Trustees expence next fryday in Capt. Daubur Ship.
4. Advertisement in the news papers orderd of 30£ received by me from an unknown hand for the use of the Colony.
5. Committee order'd to prepare an Acct. of our Receipts and disbursments to the 9 June 1733, to be given to the Ld. H. Chancellor, Ld. Ch. justice, & Master of the Rolls, as the charter obliges us.
6. Draft on the Bank & Impress to Mr. Geo. Heathcote of 1000£ for the embarkation.

7. Order that any 3 of the Common Council be a Committee of Accts.

20 June 3.

Frederick, Tho.	C	Towers, Tho.	C
Hucks, Robt.	C	Vernon, Ja.	C P
Ld. Percival	C	Coram, Tho.	T
Lapotre, Hen.	C	Smith, Saml.	T

1. An offer was accepted from Mr. Mount the Stationer, that he will give the paper, if we will let him have the printing the things we publish.
2. Some persons who offer'd themselves for a future embarkation were examined & noted down.

27 June 4.

Bundy, Ri.	C	Ld. Percival	C
Chandler, Ri.	C P	Vernon, Ja.	C
Hucks, Robt.	C	Coram, Tho.	T
Lapotre, Hen.	C	Smith, Saml.	T
LaRoch, Jo.	C		

The Annual acct. of Receipts and disbursements gone through.

4 July 5.

Chandler, Ri.	C	Ld. Limerick	C
Frederick, Tho.	C	Ld. Percival	C
Heathcote, Geo.	C Ch.	Towers, Tho.	C
Kendal, Robt.	C	Vernon, Ja.	C
Lapotre, Hen.	C P		

1. Confirmation that the Revd. Mr. Herbert Minister at Savannah died at Sea in his return to England, of the fever & bloody Flux in June last.
2. Read letters from Mr. Oglethorp acquainting us that the assembly of Carolina, had given 2000£ of their currency to forward the Settlement of our Colony this year, and that the Committee of assembly had agreed to 12000£ currency for the Service of next year, which he believed would be approved at next meeting of the Assembly. That this 14000£ currency makes 2000£ Sterl. Besides which the Town of Charlestown had raised 1000£ currency, and paid 500£ of it for buying cattel for our Settlers. That he had

hopes of converting one Indian town to christianity. That he had Sent us Seeds Skins & druggs, being a present from the Indians.

3. Order given that care be taken that no prejudice come to our Colony by an Act Sent over by the Assembly of Carolina for his Majesties approbation.

[N.B.] The Act of the Assembly of Carolina mention'd on the other Side was for confirmation of divers old Grants of land, and drawn up in So general terms, that the Trustees were apprehensive if past by his Majesty, it might endanger the Title they have to Georgia notwithstanding their charter, because Georgia was formerly granted to Sr. Robt. Montgomery. And tho by a clause in his Grant, it was declared void unless cultivated & Settled with people in 3 years time, which was not done, yet by reason of a general confirmation and the making good all defects, the Trustees thought their Title might be weaken'd. But the Committee of Lords put them out of their pain by rejecting the bill 11 July 1733. The Lords present were Ld. Wilmington, Sr. Robt. Walpole, Mr. Horace Walpole and Sr. Cha. Wager.

4. Mony imprest to Mr. Geo. Heathcote to answer a bill drawn on us by Mr. Oglethorp.

5. Powers granted to Mr. Oglethorp to Set out the 2800 acres granted in Trust 11 June last, and to dispose of them.

6. Appointment of 4 Constables.

7. Grants made & past the Seal this day
   To Tho. Fawsett 500 acres
   To Robt. Hethrington 250
   To Theophilus Hethrington 250

11 July 6.

Chandler, Ri.	C		Bedford, Arthr.	T
LaRoch, Jo.	C		Coram, Tho.	T
Ld. Percival	C	P	Smith, Saml.	T
Vernon, Ja.	C			

1. Report made that our yearly accts. were laid before the Ld. Chancellor & Ld. Ch. justice Eyres.

2. Report that 70 heads of Saltsburgers had been wrote for, to come down forthwith to Rotterdam, from whence a Ship of Mr. Simons the Mercht. would be ready to transport them to Georgia.

3. Upon private Accts. from Charlestown that Mr. Oglethorp intended to Set out in 6 Weeks for England, We directed a Special Summons of our Members to consider thereof, it being of con-

sequence that Some discreet person vested with proper authority Should be appointed to take care of the Province in his absence.

18 July 7.

Bundy, Ri.	C	Ld. Percival	C
Chandler, Ri.	C	Towers, Tho.	C P
Lapotre, Hen.	C	Vernon, Ja.	C
LaRoch, Jo.	C		

1. Persons noted down for a future embarkation, one of whom Skilfull in fencing banks, and another in mechanical Engines. Others reduced to the last extremity of want.

2. Upon consideration of the difficulties we Should find to make boards of Common Council during the Summer time, at which 8 Common Counsellors must necessarily be present to issue money, and provide necessaries for future embarkations, It was concluded that at next Common Council board a motion Should be made that the Bank Should be drawn on for a large Sum to answer occasions, by any five of the Common Council.

[N.B.] On 20 July 1733 Richard Hodges 2. Bailif of Savannah died. He went over in the 1st Embarkation and had been a basket maker by trade in England.

25 July 8.

Frederick, Tho.	C	Ld. Percival	C
Heathcote, Geo.	C	Towers, Tho.	C
Hucks, Robt.	C P	Bedford, Arthr.	T
Lapotre, Hen.	C	Coram, Tho.	T
LaRoch, Jo.	C		

1. Ld. du Ferron a French disabled Officer desired to go over with his wife and 2 children on the poor acct.

2. One Rainer Partner with the Potash makers came to acquaint us he liked not his associates and would deliver up his Grant. There were 6 of them who had taken a grant of 1200 acres, and were to have carry'd over 12 Servants, and proposed to lay out 2000£. But we found them afterwards to be most of them beggers, and with this mans resignation the Grant to them all fell.

3. Some poor persons well recommended were noted for a future embarkation.

4. Letter of Attorney Sign'd to our Accompt. to recieve of the Treasury the 10000£ granted by Parliamt.

1 August 9.

Bundy, Ri.	C	LaRoch, Jo.	C P
Frederick, Tho.	C	Ld. Percival	C
Hales, Steven	C	Towers, Tho.	C Ch.
Heathcote, Geo.	C	Vernon, Ja.	C
Hucks, Robt.	C	Coram, Tho.	T
Lapotre, Hen.	C	Smith, Saml.	T

1. The Corporation Seal broken and a new one made.

2. Mr. Martin our Secy. continued, his 1st appointment expiring 2 days hence.

3. A long letter from Mr. Oglethorp was read, giving a character of the Indians with whom he has made a Treaty, of his proceedings in Settling the Colony, and of the encouragement expected from South Carolina.

4. Grant past the Seal to Patrick Houston of 500 acres, also to Geo. Moore of 400.

5. A Saw mill order'd to be made & Sent to Georgia according to a Model presented to us by Messr. Thibbalds Timber Mercht. of London.

6. Order'd 5 guineas to Mr. Harbin for his Services.

7. Order'd 1 guinea & ½ to Mr. Brown for his information concerning Bacon als. Hog.

8. Appointed a Committee to make drafts on the Bank as far as 3000£ for defraying the expences of the Saltsburgers embarkation.

9. Order'd a new embarkation of English, and the above Committee to have the care of it.

10. Order for buying to be Sent over 160 Firelocks & bayonets.

[N.B.] 2 Aug. 1733 William Waterland 2d Bailif of Savannah was turn'd out of his Office by Mr. Oglethorp for drunkenness, whereupon he went to Carolina and never return'd. He was brother to Dr. Waterland the Kings Chaplain, and had been by trade a mercer, but breaking turn'd School master. His brother had renounc'd him & the very rich would do nothing for him, So he went over in the first embarkation on the poor acct.

[N.B.] On 5 Augst. 1733 I kist his Majestys. hand for creating me Earl of Egmont, and on the 11th of that month Set out for Bath, where I remain'd till 20 Octbr. following, and on the 24th return'd to London.

8 August 10.

Hucks, Robt.	C	Vernon, Ja.	C
Lapotre, Hen.	C P	Coram, Tho.	T
LaRoch, Jo.	C	Smith, Saml.	T
Towers, Tho.	C		

1. Read a letter from Mr. Oglethorp, with the Articles of Treaty he enter'd into with the Indians.
2. Some people examin'd for next embarkation.

11 August 11.

Lapotre, Hen.	C	Vernon, Ja.	C
Towers, Tho.	C P		

1. Memorial prepared to the Treasury for payment of the 10000£ granted by Parliament.

15 August 12.

LaRoch, Jo.	C	Coram, Tho.	T P
Towers, Tho.	C	Smith, Saml.	T

1. Persons examin'd to go to Georgia.

17 August 13.

LaRoch, Jo.	C	Coram, Tho.	T
Towers, Tho.	C	Smith, Saml.	T

1. Reciev'd the Receipt for the Parliaments 10,000£.

22 August 14.

Hales, Steven	C	Anderson, Adam	T
Hucks, Robt.	C P	Coram Tho.	T
Towers, Tho.	C	Smith, Saml.	T

1. Persons examin'd to go to Georgia
2. Rainer deliver'd up his Grant of 1200 acres, for Copartnership for Pot ash.

29 August 15.

Heathcote, Geo.	C	Towers, Tho.	C

[1733]   JOURNAL OF THE EARL OF EGMONT   33

| Vernon, Ja. | C P | Gonson, Sr. John | T |
| Anderson, Adam | T | Smith, Saml. | T |

1. The persons design'd for embarkation Sign'd their articles.
2. Dr. Warrens collection brought in 7.17.0.
3. Capt. Yoakly brought 2 barrils of Rice & 1 barril of Skins from Georgia on the Trustees Acct.

[N.B.] From the beginning to Septbr. 1733 about 40 persons Sent over by the Trust, died.

5 Septembr. 16.

Hales, Steven	C P	Moore, Robt.	C
Hucks, Robt.	C	Vernon, Ja.	C
Lapotre, Hen.	C		

1. Persons examin'd to go to Georgia

12 Septembr. 17.

Hales, Stephen	C	Burton, Jo.	T
Lapotre, Hen.	C P	Gonson, Sr. Jo.	T
Vernon, Ja.	C	Smith, Saml.	T

1. Persons examin'd to go to Georgia.
2. Power Seald to the Revd. Mr. Urlsperger at Ausburg, to collect Saltsburgers for Georgia, and instructions given him.
3. Reported to the board, that the Society for promoting Christian Knowledge, who were the Collectors for the Saltsburgers, had come to a resolution to Support a Saltsburg Minister and Catechist, if Settled in one town, or 2 ministers & 2 Cathechists if Settled in 2 towns.

19 Septembr. 18.

Frederick, Tho.	C	Gonson, Sr. Jo.	T
Lapotre, Hen.	C	Smith, Saml.	T
Vernon, Ja.	C P		

1. Examin'd people to go to Georgia.
2. Recd. Sevl. benefactions for Religious Uses.
3. Sign'd a petition to the King for instructions to his ministers at Vienna, to admit Georgian Colonists into their City till there was a Sufficient Number to embark.

26 Septembr. 19.

Hales, Steven	C P	Vernon, Ja.	C
Hucks, Robt.	C	Smith, Saml.	T

1. Recd. Several benefactions.

3 October 20.

Lapotre, Hen.	C P	Smith, Saml.	T
Vernon, Ja.	C		

1. Recd. Several benefactions.
2. John Scot examined to go to Georgia.

10 October 21.

Chandler, Ri.	C	Vernon, Ja.	C P
Hucks, Robt.	C	Smith, Saml.	T
Lapotre, Hen.	C		

1. Received Several benefactions.

17 October 22.

Hucks, Robt.	C P	Anderson, Adam	T
Vernon, Ja.	C	Smith, Saml.	T

1. Recd. of the Apothecary's Compy. 20£ for the use of Mr. Houston the Trustees Botanist.
2. Recd. a benefaction of 20£ in butter, cheese or bacon, the gift of John Child.
3. Christopher Ortman proposed to be Sent over as Parish Clerk to the Saltsburgers, & Schoolmaster to teach their children English.

18 October. 23.

Bundy, Ri.	C	Hucks, Rob.	C Ch
Chandler, Ri.	C	Lapotre, Hen.	C
Frederick, Tho.	C	Vernon, Ja.	C P
Hales, Steven	C	Smith, Saml.	T
Ld. Carpenter	C		

1. Mr. Vernon reported the muster of persons taken on board 3 Ships, viz. the Savannah, Capt. Wood, 130, [viz.] Males 73, Females 57. The London Merchant, Capt. Thomas, 5, viz. 3 males,

2 females. The James, Capt. Yoakly, 48, viz. 27 Men, 21 females, making in all 183 persons, and 139 ¾ heads.

2. Constables and Tythingmen appointed for a new intended vilage in Georgia call'd Thorp. Robt. Parker Senr. late Aldn. of Lyn was made chief Constable there.

3. Power under Seal granted to Mr. Oglethorp, or in his absence to Mr. Ja. St. Julian of S. Carolina, & Fra. Scot of Georgia Gent. to set out, limit divide & bound 2800 acres formerly granted.

4. Lease and Release of Said 2800 acres, made to John Ambrose, Isaac King Clark, & Arthur Ogle Edgcomb in Trust.

5. Lease and release of 2500 acres granted to George Buckman, Christopher Ortman and Willm. Sale in Trust for the Saltsburgers.

6. Same powers granted as in the former case to Set out &c the Said 2500 acres.

7. Seal put to the Ratification of the articles of Friendship and Commerce agreed by Mr. Oglethorp in behalf of the Trustees with the Chief Men of the Lower Creeks.

8. Grant past of 300 acres, and ground for a house in Savannah to Will. Sale.

Grant past of 200 acres & ground for a house in Savannah to Will. Terry.

Grant past of 500 acres to Patrick Tailfer, Surgeon.
Grant of 400 acres past to Andrew Grant Gent.
Grant of 400 acres past to Jo. Baillie.

24 Octobr. 24.

Ld. Percival	C	Smith, Saml.	T
Vernon, Ja.	C		

1. We order'd a Ship of Mr. Simonds to go the middle of next week to Rotterdam, to take up Saltsburgers expected to be there about the time of the Ships arrival. There go several person on board for Georgia Same time.

31 Octobr. 25.

Bundy, Ri.	C P	Ld Percival	C
Ld Carpenter	C	Vernon, Ja.	C
Lapotre, Hen.	C	Smith, Saml.	T

1. Engagement made with Christn. Ortman a German to Set out ye 2d next month on board Mr. Simons Ship the Purysburg, Capt. Fry commander, for Rotterdam, & from thence proceed

with the Saltsburgers to Georgia, and there to teach their children Englsh.

2. A letter was read, requesting that Several hundred Piedmontese Protestants who understand cultivating vines and making Silk might be transported to Georgia at the Trustees charge, they being now at Rotterdam in great distress. We order'd that as many as the Ship will hold more than the English now on board & the Saltsburgers expected Should be taken in, to fill up the Ships compliment, of 75 heads.

7 Novbr. 26.

Bundy, Ri.	C	Coram, Tho.	T
Moore, Robt.	C P	Smith, Saml.	T
Vernon, Ja.	C		

1. Letters recommending Several Piedmontese or Vaudois Protestants to be Sent over.

2. Letters recd. of numbers perishing in Georgia by drinking Rum, and of an intended rising of the meaner Sort of Inhabitants.

14 Novbr. 27.

Bundy, Ri.	C	Holland, Rogers	C Ch.
Ld. Carpenter	C	Kendal, Robt.	C
Chandler, Ri.	C	Lapotre, Hen.	C
Frederick, Tho.	C	Moore, Robt.	C
Heathcote, Geo.	C	Towers, Tho.	C
Hucks, Robt.	C	Vernon, Ja.	C

1. Grant past to Will. Stirling of 500 acres
   to Hugh Stirling of 500
   to Ja. Houston of 500

2. Powers given to Mr. St. Julian & Mr. Scot to execute in Mr. Oglethorps absence, Such powers & appointments as Shall remain unexecuted by him.

3. Power given Mr. Oglethorp and in his absence to those Gentlemen to Set out, limit and deliver possession of the 3 above Grants.

4. Powers to Mr. St. Julian and Mr. Scot to grant lycenses in Mr. Ogeltorps absence to persons to go out of the Colony.

5. Will. Lake petition'd for an addition of 200 acres intending to carry over ten Servants. The Same was granted, So that his Grant is of 300 acres.

[1733] JOURNAL OF THE EARL OF EGMONT 37

6. Resolv'd that if there are not Saltsburgers to make up the number 75, that the Same be compleated with English men.

7. A Committee of any 3 of the Common Council appointed for that purpose.

8. Order to acquaint the Society of Christian Knowledge that on their paying 3000£, the Trustees will engage under their Seal to p ann 50£ to a Saltsburg Minister, 30£ to a Catechist, and 10£ to a School master.

9. 50£ ordered to the Secy. & 25£ to the Accomp. for ye Services.

21 Novembr. 28.

Ld. Carpenter	C	LaRoch, Jo.	C P & Ch.
Chandler, Ri.	C	Towers, Tho.	C
Hales, Steven	C	Vernon, Ja.	C
Heathcote, Geo.	C	Coram, Tho.	C
Holland, Rogers	C	Page, Jo.	C
Hucks, Robt.	C	Smith, Saml.	C
Lapotre, Hen.	C		

1. Letter and proposal read for 100 German families to go to Georgia.

2. Benefactions recd.

3. Persons examin'd to go over.

4. Order past for prohibiting the drinking Rum in Georgia, & to Stave all the Rum brought thither.

5. Grant past of 150 Acres to Nathanl. Polhill.

6. Powers granted to the Revd. Mr. Boltzius to do Ecclesiastical Officer in Georgia.

1 Decembr. 29.

Bundy, Ri.	C	Towers, Tho.	C
Frederick, Tho.	C	Vernon, Ja.	C P
Kendal, Rob.	C	Smith, Saml.	T
LaRoch, Jo.	C		

1. A letter order'd, recommending Tho. Trip a Carpenter for 50 Acres on his paying 10£.

8 Decembr. 30.

Bundy, Ri.	C P	Holland, Rogers	C
Frederick, Tho.	C	Lapotre, Hen.	C

Vernon, Ja.   C   Smith, Saml.   T
Bedford, Arthr.   T

1. Recd. Benefactions.
2. Read a letter from Mr. D. Wolters at Rotterdam, with a petition of Jean Louis Poyas to be Sent to Georgia with Several Piedmontese or Vaudois.

15 Decembr. 31

Bundy, Ri.   C   Lapotre, Hen.   C
Frederick, Tho.   C   E. of Egmont   C
Hales, Steven   C   Towers, Tho.   C
Holland, Rogers   C   Vernon, Ja.   C Ch.

1. Letter orderd to Mr. Wolters, that we would receive Vaudois to the number of 40 heads, and that Mr. Poyas might chuse that number of Such as knew the Silk trade & Vine dressing.
2. Letter of thanks orderd to Mr. Von Reck for his intention to conduct 40 Saltsburgers to Georgia, & 10£ orderd him. They now were at Dover.
3. Imprest made of 500£ to Mr. Heathcote for the expence of the Saltsburg embarkation & other occassions.
4. The Saltsburgers agreed with.

22 Decembr. 32.

Bundy, Ri.   C   LaRoch, Jo.   C
Digby, Edwd.   C   P   Vernon, Ja.   C
Frederick, Tho.   C   Smith, Saml.   T
Hucks, Robt.   C

[No entry]

29 Decembr. 33.

Bundy, Ri.   C   Lapotre, Hen.   C
Digby, Edwd.   C   LaRoch, Jo.   C
Heathcote, Geo.   C   P   Vernon, Ja.   C
Heathcote, Sr. Will. C   Egmont   C
Kendal, Robt.   C   Smith, Saml.   T

1. The affair of the Jews debated, whose going Surreptitiously over offended every member present.
2. Letters read touching the Saltsburgers at Dover on board the Ship Purysburg, Capt. Fry Commander.

[1734]   JOURNAL OF THE EARL OF EGMONT   39

3. Letters read from Georgia of an accident befallen Mr. Oglethorp in Georgia, & his design to return to England.

4. Letters read from Germany, that 1000 Saltsburgers among whom are Some late converted Papists & 2 Priests, had given in their names to quit their Country.

5. Letters read that many Anabaptist have been order'd to depart Saxony, and desire to Settle at their own charges in Georgia.

5 *Jany. 1733–4.* 34.

Bundy, Ri.	C		Lapotre, Hen	C
E. of Egmont	C		Vernon, Ja.	C P
Frederick, Tho.	C		White, Jo.	C
Heathcote, Geo.	C		Bedford, Arthr.	T
Heathcote, Sr. Will.	C	Ch	Smith, Saml.	T

1. Letter read from Mr. Oglethorp dat. 15 Novr. that he was Speedily designing for England. That he Should leave the Colony in good condition but could not make up Accts. as he wish'd, because Hughes the Storekeeper was dead, and his books not to be found. That he had drawn on us for 1100£ & Should draw again for more.

2. A letter from Some eminent jews was read, excusing their Sending jews to Georgia without our Knowledge. Order'd a letter to them to return their Commissions for collecting, and make us Satisfaction by using their endeavours to recall those jews, or remove them to Some other place.

3. 600£ imprest to Mr. Heathcote for immediate Services.

[N.B.] About the month of Jany. 1733–4 Mr. Oglethorp wrote that he had 437 mouths to feed in the following Settlements

Settled in Savannah Town	259
At Ogeeky	22
At Highgate	3
At Hampstead	39
At Abercorn	33
On Hutchinson's Island	5
At Tybee	21
At Cape Bluff	5
At Westbrook	4
At Thunderbolt	28
	Souls 437

There were about 40 more dead (whom the Trustees Sent over) about Septbr. last. By this it appears that many joyn'd the Colony not Sent by the Trust, but whose maintenance Mr. Oglethorp found reason to charge the Trust with.

[N.B.] On the 23d Jan. 1733–4 Mr. Oglethorp purchassed 40 Irish transport Servants who put into Savannah in their way to Pensilvanea being in the utmost distress, which the Trustees allow'd of. But most of them proved vile rogues.

24 Jany. 35

Bundy, Ri.	C P	Moore, Robt.	C
Egmont, E.	C	Sloper, Will.	C
Heathcote, Sr. Will.	C	Ld. Tirconnel	C
Hucks, Robt.	C	Towers, Tho.	C
Kendal, Robt.	C	White, Jo.	C
LaRoch, Jo.	C	Smith, Saml.	T

1. A Debate about moving the House concerning the great Collection made for the poor Palatins in Q. Anne's reign, wch. was not paid to their use, but remain'd Sunk in the pockets of the brief Gatherers. Our design was that it Should be recover'd and apply'd to the Settlement of Georgia.

2. Letter from Rotterdam was read, desiring a Sallary for a Vaudois minister in case we Should carry any number of those people to Georgia.

30 Jany. 36.

Hucks, Robt.	C	Towers, Tho.	C P & Ch.
Lapotre, Hen.	C	Vernon, Ja.	C
LaRoch, Jo.	C	Anderson, Adam	T
Moore, Robt.	C	Coram, Tho.	T
Shaftsbury, E.	C	Smith, Saml.	T
Ld. Tirconnel	C		

1. Grant past to Joseph Wardrope of 150 acres.
2. Resolv'd that a competent allottment of Land be granted for the use of a Catechist in Georgia.

6 Feby. 37.

Bundy, Ri.	C	Hales, Steven	C
Digby, Edwd.	C	Heathcote, Sr. Will.	C
Egmont, E.	C	Holland, Rogers	C

Hucks, Robt.	C P & Ch.	Towers, Tho. C
Lapotre, Hen.	C	Vernon, Ja. C
LaRoch, Jo.	C	White, Jo. C
Moore, Robt.	C	Coram, Tho. T
Shaftsbury, E.	C	Smith, Saml. T
Sloper, Will.	C	Towers, Christn. T
Ld. Tirconnel	C	

1. Commission given to the Rector of St. Georges Parish Hanover Square to collect benefactions.

2. Resolv'd to petition the Parliamt. for the Palatin money formerly mention'd.

3. A bill drawn on us by Mr. Oglethorp refused acceptance for want of advice.

4. 500£ imprest to Mr. Heathcote to answer bills that were accepted.

5. Dr. Hales desired to preach our next Anniversary Sermon at St. Brides Church.

8 Feby. 35. [sic.]

Bundy, Ri.	C	Lapotre, Hen.	C
Ld. Carpenter	C	Moore, Robt.	C
Digby, Edwd	C	Holland, Rogers	C Ch.
Egmont, E.	C	Shaftsbury, E.	C
Heathcote, Geo.	C	Sloper, Will.	C
Heathcote, Sr. Will.	C	Towers, Tho.	C
Hucks, Robt.	C	White, Jo.	C

1. Read a petition from Several Subscribers to the Collection made for the Palatin Refugees in 1709, complaining that One Walker had taken out a great number of Briefs, by which as they were inform'd near 20000£ had been collected for Settling Palatins in America, but that the money had not been apply'd to that use. Wherefore they desired the Parliamt. would enquire into the abuse, and that what money could be recover'd might be apply'd towards the Settlement of Georgia, or Some other Publick purpose.

2. Order'd that Mr. Douglass a Sollicitor be employ'd to get hands to the petition, in order that it may be presented to Parliamt. The Speaker having Seen & approved the petition.

3. A Principal Millright for Sawing timber, now in Georgia, having apply'd that Some others of that business might be Sent over. The Same was order'd.

11 Feby. 36.

Egmont, E.	C	Ld. Tirconnel	C P
Hucks, Robt.	C	Vernon, Ja.	C
Moore, Robt.	C	White, Jo.	C

1. Committee of Correspondence consisting of Common Council men and Trustees appointed to open letters, and prepare drafts of answers to be laid before the board.

13 Feby. 37.

Bundy, Ri.	C		Towers, Tho.	C
Digby, Edwd.	C		White, Jo.	C
Egmont, E.	C		Coram, Tho.	T
Heathcote, Sr. Will.	C	P	Smith, Saml.	T
Hucks, Robt.	C		LaRoch, Jo.	C Ch.
Moore, Robt.	C			

1. Information given that what we had been told concerning the Palatine money's being Sunk is a mistake, for that Mr. Bendish Secy of those Briefs Knew of 21000£ paid into the Chamber of London, who repaid it to the Merchants who transported many of those people to America.

2. Some bills drawn by Mr. Oglethorp were accepted he having give advice of them. And other bills to the value of 250£ were likewise accepted, tho without advice, by reason that if we did not they would have been protested, which would draw great Scandal on us, have proved detrimental to the Province on many Accts. and the protesting them had been 30 *p* cent loss to us.

20 Feby. 38.

Bundy, Ri.	C P		Sloper, Will.	C
Digby, Edwd	C		Ld. Tirconnel	C
Egmont, E.	C		Vernon, Ja.	C Ch.
Eyles, Fra.	C		Anderson, Adam	T
Kendal, Robt.	C		Burton, Jo.	T
LaRoch, Jo.	C		Coram, Tho.	T
Moore, Robt.	C		Smith, Saml.	T
Shaftsbury, E.	C			

1. I acquainted the Board that Ld. Bathurst would give Sr. Francis Bathurst 100£ to go to Georgia, and that he had 2 daugh-

ters and a son 16 years old. I was desired to let me Ld. know Sr. Francis Should have 50 acres for every Servant he carry'd, and that his Son Should be admitted as a Servant.

2. Order given for publickly advertising a legacy of 100£ left us by a Broker in Exchange Ally.

3. A Benefaction for the maintaining a Catechist, 10£ presented by Mr. Burton who desired the persons name might be conceald, and the Same promised to be continued 5 years.

4. Mr. Miller a Surgeon, recommended by Sr. Hans Sloan, was accepted Botanist in the room of Mr. Houston deceased, and he agreed with us on the Same terms made with Mr. Houston. He proposes to Sail in 2 months. Particular persons having Subscribed to him 195£ we engaged to make it up 200£ p ann.

5. Order given for Securing the Collections made for Georgia by Mr. Houston.

6. Mr. Douglass the Sollicitor reported, that the Collections made for the Palatins before they went over had been paid into the chamber of London & amounted to about 21000£. But that the Letters Patents for collecting were in force till the Michelmass following, and from the time the Palatine went no briefs had been return'd.

7. Some Bills of which we recd. advice were accepted.

8. Letter order'd to Mr. Oglethorp to Send us advice when ever he draws on us, and in his absence to Mr. St. Julian & Mr. Scot.

27 Febry. 39

Bundy, Ri.	C		Sloper, Will.	C	
Digby, Edwd.	C		Ld. Tirconnel	C	Ch.
Egmont, E.	C	P	Towers, Tho.	C	
Holland, Rogs.	C		Vernon, Ja.	C	
Hucks, Robt.	C		White, Jo.	C	
Lapotre, Hen.	C		Coram, Tho.	T	
Moore, Robt.	C		Page, Jo.	T	
Shaftsbury, E.	C		Smith, Saml.	T	

1. Resolv'd that application be made to the Ld. Chancellor in favour of the Revd. Mr. Saml. Smith, for Some Ecclesiastical Preferment on acct. of his great Service to the Trust.

2. Ld. Tirconnel paid in a benefaction of 225.1.6 collected in St. George's Parish Hanover Square, where Dr. Rundall preach'd.

3. Mr. Gordon 1 Bailif of Savannah lately come over to be cut for a fistula, attended, and presented a draft of Savannah wch. We

orderd to be engraved. He gave us an acct. of the State of the Colony.

[N.B.] Mr. Gordons acct. of the Colony at the time he left it, November last, was, That there were about 500 Souls, and of them 100 fighting Men. That 40 houses were already built of Timber & Clap board, with Shingled roofs, but Mr. Oglethorp Still lay in his Tent. That the town was intended to consist of 6 Wards, each Ward containing 4 Tythings, and each Tything 10 houses, So that the whole number of houses & Lots would be 240. That there is a battery of 12 guns on the River and over them a Guard Room, besides which 2 block houses at the Angles of the town had each 4 guns. That a Town house is erected where Mr. Quincy perform'd divine Service. That under the town the river is 12 foot deep at low water, and at high water 19 or 20. But the Bluff on which the Town is built was 40 foot higher than high Watermark. That the kitchen roots and herbs Sent over by the Trustees did not Succeed So well as was expected, nor did the people apply themselves So much as was hoped to clear and Sow their land for garden roots & corn, because taken up with building their houses, which would oblige the Trustees to give another years maintenance above what had been engaged for. That he had great hopes the cultivation of Madera grapes would bring employment & profit to the Inhabitants by producing wine, and that the growing of Silk would do the Same. That the Indians of the neighboring Town were 40 Souls, and lived in great friendship with our people as they do with them. That Several Inhabitants were fallen Sick by drinking as was Supposed the River water. But Mr. Oglethorp had Sunk a Well in the middle of the Town, which produced a Sufficient quantity of good water. That the River had a great quantity of Several Sorts of fish, particularly mullet & Sturgeon. That the people were orderly and healthy when he came away, and Mr. Oglethorp indefatigable in carrying on the affairs of the Province, conducting the building the Town, Keeping peace, laying out land, Supplying the Stores with provision, encouraging the faint hearted &c.

4. Mr. Douglass the Sollicitor acquainted us that he had wrote to Mr. Walker concerning the Palatin mony in his hands unaccounted for, (which Mr. Bendish who likewise attended Said was 1300£) and that he had received no answer. We thought it proper to move the House of Commons for a Committee to enquire into this matter.

[N.B.] Sr. Rogr. Meredith deliver'd the petition, and a Committee was appointed 28 of Feby. but Mr. Walker was grown

Senseless by old age and no Satisfaction could be obtain'd concerning the money his books being mislay'd.

5. Thanks order'd for 62£ collected for us in a Parish in London.

6. Final agreemt. made with Mr. Miller the Botonist.

7. Grant past to Ja. Hazlefoot of 150 acres.

6 March 40.

Bundy, Ri.	C		Moore, Robt.	C
Digby, Edwd.	C		Shaftsbury, E.	C
Egmont, E.	C		Tower, Tho.	C
Eyles, Fra.	C		Vernon, Ja.	C
Heathcote, Geo.	C	P	White, Jo.	C
Heathcote, Sr. Will.	C	Ch.	Belitha, Will.	T
Holland, Rogers	C		Coram, Tho.	T
Hucks, Robt.	C		Smith, Saml.	T
LaRoch, Jo.	C			

1. Agreed that the new Members to be chosen next Anniversary day be balloted for; and that if any two Members objected to the election, they Should have a weeks time to give their reason.

2. Order'd that the first Meeting of the Committee of Correspondence be this evening.

3. Instructions given Mr. Miller for his conduct in the Several voyages he is to make. He was agreed with 6 March.

4. Order'd an advertisment against certain persons who in the Trustees name, kidnap people to Send to the West Indies under promise of money or land.

17 March 41.

Bundy, Ri.	C		Shaftsbury, E.	C
Digby, Edwd.	C		Ld. Tirconnel	C
Egmont, E.	C		Vernon, Ja.	C
Frederick, Tho.	C		White, Jo.	C Ch.
Hucks, Robt.	C		Coram, Tho.	C
Lapotre, Hen.	C		Smith, Saml.	T
Moore, Robt.	C	P		

1. A By law proposed that all our Members be balloted for.

2. A By law proposed that upon any question proposed, a member may have leave to enter his dissent in writing, & that both be offer'd the ensuing Anniversary meeting.

3. Mr. Vernon proposed a law that heirs female & collatoral branches may Succeed to lands by will of the deceased. He Said many families were discouraged from going over for want of this permission. The debate was adjourned to the next Common Council day.

4. Ld. Tirconnel proposed the recommendation of our Secrety. to the Govt. for Some recompence of his Services to us.

5. A letter was read from one Peter Flower dated at Purysbury 7 Jany. last, giving Acct. that Georgia was in a thriving way.

[N.B.] The principal contents of Peter Flowers letter was, that about 600 persons were in Georgia. 10 families Settled at Thunderbolt 6 miles up St. Augustin Creek, and 4 below by water from Savannah, & as many by land. 10 familys on Tibee Isld. where a lighthouse was intended to be built. 10 families at the Ogeeky, 40 miles by land behind Savannah, and 80 by water. 10 families at Cornhow Creek 8 miles below Purysburg. 10 families at a village call'd Highgate 4 miles from Savannah, and 40 houses intended to be built for a vilage above Purysburg.

6. Another letter from Charlestown giving Some Acct. of Purysburg.

[N.B.] The letter from Charlestown added that Kilbury the most active man we had died 8 December last, that the people of the first embarkation do now work quietly and industriously, & that there were 48 houses in Savannah built, and good bricks made in Purysburg.

7. A letter the Committee of Correspondence to Mr. Oglethorp was approved, wherein we complain of his neglect to write frequently to us, whereby we are not able to acquaint the Great officers with our proceedings as we are obliged by our Charter. We therefore desire him to find a person proper to correspond with us, and promise him a recompence. We also complain of his drawing bills of 250£ upon us wth.out giving advice.

8. Finding our cash low, we order'd a letter to countermand the Vaudois who were expected from Rotterdam.

9. Grant of 75 acres made to Will. Bateman.

21 March 42.

Bundy, Ri.	C	Egmont, E.	C Ch
Ld. Carpenter	C	Hales, Steven	C
Chandler, Ri.	C	Holland, Rogrs.	C P
Digby, Edwd.	C	Hucks, Robt.	C P [sic]

Laroch, Jo.	C	Anderson, Adam	T
Ld. Tirconnel	C	Bedford, Arthr	T
Towers, Tho.	C	Burton, Jo.	T
Vernon, Ja.	C	Coram, Tho.	T
White, Jo.	C	Smith, Saml.	T

1. This being our Anniversary day, We met in the Vestry of St. Brides Church, and after the transaction of Some business, heard a Sermon preach'd by Mr. Hales, and then din'd together at the Castle Tavern. Mr. Hucks was President for a time, but being obliged to leave us, Mr. Holland took his place.

2. A benefaction of 20£ from Dr. Rundal (Since Bi. of Derry) was reported, who promises the like Sum 4 years more to come.

3. We past a By Law for balloting for elections of Members, & for permitting Members who approve not of any resolution to enter his dissent in Writing, without giving his reasons.

4. Mr. Verelts laid before us an Acct. of our Expences Since 9 June last, which amounted to upwards of 6100£ and it appear'd that above 600 persons including Foreigners and others who went over at their own charges were at this time in the Colony.

5. A draft of 150£ made by Mr. Oglethorp was order'd to be paid, and

6. 500£ was imprest to Mr. Heathcote to answer other Bills expected.

7. New Trustees elected this day were
   Thomas Archer Esq
   Henry Archer Esq
   Richd. Coop Esq Director of the South Sea Compy.
   Robt. Ayers Esq. eldst. Son to the Ld. Ch. justice Ayers
   Dr. Rundal Prebd. of Durham, Since Bi. of Derry
   Mr. Talbot, eldest Son to the Ld. Chancellor
   Robt. Tracy Esq.
   Woolaston (Willm.) Esq
   Woolaston (Fra.) Esq

27 March 43.

Bundy, Ri.	C		Heathcote, Sr. Will.	C
Digby, Edwd.	C Ch.		Kendal, Robt.	C
Egmont, E.	C		Lapotre, Hen.	C
Eyles, Fra.	C		LaRoch, Jo.	C P
Hales, Steven	C		Shaftsbury, E.	C

Ld. Tirconnel	C	Burton, Jo.	T
Towers, Tho.	C	Coram, Tho.	T
White, Jo.	C	Towers, Christn.	T
Bedford, Arthr.	T	Wollaston, Will.	T
Belitha, Will.	T		

1. Letters from Mr. Oglethorp dat. 17 Septbr. to the Trustees and Mr. Tho. Towers were read.

2. Letter also from Mr. Causton one of the Bailifs of Savannah, that Since the 1. Embarkation 8 children were born and 33 persons dead.

3. The Widdow Warren who lost her husband and 2 of her children in Georgia, and return'd to England with Mr. Oglethorps recommendation, appear'd, and being poor, most of the gentlemen gave her each a guinea, and told her She Should return to the Colony with her new husband, when we could get him from the Ship on board which he was prest. Her house was converted into an Infirmary at her coming away, but the timber on her lot preserv'd for her remaining Sons use.

4. Resolv'd that any younger child, male or female, Shall on their marriage to any person who has not lands already in Georgia and will covenant to reside there, have a grant of land to descend to their heirs male.

5. Impress made to Mr. Geo. Heathcote of 500£ for the Colonies use.

6. Order given to the Committee of Correspondence to prepare an answer to the letter wrote to us by one Monsr. Dumont a foreigner, wherein he complains of the great inconveniencies and discouragement to persons who would Settle in Georgia by not Suffering females to Inherit. He was to be told, that it was in our power to let females inherit Estates when we thought it proper, and we Should do it in the general, but it would not be convenient to put that matter entirely out of our power by making an order that we would always do it. That our aim was to fix the number of residents in the colony, and if the girls of Parents grew up and marry'd, their husbands Should have lands And as to marry'd women, they by the laws of England Succeed to the Thirds of their husbands estates, and the law is the Same in Georgia.

7. Thanks order'd to the Revd. Mr. Ven for preaching & collecting for us in his Parish 34£.

3 April 44.

Bundy, Ri.	C	Vernon, Ja.	C P
Digby, Edwd.	C	Ayers, Robt.	T
Egmont, E.	C	Coram, Tho.	T
Lapotre, Hen.	C	Rundal, [Thomas]	T
Ld. Tirconnel	C	Smith, Saml.	T
Towers, Tho.	C		

1. Mr. Vernon inform'd us that the Saltsburgers declined going to Georgia: and that the Collectors for their releif, had thereupon agreed to lay out the mony design'd for their use upon Vaudois who Shall be willing to go over. The Trustees therefore resolv'd to Send Monsr. Poyas & 40 of these people now in Holland, and approved of the letter prepared in answer to Mr. Dumont french Minister at Rotterdam, wherein we clear'd up the difficulties objected by him agst. our tenure in Tail male.

2. A letter was produced wrote by Mr. Bofin from Purysburg to Mr. Simons the Mercht. dat. 23 Jany. last, wherein he gives a very advantagious Acct. of the town Savannah, & of other Settlements, and highly commends Mr. Oglethorps application.

6 April. 45.

Chandler, Ri.	C P	Shaftsbury, E.	C	
Digby, Edwd.	C	Ld. Tirconnel	C	
Heathcote, Geo.	C	Towers, Tho.	C	Ch.
Lapotre, Hen.	C	Vernon, Ja.	C	
LaRoch, Jo.	C	Towers, Christn.	T	

1. Half years Sallary due 23 Feb. last to Mr. Verelts, order'd to be pd. him.

10 April 46.

Bundy, Ri.	C	Vernon, Ja.	C
Heathcote, Sr. Will.	C	Burton, Jo.	T
Lapotre, Hen.	C P	Rundal, [Thomas]	T
Ld. Tirconnel	C	Smith, Saml.	T

1. Recd. 5.6.3. for Skins Sold, which were Sent us from Georgia.
2. A Benefaction for Religious uses reported.
3. Commissions granted to 2 Parish Ministers of London to collect for us.

17 May 46.

Frederick, Tho.	C P	Coram, Tho.	T
Wallaston, Will.	T	Smith, Saml.	T
Bedford, Arthr.	T		

1. Benefactions recd. of 71.1.6. & 34£.

22 May 47.

Bundy, Ri.	C	Bedford, Arthr.	T
Chandler, Ri.	C	Coram, Tho.	T
Frederick, Tho.	C	Egmont, E.	C P
Hucks, Robt.	C		

1. Mr. Bedford reported that the Society for promoting Christian Knowledge declined assisting us with money towards the expence of the Vaudois to be Sent over, and that all he could obtain was, that they would take no resolution till Mr. Vernon Should come to town.

2. Monsr. Poyas Conductor of the Vaudois intended to be Sent over, appear'd, and Said he had chosen 40 of them who understood the Silk business as also vine dressing & agriculture, but that they were unwilling to go unless their wives & daughters might Succeed to their Grants as well as their Sons. This occasion'd a debate, and the further consideration thereof put off to the next meeting of Common Council, and in the meantime letters were order'd to be written to Several absent Members for their opinion.

[N.B.] The point insisted on by the Vaudois to alter the Tenure in Tail Male in favour of female Issue caused frequent debates. This day there were none against it but Mr. Hucks & I. We were of opinion that Such alteration in favour of the Vaudois, would create un-easiness in the English and Saltsburgers who went over on the foot of Tale male only, and raise their jealousie that more Should be indulged to the Italians than to them. That when this desire had been exprest on former occasions, we had opposed it upon just apprehension that the female might marry a Man who would not live on the land, wch. of course would remain uncultivated, and Men inhabitants who are the Strength of towns and Countries be lessen'd. That this once obtained, it would be followd by a liberty to Sell, which would make our Grants become a bubble in Exchange Ally. That it was unnecessary the Vaudois

Should insist on it, Since we Should not refuse any particular female her desire when judged reasonable, and for the good of the Colony, but because Such application might Some times be hurtfull it was fit [we] Should re[tain] the power in our own hands. Mr. Chandler Said he doubted if our restraining females from Succeeding is good in law, being contrary to the law of England. To wch. we reply'd that Grants are a gift which may be qualified as agreed on between the Parties, that we were not altering an ancient property, but giving a new one. Capt. Coram and Dr. Bundy Said the Vaudois Seem'd peremptory on this head, & it would be a great pity to lose the opportunity of Sending Such a number of usefull and experienced hands in the Silk trade. That it was no objection to Say that the Inhabitants now in Georgia will expect the Same favour, for it will be necessary to give it to them likewise, or else they will all go away as soon as the years Subsistance allow'd them is out, and the Neighboring Colonies will tempt them to it where the Proprietors have large Tracts of land uncultivated, where on they will give them encouragement to Settle.

We Said the debate must be defer'd we being not a Common Council to resolve the thing, and it would be fit the absent Gentlemen should be acquainted with it, particularly Mr. Digby, Ld. Tirconnel, Towers & Holland who Should be wrote to. Capt. Coram Said, we that are here might agree to it & engage to Support it, but we desired to be excused.

3. Our Secretary acquainted us that Mr. Oglethorp was gone to Charlestown in order to embark for England in feby. last: but twas believed he would return to Georgia to take care of the Saltsburgers just arrived.

29 May 48.

Bundy, Ri.	C	LaRoch, Jo.	C
Chandler, Ri.	C	Towers, Tho.	C P
Egmont, E.	C	Coram, Tho.	T
Frederick, Tho.	C	Page, Jo.	T
Hucks, Robt.	C	Smith, Saml.	T

1. No answer could be made to Monsr. Poyas who attended, concerning female inheritance, because we were not a board of Common Council. But because the poor people were in great want at Rotterdam, we acquainted him they Should have 8£ allow'd them, (being with their wives & children about 50) weekly, till Such time as they Knew the resolution taken therein. NB.

This 8£ weekly allowance was not to be taken out of the Trustees Cash, but out of 50£ given by Ld. Tullamore for Such purposes the Trustees Should judge proper.

2. The debate revived concerning the Vaudois demand that their daughters might inherit. But nothing could be determin'd because we were not a Common Council Board.

[N.B.] Two letters received from Mr. Digby & Ld. Tirconnel, occasioned the revival of the debate mentioned in the foregoing folio concerning the allowing the Vaudois daughters to inherit. The former was much against it, & the latter as Strenuous for it. Mr. Towers opposed it warmly, and fell Severely on Capt. Coram for being the occasion of the dissatisfaction which was risen against the exclusion of female heirs. He told him he was only a Trustee, and ought to [justify?] to the publick as he did in all places a resolution taken upon wise grounds by the Common Council. That we Should hear his opinion at all times with pleasure, but he ought to know himself bound by the decisions of the board. That it was Strange the Vaudois who are banish'd naked out of their Country for Religion Should Scruple to take lands in Georgia on the Same foot as the English and Saltsburgers have done. That our present Grants are only to Settle Inhabitants till a body of laws Shall be made, which very likely may alter the present tenure more to their mind and advantage, but these laws will take time to make and must be well considered, and must also pass the approbation of the King and Council. But to grant what the Vaudois desire, would be giving them Estates absolutely in Fee Simple, which his Majy. & Council might not approve. Nevertheless, Mr. Towers hastily drew up Some further encouragements to be consider'd of at the next Common Council board, and to be Shewn to Monsr. Poyas for his opinion whether that would Satisfy the Vaudois: Such as granting 50 acres of land to the Widow over & above her Thirds of her deceased husbands 50 acres, in case She remarrys a Man who will Settle on it. As also 50 acres to every daughter when She marrys.

7 *June* 49

Bundy, Ri.	C	Towers, Tho.	C
Chandler, Ri.	C	Vernon, Ja.	C
Egmont, E.	C	Bedford, Arthr.	T
Frederick, Tho.	C	Coram, Tho.	T
Heathcote, Geo.	C	Smith, Saml.	T
LaRoch, Jo.	C P & Ch.		

1. The Vaudois having presented a Memorial that exceeded the demands contain'd in the former, as that their lands might descend in Fee Simple on female heirs, together with other articles that if granted would cause a mutiny in the Colony, it was unanimously rejected, and Mr. Poyas civily dismist. Mr. Bedford gave a good character of them out of the Book of Revelations, and desired Something might be done for them. So we order'd them a full months Subsistence at 9£ per week, and that Mr. Poyas's charges of coming & going back Should be paid.

2. We past a grant to Sr. Fra. Bathurst Bt. but he desiring Some alterations in it, it was afterwards cancell'd for a new one.

The Number of Trustee Boards held this 2d Year were 48, and of Common Council 21. The number of days the Gentlemen met on were 49, and the number of times each of them attended were as follows:

Common Councillors		Trustees	
Bundy, Ri.	23	Anderson, Adam	6
Ld. Carpenter	6	Archer, Tho.	0
Chandler, Ri.	12	Archer, Hen.	0
Digby, Edwd.	13	Ayers, Robt	1
Egmont, E.	28	Bedford, Arthr.	10
Eyles, Fra.	4	Belitha, Will.	2
Frederick, Tho.	18	Burton, Jo.	9
Hales, Steven	11	Coop, Ri.	0
Heathcote, Geo.	12	Coram, Tho.	25
Heathcote, Sr. Will.	10	Ld. Darcy, Ja.	0
Holland, Rogers	10	Derby, E., Ja.	0
Hucks, Robt.	28	Gonson, Sr. Jo.	3
Kendal, Robt	8	Page, Jo.	3
Lapotre, Hen.	30	Philips, Erasmus	0
LaRoch, Jo.	23	Rundal, Tho.	2
Ld. Limerick	4	Hanbury, Will.	0
Moore, Robt.	14	Smith, Saml.	39
Oglethorp, Ja.	0	Talbot, Will.	0
Shaftsbury, E.	9	Towers, Christn.	3
Sloper, Will.	5	Tracy, Robt.	0
Ld. Tirconnel	12	Tyrer, Geo.	0
Towers, Tho.	29	Wollaston, Will.	2
Vernon, Ja.	42	Wollaston, Fra.	0
White, Jo.	12		

The Persons Sent this 2d Year at the Trustees charge were 208 Men, 133 Women, in all 341. Which added to 93 men and 59 women Sent the 1st year makes 301 men and 192 women: in all 493.

The Country Lotts granted this year were

	ac.	
In Trust, to be disposed for vilages or particular persons under Mr. Oglethorps direction	2800	11 June 1733
To Thomas Fausset	500	
To Robt. Hethrington	250	4 July 1733
To Theophs. Hethrington	250	
To Patrick Houston	500	1 Aug. 1733
To George Moore	400	
In Trust for the Saltsburgers Township	2500	18 Aug. 1733
To William Sale	300	
To William Terry	200	
To Patrick Tailfer	500	18 Oct. 1733
To Andrew Grant	400	
To John Baillie	400	
To William Stirling	500	
To Hugh Stirling	500	14 Nov. 1733
To James Houston	500	
To Nathl. Polhill	150	21 Nov. 1733
To Joseph Wardrope	150	30 Jany. 1733–4
To James Harlefoot	150	27 Feb. 1733–4
To William Bateman	75	17 March 1733–4
	11025	
Add the Acres granted the 1. year	10460	
Total of 2 years grants	21485	

The Several Embarkations made this year were as follow:

				Males	Females
On the Georgia Pink	Capt. Danbur	—15 June	1733	57	31
Savannah	Capt. Wood	—10 Sept.	1733	73	57
London Mercht.	Capt. Thomas	—21 Sept.	1733	3	2
James	Capt. Yoakly	—28 Sept.	1733	27	21
Purysburg	Capt. Fry	—15 Dec.	1733	45	25

[1734] JOURNAL OF THE EARL OF EGMONT 55

N.B. Of these 40 were Saltsburgers: 2 Germans, the rest English

Hopewell	Capt. Miffant	—28 Dec. 1733	1
Friendship	Capt. Compton	—11 April 1734	2
			205 136

The Number Sent this year on the poor account was 341, which with 152 Sent in 1733 makes 493, of whom males 299 Females 194. In Jany. 1733–4, 40 Irish Transport Servants put in to Savannah harbour in great distress, whom Mr. Oglethorp purchassed, and in April 1733 Six were Sent from England, So that at this time we had 46 Trust Servants in the Province.

1734-1735

Transactions of the 3d Year
from
9 June 1734 to 9 June 1735

19 June 1.

Egmont, E.	C	Lapotre, Hen.	C
Frederick, Tho.	C	Vernon, Ja.	C P
Hucks, Robt.	C	Smith, Saml.	T
LaRoch, Jo.	C		

1. The Accomptant lay'd before us the yearly Acct. of Receipts and disbursments to the 9th June 1734.

[N.B.] By the Annual Acct. of Receipts and disbursments, it appear'd that from the beginning to 9 June 1734 which comprehends 2 years, The Trustees had reciev'd 15226.12.10, and had expended 9117.18.7. So that there remaind in Bank 6108.14.3. But Mr. Oglethorp had drawn on the Trustees bills to the amount of near 5400£, not brought into this Account: So that it became necessary to apply for further assistance from Parliamt.

2. Letter read from Mr. Oglethorp dat. 16 inst. from Cows in the Isle of Wight that he was landed there after 6 weeks passage with the Chiefs of an Indian Nation Settled near Savannah.

21 June. 2.

Chandler, Ri.	C P	Towers, Tho.	C
Egmont, E.	C	Vernon, Ja.	C Ch
Frederick, Tho.	C	Anderson, Adam	T
Heathcote, Geo.	C	Ayers, Robt.	T
Hucks, Robt.	C	Gonston, Sr. Jo.	T
Kendal, Robt.	C	Page, Jo.	T
Lapotre, Hen.	C	Smith, Sam.	T
Oglethorp, Ja.	C		

1. Thanks given to Mr. Oglethorp for his great care and pains in Settling the Colony, and congratulation on his return.

2. The Annual Acct. of Receipts & disbursments to be laid before the Ld. Chancellor &c approved.

[1734] JOURNAL OF THE EARL OF EGMONT 57

3. 5400£ imprest to Mr. Heathcote to answer the bills drawn on us by Mr. Oglethorp for the use of the Colony.

4. Order given to bring Tomachaki and the Indians on Shipboard with him, to our Office & to lodge them there, and that our Housekeeper let not the Mob in to See them, nor take money of Gentlemen who Should come out of curiosity.

[N.B.] The Indians brought by Mr. Oglethorp were Tomachaki chief of the Yamacraws, and his wife, Toonaway his Gr. Nephew, and 5 others, besides an Interpreter. They came to confirm the Treaty made with them & 8 Nations their Allyes last year. And Mr. Oglethorp was willing they Should See the Magnificence wealth and Strength of England. They were very decent in their behaviour, and no less observing of what they Saw. Their Chief was 90 years but as hearty as any Man of 50, and had a good understanding.

This nation consists not of above 50 fighting men, but are a branch of the Creek nation who make above 600. They have lately been much reduced by the Small pox. They are of a revengefull nature, but not apt to be the aggressor, and the reason they give why they revenge themselves is, that they have no law to punish by the magistrats hand. Adultery they punish by cutting off the womans ears and hair, and cutting the mans throat. A theif or coward in battle they banish. They live by hunting when the Season is in, and in the other Season Sow corn. They are So charitable that they cant bear to See another want, & not give him what he desires, and their houses are always open to Strangers.

26 June 3.

Ld. Carpenter	C		Lapotre, Hen.	C
Chandler, Ri.	C	Ch.	LaRoch, Jo.	C
Egmont, E.	C		Oglethorp, Ja.	C
Hucks, Robt.	C		Vernon, Ja.	C
Kendal, Robt.	C			

1. 200 blank Bank forms of Receipt order'd to be printed.

2. Order repeated to bring up the Indians from Graves End to our Office.

3. Order'd that 8 blankets be bought for their bedding.

4. Order'd that the Accompt. apply at the Custom house, that the wine they brought over may be excused paying duty.

3 July 4.

Ld. Carpenter	C	Kendal, Robt.	C
Egmont	C P	Lapotre, Hen.	C
Heathcote, Geo.	C	Vernon, Ja.	C
Hucks, Robt.	C	Ayers, Robt.	T
Hales, Steven	C	Smith, Saml.	T

1. Audience given to the Indians, Tomachachi Spoke in the name of the rest, and I answer'd him.

[N.B.] When we were all Seated, Tomachachi advanc'd to the lower end of the table the rest of the Indians Standing round, and made us a formal Speech, which at proper periods the Interpreter explain'd. He began by excusing himself, if he did not Speak well and to right purpose, for when he was young he neglected the advice of the wise Men, and therefore was ignorant. That he now was old and could not live long, wherefore he desired to See his nation Settled before he died. That the English were good men, and he desired to live with them as good neighbours, for which reason he came over to talk with us, but he would not have done it were it not for Mr. Oglethorps Sake, whom he could trust, and who had used him and his people Kindly. That he thank'd the Great Spirit (at which word he pointed & look'd upward) that had brought him Safe hither, and he hoped would carry him Safe back.

I answer'd him in the Same manner paragraph by paragraph that the Interpreter might explain, That we all had the Same God & fear'd him, that we lived under a good and gracious King, who dos justice to all his Subjects, and will do the Same by his friends & Allyes, as we would do on our parts. That we will look upon their children to be ours, and ours theirs, and Should be ready to hear any proposition they would make when they thought proper. After this, We all rose, and took each of them by the hand, which I Saw delighted them, & then call'd for wine and tobacho to entertain them.

23 July 6.

Bundy, Ri.	C	Hucks, Robt.	C
Ld. Carpenter	C	Lapotre, Hen.	C Ch.
Egmont, E.	C	LaRoch, Jo.	C
Frederick, Tho.	C	Oglethorp, Ja.	C
Hales, Steven	C	Vernon, Ja.	C P

[1734]   JOURNAL OF THE EARL OF EGMONT   59

1. A Memorial drawn up to the Treasury, & Seal put to it representing that our Accompt. had Served us hitherto without a reasonable Sallary, which is out of our ability to give him, and therefore praying their Lordships to confer upon him the place of a Kings Waiter in the Customs when vacant. NB. This was not regarded by them.

2. 1500£ Imprest to Mr. Heathcote, which left us but 400£ in bank.

3. Grant of 100 Acres past to George Brigham.

31 July 7.

Egmont, E.	C	Vernon, Ja.	C
Frederick, Tho.	C P	Smith, Saml.	T
Oglethorp, Ja.	C		

1. Acct. recd. that the Saltsburgers go prosperously on, & have cut a road 5 miles in length from Ebenezar their Settlement to Fort Arguile one of our new towns.

2. Mr. Vernon reported that the Christian Knowledge Society had resolved to Send 50 more Saltsburgers and pay their transportation to Georgia, if we would only give them lands and pay their Minister. Thanks were order'd them, and the consideration thereof refer'd to next Common Council board. The expence of what they offer will come to 2500£.

[N.B.] This month one of these Indians died of the Small pox. Sr. Hans Sloan attended him. He was Cosen to Tomachachi. They Sat up all night bewayling his loss. On this occasion Tomachachi told Mr. Verelts that his Relation was gone to the Great Spirit, that he would See us no more, but he Should See him, and believed he Should be the first.

7 Augst. 8.

Egmont, E.	C P	Ayers, Robt.	T
LaRoch, Jo.	C	Smith, Sam.	T
Vernon, Ja.	C		

1. Mr. Von Reck attended, & offer'd his Service to conduct 50 Saltsburgers to Georgia, which had been wrote for by the Christian Society, and are expected in Six weeks at Rotterdam.

2. One Lownds a half crack brain'd man Sent a proposal for raising a considerable Sum without applying to Parliament, which if hearkend to by the Trust and 8 *p* cent promised him on the

Success thereof, he then would discover his Scheme, but the Board was first to declare their approbation of it. This was very extraordinary to expect we Should approve a Scheme before we knew it. However for his Satisfaction we resolv'd to acquaint the next Common Council board with it.

3. Andreas Gotfred Dietsius a german Gentleman who had got money at Batavia and Settled at Anhalt, being opprest there, attended us to express his desire of going to Georgia with Servants at his own expence. We told him that if he liked our Tenure in Tail male, and would carry 10 Servants, he Should have a grant of 500 Acres, and gave him a form of our grants to consider of.

14 Aug. 9.

Egmont, E.	C	Vernon, Ja.	C
Hucks, Robt.	C	Ayers, Robt.	T
Lapotre, Hen.	C	Smith, Saml.	T
LaRoch, Jo.	C	Towers, Tho.	C
Oglethorp, Ja.	C P		

1. A Representation was read from the Govr. of South Carolina and the assembly, to his Majesty, dat. 9 April last Setting forth the great encroachment of the French at Messasippi, and the danger that Province is in, if not timely assisted by his Majesty, they not having money or men to defend themselves in case of a War with the French, who endeavour to debauch from us the Creek Nation, which if they effect will bring certain ruin on their Province. They also acquaint him with the great protection the Settlement at Georgia gives them, and thank him for his wise & carefull establishment of that Province.

2. We order'd an Application to be prepared to his Majesty for money to Subsist the Indians now here, and to make them presents in order to Secure them to the Interest of Great Britain.

3. Mr. Vernon acquainted us that Monsr. Von Reck was Set out for Germany to bring more Saltsburgers.

[N.B.] The beginnings of this month The King gave audience to The Indians in great form. Tomachachi made him a Speech, and returnd well Satisfied, only he wished his People had been allow'd to dance their War dance, which was the highest compliment they could make. The King order'd them one of his Coaches, and that they Should be treated in the Same manner the 5 Iroquois Chiefs were in Queen Anne's reign. Tomachachi being afterward ask'd what he observed at Court, reply'd, They carry'd him thro a great many houses (by which he meant rooms) to make him believe the Kings Palace consisted of many, but he was Surprised to find he return'd by the Same Stairs he went up, by which he found it was Still but One house. He observed we knew many things his Country men did not, but doubted if we were happier, Since we live worse than they, and they more innocently. After the audience was over, the Queen ask'd for Toonaway, Stroked his face, and told him he must come again to her, for She had a present for him. He answer'd her in English, and was forward in his learning, Mr. Smith of our board taking great pains to instruct him in reading, writing & the principles of Christianity. The Prince presented him with a gun and a gold watch.

The 18th of August, They all paid the A.B. of Canterbury a visit and were extreamly pleased with their reception. They at first apprehended he was a Conjurer, but his behaviour undeceived them. He would have put them Some questions about their religion, but they have a Superstition that Some calamity attends the disclosing their thoughts of those matters, and attributed the death of their companion to their having too freely Spoke thereof Since their arrival. They therefore refused to answer. Nevertheless Tomachachi was So taken with the A. Bishop, that he Said he must come again aloan to talk with him, and added that he now really believed Some good man would be Sent to instruct them and their children. The A. Bishop was So polite that he would not Sit down all the time they were with him, tho so weak as to be Supported on the arms of two Servants, which Tomachachi observing, forebore to make a Speech he had prepared, and Said he would Speak it to his Servants, meaning Some Clergymen who were present.

On the 19th they all dined with me at Charlton. I entertained them wth. dancing, & Musick, made them presents and walk'd them in the wood, which much delighted them as it put them in mind of their own Country. At table I ask'd Tomachachi what dish I Should Serve him? He reply'd, that he [would] eat what ever was Set before him, meaning a civility thereby that he would not refuse any thing I should offer him. They also had the respect not [to] eat when Served until my wife and I had taken the first mouthfull. They had learn'd the way of drinking and bowing to the company, and behaved with much decency, making no noise or interupting any one that Spoke, and the Same is observed by them when they Sit in Council. I presented Tomachachi with a guilt carved Tobacho box, who on receiving it Said, he would get a ribband and hang it at his breast next his heart. At parting, he told me that he came down to See me with a good will, and return'd in friendship. That God above would continue it, and he hoped we would take care to make their children Christians.

21 Aug. 10.

Ld. Carpenter	C		Towers, Tho.	C	
Egmont, E.	C		Vernon, Ja.	C	P
Kendal, Robt.	C		Smith, Saml.	T	
Oglethorp, Ja.	C				

1. Mr. Oglethorp, Towers, and Vernon were desired to have a conference next Fryday with Tomachachi to know of him what are the things he desires of Majesty and us, in order to perfect the Treaty and cement the amity between us.

28 Aug. 11.

Ld. Egmont	C		Towers, Tho.	C	
Hucks, Robt.	C		Vernon, Ja.	C	
Kendal, Robt.	C	P	Ayers, Robt.	T	
LaRoch, Jo.	C		Smith, Saml.	T	
Oglethorp, Ja.	C				

1. The Committee appointed to confer with Tomachachi, reported, that he required two things in behalf of himself and people. 1. That we would make their youths Christians. 2. That we would Settle conditions of Trade. That as to the first: he proposed as the most effectual way, that a youth might be Sent over to instruct his Gr. Nephew Toonaway in our religion, whose example would be follow'd by their own youth. That as to the Second, That we would take care that our people use equal weights, for that they are used to give 12 Ounces to the pound, but at other times but 8. That we would forbid the Selling of Rum. That we would furnish them with English Stockings, garters, Knives, Seizers, needles, thread, brass pots, hatchets, nails, powder, guns, flints, Strong beer and Small &c at Such reasonable rates as they could afford to give, and favour them more than any other nation in the price as being our nearest neighbours. That we would present them with the picture of the Great Lyon they Saw at the Tower, to Set up in a great hall they intended to build. We told them that when there was a Sufficient number of Gentlemen we would take these matters into consideration, which we thought reasonable.

2. I then communicated Mr. Lownd's desire, that if he should offer us a Scheme for gaining a large Sum of mony without assistance of Parliament, he might be rewarded with 8 *p* cent of the money, provided we pursued and effected his Scheme, otherwise he expected nothing. The board unanimously agreed thereto, and orderd he Should be told it.

11 Septembr. 12.

Egmont, E.	C P	Oglethorp, Ja.	C
LaRoch, Jo.	C	Smith, Saml.	T

1. I open'd to the board Mr. Lownds proposal, which was to apply to his Majesty for permission to erect a Lottery in Edinburgh or Some other Town in North Britain. We enter'd it in our Minutes to be considered of by a Common Council board, and noted it to be the first proposal of the Kind, Mr. Lownds So desiring.

2. We past the Evening in conference with the Indians about Settling the weights, measures, goodness, Species and prices of commodities to be traffick'd in, wherein we found them reasonable and Sagacious. They desired there might be but one English dealer to every town, and he to be lycensed, that they might know who to complain of, and be Sure of redress if ill used, for multitude of Traders only bred confusion and misunderstanding. They sayd, when they came over, they expected Mr. Oglethorp would return with them, but Since that could not be, they desired our King would Send over Some gentleman or that one of our board would go, to assure the other nations, that the Word they brought from England was all true, otherwise those Nations would not believe them.

We reply'd that could not be, neither was it necessary, for the Magistrates of Georgia had all the necessary power to make good our agreements, and were obliged to follow our directions, and the Interpreter here present Should go to all those Nations. Mr. Oglethorp added, that if any of our people abused them, and they found no redress, he would go over on purpose to punish the guilty.

They desired the prices of goods might now be Settled, but we told them that could not be done, for what we Shall Send passes thro many hands, before the goods are made, each of whom must be gainers, after which the freight must be consider'd, and the living profit of the Trader who Sells to them. They reply'd their desire was that both Sides might have a living profit. That in England they Saw nothing was done without money, but with them, if they had but two mouthfulls, they gave away one. So that he who Should Sell to them would not be at great charges while Sojourning with them, which they desired we would consider.

Then the Chief Warriour Said he had news the Vice warriour was dead, and had left two daughters helpless and without clothes. That they were become his children, and he wished he was at home to provide for them. That he knew he could not go but by Ships, but were the passage by land, he would make nothing to go on foot tho all the way was thro Woods, and the night as dark as now. We understood this declaration of his love to those children & their wants to be a modest way of begging Some blankets, and therefore promis'd we would give them clothes.

Toonaway also ask'd 6 guns for his brothers. A book lying accidentally on the table, he read tolerably out of it, and afterwards of his own accord repeated the Lords prayer & Apostles Creed.

18 Septbr. 13

Egmont, E.	C	Anderson, Adam	T
Heathcote, Geo.	C	Coram, Tho.	T
Oglethorp, Ja.	C	Smith, Saml.	T
Towers, Tho.	C P		

1. Mr. Tillard, Mr. Newman, and a Clergyman attend us from the Christian Knowledge Society to Know what would be the expence of Sending to Georgia the Saltsburgers they had wrote for. We told them it would cost at least 20£ p head, but refer'd them to Mr. Oglethorp who promised to wait on them to morrow.

25 Septbr. 14.

Egmont, E.	C P	Coram, Tho.	T
Oglethorp, Ja.	C	Smith, Saml.	T
Belitha, Will.	T		

1. A letter was read from Mr. Quincy, that he was on his return from New England to Georgia, where he had been to See his friends. That the New Englands do not deserve the character of being religious hypocrites. That the town of Boston encreases much, having at present 20000 Inhabitants, & of them 600 horse and 7 or 8000 foot fit to defend themselves on occasion.

2. Mr. Newman Secy, to the Society for promoting Christian Knowledge, communicated to us a letter he had received from Mr. Urlespieger Lutheran Pastor at Augsburg, acquainting him that 54 chosen Saltsburgers had enter'd their names to go to Georgia, and were Set out the 23 of this month N.S. for Rotterdam, in order to be Shipt for England, & from hence to joyn their Countrymen in Georgia; & that he had on their Acct. disbursed 1000 florins. Mr. Newman desired from us an Acct. of the expence of Sending those people over, which we promist he Should have next fryday. We also told him that we hoped they would be here next tuesday Sennit in order to embark with the Indians.

2 Octobr. 15.

Egmont, E.	C	Hucks, Robt.	C
Hales, Steven	C	Oglethorp, Ja.	C P
Heathcote, Geo.	C	Vernon, Ja.	C

1. The Accompt. acquainted us that Warrants were gone from the Treasury for his Majesty to Sign. One for repaying us 1500£ we had disburs'd in building & Furnishing Forts for the Security of that part of his Majesties Dominions; and another for 1000£ part whereof 600£ was for the maintenace of the Indians whilst in England, & the remainder to be laid out in presents for them.

7 Octobr. 16.

Egmont, E.	C	Kendal, Robt.	C Ch.
Eyles, Fra.	C	Lapotre, Hen.	C
Hales, Steven	C	Oglethorp, Ja.	C P
Heathcote, Geo.	C	Vernon, Ja.	C

1. Agreed with Mr. Simons the Mercht. to carry 75 persons to Georgia, including the Saltsburgers daily expected from Rotterdam. The Charter party was Sign'd. Each head was to be allow'd ¼ of a Tun for his bagage.

2. Agreed that Hen. Bishop a charity School boy, Should be Sent Apprentice, and Servt. to the Revd. Mr. Boltzius one of the Saltsburg Ministers now in Georgia.

3. Agreed that one Milledge Should have his brothers house in Georgia, the brother having consented thereto till he Should come of age.

4. Resolv'd that the 3 Bailifs of Savannah Shall have each of

them a Servant allow'd at the Trustees Expence because their attendance on the duty of their Office took them off from cultivating their lands.

5. Grant past to Sr. Fra. Bathurst Bt. of 200 acres.
to Bullfinch Lamb of 500 acres
to Andreas Gotfred Dietzius of 500 acres
to Edward Wade 100 acres.

[N.B.] Bullfinch Lamb never went over, and forfeiting his Grant for non-performance of Covenants it was taken from him and declared void 2 June 1736.

Mr. Dietzius went over, but being desirous to Settle at Purysbury obtained leave to Surrender his Grant.

9 Oct. 17.

Egmont, E.	C	Lapotre, Hen.	C
Eyles, Fra.	C P	Oglethorp, Ja.	C
Hales, Steven	C Ch.	Vernon, Ja.	C
Kendal, Robt.	C	Heathcote, Geo.	C

1. Letter of Attorney Sign'd to our Accompt. to receive of the Treasury the 2500£ order'd by his Majesty: but we made the Sum run for 2561. expecting the Clerks and Officers would remit their fees.

2. Agreed with Mr. Simons to leave 6 cannon being 3 pounders for the defence of the Saltsburg Settlement.

3. Direction given for purchasing & Shipping off powder, bullets & Sundry necessarys.

4. Order for defraying the passage back to Georgia of Peter Gordon 1. Bailif, together with his wife & 2 Servants.

5. The Indians attending, to settle with us the prices of Goods that our Traders may not impose on them, we enter'd on that difficult affair, but the Interpreter Musgrove was so drunk we could neither Side understand our meanings. So we left it to Mr. Oglethorp to conclude with them the next day when Musgrove Should be Sober.

[N.B.] Upon enquiry we found the Indians had been much imposed on in their trade, for the Pedlar or Trader who furnished them with English Goods gives no more at Charlestown for a piece of blanketting containing 16 blankets than 80 pounds of leather, yet afterwards makes the Indians pay for that piece 160 pds. of leather, So that he gets cent *p* cent profit including his charges of Sending to Charlestown for the blankets. We therefore taking this into our consideration, enquired of Mr. Simons the Mercht. How low he would take for a piece of blanketting, who Said he would be contented with 75 or 80 pd. of Leather, and deliver them not at Charlestown, but on the Spot in Georgia. We then exposed to Musgrove the Interpreter who is likewise an Indian Trader, that if blanketting were deliverd him on the Spot for 75 or 80 pd. of leather, he ought to be Satisfied with a lower price than 160 pd. of leather *p* piece, or 10 pd. *p* blanket, Seeing his charge of bringing from Carolina would be Saved, as also the risque of rogues running away with his goods in the passage, which case Sometimes happend. He reply'd he then would ask but 144 pd. of leather for a piece, or 9 pd. for one blanket, but at the Same discover'd that the Indian pound is a pd. & half of ours, by which we found that if our Traders were allowed to take but 6 pd. of leather Indian weight for a blanket, the gain would be more yn. Sufficient, for that 6 pd. answering to 9 of ours, by computation they would receive 144 pd. of leather for 16 blankets, which would cost them on the Spot to buy, but 75 pd. The Indians had therefore great reason to complain of hard wage when they were obliged to pay 160 of their pds. which makes 240 English pounds for what cost the Trader but 80 English pound.

16 Octobr. 18.

Egmont, E.	C		Towers, Tho.	C
Eyles, Fra.	C		Vernon, Ja.	C P
Hales, Steven	C		Bedford, Arthr.	T
Hucks, Robt.	C		Smith, Saml.	T
Lapotre, Hen.	C		Heathcote, Geo.	C
Oglethorp, Ja.	C	Ch.		

1. Our Accomptant reported that he had received at the Treasury the 2561£ and paid it into the Bank. That the Fees of the Offices thro which it past came to 140£ but were forgiven by the Several Officers.

2. The Want of a good Interpreter prevented our Setting a tariff of trade with the Indians. But 100£ was order'd to Musgrove for his trouble in coming over with them.

3. A Grant of 2500 acres past for the use of the Saltsburgers now going over.

4. Sign'd the Charter party with Mr. Simons whose Ship is to carry them, to the number of 85 heads inclu. Some others Sent at the Trustees expence.

5. About 1700£ being drawn on us from Georgia part thereof was orderd to be accepted, because we knew the uses to which the Magistrates apply'd it, but the rest was defer'd till further advice.

6. The Unladers of coal in London being opprest by a Set of Alehouse keepers who have erected themselves into a Society and lower their wages, made us a proposal that if we would procure them an act of Parliament to regulate the abuse they complain'd of, they would pay us Such a Sum on every chaldron of coals as would arise to 26000£ p ann, to be apply'd to the Service of our Colony. We took a fortnights time to consider of it.

7. Tho. Causton 3d Bailif of Savannah appointed 2. Bailif in the room of Ri. Hodges deceased.

8. Henry Parker appointed 3. Bailif in the room of Tho. Causton. The Seals put to both.

9. Seal put to the deed of Lease and release of 2500 acres for the use of the Saltsburgers going over, in trust to Peter Gordon, Tho. Causton & Henry Parker and Tho. Christie Recorder.

26 Octobr. 19.

Ld. Carpenter	C		Oglethorp, Ja.	C
Eyles, Fra.	C		Towers, Tho.	C Ch.
Hales, Steven	C	P	Vernon, Ja.	C
Hucks, Robt.	C		Smith, Saml.	T
Lapotre, Hen.	C			

1. Powers Seal'd to Peter Gordon, Tho. Causton, Hen. Parker, & Tho. Christie to Set out Limit & bound the 2500 acres granted for the use of the Saltsburgers & others.

2. John Vatt the Conductor of this new Embarkation of Saltsburgers appointed Secy. for the Saltsburgers under direction of their Ministers, with orders to write to the Trustees from time to time all transactions relating to them. Which NB. he did not obey but neglected. Orderd also that he keep Such accounts and write Such letters as Mr. Tho. Causton the Store keeper at Savannah Shall require.

3. Ordered a Lot in Savannah to him.

[N.B.] On the 31 Octbr. 1734 The Indians Saild for Georgia on board the Princess of Wales Capt. George Dunbar Commander; and with them went 57 Saltsburgers under the conduct of Mr. Vatt a Swiss. There went also on board the Same Ship 27 English. And all happily arrived in December following at Savannah. Peter Gordon 1. Bailif of Savannah return'd with them.

[1734] JOURNAL OF THE EARL OF EGMONT   69

6 Novbr. 20.

Egmont, E.	C		Vernon, [James]	C	
Lapotre, Hen.	C	P			

1. Letter wrote to Mr. Von Reck to Stop the coming over of 100 Moravians, whom he wrote word to the Society for promoting Christian Knowledge were coming over under his conduct to England, in order to be Sent to Georgia. Of this we had no manner of previous notice, nor had he when he left England the least encouragement to do this.

11 Nov. 21.

Ld. Carpenter	C	P	Hucks, Robt.	C	Ch.
Chandler, Ri.	C		Lapotre, Hen.	C	
Bundy, Ri.	C		Vernon, Ja.	C	
Eyles, Fra.	C		Tower, Tho.	C	
Heathcote, Geo.	C				

1. Little business done only an Impress made to Mr. Heathcote. I was prevented attending.

2. Benefactions recd. 100£ collected at Leverpool, and promise of 50£: which was never paid. 42£ from a person unknown. Books for the Saltsburgers.

3. A Present received of 25 buckskins, 1 Tyger Skin and 6 Boufler Skins from Tomachachi to the Trustees.

20 Novbr. 22.

Bundy, Ri.	C		Hucks, Robt.	C	
Ld. Carpenter	C		Oglethorp, Ja.	C	
Egmont, E.	C		Towers, Tho.	C	
Heathcote, Geo.	C		Vernon, Ja.	C	Ch.

1. 50£ gratuity order'd to our Accompt. for his trouble in attending the Indians, and 12.12.0 to our Messenger on the Same account.

2. 400£ imprest to Mr. Heathcote.

27 Novbr. 23.

Egmont, E.	C		Towers, Tho.	C
Holland, Rogers	C	P	Vernon, Ja.	C
Hucks, Robt.	C		Archer, Tho.	T
Oglethorp, Ja.	C		Smith, Saml.	T

1. A letter from Ld. Harrington Secy. of State enclosing another from Mr. Walpole at the Hague was read, importing that 50 families of Swiss were come to Holland with intention to embark for England, in hopes to be sent to Georgia. His Lordship desired to know what Should be done with them. We Sent his Lordship an answer in writing, that they were not Sent for by us, and that when we write for foreigners we take care to condition for them. That however we would do what we could for them if his Majesty Should think fit to Send them to Georgia, and would enable us thereto, we having Spent all our money in the late Embarkations.

2. A letter from Mr. Von Reck was read acquainting us, that on receipt of our letter of 6th inst. he had Stopt the Moravians from coming, in hopes that next Spring we Should have money to transport them to Georgia.

4 Decbr. 24.

Bundy, Ri.	C	Oglethorp, Ja.	C
Holland, Rogers	C	Tower, Tho.	C
Hucks, Robt.	C	Vernon, Ja.	C
Kendal, Robt.	C	Smith, Saml.	T
Lapotre, Hen.	C P		

1. Benefactions reported: 50£ given by Tho. Archer Esq. and 100£ Collected at Leverpool and Preston

2. A Committee appointed to prepare an estimate for building a Church in Savannah.

3. Recommended to the Common Council to order Mr. De Ferrons lot at Highgate to be Sold for the use of the Trust, in consideration of our paying 8£ towards putting out his daughter Apprentice.

11 Decbr. 25.

Bundy, Ri.	C P	LaRoch, Jo.	C
Egmont, E.	C	Oglethorp, Ja.	C
Heathcote, Geo.	C	Towers, Tho.	C
Hucks, Robt.	C	Vernon, Ja.	C
Lapotre, Hen.	C Ch.		

1. Suspended payment of a bill drawn on us by Jenys and Baker of Charlestown for 238.9.8, being drawn at *p* advice, and advice not yet come.

2. Order'd 101.13.4 to Mr. Simons for the freight of 20 heads (one third passengers) on board of the Pr. of Wales: 70£ for the freight of the 8 Indians in the great Cabin, and other expences on that embarkation.

3. Orderd that Mr. Bulfinch Lamb have 500 acres So laid out as that part may bound upon a river, he intending to build Ships.

4. Orderd that 43.13.4 be apply'd out of the money contributed towards Religious uses, for enclosing the glebe for the Minister of Savannah; That Mr. Tho. Causton do See the work done and draw on the Trustees as the work goes on, and that Mr. Quincy do certify each draft what work is done.

5. Order'd that Mr. Quincy do constantly Send us duplicates of the Accounts he Sends to the Society for propagating the Gospel in foreign parts of the State of his Parish: & that he likewise Send us copies of that duplicate by the next Ship.

18 Decbr. 26.

Bundy, Ri.	C	Towers, Tho.	C
Heathcote, Geo.	C P	Vernon, Ja.	C
LaRoch, Jo.	C	Smith, Saml.	T
Oglethorp, Ja.	C		

1. Benefaction of 20£ reported, given towards building a Church.

7 Jany. [1735] 27.

Bundy, Ri.	C	Hucks, Robt.	C P
Ld. Carpenter	C	Lapotre, Hen.	C
Chandler, Ri.	C	LaRoch, Jo.	C
Egmont, E.	C Ch.	Ld. Limerick	C
Eyles, Fra.	C	Oglethorp, Ja.	C
Heathcote, Geo.	C	Vernon, Ja.	C

1. Letters read from Mr. Eveleigh concerning the State of Savannah.

[N.B.] Mr. Eveleigh Mercht. of Charlestown acquainted the Trustees that he had been at Savannah and found 80 houses already built, and 40 more in hand, besides additions making to those that were finish'd. That the houses Set for 15£ Sterling *p* ann, tho they cost but 15£ to build, and the gardens Sat for 20 Shill *p* acre. That the people are in good health, but unneasie they are not allow'd the use of Negroes. That the Lacys and Hethringtons Seated at Thunderbolt have built a Fort Mounted with cannon, and go on Successfully in making pot ash. He advised the building Several Forts, particularly on the South of the River Allatahama; but that River being the Southern boundary of our Province, to build on the South Side thereof was without our Limits. His reason was, that if we built not a Fort there, the Spaniards would, which could not fail of anoying any fort we Should erect on our Side the River, and disturbing the passage of that River. He added that a Spanish Capt. with Soldiers had been Seen thereabouts, probably to observe our proceedings. He advised the bringing more Indians near to Savannah: That he had found out a way to preserve the eggs of the Silkworm. That above 100000 Mulberry trees planted by the Trustees Order were come up. That there is a vast quantity of Masts & crooked timber for building Ships. That Joseph Watson Indian Trader and Partner with Musgrove the Interpreter, had Kept an Indian Warriour belonging to us, in his house, and So ply'd him with drink that he died there, which might prove of dangerous consequence, the Indians alledging he was kill'd by Watson & demanding Satisfaction, which Mr. Causton the eldest Bailif at that time on the Spot was unwilling Speedily to give them, being desirous he Should first be heard and proceeded against according to the law of England. This affair gave much trouble to the Magistrates of Savannah and to the Trustees.

2. Agreement made with Capt. Thompson of the Two Brothers, for transporting to Purysburg 200 Swiss & German Protestants at the Kings expence, he having orderd 1200£ for that Service at the request of the gentlemen concern'd in Settling that Plantation in South Carolina. He was pleased that our Board Should take the care of their embarkation. This mony was only to be a loan, and was to be repaid as the poor people Should be able: and when repaid it was to be employ'd in establishing an English School in Purysburg under our direction. But Soon after his Majy. determin'd to lend but 600, So that but 112 persons could be Sent, of whom there were now arrived about 80, & the rest every day expected.

3. John Roberts Esq. laying claim to a Barony consisting of 12000 acres within the Province of Georgia, Sent the Trustees a memorial of his case. Upon which we drew up reasons to Shew that his pretentions were entirely groundless.

4. Ten Moravian brethren appear'd, desiring to go to Georgia: They are Subjects to Ct. Zinzendorf a nobleman of that persuasion, and his Steward came over wth. them to See them embark'd.

[1735] JOURNAL OF THE EARL OF EGMONT 73

They are to be follow'd by more. We promis'd their Master Should have a Grant of 500 acres, and their Minister a garden and Plot to build on in Savannah. And that for their encouragement, when they had improved their masters land, or were out of their time, they Should have a Grant of 20 acres each. That they Should go over when the Swiss did.

5. Mr. Chardon the Mercht. at Charlestown's Accts. and letter accompanying them were read. The former were refer'd to the Committee of Accts. to examine, and the letter to the Committee of Correspondence to answer.

6. Impress of 400£ made to Mr. Heathcote, So that now we have left but 300£ to carry on our designs, 3 benefactions excepted which came in this day, viz. from the Dean & Chapter of Westminster 20£, from John Temple Esq. 10.10.0, and from Mr. Watts 50£.

9 Jany. 28.

Bundy, Ri.	C	Vernon, Ja.	C
Eyles, Fra.	C	Coram, Tho.	T
Lapotre, Hen.	C	Rundle, Tho.	T
Moore, Robt.	C	Smith, Saml.	T
Oglethorp, Ja.	C	Talbot, Will.	T
Sloper, Will.	C P		

[No entry]

10 Jany. 29.

Bundy, Ri.	C	Moore, Robt.	C
Ld. Carpenter	C Ch.	Oglethorp, Ja.	C
Lapotre, Hen.	C	Sloper, Will.	C
LaRoch, Jo.	C	Vernon, Ja.	C
Kendal, Robt.	C		

1. Grant past to Nics. Lewis Ct. Zinzendorf of 500 acres.
2. Grant made to David Nitchman one of his Moravians of a town lot in Savannah.
3. A Committee of Trustees appointed to take care of the Embarkation.

15 Jany. 30.

Bundy, Ri.	C	Chandler, Ri.	C
Ld. Carpenter	C	Egmont, E.	C

Eyles, Fra.	C	LaRoch, Jo.	C P
Heathcote, Geo.	C	Moore, Robt.	C
Heathcote, Sr. Will.	C	Oglethorp, Ja.	C Ch.
Holland, Rogers	C	Ld. Tirconnel	C
Hucks, Robt.	C	Vernon, Ja.	C
Digby, Edwd.	C	White, Jo.	C

1. Some Benefactions reported.

2. A debate about petitioning the Lords of the Treasury for grant us the Office they now meet in, when the New office is built: resolv'd not to proceed therein.

3. The Same Mr. Lown'ds formerly mention'd made a new proposal to discover us a project whereby we might raise a large Sum in present and annually for the Service of the Colony, without expence to the publick but to its great advantage, for which he demanded 6 p cent of the money if put in execution & it Should prove effectual. Orderd at his desire that Mr. Oglethorp, Sloper, Vernon & I discourse him thereon.

4. Mr. Oglethorp inform'd the board that the Swiss design'd for Purysburg on his Majesties loan to them, made three objections to the terms on which they were to go. 1. That they liked not to be bound one for tother for repayment of the money. 2. That they liked not the double penalty of their bond, a form they were unacquainted with. 3. That it was too hard to pay 10 p cent Intst. when the English Interest is but 5 p cent. We resolv'd to make them easie as to the 1st objection and to take their Single bonds. That they Should be told as to the Second, that becoming Subjects of England, they must comply with the form used by Englishmen. And lastly as to the third, that the Interest they were to pay was Carolina money, and to be recover'd if necessity obliged by the laws of that Province, which constraind us to follow the Interest established there. On this occasion we Suspended Signing the Charter party for their passage till we knew their further resolution.

21 Jany. 31.

Ld. Carpenter	C	Hucks, Robt.	C
Digby, Edwd.	C	Moore, Robt.	C
Egmont, E.	C P & Ch.	Ld. Tirconnel	C
Heathcote, Geo.	C	White, Jo.	C
Heathcote, Sr. Will.	C		

[1735]   JOURNAL OF THE EARL OF EGMONT   75

1. Our Cash being almost all expended, and divers benefactions being made not for the general but particular uses of the Colony, We orderd a Ledger after the Italian manner to be added to our Acct. Books that it might readily appear what Sums were recd. for particular purposes in order to prevent the misapplication thereof to other purposes than those for which they were given.

2. His Majesty having resolved to lend the Swiss and Grisons but 600£ instead of 1200£ he at first intended, We were obliged to reduce the number intended to be Sent, & this day Sign'd the charter party for transporting 87, the difficulties they objected to being removed. Afterwards they amounted to 112, which with Ten Moravians who went on board the Same Ship at their own expence (but whose passage we advanced to be repaid) made 122 Souls and 100 heads.

3. Letter of Attorney given to our Accompt. to receive at the Treasury the 600£ above mention'd.

[N.B.] On the 23d Jany. 1734–5 The 122 foreigners mention'd on the other Side Set Sail for Savannah on board the Two Brothers Capt. Thompson Master.

29 Jany. 32.

Ld. Carpenter	C	P	Shaftsbury, E.	C	
Egmont, E.	C		Ld. Tirconnel	C	
Lapotre, Hen.	C		Smith, Saml.	T	

1. Report made of the Shipping 122 foreign Protestants making 100 heads.

5 Feby. 33.

Bundy, Ri.	C		Ld. Limerick	C	
Ld. Carpenter	C		Oglethorp, Ja.	C	
Chandler, Ri.	C		Shaftsbury, E.	C	
Digby, Edwd.	C	Ch.	Ld. Tirconnel	C	
Egmont, E.	C		Towers, Tho.	C	P
Hales, Steven	C		Vernon, Ja.	C	
Heathcote, Sr. Will.	C		Coram, Tho.	T	
Holland, Rogers	C		Smith, Saml.	T	
Lapotre, Hen.	C		Tracy, Robt.	T	
LaRoch, Jo.	C				

1. Resolv'd that all the members of the Common Council be of the Committee of Accts.

2. Mr. Oglethorp deliverd his Acct. of Receipts & disbursmts. for the Service of the Colony, which were refer'd to a Committee to examine.

3. Power given to a Parish to collect money.

4. Dr. Bundy excused his not preaching the next Anniversary Sermon, but promised to procure another Clergyman in his Stead, and he hoped to engage Dr. Thomas.

5. Capt. Coram moved that a day might be appointed to consider the expediency of excluding heirs female from Succeeding to lands, but he was not Seconded. Mr. Oglethorp & Mr. Vernon Strongly Set forth the inconveniencies That would arise from it in the infant State of the Colony.

6. Mr. Oglethorp read a Short account of the present condition of the Colony, but being imperfect, it was return'd to him to finish.

12 feby. 34.

Egmont, E.	C	Ld. Limerick	C
Hucks, Robt.	C	Ld. Tirconnel	C
LaRoch, Jo.	C P	Vernon, Ja.	C

1. A Duplicate of Bailif Caustons accts. being arrived, was refer'd to a Committee to report on.

2. A letter to Mr. Hucks from an Inhabitant of Georgia was read which gave a good Acct. of the Colony.

19 Feby. 35.

Egmont, E.	C	Ld. Limerick	C P
Heathcote, Sr. Will.	C	Oglethorp, Ja.	C
Hucks, Robt.	C	Ld. Tirconnel	C
Lapotre, Hen.	C	Smith, Saml.	T
LaRoch, Jo.	C		

1. Appointed a Committee to draw up a petition to Parliamt. for a Supply of money.

26 Feby. 36.

Digby, Edwd.	C	Holland, Rogers	C
Egmont, E.	C P	Hucks, Robt.	C
Heathcote, Geo.	C	LaRoch, Jo.	C
Heathcote, Sr. Will.	C	Ld. Limerick	C

[1735]   JOURNAL OF THE EARL OF EGMONT   77

Moore, Robt.	C		Towers, Tho.	C
Oglethorp, Ja.	C		Vernon, Ja.	C
Shaftsbury, E.	C	Ch.	Anderson, Adam	T
Sloper, Will.	C		Ayers, Robt.	T
Ld. Tirconnel	C		Smith, Saml.	T

1. The Seal put to our petition to Parliament for money.
2. Mr. Fury Agent for Carolina attended, to desire our Board would favour that Province in promoting the passing of a bill this Session for prolonging the time, for their exporting of Rice without calling at England, as also for extending their trade to the French Dutch & Spanish Settlements in America. We reply'd in writing, that we Should always contribute our endeavours for advancing the Interest of Carolina.
3. Some letters recieved from Georgia & Carolina giving an acct. of the State of the Colony, together with a book of the Proceedings of the Court of Justice at Savannah, were refer'd to the Committee of Correspondence.
4. Imprest 600£ lately recieved from his Majesty for the use of the Swiss Sent to Purysburg, to Mr. Heathcote, he having advanced the Same.

5 March 37.

Bundy, Ri.	C		Ld. Limerick	C
Egmont, E.	C		Moore, Robt.	C
Eyles, Fra.	C		Oglethorp, Ja.	C
Heathcote, Geo.	C	P	Shaftsbury, E.	C
Holland, Rogs.	C		Ld. Tirconnel	C
Hucks, Robt.	C		Vernon, Ja.	C
Lapotre, Hen.	C		Smith, Saml.	T
LaRoch, Jo.	C			

1. Some alterations were thought proper to be made to our petition to Parliamt. and order'd that the Seal be put there to tomorrow.
2. Advice recieved by letter from Capt. Dunbar to Mr. Simons the Mercht. that he arrived with the Indians and Saltsburgers at Savannah in 50 days passage, & that he was but 39 days between land and land.
3. The Committee of Correspondence reported their remarks and heads of answers to the Bailifs of Savannah upon their Accts and letters.

4. Mr. Oglethorp Shew'd us an estimate of Expences by him drawn up, on which to ground our demands of a further Supply from Parliament. The whole demand is 25800£ for which he proposes to erect 2 Forts of 80 men each, and 18 Forts of 40 Men each, to be built on the banks of a certain river in Such a manner as to defend the County of Savannah, from incursions or Spaniards by land.

5. He told us also that the French Govr. of Mobile had wrote to Govr. Johnson of South Carolina, demanding Satisfaction for his harbouring 2 Deserters, otherwise that he would march and take Satisfaction himself. That the Government only Knew this, and it is not to be Spoken of.

[N.B.] On the 10th March 1734–5 Mr. Oglethorp presented our petition to Parliament. Sir Orlands Bridgman Seconded it, and the House refer'd it without any difficulty to the Committee of Supply.

12 March 38.

Ld. Carpenter	C	Ld. Limerick	C	
Digby, Edwd.	C	Vernon, Ja.	C	P
Egmont, E.	C	Smith, Saml.	T	

1. Very little done this day, The Members of our board who are of the house of Commons attending the Committee of Supply, which Sits this day.

17 March 39.

Bundy, Ri.	C	Hucks, Robt.	C	
Ld. Carpenter	C	Lapotre, Hen.	C	Ch.
Digby, Edwd.	C	Oglethorp, Ja.	C	
Egmont, E.	C	Shaftsbury, E.	C	
Heathcote, Geo.	C	Sloper, Will.	C	
Heathcote, Sr. Will.	C	Ld. Tirconnel	C	
Holland, Rogers	C	Vernon, Ja.	C	

1. An Answer agreed on to a letter lately recieved from Mr. Causton 2d Bailif of Savannah. And orders issued to all the Magistrates to take from Joseph Watson his Lycense for trading with the Indians, and to confine him as a lunatick, till having recover'd his Senses, he Should be brought to tryal for drinking to death Skea an Indian Warriour, which he first gave out he would do, and afterwards glory'd in.

2. Order'd a present to the Relations of Skea to pacify their resentment.

3. Order'd amends to be made Mrs. Watson for the loss of one Justus her Servt.

4. 50£ order'd to the Accompt. and 50£ to the Secrety. for their Services.

[N.B.] 17 March 1734-5. The Committee of Supply voted 26000£ for the Colony of Georgia.

About this time the Government being under apprehension at the danger our Colony's are in from the Strong Settlements of the French at Messasippi, prest Mr. Oglethorp to accept the Goverment of South Carolina, which he refused, but offer'd to go over and undertake the defence of Carolina and Georgia, if the power of the militia of both Provinces were given him, which now is in Mr. Johnson the Govr. of South Carolina's hands. For his Majesty when he granted our Charter reserved to himself the appointing the chief Military Officer in Georgia, and had given it to the Govr. of South Carolina.

26 *March* 41.

Egmont, E.	C	Ch.	Sloper, Will.	C
Holland, Rogers	C		Ld. Tirconnel	C P
Hucks, Robt.	C		Towers, Tho.	C
LaRoch, Jo.	C		Vernon, Ja.	C
Oglethorp, Ja.	C		Belitha, Will.	T
Shaftsbury, E.	C		Smith, Saml.	T

1. Benefactions reported: Collections at Several Churches amounting to 27£ at St. Andrews Holburn 134.14.0. and a clock and dyal for the Church of Savannah valued at 40£ presented by Mr. Tuckwell.

2. Order'd an extract of Capt. Dunbars letter to Mr. Simon to be printed in order to prevent the ill impression false accounts of the Colony may make on the people.

3. An application from 26 Protestants & their families Natives of Carinthia and under popish persecution was read, desiring to be transported to Georgia.

4. Also was read an application from a number of french Protestants of Languedock retreated to Geneva desiring to be Sent over.

5. Also was read a Memorial from Ct. Zinzendorf presented us by his agent here desiring more of his people might go over at their own charges, We advancing them 500£ to be repaid in time.

These and other matters were refer'd to future consideration, it being necessary in the first place to determine the disposal of the 26000£ given us by Parliamt.

31 March 42.

Bundy, Ri.	C	Sloper, Will.	C
Chandler, Ri.	C	Towers, Tho.	C
Egmont, E.	C	Vernon, Ja.	C
Oglethorp, Ja.	C		

1. The Summons was for a Common Council to consider and order the application of the 26000£ given us by Parliamt. but not beg. a board, we could only give our opinions thereon: and we agreed that it would be necessary 1. To Set a part 3000£ to answer bills drawn upon us not yet paid. And 2. 4000£ to defray the expences of person now in Georgia on the charity account, who must be Supply'd out of our Stores, & to answer presents to and entertainment of Indians & Strangers for the year to come. And 3. 300£ for building Churches.

2. We also approved a proposal made by Ct. Zinzendorf's Agent for lending money to 55 heads of his people whom he is desirous to Send to Georgia. We had before lent him 60£ to Send the 10 Moravians who went before, and upon making that Sum up 500£ he offers to Send 55 whole heads more. The mony to be repaid in 5 years time, and he to bring them to Rotterdam, and maintain them in Georgia, and their freight to be deducted out of the 440£ by us to be lent.

2 April 43.

Egmont, E.	C	Shaftsbury, E.	C
Heathcote, Sr. Will.	C P	Sloper, Will.	C
Hucks, Robt.	C	Vernon, Ja.	C
LaRoch, Jo.	C	Smith, Saml.	T
Oglethorp, Ja.	C Ch.		

1. Commissions given to 2 Parishes in London to Collect.
2. The Memorial of Ct. Zinzendorf mentioned last meeting agreed to.

5 April 44.

Holland, Rogers	C	Kendal, Robt.	C
Hucks, Robt.	C P	Lapotre, Hen.	C

[1735] JOURNAL OF THE EARL OF EGMONT 81

Oglethorp, Ja.	C	Vernon, Ja.	C
Ld. Tirconnel	C	White, Jo.	C
Towers, Tho.	C		

1. This was neither a board of Trustees nor Common Council, but a Committee that met to consider how to appropriate the 26000£ given by Parliamt. to particular uses. And they resolved it to be their opinion
   1. To reserve for paymt. of bills out Standing £3000.0.0
   2. To reserve for the further Support of the people in Georgia   4000.0.0
   3. To apply for 3 ten oard boats, wages & victualling of men at 227.8.7 each   682.5.9
   4. For purchasse of Said boats at 29£ each   87.0.0
   5. To apply for 50 Rangers on horseback, who drive up cattel, kill deer & open communications   1159.8.8
   6. To apply for 100 working Men to cut roads & fortify at 50 Shill. each man p month   1200.0.0
   7. To an Agent to bring men from Switzerland   150.0.0
   8. To an Agent to bring men from Germany   150.0.0
   9. For Presents to the Indians to purchasse lands   1000.0.0
   10. For Building Churches in Georgia   175.5.7
       12800.0.0

   Remainder of the 26000 not yet adjusted   13200.0.0

2. Mr. Martin our Secretary acquainted us, that Sr. Tho. Lomb Aldn. of London the great Organizer of Silk, had recieved the 30 pound of Raw Silk Sent us from Georgia, and had promised to organize it at his Mill at Derby without expence, in order to our weaving it into a Suit to present the Queen. Sr. Thomas added that tis as good raw Silk as ever he had Seen, and that considering how cheap we can aford it from Georgia, we may not only beat out the Italian Silk, but even Send Silk thither. That if we could procure the China Silk worm, it were of all the best, because the Silk they produce never changes its colour.

9 April 45.

Ld. Carpenter	C		Hucks, Robt.	C
Digby, Edwd.	C		Lapotre, Hen.	C
Egmont, E.	C	P	Smith, Saml.	T

1. Sign'd a Commission to the Minister of St. Gyle's Parish to collect.

16 April 46.

Ld. Carpenter	C	Oglethorp, Ja.	C
Egmont, E.	C	Shaftsbury, E.	C
Hales, Steven	C	Ld. Tirconnel	C
Holland, Rogs.	C P	Towers, Tho.	C
Hucks, Robt.	C Ch.	Vernon, Ja.	C
Kendal, Robt.	C	White, Jo.	C
LaRoch, Jo.	C	Smith, Saml.	T
Ld. Limerick	C		

1. The petition of Thomas Pratt newly come over from Georgia desiring permission to Sell his lot to Mrs. Bovey, was refer'd to a Committee.
2. One Littel whose Son died in Georgia, came to complain that Willm. Littel his Grandson was unjustly kept out of his fathers house & Lot in Savannah. Order that all the justice Shall be done him the Law will allow.
3. Refer'd Mr. Chardons Accts. to a Committee to examine & make a report.
4. Order'd that instructions be Sent to the Magistrates of Savannah, to enquire whether any Guardians have been appointed by the Will of Willm. Littel Senr. deceased at Savannah, and if not to assign Saml. Mercer for Guardian to Willm. Littel junr. an Orphan. That the Rent of the house must in the first place be apply'd to the childs maintenance, and the residue thereof to the improvment of his Lot.
5. Other directions given relating to personal Estates.
6. Refer'd to Mr. Oglethorp, Mr. Holland & Mr. Tho. Towers to consider of proper grants to be made of Glebes for the Ministers of Savannah.

23 April 47.

Bundy, Ri.	C	Sloper, Will.	C Ch.
Egmont, E.	C	Ld. Tirconnel	C
Heathcote, Sr. Will.	C	Towers, Tho.	C
Holland, Rogers	C	Vernon, Ja.	C
Kendal, Robt.	C	White, Jo.	C
Oglethorp, Ja.	C	Bedford, Arthr.	T
Shaftsbury, E.	C P	Smith, Saml.	T

1. It appearing that Tho. Prat return'd from Georgia without Lycense, we rejected his petition for leave to Sell his lot, and de-

clared it forfeited for not abyding by the condition of his Grant; and then order'd it to Mrs. Bovey.

2. Three laws, the 1. for maintaining Peace with the Indians of Georgia; the 2. for preventing the importation of Rum and Strong liquours into the Province; and the 3d for prohibiting the use of Negroes there, having been approved and past by his Majesty and Council, the Same were order'd to be printed.

3. Order'd 1000 weight of copper farthings for Georgia.

4. Agreed to the proposal of George Lewis Wentz to bring from Germany 100 protestant Servants, at 4 Shill. a head for himself, and 4 Shillgs. a head to the Captn. who Shall bring them over from Rotterdam. And to pay him at Setting out 20£, 20£ more at Worms, 20£ at Cologne, 20£ at Rotterdam, and 20£ for the Captain in case he brings 100 Servants, otherwise as has been Said 4 Shillgs. per head for as many as he brings.

5. Refer'd to Mr. Holland and Mr. Towers to prepare a Sumptuary law agst. wearing gold or Silver in aparel, or using it in furniture & equipage in Georgia.

6. Also to prepare an act for obliging Ships that clear out of Savannah River to pay a pound of pistol gunpowder p Tun duty.

7. Mr. Oglethorp acquainted us that this morning he had in the house offer'd a clause in the Carolina Rice Act to declare Savannah a Port town, and that the house had received it.

30 April 48.

Bundy, Ri.	C	Towers, Tho.	C
Egmont, E.	C	Vernon, Ja.	C
Heathcote, Sr. Will.	C	Page, Jo.	T
Oglethorp, Ja.	C	Smith, Saml.	T
Ld. Tirconnel	C	Lapotre, Hen.	C P

1. Letters read of an intended insurrection Supprest, wherein divers of the Inhabitants were concern'd, to murder the rest, plunder their goods, and carry their wives & children to the next Spanish Settlement Fort Augustine; and that the Magistrates had committed Some of them to prison. That Robert Parker junr., Earl Piercy Hill, Joseph Watson who was to be try'd for killing Skea the Indian and others were of the number. We order'd they Should be detain'd, till a Special commission was Sent to try them.

2. A letter from Elisha Dobré was read, complaining that Tho. Causton Bailif had used him ill, that he endeavour'd to monopolize the trade, and would make Strange Accompts up.

3. Informations Sent the Trustees that Tho. Christie the Recorder retails Rum, tho the Trustees had forbid the use of it.

4. Complaints from Amatis the Silkman were read against our publick Gardiner Joseph Fitzwalter.

5. A long letter was wrote to the Magistrates touching these matters.

6. Benefactions recd. 100£ for the Saltsburgers use from an unknown hand. 5£ from Mr. Askew for the general uses of the Colony, & 40.8.6 collected in a Parish of the City of London.

7. A Reward of 20£ order'd to Mrs. Musgrove the Interpreters wife for her Service in preserving the Indians friendship to us.

8. Order'd that the Magistrates & their Servants Shall be Subsisted one year longer out of the Publick Stores, as a reasonable encouragement to them for the loss in cultivating their land, by reason of their attendance in the publick affairs of the Colony.

5 May 49.

Egmont, E.	C P	Lapotre, Hen.	C	
Eyles, Fra.	C	Oglethorp, Ja.	C	
Hales, Steven	C	Ld. Tirconnel	C	
Heathcote, Geo.	C	Vernon, Ja.	C	Ch.
Holland, Rogers	C	Anderson, Adam	T	
Hucks, Robt.	C	Bedford, Arthr.	T	
Heathcote, Sr. Will.	C	Smith, Saml.	T	

1. Several new letters from Elisha Dobre were read, giving acct. of his improvments in raising divers Sorts of fruit trees &c and of his taking the lots of Several people to improve on. Order'd a letter in answer to his former letters, and exhortation to pay due obedience to the Civil Power.

2. Several persons admitted to go to Georgia and take up land.

3. Grant past to Margt. Bovey of Tho. Pratt's late Lot in Savannah.

4. Order given for Shipping on board the James, Yoakly commander who is Speedily to Sail for Georgia, 300£ weight of gunpowder for the use of the Province.

5. New agreement made with Geo. Lewis Wentz for bringing over 100 German Servants, at 20 Shill. *p* head for all who are above 16 years old, and as many of them as can be, to be Batchellors. We order'd he Should have 20£ in hand, and 20£ at Worms, Cologn, and Rotterdam. The remaining 20£ to be kept in our

[1735] JOURNAL OF THE EARL OF EGMONT 85

hands to pay the Captn. who brings them from Rotterdam to England. He is to be here with them in July next.

7 *May* 50.

Egmont, E.	C		Shaftsbury, E.	C Ch.
Heathcote, Sr. Will.	C		Towers, Tho.	C
Holland, Rogers	C	P	Vernon, Ja.	C
Lapotre, Hen.	C		Smith, Saml.	T
Oglethorp, Ja.	C			

1. Mr. John Tuckwell who presented us with a Dyal & clock for a Church, presented a Memorial that he and Two others might have a lycense to furnish the Colony with Iron ware, linnens, blankets &c. We let him know it could not now be consider'd. We Suspected his design was to obtain an exclusive lycense.

2. Being inform'd that Peter Gordon 1. Bailif of Savannah a conceited unsteady Man, and favourer of the malecontents in the Colony, was again return'd to England, We orderd he Should attend the board next Satturday.

3. A Committee appointed to meet next Satturday afternoon to consider of furnishing the Colony with meal from Pensilvanea.

4. The Articles of agreement with Mr. Wents for bringing over German Servants Sign'd.

5. Bedding order'd for the foreign Servants and English passengers now going over with Capt. Yoakly.

10 May 51.

Bundy, Ri.	C	Ld. Limerick	C Ch.
Ld. Carpenter		Oglethorp, Ja.	C
Heathcote, Sr. Will.	C	Towers, Tho.	C
Holland, Rogrs.	C	Vernon, Ja.	C
Lapotre, Hen.	C		

1. Peter Gordon attended as he was order'd, and deliver'd a Memorial against Mr. Causton the 2d Bailif, as also Several Letters from particular Inhabitants of Georgia complaining of that magistrates conduct & behaviour.

2. Seal put to the Indenture of Trust Servants, who with other passengers are to Sail the 14th inst.

[N.B.] On 14 May 1735 Capt. Yoakly of the James, Saild for Georgia with 30 passengers, viz. 15 Males and 15 females, of whom

18 were Trust Servants besides their 6 children. Of these Trust Servants 3 men were English; the rest were germans. 29 of the 30 went on the Trust acct.

21 May 52.

Ld. Carpenter	C	Ld. Tirconnel	C
Egmont, E.	C P	Coram, Tho.	T
Hucks, Robt.	C	Smith, Saml.	T
Oglethorp, Ja.	C		

1. Order'd that application be made to the Treasury for payment of the 26000£ given us by Parliament.

2. Mr. Case Billingsley attended with a proposal for raising a large Sum of money for the Service of our Colony, provided we would agree to give him half the proffits thereof, but refused to tell us his Scheme, unless we previously agreed to give him that allowance. We appointed him to come again fryday next when we hoped to be a fuller board, our number at present not being Sufficient to resolve any thing on that head.

3. John Brown Esq, a young gentleman of 25 years having ran out his fortune of 400£ *p* ann & his wifes portion of 1500£ apply'd by a friend this day to have a Grant of land in Georgia, and to go over at his own expence.

23 May 53.

Ld. Carpenter	C	Lapotre, Hen.	C Ch.
Frederick, Tho.	C	Ld. Limerick	C
Heathcote, Geo.	C	Oglethorp, Ja.	C
Heathcote, Sr. Will.	C	Shaftsbury, E.	C
Hucks, Robt.	C	Ld. Tirconnel	C
Kendal, Robt.	C	Towers, Tho.	C

1. The Accompt. reported that by the muster taken on board the James Capt. Yoakly 14th inst. the Passengers on board were 29 on acct of the Trustees, making 23 heads 2 thirds, and 1 Servant belonging to Mr. Ri. Mellichamp in Georgia.

2. Seal put to more Indentures of Servants.

3. Report made from the Committee for Settling the providing of provisions in Pensilvanea for the use of this last embarkation.

4. Order'd the purchasse of ½ Tun of halfpence at the Tower for the use of the Colony at 10.14.0 *p* C pound weight.

4 June. 54.

Bundy, Ric.	C	Oglethorp, Ja.	C P
Egmont	C	Smith, Sam.	T

1. Some persons minuted down for town Lots.
2. We digested a particular of the conditions on which Several Classes of Persons shall be sent to Georgia, to be laid before a board of Common Council for their consideration.

[N.B.] The Number of Trustee Boards held this 3d Year were 48, & of Common Council 26. The Number of days the Gentlemen met upon were 54: and the number of times each of them attended were as follows:

Common Counsellors		Trustees	
Bundy, Ri.	19	Anderson, Adam	5
Ld. Carpenter	21	Archer, Tho.	2
Chandler, Ri.	8	Archer, Hen.	1
Digby, Edwd.	8	Ayers, Robt.	7
Egmont	46	Bedford, Arthr.	3
Eyles, Fra.	10	Belitha, Will.	2
Frederick, Tho.	5	Burton, Jo.	1
Hales, Steven	10	Coram, Tho.	6
Heathcote, Geo.	18	Coop, Ri.	0
Heathcote, Sr. Will.	13	Derby	0
Holland, Rogers	15	Gonson, Sr. John	1
Hucks, Robt.	33	Hanbury, Will.	0
Kendal, Robt.	13	Page, Jo.	2
Lapotre, Hen.	30	Philips, Erasmus	0
LaRoch, Jo.	22	Rundal, Tho.	1
Ld. Limerick	11	Smith, Saml.	34
Moore, Robt.	6	Talbot, Will.	2
Oglethorp, Ja.	43	Towers, Christn.	1
Shaftsbury	11	Tracy, Robt.	1
Sloper, Will.	9	Tyrer, Geo.	0
Ld. Tirconnel	18	Wollaston, Will.	0
Towers, Tho.	25	Wollaston, Fra.	0
Vernon, Ja.	44		
White, Jo.	6		

The Persons Sent this year at the Trustees charge to Settle in Georgia, were 54 Males & 27 females, which with 301 males, &

192 females Sent the foregoing years make the full number of 355 males and 219 females: in all 574. These are exclusive of Trust Servants & others who went over on their own Acct. or joyn'd the colony.

The Country Grants past this year were

	ac	
To George Brigham	100	23 July 1734
To Sr. Fra. Bathurst, Bt.	200	7 Oct. 1734
To Bullfinch Lamb	500	7 Oct. 1734
To Andrew Godfret Dietzius	500	7 Oct. 1734
To Edward Wade	100	7 Oct. 1734
For the Saltsburgers, a further grant	2500	16 Oct. 1734
To Ct. Zinzendorf	500	18 Jan. 1734–5
	4400	
Add the acres granted the 1 & 2 years	21885	
Total of 3 years Grants	25885	

By the 3d Years Accompt of Receipts and Disbursments, it appeard The Trustees had recieved on various Accts. 5416.7.7 which added to 15226.12.10 Received the 2 years before made 20643.0.5. And that they had expended 10396.12.9½, which added to 9117.18.7 expended the 2 years before made 1914.11.4½. So that there remaind in Bank 1128.9.0½. But it is to be noted that at the making up this 3d years Acct. there was depending on Several persons in America to Accompt. There remain'd 797.16.4½ to be deducted out of the 1128.9.10½, which reduced the money remaining in Bank to 330.12.8, exclusive of the 26000£ granted this year by Parliamt., which is not brought into this years Acct. because not yet recieved.

Abstract of the 3d Years Accts. of Receipts & Disbursments endg. 9 June 1735

CHARGE

To Cash depending to be accompted for on the determination of last years Acct. endg. 9 June 1734: Being the value of Bills of Exchange

[1735] JOURNAL OF THE EARL OF EGMONT 89

drawn on the Trust by Mr. Oglethorp for defraying charges in America, and accompted for & discharged in this Accompt	2269.16. 0
To Cash remaining unapply'd 9 June 1734. viz. For establishing the Colony 5852.18.7 For the Religious uses of the Colony 207.15.8 For encouraging Botany and agriculture 48. 0.0	6108.14. 3
To Cash in Sterlg. mony, the amount of private Collections made in South Carolina, together wth. the Rum Duty	464.18. 2
To Do. Recd. for 2 barrils of Rice Sent from Georgia	7. 1. 6
To Do. Recd. at the Treasury on Acct. of the Indians brought over	2561. 0. 0
To Do. Recd. his Majesties loan to the Swiss Sent to Purysburg	600. 0. 0
To Do. Recd. by Collections made & voluntary Gifts for the general uses of the Colony	922.17.11
To Do. Recd. the Consideration mony of Grants past	5. 5. 0
To Do. Recd. of the Society for promoting Christian Knowledge, For Sending over and Settling 57 Saltsburgers under the care of Mr. Valt October 1734	748.19. 0
To Do. Recd. to be apply'd to Religious uses	46.16. 0
To Do. Recd. to be apply'd to Bottony & Agriculture	59.10. 0
Total	13794.17.10

DISCHARGE
Disbursments in England

By a Sealing Press, and Charges of Commissions to collect Benefactions	4. 6. 6
By Stationary Ware and printing	18. 7. 2
By Charges of Sending 81 persons on the Charity Acct. viz. 58 foreign Protestant & 23 British, as follows: viz.	

For Stores, Working tools, accessaries and passage	240. 1. 6½	
For Refreshmts & 3 months provision after arrival	296.19. 2	
For Ordenance, munition, Accoutremts & cloathing	119.19. 5	1173. 2. 2½
For Watchcoats and bedding for the passengers	66.11. 0	
For freight & charge of Shipping Said passengers	449.11. 1	
By Charge of Sending Servants to Georgia		36.10. 1
By Charge of passage and necessarys for 122 Grisons and Swiss Sent to Georgia and Purysburg		600. 0. 0
By Further assistance to 18 of them, Moravians		10. 0. 0
By Disbursmt. on Acct. of Vaudois who came to Rotterdam to be transported to Georgia, but did not go		48.12. 0
By Freight and charges on Commodities rec'd from Georgia		6. 6. 1½
By House Rent for the Trustees Office, necessaries for the House, & incident Charges		93. 1. 9
By Wages to the Messenger & Housekeeper, Rewards to Several people on the Embarkations, and other Services for the Trust, and for extraordinary Clerkship		189.19. 8
By Charges on Acct. of the Indians & their Interpreter	723. 1.5	1145.18. 6
And disburst. for presents for their nations	422.17.1	
Total of Disbursmts. in England		3326. 4. 0

Disbursments in America

By Charges in debarking Passengers & Goods in Georgia	100. 2.10¼
By Charges of Surveying and Setting out land	116.13. 4½
By Provision for the Inhabitants from 30 Jany. 1732 to 22 June 1734	2342.12. 4½

[1735] JOURNAL OF THE EARL OF EGMONT 91

By Live Cattel for the use of the Colony	273.18. 7¾	
By Stores, working tools & necessaries for the Colony, besides what Sent from England	537. 5. 1½	
By General Works in the Colony, fortifying, clearing ground, buildg. a Storehouse, a beacon, & fencing a publick garden	621.11. 0	
By Charges of Servants in Georgia	220. 0. 7½	
By Ordenance, amunition, cloathing purchass'd in Georgia	297.17. 1¾	
By Presents to Indians purchass'd in Georgia & othr. charges	658. 8. 3¾	
By Charge of the Compy. Sent to build & garison a Fort in the Creek Nation	518. 6. 7½	
By Incident charges disburst in Georgia	209.11. 2¼	
By rewards of Sundry Sorts, for labour, takg. outlaws &c	342.14.10	
By Disbursments for the production of raw Silk	202.11. 2	
		6945. 0. 6¼
By Money advanc'd persons to Set up their callings &c to be repaid to the Trust	271.14. 7½ ⎫	
By Mony advanc'd persons on acct. of further Supply of the Colony, for wch. they are accomptbl. to the Trust	2689.18. 0 ⎬	3067.12. 4½
By ½ Tun of farthings Sent to Bailif Causton for wch. he is accomptable to the Trust	106. 0. 0 ⎭	
By Charge of building a Tabernacle for Divine Service, a house for the Minister, and payling in his garden &c.		50. 8. 3¼
By Pd. the ½ years Sallary of		

Robt. Millar Botanist to Lady day 1735		75. 0. 0
Total of Disbursmts. in America		10138. 1. 2
Disbursmts. in England		3326. 4. 0
Total of disbursmts. in England & America the year endg. 9 June 1735		13464. 5. 2
Money remaining		
For Bottany	32.10. 0	
For Religious Uses	204. 3. 4½	330.12. 8
For the general Uses of ye Colony	93.19. 3¼	

1735-1736

Transactions of the 4th Year from 9th June 1735 to 9 June 1736

11 June. 1

Egmont	C	Towers, Tho.	C P
Oglethorp, Ja.	C	Smith, Saml.	T

1. Some proceedings made in the Rules to Serve this present year, for Sending persons to Georgia.

13 June. 2.

Egmont	C	Oglethorp, Ja.	C
Hales, Steven	C P	Towers, Tho.	C
Holland, Rogers	C	Anderson, Adam	T
Lapotre, Hen	C	Smith, Saml.	T

1. Letter of Attorney given our Accomptant to recieve at the Treasury the 20000£ granted by Parliamt.

2. Benefaction reported for 50£ for the conversion of Indians in Georgia.

3. Persons named for receiving Benefactions towards building Churches in Georgia.

4. Order that Mr. Wells furnish the Trustees with 40 pieces of blanketing, each of 30 yards.

5. Proceeded in finishing the conditions & Rules on which persons Shall be admitted to go to Georgia to form a new town & new Vilages, and orderd that Such persons as are desirous to go over be acquainted therewith.

6. Mr. Case Billingsley attended to acquaint us with his proposal and Scheme for improving the Colony. And he desiring that We would enter into agreement with him before he communicated it to give him 15 p cent of the clear profits arrising from it, on which condition he offer'd to lay out 600£ of his own money to commence it, and also to give him 5 p ct. more in case his own charges in prossecuting the affair, employ'd the 15 p ct. to him reserved, We left it by his consent to Mr. Towers to draw up such an agreement as might secure both Parties.

7. Capt. Dunbar return'd 2 days ago gave us this day a very Satisfactory Acct. of Georgia.

[N.B.] 13 June 1735. Tho. Gapan Butcher at Savannah wrote to the Trustees a description of Arguile Island, and the adjacent land, and proposed the fixing a Cow Pen there where Cattel would daily improve in goodness, the meat Sweeter, and the Colony might have a constant Supply without the assistance of Carolina; For there was naturally fine grass and a good honeysuckle bottom, with plenty of fresh water for ponds. Hogs might also be bred in great numbers there, and at Small charge, the land bearing mostly Oak and hickery trees, wth. abundance of Chinkampen Trees whose nutts are the most delightfull food the hogs feed on.

[N.B.] 20 June 1735. Mr. Robt. Miller our Botonist wrote us from Jamaica that he had found the Balsom Capivi tree and Ipicurna plant at Ayapel in the Province of Antiochia on the river St. George. And the balsom Tolu Tree at Coloso 40 leagues distant from Gegua. He gave us a description of them, and how managed, and doubted not their Suceeding in Georgia, the natural heat where they grow, Seldom exceeding 45 degrees. But he willed the proper Season for collecting the plants and Seeds.

25 June. 3.

Ld. Carpenter	C		Hucks, Robt.	C
Egmont	C	Ch.	Lapotre, Hen.	C P
Frederick, Tho	C		LaRoch, Jo.	C
Hales, Steven	C		Oglethorp, Ja.	C
Heathcote, Geo.	C		Towers, Tho.	C
Holland, Rogers	C		Vernon, Ja.	C

1. Benefactions reported.
2. Mr. Billingsley was dismist, and his proposal rejected, he having added a clause at the End of it unknown to Mr. Towers who drew up the Articles intended to be Sign'd by both Parties, which clause imported that We Should not recieve other proposals, in case his Should be found impracticable, or refused by us when he disclosed his Scheme. Besides, Mr. Heathcote, LaRoch, Vernon and others said it was a disreputation to treat with him on any foot, So bad was his character.
3. Proceeded on the Rules for Sending persons on the poor Acct and refer'd it to a Committee to conclude them.
4. An Embarkation voted, design'd for a new Town and Fort on the mouth of the River Allatahama the Southern Boundary of our Province.

[N.B.] 28 June 1735. Mr. Quincy wrote the Trustees that Noble Jones the Surveyor had run out the whole 300 acres appointed for Religious uses on Pine barren land lying on the road from Savannah to Highgate, not worth the fencing, tho Mr. Oglethorp had shewn him better land. At this time news arrived that Mr. Johnson, Govr. of South Carolina, was dead. The Govermt. was offer'd to Mr. Oglethorp, but he absolutely refused to accept it.

[N.B.] On the 30th this month Mr. Causton wrote that thro heat of the Season and for want of rain the people would be dissappointed of their Crop, and that they were afflicted with Fevers, agues and Fluxes, of which Some were dead, but many more recover'd.

2 July. 4.

Bundy, Ri.	C P	LaRoch, Jo.	C	
Egmont	C	Oglethorp, Ja.	C	Ch.
Hales, Steven	C	Towers, Tho.	C	
Hucks, Robt.	C	Vernon, Ja.	C	
Lapotre, Hen.	C	Smith, Saml.	T	

1. Benefactions reported: 50£ from Mrs Hungerford for the relief of persecuted Protestants. 5.5.0. for converting the Indians, & a parcel of Bamboo Seed from Govr. Adams.

2. Report of the receipt at the Treasury of the 26000£ granted by Parliament and that the Several Offices had given their Fees, amounting to near 700£.

3. The Rules for those who go to Settle on the poor Acct. agreed on.

4. A Tun of halfpence value 215£ order'd to be bought at the Tower to add to the half Tun formerly Sent.

5. Order'd the building a ten oard canoa boat, another of 8 Oares, & a third of Six oares for the use of the Colony.

6. Rules approved of for Such as go over to the Colony at their own charge, and orderd both these and the Rules for those who go on the poor Acct. to be printed.

7. Impress to Mr. Heathcote of 5258.7.8 to answer bills drawn upon us from Georgia.

8. Impress to Mr. Heathcote of 2000£ more to answer divers expences already made by him, and to be made for the next embarkation.

9. Mr. Lapotre offer'd a paper in favour of the daughters of persons Sent over, explaining to the Publick what shall be done

for them, in case their Fathers & brothers die. Dr. Bundy and I Spoke for it, as necessary to pacify the clamour of Many who think we act unjustly in excluding females from Succeeding to their Fathers estates. But Mr. Towers, Oglethorp and Vernon opposing it, and the rest Seeming to be of their mind, nothing was done in it.

[N.B.] The Arguments urged by the Gentlemen against making any alteration in the Tenure of lands were, That it was unfit the Trustees Should bind themselves down to give daughters a right to Succeed, because many cases might arise full of perplexity, So that it would be difficult to make one general Rule to Serve all. That our Grants are gifts & favours which may be made on what terms we please, and no man who accepts them on the present foot has reason to complain. That the Trustees will always do what is right, and the people Should have confidence in us. That we have already declared in our Rules that Special regard Shall be had of daughters, which is Sufficient to Satisfy the world on that head, and Should we be more explicite, the general welfare of the Colony might Suffer by it by dispeopling it, For persons not inhabiting the Colony might marry Such daughters. That we know our own minds, that if Such daughters marry persons approved of by us who will Settle on the fathers grant, we Shall give it anew to her and her husband and her heirs male, Or we will Sell the Estate to one who will reside, and give the daughter the profit.

10. Will. Kilberry Commander of our Sloops in Georgia being dead, 50£ was order'd to his wife for his 10 months service.

11. Order to the Accompt. to make an estimate of what money will probably be required to maintain the Colony as it Stands at present, that we may know when that Sum and the Several drafts already made out of our 26000 are deducted, How much will be left for Settling the New County, and Town design'd forthwith at the Mouth of the Allatahama.

12. Advice reciev'd that Mr. Quincy has again left Savannah & is gone to Charlestown. He has long appeard unfit for his Employmt. He is in League with the Malecontents of our Province, and writes us no account of himself, of the place, or of the performance of his duty, tho require of him both when he went over, and frequently Since by letter, So that he seems to Slight us, and not value his cure.

[N.B.] 5. July. A letter of this date inform'd us of the State of the Publick Garden, and that 4 Servants there would be necessary, 2 of whom to water the plants. He complains of Fitzwalter the publick Gardiner and of Mr. Causton and threatens if not redrest to leave the Colony. This was wrote by Paul Amatis.

[N.B.] 6 July. Noble Jones Set forth his Services to Mr. Oglethorp, a copy of which was Sent us. But the people made great complaints of his neglecting to lay out their Lands, and afterwards we dismist him from being Surveyor.

[N.B.] 7 July. By a letter from the above Paul Amatis dat. 30 June with a Postscript of this days date, he continues his complaint of Causton, and hints he will make up bad Accts and Says further that he had taken the Trust Servants out of the Publick garden under pretence of working at the Crane, but employ'd them in making pitch & Tar for his own & Compy. use. That we may depend that if the Silk Manufacture be encouraged it will do extreamly well, but that Some Small additional is required as it advances, and without money he could do nothing. That he would not concieve we will Suffer So beneficial an Undertaking and which has So great a prospect to fail for want of our countenance, encouragement and Supply of money. He adds that he is upon leaving the Colony & going to Purysubr on acct. of Causton's ill usage of him. That if he Stayd he should want 30000 bricks to build a Fabrick in the manner as is done in Italy.

[N.B.] 7 July. Letter of this date from Elisha Dobree, complaining of Mr. Caustons turning him out from being employ'd in the Stores, and offering himself to be a Commissionr. to examine into the Store accounts and management of the publick money, and he would undertake to find Caustons Accts. neither exact or true.

[N.B.] 8 July. Another letter from the Same, giving acct. of Several persons dead, the place being at this time very sickly; Also that 16 Indian Traders had been at Savannah to take out Lycenses.

9 July. 5.

Egmont	C	Towers, Tho.	C
Lapotre, [Henry]	C	Smith, Saml.	T
Oglethorp, [James]	C		

1. We could not make a Common Council, and we had no Trustee business to do: But as a Committee of Embarkation we drew up Several directions for buying Shoes, and Swords, printing advertisments &c and prepared instructions to Capt. Mackay and Capt. Dunbar to furnish us with 100 Highlanders to go over and Settle in the South.

16 July. 6.

Bundy, Ri.	C	Oglethorp, Ja.	C
Egmont	C	Towers, Tho.	C Ch.
Frederick, Tho.	C	Vernon, Ja.	C
Hales, Steven	C	Anderson, Adam	T
Lapotre, Hen.	C	Smith, Saml.	T
LaRoch, Jo.	C		

1. Letters recd. from Bailif Causton complaining of Bailif Gordon now in England, and informing that there will be 500 acres this year under corn.

2. Journal received of Mr. Macoys expedition to the Ugeeky, Creek and other Indian nations to Settle amity with them.

3. Letter recd. from Mr. Miller gardiner at Chelsea, that his namesake our Botanist had found at Cartagena the true Balsam Cavivi, & Ipicuana roots.

4. Order for acquainting Sr. Hans Sloan therewith.

5. Order'd the ¼ Sallary due to the Botanist Midsummer last be paid him.

6. A project of issuing Sola Bills for the Service of the Colony was entirely approved: but a difficulty arising whether the Act of Parliament allows any Corporation but the Bank to issue notes, we order'd that Corporation Should be apply'd to, to know if they had any objection thereto. It was hoped that as our bills were only designed for Georgia and to be issued there, they are not prohibited by the act.

7. A bill for 200£ drawn by Mr. Causton accepted.

8. A Town lot ordered to Archibald Macgilivray.

9. Resolv'd to advance the Christian Knowledge Society the money necessary for bringing persecuted Protestants from Germany to Rotterdam, they promising to repay us.

10. Order'd 10£ gratuity to each of the 2 Bailifs now in Savannah, 40£ to the Storekeeper, and 10£ to each of the Constables.

11. Order'd a Register book for the use of the Register in Georgia to incert all Grants made.

12. Instructions and powers Seal'd to Capt. Hugh Mackay to procure 100 Highland Men, 50 wives and children, & 10 male Servants to Settle on the Allatahama, with an allowance to him of 20 Shillgs. *p* man for engaging and marching them to the Ship that carry's them over. Agreed also that 40 English men with their wives and children be Sent. Agreed also that 100 Carinthians and

Austrians including their wives & children be Sent, being persecuted Protestants. Agreed also that Mr. Wents be wrote to, not to bring over more than 80 Palatins, design'd for Servants. Agreed also that 28 Swiss and Grison Servants be Sent, with 11 wives and 4 children. Agreed also that 40 Moravians with 15 wives & children be Sent.

13. Resolv'd that 600 double Sighted guns be bought for the Indians, being part of the presents intended to be made them.

14. Order'd a letter to Coll. Bull Who acts as Deputy Govr. of South Carolina till a Govr. is appointed, to desire him to purchasse for the use of our Colony 4 or 500 Cows.

23 July. 7

Hucks, Robt.	C	Vernon, Ja.	C
Lapotre, Hen.	C	Anderson, Adm.	T
Oglethorp, Ja.	C	Smith, Sam.	T
Towers, Tho.	C		

1. Number Settled of English to be Sent over, viz. 24 Men, 19 Women, 16 boys, 11 girls in all 40 Males & 30 females making 58 heads ⅓. But room was left to Send a few more.

2. Recd. a quartr. of a hundred of Bark from Georgia by Capt. Dunbar.

24 July. 8.

Egmont	C	LaRoch, Jo.	C	
Hales, Steven	C	Oglethorp, Ja.	C	
Hucks, Robt.	C	Towers, Tho.	C	
Kendal, Robt.	C	Vernon, Ja.	C	Ch.
Lapotre, Hen.	C			

1. Mr. Towers reported that the Bank made no objection to our issuing Georgia bills in Georgia to the value of 4000£ provided we alter'd the word *Note* to *bills of Exchange*.

2. Orderd that Bills of Exchange issuable in Georgia to the value of 4000£ be made, payable in England 30 days after Sight viz. 500£ in 20 Shillg. bills, 1000£ in 40 Shillg. bills, 500£ in 5£ bills, 1000£ in 10£ bills, and 1000£ in 20£ bills. In all 1250 bills.

3. Mr. Oglethorp acquainted the Trustees that he intended to go over with this embarkation.

4. Order'd that application be made to the Treasury, for leave

to Send over with Mr. Oglethorp 1000£ in Shillings and Sixpences to circulate 1000£ in bills, part of the above 4000£.

5. Order'd a petition to be prepared to her Majesty in Council for allowing our new intended Settlement at Frederica Some Cannon from the Ordenance Store.

6. Order'd the Surveyor of Georgia Noble Jones to make a Report what land has been taken up in pursuance of the respective Grants made, and how far the Same have been cultivated.

7. Order'd that a Register book, a case of Mathematical Instruments, and a Spirit Level be provided for the Survey of Georgia.

8. Order'd that a bill of Mr. Chardons for 200£ brought for acceptance, be not yet accepted, there being more than that Sum due to as from him, he having overcharged us.

9. Grant of 500 acres past to Lieut. Hugh Mackay.

10. Grant past to William Woodrope of 50 acres who likewise goes over on his own account.

[N.B.] 24 July. Mr. Amatis wrote his Satisfaction that the Sample of Silk Sent by him was So much approved, and he defied the Fabricators of Piedmont to produce better than he was able to do. That if we resolved to go on in improving Raw Silk, and to have the Silk drawn and prepared in the best manner, it would cost Some money. But in about 2 years the Mulberry Trees would be in the greatest forwardness, and in that time would be Seen the effects of Industry. That then most if not all the families in the Province would be Supply'd with as many Trees as would be necessary for them, and old and young, Small and great reap the pleasure gathering & improving the raw Silk. That the Trees & plants in the garden encreast prodigiously.

[N.B.] 30 July 1735. The Trustees petition'd the Queen and Council for Ordenance, which was refer'd to the board of trade 14 Augst. following, who made no Report thereon.

31 July. 9

Egmont	C	Oglethorp, Ja.	C
Hales, Steven	C P	Lapotre, Hen.	C
Hucks, Robt.	C	Towers, Tho.	C

1. Seal put to the Memorial to the Treasury, for his Majesties lycense to Ship off for Georgia 1000£ in Shillings & sixpences.

2. Seal also put to the Indentures made with the Trust Servants who go tomorrow to Georgia on board the Georgia Pink Capt. Danbur. These were Grisons.

[N.B.] Regularly the Common Council, and not the Trustee board, Should have put the Seal to the Trust Servants Indentures, but the time So prest that we could not Stay for a Common Council board.

6 *Augst.* 10.

Egmont	C		Oglethorp, Ja.	C
Hales, Steven	C		Towers, Tho.	C
Lapotre, Hen.	C	P	Vernon, Ja.	C
LaRoch, Jo.	C			

1. The Grisons to whom we Seald Indentures the last meeting appeard and Scrupled Some of the conditions on which they were to go Servants. The principal objection was that their wives were not to have lands. We told them we Should do by them as by others but could not break Settled Rules. 10 of them including their 4 children were contented, and embark this night. Others were not. We promis'd them 5 acres in present, and 15 more when their time of Service is expired, or Sooner if possible, and that their tools Should be given them at the expiration of their Service.

[N.B.] On the 6th August 1735 embarked on board the Georgia Pink Capt. Danbur 15 Males & 12 females, in all 27 of whom 10 were Trust Servants including their 4 children: these were Grisons. About the same month Capt. Dicker of the Allen, carry'd 12 persons from Bristol.

13 *Aug.* 11

Bundy, Ri.	C	P	LaRoch, Jo.	C
Ld. Carpenter	C		Oglethorp, Ja.	C
Egmont	C		Towers, Tho.	C
Frederick, Tho.	C		Vernon, Ja.	C
Hales, Steven	C		Anderson, Adam	T
Hucks, Robt.	C		Smith, Saml.	T
Lapotre, Hen.	C	Ch.		

1. Resolv'd that a Town Court & Civil Judicature be erected for the new Settlement on the Allatahama, that it be in the Same form as the Town of Savannah, and that the new Town bear the name of Frederica in honour of the Prince if he will approve it.

2. Petition of Peter Gordon 1. Bailif read, desiring leave to Sell his lands town lot and cattel in Georgia, being determined to remain in England & not return. We order'd the accompt. to tell

him we Should consider upon it, till Mr. Oglethorp was return'd to Georgia and had enquired into his behaviour. That he had behaved ill in returning again to England without our permission, had encouraged the faction there by countenancing complaints against the Magistracy, and that it was of ill consequence to let people Sell their Grants, who by their voluntary absence had forfeited them. That as 1 Magistrate he ought to have Staid in the Province to discharge his duty.

3. John Bromfeild appointed Register of the Province during pleasure, and to take no other Fees for the Grants enter'd in his Office than what the Trustees Shall order.

4. The Resolutions of the Committees of Accts. 15 feb. 1734 and 21 July 1735 were reported and approved.

5. Resolved that Agreement be made with Mr. Simons the Mercht. to furnish the Colony with 650 barrils of beef, & 200 firkins of butter from Cork.

6. Report of the Muster made on board the Georgia Pink Capt. Danbur, that there embark'd 17 persons making 13 heads & ½ and 10 persons making 7 heads ⅓d.

7. Order for preparing a Charter Party with the Princess of Wales Capt. Dunbar to carry over 130 heads from Scotland.

8. Imprest 3000£ to Mr. Heathcote for the charges of Embarkations.

9. Accompts received from Paul Amatis the Silk man, together with complaints against Bailif Causton. Order'd to defer payment of his bills drawn on us till Mr. Oglethorp arrive in Georgia.

10. Grant ordd. to Mrs. Mary Pember of 50 acres to her & her heirs male, being a lot in Savannah purchassed by her of a person who had left the Colony. N.B. She afterwards marry'd Sr. Fra. Bathurst.

11. Grant also order'd of 10000 Acres for the County of Frederica.

12. Order'd also that Tho. Proctor, Jo. Bromfeild, and Samuel Perkins be Trustees to receive the Same in behalf of the people to whom they are to be divided.

[N.B.] This 13 August 1735 Sr. Tho. Lomb Aldn. of London carry'd the Silk received from Georgia to her Majesty, and took her direction how She would have it work'd up into a Suit of Cloathes for her. She appear'd much pleased with it, and Sr. Thomas declared to her that he prefer'd it to the Piedmontese Silk in every respect, and particularly that it has less wast.

[N.B.] 15 Aug. Paul Amatis wrote word that all differences with him were reconciled, and he hoped we Should hear of no more complaints from him. That he intended the latter end of Jany. to go to England to acquaint us himself in relation to the raw Silk, and that there was no doubt of meeting with Success in it and to the utmost perfection, as well as in any part of the Universe. That he expected in the Fall to give the Freeholders many thousand fine Mulberry Trees to be transplanted, while they improve their land for that purpose.

[N.B.] 20 Aug. Mr. Quincy Minister at Savannah desired we would appoint him a Successor his wife not inclining to leave England & go to him. His letter contain'd Suggestions against Causton.

[N.B.] About last June, Patrick Tailfer (a proud busie fellow) wrote a long letter for the introduction of Negroes into the Colony, which arrived 27 Aug. 1735.

27 Aug. 12.

Egmont	C		Oglethorp, Ja.	C
Hucks, Robt.	C		Anderson, Adam	T
Lapotre, Hen.	C	P	Bedford, Arthr.	T
LaRoch, Jo.	C		Smith, Saml.	T

1. The years accts. endg. 9 June 1735 (See in the last year) Settled in order to be presented to the Ld. Chancellor &c.

2. Letters recd. giving a good Acct. of proceedings in Georgia.

3. The talk with the Upper Creek Indians Sent us wrote on the Inside of a buffaloe Skin. It gives a curious Acct. of the traditional history of those nations, which Says they came originally out of the Earth, and they end thus: *Some Men may have more knowledge than others, but let them remember the Strong and the weak must one day become dirt alike.* They acknowledge Tomachachi to be of their nation, and of the ancient Line, and promise to do the Same by Toonoway his Gr. Nephew when he Succeeds him.

3 Sept. 13.

Bundy, Ri.	C	Ch.	LaRoch, Jo.	C
Egmont	C		Oglethorp, Ja.	C
Hales, Steven	C		Towers, Tho.	C
Heathcote, Geo.	C		Bedford, Arthr.	T
Hucks, Robt.	C		Burton, Jo.	T
Lapotre, Hen.	C		Smith, Saml.	T

1. A Review of 40 families design'd to be Sent on the charitable Account this Embarkation, of whom there are about 46 Men.

2. The Scots Settled at Josephs Town having apply'd for liberty to use Negroes, we Shew'd them the Act which his Majesty was pleased to pass whereby they are prohibited.

3. Then they apply'd that their Settlement might be independent of Savannah, and that they might have a Court of Record of their own, and 3 Bailifs to rule for one year and annually descend according to Seniority. This was debated, but at lenght refused, it not being thought proper to errect petty Independent Goverments in the Colony. None but Mr. Oglethorp were for it.

3. Officers appointed for executing that part of the Carolina Rice act which gives Georgia liberty to export it. John Fallowfeild made Collector, Bailif Causton Comptroller, Jo. Vanderplank Searcher, & John Bromfeild the Register Naval Officer.

4. Resolv'd that Tho. Causton Bailif and Jo. Vanderplank be appointed Officers to put the Act in execution for preventing the importation and drinking Rum.

5. Resolv'd that the Constables for the time being be the Officers to put the Negro Act in execution.

6. Resolv'd that Mr. Oglethorp be the Commissioner for putting the Act in execution for maintaining Peace with the Indians.

7. Resolv'd that Austin Weddal be appointed Treasurer for the Indian Affairs.

8. Thomas Causton promoted to be 1. Bailif in Peter Gordons room; Henry Parker promoted to be 2d Bailif, and John Dearn made 3d Bailif.

9. Application from the Scots of Josephs town above mention'd to be given 2 years provision: the Same was refused, not being granted to any who went over on their own Acct. except the Lacys Settled at Thunderbolt who were the first who went at their own expence & were a frontier garison, which obliged them to avocation from their private affairs, than others.

10. Order past for granting Lots to the Scots Settlers at Josephs town.

11. Mr. Eveleigh Sent over timber from Georgia to be Sold in London, and this being the first venture of that traffick from our Province we order'd for his encouragement that the freight Should be Set down to the Trustees acct.

12. Agreed to a proposal made by Will. Bradley to cultivate 100 acres of Trust lands within one year, allowing him the use of

30 Trust Servants, conditionally that the Trustees will maintain him 10 more Servants to cultivate his own land for one year, and the Said 10 Servants to remain afterwards his own Servants. Conditionally also that he be paid 100£ out of the produce of the 100 Acres of Trust land cultivated by the 30 Trust Servants under his direction, or what is made of the corn as far as 100£ if it yeilds So much, but no more than what the corn yeilds, if it Should happen the corn did not yeild 100£ So that he Stands the hazard. And the 100£ is not to be made good to him out of the future crops of the land. He was also obliged to teach the Inhabitants how to cultivate their lands. On this foot the Trustees agreed with him, and order'd a Writing to be drawn up pursuant there to and mutually Sign'd.

13. The Seal put to the Grant of 10000 Acres for the new Province Frederica.

14. Power granted to Mr. Oglethorp to Set out limit and divide them.

15. Seal put to the lease & release of the Said 10000 Acres, in Trust to John Bromfeild, Saml. Perkins & Tho. Proctor.

16. Power granted Mr. Oglethorp to give Such orders as he thinks fit for granting and disposing lands.

17. Also power given him to grant lycenses under his hand and Seal to persons to depart the Colony. The Seal was put to all these.

18. The Power of the Militia granted Mr. Oglethorp, to which the Seal was also put.

19. Two bills of 30£ and 24£ drawn on the Trust by Amatis the Silk Man were refused acceptance, he not having a power to draw.

20. Bill of Bailif Causton drawn on the Trustees for 174£ disburst for cattel, were orderd to be paid.

21. Report made by the Accompt. of the State of our Coll: that 9350£ had been imprest for Services in Georgia Since 9 June 1734 to 5 May 1735. That there 1379.11.0 private Benefactions. That there had been contributed and recieved from 9 June 1734 to 9 June 1735 4951.9.5. That on the 9 June 1734 there remain'd unapply'd in the Bank 6108.14.3, and on the 9 June 1735 a Ballance in our hands of 330.12.8.

22. Grants past to the Scots Settlers at Josephs Town, viz.
    500 acres to Patrick Mackay, Esq.
    500 acres to John Mackay, Esq.
    500 acres to Capt. Geo. Dunbar

500 acres to Jo. Cuthbert
500 acres to Tho. Baillie
50 acres to Archibald Macgilvray.

[N.B.] 10 Sept. Mr. Samuel Eveleigh wrote our Secy. word that he had left Georgia to Settle again at Charlestown, being disappointed in his expectations, which was to be allow'd the use of Negroes, without which our Colony can never be of great consequence. That Lumber cost him there (being cut by white men) 4 times as much as if he had taken it in Carolina. That there is in Georgia great quantity of Rice land, but only Negroes can undergo that labour. That he went to See the Island of Ossebaw about 40 miles to the South of Savannah, where he saw a vast quantity of live Oak timber, and very convenient places for building Ships, and he was inform'd there was what would build 1000 sail of good vessels. That he went about 8 miles up the Creek into the heart of the Island, where he came to an open Savannah as level as a die and not a tree in it, except a few Sassafras and them no bigger than ones thigh. It was Supposed these were formerly Indian feilds and that they would bear both corn & rice, and were also good for cattel, there growing upon it canes, grass and other weeds as high as ones head; for which reasons he look'd on that Island as most valuable. That what he Saw of it was about 3000 acres, and he was inform'd that at the S.W. end there is a great deal more of the Same Sort, which land if burnt in the Spring, and planted for 2 or 3 years, would make extraordinary good meadow land, and it would be easie to do because there is no Stumps or Stones. That all the Islands Small and great, and the main land next to the Sea, are plentifully Stored with Live Oak timber. That he had Seen the Grant of Capt. Pennifeathers land for 300 acres in Georgia, and found the Terms so unreasonable, he would not lay any money out in improving land there.

17 Sept. 14.

Egmont	C	Oglethorp, Ja.	C
Hales, Steven	C	Towers, Tho.	C
Hucks, Robt.	C	Burton, Jo.	T
Lapotre, Hen.	C	Smith, Saml.	T
LaRoch, Jo.	C P		

1. Benefaction reported of 174.18.6 collected by Mr. Wilson in Hackney Parish, for which thanks was orderd him with desire that he would print his Sermon.

2. Order'd that the Commissioners of the Customs be desired to Make out bonds & Lycences for a Collector, Comptroller and Searcher at Savannah Port to be named by the Trustees.

[N.B.] It was 4 years before the Trustees could prevail with the Commissioners of the Customs to allow them a right to nominate their own Officers. At length in 1739 they came to a compromise that they Should name them, but the Commissioners give them instructions.

3. One Berry recommended by Sr. Paul Methuen and Sir Jacob Ackworth presented a Memorial, offering to go to Georgia to Survey the Oak there, and teach our people to convert it into proper pieces to Serve his Majesties Navy. But his demands were too exorbitant for us to comply with: Namely 200£ p ann, His passage over and return to be paid by us if he Should not care to Stay there, 40 Axe Men and Six payr of Sawyers to be found by us, 50£ in hand, and 6 Shill. p day when travelling the Country.

4. Agreed with Capt. Thomas of the London Merchant to carry Mr. Oglethorp over with 90 persons.

5. Mr. Burton acquainted us that two gentlemen, brothers, Wesley by name, One a Clergy man & both bred at the University had resolved to go to Georgia out of a pious design to convert the Indians. Willm. Horton Esq. who had been Subsherif of Herefordshire and was worth 3000£, presented himself to go over and Settle on the Allatahama on a Grant of 500 Acres.

[N.B.] Mr. John Wesley A.M. was and is Still fellow of St. Johns Coll. in Oxford. He and his brother Charles likewise in orders are of the New Sect call'd Methodists, Strict adherers to the Church of England, but Enthusiasts, with Some mixture of Quakerism, and fancy themselves led by the Spirit in every Step they take. John Stay'd not long in Georgia but Stole away for fear of being put on his Tryal for refusing the Sacrament to Mr. Caustons niece with whom he was in love, but who dissappointed him and marry'd another. He also refused to baptise a child because a dissenter Stood Godfather. He was for confession and brine imersion. And at his return to England preach'd as he continues to do in the feilds. Charles his brother now does the Same. In Georgia Mr. Oglethorp made him Secretary of the Indian affairs.

6. Mr. West formerly Bailif of Savannah attended. His desire was to obtain a Grant of 500 acres and to have leave to part with his House in Savannah and 50 acre lot, and in return for Gods Providence in raising him from poverty to good circumstances, he desired we would charge him with what Sum of money we

pleased towards the relief of other distrest persons who go to Georgia.

[N.B.] Mr. John West quitted the Magistracy at his own desire, that he might more closely follow his trade of a blacksmith, by which he got 10£ a week, and being grown rich desired a Grant of 500 acres. He gave us a very good Acct of the state of the Colony: that it went prosperously on. That this year there will be corn enough to Subsist all the Inhabitants, and that there is no body there but may comfortably Subsist if diligent and laborious. That Mr. Causton (now Head Bailif) is a passionate man, but resolution is necessary to repress the insolence of many of the people. That Tomachachi is a very prudent Man, and of great use in pacifying differences, and making other Indian Nations our friends. That Mr. Quincy the Minister does not attend his duty as he ought, and the religious disposition of the people So cool, that Some Sunday, there are not 10 at Church. NB. On the 10 Octbr. this year we by letter to him revok'd his authority to do Ecclesiastical Offices in Georgia. But he prevented the publick Knowledge of that disgrace by his own desire to be recall'd, exprest in a letter dat. 28 Aug. preceding. Mr. John Wesley was appointed to Succeed him.

24 Septbr. 15.

Bundy, Ri.	C		Lapotre, Hen.	C P
Egmont	C	Ch.	LaRoch, Jo.	C
Frederick, Tho.	C		Oglethorp, Ja.	C
Hales, Steven	C		Towers, Tho.	C
Heathcote, Geo.	C		Burton, Jo.	T
Holland, Rogers	C		Smith, Saml.	T
Hucks, Robt.	C			

1. Mr. Von Reck appeard, who arrived yesterday with 46 Saltsburgers and 11 other Germans besides his brother. In all himself included 33 males and 26 females: none of the men 48 years old, nor under 17.

2. Arrived also 25 Moravians pt. of Ct. Zinzendorfs people who are to joyn their Brethren at Savannah.

3. Orders given to take care of these people till they Set Sail for Georgia.

4. The Seal put to Several appointments, viz.

5. Of Tho. Causton 2d Bailif of Savannah to be 1. Bailif.

6. Of Hen. Parker 3d Bailif to be 2 Bailif.

7. Of John Dearn to be 3d Bailif.
8. Of the 3 Bailifs and Tho. Christie to be Granters of Lycenses in open Court of Publick Houses.
9. Of Tho. Causton and in his absence John Vandeplank to be the Officer in whose presence Rum is to be Staved.
10. Of the Constables for the time being or any of them to Seize Negroes entering Georgia.
11. Of Austin Weddal to be Treasurer for receiving the Lycense money from the Indian Traders.
12. Of Mr. Oglethorp to be Sole Commissioner to grant Lycenses to trade to the Indian Nations.
13. Of Mr. Oglethorp to be first Commissr. for putting in execution the Act for maintaining peace with the Indians.
14. Of Charles Wesley A.M. to be Secy. of the Indian affairs.
15. Seal put to a Lease and Release of 10000 Acres to the 3 Bailifs & Tho. Christie Recorder, in trust for the use of the new County Frederica.
16. Powers granted to Mr. Oglethorp to dispose of Said Acres, & to dispose of Said Acres, & to Set out, limit and divide them.
17. Seal put to the Indentures of Jo. Ridley & Cha. Carter to be Trust Servants.
18. A Bill for 100£ drawn on the Trustees by Patrick Mackay Capt. of the Independent Company, for provisions for his Men, was refused acceptance, having no instructions or power to make drafts. It was dat. 18 July 1735.
19. A bill drawn on the Trustees for 500£ for wages and charges of the Independent Company, was noted by us, but not accepted, because Special advice was not received thereof, as the bill had exprest.
20. Grant past of 500 Acres to Walter Augustin, late of Cat Isld.

Grant past of 500 Acres to John Musgrove, the Indn. Interpreter.

Grant past of 500 Acres to Ja. Gascoign, Capt. of the Kings Ship.

Grant past of 500 Acres to Willm. Horton, Esq.

[N.B.] John Musgrove died 12 June 1735, But this grant was promised him, and his Son will enjoy it. In the meantime Mary his widow enjoys it, and has good Improvements on it. The place is call'd Grantham. Mr. James Gascoign was Capt. of an 18 gun Sloop, Station'd for 3 years at the Allatahama for defence of the Province.

21. Memorials orderd of these Grants, in order to be registered in the Auditor of Plantations Office.

22. Order to Mr. Harbin to bring from Holland 50 Men Servants at 1.5.0 *p* head.

26 *Septbr.* 16.

Egmont	C P	Lapotre, Hen.	C
Hales, Steven	C	LaRoch, Jo.	C
Heathcote, Geo.	C	Oglethorp, Ja.	C Ch.
Holland, Rogers	C	Towers, Tho.	C
Hucks, Robt.	C	Burton, Jo.	T

1. Name of Frederica given to the New Town to be erected in the South of our Province.

2. Seal put to the appointment of the Several Officers for Frederica following, viz.

3. Of Tho. Hawkins Surgeon & Apothecary to be 1. Bailif.

4. Of Saml. Perkins Coachmaker to be 2d Bailif.

5. Of Edwd. Addison Miller & Farmer to be 3d Bailif.

6. Of 3 other persons to be Bailifs in case of Mortality Or removal of the former, viz.

 Richd. White, a Clergymans Son

 Samuel Davison, a Chairman

 Richd. Cooper

7. Of Fra. Moore, to be Recorder and Storekeeper

8. Of John Brooks to be 1. Constable

9. Of Samuel Davison above mention'd to be 2d Constable.

10. Of John Calwell, Tallow Chandler to be Tithing Man.

11. Of Will. Allen, Baker, to be Tithing Man.

12. Powers granted to Mr. Oglethorp to administer the Oathes of Allegiance and Supremacy and abjuration, and the oathes of Office to the Several Officers appointed as above.

13. Granted the petition of John West late Bailif, & Elizabeth (late Hughes) his wife, for lycense to alienate their Town lot in Savannah to Such person as they Should nominate, provided the Said person hath not lands already in Georgia in possession or expectancy.

14. Order for making out a grant of 500 Acres to John & Elizabeth West and the heirs male of their bodies, in consideration of her paying 10£ for the use of the Trust, and making over her right in the 50 acre Lot.

15. Order for Sending 25 persons, Moravians lately arrived under the Conduct of Mr. Nitchman, to Georgia, on the terms agreed on by the Common Council 2 April 1735.

16. Order for distributing to them 32.0.0 being part of 200£ a benefaction from a person unknown.

17. 20£ order'd to John Bromfeild for his Services done the Trustees in drawing Mapps.

18. Imprest 3000£ to Mr. Heathcote on account.

[N.B.] Mr. Robert Millar the Botanist, wrote us that the Ipicuana Plants he brought with him from Cartagena to Jamaica, and which had Such a bad appearance in June, were by the favour of the Rainy Season Shooting out all fresh from the Roots, and in a very promising way. That he had also planted Some of the Balsom Capivi Seeds which came up. But those of the Balsom Tolu had not yet appear'd above ground; however he had still remaining Some of the best Seeds of both of them, which he kept for the Colony of Georgia.

2 *Octbr*. 17.

Egmont	C	LaRoch, Jo.	C
Hales, Steven	C	Oglethorp, Ja.	C
Heathcote, Geo.	C P	Towers, Tho.	C Ch.
Hucks, Robt.	C	Vernon, Ja.	C
Lapotre, Hen.	C	Smith, Saml.	T

1. Benefaction reported of 100£ from a person unknown to be apply'd to the conversion of the Indians to Christianity. Also 20£ in books given by Ladys unknown. Also of 10£ given by the A.B. of Canterbury for the Conversion of ye Indians. Also of a Cambridge Concordance & Some Hymns given by one Williams a poor blind man.

2. The Seal put to Sola Georgia Bills to the value of 4000£, and order'd that 4000£ be apropriated in the Bank for the answering them, purs. to ye order of Common Council 24 July 1735.

3. Order'd 1000£ in Silver to Mr. Oglethorp to take over with him, to make current the Said 4000£ in Sola Bills, and another 1000£ in Sola bills when Seal'd.

4. Orders Sent to the Magistrates at Savannah repeating former directions not to draw any bills on the Trustees without giving advice of the Said bills, and that they do not pretend upon any account what ever to draw bills except for answering ordinary

Services, before they have communicated the reason and necessity of the extraordinary Services for which they must be drawn, & have received from the Trustees leave to make Such drafts.

5. Charter Party Sign'd with ye Ship Simons, Capt. Cornish, for carrying over 124 persons to Georgia with Mr. Oglethorp.

6. 50£ given to Mr. Von Reck for his trouble in bringing over the Saltsburgers & Germans.

7. Orderd that a Memorial be prepared and Sign'd, of the Grants and Conveyances past the Seal last year, that have not been register'd by particular Memorials, in order to be register'd with the Auditor of the Plantations.

8. 1000£ imprest to Geo. Heathcote on acct.

9. Grants past as follows:

500 Acres to Paul Jenys Esq., Speaker to the Assembly of Charlestown.
500 Acres to Jo. Baker of South Carolina, Esq.
100 Acres to John Brown Esq., of London.
50 Acres to Jo. Tuckwell Ironmonger of Wallingford.
500 Acres to Rowland Pytt Ironmonger of Gloucester.

10. Lycense given to Mr. Tuckwell & Mr. Pytt to reside in England, notwithstanding their Grants.

7 Oct. 18.

Egmont	C		LaRoch, Jo.	C Ch.
Eyles, Fra.	C P		Oglethorp, Ja.	C
Hales, Steven	C		Towers, Tho.	C
Heathcote, Geo.	C		Vernon, Ja.	C
Hucks, Robt.	C		Anderson, Adam	T
Lapotre, Hen.	C		Smith, Saml.	T

1. Benefactions reported. Among the rest 20£ from a person unknown to be apply'd to the erecting Churches in Georgia.

2. The bill of 500£ for payment of the Rangers of Independent Company was now orderd to be accepted & paid, the Govermt. of Carolina having Suspended the promise they made to pay them.

[N.B.] Now began the Province of South Carolina to be our Enemies, and to grow exceeding jealous of us, especially on account that we do not suffer their Traders to traffick in the Province of Georgia with the Indians without taking lycenses from our Magistrates or Commissioners, pretending that by an Act of their Assembly approved by Q. Anne, their Traders have liberty to traffick over their whole Province wherein at that time Georgia was comprehended, and therefore tho Georgia has Since been Seperated from it they have a right to traffick in Georgia. Our letters recd, about this time also inform us, that they have stopt payment of the 8000£ currency formerly granted by their Assembly to us, on pretence we have not built a Fort, for which they Say they gave it. They also demand a Satisfactory Acct. of the death of a Spaniard by one of our Indians, and assert that the Militia of Georgia is in them (which is true as far as their Govr. but not in their Council and Assembly).

I advised the Attorney General's opinion might be taken thereupon, for if their assertions had ground, our disputes with them might have had consequences, and accordingly it proved So.

3. The Moravians now going over desiring to know whether their wives & children who are to follow them Shall be transported at the Trustees charge, or at Count Zinzendorfs, they were answer'd it could not be at our charge.

4. Order'd 40£ gratuity to Mr. Winants for his trouble about the Moravians.

5. Order'd that 3 of the Common Council draw up instructions for the magistrates of Savannah touching Several points contained in Bailif Caustons Letters.

6. Appointment of John Bromfeild to be Register of Lands in Georgia.

7. Appointment of John Vandeplank to be Naval Officer.

8. The appointment of 3 Bailifs to ly dormant, and to Succeed the present 3 in case of mortality or removal (see 26 Septbr.) was reconsider'd, and the 3 following appointed in the place of Ri. White, Saml. Davison & Ri. Cooper, viz.

 Ensign Ri. Johnson—to Succeed 2d Bailif to Tho. Hawkins.
 Danl. Cannon—to Succeed 2d Bailif to Saml. Perkins.
 Jo. Calwell—to Suceed 3d Bailif to Edwd. Addison.

9. Also appointed in like manner and in the like cases,
 Willm. Abbot to Succeed—1st Constable to Jo. Brooks
 Jo. Flower to Succeed—2d Constable to Saml. Davison.
 Jo. Levally to Succeed—1 Tithing Man to Jo. Calwell
 Danl. Parnell to Succeed 2 Tithing Man to Will. Allen.

10. Grant past of 500 Acres to Philip Von Reck of Ratisbon
11. Grant past of 500 Acres to Eliz. West.

[N.B.] Mr. Sterling Settled with a party of Scots in the County of Savannah, having received a letter full of Invectives against the Trustees, accusing us of pursuing our private Interest at the expence of those we Send. That our Constitution is military, arbitrary and Tirannical, and that in a little time we Shall by our management destroy the Colony, he honestly gave it to our Bailifs to peruse, who Sent us a Copy of it. But the name of the Writer being Scratch'd out, we could only guesse the Man, which Some believ'd to be Capt. Coram one of our Trustees, who on account of our not giving liberty to Females to inherit is so disgusted that he very rarely comes among us, and prejudices every body he can against us. He was the rather believed the Man, because mention is made in that letter of a New Settlement in another place, which the King and Council have been apply'd to grant, and all the Steps therein taken, related, Which none could tell but Capt. Coram, he being the person who is now applying for erecting a new Settlement at a considerable distance from Georgia.

[N.B.] 14 Oct. 1735. Mr. Oglethorp embark'd at Gravesend on board the Simons, Capt. Cornish, and with him Mr. John Wesley A.M. in Priest's orders, and Charles Wesley his brother in Deacons Orders, who is to be Minister at Savannah whilst his elder brother endeavours to convert the Indians. The whole number that went in his Ship were 125 of whom 102 at the Trustees charge. On the 20th of the same month, Mr. Oglethorp was joyn'd by 136 persons more in the Downs, on board the London Merchant, Capt. Thomas, of whom 129 went at the Trustees charge. The Saltsburgers that went with him were 59. And about the 29th of same month Capt. Geo. Dunbar of the Princess of Wales carry'd from Scotland 180 persons, of whom 130 were contracted to be at the Trustees expence, but our Accompt. believed these last would be but 120.

[N.B.] On the 10 Oct. 1735 Patrick Mackay Capt. of a party of Rangers, and employd to Settle a Fort in the Indian Nation was turn'd out of our Service for notorious ill behaviour.

29 Oct. 19.

Egmont	C	Towers, Tho.	C
Hucks, Robt.	C	Vernon, Ja.	C
Lapotre, Hen.	C P	Smith, Saml.	T
LaRoch, Jo.	C		

1. Benefactions reported: 20.2.0 from an unknown hand towards building a Church. 2.2.0 from an unknown hand for the Same purpose, and 20£ from Mr. Holden for the genl. uses of the Colony.

[1735] JOURNAL OF THE EARL OF EGMONT 115

2. Letter of lycense granted to Mr. Hugh Macleod a Scots Minister to perform divine Service to his Countrymen in Georgia.

3. Orders Sent to Mr. Harding to Stop the coming of 50 Servants we had directed him to bring from Holland, our Cash beg. low.

4. Peter Gordon late Bailif applying for an answer to his letters and Memorial agst. Mr. Causton, we told him no answer could be given till Mr. Oglethorp had enquired into those complaints.

5. Report of the Muster on board the Simons wch. Sailed with Mr. Oglethorp 14th inst. That there were on board 121 persons.

6. Report of the Muster on board the London Merchant which Saild the 20th inst. That there were on board 136 persons.

7. Report that the Scots going on board the Princess of Wales were already 160 persons.

7 *Novbr.* 20.

Ld. Carpenter	C		Lapotre, Hen.	C	
Egmont	C		LaRoch, Jo.	C	
Eyles, Fra.	C	P	Towers, Tho.	C	
Chandler, Ri.	C		Vernon, Ja.	C	
Hales, Steven	C		Anderson, Adam	T	
Heathcote, Geo.	C		Smith, Samuel	T	
Hucks, Robt.	C	Ch.			

1. Benefactions 13.13.0 given for the use of the Mission by a person unknown.

2. The Account of beef and butter Ship'd from Corke for Georgia arising to more than we agreed for with Mr. Simons the Merchant, we nevertheless order'd it to be allow'd, because after the Agreement made we directed that the beef & butter should be of the best Sorte, which Merchants do not in the common course Send.

3. Order'd that 20£ be given to the 10 Moravians who first went over, out of the 200£ given 26 Sept. last by a person unknown for the use of persecuted Protestants.

4. Agreed with Capt. Thompson to carry over 50 tun of goods at 1.10.0 *p* tun, which the 2 last Ships had not room to take in.

5. 50£ given the Accompt. for his trouble in the late embarkations.

6. Mr. Lapotre reported that Sola bills to the value of 4000£ had been Seald between the 2 & 9 October last.

7. Two Reports from the Committee of Accts were reported & agreed to.

8. Received the Report of the Musters on board the Simons, Capt. Cornish, and the London Merchant, Capt. Thomas. That the former carry'd 121 persons, of whom 102 were at the Trustees charge making 93 heads & ½, And 19 at their own. And that the London Merchant carry'd 136 persons, of whom 129 at the Trustees charge making 112 heads 2 thirds.

9. Reported by the Accompt. that 180 persons from Scotland were ready to Sail on board the Princess of Wales, Capt Dunbar making 166 whole heads, of which number the Trustees had contracted to Send at their charge 130, but by looking over the list he apprehended there were but 120 to be charged to the Trustees Acct. He added that 36 of the others had taken grants and were to pay their own passage.

10. Application being made by a person at Geneva, to bring over 100 persons of that City & Teritory on certain conditions: We answer'd his Agent that our embarkations for this year are over, and that our Mony will not answer to Send any more: But that if he will apply next April and the Parliament give us money we will recieve and consider his proposal.

11. Imprest 3000£ to Alderman Heathcote, there being great bills to pay, and other demands not expected made on us.

12 Novbr. 21.

Chandler, Ri.	C P	Towers, Tho.	C
Egmont	C	Vernon, Ja.	C
Hucks, Robt.	C	Smith, Saml.	T
LaRoch, Jo.	C		

1. 10.0.0 Given by Mr. Chandler towards the Religious uses of the Colony.

2. Agreed upon Sr. Cha. Hothams recommendation that Michl. Wilson and his wife be admitted to go to Georgia, he paying 10£ for his and his wifes passage.

3. One Stayley a potter, having taken the Kings money to go to Georgia in company of the Swiss, and having Suddenly withdrawn himself when the embarkation came on, and begging now about the Streets, Order was given to take him up when found, and carry'd before a justice of Peace to answer for the fraud.

4. Mr. Creswick Dean of Bristol having wrote a letter (in wch. there were 7 false Spellings in Six lines) desiring that a person

belonging to that City recommended by Col. Yates might be admitted to go to Georgia, he paying 10£ for his and his wifes passage, We declin'd it on acct. of the expence of maintaining them when there, Our Cash running low, & the City of Bristol not having yet in any manner countenanc'd our designs.

5. Advice from Portsmouth that Mr. Oglethorp was Still there waiting for his Majesties Sloop, Capt. Gascoign, which troubled us much, because he will arrive at Georgia too late for the planting Season, whereby we Shall have two years provision to furnish the Passengers instead of One. Besides the Wind is turn'd against them, and we pay almost 100£ p month demurrage.

6. Order'd to respit the Selling 200 barrils of Tar arrived from Georgia, by reason of the low price it bears.

7. Letters arrived from Capt. Dunbar in Scotland, that he had on board 179 Scots, of whom 55 pay their own passage, and that of their Servants, and the rest are at the Trustees charge.

17 Nov. 22.

Ld. Carpenter	C	Lapotre, Hen.	C P
Chandler, Ri.	C	LaRoch, Jo.	C
Bundy, Ri.	C	Towers, Tho.	C
Egmont	C	Vernon, Ja.	C Ch.
Hucks, Robt.	C		

1. Benefactions reported.
2. The Seal was put to a petition to his Majesty not to permit the running out of lands or granting of land Southward of the Allatahama River, because So near a neighborhood to the Spaniards might involve us in a War with them or their Indians.

[N.B.] The cause of our petitioning the King was this. By a Treaty between South Carolina and the Indians on conclusion of their War about 18 years ago, all the lands Southward of the River Savannah were allow'd to be the Indians property. But when the King regardless of that Treaty granted the greater part of that land to us & erected it into a new Province, and in his grant mention'd it to be pt. of South Carolina, and the Carolinians found they were protected by our settlement, they raised a doubt whether they could lawfully yeild up to the Indians lands asserted by his Majesty to be part of Carolina, and look'd on the Treaty to be Superseded, and were preparing to get Grants of what remaind of those lands Southward of the Allatahama our most Southern Boundary. Which had they Succeeded in, might have exasperated the Indians & given the Spaniards jealousie by drawing down So near to them. We therefore opposed their design, and upon our Representation of the matter, His Majesty forbid the Carolinians to take up grants there, which encreased their ill will towards us.

3. A Letter from Mr. Saml. Eveleigh was read acquainting us that he had quitted his purpose of Settling in Georgia, and was return'd to Carolina, because we allow not the use of Negroes, nor females to inherit. That Robert Parkers Saw Mill would not Succeed, but there was better hopes of that Walter Augustin design'd to erect. That he had been at Osebaw Island, 40 miles South of Savannah Town, and went 8 miles up a creek into the heart of it, where he saw about 3000 acres fine land fit for meadow, and was inform'd that Southward there were other great plains: And that on the Shoar and in most places there were live Oaks Sufficient to build 1000 Ships.

4. Report made that Ri. Lawley had paid us 10£ for the use of his Son in Georgia. That Michl. Wilson had paid us 10£ towards the expence of Sending him and his wife to Georgia.

5. Order given to ensure Ri. Lawleys goods to Georgia.

6. Ri. Faulcon an able Millwright and Jeremy his Son admitted to go to Georgia on the poor account.

7. Received a Report from the Committee of Embarkation and agreed to it, touching the beef & butter Sent to Georgia from Ireland, and we agreed to Mr. Simons demands.

8. Received the Report of the Committee of Accts. concerning disbursments made in America from 30 Jany. 1732 to 30 Jany. 1734.

9. Received the Report of the Committee of Accts. of the genl. Acct. of Receipts and disbursments, from 9th June 1734 to 9 June 1735.

10. Orderd fair copies to be made thereof, and given to the Lord Chancellr. &c as the charter obliges.

11. Order'd that the expence of transporting 17 male & 6 female Servants for the use of private persons in Georgia be advanc'd by the Trust, and that Bonds be made out for their Masters to repay the money when the Servants Shall arrive, and that Mr. Oglethorp be wrote to, to take care therein.

12. Agreed among our Selves to Subscribe 10£ each towards erecting Churches, our Fund appropriated for that purpose being too Small. Some Subscribed, others declined it.

13. Grant of 500 Acres past to Willm. Bradley.

[1735] JOURNAL OF THE EARL OF EGMONT 119

[N.B.] 22 Novbr. Mr. Robert Millar our Botonist Wrote us from Jamaica, That he would have Sent the Ipicuana Plants, and Balsoms of Capivi & Tolu Trees before now to Georgia, but being Winter there, and the Plants young, he judg'd it Safe to keep them till next Spring. He added that he was Speedily going to Campeachy and La Vera Crux, and would as directed, use all possible means to procure Some plants of the Jalap, Sassaparilla, Contrayerva and the Cochineal plants with the animals, the Seeds of the gum Elemi Trees, and all other useful plants that are to be found in those parts, none of them being to be found in the parts where he had yet been.

[N.B.] 27 Novbr. the Georgia Pink arrived at Savannah with the passengers from England.

[N.B.] On the 2d Decembr. 1735 Capt. Thompson of the Two Brothers Saild for Georgia wth. 11 Males & 4 females, in all 15, of whom 13 went at the Trustees charge on the poor Account.

3 Decbr. 23.

Egmont	C	Bedford, Arthr.	T
Vernon, Ja.	C	Smith, Saml.	T
Anderson, Ad.	T		

A Common Council was Summond to receive an Acct. of the freight of goods & passengers lately gone or Georgia on board Capt. Thompsons Ship, but we were not a board.

1. Benefaction reported of 5.5.0 from Mr. Huddy for the use of the mission.

2. Report made of 196.15.8 repaid us by the Society for promoting Christian knowledge, being expences of bringing the Saltsburgers from Augsburg and keeping them at Rotherhithe till Ship'd for Georgia wth. Mr. Von Reck.

3. One Taylor haveing printing an advertisment inviting people to go to Georgia, we orderd an advertismt. that he did it without our orders or knowledge.

10 Decbr. 24.

Bundy, Ri.	C		Hucks, Robt.	C
Ld. Carpenter	C	P	Lapotre, Hen.	C
Chandler, Ri.	C		LaRoch, Jo.	C
Egmont	C		Towers, Tho.	C
Hales, Steven	C	Ch.	Vernon, Ja.	C

1. Benefactions reported towards building Churches.
2. Letter read from Mr. Quincy, desiring another Minister might be appointed in his room at Savannah, he designing to return to England, because he could not prevail with his wife to go over to him.
3. A Memorial drawn up to be presented the Incorporate Society for propagating the Gospel in foreign parts, desiring they would confer their salary of 50£ which Mr. Quincy enjoy'd, upon Mr. John Wesley who is on his voyage to Georgia, and whom we would appoint Minister at Savannah.
4. Letter from Mr. Oglethorp dat. at Cowes in the Isle of Wright the 3d inst. informing us he had been ill of the Fever, and that the Passengers were sickly, and lamenting the loss of a fair Wind by waiting for his Majesties Sloop. He desired a horse and mare might be sent after him by way of Charlestown, but not the Saw Mill, lest the person who go over to erect it should be debauch'd to Stay there, wherefore he advised the Sending it directly to Frederica.

[N.B.] The negligence of the Officer at Plymouth in not dispatching the Kings Sloop put the Trustees to a very great expence, for thereby a fair wind was lost, So that Mr. Oglethorp who embark'd the 20 Octbr. was not able to Sail till 8 Decbr. following. Mr. Oglethorp made a Remonstrance thereof to the Admiralty, and the Officer was turn'd out.

5. Letter from Mr. Abercromby Attorney Genl. of South Carolina was read, containing his opinion on the late Act that past in England for prolonging the time for allowance of Rice to go from South Carolina without calling at England, and his doubts whether by the clause contained in that Act that respects Georgia, the Parliament intended that Georgia Should have the Same liberty of exporting rice.
6. Letter from Bailif Causton was read dat. 8 Septbr. justifying himself from insidious complaints, and acquainting us that the Colony is in good order. That he had staved a Barril of Rum privately landed from Charlestown under colour of being Cyder. With this, came a duplicate of the moneys taken up by him, and paid, Sign'd by the persons concern'd. And a list of the Improvments made. And a Register of the deaths, marriages, births and desertions from 1 feby. 1732–3 to 13 Sept. 1735 which were as follows:

   Dead within that time 172
   Banish'd run away or executed 31

Married 66
Born 34

7. Letter read from Mr. Chardon touching his Accts.

8. Letter from Elisha Dobre read, desiring encouragemt. to Set up a Salt pan, and to have land for that purpose.

9. Letter from Tho. Christie Recorder of Savanna, justifying himself from selling or encouraging the use of Rum of wch. Some had accused him, and desiring he may Sell his Town Lot and have a Grant of 500 Acres.

10. A Letter from Mr. Bolzius Minister at Ebenezar was read thanking the Trustees for their favours to the Saltsburgers, but modestly insinuating their land was bad.

11. Letter from Dr. Stanley to me was read, desiring 5 persons may be Sent over, for the 80£ collected by him at Leverpool and the 20£ at Preston. I was order'd to let him know that 4 persons Shall be Sent over at his and the Corporation of Leverpools recommendation, but that the 5th had already been Sent on the score of the Preston collection.

12. A Letter from Mr. Broughton. Pressdt. of the Council of South Carolina to me was read, Complaining of our Magistrates, and of Capt. Mackay their forbidding the Carolina Indian Traders to traffick with the Indians within Our Province. This letter was accompany'd with a large packet of Memorials depositions, &c. He Sent at the Same time a duplicate of these papers to the Board of Trade, who desiring to discourse with us thereupon, Mr. Hucks and Mr. LaRoch were immediatly deputed to inform them, that these papers are now under our consideration and when we had digested our reply, we would impart it to them.

13. The Accomptant reported the Muster of passengers that Saild for Georgia on board the Two brothers, Capt. Thompson, 2 inst. which were in all 15, 11 males & 4 females, of whom 13 went at the Trustees charge making 11 heads & one third.

14. Some bills drawn by Bailif Causton were accepted.

15. Imprest 1600£ to Alderman Heathcote.

16. Order'd that Mathew Brown and his Servant be Sent over by the way of Bristol, and to Stand part of the late embarkation.

17. Resolv'd to Send no more persons on the charity till the Trustees are enabled by a new Supply from Parliament.

18. Order past for Sending over an Auger to boar Earth.

19. Order'd that the weekly allowance to our Messenger and house keeper be encreased to 4 Shillings p week to each, and that 5 guineas be given the messenger.

20. Order'd that 250 Copies of the Years Accts. & disbursmt. to 9 June 1735 be printed.

13 Decbr. 25.

Bundy, Ri.	C	LaRoch, Jo.	C
Egmont	C	Towers, Tho.	C
Hucks, Robt.	C	Vernon, Ja.	C

1. This was a Committee of Correspondence, wherein the whole day was Spent upon the letter and papers Sent by President Broughton, which having carefully perused, together with our Act of trade, and Our charter, We drew up an answer to the Presidt. to the effect following: That Capt. Mackay complain'd of, acted in matter of Trade by authority of the late Govr. of South Carolina Mr. Johnson. That Mr. Oglethorps Commission to him related only to the Fort that was to be built in the Creek Nation. That orders are Sent to Mr. Oglethorp to enquire into the Captains conduct, and the murder of the Spaniard, and that when we know Where the crime ly's, the persons Shall be punish'd. That we have no design to exclude the Carolinians from trading within our Province, but he must needs think it reasonable that the Trade Should be under proper regulations, and accordingly his Majesty had past an Act to that purpose, which we Send him. That we know our Charter vests the chief command of the Militia in the Govr. of South Carolina for the time being, but this to be exercised only on extraordinary occasions, for in ordinary ones the Militia is in us as may be seen by a previous clause. That we Shall always cultivate a good correspondence with his province to which we Stand obliged, but wish'd him to consider the fatal tendency of his threatening our militia to keep home, which may happen to endanger both Provinces in case of a rupture with our Neighbours.

17 Dec. 26.

Egmont	C	Anderson, Adam	T
Vernon, Ja.	C P	Smith, Saml.	T

A Common Council Summond, but No Board.

1. Letter read from Mr. Oglethorp that he was the 8th inst. Saild from Cowes.

2. Commission given Dr. Lavington to preach & collect for us at St. Michl. Bareshaw.

3. Agreed that a Memorial be consider'd of to present the Citie Companies for obtaining of them encouragemt. towards establishing our Colony.

4. The letter prepared by the Committee of correspondence 13 inst. in answer to Presidt. Broughtons complaints was approved, and then we waited on the board of Trade therewith, who read it together with Presidt. Broughtons letter, and a letter wrote by us in August last for dismissing Capt. Mackay. Of these the Board desiring Copies we promised they Should have them.

24 Dec. 27.

Bundy, Ri.	C		LaRoch, Jo.	C
Egmont	C		Vernon, Ja.	C
Kendal, Robt.	C		Smith, Saml.	T
Lapotre, Hen.	C	P		

A Common Council was Summond to consider of the Acct of demurrage and victualling the Simond & London Mercht. while at Cowes, and other business. But we were not a board.

1. Benefaction of 5.5.0 from a Lady unknown, for buildg. Churches.

2. We read the Accompt of Mr. Simons and Mr. Ragg for demurrage of the Simons and London Mercht, but resolv'd nothing till Some London Merchts. were talk'd to thereon.

3. Mr. Willm. Bradley who was Sent to instruct our people in Agriculture appear'd, and acquainted us he had lost his passage on board the London Mercht. by going from Cowes to Portsmouth to Seek for a Midwife, there being 6 women on board who will ly in in a month, and nobody to assist them. That a few hours after he left the Ship the wind turn'd fair, and it Saild away without waiting his return. That there upon he hired a Ship & follow'd but could not overtake her, so was obliged to put into Plymouth, from whence he and his Son and another person were come to London in the Stage coach. He desired his expences might be allow'd him, and that we would pay his and his Sons passage, there being a Ship to go to Carolina within a week, which we judged reasonable, and resolved to recommend it to the Common Council.

[N.B.] 10th Jany. 1735–6. The Pr. of Wales Capt. Dunbar arrived at Savannah with the Scots Highlanders. And Mr. Hugh Mackay with many of them went for Barnwells Bluff to take possession thereof and erect covering for the rest. In Feby. following they call'd their Settlement Darien. Afterwards they changed it to New Inverness. The Same day arrived the Peter & James Capt. Diamond. The Allen, Capt. Dicker, arrived also.

12 Jany. 1735–6. 28.

Bundy, Ri.	C	Heathcote, Sr. Will.	C P
Egmont	C	Bedford, Arthr.	T

A Common Council was Summond to Seal Agreement with Will. Bradley, to order the payment of bills of Exchange, & to receive a Report of the Committee of Accompts: But No Board.

1. Benefaction of a Stonehorse presented by Mr. Oglethorp for a Stallion to be Sent to Georgia. Order'd that 2 Cast off mares Should be look'd out to Send after it.

3. Mr. Verelts reported that Sr. John Barnard, Aldn. of London declined being Umpire in our difference with Mr. Simons the Mercht. concerning his demand for demurrage, whereupon Col. Raymond had been apply'd to, and his answer was expected. That in the mean time Mr. Simons takes offence, and insists on our paying his demand, being Settled by Mr. Oglethorp, before he left Cowes. But we apprehended Mr. Oglethorp was Surprised in that affair by Mr. Simons book keeper, Mr. Pury, who went on board the Ship to Settle that account with him.

4. Dr. Bundy was desired to preach our Anniversary Sermon this year, but he refused it as he had done the year before.

16 Jany. 29.

Bundy, Ri.	C P	Ld. Tirconnel	C Ch.
Egmont	C	Towers, Tho.	C
Holland, Rogers	C	Vernon, Ja.	C
Hucks, Robt.	C	White, Jo.	C
LaRoch, Jo.	C		

1. Mr. Vernon reported that the Incorporate Society for propagating the Gospel in foreign parts had yeilded to our desire to pay the 50£ p ann which Mr. Quincy had to Mr. John Wesley who Succeeds him in Savannah.

2. Mr. Simons demand for demurrage of the 2 Ships that went with Mr. Oglethorp was taken into consideration, and upon reading Col. Raymonds publick opinion, and receiving Sr. John Barnards private opinion, we resolved to pay his full demand. This was near 500£, all owing to the loss of a fair wind, occasioned by

the delay of Mr. Oglethorps delay of departure on account that the Governts. Sloop was not ready to Sail with him.

3. Mr. Fury Agent for South Carolina having 600£ Sterlg. due to him there for his Services, which that Province was not able to pay him for want of Bills, he apply'd to us to direct Mr. Oglethorp to recieve his money in Georgia, and to return it to him here by a bill upon us. We readily consented to it as a matter that would give credit to our Sola bills, and was no inconvenience to us. Besides that it was a friendly action, and might render Mr. Fury a friend to our Colony.

4. A letter from Mr. Miller our Botanist was read, dat. from Jamaica 27 Sept. 1735, wherein he acquainted us what collections he had made of valuable plants & roots to Send to Georgia, & that he design'd for Campeachy Bay & Carthagena. We orderd that a quarters Sallary Should be paid him as Soon as the Subscriptions of Ld. Peters Sr. Hans Sloan &c come in: But that his Christmass Quarter Should be postponed till we heard of his being alive at the end of the Said Quarter.

5. Received the Report of the Committee of Accts. drawn up 24 Decbr. last.

6. The Articles of Agreement made with William Bradley to instruct our people in agriculture 7 Oct. last were read & the Seal put to them; and at his desire 31.10.0 was advanced him to be repaid out of the money arising to him by the Sale of turf in England.

7. We granted Mrs. Hazlewoods petition, that James Hazlefoot her husband might have leave to dispose of his Town lot to Such person he Should recommend for a grant thereof, and take 150 acres further up in the country. Order'd also that Mr. Oglethorp Should furnish him with 2 Servants, he repaying the Trustees as he Shall be able.

[N.B.] I know not how it happend that Ja. Hazelfoot apply'd now for a grant of 150 acres, there having been past to him a grant of the Same number on the 27 feb. 1733-4.

8. Committee appointed to consider of a proper method to raise a provision for the maintenance of a minister in Georgia.

19 Jany. 30.

Ld. Carpenter	C	Heathcote, Geo.	C
Bundy, Ri.	C	Hucks, Robt.	C
Egmont	C	LaRoch, Jo.	C

Shaftsbury	C	Vernon, Ja.	C
Ld. Tirconnel	C P	White, Jo.	C
Towers, Tho.	C	Smith, Saml.	T

This meeting was only a Committee to consider of a proper Settlement of Incom for a Minister in Savannah, but it was better attended than many Common Council boards, Several Gentlemen being averse to granting land in glebe, and apprehending the others would make too good a provision for the Minister.

1. Three minutes were read concerning Steps taken for a provision for a Minister, dat. 8 Nov. 1732, 11 Dec. 1734 & 16 Apr. 1735. The 2 last of which expressly mentioned a glebe to be laid out: On which a debate arose, whether to grant a Glebe, or pay the Minister a Sallary in money. It was Said that if we should grant land in glebe, it would be a Freehold to the Minister, out of which let him behave ever so ill, we Should not be able to remove him, without tedious proceedings at law; whereas if he were removable at pleasure, he would be carefull to behave as he ought.

2. On the other hand it was argued, that our intention was always to Settle a Glebe, the Minutes Shew it, and the very Situation was Set down in our Map. That the number of acres, 300, had also been allotted, mony order'd to fence them in, and that the Incorporate Society allow'd our Minister 50£ Sallary on that account. That our honour was concern'd to See it done, and our Interest too, for when it Shall be Known that we will grant no Glebe, the Incorporate Society will withdraw their Sallary, and others forbear to Subscribe to our religious designs because the Ministers residence is precarious, and only at will, and being Subject to a removal on the complaints of ill minded people there, no Clergyman of good character will ever be prevail'd on to enter our Service.

To this it was reply'd, that what the minutes had mentioned of *Glebe* ought to go for nothing. Since there had no actual grant or Settlement of Glebe past the Seal. That a worthy Minister would never fear being turn'd out or ill used by us, and they had rather allow him 100£ in money than 50£ in glebe. That this would Save the honour of the Trustees, and very likely content the Incorporate Society to whom no promise had been made that they knew of, of granting land in glebe, but only that provision Should be made as Soon as possible to ease that Society of the 50£ Sallary. That 300 Acres might hereafter be worth 300£ *p* ann, which being more than we ever design'd for a Minister, the overplus

Should go to defray other charges of the Publick. That if this were agreed to, our Covenanted Servants there, might immediately Set about cultivating the 300 Acres laid out, and So the Minister would Sooner come into his Sallary to be paid out of it, and the Incorporate Society eased of the 50£ p ann. Whereas, if this proposal Should not be approved, those Servants will be employ'd on Trust lands, and it will be long before the Minister will be provided for.

In conclusion we agreed to put off this affair for a fortnight and then reasume the debate in Common Council.

[N.B.] 20 Jany. 1735–6 Mr. Causton wrote to the Trustees that Capt. Yoakly was return'd from the Allatahama, and reported he found the middle Inlet to that River not Safe for any Ship to enter by; but his Acct. being imperfect he had Sent other persons with orders to Sound the mouth Southern mouth & inlet, and that these found the Same very good, having 2 Fathom & ½ water on the Bar at low water, and very Safe for Ships to enter and lye, either at the South End of St. Simons Island, or 8 Miles further up well landlock'd.

2 *Feby.* 31.

Bundy, Ri.	C	Shaftsbury	C
Egmont	C P	Ld. Tirconnel	C
Eyles, Fra.	C	Towers, Tho.	C
Digby, Edwd.	C	Vernon, Ja,	C
Heathcote, Geo.	C	White, Jo.	C Ch.
Hucks, Robt.	C	Tracy, Robt.	T
LaRoch, Jo.	C		

1. Benefactions reported of 56.15.0 given for the Religious uses of the Colony. Also 10.10.0 Subscribed by John Temple Esq. towards building a Church.

2. A bill drawn on us for 150£ order'd to be paid.

3. Other bills drawn by Bailif Causton refused acceptance for want of advice, but order'd our Accompt. to acquaint the Merchant that we will allow Interest from the time they were due until advice came of them, & then we would pay them.

4. Report of the Selling 240 barrils that came from Georgia.

5. The Common Council then enter'd on the consideration of a provision to be made for a Minister, and report was made how far the Committee that sat the 19th Jany. had proceeded therein. The E. of Shaftsbury, Aldn. Heathcote, Mr. LaRoch and Mr.

White were of the Same opinion they exprest in the Committee, for granting no land in glebe but giving the Minister a fixt Sallary; and the Alderman added that 300 acres was too much to apply to religious uses alone, and therefore Should not be vested in Feofees for that only purpose, because it would tye up our hands from employing the overplus of the profit arising from the land (after the Religious purposes were answer'd) to the Civil Services of the Colony. But Dr. Bundy, Ld. Tirconnel, Mr. Vernon and others thought that the Sallary of a Minister, and School master, with the erecting a Church and keeping it in repayr would in all probability employ the whole proffits arrising from these acres when cultivated. That unless it appear'd we did handsomly by the Church, we could not expect any considerable Sums would be contributed towards religious uses. That this land was to be cultivated out of the moneys given to those purposes, and we could neither in conscience or honour employ it to any other than what the Givers intended it, which would be the case if any part of the profits of these acres were apply'd to the civil concerns of the Colony. And as lands were to be cultivated by this money, it was necessary they Should be appropriated to religious uses and vested in Feofees.

This being at length agreed we resolv'd and accordingly enter'd it in our books, "That 300 Acres of Land be granted to proper Trustees (who are to be changed at the will and pleasure of the Common Council of Trustees) to be cultivated out of the moneys which are or Shall be received for Religious uses. And that out of the clear moneys arising out of the proffits of the Said lands so cultivated, Such Sum as the Common Council of the Trustees Shall think proper, be in the first place paid to the Minister, who Shall from time to time be appointed by the Common Council, for the time being to officiate in the town of Savannah. That Such a Sum as the Common Council Shall think proper and direct be then paid to a Schoolmaster, and that the remainder Shall be apply'd to the repayrs of the Church, and Such other Religious uses and purposes, as the Common Council Shall think proper and direct."

N.B. Here it is to be noted that Mr. White the Chairman Struck out (unobserved by the Gentlemen) the word Religious, And giving the resolution they alter'd by him to the Secretary it was accordingly enter'd without that word, which was diametrically opposite to what the board had resolved upon debate.

[N.B.] 2 Feb. 1735–6 arrived at Savannah the Two Brothers, Capt. Thompson. 5 Feby. arrived Mr. Oglethorp at Savannah with his people on board the Simons, Capt. Cornish.

11 Feby. 32.

Bundy, Ri.	C	Ch.	Shaftsbury	C
Ld. Carpenter	C	P	Ld. Tirconnel	C
Egmont	C		Towers, Tho.	C
Holland, Rogers	C		Vernon, Ja.	C
Hucks, Robt.	C		White, Jo.	C
LaRoch, Jo.	C		Smith, Saml.	T

1. It coming to the knowledge of gentlemen that the Order of last meeting had been enter'd in our books, and the material Word Religious left out, Mr. Vernon made complaint thereof, and Said he knew not how it happen'd, for when he left the board, the Gentlemen had agreed that no mony given to us for Religious Uses Should be apply'd to other purposes of the colony: that it was a plain breach of Faith to those who gave us money for religious uses, and would infalibly put a Stop to all future gifts.

Ld. Tirconnel Spoke to the Same effect, and in Some words that gave Mr. White Offence exprest his Surprise how it could happen, but insisted that the minutes Should be alter'd by again inserting the word Religious.

Ld. Carpenter Said we Should take care how we hazarded the continuance of the 50£ p ann Sallary allow'd our Minister by the Incorporate Society, by not restoring the word *religious* for Should they take offence it would fall upon us to pay our Minister, which We have not ability to do.

Lastly, I Said, that I Staid till the breaking up of the board that day and took the Sense of all the gentlemen to be that the Word *Religious* Should Stand part of the resolution, as Securing the thing So long debated and at last given up, that the profits of land cultivated by money Solely given for religious uses, Should be apply'd to no other use. That I thought honour, conscience and prudence required it, and that I had a considerable gift in my pocket to present the Trustees for this end alone, which if the Word *Religious* were not restored, I Should not let them have.

Mr. White in his justification Said, he Scratch'd out the Word Religious, upon the debate of that day, and thought he had thereby exprest the Sense of the gentlemen, Seeing that after the minute was thus alter'd, the Secretary read it publickly, and was order'd to enter it as the Resolution of the Board. That for the rest, it was his judgment the alteration was reasonable.

I reply'd the Secretary might have read the resolution but I did not hear it. That it was customary with Gentlemen, when a thing was agreed to, to leave it to their Secretary to put into form and express it in proper words, and in that confidence all debate being over, to talk of other matters with the friend that Sat next. That I was So persuaded the word *Religious* was in, that I exprest my Satisfaction at the matters passing in the way I had argued for.

Mr. Towers Then Said he must Speak to this point, because he drew up [the] minute. That he had inserted the Word Religious, but Some gentlemen objecting to it, he took it to be the general opinion & Scratch'd it out. That without doubt money given for religious uses ought to be So apply'd, But when the purposes for wch. that money were answer'd, namely the allowance to a Minister & a Schoolmaster, and Church repayrs, the Overplus Rent of the Acres cultivated, if any, ought to go to what other uses the Trustees Should think fit: Otherwise there might be more apply'd to religious uses than is necessary. 300 Acres cultivated might in time yeild 1500£ p ann. and Should all this go to Religious uses?

Mr. LaRoch, Spoke to the Same purpose, adding, that there was no need of this precise care of Religious uses, for doubtless the Trustees would always do in that what Should be proper, and we Should not ty ourselves down.

Mr. Vernon answer'd, that was not the question: the question was whether money given for religious uses can in good faith be apply'd to other uses, or ought to be render'd precarious, for even the leaving that matter open was a degree of breach of faith.

Mr. LaRoch reply'd the money given for Religious Uses might possibly not Suffice for the Ends proposed, in which case the Parlimt. mony must go in aid, but then it was reasonable that the produce of land cultivated by the Assistance of Parliament Should go in part to other than relgious Uses.

To which it was reply'd that the Parliamt. could not mean to exclude religious uses out of their design, & it was a Strange Suggestion that they Should intend no religion to be Supported in Georgia. That the right way of thinking was that what private persons gave for religious uses Should be understood to go in aid of what the Parliamt. intended Should be apply'd out of their money for those purposes.

Mr. White then made a Second Speech resenting that it Should be Suggested he had Surprised the Gentlemen by the alteration of the minute, wherein he So far Said true that it was not his doing alone, but that of Mr. Towers & Aldn. Heathcote in conjunction with him. He Said it was a heavy charge and a great deal of that Sort, and in conclusion moved, that upon every question, the member who went away before it was over Should be noted down by the Secretary. This I opposed as being a needless trouble, for the greatest number of questions were too trivial to remark it, and it would be Sufficient if the chairman thought fit to give the Secrety. order to do it. Mr. White agreed thereto, But afterwards it was resolved that no Order needed to be made of this, But Gentleman Might understand the Sense of the Board to be So, without the formality of entering it in our books.

After So long and warm debate I was for coming to a resolution this day, because I was Sure if put to the vote we Should have carry'd it, whereas a delay was dangerous. Absent gentlemen of the contrary opinion might come down, and the ill blood this affair had occasion'd would encrease by renewing the dispute. But Mr. Towers labour'd to unite our Sentiments, assuring me that the opposing Gentlemen intended at the next meeting to accomodate the matter and gently drop their purpose, which Mr. Hucks confirm'd, and Ld. Tirconnel and Mr. Vernon acqueseing thereto, I also yeilded, but at the Same time assured him that unless they did as he said, Some of the Trustees would quit the Common Council, which could not but be reported in town, to the Striking a great damp on our Proceedings. He reply'd it was a great pity, We who from the beginning proceeded with constant unanimity Should break on this occasion.

Mr. Vernon told me afterwards that if the point were lost next meeting he would resign. I Said I would do the Same, but beg'd him not to do it, till Mr. Oglethorp Should be return'd to England, for it would be a great Shock and discouragement to him, to See the Trust deserted by those who hitherto had Shewn the greatest Zeal for the Colony's Success.

2. Grant of 200 Acres agreed to be past to Mr. Tho. Ormstone in case he carrys over 4 Servants.

[N.B.] 14 feb. 1735-6. Mr. Jo. Wesley relates in his journal, that on this day Tomachachi, Toonahowy, Senawki Tomachachi's wife, and the Micho or king of the Savannah nation with 2 of their chief women and 3 children came on board to visit him. That Tomochachi, Senawki, and Toonahowy were in an English dress, the other women had on calicoe petticoats, and loose wollen mantles. The Savannah King whose face was Stained red in many places, his hair drest with beads and his ear with a Scarlet feather, had only a large blanket which cover'd him from his Shoulders to his feet. Senawki brought a large jar of milk and another of honey, and Said She hoped when we Spoke to them, we would feed them with milk for they were but children, and be Sweet as honey towards them. At our coming into the cabin They all rose, & Tomochachi Stooping forwards, Shook us by the hand, as did all the rest Women as well as Men. This was the more remarkable, because the Indians allow no man to touch or Speak to a Woman, except her husband, not tho She be ill, and in danger even of death. When we were all Set down, Tomochachi by his Interpreter one Mrs. Musgrove Spoke to this effect:

I am glad to see you here When I was in England I desired that Some might Speak the great word to me, and my Nation then desired to hear it; but Since that time We have all been put into confusion. The French have built a Fort with 100 Men in one place, and a Fort with 100 Men in another place, and the Spaniards are preparing for War. The English Traders too put us into confusion, and have Set our people against hearing the great word, for they Speak with a double tongue: Some Say one thing of it, and Some another. But I am glad you are come. I will go up and Speak to the wise men of our Nation, and I hope they will hear. But we would not be made Christians after the Spaniards way to make Christians. We would be taught first, and then baptized. All this he Spoke with much earnestness, and much action both of his hands and head, and yet with the utmost gentleness both of Tone and manner.

[N.B.] 16 feb. 1735–6. The Revd. Mr. Benj. Ingham who went over with Mr. Oglethorp to Georgia, departed from Savannah to Frederica, and in his journal gives the following description of his passage.

Monday 16 feby. about 7 this Evening, I went forward with Mr. Oglethorp, and Some others in a 10 oar'd boat for the Allatahama the Southermost part of Georgia. At 11 we arrived at a place call'd Skidawa, where we went ashoar into the Woods, and Kindled a fire under a lofty Pyne Tree. Having wrote Some letters and eaten Something, we laid down to Sleep on the cold ground, without either bed or board, having no other covering besides our cloathes, but a Single blanket each, and the Canopy of Heaven.

About 8 next day, we Set forward again, passing Several Marshes beset on both Sides with trees of various Sorts, whose leaves being guilded with the glorious rayes of the Son, yeilded a beautiful prospect. About 12 the wind blew So high, that we were driven upon an Oyster bank, where we could not get a Stick to make a fire. Here we dined very comfortably. Near 2 We set forward again, and with great difficulty crost over the Mouth of the River Ogeeky. The Wind was exceeding high, and the water rough, almost every wave drove over the Side of the boat, So that every moment we were in danger of our lives; and truly, if Mr. Oglethorp had not roused up himself, and Struck life into the Rowers, I do not know but that most of us might have here made our Exit. Towards 6 we got to a little place called Bears Island, where we encamp'd all night round a roaring fire, in a bed of canes, where the wind could not reach us. Here also we came up with a large boat call'd a Pettiague, loaded with people for the Allatahama, who had Set out before us.

Next morning after prayers, on Mr. Oglethorps proposal, I went on board the Pettiagua, and in the Evening we lay upon St. Catherines, a very pleasant Island, where we met with 2 Indians hunting. I took one of them on board the Pettiagua, and gave him Some biscuit and wine, and he in return Sent us the greatest part of a deer.

On Sunday morning 22 feby. We arrived at the Island of St. Simons, on the River Allatahama, Where Mr. Oglethorp had reach'd the thursday night before.

18 Feby. 33.

Bundy, Ri.	C		LaRoch, Jo.	C	
Ld. Carpenter	C		Moore, Robt.	C	
Egmont	C	Ch.	Shaftsbury	C	
Hales, Steven	C		Ld. Tirconnel	C	
Heathcote, Geo.	C		Towers, Tho.	C	
Holland, Rogs.	C	P	Vernon, Ja.	C	
Hucks, Robt.	C		White, Jo.	C	
Lapotre, Hen.	C		Anderson, Adam.	T	

1. The form of a Petition to Parliamt. for a further Supply was read & approved, and Ld. Shaftsbury, Ld. Tirconnel, Mr. Holland and Mr. Towers were desired to Shew it to the Speaker & Sr. Robert Walpole on fryday next.

[N.B.] When the E. of Shaftsbury, and the other gentlemen waited (as appointed) on Sr. Robert Walpole to Shew him our petition to Parliamt. and acquainted him we Should want 20000£, he ask'd how they could expect it, Seing Mr. Hucks, White and Heathcote had Spoken and divided against the Parliaments giving 4000£ towards repaying King Henry the 7th Chapel. He added it was indiscreet in Gentlemen who were themselves applying for money, to refuse it to others. That we Should find a great difficulty, Sr. Cha. Wager & Ld. Sundon being determin'd to oppose us, and Himself had had Strong Sollicitations to be out of the way when we offer'd our petition, for then they thought they Should be able to reject it.

Ld. Tirconnel reply'd that he both voted and Spoke for giving the money, wherefore the opposition given by Some of our number was not to be taken for an act of our Board. And Ld. Shaftsbury Said, Our Affair was the Publick's not our own, who got nothing by it, but the trouble of carrying on a design that had been hitherto approved by King and Parliament. In conclusion, Sr. Robert told them, that he would be favourable, but advised the asking as little as could be, that being the most likely to Succeed. Thereupon they proposed 15000£, and at last fell down to 10000, on Supposition they might have 10000£ more next year. The pleasure the Gentlemen mentioned by Sr. Robert, and others of our board take in Shewing the World that they are averse to any thing that bears relation to the establish'd Church, brought Such Suspicion that we were Enemies to the present Constitution, & to a church establishment in Georgia, as cool'd the minds of very many towards us.

2. We also prepared an Estimate of the Supply wanting this year which exclusive of religious uses amounted to 19850£. It was not intended to lay it before the Parliament, for that would have obliged us to be accomptable to Parliamt. and ty'd us down to lay no more out on each head of expence than what was set down in the Estimate in the nature of appropriation, which was not convenient, our calculations being built on probable conjecture, not on absolute certainty, and there might be occasion for Some expences not considered of as not foreseen.

3. We then reasumed the Grand debate touching a provision for the Minister of Savannah. Ld. Carpenter, Dr. Bundy, Ld. Tirconnel and Mr. Vernon gave their opinion as they had done before that the word Religious Should be replaced in the minute. But Mr. White, Mr. Hucks, Mr. LaRoch, Ld. Shaftsbury and Aldn. Heathcote were urgent for Suspending the consideration of this affair to a further time, with whom Mr. Moore joyn'd, for which the only reason they gave was, that an affair of Such importance

required Some time to unite the opinions of gentlemen, who were not yet agreed, that we might afterwards act as unanimously as we had hitherto done; that there was no doubt we Should at last be all of one mind, all being disposed to apply the land in question Solely to religious uses, only we disagreed about the manner.

This was consented to, and it was agreed to meet tomorrow Sennit, when it was told them we hoped they would come to a final resolution.

Soon after, Mr. Towers, who in this affair Sought to please both parties took me aside, and Said, the opposite gentlemen would agree that the land cultivated by money given for religious uses Should be wholly apply'd to that end, but they resented Some words that fell from Ld. Tirconnel last Wednesday that Seem'd to cast a reproach on Mr. White, and therefore intended to propose that the land Should be apply'd in general to religious uses, but not to Specify the particular designs, as for a Minister, a Catechist and building a Church. That by this means there would be a general consent to alter the minute, and being thus alterd, a reflection would not remain on Mr. White that we had done on account of his having Scratch'd the word Religious out.

I told him I did not See how this acquitted Mr. White of what he apprehended himself accused, but it rather look'd as if he and those other gentlemen were against a Church establishment, Seeing they proposed to drop the mentioning provision for a Minister, the building a Church, or keeping a Catechist, whereby they put the Church of England on no better foot than the Dissenters, So that the profits arrising from the land might all be apply'd to the maintaining of Schism for any thing I Saw in their proposal, for Still in that case religious uses would be follow'd. I thought this would have an ill appearance to the Incorporate Society & to the Clergy in general. However, as the main point was gain'd of applying the land Solely to religious uses, I Should be Satisfied, especially Since by not confining the profits to the use of one Minister & Church, there was room for maintaining more in case the profits allow'd it.

Soon after Mr. White came up to me and Said our naming a Minister and Church in our resolutions would endanger our obtaining mony from Parliament. I ask'd him whether he knew that Deists and Dissenters were a majority in the house. He only answerd with a Nod, that I would find it So.

[N.B.] On 21 feby. (as the Accompt. inform'd me) Twelve

Gentlemen of the Trust Supp'd together, and Settld among themselves that the Sum to be ask'd of the Parliament Should be 15000£. They were, Aldn. Heathcote, Mr. Holland, Mr. Hucks, Aldn. Kendal, Mr. La Roch, Mr. Moore, E. of Shafstbury, Mr. Towers, Mr. White, Mr. Tho. Archer, Mr. Hen. Archer and Mr. Tracy; 9 Common Counsellors, and 3 Trustees.

Afterwards they discoursed the affair So long contested concerning the lands for Religious uses. Mr. Towers who Saw the Inconveniences that must follow a breach among the Trustees, began the Argument in favour of our opinion, and as a Lawyer insisted on the justice of not applying the Rents of lands cultivated by money given for religious uses, to purposes foreign thereto, for it Seems they yet were not determin'd to give that matter up. Mr. Holland, likewise a Lawyer, declared himself of the Same opinion, and Alderman Kendal urged the Indiscretion of disgusting So many Gentlemen as thought that way, and who So zealously apply'd themselves to the Service of the Colony. Upon this the Gentlemen yeilded, and it was agreed to acquiesce next meeting, which was to be the thursday following.

26 Feby. 34.

Bundy, Ri.	C		Holland, Rogers	C	
Ld. Carpenter	C	Ch.	Hucks, Robt.	C	
Chandler, Ri.	C		Shaftsbury	C	
Egmont	C		Towers, Tho.	C	
Eyles, Fra.	C	P	Ld. Tirconnel	C	
Hales, Steven	C		Vernon, Ja.	C	
Heathcote, Sr. Will.	C				

1. Mr. Towers acquainted the Board, that the Gentlemen who So long opposed the appropriating 300 Acres to Religious only, had given the matter up, And then offer'd a draft of a resolution on that head for our approbation, which we agreed to without amendment, and order'd it to be enter'd in our books as the Resolution of our Board. It was as follows:

"The Board took into consideration the Committees Report concerning a maintenance for a Minister in Georgia, and resolv'd that a Grant be forthwith made under the corporation Seal of 300 Acres, to Trustees to be appointed and from time to time alter'd as the Common Council Shall think fit; and that all moneys as have been or Shall be recieved for Religious uses of the Colony Shall be apply'd with all convenient Speed, towards the cultivating and improving the Said 300 acres; And that the neat produce and profits thereof Shall from time to time be apply'd to the Religious Uses of the Colony in general only, in Such manner as the Common Council Shall think fit and proper."

Order'd that Mr. Oglethorp be acquainted with this Resolution, and desired forthwith to cause to be Survey'd either together or in parcels 300 Acres in the best Spot of land unsurvey'd in the Neighborhood of Savannah Town. And that he be desired to propose a method for the cultivation, and to Send over a Plan and Estimate for a Church to be built.

2. Order'd that this resolution be publish'd in the Newspapers to clear ourselves of the ill opinion taken up agst. us on Acct. of this long and unreasonable opposition made thereto.

3. Order'd payment of a bill.

4. Grant of 150 acres ordd. to Mr. Reas Price of Landovery in C. Carmarthen under the usual limitations & conditions.

5. Seal put to our petition to Parliament for money, which the Lord Baltimore is to present tomorrow.

[N.B.] At this time we found many Enemies among the Court Members, because they Saw most of the Trustees who are in Parliament Stick together in opposing the Court measures. They Said, We gave a turn to elections, and if encouraged would ruin the Whig cause. They had rather See the Colony perish than that one Election on their Side Should be lost by our means. When Col. Bladen was desired to Speak in favour of our petition, he declined it, owning, which was very indiscreet, that he was chid for doing it the last time. The Same request being made to Sr. Joseph Jekyl, who once had presented a petition for us, and given us 500£ likewise refused. Some pretended we were a prejudice to the Plantations, and the Tories were displeased at our Members opposing the Interest of the Church. Tho Some of our own Body deserted us not long after this long debate about applying lands to religious uses, because they thought we took too much care of the church, and this very next day Mr. White declared to a gentleman that he would resign on the Anniversary Day.

[N.B.] 27 feby. Ld. Baltimore presented our petition to Parliament, and Ld. Tirconnel Seconded it. It was refer'd to the Committee of Supply, and no body opposed it.

[N.B.] 28 feby. Mr. Boltzius Minister to the Saltsburgers wrote large complaints agst. Mr. Vatt, and Shew'd him to be a Silly busie and Domineering fellow. On 10 March following he wrote to the Trustees to be discharged. On 26 May we recall'd him.

[N.B.] 7 March, Mr. Von Reck wrote to Mr. Oglethorpe (then at Frederica) the deplorable State the Saltsburgers of Ebenezer were in, as also complaints agst. Mr. Vatt.

[N.B.] 11 March 1735–6. Mr. John Hamilton came to me with a discovery of 12000£ p ann Lands made over by Papists for pious Uses, which he proposed the Trustees of Georgia Should Set about recovering, by petitioning his Majesty, and obtaining an Act for Settling the Same to the Uses of our Colony. He Said Some Corporations were Solliciting for it, but he rather chose that we Should have it. That these lands were discover'd in King Williams Reign, & a Commission of Inquisition was granted for finding them, the Thirds of the profits to be assign'd to the Informers. That the Lords Commissioners of the Treasury order'd a minute thereof to be taken and enter'd. That the Informers thereupon proceeded by due course of law at their own expence to find and take Inquisitions in Several Counties of England to the amount above mention'd, or thereabouts, which they return'd into the Petty bag Office, and are now upon Record. That the Right and Title of all the Discoverers is now devolv'd Upon him, and he was desirous his Majesty Should grant these Estates to us for the use of Georgia, and that the Parliament would appropriate them for that use.

I told him the Trustees were obliged to him for making them the option of obtaining these lands, but Supposed he had Some proposals to offer of a Suitable consideration to him. He reply'd that could not be doubted, but he would Say nothing as to that till he found we would concern ourselves in it.

I Said these were matters wholly out of my Sphere, and belong'd to Lawyers, wherefore if he gave me leave, I would consult Mr. Towers and Mr. Holland, both Lawyers of our Board, and Parliament Men. To this he agreed, desiring that if they found any difficulty in the thing I would procure him a meeting, that he might explain the matter further. That in the mean time he would tell me, that Col. Selwyn his great friend had often Spoke of it to Sr. Robert Walpole, who did not dissapprove its being brought into Parliament, but declined being himself concerned in it by reason of the Struggle the foreign Popish Ministers at our Court would make to oppose it. He Said he had also Spoke of it to Mr. Philip Gibbons, who is very desirous it Should come into Parliament, and that Mr. Sands approves it no less, but he would not be the man to introduce it because it might divide his Party, there being among them Several Jacobites who would certainly oppose it.

I ask'd him whether in his opinion Sr. Joseph Jekyl was not a proper Man, he having [spoken] So lately as but yesterday against Pious Uses bequeath'd by Protestants, and therefore the more likly to be zealous against Popish Pious Uses. He thought him proper.

Some days after Mr. Holland, Mr. Towers and I had a meeting with this gentleman, When it appear'd that there [were] difficulties in prossecuting this affair not to be got over. For the persons are dead who first gave information of these lands in 1692, & Mr. Towers thought the Inquisition taken of them and their return into the Petty bag Office was no authority for the Trustees of Georgia to petition his Majesty to grant them to Georgia. Besides, Supposing his Majesty Should grant them, a Suit of law would follow upon ejecting the present Occupyers, and it did not appear there were any living wittnesses to prove the Kings Right.

Mr. Hamilton reply'd, that he was inform'd the Parliament had gone So far as to engross a bill for recovering these lands, and he conceived this might be a ground for petitioning the Parliament, which if done, he doubted not but Several who now are Tenants would upon passing an act turn to the Trustees, and make discoveries. Mr. Towers Said he would look into the journals of those times, but doubted tho he Should find it there whether the Parliament would revive the matter, without Wittnesses to prove the illegal Application of those Rents.

After this Conversation, Mr. Hamilton came to my house to inform me that Since our meeting, he had got further lights. That he had been with Mr. Towers and informed him, that Mr. Jerningham the Goldsmith had own'd to a friend of his, that he was the person who transmitted those Rents to Popish Seminaries abroad, and that he believe he could produce a person who would furnish us with authentick Copies of the Original deeds of Gifts kept in a particular Office in Rome. That Mr. Towers Said if he could produce them it would be matter to go upon, but who should defray the charge? The Trustees could not do it, for it would be a misapplication of their money. That he reply'd neither could he do it, but perhapps charitable persons might be moved to contribute thereto.

Upon discoursing this matter with Mr. Towers and Mr. Vernon it appeard to them more rational than feazable. They Said it would be necessary that authentick copies of the original deeds and legacies Should be obtained from Rome, and the Same proved authentick, before we could proceed therein. But then, where to get money we knew not for defraying the charge. For if the design Should take wind we Should be defeated, but it must take wind, if we apply to others to contribute to it. And as to the money under the Trustees care we could not apply any of it thereto. That were we to undertake it, nothing could be done therein this Session. Mr. Towers added, that he found Mr. Hamilton was for laying all the load and expence on the Trustees, but he had Staved it off, the rather because we had hitherto kept entire a reputation of prudence in all our proceedings, and it would be pitty we Should forfeit it by engaging in an unsuccessfull attempt.

Thus ended this negotiation, which I have put together that the thread of it might be kept, tho reasum'd at different times. It were certainly of publick benefit (and I think if a national concern) that the Revenues which Supply England with Such a number of Regular and Secular Priests of the Romish Church, were thoroughly enquired into, and forfeited to the publick, but it Seems this is not the time.

[N.B.] 16 March 1735–6 I recd. a letter from Mr. Oglethorp dated 1 feby. last and wrote when he was 30 leagues from the Coast of Georgia. In it he recommends

1. The procuring a Supply from Parliament this Session, to Supply the following occasions:

Two years provision for the people he carry'd over, the Season for planting being lost, by Staying So long at Cowes for the Kings Sloop to convey them. N.B: This extraordinary expence with the demurrage of the Ships cost the Trustees near 3400£ allowing to the negligence of the Officer in not dispatching Capt. Gascoign.

Continuation of Rangers, otherwise the new Settlements would have no communication by land, or Support, & were Subject at pleasure to be Surprised by the French Indians.

The keeping 100 Workmen at pay to make communications.

The Entertainment of boats to keep open Communications by water.

Presents for the Indians more than ever, the French and Spaniards labouring to debauch them from us.

Pay of Agents to bring more Settlers from Swizerland & Germany.

He added that we have already 1200 Foreigners Settled in Georgia and the Neighborhood (I Suppose he meant Purysburg) Most of them Settled at their own expence and putting the Colony to no expence.

At the Same time came a letter from Mr. Causton to the Trustees giving acct. of the arrival of Capt. Dunbar with his Scots, Capt. Diamond with provision from Ireland, and Capt. Dicker with Servants from Bristol, all which Ships tho Saild from different parts arrived the Same day 10 Jany. at Savannah.

He mention'd also a jealousie infused into our neighboring Indians that we had agreed with the Northern Indians to write and cut them off. Which was occasion'd by Some ill designing persons, and partly by a man's going to them with a red flag (we Suppose from Carolina) Which is with them a Token of War. But he convinc'd Tomachachi of the malice & untruth of that report, & obtain'd of him to Send to those Indians two of his Men who had been here in England to undeceive him.

He further writes that he had caused the mouths of the Allatahama to be Survey'd and Sounded; that the middle opening was impeded but the most Southern mouth was found to have 2 fathom & ½ over the bar at low water, and the bay within very Secure for Shipping, being land lock'd from the Winds.

[N.B.] On 6 March 1735–6 Mr. Jo. Brownfeild Register of the Province wrote the Trustees, yt. at his arrival at Savannah he found the Town at a very low Ebb, and overstock'd wth. goods of Trade. That the people were harrast with executions for debt & imprisonment. That these means were chiefly used by a number of Scots Gentlemen (these were the Stirlings, Tailfer &c who afterwards made Such noise for negroes and change of Tenure of lands) who arrived there Soon after Mr. Oglethorp went for England in 1734, and instead of cultivating their land fell into Trade, and thereby dispirited the poor Inhabitants from any attempts that way. These when they had engros'd most part of the Trade, advanced their prices, and by fair outward pretences drew abundance of people into debt, Soon after which, they threaten'd to Serve executions in order to get houses and lands morgaged to them, and Succeeded with a few weak men. That giving Credit proved hurtfull to those who received it, for they quitted all labour finding that goods could be had without, and fell into a habit of idleness. But those who lived independent of the trading people by keeping out of debt, made most Improvment on their lands.

[N.B.] On the 13 March O.S. Don Francisco de Moral Sanchez Govr. of St. Augustine, complained in a civil manner to Mr.

Oglethorp, that we had extended into his mastr. the K. of Spains Dominions, by going out of the bounds mark'd out to each King by ancient Treaties with his Predecessors. On the 19th he repeated the Same. On the 18 March and 5 April 1736 Capt. Dempsi wrote an Acct. from St. Augustine to Mr. Oglethorp of his negotiation with the Govr. to preserve a good understanding. On 14 April he inform'd him of preparations of War making by the Governor. On the 17th Mr. Oglethorp wrote the Trustees that he had advice 1500 men and 3 men of war had left the Havannah to dislodge the Southern Settlement as was apprehended, and that he had Sent the D. of Newcastle a Memorial of our Kings Right to Georgia.

[N.B.] On 16 March Mr. Oglethorp wrote the Trustees that he was to go the next day with Tomachachi to hunt the Buffaloe, as far as his utmost extend of Dominions towards St. Augustine, by which he Should know how far the lands possest by the English Confederate Indians extend. That Tomachachi was willing we Should settle upon any place within his lands, provided the Lower Creek Nations agreed to it. That he allow'd us possession of St. Simons Island, but reserved the Islan of St. Catherine to the Indians.

18 March. 35.

Bundy, Ri.	C	Ld. Tirconnel	C
Ld. Carpenter	C	Towers, Tho.	C
Egmont	C	Vernon, Ja.	C P
Hales, Steven	C	White, Jo.	C
Heathcote, Sr. Will.	C	Archer, Tho.	T
Holland, Rog.	C	Archer, Hen.	T
Hucks, Robt.	C Ch.	Burton, Jo.	T
LaRoch, Jo.	C	Smith, Saml.	T
Sloper, Will.	C	Heathcote, Geo.	C

1. This being our Aniversary day we met at St. Brides Church, where Dr. Watts gave us an excellent Sermon, which we obtain'd leave from him to print.

2. The Accompt. layd before us a State of Receipts & disbursments from 9 June 1735 to this day.

3. Sundry bills of exchange drawn upon the Trustees were order'd to be paid amounting to 700£.

4. Imprest 1500£ to Aldn. Heathcote.

5. After this most of us dined together at the Castle Tavern,

and with Some Strangers. But Mr. White had bespoke a dinner at home and carry'd with him away Aldn. Heathcote and Mr. Hucks. He also ask'd Mr. LaRoch, but he chose to remain with us. It was Supposed that Mr. Moore and Ld. Shaftsbury were of that Company, for they came not to us. This was esteem'd by Some Studied Slight of us, and a very mean mark of his resentment and discontent that he could not carry his point relating to the lands Set out for Religious uses.

[N.B.] 24 March 1735–6. Mr. Eveleigh wrote our Accompt. that on Mr. Oglethorps arrival at Tybee he imprison'd and threatened to hang the Chief Undertakers for building the Light House, whereupon he undertook to finish it in 5 weeks, and in 16 days, had done more than in 16 months before.

That the Red Bluff where the Saltsburgers were removed from their first Settlement (calld as the former was, Ebenezar) is good land for planting and timber, and that it Stands 2 miles up a creek that falls into Savannah River, 3 miles above Purysburg, on the Georgia Side.

That the Merchants of Charlestown had joyned in a Memorial to the Govr. & Council in relation to the Indian Trade, which they apprehend Savannah is likely to take from them, and that it was refer'd to the Assembly where hot debates arose, and that they came to Several resolutions resolving to defend the Indian trade to the utmost of their power.

25 *March 1736.* 36.

Egmont	C	Vernon, Ja.	C
Towers, Tho.	C		

There being nothing of moment to order this day, we made no board.

[N.B.] 26 March 1736. This day Ld. Baltimore moved the Committee of Supply for 10000£ to carry on our designs, and Ld. Tirconnel Seconded him. There were a few noes, but no body Spoke against it, and the Sum was granted.

[N.B.] 28 March 1736. Mr. Oglethorpe wrote Govr. Broughton that he had been to view the Spanish Out Guards South of St. Juans River, and gone round the Southernd most point of his Majesties Dominions in N. America, which he named St. Georges Point, and is over against the Spaniards Lower Lookout, from which it is Seperated by the mouth of St. Juans River, which is there about a mile broad. That returning, he found the Highland

Men whom he had left upon an Island at the Southward most Entrance of Frederica Post had fortified themselves there, and that he named this new Fort St. Andrews, and the Island it Stands in, The Highlands. The Island is call'd by the Spaniards St. Pedro, and is much larger than St. Simons.

29 March 37

Ld. Carpenter	C	Towers, Tho.	C
Heathcote, Sr. Will.	C	Vernon, Ja.	C
Egmont	C		

1. This was only a Committee of Correspondence. We agreed it to be impossible to proceed on the new Settlement on the Allatahama River, Since the Parliamt. had given us this year but 10000£, which will barely Suffice to feed the people fed from our Stores, in number near 1300, including those who went with Mr. Oglethorp. We therefore drew up a letter for the Common Councils approbation, to inform Mr. Oglethorp of the case, and to abandon the design of that new Settlement, and to Settle the new people either on the Ogeeky river, or at Savannah.

2. A Benefaction reported of 50£ in Iron ware towards building a Church and Ministers house.

[N.B.] 29 March. Mr. Eveleigh wrote to Mr. Oglethorp from Charlestown, that Capt. Watson brought an Account. there from St. Augustine, that the Governr. Shew'd him a letter from Monsr. Bienville General of Louisiana, in which he offers that in case he Should be attack'd by the English, he would Send him 5000 Men for his assistance.

31 March 38.

Bundy, Ri.	C		Shaftsbury	C P
Digby, Edwd.	C		Sloper, Will.	C
Egmont	C		Ld. Tirconnel	C
Heathcote, Sr. Will.	C		Towers, Tho.	C
Holland, Rogers	C	Ch.	Vernon, Ja.	C

1. Agreed to the letter prepared by the Committee of Correspondence the 29. inst. to Mr. Oglethorp for recalling him from the Allatahama and Settling the people he carry'd over, either on the Ogeeky or at Savanna, which letter is to be dispatch'd away next tuesday by a Ship going from Bristol to Georgia. Some of the

reasons have been given before, to which we added, that at the Ogeeky or Savannah provisions will be cheaper and Sooner come at, that the Inhabitants would be more compact and a Stronger Support to each other. That we Should thereby Save the charge of a Company of Rangers, and of cutting roads, of 3 new Sloops destin'd for the new Settlement, of presents to the Indians for purchassing new lands. That our disappointment in being granted but 10000£ instead of 20000£ which we expected made the utmost frugality necessary, especially as there would be 2 years Subsistance necessary for 491 persons gone this year, and 500 others Still a charge on the Stores and till their lands can Subsist them. That nevertheless, for the Security of the Southern part of our Province, We would when the Parliament is up Sollicite the Ministry, that the late demolish'd Fort at the Forks may be rebuilt by his Majesty, and the Independent Company paid by the Government, and now at Charlestown may be remanded thither. That the reason why the Ministry were disposed to give but 10000£ was the assurance of a General Peace, which would Secure our Province from molestation either from French or Spaniards, Whereas when he embark'd for the Allatahama it was uncertain whether we might not have war with the Spaniards.

2. Seal put to a Grant of 300 Acres for religious uses, and Tho. Causton, Hen. Parker, Jo. West & Tho. Christie made Feofees in trust.

[N.B.] It was remark'd that the E. of Shaftsbury went away when we came to put the Seal to the Grant of land for religious Uses. He was one of those who opposed it before, being led away by his friendship with others, but otherwise a Nobleman of great virtue and worth.

3. A Second Letter order'd to Mr. Oglethorp, desiring him to Set out the Said 300 acres in whole or in parcells near Savannah town, and that it be of the best land. That it be enclosed and cultivated as Soon as possible that a Rent may be raised for maintaining a Minister, a Catechist, and for repayring the Church intended to be built, which Church to be of brick, and made Strong, So as to be capable of defense in case of Sudden Surprise. That the Church yard be enclosed and also made defensible, and an estimate of the charge of this to be Sent by him to the Trustees as Soon as possible.

4. Resolv'd that a Catechist be appointed at Savannah, That Mr. Oglethorp be desired to find out a proper person to be Catechist, and that the 10£ annual benefaction pd. by Mr. Burton for

5 years certain or during the life of the benefactor be apply'd as intended to the use of Such Catechist.

A third letter order'd to be wrote to Mr. Causton our 1 Bailif and Storekeeper, to Send us a particular acct. of the people now Subsisted out of our publick Stores, and their pretentions be continued thereon; And that he Strike off all who have been Subsisted there out two years, unless in very particular cases whereof he must inform us; and to let him know that if we find reason to dissapprove his proceedings therein he will incur our highest displeasure.

5. I presented 3 benefactions from Mrs. Southwell of 100£ towards building a church at Savannah, and 100£ for cultivating lands for a Minister, and 100£ towards a Fund for maintaining a Catechist. I was desired to return her thanks, and with all to represent that as we had not Sufficient money to cultivate lands for the Ministers Maintenance, it were better, if She thought fit, to let the last mention'd 100£ go to that Service as well as the first hundred pounds for the Same land intended for the Minister will when cultivated yeild a perpetual maintenance for a catechist too.

6. Grant past the Seal of 200 acres to Tho. Ormston of Edingburg Mercht.

7. Grant of 150 acres past the Seal to Reas Price of Landovery in Carmarthenshire.

[N.B.] I know not if Mr. Price ever took out his Grant.

8. Order'd that Memorials of the Grants made this day be registerd in the Auditor of the Plantations Office.

7 April 39.

| Bundy, Ri. | C P | Holland, Rogers | C |
| Egmont | C | Vernon, Ja. | C |

1. Report made of the 200£ benefactions of Mrs. Southwell, one for cultivating land for a Minister, the other for building a Church. This was appointed a Common Council for fixing resolutions to prevent unnecessary applications for going to Georgia.

[N.B.] 9 April 1736. Mr. Brownfeild wrote the Trustees that he was inform'd St. Juans River is 60 miles South of Frederica, on a Streight line, and 30 North of St. Augustine.

[N.B.] 12 April, Accounts came of the progress made at Frederica: That the Town Lotts were already given out to each family, Those on the Strand consisting of 30 feet in front, and 80 feet in depth. Those further from the River of 60 feet in front, & 90 in

[1736] JOURNAL OF THE EARL OF EGMONT 147

depth. That the garden lots, each one acre, were mark'd out, and possession would be given the next day. That the people planted corn in common in an old Indian feild of about 60 acres. That Some barly and Lucern grass was come up well. That a Fort was near finish'd consisting of 4 bastions and a ditch with Some bulwarks fraized round with Cedar Posts; the Works faced with Greensod, which grew very well.

That Capt. Mcpherson was come over by land from Savannah to Darien (which ly's 16 miles from Federica by water and is 3 hours in rowing) and that by a travers line Darien is distant from Savannah 70 miles, but go by the places where the Swamps are passable.

That the first day Mr. Oglethorp departed from Frederica to view the extent of his Majesties Dominions Southward, the Indians carry'd him to an Island at the mouth of Jekyl Sound, where on a high ground commanding the passes of the River, he left a party of Highlanders under the command of Lieut. Hugh Mackay, who mark'd out a fort & call'd St. Andrews, and Toonahowy pulling out a watch given him by the Duke when in England named the Island in memory of him Cumberland. This is the Same with Pedro Island, before named the Highlands by Mr. Oglethorp.

That the next day they past the Clothogotheo, another Branch of the Allatahama, and discover'd another fine Island about 16 miles long, with Oranges, myrtles and vines growing wild to which he gave the name of Amelia, in memory of her Highness the Princess.

That the third day, he arrived near the Spanish Look out, and having run down the River St. Juans or St. Wanns, doubled point St. George, being the North point of St. Juans River, and the Southernmost point of his Majesties Dominions on the Sea Coast of N. America, The Spaniards being in possession, & having a Guard call'd a Lookout on the other Side of that River.

That returning, he call'd at St. Andrews and was agreably Surprised to find the Fort in a State of defence. He profer'd the Highlanders to transport them back to Darien, but they chose to remain there.

14 April 40.

Egmont	C	LaRoch, Jo.	C
Kendal, Ri.	C	Towers, Tho.	C

This day was appointed a Common Council for the purpose above mentioned but we could not make a board. Mr. Towers went himself to the House of Commons to desire Aldn. Heathcote, Sr. William Heathcote, Mr. Hucks and Mr. White to come to us that we might be able to transact business, but the two last refused without giving any reason, Sr. Willm. was obliged to Stay there on business, and Aldn. Heathcote promised to come but faild.

1. All we therefore did was to read two letters, one from Mr. Causton dat. 15 feby. that Mr. Oglethorp had Settled every thing to Satisfaction in and about Savannah, and was then on board with the Indians to proceed to the Allatahama to make the new Settlement there.

2. The other was a letter from a Gentleman in Jamaica to Mr. Pyne of London, Engraver, wherein that Gentleman gave excellent reasons why the Settlement at Allatahama ought to be pursued.

20 April 41.

Egmont	C P	Lapotre, Hen.	C
Heathcote, Geo.	C	LaRoch, Jo.	C
Heathcote, Sr. Will.	C	Ld. Tirconnel	C

A Common Council was Summond this day upon business that required dispatch yet we could not make a board, for tho Mr. White and Mr. Moore were Sent for to the House of Commons they excused themselves being desirous to hear the debates on the Mortmain bill, tho we might have finish'd our business before that came on. The Business before us was to consider of an Acct. recieved by Mr. Simons the Mercht. from Mr. Oglethorp of the Ballance of freight, victualling and demurrage and pilotage of the Ship Princess of Wales, Stated at Tibee Road the 13 feby last. To order the acceptance and payment of bills, and to issue money to compleat the amount of them.

21 April 42.

Ld. Carpenter	C		Heathcote, Sr. Will.	C
Chandler, Ri.	C		Lapotre, Hen.	C
Digby, Edwd.	C	P	LaRoch, Jo.	C Ch.
Egmont	C		Shaftsbury	C
Heathcote, Geo.	C		Ld. Tirconnel	

A Common Council was Summond for the purposes mention'd above.

1. Benefactions recd. I paid Mrs. Southwells 3d 100£ to be apply'd as Gentlemen had desired to the cultivating lands for maintenance of a Minister at Savannah. I also paid 25£ given by Sr. Philip Parker Long my brother in law for the Same purpose.

2. Resolv'd that a Catechist at Savannah be maintained out of the 300 Acres granted for Religious uses.

3. Resolv'd to Send 4 persons on the poor Acct. from Liverpool recommended by the Revd. Dr. Stanley and the Inhabitants of that Town, and that no more persons be Sent over this year 1736 on the poor account our money not holding out to Subsist them.

4. Resolv'd to accept the following bills drawn on the Trustees by Mr. Causton for necessaries in Georgia, viz.

His bill to Mr. Eveleigh for 272.0.0
His bill to —————— for 200.0.0
His bill to Col. Bull for 342.17.2 the purchasse of Cattel.

5. Defer'd acceptance of 2 other bills of Mr. Causton, advice not being come thereof.

6. A bill of Mr. Chardons for 38.17.2 was refer'd back to Mr. Oglethorp, there being a difference between the draft, & the Acct. Sent us.

7. An Acct. of Mr. Oglethorps was refer'd to the consideration of a Committee of Accompts. it was for 246.1.4.

8. Imprest 600£ to Aldn. Heathcote towards payment of the bills accepted, he having in his hands Sufficient to pay the rest.

9. Observing that Mr. White & Mr. Moore had totally withdrawn their attendance the last ever Since the 18 feby. and the former Since the Anniversary day, I took notice this day how difficult it was to proceed on business for want of a due number of Gentlemen, and laid it home to the consciences, honour, & humanity of all who had taken a Trust of this publick nature upon them not to be careless in their duty of attendance. That the lives and well being of near 2300 people are concerned, and if anything amiss Should fall out by our negligence, the Parliament would certainly call us to account, which had given So much for erecting this Colony. I Suppose what I Said was told those two gentlemen by Some of the Company present, and that it quicked their resolution to quit us, wch. I was inform'd they long had design'd, for the next meeting they both resign'd their Office of Common Counsellors.

[N.B.] 30 April 1736, A letter was wrote from Charlestown

expressg. great jealousie that the Province of Georgia would deprive them of the Indian Trade for Skins, & reproaching them with Ingratitude.

[N.B.] 1 May 1736. The people of Charlestown made heavy complaints the Magistrates of Savannah Staved their Rum that was only passing up the River, & imprison'd the Patrons.

This month Mr. Oglethorp Sent Mr. Horton and others to the Govr. of St. Augustine to preserve friendship but apprehended he had made prisoners of them.

5 May 43.

Egmont	C	Vernon, Ja.	C P
Moore, Robt.	C	Anderson, Adam	T
Tirconnel	C	Bedford, Arthr.	T

A Common Council was Summond. for this day, to recieve a Report from a Committee of Accts. relating to the freight victualling and demurrage of the Ship Pr. of Wales: but we could not make a board.

1. Benefactions to Religious Uses reported.

2. Report made to us, of a bill of 100£ drawn by Mr. Oglethorp, of which advice was not yet arrived. This both Surprised and troubled us. He carry'd with him 5000£ in bills and money, and if draw upon us notwithstanding, we Shall quickly be bankrupt. He knows not how low we are in Cash.

3. Another thing that much displeased us at first, was a bill for 100£ drawn on us by Mr. Causton, notwithstanding orders had long Since been Sent him not to draw bills anymore, Mr. Oglethorp having money to answer all occasions. But by computing the date with the time our orders above mentioned were arrived, we found the bill was drawn two days before.

4. Letters received from Mr. Eveleigh, and John Bromfeild our Register were read.

[N.B.] Mr. Eveleighs letter contain'd, a very advantagious Acct. of St. Simonds Island wch. lys before one of the branches of the Allatahama, the ground of which he says is richer even than that of Rhode Island. He likewise confirm'd that the middle branch of the Allatahama is not navigable for large Ships.

John Bromfeild wrote that the Scots which went with Capt. Dunbar had Settled on St. Simonds Island, and had already built a Fort and 8 hutts, which So pleasd Mr. Oglethorp that in compliment he Some times wore the Highland dress. That the Assembly of South Carolina had Sent a Deputation to compliment him on his arrival at Savannah with offers of their assistance. That great care was taken to prevent the Introduction of Rum, and the 3 Acts Sent over were to be publickly read & proclaymed next day to the Inhabitants.

5. After this Mr. Moore presented his and Mr. Whites resignation of their Office of Common Counsellors. It was respectfully drawn up, expressing their incapacity of continuing by reason of their absence from town the greatest part of the year, and when in it, their attendance on Parliament. They profest this to be the only reason for resigning, and declared they were Still most cordial well wishers to the Colony, whose good they Should continue to promote, being persuaded it was one of the most usefull & noble designs that could have been thought on. Afterwards Mr. Moore Said that one of the main reasons for their quitting (though they did not mention it in their resignation) was the coldness which the Ministry Shew towards the Colony.

That the Ministry were cold to us we all knew, but if that were a justifiable reason for their quitting it was the Same for every Member. And as to their not being able to attend because of their avocations in the Country, Many Gentlemen who did not quit had the Same plea. And they knew we did not expect their attendance at Such times of the year; but it might have been expected when they were in town, for our business generally was over before the Parliamt. Set to business, and our Office adjoining to the two houses. But the true Secret was, they never could be reconciled to us after losing their point concerning the lands Granted for Religious uses; and tho they made Such professions of being cordial Well wishers to the Colony, they never assisted as Trustees to carry it on, nay one year that the motion was making to grant us a further Supply Mr. White rose from his Seat and left the house with another of our board, as if he had a mind publickly to Shew the house he was against a Supply.

12 May 44.

Egmont	C	Towers, Tho.	C
Sloper, Will.	C	Vernon, Ja.	C
Ld. Tirconnel	C		

1. A Common Council was Summon'd this day for granting lands to persons going over at their own expence, but we were not a board.

[N.B.] 18 May. Mr Oglethorp wrote the Trustees that the Govr. had released Mr. Horton being advised by his Officers & by the Bishop to live in amity with us. He also Shew'd why Causton Staved ye Caroline Rum, the Sloop not Keeping to the Carolina Side of the river, but coming up the channel formd by Hutchinsons Island nearest Savannah, which made it reasonably Suspected the Rum was design'd to be run into Georgia.

19 May 45.

Ld. Carpenter	C		Towers, Tho.	C
Egmont	C	P	Vernon, Ja.	C Ch.
Lapotre, Hen.	C		Anderson, Adam	T
LaRoch, Jo.	C		Smith, Saml.	T
Ld. Tirconnel	C			

1. Capt. Thompson of the Two Brothers lately arrived from Georgia, attended, and acquainted us that the people are all well, and industrious in clearing their lands. That almost all the 5 acre lotts are clear'd, and now they are busie in clearing their 45 acre lotts. That they are quiet & orderly, and Williams who lately went over on his own account had already freighted a Ship load of timber, which paid the charge of the Servants he carry'd over.

2. He demanded 12 days consideration for demurrage beyond the time agreed for at 40 Shill. *p* diem, which we promised to take into consideration.

3. Letters from Mr. Oglethorp enclosing divers others were read, which contained matters of importance, were referd to divers of our Members to prepare answers to, who are to meet next tuesday for that purpose.

[N.B.] By Mr. Oglethorps letters and others we find the Saltsburgers were not pleas'd with their Settlement at Ebenezar, and therefore obtain'd leave from Mr. Oglethorp (tho much against his grain) to remove lower near the mouth of Ebenezar River, opposite to Purysburg. That they were at difference among themselves, and that the last embarkation of them under the Conduct of Mr. Von Reck which were to Settle at Frederica were gone to Settle with their Countrymen which carry'd 50 Stout Men away from the defence of the South, So that Mr. Oglethorp had with him only 200 effective men, only the Scots at Fort Arguile were near at hand. But this removal of the Saltsburgers from the South had occasion a vast expence for provisions.

That he had already begun the Settlement on the Allatahama.

and traced out a Fort on which Men were at Work. That others were employ'd in cutting a road from Frederica to Georgia, a length of 90 Miles. That Frederica Town was mark'd out and a good part of the peoples lands. That Tomachachi and his Indians were come down thither from Savannah, and So eager to assert their right to the land as far as St. Augustin, that Mr. Oglethorp was obliged to keep a boat on the River St. Juan to prevent their going over and making War on the Spaniards. That the Governor of St. Augustin had Sent him a very civil Message, but it was Suspected he had Sent a Ship to get Soldiers to drive us from our new Settlement.

4. A letter from Ld. Harrington Secy. of State was deliver'd us, enclosing one from Mr. Horace Walpole at the Hague to him, And an application from 300 Palatin Protestants to be transported to Georgia, who were to be follow'd by 1100 more. My Lord desired to know what we would do therein. We instantly drew up an answer to his Lordship, that with the money remaining in our hands and the 10000£ given us this year by Parliament we were not able to Support the Settlement already made, wherefore we desired him to represent to his Majesty the impossibility we were under to engage in any new expence for transporting Foreigners.

5. Benefactions reported: 10£ given for Religious Uses. 10£ for a Catechist, and 15£ for a Botanist, and Agriculture.

6. Then the Common Council took into consideration Two bills drawn upon us by Mr. Causton for 400£. There was no advice come of them, but the time of payment being expired, and the Merchts. threatening to protest the bills unless accepted, we comply'd with them to be pd. when advice comes.

7. There were also bills to the value of 700£ drawn by Mr. Oglethorp, but the time of payment not being due, we postponed the consideration of them. We admired at these drafts, so Soon after Mr. Oglethorps arrival who, as has formerly been observed carry'd with him 5000£.

8. Order'd 20 Tun of Strong beer and Some Spices to Supply the Stores in Georgia, and to go by the next Ship.

9. Refer'd the demand of Mr. Simons for demurrage of the London Merchant to a Committee of Accompts.

10. Refer'd also a letter of Capt. Thompsons dat. 19th inst. to the Said Committee.

11. Grant of 100 Acres past & Seal'd to Patrick Graham Surgeon and Apothecary of Crief in Scotland.

12. Grant of 100 Acres past and Seal'd to Hen. Pitts of Carlile, Carpenter.

[N.B.] I do not find that Hen. Pitt took out his grant, or ever went over.

[N.B.] 19 May, the Govr. of St. Augustine Sent Plenipotentiaries to Mr. Oglethorp to Know why he Settled a garrison at the Fort St. George and on St. Simons Island, and to agree a Treatie of Amity.

[N.B.] 22 May, Mr. Oglethorp wrote to the Govr. and Shew'd his Majesties of Gr. Britains right to make those Settlements.

[N.B.] 22 May, Mr. Eveleigh wrote to our Accompt. that the Forts at Frederica & St. Andrews were Strong and compleat. That Olive trees thrive wonderfully in S. Carolina & therefore must certainly Succeed well in Georgia. That a gentleman of the Same Province had made as much Silk last year as he Sold for 100£ currency, and that he kept an exact acct. of his Negroes labour about it, and found that they got Seven & Sixpence *p* day, which is much as they could have done at any other work, and he hoped this would encourage the Planters to go upon it. That the assembly were passing a law for giving 4 pds. *p* hundred premium for hemp. 40 Shill. for Flax, and 20 Shillgs *p* pound on Silk.

That by Mr. Oglethorps order he had bought up at Charlestown arms to the value of 500£ to prevent the Govr. of Augustin from buying them to present the Upper Creeks.

[N.B.] 24 May, he wrote another letter, that Monsr. Bienville Govr. of Lousiiana had Sent for 800 Illinois Indians, who came down the River Messasippi, & March'd 10 weeks ago with 2500 White Men agst the Chickesaws (who are in friendship with the English) who are a Nation only of 400 fighting Men, but bold warriours & good Hunters. That the reason given is that they protected Some Scatterd Nauchees, who took a Fort and kill'd a great number of French Some years ago on the Messasippi. That the Genl. would not take with him any of the Chocktaws, tho a nation of 3 or 4000 Men, because they are not reckon'd Stout, for they have had war these Several years with the Chickesaws & it is not Known which had the best. That Some believed these latter will be obliged to remove either to the Cherikees who live beyond the Appalachee Mountains, or down to the Creeks.

26 *May* 46.

Egmont	C	LaRoch, Jo.	C
Kendal, Robt.	C	Lapotre, Hen.	C

Shaftsbury	C	Anderson, Adm.	T
Towers, Tho.	C P	Bedford, Arthr.	T
Vernon, Ja.	C		

A Common Council was Summond for this day to Grant land to a person who goes by the Two brothers at his own expence, to receive Reports from the Committees of Correspondence and Accts. and other business. But we could not make a board.

1. It was debated whether a new letter Should not be wrote to Mr. Oglethorp, to reinforce our former wherein we advised his abandoning the design of Settling a Town to the Southward of our Province, being unprovided of Cash to carry it on. But Mr. Towers moved we would defer our final resolution thereon till the next meeting, it being his judgment that it ought to be left to Mr. Oglethorps discretion, and that Since the people are now Settled there at a very great expence, it may be Sufficient if we Send no more persons thither. That the removing them will be a new expence, and by it all the Sums already disburs'd on this Settlement be lost.

2. Agreed a letter be wrote to Mr. Boltzius the Saltsburg Minister, and therein to recall Mr. Vat Secrety. of their affairs, Since he represented him to be a very troublesome fellow.

2 June. 47.

Chandler, Ri.	C	Ld. Tirconnel	C
Egmont	C	Towers, Tho.	C P
Hucks, Robt.	C	Vernon, Ja.	C
Kendal, Robt.	C	Anderson, Adm	
Lapotre, Hen.	C	Bedford, Arthr.	
LaRoch, Jo.	C	Smith, Saml.	
Shaftsbury	C Ch.		

1. Benefactions reported.
2. Approved of a letter to Mr. Oglethorp containing matters of great importance.
3. Approved a letter to Mr. Boltzius.
4. Received & approved the Report of the Committee of 5 May, that Mr. Simons Acct. of freight demurrage &c of the Ship Pr. of Wales cannot be Settled until Capt. Dunbar be examin'd thereon.
5. Recd. the Said Committees report of 26 May, and approved the Same that Mr. Simons demand above mentioned ought to be paid.
6. Recd. the Report of Said Committee 26 May & approved the

Same, that Mr. Simons demand of demurrage &c of the Ship London Merchant ought to be paid.

7. Received and approved the Said Committees Report upon Capt. Will. Thompsons Memorial of 19 May being a demand for demurrage of the Ship Two Brothers, And order'd 26.16.0 to be paid the Owner thereof.

8. Letter from Mr. Oglethorp dat. 27 feby. was read, informing us that the Scots under the leading of Lieut. Hugh Mackay had Settled themselves at 3 hours distance from the mouth of the Allatahama, & call'd their Town Darien; that they had built themselves hutts, laid out ground for a church and traced a Fort of 4 bastions. They are 177 persons.

9. Resolv'd that 6 Reams of paper for printing off Sola bills be provided.

10. Orderd that the Skins Sent us as a present from Tomachachi be drest and Sold for the uses of the Trust.

11. Order'd that out of the 10000£ granted last Session of Parliamt. 100£ be given to our Accomptant.

12. Order'd that out of the Same 100£ be given to our Secrety for their Services.

13. The Widow of William Calloway (deceased in Georgia 4 June 1735) complaining of injury done herin relation to her late husbands effects, Order'd that Enquiry be made into it.

14. Resolv'd that the Grant made to Bullfinch Lamb 7 Oct. 1734 of 500 Acres is void, he not having perform'd the condition of his Grant of going over within the time limmitted.

15. A Bill drawn by Mr. Causton accepted.

16. Two bills drawn by Mr. Oglethorp, one for 200£, being the making 2 wood houses in Carolina for Frederica Town, the other for Supply's furnish'd by Mr. Cha. Pury, were orderd to be accepted & paid.

17. Three other bills drawn by Mr. Oglethorp of which we have received no advice, amounting to 500£ Orderd Suspension of acceptance.

18. Two other bills drawn by Mr. Oglethorp amounting to 300£, were voted not to be accepted, and we were all extreamly displeased that having taken with him 5000£ he Should continue to draw bills on us & not employ that money.

19. Order'd thereupon that it be advertised in the News papers here and in Carolina, that having Sent Sola bills over to answer expences in Georgia, we will pay no bills drawn upon us.

20. Order'd that 1000£ more Sola bills be made out and Sent by the first opportunity to Georgia.

21. Impress of 351.9.11 to Aldn. Heathcote.

22. Order'd that after the 5th inst. any 5 Common Counsellors may draw upon the Bank to pay our Georgia Sola Bills. We found this necessary because during the Summer time it is very difficult to make a board of Common Council.

23. Order'd that the Accompt. do take an Acct. of the Cash remaining of what was recd. last year, and that he make an estimate of the Services in which the 10000£ given this year is to be employ'd, and that the Same be layd on the table.

24. The Accompt. observed that there were 590 persons fed by our Stores before Mr. Oglethorps embarkation, and that 5818£ would be necessary to maintain them, and those who went last year with Mr. Oglethorp.

25. Grant of 100 Acres past to Will. Aglionby of Westminster.

26. Grant of 100 Acres past to Isaac Young of Gloucestershire.

27. Grant of a 50 acre Town Lot in Savannah to Mr. Hugh Anderson: and assurance given him, that when he has a mind to part with it, a new Grant Shall be made him of a Country Lot, in proportion to the Servants he Shall be able to employ in cultivating it.

28. The Same Gentleman appointed Inspector of the Publick Garden and Mulberry plantations.

[N.B.] 2 June 1736. This day Capt. Cornish who carry'd over Mr. Oglethorp acquainted us that before the Middle mouth of the Allatahama there is a bar of about 7 miles broad, with 11 foot water at low water and 21 at high. He Said St. Simons Island where Frederica was to be built is about 8 miles long, and 5 broad, that there are there 3 great bluffs about 11 feet high above high watermark, and within the Island a great deal of good Savannah or open grass plains.

This Captn. was in company with Capt. Chambers, Capt. Dunbar, Mr. Oglethorp, & Mr. Barnes of New York when the Inlet at St. Simons (the middle mouth of the Allatahama) was Sounded; and, as Mr. Saml. Eveleigh wrote Mr. Verelts from Charlestown 5 March 1735–6, they could find but 10 or eleven feet at low water, so that the larger vessels that transported the people were not capable of going to the place where they design'd to build a fort which was about the middle of that Island.

Mr. Barnes acct. to Mr. Eveleigh of St. Simons Island was, that the goodness of the land Surprised him, that he never Saw Such in his days, and that it is far Superior to Rhode Island which is look'd upon to be so fine.

And by letter to the Trustees from Mr. John Brownfeild the

Register dat. 6 March 1735–6, we were inform'd that the land is exceeding good; that there are near 20000 acres on that Island, and at least 1000 clear, Supposed to have been done Some years Since by the Indians.

[N.B.]——June, Mr. Oglethorp wrote a particular Account of the Spaniards design to dislodge the Settlers in the South, and of the method he used to make them lay aside that purpose.

He also takes notice of the distress of the people at Savannah by reason of their debts, by which 300 labouring hands are lost to the Province, they not caring to work only to pay their Creditors who they Say extorted upon them in the goods they Sold. He advises Stopping Credit.

He takes notice of the vast expence the Spaniards had put the Colony to, and the Estimate not having provided for it, he advised the Sending but few more this year, not above 400 Servants.

He also Says that the Indians & Traders and Cherokees had been down at Savannah and claim'd the Protection of the Trustees (Those Indians all living in Georgia) that they offer'd to build a Town at their own expence 300 miles up the River to consist of 40 families the first year, and desired no provisions or any other expence from the Trustees. Vid. more of this Fol. 131.

He also explain'd the reason why he drew bills of Exchange upon us (not withstanding the 4000£ Sola bills he carry'd over, namely, that the people of Charlestown had for the present run down the Sola Bills.

[N.B.] 4 June. Mr. Eveleigh wrote to one Mr. Morley that the French Men & Indians had attack'd the Chickesaws in their nation, who afterwards attack'd them in their turn, and kill'd 40 french, 9 Indians, & took 10 horses loaded with amunition & Some Goods.

[N.B.] 5th June, Mr. Oglethorp in a letter to Lieut. Govr. Broughton answer'd his complaints concerning the injuries Supposed to be done by the Georgia Act for Regulating the Indian Trade, to Carolina, and Shew'd him it was no loss to the Province of Georgia deprived her of it, but nevertheless the Act was not exclusive, and he would lycense any person coming from Carolina, he Submitting to the wise regulations of the Act.

The Same day he explain'd more largely to Paul Jenys Esq., Speaker of the Assembly of S. Carolina the wisdom of the Georgia Act above mention'd, the advantages it is of to S. Carolina, and the necessity he is under to put it Strictly in execution. That hitherto the Publick of Carolina had been loaded with Taxes

Presents to the Indians, Allarms and Men raised at large charges, Agents with Sallaries &c on Acct. of the Indian Trade, and with a garison at Pallachocolas to oppose the Indians when Seeking revenge for injuries done them by the Carolina Traders, whereas by drawing the trade to Georgia, the Indians if wrong'd would Seek revenge only on this latter Province. That all their care could not prevent the Indian Traders lycensed by them from bringing on an Indian War, whereas the Georgia Act is well regulated to the Satisfaction of the Indians. That in this critical juncture when the French & Spaniards are Striving to debauch our Indians it is absolutly necessary not to Suffer any to go among them contrary to our Act, which being express, he would be answerable for any inconveniencies that might arise by dispensing with it, when by adhering to it and obeying his Majesties orders he might have prevented it. That the Act does not make the Trade exclusive but if any Carolina Man Shall take Lycense out in Georgia, he Shall be well recieved.

On the 6th of Same month, Mr. Richd. Allen gave his thoughts in writing on this dispute to Col. Willm. Bull of S. Carolina, and Set forth the inconveniences to Carolina by the Loss of the Indian trade, and what ought to be yeilded to by Mr. Oglethorp to reconcile the dispute arisen between the two Provinces.

1. That the profit to S. Carolina by the Indian Trade is comm. Annis Six or 7000£ p ann.
2. That the Clergy's maintenance is paid out of it.
3. That the 3 Staple Commodities, pitch Tar and Rice is become Such a drug as to be a loss to the Province, & is only made up by the gain on Skins & Furrs.

He then puts Several Quys. as 1. Whether the Upper & Lower Creeks & Cherokees, are within the Province of Georgia; 2. if So, whether Georgia has an exclusive right to trade wth. them; 3. Whether the Crown itself has power to compel S. Carolina to trade on the foot of the Georgia Act; 4. Whether if any of those Nations Should be found to be out of the limits of Georgia, the Traders of Carolina are obliged passing to them thro Georgia to obey the Georgia Act; 5. Whether the Indians, tho within Georgia, are not a free people, and may not trade with whom they please, even the French and Spaniards; 6. How the Creditors of Indian Traders (if Such Traders Shall take lycenses in Georgia) will come at their debts. He then gives his thoughts on the Rum Act, and Says the Savannah river being the boundary of both Provinces, is as free for navigation for one as for the other. That it was wrong to lay the penalty on importation, but it Should have been on the landing & laying ashoar in Georgia. That Carolina had Settlements on their Side of the River where rum was to be carry'd, and their passing thither without breaking the bulk in Georgia ought not to be deem'd an importation. That to restrain the Indians from having Rum will only cast them on the French who will Supply them from Moville, & So get all the Trade. That the Indians get more by hunting than what buys them cloathing, which they Spend in Rum, & if debard from it, they will hunt less, and So the Skin trade be reduced, and they become less dependant as their wants are less. Lastly to reconcile all differences between both Provinces he proposed, 1. That the Trade with the Indians Should be free open and in common to Georgia & South Carolina; 2. That the Georgia Act Should be declared not to extend to the Traders of S. Carolina & Virginia, who may without restraint carry their goods &c to the Creeks & Cherikees by Liecense from their own Governments; 3. That no Traders endebted in Carolina may be lycensed in Georgia till they have paid their debts; 4. That if S. Carolina be allow'd to Send an Agent among the Indians there Should be but One for both Provinces, and but One Talk given to the Indians to be agreed on by both Provinces; 5. That both Provinces agree on the price of goods to be furnish'd the Indians, otherwise the Traders will undersell one another to get the most Skins, till the trade become of no benefit to either Province; 6. That the law to prevent giving credit to the Indians be Strictly put in execution.

The Number of Trustee Boards held this year were 40; & of Common Council 26. The Number of days the Gentlemen met on were 47, And the Number of times each of them attended were as follows:

Common Counsellors		Trustees	
Bundy, Richd.	19	Anderson, Adam	14
Ld. Carpenter	12	Archer, Tho.	1
Chandler, Ri.	8	Archer, Hen.	1
Digby, Edwd.	3	Ayers, Robt.	0
Egmont	46	Bedford, Arthr.	7
Eyles, Fra.	4	Belitha, Will.	0
Frederick, Tho.	4	Burton, Jo.	4
Hales, Steven	19	Coram, Tho.	0
Heathcote, Geo.	13	Coop, Ri.	0
Heathcote, Sr. Will.	6	E. of Derby	0

[1736] JOURNAL OF THE EARL OF EGMONT   161

Holland, Rogers	11	Gonson, Sr. Jo.	0
Hucks, Robt.	27	Hanbury, Will.	0
Kendal, Robt.	6	Page, Jo.	0
Lapotre, Hen.	29	Philips, Erasmus	0
LaRoch, Jo.	32	Rundal, Tho.	0
Ld. Limerick	0	Smith, Saml.	24
Moore, Robt.	2	Talbot, Will.	0
Oglethorp, Ja.	18	Towers, Christn.	0
Sloper, Will.	3	Tracy, Robt.	1
Ld. Tirconnel	14	Tyrer, Geo.	0
Towers, Tho.	39	Wollaston, Will.	0
Vernon, Ja.	34	Wollaston, Fra.	0
White, Jo.	6		
Shaftsbury	9		

The Persons Sent this 4th Year at the Trustees charge were 324 Males and 146 females, in all 470, of whom 129 Foreign Protestants. Which with 574 Sent before makes 1044; whereof Foreigners 302, and British 742.

Private Grants past this year

		Ac.
Lieut. Hugh Mackay	24 July 1735	500
Will. Woodrose	" " "	50
Mary Pember	13 Augst. "	50
Patrick Mackay, Esq.	3 Septbr. "	500
Jo. Mackay Esq.	" " "	500
Capt. Geo. Dunbar	" " "	500
Mr. Jo. Cuthbert	" " "	500
Tho. Baillie	" " "	500
Archibald Mcgilivray	" " "	50
Walter Augustin	24 Septbr. "	500
Paul Hamilton	" " "	500
John Musgrove	" " "	500
Capt. Ja. Gascoign	" " "	500
Willm. Horton, Esq.	" " "	500
Paul Jenys, Esq.	2 Oct. "	500
Jo. Baker, Esq.	" " "	500
Rowland Pytt	" " "	500
Jo. Tuckwell	" " "	50
Jo. Brown, Esq.	" " "	100
Eliz. West	7 Octbr. "	500
Phil. Geo. Fred. Von Reck	" " "	500

Willm. Bradley	17 Novbr. "	500
Tho. Ormstone	31 March 1736	200
Patrick Graham	19 May "	100
Henry Pytt	" " "	100
Will. Aglionbee	2 June "	100
Isaac Young	" " "	100
Reece Price	31 March "	150

General Grants past this 4th year

		Ac
3 Sept. 1735	The Township of Frederica	10,000
	Soldiers of Col. Oglethorps Regimt.	3,000
	Religious Uses of Savannah	300
		13,300
	Private Grants past this year	9,550
	Grants past the 3 foregoing years	25,885
	Total of Publick & Private Grants past in 4 years	48,735

ABSTRACT of the 4th Years Acct. of Receipts and Disbursments, ending 9 June 1736

CHARGE

To Ballance of last years Acct. remaining unapply'd 330.12.8, viz.		
For Establishing the Colony	65. 2. 3¼	
For the use of particular persons	28.17. 0	
For building Churches in Georgia	76. 1. 0	
For the Religious Uses of the Colony	128. 2. 4¾	
For encouraging Botany & Improving Agriculture	32.10. 0	330.12. 8
To Money depending to be accounted for in Georgia 9 June 1735		3067.12. 4½
To Money recieved in America reduced to Sterling	411. 1. 1¾	
To the Parliamt. Grant, includg. Fees of Offices	26000. 0. 0	
To Private benefactions for establishg. ye Colony	381. 2. 0	
		26792. 3. 1¾
To Money reciev'd for the use of particular persons		407.16. 8
To Money reciev'd for Religious Uses		899.19. 9

[1736] JOURNAL OF THE EARL OF EGMONT 163

To Money recieved for encouraging Botany &
Improving Agriculture   65. 0. 0
               Total Charge   31563. 4. 7¼

DISCHARGE

Apply'd in England as follows:

By Charge of Stationary Ware & printing	113. 3. 8½	
By House Rent for the Trustees Office, necessaries for the house, and incident charges on Embarkations, and other occasions	152.14. 8½	
By Wages to the Messenger & housekeeper, Rewards to the Secy. & Accompt., and to Several persons in the embarkations, and other Services for the Trust, and for extraordinary Clerkship	541. 5. 0	807. 3. 5
By Charges of Sending over on the charity 470 persons, and finding them tools, necessaries, Stores &c Refreshment in passage, and provisions for 3 months after arrival	3491. 7. 6½	
By Ordenance Arms cloathing &c	684. 0. 3	
By Watchcoats & bedding for passengers	195. 7. 6	
By Freight and charge of Shipping them and their baggage together with other lading, and demurrage	3782.18. 2	8153.13. 5½

By Charge of Sending Trust Servants, exclusive of their bedding & passage	22. 8. 2	
By Charge of conducting foreign Protestants to Georgia	102.10. 0	124.18. 2
By Freight and Charges on Several Commodities brought from Georgia		112.13. 0½
By Interest and charges of bills of Exchange drawn on the Trust from America, and charges of the Sola bills of Exchange Sent to Georgia to be issued there instead of drawing bills		120. 6.11
By a year and half allowance, part of the 3 years contracted for with the Botanist for collecting plants &c for Georgia at 10£ p ann.		15. 0. 0
		9333.15. 0

Disbursments in America

By Charges of Surveying the Coast, & Setting out lands		116. 0.11
By General work in fortifying, clearing the ground, Sawing timber, building a Beacon, a Corn Mill, and making a large garden to Supply the Inhabitants with Mulberry trees, &c		849. 3. 8
By Charges of the Company Sent into the Creek Nation to build & garison a Fort there, And for Saddles for the Rangers		778. 2.10
By Incidental Charges		64. 0. 6¼
By Provisions for the Inhabitants from 22 June 1734 to 8 Decbr. 1735	5063. 7. 9¼	5365.14. 2¼

[1736] JOURNAL OF THE EARL OF EGMONT

By Cattel bought for the Colony	302. 6. 5	
By Stores, Working tools & necessaries bought in the Colony besides those sent from Engl.	287. 8. 4½	
By Ordenance, Ammunition & cloathing besides those Sent from England	192. 4. 11½	479.13. 4
By Charges of Periaguas & freight, & charges of persons and goods from Carolina to Georgia	240. 5. 8	
By Presents to the Indians, charges of Indians, and purchassing land of them	937.16. 6¼	
By Rewards for Services in Georgia	298.11. 7½	
By Production of Raw Silk in Georgia	471. 3.11½	
By Expended for Encouraging Botany & improving Agriculture	97.10. 0	
By Expended on the Missionaries	107. 3.10½	
By Application of particular Benefactions	281. 7. 8	
Depending to be accounted for in America	6344. 7. 1	

Disburst in America   16431. 2.10¼
Total Disburst in England & America   25764.17.10¼
Charge 31563. 4. 7¼ – – – Ballance remaining, 9 June 1736
                                                                                                                                  5798. 6. 9

Particulars of the Ballance carry'd to next years Acct.

Remains for the General Uses of the Colony	474.15.10¾
For the Use of particular persons	155. 6. 0
For the building Churches	488. 0. 4
For the Use of the Missioners	243. 9. 1½
For the Saltsburg Ministers	50. 0. 0

For the Religious uses of the Colony
in genl. } 386.15. 4¾
For Botany and Agriculture   0. 0. 0
Appropriated to answer Sola Bills   4000. 0. 0
                                                5798. 6. 9

1736-1737

Transactions of the 5th Year
from 9 June 1736 to 9 June 1737

[N.B.] On the 4th & 11 of June 1736 Mr. Oglethorp in Support of the Act for keeping Peace with the Indians, issued divers Orders Instructions and Commissions to take up and Seize the goods of all Traders within the Province of Georgia, who had not taken Lycenses therein, which kept up the base of contention between S. Carolina and Us.

9 June. 1

Egmont	C	LaRoch, Jo.	C
Hucks, Robt.	C P	Towers, Tho.	C
Lapotre, Hen.	C	Vernon, Ja.	C

A Common Council was Summon'd for this day to consider if anything further was necessary to be wrote before Capt. Thompson's departure who was to Sail this week for Georgia. But we were not a board.

1. Benefactions were reported: 20£ from an unknown person, for the Ministers; 50£ from the Society for promoting Christian Knowledge, for paying the Saltsburg Ministers; 30£ from the D. of Richmond towards Mrs. Millar the Botanists Sallary; and Some lesser benefactions.

2. Approved a letter from Mr. Verelts to Mr. Oglethorp in the name of the board insisting on frugal management, & that he draw no bills on us.

3. A calculation was Sent him amounting to 9500£ to be defrayed out of the money remaining in our hands & the 10000£ given by Parliamt. desiring that if any thing could be Saved out of it, it Should be apply'd to the cultivating Trust lands.

4. We computed to him that the charge of provision next year for those who are now in Georgia on the poor Acct. will amount to 3269£.

5. We agreed it to be our opinions that 50£ *p* ann. ought to be the respective Sallary's of our 2 Ministers, the 3d Minister being

as yet paid by the Incorporated Society for propagating the Gospel.

6. We also agreed it to be proper that more Sola bills Should be made out to the value of 3150£ to be fill'd up by Mr. Oglethorp as he Shall See occasion; and that these bills be 1150£ in 5 pounds, 1000£ in 10£ pd. bills, & 1000£ in 20 Shillgs. bills.

7. Draft made on the Bank to Mr. Heathcote of 500£ to pay Sola bills lately come over, and to pay others as they Shall come.

[N.B.] On the 14th of Same Month Mr. Oglethorp directed Noble Jones, Surveyor to the Trust to Lay out a new Town call'd AUGUSTA on the Savannah 250 miles from the Sea, for the convenience principally of the Indian Traders. He order'd it Should consist of 40 House Lotts each of an Acre, the largest Streets not narrower than 25 yards; a Square in the Center, & Lotts for Publick Buildings on each Side the Square. All the Publick Lotts together not to consist of less than 4 acres. The Common to consist of 600 acres, and the Lotts next the Town to be 50 acres, but only to each of those who have 500 acres. That a house in town and a 500 acre Lot Should be mark'd out to the following Indian Traders,

Saml. Brown	Gregory Haines	Joseph Pavey
George Currie	Lochlane Macbane	
Cornelius Doehorty	Kenedy Obryen	

50 Acre Lotts were at the Same time order'd to Such persons as Mr. Roger Lacy Should think proper: the whole under the Same conditions as the rest of the Colony of Georgia were.

N.B. On the 14 Sept. 1739 there was a paragraph in one of the Publick papers, that there was a pretty little town there, protected by a Fort, & inhabited by English. That there were Several Traders Settled, with large Warehouses of goods, and a great trade drove with the Indian nation. And that Mr. Oglethorp who arrived there the 5 of that month, granted lands to Several people who desired to Settle there.

[N.B.] 14 June. The Grand jury presented the Memorial Sent over by the Assembly of S. Carolina against the proceedings of the Magistrates of Savannah as containing unjust assertions, unwarrantable Presumptions, and Aspersions highly reflecting on the King, The Trustees, the Magistrates and the whole body of the Colony, and gave a detail wherein.

16 June. 2.

Ld. Carpenter	C	Lapotre, Hen	C P
Egmont	C	LaRoch, Jo.	C
Hucks, Robt.	C		

An Urgent Common Council was Summond for this day to issue money out of the Bank for payment of accepted Bills of Exchange, for Provisions & freight of Goods & Passengers on board the Two Brothers, Capt. Thompson, there being no money but what is in the Bank for that purpose, & 200£ to be paid the next day. But Still we were not a board. We therefore order'd another Summons for tomorrow, the affair being of great consequence. In the mean time we read divers letters from Mr. Oglethorp, mention'd in the foregoing year, & relating to his negotiations with the Govnr. of Augustine.

17 June. 3.

Ld. Carpenter	C	Lapotre, Hen.	C
Egmont	C P	LaRoch, Jo.	C
Heathcote, Geo.	C	Vernon, Ja.	C
Hucks, Robt.	C		

Notwithstand the necessity of a Common Council, and the particular Summons order'd yesterday, we were not a board.

1. Read the letters & papers enclosed in Mr. Oglethorps Packets, and desired Mr. Vernon to present to the D. of Newcastle the Memorial of the Kings right to Georgia Sent over by Mr. Oglethorp, together with the depositions of Several persons who had visited the North Side of St. Juans river and found no Spaniards occupying the Same. He was also desired to acquaint his Grace that there were matters of great consequence in other letters Sent his Grace, and particularly where mention is made of orders & instructions recieved from his Majesty by Mr. Oglethorp, to which the Trustees were Strangers, wherefore they Submitted the whole to him to Send Such orders as he Should judge necessary.

N.B. When Mr. Oglethorp Saild to Settle the Southern Province, the Trustees were not aware it would give umbrage to Spain, which had they been, they would have made the Settlement more northward, for a contest wch that Nation about bounds, and the defence of our Settlement when made, in case of an attack, would necessarily create an expence far beyond our ability to defray. I was not therefore displeased that his Majesty had given orders to Mr. Oglethorp for him to pursue, because thereby it lay on the Crown to justify and Support him in his conduct. But it Seem'd Strange to us that Mr. Oglethorp conceal'd those orders from us when he went, for nothing ought to be a Secret to our board, relating to our Province; and besides it might happen that we Should give Mr. Oglethorp directions contrary to those his Majesty had given him. On this occasion, Mr. Vernon Shew'd us the very letter He wrote to the Duke, being By Mr. Oglethorp Enclosed to him open, with desire that he would Shew it to Mr. Towers and then Seal and deliver it to the Duke, thereby passing by the Trustees, and leaving them in ignorance of what they ought to know as being materially concerned therein.

[N.B.] 17 June 1736. I was privately inform'd this day that Tho. Frederick, Esq., a Member of the Common Counsel designs to come no more among us, he being very intimate with Sr. Robert Walpoles Lady who is a great enemy to our Colony. Neither is Sr. Robert and the Employment Men friends to us, because Some of our Board vote in Parliamt. against the Ministerial measures. They also pretend our Charter gives us too much power, and makes us Independent of the Crown.

[N.B.] 18 June 1736. Capt. Thompson of the Two brothers Saild for Savannah with 5 males and 1 Female Sent at the Trustees charge. Two of them were able Millrites intended to erect a Saw Mill framed partly in England, & which cost near 500£.

23 *June*. 4.

Ld. Carpenter	C	Lapotre, Hen.	C Ch.
Egmont	C	LaRoch, Jo.	C
Heathcote, Geo.	C	Towers, Tho.	C
Hucks, Robt.	C	Vernon, Ja.	C
Kendal, Robt.	C		

1. Seal'd a letter of Attorney to Mr. Verelts for receiving at the Treasury the 10000£ granted by Parliamt.

2. Mr. Vernon reported he had laid our papers & Mr. Oglethorps letter to the D. of Newcastle before his Grace, but as yet had recd. no answer.

3. A letter was orderd to Mr. Tho. Christie Recorder to Send Copies of the Court Proceedings of Savannah Since Novbr. 1734 hither to neglected to be done by him, that he do the Same quarterly, and also certify whether any Fees and what have been taken

for issuing and executing Processes, and what Fees are taken in Gaol, and at the discharge of persons from thence.

4. Letter orderd to Mr. Tho. Causton Bailif to acquaint the Trustees with all proceedings in the Province notwithstanding Mr. Oglethorp is there. That he prevent as much as he can the peoples running in debt by putting them on labour, and not letting them Supply their necessities by Credit. That he Send particular Accts from time to time of the Settlers, and their progress and behaviour.

5. Letter orderd to Jo. Bromfeild Register of Georgia commending his diligence in informing the Trustees of what passes, and desiring he will continue to do the Same.

6. Order'd 500£ to be insured on Capt. Thompson on acct. of the Saw Mill carry'd Over.

7. Resolv'd that any 5 of the Common Council may draw on the Bank for a Sum not exceeding 1133.17.8½ (prt of the 10000£ given by Parliament for payment of divers expences that may acrue).

8. Imprest to Mr. Heathcote 447£ to pay Bills when they come to hand. The uncertainty of Common Council Boards during the Summer obliged us to take these measures.

[N.B.] 25 June 1736. A Committee of the Assembly of South Carolina made Report, concerning Mr. Oglethorps letters relatg. to the Indian Trade: 1. That Nothing contain'd in the Georgia Act for maintaining Peace with the Indians, excludes, in their apprehension, the Traders of other Provinces from trading with the Indians within Georgia, there being an act of S. Carolina Subsisting and unrepeal'd by his Majesty, that gives liberty to Traders of S. Carolina to carry goods & barter with those Indians, & no *Non obstante* in the Georgia Act. 2. That the heads of the Savanna & Allatahama Rivers (the N. & S. boundaries of Georgia) are not Known, but by what maps & information could be got, it appear'd that but a Small part of the Creek & Cherokee Nations are included within the bounds of Georgia, So that Supposing the Georgia Act were in force to oblige all Traders with Indians in Georgia to take out Lycenses in Georgia, it could not oblige them to take Lycenses there who trade with Creeks and Cherokees dwelling out of the limits of Georgia. Wherefore they recommend to the Assembly to assert the right of their Traders to trade with the Several Nations of Indians in amity with the English, without taking Lycences in Georgia and to indemnify them for loss of goods or imprisonment incurred thereby to the amount of 2000£

Sterlg. And also to bring in a bill for removing Such discouragements as the Indian trade of their Province lyes under with regard to the Lycense Money, and the duties imposed on the Trade.

Upon this the Council and Assembly past the Same day an Ordenance for ascertaining the right of their Traders to trade with the Creeks, Cherokees & other nations in amity with the English, without being obliged to take Lycences in Georgia. That 2000£ Sterl. Shall be appropriated out of the next Genl. Tax for indemnifying them for their Losses. And that all additional duties not heretofore laid upon Indian drest deerskins or other Skins or furrs Since 25 March 1730 Shall be remitted. And that but 10 Shillgs. Shall be hereafter paid for taking out a Lycence to trade with the Indians. This ordenance was to remain in force for 2 years & to the end of the next Session of the General Assembly. But his Majesty annull'd it.

[N.B.] 27 June 1736. Chigilli Chief of the Lower Creeks with the Chiefs of 7 Towns and their Attendants to the number of 60, came down to Mr. Musgroves Cow pen to have a talk with Mr. Oglethorp, who caused them to be conducted to Savanna in boats and recieved them Kindly.

[N.B.] 28 June. Mr. Jenys Speaker of the Assembly acquainted Mr. Oglethorp by letter how irregularly and basely the Ordenance above mention'd past, and how thin the lower house of Assembly, there being but 19 Members present & 9 agst. it. He added that he believed the differences of the Two Provinces might be made up, if it would content him (Mr. Oglethorp) that the Agent for Indian affairs Should be named by him, and their Traders Subject to him, and their conduct under his inspection.

[N.B.] On 29 June 1736 Mr. Saml. Eveleigh wrote to Mr. Verelts a particular Acct of the Engagement between the French and their Indians, and the Chickesaws. That in the Month of Jany. 1735 the Savannah Indians met the Chickesaws in their winter Hunt and inform'd them the French intended in March to destroy their Nation. That upon this the Chickesaws put themselves on their defence. That on the 8 March they heard Some guns, and concluding the French were coming, they on the 9th went out in Scouts and in 3 different paths about half a mile distance one from the other, and about the Same distance from Chocolissa their chief town. That they found bread in their way which they Supposed thrown there by the French Indians to give them notice, for the French had a Chickesaw Slave (afterwards taken) who inform'd that the French and the Indians had Some difference in their March. That on the 10th March, by break of day, the French being about 150 and their Indians about 400, attack'd the aforesaid town (where the Chickesaws were retired) very courageously, but these being well prepared for them, after an hours firing very close at each other, the French Indians, tho they were 5 times as many in number, retired, and the French Seeing them gone immediately follow'd them to their Camp, which was about 3 quarters of a mile from the Town, where the Chickesaws pursued them and took their Governr. Monsr. Dartiquet, brother to Monsr. Bienville, Govr. of Moville, prisoner, continuing the pursuit for 8 miles taking & killing them all the way; that by their computation there were about 25 French Men and 10 of their Indians kill'd and about 23 French and 2 of their Indians taken prisoners. That they immediately burnt 19 of the French & 1 Indian, but not tortured as is the customary way among the Indians, being first knock'd on the head & then cast into the fire.

The Chickesaw Slave Said it was constantly the Governours talk to the Indians that the English were no more than Fowls, that they would make us pack their horses and their leather to their Sloop, and then deliver us to the Indians.

There were 8 of the Chickesaws kill'd viz. 4 Men, 1 Woman, & 3 children. Several Frenchmen were afterwards found dead by the Turky Buzzards.

Mr. Eveleigh added, that the Chickesaws will certainly be destroyed by the French by one means or other, wherefore he had advised Mr. Oglethorp to endeavour to move them from whence they are, down to the occony or Ochemulgy Rivers, which would be an act of humanity to a brave people, and a great Service in case of a War between us & the French to whom they bear inveterate prejudice as the French do to them. But they look upon it as a great disgrace to leave their own ground.

He had the Acct. of the above mentioned Engagement from Mr. Willm. Macmullane a Trader with the Chickesaws who was present and Saw it.

[N.B.] On the 1. July 1736 Mr. Oglethorpe wrote another letter to the D. of Newcastle, importing that in October last the French upon the Messassippi River recd. advice from Europe to prepare for War the Spring following, and accordingly Spent the Winter in drawing together 2500 French, and 800 Indians. That they also attempted to gain over the Creek Indians through whose Country the road to Charlestown lay. That they had provided pack horses Sufficient to carry 70 days provision, and made Magazines upon the Moville River at a Fort call'd Albam as otherwise Fort Tholouse, which is the nearest they possess to Carolina, and to which the Pack horses go from Charlestown in 27 days. That they were to Rendevouz in Jany. and take the field in March. That in Jany. Monsr. de Bienville arrived there, but that on the 10th of that month orders arrived to him to lay aside the design, upon which he gave out his preparations were against the Chickesaws, a Nation of Indians in allyance with the English, and nearer by Some hundred of miles to the quarters His troops came from than the Moville.

He then relates the Engagement with the Chickesaws (mention'd by Mr. Eveleigh) and adds, that the Chickesaws pursued the French 3 days, till they met with another Body of French consisting of Some hundreds, who guarded the boats, on the Messasippi river, but no Indians. That the engagement was very Short, The French immediately taking to the Stream, where most of them were drown'd, their boats having been in the beginning of the Action Sunk, or burnt by the Indians.

That the Creeks had carry'd him down to the Frontiers of the Kings dominions in America which are divided from the Spanish by the River St. Juan, & of which the English or their allyes have been in possession quiet, before the Treaty of Utrecht. That the Govr. of Augustin disputed our right to St. Simons Isld. & the Allatahama river, but at last offer'd to leave all differences concerning the Limits of the Two Provinces to the determination of the Courts in Europe provided he would deliver up the Fort at St Georges Point on the N. Side of St. Juans River over against their garison which he would not do without the kings orders.

That the people of Charlestown are angry wth. him for insisting on their obeying his Majesty's Orders, particularly that relating to the Treaty with the Indians, Some of their Merchants carrying on a clandestine Trade with the French & Spaniards and very zealous against every thing that Settles the Indians in his Majesties Interest; for if the Indians go to the French & Spaniards these Merchants gain by it, because they Sell to these Nations at vast prices, Goods to present and trade to those Indians. By the Georgia Act, no person can go into the Country of the Indians without giving Security for his behaviour, and obtaining a Lycence thereupon, a precaution absolutly necessary, since if Men without Security given went into Country's where are no Magistrates to do justice to the Indians, they would be apt to commit all Sort of Offences, and if we Suffer'd the Indians to distroy them for

Such Offences, we Should give them the Governmt. from the King, and if we did not, they would take a national revenge on us all and be therein Supported by the French and Spaniards.

[N.B.] On the 3. July 1736 The Upper and lower Creek Indians had a Talk wth. Mr. Oglethorp at Savannah where they came to complain of abuses recd. from Joseph Watson for beating them and drinking one of their people to death. They Said the Spaniards told them Mr. Oglethorp would cut off their heads, and the Carolina people that he was come to Steal their lands. They complain'd that while they were at War wth. the Cherokees, the Cherokee Traders came out on horseback to help their Enemies. They desired Mr. Oglethorp would order those Traders to Stay at home, and they on their Side would not let the Traders help them. That the Uchees and they were friends, but if they met with any Cherokees, they must die, for they had made peace with them and yet they kill'd their women & children, that they were mad men. That the French enlarged the Fort Allamos last autumn, & had made it much Stronger, tho they promis'd the Indians, that if they would not pull it down they would never repair it. Then Mr. Oglethorp made them presents, and they departed, Saying all was good, All Should be Straight between us always, & Chegilly their chief Said he was never So well pleased in his life as wth. this Talk.

7 July. 5.

Egmont	C	Vernon, Ja.	C
Lapotre, Hen.	C P	Smith, Saml.	T
LaRoch, Jo.	C		

A Common Council was Summond, but we could not make a Board.

1. Mr. Verelts reported that he had recieved at the Treasury the 10000£ granted by Parliament, and lodged it in the Bank, and that the Several Offices had forgiven their Fees amounting to 257£.

2. The Impress to Mr. Heathcote order'd last meeting of 1133.17.8½ and 447£ and 500£, in all 2080.17.8½ was Sign'd by the 4 Common Counsellors present, and Mr. Verelts order'd to procure another hand to it.

3. Thomas Boyde and David Blair, Scots Gentlemen, apply'd by letter from Edinburgh for grants of lands in Georgia, & each to carry 10 Servants.

4. Mr. Vernon reported, that he waited on the D. of Newcastle to Know his pleasure on the letter Mr. Oglethorp had wrote him, and on the papers we had communicated to him. That his Grace observed by the Copy of our order for his attending his Grace, that the Trustees would not charge themselves with, or be accountable for Mr. Oglethorps conduct in going out of the limits of Georgia to build Forts. His Grace Said he had written to Mr. Oglethorp, & Mr. Stone would bring the letter for the Trustees to forward. Accordingly that Mr. Stone would have come but Mr. Vernon chose to go to him who read to him the contents of the Dukes letter but refused to let him have a copy of it. That the contents were to recommend to him not to fall out with the Spaniards, but to follow the things recommended to him when he left England, which Mr. Vernon Supposed related to S. Carolina; that it ended with many compliments.

5. Order'd that Mr. Vernons report be enterd in the minutes, & agreed on a letter to Mr. Oglethorp, expressing the impossibility of our disbursing the Publick money upon any undertakings of his beyond the Limmits of our Province which we could not answer. We therefore recommended to him to act with the greatest caution & prudence, & Sent him a copy of the minute we made when Mr. Vernon was Sent to the Duke of Newcastle (the Duke having Sent the Same to him) because Mr. Oglethorp Should not think that we had been accusing him of indiscretion to the Duke, & were ashamed of it afterwards.

6. Mr. Millar our Botanist who was Seized in his passage from LaVera Crux to the Havannah, and Sent to England by order of the Governour of La Vera Crux, being arrived the 26 of last month, attended, & presented a Narrative of his proceedings in America. He brought us no Seeds or Plants for Georgia, as we expected, but Said he left them in Jamaica, where he heard they thrived.

[N.B.] On the 7 July 1736 Robt. Millar Botanist gave us his narrative of proceedings to collect plants &c for Georgia.

[N.B.] On the 10th July 1736 Opayhatchoo K. of the Upper Creeks, and a beloved Man of the Abecoes, and a head Warriour of the Cussaboes of the Lower Creeks were Sent for to come to Charlestown, and the first in his Talk wth. Presidt. Broughton and Council Said he wish'd that the Traders might go abroad in peace amongst them from Carolina as they did before. That he would not have the River that goes round (Savannah) to be Stopt for the carriage of Rum. That he chose Charlestown to deal with as his friends. That he was a red Man, and the ground did belong to them, but they had parted with their land on this Side the River, and had no pretention to it, But That on the other Side (Georgia) was for the Red people, and was their land. That Mr. Mackay had built a Fort there by his consent but had not reach'd him, and whoever Should build another Fort on his land Should be a better Man than he.

[N.B.] On the 10th [July] Mr. Jo. Wesley had a conference with the Chickesaws touching their notions of Religion, wherein they profest to believe there are 4 Beloved things above, the Clouds, the Sun, the Clear Skie, and He that lives in the clear Skie. That there is One lives in the clear Skie, & Two with him, Three in all. That he made all men at first out of the ground. That he had often Saved them in battel, and would not let the bullets hurt them, and tho Some then present had bullets went into them, they Still were alive. That he might Save them from their Enemies now, but who knew if he would have mercy, that if they are to die, they must, but if he will have them live, they Shall tho they have never So many Enemies, he can destroy them all. That he had on occasions made the beloved Clouds, and rain and hail fight for them, and that in a very hot day; and the ground had made a noise under their Enemies and the beloved ones behind them, which drove them away. That often, before & after almost every battel they heard the noise of drums & guns and Shoutings, and Postubee (one of the Chiefs) Said this happen"d after their last battel with the French. That the night before he dream'd he heard many drums beating up there, and many trumpets Sounding with much Stamping of feet and Shouting. That before this, he thought they Should all die, but then he believed the beloved Ones were come to take their parts. That the next day he heard above 100 guns go off before the battel began, (the Interpreter Said he heard them too) and he Said when the Sun is there the beloved ones will help us, and we Shall conquer our Enemies, and they did So. That they thought of the Beloved Ones always, and wherever they were talk'd of them & to them, at home, abroad, in peace, in war, before and after fight, and indeed when ever & where ever they met together. He added that they thought the Souls of Red Men (Indians) walk'd up and down after death near the place where their bodies lye, for they often heard cries and noises [near] the places where any prisoners had been burnt; that this was the general belief of his Nation, but for himself he thought only the Souls of bad men walk'd, but that the good went up. Mr. Wesley told him, We white men had a book which Says many things of the beloved ones above, and ask'd him if he would be glad to know them? To which he reply'd their Enemies were all about them, and they had no time but to fight. But if they Should ever be at peace they Should be glad to know. That the Old Men of his nation know more of these matters than himself and would tell him more than he had done. That there are only a few whom the beloved One chuses from a child, and is in them, and takes care of them, and teaches them, and they know these things, and their Old Men practiced, therefore they knew, but I (Said Postubee) do not practise, therefore I know little.

[N.B.] On the 12 July 1736 the Assembly of S. Carolina, being extraordinarily assembled, to consider of letters and papers Sent to their Lieut. Governor Mr. Broughton, by Mr. Oglethorp, wherein he adhered to his resolution of executing in full force the Acts for maintaining peace with the Indians, & for prohibiting Rum to come into the Colony, met and on the 17th drew up a Representation to his Majesty, against the Trustees of Georgia and their Magistrate there. In it they complain'd that we pretend to the Sole navigation of the Savannah river, tho it is only a boundary between both Provinces, and consequently free to both. That in consequence thereof we Seize and Stave their Rum, tho not intended to be landed in Georgia, but at their remote Settlements on the Same river. That the moderate use of that liquor is wholsome, and the Indians like it, and if they cannot have it from the English will go over to the French and purchasse it of them. That they must be presumed to know better how to carry on the Indian Trade than new people Such as the Trustees and magistrates of Georgia, and that the Safety of S. Carolina depended on a right management of it. That they cannot conceive his Majesty design'd when he past the Georgia Act for maintaining Peace with the Indians, that Georgia Should have an exclusive trade with them, for that Two Acts giving liberty to S. Carolina to trade with the Cherokee and Upper & Lower Creek Indians, past by his Majesty were Still in force, yet the Trustees will Suffer none to go up to them unless they take out Lycences in Georgia, which was a great hardship on the Indian Traders of S. Carolina, in as much as it obliged them to come down 3 or 400 miles to take those Lycenses and give Security. That if they refused So to do, their persons were threaten'd to be imprisoned and their Goods Seized, which was an ill return for the aid the Province had given towards Settling the Colony of Georgia. That having represented these things to the Trustees and their Magistrates, and found no redress, they beseech'd his Majy. to declare the Rights and libertys of S. Carolina to an open and Free trade with all the Nations of Indians in amity with the English, according to the Regulations for the Same by the Laws of S. Carolina, without being Subject to the Laws & Regulations of Georgia, and that the passage of the Savannah river may be declared free and open to all his Majesties Subjects of S. Carolina, and that the Magistrates of Savannah be order'd to make reparation for all the violences they have done to the Traders of S. Carolina.

[N.B.] 12 July 1736, Mr. Paul Amatis wrote us there was no doubt of Succeeding in raw Silk in Georgia, to the utmost perfection as Soon as there are a Sufficient quantity of balls or Coquons, a building erected for the purpose, and Spinners enough. That Rome was not built in a day. When he first came there was not a white Mulberry tree in the Province, but he brought 40000 plants in Carolina & transplanted them thither in to the Trustees garden for a nursery. That at Mr. Oglethorp's arrival he gave out to the Inhabitants 15000, and he had 25000 Still in the garden, the greatest part of which were to be distributed this Autumn, and he hoped in two years they would receive the fruits of their labour.

[N.B.] On the 13 July 1736 Mr. Oglethorp had a talk with the Chickesaw Indians who came to Savannah to request guns powder & Shot to defend themselves from the French and the Indians their Enemies. They first produced commissions whereby it appear'd they had been declared Subjects to the King of Great Britain by the Governr. of Carolina, and were as Such entitled to the help and protection they Sought for. Then they Said the S. Carolina Traders told them Mr. Oglethorp was a Red womans child, but now they had Seen him, he believed he was as white a body as any in Charles Town. That they told them many other talks, but he Saw by their coming, they did not believe them. However they believed him a Red Man in his heart. That they were come into their own town & their own people, and had they not So many enemies would Stay with him till winter. That the people of Old Savannah town (in South Carolina 300 miles up the Savannah river built 24 years ago) Said they were going to a French town and a French Man, and the Creeks, Chickesaws, Obehatchee and the White Men told them So, and that they Should be tied & never return, but they had Seen him and were Satisfied. That they had heard of Georgia in their own Country, that the Abeenchee King Said He was French, but they were resolved to take his talk, and they had taken it and their heart was as glad as his. That they were come to their great Micho for assistance wanting powder and bullets. That it was the English first came to their nation, not the French. That they could not tell the names of all their Enemies they were So many, The Chocktaws, Towasiaws, Movilles & Tomos, who were not concern'd in the late Invasion; the Yungusees, Tomolohaws or Illinois, Nawtowees and Wrawtonos, these were with the French that had just now fallen on them. That 700 Men came into their Towns twice, but had not killed them all. That the French had Forts in all those Nations, and kept them always in readyness to Send against them. That the Great Micho (K of Gr Britain) had a long time ago promised them white Men and arms, and to Send white Men and Writings. The people of Carolina had promised them too, but never Sent them. They ask'd nothing but powder and bullets, and he Mr. Oglethorp had a heart. That their nation was So big (making a Small circle with their fingers) You English So big (making a larger) but the French were quite round them all (Stretching out their Arms) & kill'd them like hogs or fowls. That only the Cherokees were their friends, the Creeks were almost So, but the Albamos entirely French, and the Chocktaws were also their Enemies, tho they came not against them in the late invasion, except Some few Stragglers. That of the Cherokees, their most beloved Towns were Tanasee and Great Telliquo, till the Creeks kill'd their Chief Warriour. That the French threaten'd to bring great guns against them, but they did not believe they could.

Mr. Oglethorp presented them with what they wanted, and Sent them away contented. When he gave them the gunpowder, he bid them See and try if it was good, to which they Said the French had told them our powder made no noise & that the bullets dropt down as Soon as they came out of the guns, but they knew wt. he gave them would be good, and they would not look upon it.

[N.B.] On 20th July 1736 Will. Drake Esq. wrote from Santee to Cha. Pinkness Esq. his thoughts of the importance of rightly Settling the bounds of the British Dominions in America, with Spain. That he Should be Sorry to find the Rumor true, that the bounds were to be from the head of the Allatahama westwards to the South Sea in a Streight line, by which the importance of those Countries which ly South and West of that River would be overlook'd. That K. Charles the 2ds Charter to the Proprietors of Carolina the Latitude of 29 degrees was fixt as the Southern boundary, which includes also the mouths and Entrances of the Apalachee, Catachuchee, and almost all the other rivers that empty themselves into the Gulph of Mexico to the East of the Messasippi River. Whereas Should the Allatahama be Settled as a boundary, we Should thereby lose at least 100 miles extent of Dominion, and what would in process of time be of infinite worse consequence, we Should be excluded from the mouths of those Rivers aforemention'd, which would effectually hinder the Settlement of the Inland Shoars of those rivers by the English. For if the Allatahama must be the boundary to the head thereof, and a west line be Struck from thence to the South Sea, it will certainly render those parts of the Catachuchee which ly to the north of that line of no manner of consequence to us, Since it will be in the power of the possessor of the mouth of that river wholly to command the navigation of it. That in 1735 he was appointed Commissioner of the Indian Trade to perform an Agency to the Creek Nation, and during his Stay among them inform'd himself of what he thought he might concern the British Interest in those parts. That in his journey he crost 5 or 6 Rivers before he came to the Nation, and rode through a body of good rich lands for near 200 miles in length, among which there was hardly any intermixture of that which could be call'd bad. And after a journey of about 400 miles from Charlestown came to the Catacuchee River before mentioned, a place and Country by far the pleasantest he had Seen in America, tho he had been in Several other parts besides Carolina. But the agreableness of the Situation was the least part of its value, its exceeding richness & fertility of Soil, and its being capable to produce every necessary of life made its value inestimable. That Upon this River live the Lower Creek nation and from thence the Indians Sometimes go down to the Sea, and Some of their Chiefs who had been down inform'd him it took them up a whole month to return in their Canoes, from whence he concluded that from the part of the river where he had this information it was 200 or 300 miles down to the Sea, whereafter watering a fine Country it empties itself at the Bay of St. Joseph in the Gulph of Mexico.

That this River is more deserving consideration than any that falls into that Gulph, not excepting even the Messasippy, tho it leads into a greater extent of Country. For Capt. Hen Isaac, an Englishman who had lived many years with the French on the Messasippy, and whom he found among the Creeks, Said the Messasippy is So full of flats at the mouth & Shallow, and its Stream

So exceeding rapid, that its navigation is render'd extreamly difficult. But the Catahuchee has 12 or 12 fathom water at its mouth, and carrys its depth a considerable way up into the Country, and is adorned with Several noble and bewtiful Islands which it Surrounds, and is not at present possest by any Europeans from one End of it to the other, So that there is no obstacle to hinder us, if So minded, to take possession of it.

That the advantages which would accrue to the English by possessing this River, would be,

1. The immediate possession of a fine Port & Harbour in the Gulph where now we have not an inch of Teritory.

2. The Ships that use the Same would ly in a Fresh water River free from the Worm, which So much injures the Shipping at Jamaica & the West Indies.

3. They might here be very easily Supply'd with Masts and all other Naval Stores.

4. The Country would in a little time Supply them with provisions.

5. It would be a more convenient receptacle for our West India Squadron than Jamaica, there being (as the Indians inform'd him) no Hurricanes or hard Gales of Wind that ever blow down their Trees, and from thence they might as easily obstruct the Spanish Flota in their voyage to old Spain as from Jamaica, and as well protect our trade.

6. It would render the French Settlement at Moville of little use to them, and it would prevent their encrease & Spreading in those Countries.

7. But above all it would be the best Barrier we can possibly have against the encroachment of the French at Messasippi, of which they were So Sensible, that as Capt. Isaac inform'd him, wilst the Capt. was at New Orleans (at which time the Settlement of Georgia was first talk'd of) The French were under a good deal of concern about it, and concluded the Settlement was to be on the Catahuchee River, whereupon the French Genl. Monsr. Bienville Sent a vessel from thence to the mouth of the Catahuchee to learn the certainty of it, with design no doubt to give what obstruction he could to it.

He further observed, that the French were endeavouring to unite their Strength and joyn their hands from all their Settlements from Canada & the Bay of St. Lawrence in the North through the Messasippi and the Gulph of Mexico in the South, by which means they will in time either gain all the Indians from

St. Lawrence to the Messasippi to their Interest, or destroy & root out all those Indians who will not come into their Interest, as they are now attempting wth too much probability of Success agst. the Chickesaws. From which a very possible consequence is to be fear'd, that in process of time they will be able to push the English in N. America into the Sea, unless proper Stands & Barriers be in time (even now when they are to be had) made against them.

[N.B.] 20 July 1736 Mr. Saml. Eveleigh wrote to Mr. Verelts that the Assembly of Carolina had Sent a Committee to Settle disputes between the 2 Provinces with Mr. Oglethorp, and that Mr. Oglethorp design'd to build a Fort and call it Augusta as high as the near the head of the Savannah river is navigable by pettiaguas which is at a place 3 miles above Fort Moor call'd Kinyans Bluff on the S. Side of the River.

21 July. 6.

Bundy, Ri.	C		LaRoch, Jo.	C
Egmont	C	P	Towers, Tho.	C
Lapotre, Hen.	C		Vernon, Ja.	C

A Common Council again Summon'd to consider of Bill whether to accept or not: but no Board.

1. Letters lately arrived from Mr. Oglethorp containing his negotiation with the Govr. of St. Augustine, and from Mr. Eveleigh were read.

2. Several bills drawn on us were refer'd to the next meeting.

3. Mr. Wants the German who was employ'd above a year ago to Select persons to Send to Georgia, appear'd, and told us that many of them were come to Rotterdam: We answer'd that having fail'd in bringing them at the appointed time, they were come too late. Besides we put him in mind that when he many months ago return'd, that if any came we could not accept them for want of money.

4. Capt. Thomas, and Capt. Dunbar appear'd & gave us a good Acct. of Georgia.

5. Capt. Dunbar apply'd to be paid by the Trustees for 31 Servants he carry'd over, not on the Trustees acct. for on that of private Men, and he produced a letter from Mr. Oglethorpe recommending the Same. He Said he did not desire we Should pay the freight, but take them as our Servants till their work Should discharge it, and he believed Mr. Oglethorpe had already actually taken them into our Service. We answer'd it was more than we Knew, but if

it were So, then the proper Owners wanting those Servants could not perform their agreement to cultivate their lands according to their Covenants. That these Servants freight was no concern of ours, but as he was to answer it to Mr. Simons his Owner, we would recommend to Mr. Oglethorpe, that if they have been employ'd in our Service the 5£ for their respective passages be Stopt out of their wages, and paid to Mr. Pury Agent to Mr. Simons in Georgia. He made Some other demands about Canon &c with wch. he furnish'd Mr. Oglethorpe, whereto we could Say nothing, not being a board of Common Council.

6. A letter order'd to Mr. Oglethorp on these heads.

N.B. Our Situation was now bad. Great drafts & little money to answer them. Few accts. from our Magistrates of proceedings in the Province, & but Short ones from Mr. Oglethorp. Two Forts building beyond the limits of our Province, danger of the Spaniards resenting it and in that case a vast expence accruing to defend ourselves. The Carolinians fallen out with us, and our own Members backward in attending. The Ministry giving us no countenance &c.

[N.B.] 24 July 1736 Mr. Oglethorp wrote the Trustees that he had drawn on us for 700£ which was employed in presents to the Indians, fitting out 2 Agents, one for the Creek the other for the Cherokee Nation to prevent them from falling upon us, to which they had been Sollicited not only by the French and Spaniards but by Some who are nearer to us (S. Carolina) as might be Seen by Hoboihachi's Speech; in advancing Credit to people who wanted it, and in Cash put into Bailif Caustons hands for circulating our Georgia Sola bills.

[N.B.] 26 July 1736 Mr. Oglethorp wrote to me the opposition made by the Assembly to the execution of our Georgia Act for maintaining Peace with the Indians, and that Some of the Indian Traders Sent from S. Carolina had with much difficulty obtained of One Indian Chief Opayhatchoo to deny the concession of those lands which he himself had before consented with the rest of the Nation to grant us. He also desired to know what he should do with relation to assisting the Chickesaws.

[N.B.] This month of July 1736 Mr. Oglethorp wrote to the Trustees in answer to theirs of the 1 April wherein they advised him to lay aside his design of making a Settlement on the Allatahama by reason of their want of money to pursue it, That The Town there was already Settled, the Kings Independent Company fix'd there, Two Forts build beyond it, and the Kings Sloop Station'd.

That Servants were much wanted, & if Some hundreds were Sent by the next Ships, there were persons enough at Savannah and Frederica who would be glad to purchasse them immediately.

That he would reduce the Expence by all possible means, especially by discouraging the Lazy to Stay, tho when gone they would abuse the place as many already had done.

That he had engaged 100 Workmen from various places for 6 months, and 50 Rangers for a year, before he reciev'd our letter. That the Spanish Frontier had occasion'd many large and new expences, as also large presents to the Indians which the opposition from Carolina obliged him to make, to procure the Confirmation of the cession of the Islands.

That They had refused as yet to give leave to Settle the In-land Parts up the Allatahama.

That if the Act for the Peace with the Indians be not Supported, not only our Province but Carolina too must be undone, and an Indian War follow.

That our resolution was wise of Sending over no more people on the charity, for there were too many mouths, and not labouring hands in proportion.

That it would be very necessary to Send Some more persons to form the Morals of our people and instruct them in Religion. The change Since the arrival of the Missioners was very visible with respect to the increase of Industry, love and Christian charity among them; but Should they remove to the Indians, we Should be left entirely destitute, and the people by a relapse become if possible worse than before.

28 July. 7.

Egmont	C P	LaRoch, Jo.	C
Hales, Steven	C	Towers, Tho.	C
Lapotre, Hen.	C	Vernon, Ja.	C

A Common Council was Summon'd to recieve a Report from the Committee of Accounts: to consider of Mr. Oglethorps letter and Bills presented: and to issue money for paymt. of what is due to Mr. Simond. But we were not a board.

1. Impress to Mr. Heathcote to pay Sola bills return'd from Georgia—300£.

2. Capt. Dunbars Memorial was read, as also his Sailing orders given by Mr. Oglethorp, by which he would have us understand it was by his orders he took over to Georgia the Servants of Mr. Mackay and Cuthbert. So that he expected we would pay their freight to the Owners of his Ship, altho they belong'd to Gentlemen who went over at their Own expence, and we might repay our Selves out of Work done by them for the Trust. We order'd our Accomptant to prepare a State of the case to lay before the next Common Council board.

3. A person from Mr. Baker the Merchant attended, to know if we would accept Mr. Oglethorps bill on us for 500£, payable to Mr. Saml. Eveleigh of Charlestown, & by him assign'd to Mr. Baker. We told him we were not a board & could order nothing in it. But we directed our Accomptt. to go to him before our next meeting & talk the matter over to See if he could prevail with him for Mr. Oglethorps Sake not to protest the bill tho we Should not accept & pay it, which we did not think we ought to do, that money having been disburst by our Province, namely for buying Arms for defence of Forts erected South of the Allatahama. The charge on Mr. Oglethorp on protest of his bill would have been 30 p cent.

[N.B.] On the 2d August 1736 the Committee of the Assembly made the following proposalls to Mr. Oglethorp for restoring harmony between the Two Provinces, to which soon after Mr. Oglethorp reply'd as underneath.

1. That a certain number of Traders with the Indians be licenc'd from both Provinces purusant to the laws thereof: and that Such Traders observing the laws and instructions of both Provinces do pass and re-pass through the Said Provinces equally unmolested.

Oglethorp. I Shall come into any measures not inconsistent with the Laws of the Province, and without disobeying them. I refused no Carolina Traders who conform'd to the Act: I granted Lycences to none but those who had been employ'd by Carolina, and I gave them the Same Rules and Instructions as had been given them by Carolina, and at your desire I Shall give Such further instructions as are necessary on the present emergency. I desire the names of Such persons as have been lycenc'd by Carolina may be Sent me. And then if it is proved that any Indians do live beyond our without the Limits of Georgia, with whom these persons Shall be lycenc'd to trade, I will give orders to the Officers of Georgia not to molest those Traders, but give them aid.

2. That there will be no distinction or difference of instructions, but one Set agreed on by the Two Provinces for the regulation of the Traders of both.

Oglethorp. I have and Shall continue to give Such instructions to the Georgia Traders as have formerly been given by the Province of Carolina to theirs. And if Carolina Shall give new Instructions to theirs, and they appear for the benefit of both Provinces I will add them to the Instructions of Georgia.

3. That the Same form of Instructions Shall be Sent to the Agent or Commissionr. Sent into the Indian Nations.

Oglethorp. The Georgia Act has appointed the manner in which an Agent or Commissioner is to act in Georgia, and I cannot alter or dispense with it.

4. That no distinction Shall be made between the Traders of either Province and that all discourses with the Indians Shall be in the name & behalf of his Majesty, and for the benefit of all his Subjects without distinction of Provinces.

Oglethorp. I will give orders to all our Officers & Traders as is here desired.

5. That the Agent or Commissioner Shall be directed to act with equal justice in all complaints against any Trader or Indians, as well to the Traders of One Govermt. as the other, and that if any Trader Shall act amiss, he Shall be punished according to the laws of that Province from which he was lycenced.

Oglethorp. If any Trader or Indian be complaind of, I will act with impartial justice, and if any Trader act amiss he Shall be punish'd according to the Laws of the Province wherein he acted amiss.

6. That the Agent be obliged to enter into Bonds with his Majesty, and take an Oath for the due execution of his charge.

Oglethorp. The Georgia Act expresses the obligations under which the Agent is to act.

7. That any Traders who have well behaved heretofore Lycenc'd by Carolina, Shall have liberty to trade being again lycenc'd by Carolina, and if it be desired, to the particular town or towns where they traded before, and in Such case that a Trader from Georgia Shall withdraw from Such town or towns with his effects. Provided the number of Traders lycens'd or to be lycenc'd

from [Carolina] do not amount to more than one half of all the Traders that have been usually lycenced.

Oglethorp. To answer this, I must first know the number and names of the Traders which Carolina have lycenc'd. and to what towns they are lycenc'd.

8. That Orders be immediately Sent to the Agents lately Sent from Georgia not to molest any of the Traders licenc'd from Carolina.

Oglethorp. I doubt not but the Commissioner of Carolina will take care to prevent any Trader licenced by him from disturbing the Peace of Georgia, by entering the Same in defyance of the Laws thereof. But as the Western lines from the Heads of the Savannah and Allatahama Rivers have not yet been run, whereby the bounds of Georgia to the West of those rivers are yet unknown; and that no dispute may arise in the Indian Nations which ly beyond the Same, between the Traders of the Two Provinces, I will dispatch orders to the Agents Sent up into the Said Indian nations, not to molest the Traders already there licenced from Carolina, until boundary Lines are Settled, or his Majesties pleasure be Known.

9. That the Use and Navigation of the Savannah River be left open and free for all his Majesties Subjects of Carolina to all parts & places within the Province of Carolina, without molestation or hindrance whatsoever. And that an agreement pursuant to the above Propositions be enter'd into by Mr. Oglethorpe in behalf of Georgia, & this Committee in behalf of S. Carolina to Subsist till his Majesties pleasure be declared on the petition and Representation of the Assembly to his Majesty, and that the Said agreement be exchanged. Jo. Hamerton, Cha. Pinkney, Oth. Beet.

Oglethorpe. It would be presumption to determine any thing finally till his Majesties pleasure is known: But the Officers of Georgia must continue to act according to the laws thereof within the Said Province till his Majesties pleasure be Known. However, till that be known there, I Shall Suffer all boats and Pettiaguas from Carolina to pass up the Same, They delivering a Manifest of their Cargo and of the place or places to which they are bound in Carolina upon Oath to the proper Officer or Officers of Savannah, and at the Expence of the Trustees putting an Officer on board Such boats, to See the Same deliver'd at the place or places exprest in the Manifest.

4 Aug. 8.

Ld. Carpenter	C		Heathcote, Geo.	C
Cates			Lapotre, Hen.	C
(late Kendal),	R. C	Ch.	LaRoch, Jo.	C
Chandler, Ri.	C		Towers, Tho.	C
Egmont	C		Vernon, Ja.	C
Hales, Steven	C			

1. Letter from the E. of Derby was read, promising to perform the late Lords intention of paying 50£ to Mr. Millar the Botanist, but excusing himself from continuing it.

2. Order'd that Mr. Millars Sallary be paid him to Midsummer 1736, being 75£ at which time his contract with the Trustees ended.

3. Received two Reports from the Committee of Accts. & agreed thereto.

4. Order for Speedily making out 3150£ in Sola bills to be issued in Georgia by Mr. Oglethorp for the Services appointed by our letter of the 15 June, viz. 1000 bills of 1£ each, 1150£ in bills of 5£ each, & 1000£ in bills of 10£ each.

5. Draft made on the Bank to pay Mr. Simond the Merchant 469.9.10 for charges of freight &c of passengers.

6. Impress to Mr. Heathcote of 1000£ to pay bills that may come over.

7. Seal put to Mr. Hugh Andersons Commission to be Inspector of the Publick Garden and Muberry Trees.

8. Order for payment of Mr. Caustons bill drawn on us 14. May last viz. 173.7.9.

9. Agreed unanimously not to accept or pay Mr. Oglethorps bill to Mr. Eveleigh for 500£ dat. 11 May last, being for arms bought by him at Charlestown to prevent the Spaniards buying them, but for the Service of Forts built by him without the limits of our Province, which we apprehended was a misapplication of our money given only for Services within the Province. For tho the Forts built (which gave the Spaniards Such jealousie) were on land part of Carolina Southward of our bounds, and did ascertain his Majesties right thereto, yet the Parliament did not design we Should defend Carolina with the money given us, but only establish and Support our own Colony. Ld. Carpenter only objected that by our Charter we are to defend our Colony, and as Mr. Oglethorp apprehended the Spaniards design'd to dislodge

us, he might Say the purchasse of those arms was to prevent the Spaniards in their purpose. Besides, the not accepting this bill would bring us under disrepute. To which Mr. Vernon, Mr. Towers, Alderman Cates and Aldn. Heathcot reply'd, that had not Mr. Oglethorp built those Forts the Spaniards would in all probability enterd into dispute with us, that the maintenance & defence of those Forts was the Govermts. concern, not ours, and we neither did nor could give orders for erecting any beyond our own bounds. And as to refusing to pay this bill, it would prove So contrary to bringing us under disrepute, that nothing could more preserve our Credit, for the reputation of Merchants lay in not paying Bills they had no right to pay, and Shewing caution therein.

10. Grant Seald to Mr. Tho. Boyde of Piteon in Scotland 500 ac.

11. Grant Seald to Mr. David Blair of Gifford in Scotld. of 500 ac.

12. Order'd that the Accompt. write Mr. Oglethorp the reason why we refuse to accept his bill for 500£ to Mr. Sam. Eveleigh, and that we will not charge ourselves wth. 31 persons who went over with Capt. Dunbar from Scotland, viz. Mr. Jo. Cuthbert, his 10 Servants, 10 Servts belonging to Mr. Patrick Mackay, and 10 Servants belonging to Mr. John Mackay, whose freight was payable by those 3 Grantees of 500 acres. But it appearing that he had lent those people their passage to be repaid to the Trust by their labour in the publick works of the colony, or in Such provisions as they Should raise more than would Support themselves, and Should carry into the Publick Store, We had payd Mr. Simond the Said 155£, with which they charged him (Mr. Oglethorp), which he was to discharge himself by Sending an Acct. of those peoples labour.

[N.B.] On the 7 Augst. 1736 Mr. Eveleigh wrote our Accompt. a more particular acct. of the 2d Engagemt. between the French and Chickesaws, mentiond by Mr. Oglethorp in his letter of 1 July which Augustin Smith lately came down from the Chickesaw Nation related as follows.

That about 20 days after the first engagement, the French came before that place (Chocolissa) in the night time undiscovered, and tis supposed Monsr. Bienville himself commanded them. They were in number 600, 800 Chocktaws & 400 Negroes. In the night time they threw up an Intrenchment just before the Town in the form of a half Moon, & just before break of day 3 Indians came into the middle of the Town, Set up the Warr-Hoop, and So ran off, in expectation that the Indians would have follow'd them, and So have fallen into their Ambuscade. But the Chickesaws being dubious of Some Such design forebore it. The French finding them were dissappointed in that design Set the Indians to fireing upon the town, which they did without any execution, and then flew off out of the reach of their guns, and lay on their arms. Then the French went into the Town, and attempted to pull down the pallasadoes of their Fort, wch. gave the Chickesaws an opportunity of firing on them and killing several, upon which the French fled leaving about 30 of their number dead & wounded on the Spot and in the Intrenchment. Amongst the wounded was a gentleman very richly cloath'd, he had a fine gun, cuttlass & Snuffbox. The two latter Augustin Smith Saw, and the Cutlass was inlaid with Gold as he took it to be. It is Supposed to be Monsr. Bienville. There were also kill'd in the battle 8 Choctaw Indians, with only the loss of 2 Chickesaws & one Nauchee.

This Body of Troops came up the River Tholouse (or Alabamas) in pettiagua boats and Canoes, and landed about 10 miles from the Chickesaw Town. The Indians follow'd them down to their landing place, and in their retreat kill'd about 60 of the French, So that in the whole they lost about 100.

Augustin Smith was about 10 Miles distant from the Nation, which the Indians understanding, they immediately Sent out a Party to guard him in, and likewise Sent 8 Indians with him to guard him back to the Creek Nation. They appeard finely drest with White ruffled Shirts and other fine cloaths they had taken from the French, and were very earnest to go back for fear of another attack, tho Mr. Eveleigh believed these two losses would very much discourage them.

There are 3 Towns in the Chickesaw Nation, the chief of which is called Chocalissa. When this town was attack'd in the first engagement, the Women march'd from the other two to its assistance at the head of the Men & boys with their hatchets in their hands Singing, and the boys with bows and arrows, which frighted the French Indians & made them run.

Tis very usual when the Indians take any prisoners whether white Men or their own colour to put them to the torture, which is a very cruel death, but the French they took they knock'd on the head, and then threw them into a very great fire. But they burnt one Indian after the first engagement after a most cruel manner: they ty'd him to a Stake naked, and having a fire by, heated barrels of guns, & thrust them into his privy parts, his face and neck, and this they continued to do 3 or 4 hours before they kill'd him.

Upon examination of an Indian that was taken, they found, that if the French had had the better of it, The Traders among the Chickesaws had been deliver'd up to their Indians to be Served after the Same manner.

These Chickesaws are not in the whole 300 fighting Men, but are esteem'd the bravest Indians upon this Main.

[N.B.] About this time the journal Willm. Stephens Esq. (Since Secy. of the Province of Georgia) was communicated to the Trustees, giving account of his proceedings in taking up lands in Carolina in behalf of Col. Horsey, granted to him this year. His description of the River Savannah for 300 miles from our principal Town Savannah up to Old Savannah otherwise call'd Fort Moor and now New Windsor is very proper to be here incerted, & the more So as it Shews the distances of our Settlements one from 'tother on that River.

Satturday, July 5. He Set out in a Canoe & 6 hands, 4 of which were to row at a time, pretty late in the day, and lay at Josephs town, where 4 or 5 families of 500 acres to each (Scots) were at Work on their plantations. This place is 10 or 12 miles above Savannah town, and the Tide flows about 6 miles higher.

Sunday, July 6. He Set out early and about noon reach'd Purysburg, where he rested that day. This place is on the Carolina Side of the River, inhabited by Swiss, and about 14 miles above Josephs town.

Monday, July 7. He Set out very early. Now the current was very Strong against them and every day they were to expect the Same. They past by Abercorn which ly's up a creek on the Georgia Side, and at noon Stopt in the Woods to dine. About Sun-Setting they arrived at New Ebenezar, reckond about 12 miles above Purysburg. This was a hard days work.

Tuesday, July 8. He Set out before Sun-rising and had a Strong current agst. him all day. He met with no Inhabitants or anything remarkable but high close woods on the sides of the River. At Noon they Stopt to dine in them, and proceeding, lay in them, making fires near them to keep off vermin and the Musketas which were exceeding troublesome. They judg'd themselves about Midway between Ebenezar and Palachocolas.

Wednesday, July 9. He Set out very early, Stopt at Noon to dine in the Woods, and at 5 arrived at Palachocolas, computed 24 Miles by water from Ebenezar, and about 60 or 62 from Savannah. This is a Fort on Carolina Side of the River, maintain'd formerly at the expence of that Province, but upon a Colony being Settled in Georgia, they thought themselves Secure, and gave this Fort up to Mr. Oglethorpe and all the Artillery which belong'd to it, he promising to maintain it, which the Colony of Georgia Since did with a garison of 10 Men, and Capt. MackIntosh the Governor.

Thursday, July 10. He Set forward from Palachocolas about 10, and Stopt at Noon at a town of the Uchee Indians on the Georgia Side about 5 or 6 miles above Palachocolas where he dined with an Indian Trader who lived there, and proceeding, lay at night in the woods. This days work was reckon'd about 10 miles.

Fryday, July 11. Proceeded early and Saw nothing all the day, but high close woods, with here and there a little opening where Some Indians formerly lived. Stop'd as usual to dine, and at night lodged in Some old Indian hutts which had been forsaken Some time.

Satturday, July 12. They rowed about 3 or 4 hours, very leasurly, and found the Mark where the vacant lands began, which gave him great pleasure, having now the whole River before him upwards, to fix on. So that from thence forward they row'd Slowly, often Stopping to look into the land, and the nature of the Soil, which he found very good, but flat, mostly on the river & Swampy; in Some places Subject to overflowing, in others not; frequently full of canes which is allow'd to be the best token of fertility. The timber generally Oak either white, red, water oak or live Oak (call'd in Europe ever-green) Hickory, Gum, Cypress with many others, but very rarely any Pyne or Fir. This day was Spent resting a While at noon, and at night he lay in the Woods.

Sunday, July 13. Row'd up a few miles further to examine land & Stayd all day. About 2 furlongs further was an Indian hut where a family or two lived.

Monday, July 14. He proceeded Still up the River which hitherto winded & doubled So much from the beginning of vacant or ungranted land, that it was double the length by water, as in a Streight line cross the land. This day he found a firm Bluff on the Carolina Side above 30 foot higher than the Surface of the Water And there fixt his choice for a Grant for Col. Horsey whose design was when in his Post (for his Majesty had newly made him Governr. of S. Carolina) to erect a considerable Town on his land.

Here Mr. Stephens Staid a week lodging in a Tent, to See the land run out and Survey'd, and in that time a Scout boat of 8

Oars came up the river with an other of 4 Oars wherein was 12 hundred weight of powder. They were going as far as to Old Savannah or Moors Fort, new named by the Province of Carolina in which it Stands, this very month, New Windsor. It is by land but 150 miles from Charlestown, but the communication that way is very little, & therefore these latter Send their trading vessels thither up the Savannah River, from the mouth of which they must row near 300 miles. In this Town are 100 white Inhabitants among whom are Several Traders who have warehouses and Supply the Indians of Divers Nations and Towns with European Goods, either by carrying them to them, or Selling them to the Indians who come to purchasse them, So that it is the great Mart of S. Carolina for the Indian trade in these parts. And as Rum is One of the Commodities they Supply the Indians with, the prohibition thereof to enter the Province of Georgia by the Georgia Act, and the rigerous execution of it by not Suffering Rum to come up the River Savannah, least it Should clandestinly be landed on the Georgia Side (of which there were frequent instances) extreamly irritated the Province of Carolina and will continue So to do until the matter be amicably adjusted between both Provinces, Carolina being apprehensive that it is Mr. Oglethorpes design to engrosse all the Indian Trade to Georgia, and cause enough they have for this jealousie. For thus Mr. Stephens goes on, and Says:

Opposite to this Town of Old Savannah, Mr. Oglethorpe has lately order'd the Plan of a Town to be laid out (named Augusta) which the Indian Traders have undertaken to build upon Mr. Oglethorpes assigning to them a reasonable quantity of land. (500 acres to each). These Indian Traders are all Europeans, English, Scots or Irish, who plant themselves here and there among many Nations of the Indians, Several hundred miles beyond Old Savannah and many miles asunder. There they trade for Skins Furrs and Such commodities as are of value with us, and in exchange for it they dispose of Blankets powder & Shot, and many other things of Small note, by which trade many of them grow rich, and indeed they earn it dearly. For tho the Several Nations they So live among and deal with, are at present our Friends, yet they are almost at continual War wth. one another. And were it in the power of the French Settlements on the Messasippi to incite them against us (wherein their endeavours are not wanting) those Indians would not be our Friends long. This trade has hitherto been carry'd on by the way of Charlestown, But Mr. Oglethorpe by virtue of a power vested in him by the Trustees for Georgia, *intends from hence forth it Shall take its course that way* and in order thereto, all are prohibited from being Indian Traders, but Such as take Licence from him. Upon which occasion, most of them have lately been with him at Savannah Town, and taken out Such Licences. So that the whole Indian trade hereafter is So meant to be carry'd on by the Savannah River; which River as it is the boundary betwixt Carolina and Georgia, it may be proper to observe, that its entrance from the Sea its course is near East and West, but after a few miles above Savannah Town it alters more to the North, and with abundance of windings, runs in many places almost North and South, by which means it contracts the extent of Carolina pretty much westerly, and they having but little communication (as has been Said) with Old Savannah or Moors Fort by land whereby any traffick can be carry'd on by land, they have been obliged to Send their trading vessels quite round to the River Savannah, from whence they must go afterwards near 300 miles further by water, which Shews how much they are encompassed. But So valuable a trade few would grudge to go far for, which may in Some Sort be guest at, when we Know, that the Cargo of one of their trading boats, wch. commonly go with only 4 Negroes to row, and a white Man to Steer who is Master, is Seldom less worth than 1000£ Sterlg. *all which Trade from what is Said is now likely to center in Georgia,* and hereafter the Indian Traders, instead of Sending their goods over the mountains to Old Savannah, will Send them to their own Town Augusta, where they will also be provided with all Such commodoties from the Colony of Georgia, as their Trade requires. Thus in all Events the River Savannah is likely to become as noted in few years as any River in America whether Carolina or Georgia are mostly benefitted by it, Few if any Surpassing it in Such a depth of Water as to be navigable from the Sea to old Savannah Town upwards of 30 miles. And notwithstanding the great body of water it consists of, it Shews no extraordinary rapidity any where, but glides Smoothly on as the River Thames at Putney, and in many places confined within as little Space of breadth, but then tis far deeper.

18 Augst. 9.

Egmont	C P	Lapotre, Hen.	C
Hales, Steven	C	LaRoch, Jo.	C
Hucks, Robt.	C	Towers, Tho.	C

A Common Council was Summond to recieve Mr. Quincy's account of the State of Georgia being lately arrived. To read letters from Mr. Oglethorp of the 18 May, and to consider of the acceptance of bills of Exchange drawn by Mr. Oglethorp for provisions, for 500£ Sterlg. But we were not a Board.

1. Letters were read from Mr. Oglethorp and Fra. Moore Recordr. of Frederica, dat. 18 May. The former acquainted us that Capt. Green of Charles Town had tempted the Uchee Indians to fall upon the Saltsburgers at Ebenezar, because these last had past the River and put their Cattle on the Indian lands on the Carolina Side, but that the Indians refused. That the dispute with the Govr. of Augustine was happily over, who was prejudiced against us by letters he received from Charlestown.

Mr. Moors letter related chiefly to accompts.

2. Bills lately drawn on us by Mr. Oglethorp to the amount of 2700£ a great part of which was for provision astonish'd us, considering the number of Sola bills he carry'd with him.

3. We hoped to put an end to this drawing bills on us, by ordering an advertisment for the gazet & other Newspapers, that we will answer no bills from Georgia but our own Sola bills, which Should be duly paid.

4. Mr. Quincy who brought these letters, gave us a very unsatisfactory Acct. of Savannah. He Said the people employ'd themselves in building their houses in order to Set others to advantage, & neglected cultivating their lands, So that he did not believe the first Settlers would be able to maintain themselves, but must Still live at the Trustees charge on the Stores, altho they have been 3 years there. That very few had cultivated any thing worth, but he heard the Tithing men had lately enter'd into agreement to cultivate in common. That he believed there were about 200 houses in the Town besides hutts and 600 Inhabitants. That a new Town house had lately been built capable of holding 200 persons, which was likewise made use of for a Church. That he left the place very healthy, but many of the new born children died, he supposed for want of milk, because the land adjoyning to the Town was Pine-barren, yeilding no grass for above 8 months of the year, So that the cattle run wild into the woods, & among the Sugar cane Swamps.

26 *Augst.* 10.

Egmont	C		Lapotre, Hen.	C
Hales, Stevn.	C		LaRoch, Jo.	C
Heathcote, Geo.	C	P	Towers, Tho.	C

[1736] JOURNAL OF THE EARL OF EGMONT 197

No Board again this day tho a particular Summons was orderd for going into a Committee of Correspondence & Accts. and to recieve their reports, Capt. Yoakly being to attend. For ordering the acceptance of Several bills of Exchange, and for other business necessarily to be dispatch'd this day.

1. Capt. Yoakly appeard & demanded 378.13.4 for demurrage in Georgia, in complyance with Mr. Caustons directions, and as certified by Mr. Moore Recorder of Frederica. We concluded we Should be obliged to pay it, but could not order it being no Common Council. We highly condemn'd Mr. Causton for creating this expence.

2. Mr. LaRoch acquainted us that his brother a Mercht. at Bristol would credit all the Sola bills deliver'd out by Mr. Oglethorp, which would prevent the Carolina people from running them down, and Mr. Oglethorp would by circulating them be free'd from the necessity of drawing on us.

3. Order'd a letter to Mr. Oglethorp to acquaint him therewith, and with the low State of our Cash, and with the reason of not accepting his bill on us payable to Mr. Eveleigh for arms &c.

4. Order'd also a letter to Mr. Causton Severely reproving him for Sending over imperfect Accts. and for not writing any thing to us from 14 April to 8 June. For not answering Queries Sent him, and for employing Capt. Yoakly in Sounding the Allatahama and continuing him on demurrage til Mr. Oglethorps arrival, which came to 60£ Sterlg. p month.

[N.B.] On 30 Aug. 1736, it was wrote in the S. Carolina Gazet, that a Commissioner from the Governr. of Havana was Sent to Frederica, Solemnly to demand that the English Should evacuate all to the South of St. Helena Sound; and that the Town of St. Augustine was reinforced by 3 companys of foot from Havana.

8 Sept. 11.

Ld. Carpenter	C	Lapotre, Hen.	C
Egmont	C	LaRoch, Jo.	C
Hales, Stevn.	C	Towers, Tho.	C
Hucks, Robt.	C	More, Robt.	T
Heathcote, Geo.	C P		

Tho we were enough to make a Common Council being 8, yet the pressing hast with which Ld. Carpenter and Aldn. Heathcote made to go away, prevented us from very necessary business, one of which was ordering the acceptance & payment of 2141.14.0 bills of exchange, which if return'd for want of a board would be near 30£ ⅌ cent expense.

The negligence of our Gentlemen in attending was now become great matter of complaint.

1. Robert Parker a Saucy fellow who formerly was an Alderman of Lyn in Norfolk and transported on the charity acct. to Georgia, having lately run away from the Colony appear'd, and made heavy complaints against Mr. Causton that he had ruin'd him by not advancing him money to compleat a Saw Mill which would have yeilded him 1000£ ⅌ ann. Also that he would not Suffer him to leave the Province. He concluded with desiring the Trust to advance him money, being in debt, and in danger of arrest. We bid him put his request in writing & bring it next fryday. He told us the land of Savannah was very indifferent, and he could not Speak much for the place; and is very detrimental to the Inhabitants, who for want of molasses to make beer, had for 6 months drank nothing but water.

2. Imprest 500£ to Aldn. Heathcote to discharge Several Sola bills lately arrived, and to pay others that would come.

3. Captn. Yoakly attending, and offering to make oath to his Acct. for demurrage, we directed him So to do, for our better justification in paying him.

4. We agreed that Capt. Diamonds demand for demurrage be a guardship to Frederica & for freight of provisions ought to be paid when the Common Council meets, being duly certified by Mr. Oglethorpe and Francis Moore Recorder.

10 Septbr. 12.

Bundy, Ri.	C	Ch.	Hales, Stevn.	C
Ld. Carpenter	C		Hucks, Robt.	
Egmont	C		Lapotre, Hen.	C
Eyles, Fra.	C		Towers, Tho.	C

1. Order'd the 378.13.4 be paid to Capt. Yoakly for demurrage at Frederica and for Searching the harbour at the Allatahama, he having made oath to his Acct.

2. Report of the Committee of Accts. touching his demand for demurrage at Frederica freight of provisioons &c was received & approved & order'd 289£ to be paid him.

3. The Report from the Same Committee was received, toughing a bill for 13£ odd Shillings drawn us by Mr. Jeffries of Bristol, for the expence of 6 couple of Dogs Sent Mr. Oglethorp, And

[1736]   JOURNAL OF THE EARL OF EGMONT   199

agreed that payment be Suspended till we know if they were Sent on the Trust acct. But 8 Shill. and 4 pence postage of letters was orderd to be paid him.

4. Order for paying Several bills drawn on us for provisions and other uses of the colony.

5. The Board took into consideration the new Set of Sola bills made out amounting to 3150£, and concluded that if all were Sent to Mr. Oglethorpe (as at first intended before the late bills Sent us) We Should have but 1681£ remaining in our hands to answer future drafts, and all other unforeseen expences of the Colony. And Since means had been found to give currency to the Sola bills Mr. Oglethorpe carry'd over, it was judged proper to Send at present but 1500£ in Sola bills, whereby we Should have remaining on this Side 3331.12.10 including the rest of the Sola bills not to be Sent which were 1650£ which we order'd to be lock'd up. The Sola bills to be Sent we orderd Should be 1000 of 20 Shill. each, & 100 of 5£ each.

6. Order'd payment of 23£ to Mr. Bevan Apothecary, for druggs & Surgeons instruments Sent to Supply our Physical Chest in Georgia.

7. Imprest 1500£ to Aldn. Heathcote, for paymt. of bills drawn us, he having the rest of the money in his hands, and for answering Sola bills that may be returnd for payment.

8. Draft also on the Bank of 974.14.2 to pay Mr. Simonds demands, of which Capt. Yoakly's money is part.

9. Robert Parker again attended to See if he could obtain money from us, either by gift or loan. We told him he was already indebted 80£ to the Trust advanced him towards erecting his Sawmill, which by Accts. Since received we heard would not have Succeeded. That we could not justify the giving him Publick money, or lending him any more. He then desired we would contribute to him out of our private purses, but none of us were inclined thereto. He was very blustering and indecent, and again complained the Magistrates of Savanna had been unjust and cruel to him in ruining his project of a Saw Mill. We answer'd, if all was true he Said, he had his action against them, but We had only his own word for it unsupported by any manner of proof. That Mr. Oglethorpe was in Georgia when he left it, & it is Surprising, if he had been injured, that he did not complain to him, who had power to redress all wrongs, and too much honour & conscience not to do it if proved, but we had received no letter or intimation on that Subject from him or any one else.

10. Capt. Dunbar attended, to make us an offer of 150 Swiss whom he was to bring from Holland & carry to Carolina, but if we thought it for our Service, he believed they might be prevail'd on to go to Georgia. We thank'd him, but with all acquainted him we were too low in Cash to Send any more at present.

11. Two Scotsmen brothers, named Gibson attended, and desired their Grant of 100 Acres formerly made to one of them might be changed to a 50 acre town lot in Savanna. The other also desired a town lot there, but we told them it was doubtfull whether there is a town lot vacant, and advised them to take their 100 acre lotts each, promising that when they had cultivated them they Should have more land in proportion to the Servants they carry'd over, in which they acquiesced, only desired their land might be as near the town as possible.

N.B.: it dos not appear they ever went over or took out their Grants.

12. Rowland Pytt and Jo. Tuckwell Merchts. having trusted Jo. Bromfield our Register at Savannah with 2000£ of goods, petition'd that we would send instructions to the Magistrates of Savannah, that in case He Should die, they Should take an inventory of his debts & effects in order to Secure them for their use, which the Board thought reasonable, and orderd the Accompt. to write a letter to that purpose.

[N.B.] 10 Septbr. 1736. Paul Jenys Esq, Speaker of the Assembly of S. Carolina wrote the Trustees that John Baker of Charlestown Esq. was dead. He had a grant of 500 Acres, and was a good friend to our Colony, So that by his dying at this juncture when Such heats were arisen between the two colonies, was a great loss to us.

[N.B.] 11 Septbr. 1736. Mr. Jo. Wesley wrote Mr. Vernon giving account that Mr. Benjamin Ingham had made Some progress in the Creek language, but that himself chose rather to learn the Chickesaw language, the Genearality of that despised and almost unheard of Nation being humble and tractable (qualities Scarce to be found among any other of the Indian nations) having So firm a relyance on Providence and So Settled a habit of looking up to a Superior Being in all the occurrences of life, that they appear the most likely of all the Americans to receive & rejoice in the Glorious Gospel of Christ.

[N.B.] 15 Sept. 1736. Mr. Benj. Ingham wrote Sr. Jo. Philips that a School house was built on a little hill (call'd by him Irene) by a brooks Side, a quarter of a mile above Tomochachi's town, where the Savannah River divides itself into 3 Streams. That this hill had been raised Some hundred years ago, he Supposed to perpetuate the memory of Some Warriour. In digging the cellar, they found abundance of oyster Shells, and Some bones and Buckhorns. That Tomachachi favour'd the building, but the Indians ask'd him if he was not afraid to live on a hill as they were, believing Fairies haunted Hills. That the Moravian Brethren (the most holy Society of Men in the whole World), were So zealous as to help on the building at a very low price. That he design'd to live there with one of these Moravian families. That the Indians who at first were unwilling their children Should learn, were now willing to have them taught, and Some of the Men Seem'd to have the Same desire. That Chickilly the chief of the Lower Creeks was well pleased when he Saw the children Say their lessons, and Said, perhapps the time is now come when all our children are to be taught learning. That white peoples children behaved themselves like Men, we Indians who are Men, behave ourselves like Dogs. And Molatchee who is next to him, Said, if he had 20 children, he would have them all taught.

[N.B.] 18 Sept. 1736 advice was Sent from Charlestown that Roger Lacy by Commission from Mr. Oglethorp had with an armed force broke open the Stores and carry'd away the goods & Skins to the value of 3000£ of John Gardiner an Indian Trader from Charles town, in the Town of *Tunasea* on the Messasippi River, one of the most northern towns of the Cherokees, and accounted above 100 miles North of any part of Georgia. And that the Said Gardner was by Lacy order'd to depart out of the Cherokee nation in 4 days, on paid of being carry'd prisoner to Georgia. That on the 11 August he according left Tunasea, and arrived at New Windsor the 26 and leaving that town (al. Old Savannah) the 28, arrived in Charlestown 3 Septbr. Of this he made Oath. Also Joseph Griffin, another Trader lycenced at Charlestown, that he with a carriage of the Same value had undergone the Same fate, and lost everything he had by the Same people, who threatened to bind & carry him to Georgia, because he would not Sell his horses to them.

[N.B.] 20 Sept. 1736 came an Acct. that Don Antonio Aredondo the Spanish Commissary demanded that the English Should evacuate all they Stand possest of as far as St. Helena Sound, the Spaniards having formerly had Forts there. But that Mr. Oglethorp demanded of him, that the Spaniards Should evacuate as far as the 29 degree North latitude, conformable to King Charles the 2ds

Charter, the English having formerly had possession as far as that Latitude, Sr. Francis Drake having by Q. Elizabeths orders taken Augustine. That at length Don Antonio agreed that on withdrawing the Garison from the Island St. George, the Said Island Should remain unpossest by either Party, till advices Should arrive from Europe, and that no hostilities Should be committed on either Side till the determination of the English and Spanish Courts Should be known; and all other claims be defer'd till their determination.

That after this Mr. Oglethorp had gone up the Allatahama River Several days journey, and return'd by the Darien, where he marked out the Fortifications of that place, and orderd a Church, School house, and Guardhouse to be built.

That while he was there, Capt. Macpherson arrived with a drove of Cattle, which he brought all the way over land from South Carolina, and that it caused great joy in all our Settlements to find the communication for Cattel by land open'd, whereby those Southern Settlements will be Supply'd with Milk and fresh provisions of which they hitherto Stood in great need.

[N.B.] 21 Sept. 1736 Monsr. Giraldini the Spanish Minister at London wrote a letter to the Duke of Newcastle Secy. of State fill'd with false complaints agst. our Province, the Substance of which was, that Our people had attack'd a Fortress Situated on the Teritories of his Master, 8 leagues distant from St. Augustine the 3d of March last and Kill'd a Spanish Soldier in the taking it. That afterwards they built a Fort on his Masters Territories, in Florida 25 leagues to the North of St. Augustine at the Entrance of the *River St. Simons* and garrison'd it, altho the Inhabitants of Carolina who had built a Fort in the Same place, caused it to be demolished by order of the Court of England, at the request of that of Spain.

That the Govr. of the Fort *St. Mark* in the Province of *Apalache* had Sent account, that the Indians of the Provinces *Uchisses,* and *Talapuzes* Subjects of his Majesty, complain'd, that the English were building a Fort in the Territories of his Majesty inhabited by the Said *Uchisses,* and that they give acct they will build another in the territories of the *Talapuzes* to the N.W. of Augustine.

That another Party of 300 English had appeared on the Frontiers of the *Talapuzes,* and having Set up a Standard of War in a town of Indians call'd *Apalachicholo,* had Summond the chief Town of that Province call'd *Coveta* to joyn them in order to make War on the Spaniards, as[suring] them they were resolv'd to demolish the *Fort St. Mark,* and afterwards to besiege St. Augustine.

For all these things be desired the people of Georgia concerned in them might be punish'd. And added,

That the Colony of Carolina being Situated in 32 degrees of Latitude, and 294½ of Longitude, and the Colony of Georgia being to the Southward of the other, Georgia is without dispute on the Territories of the King his Master. And even the former according to the Treaty of Peace in 1670, by the 7th Article of which, the Limits were Settled precisely for the Said Province and that of Florida at 33 degrees of Latitude and 339 degrees of Longitude and 30 minutes, Tho the Town call'd Carolina (he meant Charlestown) was tolerated, because it was built before the making the Said Treaty. And as by the 8 Article of the Treaty of Utrecht in 1713 it is agreed that the Limits and Demarcations of the West Indies Should remain on the Same foot as they were in the reign of K. Charles the 2d. The king his Master hoped the Inhabitants of Georgia Should be punish'd, that due observance Should be paid to the limits that had been Settled between both Crowns, and that the Forts built on the Territories and demarcations of Florida, Should be immediately demolish'd.

[N.B.] 27 Sept. 1736. The above letter was Sent by the D. of Newcastle, acquainting the Trustees at the Same time, that twas her Majesties pleasure we Should enquire into the matter, and Send him a State of it, to lay before [her] Majesty for her commands thereon.

6 Octbr. 13.

Egmont	C	Vernon, Ja.	C
Hales, Stevn.	C	Anderson, Adm.	T
Hucks, Robt.	C	Bedford, Arthr.	T
Lapotre, Hen.	C	Smith, Saml.	T
Towers, Tho.	C P		

A Summons for a Common Council was issued, to consider of Monsr. Giraldinis Letter to the D. of Newcastle containing complaints against the Inhabitants of Georgia, and of his Graces letter to us to State the matter to be laid Before the Queen; and to make a further Contract with the Botanist. But we were not a board.

1. Seal'd a Commission to Mr. Thoresby to preach & collect for us in the church of Stoke Newington.

2. We considerd of an answer to Mr. Giraldini's letter to the D. of Newcastle.

3. A Message from the Lords of the board of Trade came desiring we would talk with them thereon.

4. Read a Memorial (formerly mentioned fol. 136) and desired Mr. Fury the Carolina Agent not to present it out of hand, hoping we might accomodate disputes wthout making noise, which he Said he would yeild to Since the depositions for Supporting the Memorial were not yet arrived

It was our opinion that the Navigation of the Savannah is free to the Carolina Traders, but that Mr. Causton Should when their Vessels come up, Send a person on board in the nature of an Officer to prevent their landing Rum.

We admired at Mr. Caustons negligence in not acquainting us with his proceedings in a matter of this consequence.

13 Oct. 14.

Egmont	C	Towers, Tho.	C
Heathcote, Geo.	C	Vernon, Ja.	C
Hucks, Robt.	C P		

A Common Council again Summond for the purposes above mentioned, as also for ordering paymt. of a bill of exchange, and to confer with the Board of Trade; But again No board.

1. Order given for transporting to Georgia a daughter of Sr. Francis Bathurst, She desiring to be Sent, her husband being lately dead.

2. Agreed on the form of a letter to the D. of Newcastle in answer to Monsr. Giraldini's Memorial or letter to his Grace.

3. Being inform'd that by Mr. Oglethorps order Mr. Causton had drawn upon us a bill payable to Mr. Abrm. Minas of 210£ being the purchasse of a whole Cargo bought on the Trust acct. and as Mr. Causton inform'd us in his letter of 22d (blank) was bought entire, because Such goods as were proper for the Stores thereby became cheaper, we thought it fit the bill Should be accepted. It was dat. 20 July. But we admired that Mr. Oglethorp did not make use of the Sola bills instead of drawing bills, and Some Suspected he kept them to answer extraordinary charges with which he did not think proper to acquaint the Trustees till over. We also were greatly displeased that Mr. Causton having So fair an occasion as the drawing this bill gave him to write to us the Transactions in the Colony wholly neglected. Mr. Vernon was ab-

solutly of opinion that Mr. Oglethorpe had forbid him or any others to write us any Accts. tho at the Same time he Scarce writes us any himself, by which we are kept in the dark. And this he thought might reasonably be interpreted one of the reasons why the Gentlemen of the Common Council fall off from giving their attendance at the Board.

4. We observed that Will. Cooksey is made debtor by Mr. Causton to the Trust for bisquet, corn, tea & Coffee, pt. of this Cargo to the value of 27.15.11, by which we perceived Luxury was introducing into the Colony. N.B. This loan or credit to Cooksey was without order of the Trustees, and a misapplication of their money by Causton.

[N.B.] 13 Oct. 1736. Mr. Saml. Eveleigh wrote to our Accompt. that Mr. Oglethorpe had taken his passage to go from Georgia to London on board Capt. Thompson who was to Sail the 18th inst. But that he design'd to Stay till the return of the Two Agents he Sent to the Cherokee and Creek nations, Roger Lacy and another.

[N.B.] 13 Oct. 1736. Mr. Boltzius Saltsburg Minister, wrote complaints to Mr. Oglethorpe, that the new come Saltsburgers had not recieved half the Tools promist them out of the Stores. That the Surveyor had not run out all the gardens & Farm lotts of the people, but was gone to Purysburg to do work there and was like to Stay there a considerable time. That Some gardens were run out on pine barren lands, and confidently hoped it Should be exchanged for better ground, of which there lies a fine Tract behind their gardens towards Ebenezar River. That the Spots in the middle of the Town reserved for Publick Buildings were not exactly laid out, wherefore none could be built. That he and Mr. Gronau his fellow labourer wanted money to build a dwelling house, having hitherto lived in hutts. Their Sallary being hardly Sufficient for their Sustenance. That they had bought a Small boat which was necessary for their Colony and hoped to be repayd. That the Schoolmaster & Dr. Swiffler were disabled to pay the building Hutts & garden Fence, which they had advanced them out of what was Sent for the poor of their Congregation. That 4 Carpenters were yet unpaid for building Mr. Gronaus house at Old Ebenezar, tho it had been promised them. That the peoples provision allowd them is too Short. Finally that they must break up & go more Southward, if deny'd their full provision on acct. of being Settled at Ebenezar. That flower and butter was wanting as well as Molassus for the Sick. That they had not received their full quantity of Cows, Sows and Poultry, and provision was necessary for the School children as also a School house.

[N.B.] 16 Augst. [October?] 1736. Mr. Eveleigh wrote our Accompt. his Surprise at the likelyhood of Mr. Oglethorpes bill to him for 500£ for purchasse of guns & duffels to be return'd protested, it being to prevent the Govr. of Augustine from purchassing them to present the Upper Creeks to come down to him, to whom he had Sent word he would give 400 guns and as much cloth as they could carry back. That it was confirm'd from many hands that the Govr. above mentioned had that design.

That the Indians were So used to presents of late years, that they expected them as a right from English, French and Spaniards who in Some measure were become Tributary to them.

That he was credibly inform'd, that 3 or 4 years Since, the Govr. of Moville gave their Indians at one time to the value of 2000£ Sterlg.

That an Indian Trader inform'd him, The upper Indians had met with a body of Frenchmen, had kill'd 4 of them, and brought one wounded into their Nation.

That in the Engagement for mention'd between the French & Chickesaws it was Monsr. Dartigut was Slayn.

He further acquaints him that Mr. Philip Von Reck Commissary of the Saltsburgers Sail'd for England the day before the date of his letter.

Octbr. 20. 15.

Bundy, Ri.	C	Towers, Tho.	C
Chandler, Ri.	C	Vernon, Ja.	C P
Egmont	C	Anderson, Ad.	T
Hales, Stevn.	C	Smith, Saml.	T
Lapotre, Hen.	C		

A Common Council again Summond, and in great distress for one, to order the matters mention'd in the former Summons but no Board.

1. Seal put to our Memorial to her Majesty, in answer to Monsr. Giraldini's letter to the D. of Newcastle. Wherein we acquaint her Majesty

a. That concerning the complaint of our peoples attacking on the 3. of March last a Spanish Fort 8 leagues distant from St. Augustine, and killing a Spanish Soldier, We could not find any English or Indians inhabiting Georgia had been concerned in the Outrage; But that it was committed by Some neighbouring Indians in revenge of a most unheard of barbarity acted by Some

Spaniards or Spanish Indians who had killed Some Indian Women and children and two Men, and after most wickedly abusing another Indian Woman, burnt her alive.

b. As to our rebuilding a Fort wch. is alledged to have been formerly demolished by order of the Court of England at the request of the Court of Spain, the Spanish Minister was misinformed therein, for that Fort having been left without the consent or Knowledge of his Majesty, was order'd to be rebuilt by his Majesty, by an instruction to the late Govr. Johnson.

c. As to the complaints of the Uchisses & Talapuzes Indians, that the English were building a Fort on the Teritories of the K. of Spain inhabited by the Uchisses, and gave out they would build another on the Talapuzes land, The Trustees never gave direction for any Settlements to be made or Forts built but within the Limits of Georgia, and if those Nations inhabit within the Same, they ought not to be Stiled Subjects of Spain.

d. As to the 300 English appearing on the Frontiers of the Province of Apalache, Setting up a Standard of War, Summoning the Capital Town Coveta to joyn them in order to make War agst. the Spaniards, and telling them they intended to demolish the Fort of St. Mark, and afterwards to beseige St. Augustine: We did not believe there is any foundation for these reports, or that any of our people could have acted So contrary to the intentions of the Trustees, who always had it at heart in making their Several Settlements to avoid all occasions of contest with their Several Neighbouring Nations.

e. That We confine our Selves within the Limits of our charter, and make no question but his Majesty has an undoubted right to Georgia, observing nothing in the Treaties refer'd to by Monsr. Giraldini that makes for the contrary.

2. Mr. Quincy late Minister at Savannah appeard & desired 3 things:

a. That we would give him an attestation of his good behaviour while he served in Georgia.

b. That we would make him a consideration for his expences and loss of 3 months time after the arrival of Mr. John Wesley to Succeed him, before his return to England.

c. That we would let him know what charges had been laid against him, and by whom, in Georgia, that he might wipe off the aspersions.

[3.] Mr. Vernon being in the chair, reply'd in the name of the Board.

a. That his behaviour had been Such in Georgia, that had he

not of himself wrote to be dismist, we Should have dismist him without it.

b. That as to his desire of a consderation for Staying in 3 months after Mr. Wesley arrived there to Succeed him, we must first know whether he made that Stay at the desire of the Magistrates or Mr. Oglethorp, for otherwise we could not justify the giving him the Publick money, merely to maintain a person to whom we had no longer relation. Then being ask'd if he had been desired to Stay, & he replying no, Mr. Vernon told him we could give him nothing.

c. As to his request that we would let him Know his accusers, we thought it better for him to rest his return on his own desire than to oblige us to give the reasons why his conduct was not approved and he thereupon dismist. That the Board always acted on good reason, and were not obliged to give him Satisfaction what we disliked concerning him. However he Should be So far indulged as to Know, that his abandoning the Colony for Six months together, and leaving a Wheelright to read Publick prayers, comfort the Sick and bury the dead, was a behaviour the Trustees could not excuse. We were Sorry he had given occasion for censure, and Supposed by accusers he meant the Magistrates of Savannah, but we could not recollect that they had wrote a Syllable against him, But indeed Several had viva voce acquainted us with his behaviour there, and his neglect of duty by the long absence above mention'd: And besides he was guilty of another great neglect in not corresponding with the Trust as enjoyned when We sent him.

He reply'd it was Sickness carry'd him to New York, but he was answer'd he Should then have taken care to have his absence Supply'd by Some other Minister, or have obtained leave to go from persons who had authority to give it.

He then Said the cause why he had raised Enemies to him in Georgia, was his representing against the great irregularities and bad administration of Affairs there. Mr. Vernon reply'd, this was a new matter which we would consider of, and therefore desired him to withdraw a while. Whereupon taking his hat he left the room, and as we thought retired into the next adjoyning, but he went quite away, & returned not.

4. Letter wrote by the Accompt. to Mr. Oglethorpe, that 1500£ in Sola bills had been Sent him by the Brook Capt. Keet; that he Should draw no more bills; that he Should Speak to Mr. Causton that he Should return Satisfactory answers to the Several queries

[1736] JOURNAL OF THE EARL OF EGMONT   209

Sent him, in order that a proper application of the moneys that have come to his hands may appear. That the Trustees make him Debtr. for the 210£ bill drawn by Causton in July last payable to Abraham Minnis, because credit had been given to Will. Cooksey for part of the Cargo. He concluded with the Trustees earnest desire that he would return to England before next Session of Parliamt. for without his presence we had no manner of hopes of a further Supply.

Octobr. 27. 16.

Ld. Carpenter	C	Hucks, Robt.	C
Chandler, Ri.	C	Towers, Tho.	C
Egmont	C	Vernon, Ja.	C
Hales, Stevn.	C		

A Special Summons for a Common Council to do Several necessary business for which former Summons were issued, but again we were no Board.

1. We only in a Committee of Accts examined the Vouchers of last years Accompts.

[N.B.] 1 Novbr. 1736. It was publish'd in the S. Carolina Gazet, that the Sloop Frederica, Capt. Goodwin Commander was lately arrived at Philadelphia from Frederica, reported, that the *furthest English Settlement* Southward lies in the Latitude of 30 degrees 30 minutes; The Town of *Frederica* in 31 degrees, and that of Savannah in 32 degrees. That he found 3 Fathom & ½ on the Bar of Frederica, and went in without a Pilot. That there are several Clapboard houses built there, and 2 brick houses one Story above ground, & preparations for a great many more. That there is a Fort with 4 Bastions, one large Store house three Stories high and another building, the Timber being all ready for the building.

That Mr. Oglethorpe was returning to England, having fix'd his people, & Secured them both against Want and Enemies, & was to Sail in a fortnight.

[N.B.] 3 Novbr. 1736. One P. Thickness a young Lad who lived with Mr. Causton and work'd for him wrote his mother that he had been over about 2 months that in Savannah were about 300 houses besides hutts. That he liked the place and would Sooner live in it than in any part of England, but not in the Town, for there was an island about 12 miles off where were about 10 lots, and 7 of them taken, and being Surrounded with salt water was more healthy, and one may keep their Cattel Safe, wch. they cant on the Main-land. That if a man had there but 20£, & laid it out in Cattel, he might clear that 20£ on Salt beef and boild Rice instead of bread. That there were a parcel of good for nothing Chapps who gave the place an ill name to all Strangers, and had like to have frighted him away when first he came. That if a man died, his child inherited his Improvements at 16 and there was no man but might live on his own Improvments if industrious. That it is a fine Country for any Sort of game, one needed not fear Shooting a deer every day, Turkeys, and wild Ducks Swimming 1000 of them in the River all the Winter. That he mounted Guard once in 17 nights.

[N.B.] 8 Nov. 1736. Joseph Cannon (Son of Danl. who was appointed 2 Bailif of Frederica in case of vacancy) wrote to Joseph Flitchcroft Esq. from Frederica the following Acct.

That the Island St. Simons (where Frederica is built) is about as big as the Isle of Wight: about 60 leagues South from Charlestown, 30 from Savannah, and about 30 N. of St. Augustine. That there were about 15 or 16 Settlements in the Colony already. That Frederica lies very well Situated on the West Side of the Island on a fine River, where a Ship of 300 Tun may come up. On the South End is a fine Inlet of the Sea, where his Majesty's Sloop the Hawk lies, and on the point of the Island was a garrison of 100 Men. On the East Side was the Sea. On the North End another fine Inlet of the Sea. That there were about 50 families in the Town wch. was laid out for 500 families. That the Island was pretty thick of Wood, and there were a great many Deer on it, but they Seldom got any, the Wood being So very thick, But the Indians very often brought them 10 or a dozen at a time, and Sometimes a whole Buffelo. That there were a great many wild fowl, Such as Turkeys, Geese, Ducks and other kinds, And abundance of fish, but having no time at present for want of getting houses over their heads, they got any of them.

That they had no lime or chalk, or Stone, and their lime was made of very fine Oysters, which they burnt 2 or 300 bushels at a time. That his father and about half the people of the Town were agreed to build themselves brick houses. The first Two were almost coverd in 3 Story high. That when first they came they built themselves little Hutts, and cover'd them with Palmetto leaves.

That they had clear'd their Acre lott about ½ a mile out of town, & their Lot is town as Soon as they knew where it was, which was not till April last. That they had clear'd and fenc'd it round with a hedge, and Sow'd it with almost all Sorts of garden Seeds of

[1736] JOURNAL OF THE EARL OF EGMONT   211

England, which grew very well, So that they were the forwardest of any person in the place, & lived as happy and as well contended as possible, and hoped So to continue if it pleas'd God they Should find their health. That his father was talking of getting 10 Men with himself to fence round their great Lots which are laid out in Tithings, and himself and 9 more had agreed to do the Same, and to put Some Cattel on to begin the Same, 1 Jany., And Mr. Oglethorpe had given them a grant for the Same.

10 Novbr. 17.

Ld. Carpenter	C		LaRoch, Jo.	C
Chandler, Ri.	C		Towers, Tho.	C
Bundy, Ri.	C		Vernon, Ja.	C
Egmont	C	Ch.	Derry,	
Hales, Steven	C	P	Bi. of, Rundall	T
Hucks, Robt.	C		Smith, Saml.	T
Lapotre, Hen.	C			

1. Col. Horsey newly appointed Govr. of S. Carolina communicated to us Mr. Stephens journal (fol. 141) who was Sent by him to take up a Grant of 40000 Acres in Carolina.

2. An impertinent letter was read from Robt. Parker formerly mention'd, the Sauceyest fool and errant knave I have met with. After many charges against Mr. Causton, he concludes with desiring the Board to lend him 3 or 400£ of the Publick money, or that We would club and do it among ourselves in our private capacities. We answer'd we would Send over his complaints to be answer'd by Causton. This fellow offer'd his Service to Mr. Fury the Carolina Agent, to appear at the Council board, and Support viva voce the Representation Sent by that Province against our Magistrates.

3. Mr. Fury above mention'd came and excused his presenting the Representation and lodging it in the Council Office yesterday, on account of the notice taken in town that he had So long delay'd to give it. We told him he did but his duty, and acquainted him we would accept and pay him bills drawn to his use by Mr. Oglethorpe for 400£, being money of his paid into Mr. Oglethorp's hands in Georgia and was his Sallary which Carolina return'd him after this manner. Our orders not to draw were not then arrived.

4. Mr. Millar the Botanist whom we agreed with to continue in our Service for 2 years from Midsummer last attended, and received from us the Articles he is to Sign, together with directions

concerning his conveying to Georgia the plants and roots he collected in his last voyage.

5. Bills drawn on us to the amount of 1800£ were accepted, being mostly for provisions to Supply the Publick Stores, the rest for Ship Goods.

6. Letters from Mr. Oglethorpe and Mr. Causton were read which contained nothing of any moment towards Satisfying our desires of Knowing what was doing in Georgia. But we expected a thorough information from Mr. Jo. Wesley who we heard was on the Sea in his return to England who we Supposed brought letters.

7. Mr. LaRoch inform'd Some of us privately that the Bristol Merchants complain Mr. Oglethorpe is turn'd Merchant, and bought up Skins at 21 Shillgs. *p* hundd. Whereas they used to give but 20 Shillgs., So that he monopolized the Trade.

And Mr. Vernon said he had obtained a Grant of 12000 Acres in Carolina.

The former was new to me, but the latter is taken notice of in Mr. Stephens journal who Says these 12000 Acres are adjoyning to Palachocolas Fort.

Novbr. 24. 18.

Ld. Carpenter	C		Towers, Tho.	C
Egmont	C		Anderson, Adm.	T
Lapotre, Hen.	C	P	Smith, Sam.	T

A Common Council was Summond, but we were not a number.

1. Benefactions received, among others 38.2.0 collected by Mr. Thoresby.

2. Drew up a letter from Mr. Verelts to Mr. Popple Secy. to the Board of Trade, renewing our application for a report from that board upon our petition to the Crown for Cannon presented in August 1735. It Seems the regular manner had been to have refer'd our petition to the Board of Ordenance, but the Ministry Sent it to the Board of Trade, very probably with intention to defeat our application: for we never obtained our request, no report being ever made.

3. We also drew up a letter to Mr. Oglethorpe to be written to him by Mr. Verelts as in his own name but by our order, complaining in Strong terms that he had given us no acct. of his proceedings in Georgia Since June last, tho the complaints agst. the managements in Georgia Sent by the Province of Carolina have

Since that time been frequent and Strong. That the Representation from Carolina was come and presented, and refer'd to a Committee of Council, and Such paragraphs were incerted in the Newspapers, as required explanation. That for want of a regular correspondence from him & Mr. Causton, of what is doing in Georgia, we are wholly disabled from giving the Publick the Satisfaction they expect. And that we cannot carry on the Settlement of Georgia, or apply again to Parliamt. with any Success unless he come over to answer objections, and give an Account of the progress already made, and justify the application of the Sums heretofore granted.

1 Decbr. 19.

Egmont	C P	Vernon, Ja.	C
Towers, Tho.	C	Smith, Saml.	T

Summons again for a Common Council: but were not a number.

1. We went thro the Genl. Acct. & Settled it, in order to its being presented to the Ld. Chancellr. &c pursuant to Charter.

2. Mr. Towers reported his and Mr. Vernons Conference wth. the Board of Trade yesterday on the Subject of our petition for Cannon. He Said the Lords present were the Ld. Fitzwalter, Mr. Pelham and Sr. Archer Crofts. That my Ld. Fitzwalter Said it was not neglect in their Board that we had for a year & half recieved no answer to our application, *but we had gone by the bow & not by the String* (meaning as our gentlemen Supposed, we had not apply'd first to the board instead of petitioning the King, but I thought differently). Nevertheless when we Should be able by new Accts. from Georgia to give them further information, they would give our application due consideration. He added, that as the Parliament had given money for the Support of Georgia, he thought the Supplying of cannon Should have been taken care of out of the Sums given by the Publick.

Mr. Vernon reply'd, that we would cease further application till we Should hear from Georgia, But as to buying cannon for the defence of that Province, the Trustees look'd on it as a matter that lay upon the Crown, the money given by Parliament being for the Settling, not defending Georgia. That it was not to be expected the Trustees would out of their own pockets purchasse cannon, they acting voluntarily for the Service of the Publick, and having no private Interest of their own in conducting this affair.

[N.B.] In the beginning of Decbr. 1736 Mr. Charles Wesley arrived from Georgia, and on the 8th made me a visit, when he told me the following particulars:

1. That the Chickesaw Indians are about 400 fighting Men, a brave people, fond of the English and utter Enemies to the French, who Seek to root them out because Situated in Such a manner as to divide the French settlements, lying between the Northern and Southern Territories, to the hinderance of their communication, & consequently their Trade and Strength.

2. That the people of Carolina are utter Enemies to Georgia, tho not the Governing part.

3. That if the Province Should Succeed in their Representation lately Sent over to the King and Council, and obtain an explanation of our Trade Act in their favour, there would be an end of all hopes of converting the Indians to Christianity, or of preserving peace with them. For if the Carolina Traders are not obliged to take their Lycences from Georgia, and Submit to the regulations of the Georgia Act, they will go on to cheat the Indians as formerly, and new Wars will follow, in which case Georgia will be attack'd by them, they making no distinction of British Subjects when once engaged in War.

4. That the Spaniards were excited to attack us by people in Carolina, & were furnished with arms and ammunition for that end, which occasion'd Mr. Oglethorps buying up all the Spare Arms that could be found at Charlestown to prevent the Spaniards having them.

5. That the people of Carolina did what was in their power to prevail on the Indian Nations to recede from their agreement with Mr. Oglethorp when he purchassed from them the lands of Georgia, and had prevaild on Opayhatchoo one of their chiefs to deny the concession of those lands which himself had before consented to with the rest of his Nation, But that at length Mr. Oglethorp had got him to confirm it again, and we have now possession by consent of all the Nations, of all the Sea Coast & Islands, and 6 miles within the Coast of our Province, Two Islands of rich land excepted that ly between Savannah and the Allatahama which the Indians have reserved to themselves.

6. That Carolina has distrest our Colony by Seducing away, Since the first Settling our people 700 persons, who were of great Service in cultivating our lands, and this had occasioned the Slow progress in that affair, and render'd labour dear.

7. That Carolina is unreasonably jealous of our injuring her

in the Indian trade for hides, for the publick Revenue arising from it is to her but 500£ Sterlg. *p* ann., and as to the Rice trade we having no Negroes Saw none of that grain So that She has no reason to fear on that head, but it is the private Interest of a few Carolina Traders which occasions all the un-easiness, and a pride not to Submit to take out lycences in our Colony, together with a desire to traffick in Rum.

8. That Carolina labours with the Indians not to Send their children for instruction, telling them we Shall detain them prisoners and hostages to keep their nations in Slavery, but one of their chiefs making a journey on purpose to know the truth, return'd satisfied of the falsehood of what had been told him.

9. That this dispute between the two Provinces, together with that between Georgia and the Spaniards had occasion'd a very great and unexpected charge, especially for presents to the Indians to Secure their friendship.

10. That the Scots at Darien are very industrious, have cultivated Surprisingly fast, and have a very honest quiet Minister.

11. That the New Settlers at Frederica are likewise very industrious.

12. That Mr. Lacy Settled at Thunderbolt has many Servants, a great deal of Indian corn in the ground past danger, and would make this year a hogshead of wine.

13. But the Moravians are the most laborious, cheapest workers and best Subjects in the whole Province, and have among them also the best Carpenters.

14. That there are about 200 houses in Savannah, and 700 Souls. That the people now Seem disposed to labour and cultivate their lands which many have been too tardy in.

15. That a New Convenient Town hall is built in the town, furnished wth. Benches, a Gallery for the Bailifs and a Pulpet for the Minister for Divine Service, and it will hold 100 people.

16. That every one of the complaints (of which there were above a hundred) against Mr. Causton, were found by Mr. Oglethorpe at his arrival absolutly frivolous.

17. That Joseph Watson who was try'd for killing an Indian by giving him Rum with intent to destroy him, and who is Still confin'd, is really disturbed in his Senses, as the Jury had found him, & this Mr. Wesley Said he learn'd from Several persons in Charlestown, who declared he had Six years before been mad on account of a Mistress that jilted him.

18. That Noble Jones our Publick Surveyor is an idle Man, and

Mr. Oglethorp greatly desired Two more Surveyors to expedite laying out the peoples lands, till when they could not pretend to Set about cultivating.

19. That Mr. Oglethorp is indefatigable, often Sleeping but 2 hours in a night, and rising at midnight would Set out on journeys of 150 miles & perform them in 2 days; yet he was never better in health.

That he had Sent large Accts. of his proceedings to the Trustees by Mr. Apie, who loiter'd his time at Charlestown where he was to take Shipping, & at last came over in the Same Ship with Mr. Wesley. Yet tho now arrived he had not Sent the packet he was charged with to the Office. Tis very probable the people of Carolina detained him till their memorial was first arrived and deliverd.

20. That no lands for Religious Uses had yet been Set out; neither did he know that Mr. Oglethorpe had taken any care of finding proper catechists for instructing the Negroes at Purysburg.

21. That Mr. Oglethorp is cutting a road from the mainland opposite to the Isld. St. Simons, up to Savannah, to open a free communication between our Northern and Southern Settlements.

22. That for the defence of Frederica Darien, and our Southern Settlements Mr. Oglethorp had erected a Strong Fort 60 Miles beyond the limits of Georgia, but Still on the lands claim'd by our Crown as part of Carolina and belonging to the Indians in Allyance with us. Which Fort is garisond by 60 Scots, who desired that Post of honour, as most exposed to the Spaniards. That there is a good ditch round the fort and a rampart palisadoed, and Cannon to defend it. N.B. This is Fort St. George, which Mr. Oglethorpe told me could not be taken but by regular approaches.

23. That when he arrived at Savannah, he found the people had been miserably neglected by Mr. Quincy our late Minister; that but 3 people partook of the Communion, and employ'd the Sunday in Shooting. But before he came away, his brother John Wesley who preaches by heart, had full Assembly's, that publick prayer was Said every morning, and at 9 at night, by reason the day is Spent in labour in the field, and that there were now 40 Communicants.

24. That Mr. Ingham our 3d Minister, dedicates himself to the conversion of the Indians, and for that end lives at Mrs. Musgroves Cow Pen or farm in order to learn their language, in which he has made a great proficiency.

That the Indians are all fond their children Should be Christians, tho the Old ones Say they are too old to learn. However these have a great notion of God and a Providence, especially the Chickesaws. That young Toonaway and his brother is learning, and much brought off from the habit of drinking which our English had taught him. That he understands & Speak English So well as in Mr. Oglethorps opinion to be the best Interpreter we have.

That there is a handsome Hall building in Tomochachi's town to Serve as a School, that the Indian children may be taught English & religion among their Parents.

25. That Mr. Delamot (a Merchants Son of London) had opend a School to teach all children who were Sent him their catechism, and the first principles of Religion, gratis.

26. That no Mulberry trees have yet been demanded out of our Publick garden by the Planters, but there is great Store of them there, and it abundantly furnishes the Town of Savannah with cowcumbers, melons and vegetables, tho ill managed as to the Nursery trees by the former gardiner, Whom therefore Mr. Oglethorp removed, and had placed Fra. Piercy who marry'd a daughter of Sr. Francis Bathurst in his room.

27. That our Georgia Sola bills have due currency, and our advertismt. to answer no bills drawn on us from Georgia, other than our own Sent over, was exceedingly pleasing to our other Colonies.

[N.B.] 11 Dec. 1736. Mr. McBane a Highlander Settled at Darien, and Sent over by Some private persons to procure them Servants, brought me the present of a bare (which I refused to accept) and gave me the following particulars of the State of Georgia.

1. That the first Settlement to the South of Savannah made by the Embarkations of last year, is Darien, So named by Capt. Dunbar, who wth. his people arrived before Mr. Oglethorpe. That there were about 45 families of Scots Settled there, besides about 30 Servants. That the Town Stands on the Continent on a fruitful bluff about 10 miles distant from St. Simons Island, and has no Fort, but Some cannon. That the people are extraordinary industrious, and will have corn sufficient not only for their own Subsistence, but to Sell. That Capt. Mackintosh has the chief command of them, and Mr. Macleod their Minister is extraordinarily beloved by them. That they first cultivated their lands, and then built their houses, which it were to be wish'd the people of Savannah had done.

2. That the next Settlement made is Frederica in St. Simons

Island where there is a Strong Fort finish'd of 4 Bastions, ditch'd and rampier'd, with double palisadoes. That it has 9 cannon with Suitable Ammunition, and the Storehouse in the middle of the Fort has a platform, on which a 100 Men may Stand & defend the place. That there are Settled there about 60 or 80 Families besides Single Men, and that many come from Carolina & other parts to fix there. That Mr. Horton has the general care of the place, Dr. Hawkins a Surgeon 1 Bailif and Mr. Moore Storekeeper. That two Streets were laid out and 15 or 16 houses already built. That the people are industrious, and there is great plenty of Fish, fine Cedar Trees, and other Timbur, and no Rum drunk.

3. That the next Settlement to Frederica is on the South extremity of the same Island, where a Fort is built that commands the Sea, and guards the Island, named Fort Arguile. It is garrison'd by the Carolina Compy. of Regular Forces commanded by Capt. Delagal consisting of 50 men. There were yet no Settlers upon lands, it being intended purely for defence of the Island.

4. The fourth Settlement made is call'd Fort St. Andrews, and Stands about 50 miles Southward of Darien, on the Continent, but Still on the North Side of the Allatahama River, & So within the limits of Georgia. It is erected on a high Bluff and commands all the Country round. Tis built like the rest, and So Strong by Situation that 30 Men, of which the Garison consists can defend it against 300. And there is a fine well in the middle of it. There are no Settlers on land, this being intended only for a Guard to the Country, and the vilages and Forts that ly within the bounds of it. Mr. John Cuthbert commands there, a Gentleman of Scotland, & of Some fortune who went over wth. Capt. Dunbarr.

5. The 5th and last Fort erected is call'd Fort St. George, and Stands in a Streight line 50 miles from Fort St. Andrews, close to St. Juans River which at that place is 3 leagues broad, tho Some way higher up, not half so much. Capt. Mackay commands there, and has generally with him 200 Men, tho they are not all upon pay, for there are many labourers & workmen, and besides, Mr. Oglethorpe enjoined all who came out of curiosity to See the place, to reside a month there, that if a Sudden occasion Should happen, they might assist in defending it. [It] has a great many cannon, but there are no Settlers on land, because So much exposed to the Spaniards, to whom it gives great umbrage being in Sight of their advanced Guard, & Fort Augustine not far beyond the other Side of the River.

This Fort is out of the Limits of Georgia, but the land belongs to Indians in our Allyance, who claym it and have given us leave to Settle there. They are mortal Enemies to the Spaniards, and many refused to accompany Mr. Oglethorpe thither, because he refused to let them attack and kill them. N.B. Mr. Macbean did not know that Mr. Oglethorp vacated this garison by agreement wth. the Spaniards in October 1736.

6. That as to Savannah, there are Some who have cultivated & are diligent to thrive, but a great number are idlers and will never come to good. Many of these were intending to leave our Colony when orders came to Strike them off the Stores, but having run themselves in debt, were not Suffer'd to depart till they had paid their debts, upon which Some had made themselves over Servants to their Creditors to work them out, and it was hoped more would do So.

7. That the people there Still get Rum notwithstanding all the care taken, by means of Carolina boats which in the night time land it in creeks unknown to the Magistrates. However that they are healthy, whereas at Ebenezar they are not So.

8. That at Frederica tho it ly's So much to the South he work'd in the midst of Summer as he would have done in England, So tolerable are the heats.

9. That the land bears good barly as it dos Indian wheat, and the beer they make of Molossus is very good. That there is plenty of horses, cattel and fish, and hemp and flax grows well.

10. That Watson who has So long layn in prison is at times mad, but rather foolish than mischievous, and when he left Savannah, there was a talk of Shipping him on board the Diamond, & making him return to his first occupation, that of a Sailor.

11. That a fair hearing had been given to all the complaints made against Mr. Caustons administration, and this by Mr. Oglethorp in open Court, and that all present Said there never were more groundless accusations.

12. That the Publick garden is now in good order, Since Piercy had the care of it, and Some had already planted mulberry trees taken out of it, on their lands, and that the Silk worm thrives & multiply's.

This Gentleman came over as has been Said to hire Servants for particular persons, and chiefly for Lycenced Traders, who offer to pay the charge of transporting & keeping them, if the Trustees will only be at the charge of Sending a Ship to Scotland,

Wales or Ireland to take them up, & if any of they who require Servants Should die or change their minds, then they desire the Trust will keep them for the Trust use.

15 Decbr. 20.

Bundy, Ri.	C		Towers, Tho.	C
Ld. Carpenter	C	Ch.	Vernon, Ja.	C
Egmont	C		Anderson, Adm.	T
Hales, Stevn.	C		Belith, Will.	T
Lapotre, Hen.	C		Smith, Saml.	T
LaRoch, Jo.	C			

1. The Committee of Accts. reported the Annual Acct of Receipts and disbursmts. from 9 June 1735 to 9 June 1736 and that they had examin'd the Vouchers, and the Acct. was approved, and 250 Copies order'd to be printed after the Same Should be presented to the Ld. Chancellor &c.

2. Mr. Philip Von Reck who conducted, Saltsburgers to Georgia being return'd to England, to go in quest of more, and not being able to attend us by reason of a Fever, we order'd him 30 guineas.

3. Mr. Wesly appear'd & gave us a journal book of Mr. Oglethorps proceedings in Georgia with other papers.

4. The Packet brought over by Mr. Apie (from which we expected much information) was at length Sent to us, but it only contained duplicates of what we found in the journal book.

5. The Lords of the Board of Trade having Sent to desire a conference with us this day upon the Memorial of Carolina refer'd to them, we Sent to acquaint them we were not prepared for it, and desired them to name Some other day. Whereupon they named the 13 Jany.

6. A Resolution that gave us very great offence both for the wording and manner of delivering it was Sent us by the Incorporate Society for propagating the Gospel, reminding us that we had formerly told them we would Settle a Glebe of 300 acres on the Minister of Savannah, and desiring we would inform them whether we had So done, but that in the mean time they had Suspended the paymt. of their 50£ Sallary to our Minister. We were all in indignation at Such a Message which condemn'd us unheard, and concluded among ourselves not to Stand obliged to that Society for a Sallary but to raise it among ourselves. But we resolv'd nothing until we Saw the process of this matter.

7. Agreed that a Committee Should meet to inspect our books, papers & letters in order to prepare our Selves for the Conference desired by the Board of Trade toughing the Carolina Memorial.

17 Decbr. 21.

Egmont	C	Towers, Tho.	C
Lapotre, Hen.	C	Vernon, Ja.	C

1. We met in Committee to prepare an Answer to the Carolina Memoriall, and Set down heads for our Council to plead, having learned that the Province of Carolina intend to be heard by Council in Support the Memorial and Representation. These heads we order'd to be wrote fair for the approbation of the next Common Council, and we pitch'd on Mr. Murray and Mr. Cha. Clarke to be our Council, and to be pd. 2 guineas each for a retaining fee Subject to the Common Councils good liking. Mr. Towers undertook to put these heads into form in nature of a Brief for the Councils Instruction.

2. Sr. Jacob Bouverie came to offer us 1000£ legacy left to him by his deceased Brother to dispose in charity as he thought fit, and Said he believed it could not be better disposed of than to further the designs of our Colony. That he Should like it were disposed to one head of our Expences, and therefore desired to know which way we would apply it. We answer'd that Some of our designs were to propagate Christianity among the Indians, the maintenance of Clergymen and Catechists, the building Churches, the cultivating lands, and for that end Sending over Servants whom we Stood much in need of, the maintenance of Magistrates, the building of Forts, the feeding a number of people, and raising usefull produces. That it did not belong to us to prescribe to him how this generous gift Should be disposed, and that twas frequent for our Benefactors to appoint under what head their money Should be laid out. He liked best the furnishing ourselves with Servants, Since we appeared to Stand in need of them, and they further'd cultivation of land, and therefore if we pleased the money Should be apply'd that way.

We answer'd it came very opportunly, for there was now come over Mr. Von Reck the chief leader of Germans to Georgia for 2 years past, and he was Speedily to Set out again for Germany to bring Servants. Sr. Jacob Said he did not know but that for his Safety it might be necessary for him to get an Act of Parliament to allow of & confirm this gift, but in that case he would be at all the charge, So that we might receive the 1000£ clear, but he hoped we would take care it might not discourage the Grant of other money by the Parliament, for in that case his gift would be in effect to the Publick not to us, if it any way lessend the Sum we expected from them. We reply'd it was true and we would think of it, but we hoped So generous a private benefaction would rather excite the Parliament to assist us hansomly, than occasion them to give us less.

22 Dec. 21 [sic].

Bundy, Ri.	C	Egmont	C
Cater, Robt.	C	LaRoch, Jo.	C P
Ld. Carpenter	C	Vernon, Ja.	C

A Common Council was Summon'd to Settle Instructions for Mr. Von Reck who was going this Week to bring Germans over, and to Settle a letter to the D. of Newcastle relating to the protection claim'd by the Chickesaw Indians against the French: both which were necessary to be dispatch'd this day. But we could not make a board, and we were obliged as Trustees to act.

1. We drew up a letter to the D. of Newcastle, and order'd our Secrety. to Countersign it, wherein we acquainted him that the Chickesaw Indians had been attack'd by the French: That Mr. Oglethorp thought this of So much consequence as to send over Mr. Wesley his Secy. to acquaint us with the conference he had with them on that Subject. That they demanded the protection and Support of Gr. Britain as at all times faithfull allyes, and that they had accepted Commissions from our Governours from the first time his late Majesty Sent Genl. Nicholson to be Govr. of South Carolina, as appeard by one of those Commissions in the year 1732 under the hand of the late Govr. Johnson, wch. they produced at the Conference, and is now Sent over to us. That in duty to his Majesty, and out of concern for the Safety of the colony we layd this matter & the copies of the Conference before his Grace for his Majesties information, not doubting but his Grace would apprehend that if that nation Should be deserted & not Supported, All the Other Free Indians which ly on the back of his Majesties Colonies will thereby be obliged to throw themselves into the hands of the French; and if the French be allow'd to destroy our Indians Nation by Nation, in time of Peace, the Settlements must meet with the Same Fate in time of War.

2. We drew up the form of an advertisment to be publish'd in

[1737]   JOURNAL OF THE EARL OF EGMONT   223

the Newspapers, for clearing the Trustees from Several imputations & malicious aspersions flung out against us & our proceedings, but agreed to defer it till our hearing against the Carolina complaints were over.

3. We drew up an answer to the Minute of the Incorporate Society (See Fol. 155.6) and orderd it Should be left at their Office, with Copies of the Resolutions taken by the Trustees for allotting 300 acres for Religious uses, & of our letter to Mr. Oglethorp thereon.

4. Agreed to a calculation for the disposal of Sr. Jacob Bouveries 1000£, and found that Sum would bring over 40 German Servants with 20 Women and children.

5. We prepared instructions for Mr. Von Reck who Sets out tomorrow for Germany, directing him to bring over the above mentioned number, the Men under 50 years old and the children above 12. We recommended to him to chuse persecuted Protestants preferable to others; and gave him 30 guineas to carry himself over.

6. Mr. Macbane (Mentioned Fol 54) attended to acquaint us that Mr. Oglethorpe had sent him over to bring Scots Servants, which Mr. Oglethorpe expected the Trustees would enable him to procure, and the charge was to be reimbursed by the Masters who Should take those Servants. We told him, we were entirely un-acquainted with the Affair & could Say nothing to it, he having brought no letter from Mr. Oglethorpe to explain the matter. But that we had compassion for his case to be Sent over on So empty an Errant. We advised him to Stay till Mr. Oglethorpe Should be returned, which we believed would be in a week or fortnight, and then we Should know what answer to make him.

[N.B.] 2 Jany. 1736–7. Mr. Oglethorpe landed from Georgia at Ilfercomb in Wales, & taking Post arrived at his house in Westminster the 6th. He was 70 days in his passage. He had a narrow escape from drowning, being caught on the English Coast for 9 days in So thick and continued a Fog, that they knew not where they were, and at last found themselves among the Breakers, which So frightened the Sailors, that Captn. Thompson could not by any entreaty get them to work the Ship, and get them out of the Hould, where they ran all down to a Man, giving themselves for lost; So that Mr. Oglethorp and Mr. Tanner who came with him were obliged to jump out of bed in their Shirts to pull the ropes.

He Said he left Georgia in good condition, the people much reformed to Industry, the Stores full, and an honourable Treaty concluded with the Govr. of Augustine, who proposed to be furnish'd from Frederica with provisions and make payment in pieces of eight, which alone would support that Southern Settlement, the allowance for the Garrison of Augustine being annually 150000 pieces of eight.

But as for Savannah, Two thirds of the people are in debt, and he thought the properest way to do by them, was to give them all leave to Sell their Town Lotts of house & 5 acres (there being Tradesmen enough to buy them,) and oblige them with the residue of their money (after their debts are paid) to Settle on their 45 acre lotts.

That Servants are absolutly [necessary] for the people to help cultivate their lands.

That last year, the French Govr. of Louisiana, upon a report that there would be a general War in Europe, drew down all his Garrisons to compose an army to invade S. Carolina, and must if he attempted it Succeeded, For they have 2500 Regular troops, besides Several thousand of Indians their allyes: But when the Govr. was on the point of marching, letters came from France commanding his forbearance, on which he remanded his Forces, but afterwards Sent a body against the Chickesaws who repuls'd them in the manner we had been informed.

12 Jany. 22.

Bundy, Ri.	C	Ld. Tirconnel	C
Ld. Carpenter	C	Towers, Tho.	C Ch.
Egmont	C	Vernon, Ja.	C P
Hales, Stevn.	C	Anderson, Adm.	T
Lapotre, Hen.	C	Bedford, Arthr.	T
LaRoch, Jo.	C	Smith, Saml.	T
Oglethorp, Ja.	C		

This Common Council was Summond to confirm the Instructions for Mr. Von Reck to be Sent after him: but it was very uncertain if they would come to his hands, Such is the inconveniences of Gentlemens not attending to make Common Council Boards. The Summons was also to meet Mr. Oglethorpe and receive his report on the State of the Colony, and his proceedings there.

1. Mr. Oglethorpe reported his proceedings in Georgia from the time of his landing in Feby. last. and presented the Treaties

[1737]   JOURNAL OF THE EARL OF EGMONT   225

he had made with the Spaniards, dat. 26 Aug. 1736. Thanks were return'd him for his many important Services.

2. Thanks orderd to Capt. Windham & Capt. Gascoign.

3. Order for Selling 260 barrils of Rice & 7 Casks of Skins.

4. A bill for 200£ dat. 29 Sep. 1736 drawn by Mr. Oglethorpe to Jo. Crockats use value recd. was ordered to be accepted & paid, tho drawn 4 days after our advertisment was printed in the Carolina Gazet forbidding the drawing more bills. For Mr. Oglethorpe assured us he was at that time at Frederica & knew not of the advertisment, and he drew the bill for Services of great importance to the Colony.

5. 100£ order'd to the Accompt. for extraordinary Services.

6. Imprest 1000£ to Aldn. Heathcote.

7. Imprest 500£ more to him for paymt. of Sola bills.

8. Order'd a letter by Capt. Nicholson to Mr. Jenys, to Send back the sola bills for 1500£ wch. we Sent to Mr. Oglethorpe but were not recieved by him before he left Georgia.

[N.B.] 12 Jany. 1736–7. Nicholas Lewis Ct. Zinsendorf landed in England.

14 Jany. 23.

This was a meeting of a Committee to consider of the Carolina Representation, which my Son Hanmers extream illness would not Suffer me to attend.

19 Jany. 24.

Ld. Carpenter	C		Ld. Tirconnel	C P
Egmont	C		Vernon, Ja.	C
Heathcote, Geo.	C		Anderson, Adm.	T
Heathcote, Sr. Will.	C		Page, Jo.	T
Lapotre, Hen.	C		Smith, Saml.	T
LaRoch, Jo.	C Ch.		White, Jo.	T
Oglethorp, Ja.	C			

1. We agreed to a Representation to be presented his Majesty this day, wherein we complain of the Lieut. Govr. & Assembly of S. Carolina's opposing our Act entitled *an Act for maintaining peace with the Indians in the Province of Georgia.*

2. Agreed that Mr. Paris be employ'd as our Sollicitor, when the hearing of this dispute by Council comes to be 3 weeks hence before the Board of Trade.

3. Agreed that Counsellor White be added to Counsellor Cha. Clarke and Counsellor Murry to plead for us, and that a Retaining Fee be offer'd to the Sollicitor Genl. Mr. Strange, in order to engage him for us, or not to be agst. us.

4. Agreed upon an answer to the Incorporate Society, wherein we acquainted them (as they desired) with what we have done & further design to do in relation to the Religious concerns of our Province, and in gentle terms exprest our resentment at their Suspending the allowance they gave our Minister, before they had heard from us on that head.

5. Imprest 600£ to Aldn. Heathcote, which was resolv'd last meeting, but we were not a board to Sign it.

6. Several bills drawn on us by Mr. Oglethorpe 22d Octobr. last were order'd to be paid amounting to 475.13.11½. We also did the Same by the 500 bill drawn by him payable to Mr. Eveleigh, for purchasing Arms & Duffels at Charlestown, which bill we on the 4th of Augst. last Suffer'd to be protested because we thought it was for Services without the bounds of our Province, and therefore that we could not be justify'd in paying it.

But Mr. Oglethorp explain'd that matter in a right light to us. He said that when he came to Settle our people at Frederica on St. Simonds Island, (which is undoubtedly within the limits of Georgia) He Sent 2 persons to Fort Augustine with a compliment to the Spanish Govr. who against the law of nations confind them, and Soon after drew out his Soldiers, and Sent to the Indians to assist him against us. That at the Same time he had private intelligence, that the Spaniards intended to fall upon him. Whereupon he immediatly Sent to Charlestown to buy up all the Arms, duffels and wollen goods that were there, to prevent the Spaniards from doing the Same, knowing that if the Spaniards were prevented in that, the Indians would want arms to hurt us, and would not assist the Spaniards, because no presents were made to engage them. That for further Security he built a Fort more Southward & nearer the Spaniards, to keep the Spaniards from interrupting his building a Fort at Frederica: but this was not unnecessarily done, or before the threatened Invasion by the Spaniards. That part of these arms & duffels had been given in presents to the Indians, and the rest were lodg'd in our Storehouse, to be disposed of as occasion Should require.

[N.B.] 19 Jany. 1736–7. Some days after the letter ordered this day to be wrote to the Incorporate Society, I was in conversation with Mr. Burton one of our Trustees (a very worthy Clergyman) and Mr. Oglethorpe. When talking of our difference with that Society on acct. of our not allowing lands in Glebe to our Ministers, by wch. means he was removable at pleasure (his living not being a Freehold) by the Trustees, and could not appeal to or be redrest by the Bishop of London, He exprest his wishes that Some expedient could be found to please both Party's. For he thought it very right that our Ministers Should be answerable to that Bishop for their behaviour, who by law has the care of all the American Clergy. Besides it was unknown to the Primitive Church that Ecclesiasticks were accountable to Laymen, and not any way to the Bishop.

Mr. Oglethorpe reply'd that the Trustees are not all Laymen, and as to the Bishop of Londons power over the American Clergy, he has no legal power, for that which he exerts dos not flow from the King, but from a bare letter Sign'd by a Secy. of State. That he cared not to mention this publickly, Since the exercise of this power has been wink'd at. That the true Diocesan of the American Clergy is the A.B. of Canterbury, and if he appointed Suffragan Bishops there, his authority would be obey'd, and things would go well.

Mr. Smith also (another worthy clergyman of the Trust) doubted if the Bishop has authority over the clergy of our Province, being erected Since the power given him by the Secretary's letter. Some time after I had discourse with Dr. Philip Bearcroft a Member of the Incorporate Society (and Since Secretary thereto) on the Same Subject. He Said the Society thought it very hard, that the Ministers in Georgia Should be the only persons without Property, and depend on a Bailif for payment of their Sallarys. That having ask'd for an allowance on engaging to Settle lands in glebe, We had broke our bargain, the Society thereby released, and we might thank our Selves. Besides Mr. John Wesley our present Minister had (as appeard by a letter of Mr. Oglethorpe to the Society) renounced a Sallary, as thinking Ministers ought to preach the Gospel without hire, and had only desired the 50£ designd for Sallary might be paid him on the foot of charity to be put into his hands to distribute to others, which the Society was not warranted to do. Lastly, that Dr. Humphrey, their Secy. had on his own head, added to their written Message the paragraph that gave our Board offence, namely that the Sallary was Suspended till we Satisfy'd the Society how we had disposed of the 300 acres.

I reply'd, Our Ministers had no hardship done them if regularly paid for their Service, which it was our absolute intention to See done, and no man in his Sences could Suppose otherwise, wherefore there was no need he Should have Such a property in land, as that we might not be able to remove him if we found him unworthy, without a tedious uncertain and expensive application to the Bishop, during which process he must come over to England to defend himself, and the Inhabitants be So long without a Minister, or he must remain on the Spot giving offence. That when we first promised to give the land in Glebe, we did not consider the consequences, and had not the instance happen'd of Mr. Quincy's abandoning the Province for 7 months, and leaving only a wheelright to comfort the Sick and bury the dead, we might have given land in glebe, but experience had made us cautious. That had land been So given at that time, Mr. Quincy would not at this [moment] been removed. That a Clergy man may be a good Parish Minister as to the discharge of his Office, and yet be so troublesome and injudicious in his conduct as not to be fit to be continued, but Such bad conduct might by the Bishop be thought no Sufficient reason for depriving him, tho a necessary & justifyable one for us. That our Colony is made up of Protestants of all denominations, and much depended on the prudence of our Clergy, but he who Should Shew himself most violent against all Protestants but those of our church, would be most favour'd by the Bishop. That if Mr. Wesley refused a Sallary, or any others, there was the less reason for the Bishop to insist on it, and it only Shew'd his desire of power. That when we Spoke of glebe we had not intention as now we have to cultivate that land, and it would cost us 1000£. That tis no excuse to Say their Secretry. added the offensive matter on his own head, for it appeard to us the Act of their Society who Speak by their Secrety. and at the bottom, we found the Society were disposed to adhere to the Sense of it unless we gave our land in glebe. Finally that we had more concern for our people than for one Minister, but the Society had more for one Minister than the people.

He appear'd Satisfy'd with what I Said, but added that the Society had a very bad opinion of the Members of our Trust, and as to himself he knew of none but Mr. Vernon and me, but what were Enemies to the Establish'd Church. I reply'd the Gentlemen were greatly injured, and named to him Ld. Tirconnel, Mr. Digby, Mr. Towers, Mr. Oglethorpe, Dr. Hales, Mr. Smith and others who were as zealous for our Church as any whatever.

[1737]   JOURNAL OF THE EARL OF EGMONT   229

24 Jany. 25.

Egmont	C	Towers, Tho.	C
Lapotre, Hen.	C	Vernon, Ja.	C
Oglethorpe, Ja.	C	White, Jo.	T
Ld. Tirconnel	C		

We were only a Committee who met to prepare instructions for Counsel in the Carolina affair.

1. Several letters and Affidavits were read manifestly proving that the people of Carolina, bring & Secretly land them in Georgia contrary to our Law, and trade with our Indians who are within our Limits without taking Licences from Us.

2. Read also a petition from the Magistrates & Inhabitants of Georgia, complaining of these abuses, and desiring redress. These and Several other papers we put into the hands of our Sollicitor Mr. Paris for forming his brief.

26 Jany. 26.

Egmont	C		E. Shaftsbury	C
Lapotre, Hen.	C	P	Towers, Tho.	C
Oglethorpe, Ja.	C		Vernon, Ja.	C

A Common Council was Summon'd to confirm the Instructions for Mr. Von Reck (See fol. 158.5). To Settle the money payable by the Soceity for promoting Christian Knowledge for the 9 months maintenance of the Saltsburgers who went to Georgia with Mr. Vatt, & for other purposes. But could not make a board.

1. A letter from Mr. Ulsperger to Mr. Hen. Newman was communicated to us, wherein he desired to know if we purposed to Send more Saltsburgers, and repeated his wishes that we would not confine our Grants of lands to Heirs male.

2. We debated upon what answer to return, and at length resolved that Mr. Ulsperger Should be inform'd we were not able at present to Send more Saltsburgers. As to not Suffering Females to inherit, Mr. Oglethorpe & Mr. Towers insisted on it, and gave Such reasons as Satisfy'd us we did right not to allow thereof, tho my Ld. Chancellor Talbot is of another mind. We desired Mr. Towers to Set his reasons down in writing, that we might Shew them to our acquaintance as occasion offer'd, to Satisfy them, there being a great clamour against us on this head.

3. Mr. Vernon inform'd us that Willm. Stephens Esq. (formerly Member of Parliament in England) the Same who went to S. Carolina to take up lands for Col. Horsey had offer'd his Service to go to Georgia, and be our Secretary for that Province, on the terms of making him a Grant of 500 acres, and paying Servants to cultivate them. This was highly pleasing to us, he being a Man of cool temper and excellent Sense, & great industry & punctualness, and by him we were sure of having constant information of the State of the Colony concerning which hitherto we had been kept too much in the dark.

4. Mr. Vatt who went Secrety. for the Saltsburgers in Octbr. 1734, and So remaind till the 26 March 1736 when we recall'd him for breeding disturbances there, attended for Some gratification for his trouble, but not being a Common Council we could dispose of no money.

5. A letter from Mr. Popple Secy. to the board of Trade to Mr. Martin our Secy. desiring him to acquaint the Trustees that at Mr. Fury's desire (Agent for Carolina) the Hearing upon the Carolina Memorial was by their Lordships put off from the 8 of next month where on it was appointed, by reason more Evidence was to come over to Support the complaints. Upon this we drew up a letter to Mr. Popple expressing our concern that the Hearing did not proceed but was defer'd Sine die, whereby our material Wittnesses might be lost. Besides that we Suffer by the calumnies raised against our proceedings, and Should continue so to do, till we had cleared ourselves.

6. Mr. Verelts our Accompt. Said before us the State of our Cash, which for the general Uses of the Colony was now reduced to 928.15.5¼. But there was owing to us from the Society for promoting Christian knowledge 287.0.1 for 12 months provision furnish'd to the Saltsburgers, and Some money was to come by the Sale of 3000 Deer Skins and a good quantity of Rice imported by Mr. Oglethorp from Georgia on the Trustees Acct. Mr. Verelts valued the Cargo at 1200£, but there would be a considerable deduction for freight duties &c.

2 *Feby.* 27.

Bundy, Ri.	C	P	Lapotre, Hen.	C
Egmont	C		Oglethorp, Ja.	C
LaRoch, Jo.	C		Towers, Tho.	C

A Common Council Summond to order payment of Several demands on the Trust, But again no Board.

1. Some letters were read, among which was one from Mr. Ellis a Mercht. of Pensilvanea, that a Ship had been freighted with Madera wine flax, wheels &c from thence to Frederica, on which Several persons were gone to See the place, and if they liked it intended to Settle there.

2. We drew up a 2d letter to the D. of Newcastle concerning the Spaniards complaints against us, deliver'd by Mr. Giraldini in a Memorial to his Grace.

[N.B.] 6 Feby. 1736–7. Mr. Oglethorp told me he was last fryday with Sr. Robert Walpole alone, who was at a loss what to do in the American affairs with respect to the Security of our Colonys, and desired his advice, with Some Scheme or Plan for defending, with his thoughts upon paper.

He Spoke with great freedom to Sr. Robert, who Said he was not used to have Such things Said to him, to which he reply'd, Yes, he was, when he was plain Mr. Walpole, but now was Sr. Robert, & chief Minister, he was Surrounded by Sycophants and Flatterers who will not tell him the Truth, incapable of advising him well, & the first who would drop him on a reverse of fortune.

Sr. Robert profest himself very Sincere to further the Settlement of Georgia, but ask'd him whether he was in earnest for carrying it on, adding the Trustees he heard were at variance, and had given the matter up.

Mr. Oglethorpe reply'd that nothing was more false, and he could not imagine who inform'd him So. But as to himself he must give it up, if not Supported by him, for he had twice crost the Sea to carry the Colony on, and not only ventur'd his life & health, to the neglect of his own affairs, but actually Spent 3000£ of his own money. That this Colony was a National Affair, and he did not pretend to be a Don Quixot for it, and Suffer in his reputation as he must do, if he continues his concern for it without Publick Countenance. If Sr. Robert was of opinion to drop it, he Should advice the making Some good bargain for it with the Spaniards who would be very thankfull to See it Surrender'd to them, But if he did drop it, he would hazard the loss of South Carolina & Virginia too. For the French would then be invited to attack those Colonies on their backs, and in 27 days were able to march up to Charlestown. That in case of Such Invasion, those who were rich would Ship themselves for England, or buy their peace, & the poor would submit themselves without a Stroke to the Conquerors.

Sr. Robert Said he was ignorant of West India affairs, but repeated his desire of Some general Sketch or out line, without entering into a detail, which he had not leasure for.

Mr. Oglethorp Said, there were but two ways of defending our Colonies from the French and Spaniards and their Indians: The One by forming a regular and Warlick Militia, The other by keeping a Regular Body of Troops. That a Substantial Militia is not to be had, for want of numbers of White Men. That he could form about 300 Men capable of bearing arms in Georgia; That South Carolina had money, but no Men; That New England had Men but no money, and New York had money but few Men. That if the defence were left to a Militia, it would cost dear, because they must be paid when in Service on account of the neglect of their own affairs, and therefore it were more eligable as well as safe to have regular forces.

Sr. Robert Said it was very difficult to Keep a Sufficient Body of Soldiers because of the Expence.

Mr. Oglethorpe reply'd the expence would amount to about 20000£ p ann. But if his Majesty would allow a draft of 2 Men out of each Company of foot, and each troop of Dragoons on the English Establishment, it would cost little more than the Expence England is now at.

Sr. Robert Said, the King would not consent to it.

Mr. Oglethorpe reply'd, then there must be a certain number new raised, and he believed if a Batalion of 500 Men were allow'd to each Colony the Colonys would themselves pay them, for the un-easiness they now are under proceeds from observing that the Company's now there are not kept full, but have only the name of a Company, the Officers putting the pay of vacant Soldiers into their pockets, So that the regular Forces there are only nominal, and of no Service.

Sr. Robert relish'd the proposal, and ask'd him if he had anything further to propose on that head?

Mr. Oglethorpe reply'd it would be necessary those Forces Should be put under Some Single persons command, otherwise they could not be rendevouz'd in time, and the particular Govrs. of Provinces, if they differ'd in judgment, or had more respect to the Safety of their own Provinces than to the general Safety of all, would defeat any measures that might be necessary for a defence.

Sr. Robert Said that was right, and ask'd him if he would be the

Man? Mr. Oglethorpe reply'd he would that he Should not desire the Title of Capt. Genl. but of Inspector Genl. of all the Forces, with power to direct & lead them forth.

Sr. Robert ask'd how that would agree with his being a Member of Parliament?

He reply'd, very well, he need not lose his Seat, this being a Military & not a Civil Employment, and there were presidents for it.

Sr. Robert ask'd if he would accept to be Govr. of South Carolina? He answer'd he would not, but he Should require that Province might be govern'd by a Lieut. Govr., and Presidt. Broughton turn'd out for the animosity he bore to Georgia.

Sr. Robert then Said, he was really a favourer of Georgia, but we had many Enemies, and we Should find them among the Gentlemen who oppose the Administration, wherefore we must Seek to gain them over.

Mr. Oglethorpe reply'd he was mistaken, our Enemies have rather been his own Creatures, whose mouths if he pleased he might Stop.

Sr. Robert hinted his dislike of the Trustees as a body that hangs together and in Parliament votes against the Governmts. measures.

Mr. Oglethorp reply'd he knew none among them were his personal enemies, and that the far greater number were constant Voters wth the Court.

Nay, Said Sr. Robert, I believe as you do, but our friends will have it otherwise, and there are Some I cant undeceive. There are others also who will not believe that any advantages can come from your Colony, and I wish you would write Something on that head to clear their doubts, but it must be done Suddenly, no time is to be lost.

Mr. Oglethorp reply'd, he had done Something that way, and if he had time might follow his advice.

Then Sr. Robert ask'd what money we Should want this year?

He reply'd 30000£, but if that could not be obtain'd we must have 20000£ merely for the Settlement of the Colony, wholly distinct from the defence of it, except the keeping a Compy. of Rangers, and finishing the Forts begun. And therefore if both the Settlement and the defence are to be provided for, there must be two distinct Estimates made.

Sr. Robert approved it. After this the discourse turnd on other topicks.

9 Feb. 28.

Cater, Robt.	C		Shaftsbury	C	
Digby, Edwd.	C		Ld. Tirconnel	C	
Egmont	C	P	Archer, Tho.	T	
Hales, Stevn.	C	Ch.	Archer, Hen.	T	
Heathcote, Geo.	C		Bedford, Arthr.	T	
Heathcote, Sr. Will.	C		Burton, Jo.	T	
Hucks, Robt.	C		Smith, Saml.	T	
Lapotre, Hen.	C		Talbot, Will.	T	
LaRoch, Jo.	C		Tracy, Robt.	T	
Ld. Limerick	C		White, Ja.	T	
Oglethorpe, Ja.	C				

1. Order'd that Mr. Oglethorpe, Ld. Tirconnel, Mr. Towers, Mr. Hucks & Mr. LaRoch be a Committee to draw up a petition to Parliament for a further Supply, and that they wait on Sr. Robert Walpole for that purpose.

2. A letter to the D. of Newcastle containing our reply to the Spanish Memorial was read & approved, and a copy of the Treaty of pacification between Mr. Oglethorpe & the Govr. of Augustine order'd to be given his Grace at the Same time with the letter.

3. Benefactions reported: 100£ from a person unknown to the use of the Missioners, and 100£ from the Bi. of Woster for the use of the Saltsburgers.

4. Order'd 10£ to Mr. Macbane for his coming to England & detainor here to collect Servants for Georgia.

5. Orderd 75£ to Mr. Verelts for his Services, being for the ½ year endg. Christmas 1736.

6. Order'd the like Sum to Mr. Martin for his Services the Same length of time.

7. Confirm'd the disposal of 31.10.0 to Mr. Von Reck, wch. Sum the Committee had Some time ago given him on his going to Germany to bring Servants.

8. Orderd 20£ to Fra. Moore Storekeeper at Frederica for ½ years Sallary due Christmass 1736.

9. Order'd paymt. of 100£ bill for Madera wine Sent to Frederica.

10. A bill of Mr. Causton for 263£ dat. 19 Novr. last, was refer'd to the Accompt. to examine, and then to be paid.

11. Imprest 700£ to Aldn. Heathcote to answer these paymts. and other purposes.

12. Accepted a bill for 120£ to be paid Lieut. Hugh Mackay in behalf of his Nephew Jo. Mackay, for 8 Servants made over to the Trust, whose Covenants are to Serve for 7 years, and are purchased at 15£ *p* head.

13. A Committee appointed to meet next monday to peruse Mr. Paris our Sollicitors brief in the cause agst. S. Carolina.

14. Our Secy. reported, that he had attended the Board of Trade to know their orders on our letter to Mr. Popple, and representation of the hardship put on us by a delay of Hearing the Cause; that they reply'd they could not yet fix the day, but it Should not wait long. Mr. Martin urged that possibly our witnesses might be dispersed, and Some returnd to Georgia. Mr. Bladen answer'd, that if we Sent our Wittnesses to make affidavit before a Master in Chancery, their evidence would be good, tho themselves were away. Mr. Martin then Said, we hoped the Carolina people would not be heard to new matter of complaint, because we could not be Supposed to be prepared against it, besides our witnesses might be gone who might be able to Speak to it, & So we Should be at an utter loss to reply to Such new matter. Col. Bladen reply'd it was not reasonable to hear new complaints, but they Should be confined to those already given in. That Some new ones had been offered by their Agent, but they were very trivial.

Mr. Oglethorpe said on this, that in case the Board of Trade reported against us, We ought to appeal to the Privy Council, & have a new hearing there, and in Such case Evidence taken before a Master in Chancery would not be allow'd good, or any notice taken of it, for Evidence recd. at the Council board must be taken by a Privy Counsellr.

15. We agreed to ask Dr. Warren Minister of Bow Church to preach our Anniversary Sermon.

[N.B.] 10 Feby. 1736–7. Commodore Dent wrote Mr. Oglethorpe that the Spaniards were Suspected of a design to attack Georgia: that he was prepared, and hoped to give a good account of them when the other ships had joyned him. That being pretty fat, the Spaniards Should have fat with their Salt, for they Should Slice him in pieces before he Surrender'd.

[N.B.] On 22 feby. 1736–7. A Man was Sent from Bristol to Georgia at the Trustees charge.

23 Feby. 29.

Egmont	C		Vernon, Ja.	C
Lapotre, Hen.	C		Anderson, Adm.	T
LaRoch, Jo.	C		Smith, Saml.	T
Holland, Rogr.	C		White, Jo.	T
Oglethorpe, Ja.	C P			

A Common Council was Summond to Seal our petition to Parliament, and to receive reports from the Committee of Accts. but we could not make a Board.

1. The complaints of the Saltsburgers wrote over by Mr. Boltzius 13 Oct. 1736 (See Fol. 147) were taken into consideration, and we came to resolutions to be offer'd to the next Common Council board for confirmation, viz.

a. That the 45 acres allow'd to each family of Saltsburgers (over & above their 5 acre lots) being not yet survey'd to them, the Allowance from the Stores for the 1 & 2 Transport Shall be continued to them from March last to September next.

b. That the boat provided for them Shall be pd. by the Trust.

c. That Noble Jones our Surveyor be immediately directed to Survey their 45 acres.

d. That the familys who went in May, Shall each of them have a Cow, Swine & poultry as the others had.

e. That the Ministers houses be built at the charge of the Trust out of the money appropriated for Religious uses.

f. That the Ministers Sallary be forthwith paid, and the Interest due for the money they were obliged to borrow be paid by the Trust out of the Said money.

g. That the Same number of Tools and quantity of other necessaries be distributed to the 3d Transport as were to the 1 & 2.

h. That the 4 Saltsburgers be pd. for buildg. a house at old Ebenezar.

i. That for the Satisfaction of the Revd. Mr. Urlesperger of Ausburg, a copy of our former order on these heads be Sent him.

2. Mr. Oglethorpe reported from the Committee appointed to wait on the A.B. of Canterbury to know his opinion of the Moravian Brethren, that his Grace declared to them, the Moravians are an Episcopal and Apostolick Church.

3. The Committee appointed to treat with Ct. Zinzendorf about furnishing 2 Moravian brethren to Serve as Catechists for the conversion of Negroes at Purysburg, and to catechise also

Such white children as the Swiss there Settled Should admit to be instructed, that he had agreed two of those people Should reside at Purysburg for a yearly Sallary to each of 15£, and houses built for them at the charge of the Associates of Dr. Bray.

4. A Letter from Mr. Causton dat. 26 Novbr. last was read, acquainting us,

a. That to the Westward of Savannah town, there had been much Sickness, but few died; but that at Purysburg they had lost 30 men that bore arms.

b. That the Saltsburgers had also been Sick, but lost few.

c. That Josephs town, most had been Swept away.

d. That a Cowpen had been erected at Old Ebenezar (wch. the Saltsburgers had deserted) for keeping our Cattel.

e. That Mr. Augustin had erected a very good Saw Mill, but it had often been blown up by the water, being ill Situated, which would be remedied. N.B., he deserted it in 1737.

f. That he had brought a Ship load of Sugar Molossus &c which would be freighted back with timber.

g. That Mr. Musgrove continued a very usefull Interpreter.

h. That the Inhabitants had raised Sufficient corn for themselves for their use next Season. That Savannah Town improved much as did Hampstead & Highgate.

i. That Mr. Lacy had improved well at Thunderbolt.

j. That Skidaway Improvmts. went not on So well.

k. That the Settlers on the Ogeeky river had made good Improvements.

l. That those on Tybee had improved nothing at all.

m. That the Settlers at Fort Arguile did not think of improving, but had all enter'd themselves into the Rangers Troop.

n. That in general the people Seem'd resolv'd to be obedient & to improve, but there were many idle who ran themselves in debt, and those who had not improved, occasioned the best planters to fall Short of the publick encouragement given by the Trustees, by reason the lands improved by them lay exposed to cattel and vermin for want of the others clearing their ground.

5. Another letter from Mr. Causton dat. 14 Decbr. 1736 was read, enclosing an Acct of Proceedings of Justice. He complain'd of the refractoryness of the Constables and Tything Men to do duty of Watch and Ward, and their irregular proceeding to elect the like Officers among themselves without consulting him. He added that Mr. Oglethorpe directed him to put the Stat. of Westminster 4 & 6 in relation to the Militia in force.

6. We drew up heads for a letter to be prepared to lay before next Common Council board, containing Several directions to Mr. Causton, and particularly that he be as easie as possible with the Constables and Tything Men, until we Should pass a Law for Settling the Militia on a proper foot.

7. A Proposal was offer'd for Settling 2000 Protestants of the Canton of Apenzel, in Georgia.

8. A Proposal offer'd also from Geneva for Sending people thither; both proposed to be Settled there on as good terms as any had before been Sent. This matter was refer'd to future consideration.

9. We prepared and directed to be wrote fair our petition to Parliament for a further Supply; as also a calculation of our Wants, and the necessary Sum to be ask'd, to be Shewn to particular Members when we present our petition. I desired an article might be inserted of 20 Men to be employ'd in cultivating lands for religious uses, which number Mr. Oglethorpe Said would in 3 years time cultivate 300 acres.

10. Capt. Jenkins who was lately at Savannah told us the people were in a happy [condition]. That he found in the woods divers plants and herbs that grew both Southward & Northward, even as far as Moscovy where he had been. That there are Trees in Georgia bearing a finer cotton than in any other parts, and that they had planted the Coffee berry. That there is a face of Industry, & the Spaniards at Augustin are in fear of us, But the people of Carolina, where he afterwards went, are exceedingly incenced against us.

[N.B.] 24 feby. 1736–7. Mr. Causton Sent the Trustees the following Account of the Inhabitants of Savannah town at the time of his writing:

Freeholders	132
Freeholders widows	9
Boys	40
Infants	8
Inmates	72
Servants	86
Freeholders absent	32
Freeholders dead	6
Freeholder run away	1
	386
Besides wives & girls	

2 *March* 30.

Ld. Carpenter	C		Ld. Tirconnel	C	
Egmont	C	Ch.	Towers, Tho.	C	
Eyles, Fra.	C		Vernon, Ja.	C	
Hales, Steven	C		Anderson, Adm.	T	
Holland, Rogrs.	C	P	Bedford, Arthr.	T	
LaRoch, Jo.	C		Belitha, Will.	T	
Ld. Limerick	C		Smith, Saml.	T	
Oglethorpe, Ja.	C				

1. Seal put to our petition to Parliament for a further Supply, and approved of the form of motions to be made for lying before the house an Account of the manner how we disburst the last years Supply.

2. Approved of the estimate & calculation of our wants to be Shewn particular Members.

3. Report was made that Mr. Timothy Wisson deceased had left part of his Estate to Charitable uses, & that half thereof being already Sold, Mr. Callard one of the Trustees had promised 400£ to our Trust, and had a prospect of giving 400£ more when the remainder of the Estate Shall be Sold.

4. Report was made, that Sr. Jacob Bouverie had quitted his purpose of procuring an Act of Parliament to Secure to use the 1000£ he promised: and that he would pay in the money tomorrow.

5. Mr. Berry (formerly mention'd Fol. 83.3) came and renew'd his proposal to go over to Georgia, and there cut timber for to Supply his Majesties navy, which would prove of advantage to our Province, and to his Majesty, by Supplying his Stores with timber at a cheap rate, & particularly with an Oak which he by experience had found would not take the worm. He demanded for his encouragement a yearly Sallary of 200£ payable Quarterly in England, 7 Shillgs. *p* diem travelling charges when in Georgia, a further gratification according to his Success, 10£ for his freight over, and as much for his return, besides other advantages.

We reply'd, his proposal was very commendable, and would be of great advantage to the Publick, but we were in no condition to bear the expence of it. That He would do well to lay it before the Admiralty, & we Should be extreamly glad they would approve of it.

6. We approved the letter drawn up at our last meeting to be Sent to Mr. Causton.

7. Order'd 50 Muskets & Bayonets to be bought, & Sent tomorrow on board.

8. In the afternoon Several of us met in a Committee of Correspondence, and prepared heads of an answer to be return'd Ct. Zinzendorf concerning his proposal to Send more Moravians over to Georgia. He is now in Holland expecting our answer, and the Common Council gave us full power to transact that affair with him.

9. The Common Council before they broke up, Resolv'd that Mr. Oglethorpe Should be desired to issue Francis Moore Recorder of Frederica (now in England) 1000£ Sterlg. in Sola bills, and that the Said bills be dated Some day in Novbr. last, before Mr. Oglethorpe and the Said Francis Moore left Georgia. And that they be Sent by the Peter and James, Capt. Diamond to Mr. Causton as Cash for the present Supply of the Colony. And that the 500£ Credit in provisions and money which Mr. Simons was desired to give Mr. Causton be countermanded.

10. Order for cancelling Sola bills paid.

11. Jacob Lopez de Crasto, a Jew in Georgia, having marry'd Siporah, widow of David Lopez de Paz, and thereby becoming possest of her 50 acre lot as well as his own, desired leave to dispose of one of them to Such purchasser as he could get. We refer'd the matter to Mr. Causton to make us a report thereon.

12. Report from the Committee of Accts. being read, concerning Capt. Thompson's demand for demurrage, freight of goods, and bring Mr. Oglethorpe over, We allow'd his demand.

13. Report from the Said Committee was read, concerning presents made by Capt. Dempsy to Several persons at St. Augustine where he was employed to negotiate the Treaty with the Govr. of that town & Fort, and the Same amounting to 83.2.0 was allow'd.

[N.B.] 7 March 1736–7. This day Ld. Limerick presented our petition to Parliament for a Supply, and was Seconded by Mr. Duncan Forbes, advoct. Genl. of Scotland. It was refer'd to the Committee of Supply without opposition, only Some gave their noes to it.

9 March 31.

Egmont	C	Towers, Tho.	C
Holland, Rogrs.	C	Vernon, Ja.	C
Oglethorpe, Ja.	C	Anderson, Adm.	T

A Common Council was Summond to dispatch business postponed last meeting, but we were not a board.

1. We did no business, only discoursed over our affairs. I Said I was Sorry that in our calculation of expences for this year, we did not Set down 3000£ for a perpetual Fund for the maintenance of Ministers in our Colony by applying the Interest of the money that way. But Mr. Oglethorpe reply'd it could not be, for that the 20000£ we propose to ask for will not answer even what we propose as most necessary, wherefore we must provide for our Ministers by Subscriptions. Mr. Vernon Said he would Subscribe 20£ p ann. Some others were also So disposed, but it was not likely this would come to much, and besides would be very precarious. It could never come to 200£ p ann., for So much would be wanting to maintain 4 Ministers, viz. 1 at Frederica, 1 at Savannah, 1 Itinerant Missioner for the distant Settlements, & 1 to be employ'd in converting the Indians.

I proposed that Mr. Whitfeild Should be appointed for Frederica, Mr. Jo. Wesley for Savannah, Mr. Charles Wesley for Itinerant Minister, and Mr. Ingham for Indian Missioner, who is now learning the Creek tongue.

14 March 32.

Egmont	C	Ld. Limerick	C
Holland, Rogrs.	C	Oglethorpe, Ja.	C
LaRoch, Jo.	C	Vernon, Ja.	C

This was neither a Common Council or Trustee Board, but an appointment at Ld. Limerick's desire to consider of Joseph Watson's case (See Fol. 62.1), One of our lycensed Traders, who glory'd in killing an Indian by drinking him to death. This Man had been try'd at Savannah for that and other offences, and found guilty but at the Same time, the Jury represented him as out of his Senses, & on that account desired we would Shew him favour. This transaction fell out the beginning of the year 1735, and as Soon as the Trustees had notice of it from Mr. Causton, they directed him to confine Watson as a Lunatice, until having recover'd his Senses, a Commission Should be Sent to try him for the Murder: for he had been indited only of a misdemeanor.

Accordingly was confined as a Lunatick and had remaind So ever Since, whereupon his wife came over & made heavy complaints against Mr. Causton, and proceeded So far as to present his case to a member of Parliament for redress.

My Ld. Limerick much concerned thereat, and ignorant of the truth, had recourse to our Office to See what we had done therein, and afterwards Shew'd the Member above mention'd, the verdict past by the Jury, wch. prevented his complaining to the house, but my Ld. Limerick was desirous we Should take the case into further consideration; the Woman continuing very clamerous, and many thinking, hardly of us.

After refreshing our memory's by consulting our books, Mr. Oglethorpe was of opinion, that if Watson were released, it would be interpreted by the unruly people of Savannah our censure of Causton for having confin'd him, and they would grow more insolent. And as he was in his conscience persuaded, that Watson not only drank the Indian dead by design (he having had a quarrel with him, and afterwards boasted he killed him) but that he poison'd his liquour, as the other Indians aledged, and appear'd by Several Symptoms on his body after he was dead, he was of opinion to Send over a commission to try Watson of murder.

But Mr. Holland who is a lawyer Said it was against law to try Men twice for the Same Fact, & with him we all joined.

Then Some Gentlemen proposed that orders Should be Sent to Mr. Causton to proceed to pass Sentence, which might be corporal punishment.

But this my Ld. Limerick opposed, as a great hardship to punish corporally a Man after 2 years confinement.

Then it was proposed that Watson Should be fined, and remain in confinement till he had found Security for his good behaviour, or else banished.

But this was not thought proper, it not belonging to us to direct what punishment the Magistrate Should inflict, and Mr. Oglethorpe added, that to banish him (tho a good thing to be rid of him) would be understood a favour done him.

My opinion was, that we Should write to know if he is Still out of his Senses, for if he is, he ought Still to remain confined, if not, the Magistrate without direction would at least fine him, and oblige him to give Security for his good behaviour for a certain number of years, if not for life. To this I think the Gentlemen agreed.

Mr. Oglethorpe Said Watson would certainly have been found guilty, of murder, if Indian evidence had been allow'd to be taken. Hereupon we all thought it proper that an Act Should pass to allow of Indian evidence, and that the Same Should be consider'd of by the Common Council.

[N.B.] 14 March 1736-7. I had private information this day (which proved true) that Sr. Robert Walpole had agreed Mr. Oglethorpe Should return to Georgia with the Commission of Genl. of the Forces of South Carolina and Georgia, but that Mr. Oglethorpe desired they might be Separate Commissions.

Also that at Mr. Oglethorpe's desire Coll. Horsey was to go Govr. of South Carolina, to the great advantage of our Province, he being a friend to it.

Also that Mr. Willm. Stephens would go over & be Secrety. of Our Province, which gave me great pleasure, as I knew it would to all the Trustees, being Sure he would regularly correspond with us So that we Should know all that post there; and that his influence and example would have great weight there, being a man of age, experience, Sober, and of calm temper.

[N.B.] 16 March. This day Ld. Limerick moved in the Committee of Supply for 20000£ to carry on the Service of Georgia, and tho there were many noes, no body Spoke against it.

The Same day Mr. Vernon and I dining with our Accompt. at the Cyder house, Dr. Hales brought a benefaction from a Gentleman unknown, of 100£ to be apply'd to the Support of an Indian Missioner.

Also came Mrs. Stanley Publick Midwife of Savannah to whom we allow 5 Shillings for every woman she lays. She lately came over to ly in her Self, not caring to trust her Self to the other Midwifes in our Province.

She Said She had brought into the World Since her going over (which was in the 1 Embarkation 3 Nov. 1732) 128 children, of whom 40 were dead.

She gave an extraordinary account of the peoples industry, and attendance on Divine Worship, and greatly commended Mr. Jo. Wesley, who went about from house to house, exhorting the Inhabitants to Religion and virtue.

She Said Some relations of her husband had promised to Send from Madera a great quantity of Vines, and her husband did not doubt of making good wine, the Vines in the Publick garden having Succeeded extreamly well and produced very large grapes.

That tho Mr. Paul Amatis was dead, and his brother run away, yet the Silk affair goes on and will Succeed, and it was talk'd at Savannah that this year a hundred pound weight of Silk would be Sent us. That when he died, his wife who had been his maid Servant gave up to the Magistrate all the machines and Eggs. That a great number of Mulberry trees had been planted out of our garden, and the worms have leaves enough for their Sustenance.

She Said her husband had cultivated his 5 acre lot entirely, & intended to go upon his 45 acre lot, but desired We would allow him two Servants, without which, it could not be done, he being Sexton of Savannah Church, which took up Some of his time: besides which he Kept a cart, and hoped to be employ'd in our Publick Works.

We ask'd her how the Inhabitants did, when Mr. Quincy was absent from his Parish? She reply'd he was frequently absent, & then a Presbiterian Minister came and Supply'd his place. That the Church is too Small, altho there are Several other Religions there, as Presbiterians, Jews, Moravians and Anabaptists who have all their Teachers.

17 March 33.

Egmont	C	Anderson, Adm.	T
Hales, Steven	C	Bedford, Arthr.	T
Holand, Rogrs.	C	Belitha, Will.	T
Hucks	C	Burton, Jo.	T
LaRoch, Jo.	C	Smith, Saml.	T
Oglethorpe, Ja.	C	White, Jo.	T

This was our Anniversary day of meeting for having an annual Sermon, and filling up vacancies in the Common Council.

1. Mr. Verelts presented an Acct. of Receipts and disbursmts. from 9 June 1736 to this day, with a particular of Expences accrued & accruing to Midsumer 1737. And then,

2. We elected 3 of our Trustees into the Common Council in the room of Mr. White & Mr. Moore who formerly resign'd, and of Mr. Hucks who resign'd this day. The Gentlemen were Mr. Talbot (now Ld. Talbot by the Ld. Chancellors death the 14 feby. last) Mr. Thomas Archer, and Mr. Robert Ayers, Son to the late Chief Justice. We also elected Sr. Jacob Bouverie a Trustee.

On this occasion Something very remarkable past between Mr. Hucks, Mr. White (whose conduct to the Trust may be Seen Fol. XCVII, CIV.5, CVIII.5, & CIX) and me. Those Gentlemen apprehensive that Some more Clergymen might be proposed for Trustees, took me aside before we enterd on business, and Said they hoped none of that Sort would be proposed, for they Should oppose it, and were therefore for chusing no Trustees at all to prevent an occasion being given.

To this I reply'd I knew of no Such design, but one new Trustee we were under a necessity of taking in namely Sr. Jacob Bouverie, who had given 1000£ to us, and had accepted to be chosen, and it would be monstrous after that not to do it.

Soon after, Mr. White (who had a mind Mr. Archer Should be elected preferable to Mr. Ayers whom most of the gentlemen were for) came again to me, and Said, that if Mr. Archer were chosen, it would not prejudice Mr. Ayers, for Mr. Hucks intended to resign, which would make room for him. But as Soon as Mr. Archer was chosen, he came a third time to me, and Said Mr. Hucks had changed his mind & would not resign. I Reply'd I was glad to hear it, tho Sorry Mr. Ayers was dissappointed who living always in town would attend more frequently than Mr. Archer could be expected to do who lived much in the Country, and we all Knew what difficulties we were under in getting Common Council boards, and how much our business Suffer'd on that account. I Spoke this wth. an air that Shew'd I did not like Such mean artifices to carry points, which he observing, went back to the corner of the room to Mr. Hucks and Mr. LaRoch, and after a Small consultation Mr. Hucks came up to the table and deliverd his resignation.

He assured us it was not out of dislike to any Gentleman, or that he grew cool in his affections to the colony that he left us, but purely because his business in trade obliged him to be absent when we met, which was prejudicial to our proceedings, as it often dissappointed us of Common Council boards. He therefore thought himself obliged to resign, and make room for a Gentleman whom he perceived every Member was desirous Should be chosen, Mr. Ayers.

I told him I was confident I Spoke the Sense of every Gentleman present in Saying, it was a great concern to us to See One who was originally appointed in the Charter and had been So constantly zealous and usefull to us, Should now quit the Common Council, and as to my Self it most Sensibly affected me. However I hoped he would Still give his attendance as often as his business would permit as a Trustee, and even on Common Council affairs would come and assist with his advice. He reply'd he would do both, But rarely did either, which was the case of most who at Several times resign'd, tho they made large promises.

3. After this, all present who were not Members of Parliamt. went to Church, the rest going away to attend the Report of the Committee upon our 20000£ Supply, but they return'd to dine with us at the Castle Tavern. Dr. Warren preach'd to us.

It was observable Dr. Bundy tho the Church was his own was not present: our not granting the Ministers land in glebe Stuck in his gizard.

4. At dinner we were the following Members; and the persons invited were Capt. Hugh Mackay, Dr. Warren, and Mrs. Whitfeild. The whole number with our Secy. & Accompt. 22.

Ld. Carpenter	C	Ld. Tirconnel	C
Cater, Robt.	C	Vernon, Ja.	C
Egmont	C	Anderson, Adm.	T
Hales, Stevn.	C	Bedford, Arthr.	T
Heathcote, Geo	C	Burton, Jo.	T
Holland, Rogrs.	C	Belitha, Will.	T
LaRoch, Jo.	C	Hucks, Robt.	T
Oglethorpe, Ja.	C	Smith, Saml.	T
Sloper, Will.	C		

[N.B.] 19 March 1736–7. Our Accompt. acquainted me that by a Ship just arrived from Carolina, that the Spaniards design'd to attack Georgia from the Havana, notwithstand our late Treaty of pacification with the Govr. of St. Augustine; and thereupon that the Commodore of the Kings Guardships in America had order'd them all to joyn him to defend our Province.

[N.B.] About the Same time arrived a letter from Mr. Horton (to whom Mr. Oglethorpe committed the care of the Militia of Frederica at his departure) that the people were resolv'd to defend themselves against the Spaniards if attack'd. That they were industrious, but wanted corn to sow.

21 March. 34.

Egmont	C		Slopes, Will.	C	
Heathcote, Geo.	C	Ch.	Towers, Tho.	C	
Holland, Rogrs.	C		Vernon, Ja.	C	
LaRoch, Jo.	C		Hucks, Robt.	T	
Oglethorpe, Ja.	C	P	White, Jo.	T	
Shaftsbury	C				

1. The Trustees took under consideration the petition presented to the King and Privy Council last week by Sarah Watson, complaining against Mr. Causton, The Trustees and in particular of Mr. Oglethorpe for an unjust Tryall of Joseph Watson her husband, & the confining him a lunatick, to the ruin of his fortune. There were diverse unfair insinuations & misrepresentations con-

tain'd in this petition. We drew up heads of instructions to be given our Lawyers against the Cause is heard before the Committee of Council & order'd that the Sollicitor & Attorney Should be retain'd on our Side.

3. [#2 omitted] A letter from Mr. Dobree at Frederica inform'd us that not one person was Sick there, & that most of them were industrious, but they are in great want of a Minister to perform Ecclesiastical Offices.

4. Resolv'd that Mr. Oglethorpe be desired to issue to Fra. Moore now in England 1000£ in Sola bills at 10£ each, to be Sent to Mr. Causton for particular uses, to be exprest in a letter that goes with Capt._____tomorrow.

5. Order'd ½ years Sallary to the Saltsburg Ministers.

6. Order'd 5 guineas to the Midwife Stanley while She Stays in England, to be repaid by her husband.

7. Order'd that Mary Cooper Widow, now here, be paid 10.10.0 being the Rent of her house let for that Sum to a Tenant in Georgia, and that her rent be paid to our Acct. in Georgia.

8. Agreed to the Committees report for gratifying Capt. Dempsy for his Services whilst in Georgia.

9. Order'd a puncheon Iron for cancelling Georgia Sola Bills.

[N.B.] 22 March 1736–7. Embark'd for Georgia at the Trustees charge on board the Peter and James, Capt. Diamond, 11 Males & 7 females.

23 March. 35.

Egmont	C	Archer, Tho.	C
Heathcote, Sr. Will.	C	Ayers, Robt.	C
Vernon, Ja.	C P		

1. Mr. Tho. Archer, Member of Parliamt. for Warwick, Mr. Ayers, Commissionr. of Excise, and Ld. Talbot, Sworn into their Office of Common Counsellors.

2. Benefactions reported: 100£ for the use of a Missioner to instruction of the Indians (mention'd 16th inst. Fol. 175) from a Gentlewoman unknown; 50£ legacy by the late Sr. Jo. Philips for the relief of the Saltsburgers or other persecuted Protestants. And Some lesser gifts.

3. A letter from Mr. Eveleigh (but without name) to Mr. Oglethorpe was readed, dat. from Charlestown, giving Acct. that the Spaniards design'd to attack Georgia, and that the Govermt. of Carolina were taking divers precautions to defend their Province

and Ours. That Ships of 86, 56. & 20 guns were building at the Havana. That a Ship was arrived thither from Old Spain with 500 Soldiers.

4. A letter was read from Dobree Clerk of the Stores at Frederica confirming the Same, adding the report was the Spaniards design'd to fall on our Province.

5. Mr. Wrag the Mercht. came to Shew us a letter he had recieved from his brother in Carolina confirming the Same, and that the Spaniards design'd to publish a Proclamation, declaring all Negroes free who Should not assist their Masters.

6. This news is come authentically confirm'd from Capt. Dent, Commodore to his Majesties Guardships in America to Sr. Charles Wager, dat. 3 Novbr. last, acquainting him, that by private Intelligence from St. Iago de la Vega, he was inform'd, that a person who had formerly been on the English half pay, but was Struck off, and thereby disgusted, was just arrived there from Cadix in 70 days. That he took on him a borrow'd name, and pretended to be an Irish Man. That immediatly on his arrival, a report ran that Georgia was to be attack'd, and preparations were making for it. That Ships were building at the Havana &c, and he had thereupon Sent for the Kings Ships to joyn him.

7. Mr. Oglethorpe recd. other letters that the Province of Carolina was much alarm'd, and had order'd the Creek Indians to go down against the Florida Indians to keep them in Play, that they might not joyn the Spaniards. This was very hasty, and might have proved of ill consequence, for it is hard to restrain our Indians from falling on the Spaniards, and in that case the latter would Say we were the first who broke the late Treaty.

8. Our condition at that time was bad: For tho we had about 700 men in our Province capable to bear arms, not above 300 could be got together to defend either Savannah or Frederica, in either of which places we had but little amunition, and no military Man fit to command.

[N.B.] 23 March 1736–7. Altho the Spaniards design to attack Georgia blew over, yet that they had Such intention, and continued it for a considerable time (not without Suspicion that the French also purposed to invade Carolina), appears by Several letters received by our English Merchants from Charlestown.

[N.B.] The 25 March 1737. Mr. Saml. Eveleigh wrote to his correspondent in London, that a Sloop was arrived from the Govr. of Providence with a packet, on reading which, it was Sent to Capt. Windham who commanded the Kings Sloops at Carolina, together with 5 affidavits made before that Govr. by 5 Englishmen who had been lately prisoners at the Havana, and were newly arrived there. These letters confirm'd the Accts. of the preparations of the Spaniards at the Havanah against Carolina.

That Capt. Dunbar was come from Georgia wth. an Acct. that at Frederica, Darien and Savannah all was well prepared, and the Inhabitants resolved to defend themselves. That the Forts at the two former Towns are Strong & regular, and a great progress was made in the 3d at Savannah.

That the night before the date of his letter Capt. Colcock was come in 15 days from the French town of *Moville,* and brought account, that a French Man of War was arived there, and that 2 more were expected wth. 1200 Soldiers: that they brought with them Several Warlick necessaries, particularly Some Small Mortars. That they design'd to make a third attack on the Chickesaws with 2000 White Men & 1000 Chacktaws. That an Acct. of this design had been given the Chacktaws, who bravely Sent down word to the French Govr. that they needed not put themselves to the trouble of coming to them, for that they would meet them half way, if they would let them know of their coming. That the Chickesaws had for a long time had constant War with the Chocktaws and had kill'd vast numbers of them wth. very little loss on their Side, insomuch that not only the Indians, but the French themselves were very much afraid of them, and acknowledge them to be the Stoutest Indians on the Main. That the French Officers dread going to War against them, & Say they dont understand Bush fighting. That the Soldiers now arived and expected, are all Roman Catholicks, & the few Switzers there who are Protestants were orderd home & there to be discharg'd.

That a gentleman there named Tarascoe, and a friend to the English was clapt into prison and put in Irons, and it was Said would be Sent home & put into the gallies.

That the Chacktaws had taken 2 Chickesaws, and carry'd them in great Triumph to Moville where they were burnt after a cruel and barbarous manner. One of them was a boy of about 10 or 11 years old.

[N.B.] On the 27 March 1737 Andrew Rutledge Esq., a Member of the Council of South Carolina confirm'd the Acct. of the Spaniards intending a Decent from Cuba, in a letter to his friend in London, and Said they were Soon expected.

In another letter of near the Same date, it was written as follows to a Merchant of London: The certain advices from the

Havanah by the way of Providence made me hurry away 100 barrils of Rice Short of my cargo, for fear of an Embargo, which I had reason to fear would be laid on in a few days. The advice which was a few days before I Sail'd, confirm'd the former, of the Spaniards arming at the Havana, and that they only waited for the Barliavento Squadron to Strengthen their Naval Force with 2 or 3 Men of War. They are to carry Six hundred Troops from thence to joyne an equal number at St. Augustine, besides Volunteers &c. On receipt of these advices, Expresses were dispatch'd by the Govr. & Council to their Agents in the Creek & other Nations to endeavour to raise 800 of them, 500 to be Sent to Georgia, and orders given to others to buy Rice and Corn for provisions for them.

That there is reason to believe the Spaniards views are not confin'd to Georgia, but extend to Carolina, where they have neither Forts nor Castles worth mentioning to Secure their Stores, provisions, Women & children in, But must leave them exposed to a more dreadful Enemy than the Spaniards, viz. their Slaves, to whom the Spaniards are to give them their freedom, and I am jealous that Some of them know it; For a few days before I Sail'd, wch. was the 23 of March, they rob'd a Store at Dorchester of Arms & amunition, So that the Carolinians have only to depend on their own courage & Strength in the feild, and if they come to engage, God only Knows the Event, & you may guess what a fright the Sight of a formidable Enemy would put them in.

Also Paul Jennys Esq. Speaker of the Assembly of South Carolina wrote to his friend in London 21 March that the Spaniards design'd to attack Georgia with 1000 land forces, but waited for the Barliavento fleet consisting of 4 Ships from 60 to 26 guns, to join two others from the Havana.

About the Same time Mr. Causton wrote us that the Lt. Govr. had inform'd him by letter that he was coming down in person with a body to the borders of South Carolina to defend Georgia.

On the 18th of the Same month Capt. Gascoign wrote Mr. Oglethorpe he believed the Spaniards persisted in their design.

The Same month Mr. Hawkins wrote the Trustees that the people of Frederica were industrious, and Since the embarkation there had died but one old woman Of 60 years, & a child of 4.

Davison the Chairman a Constable of Frederica wrote me that he had built him a brick house 3 Story high and fenced in his whole Lot, and desired a Servant without which it was impossible to cultivate.

30 March. 36.

Ayers, Robt.	C		Oglethorpe, Ja.	C
Ld. Carpenter	C		Ld. Tirconnel	C
Egmont	C		Towers, Tho.	C Ch.
Hales, Steven	C P		Anderson, Adm.	T
Holland, Rogrs.	C		Bedford, Arthr.	T
Lapotre, Hen.	C		Bouverie, Sr. Jacob	T
LaRoch, Jo.	C		Smith, Saml.	T

1. Benefactions reported: 50£ from an unknown Gentlewoman for building a Church at Frederica: 10£ from the Bishop of Gloster (Dr. Bentson) for the religious uses of the Colony, And Sr. Jacob Bouverie presented us the 1000£ formerly mentioned. Report was also made of a benefaction intended to be made us of a Town Seal for Savannah.

2. Report of 858.6.6 paid into the Bank, being the Produce of Rice from Carolina, bought by Mr. Oglethorpe when in Georgia, for the Stores. But being more than necessary, he sent it over to England to be Sold, and thereon arose a profit to the Trust.

3. A letter from Lt. Govr. Broughton to the Trustees dat. 7 Feby. last, was read, acquainting us that the Spaniards are preparing to attack Georgia, and fitting out a fleet for that end. But that S. Carolina were taking measures to march troops to their Southern borders to be near at hand to assist us.

4. A like letter came to Bristol and was read at our board that the Spaniards would attack our Province wth. 11 Ships.

5. Mr. Oglethorpe acquainted us that the French were marching 500 regular Troops to attack the Chickesaws with intent utterly to extirpate that nation, and had order'd the Albamas Fort which is the nearest to Carolina to be repaird, & then put a garison into it of 1000 Men.

6. Mr. Elisha Dobree Clerk of our Stores at Frederica, having wrote to desire his wife might be Sent over to him, we order'd her to attend, but She declined going, alledging he was a whimsical Man, and not able to maintain her & her 3 children.

7. Mr. White Council for the Trustees in Joseph Watson's business, & Mr. Paris our Sollicitor, attended us for instructions. They observed to us 2 heads of complaint, in his wifes petition to the Council board, One against Mr. Causton our Bailif for arbitrary proceedings, the Other for confining her husband as a Lunatick.

We reply'd, that as to Mr. Causton, he was chief Magistrate, and no petition had come from Watson to be reliev'd against him till last year, and without information on Cash (which we never had) we could not enquire into his conduct in that affair, for that were to Suppose a Magistrate guilty of misbehaviour, without any proof. Secondly, that as to the Trustees continuing Watson in confinement, the Jury had brought him in guilty, but out of his Senses, and Such persons are under the Magistrates care, till they recover. That there are others will Swear he is Some times out of his Senses, and Mr. Oglethorpe added Several instances of it, as his running naked about the town &c. That Men are deem'd Lunaticks tho Sometimes in their Senses, and that his confinement was a protection to his person, the Indians Seeking his life for having murder'd (as they believed) the Indian, not only by drinking him to death as Watson brag'd, but by poisoning his drink. That besides he was concerned in the Red ribbon plot of rising & killing the Inhabitants, & had Said he had been the ruin of 2 Colonies, & would be of a third, by wch. he could mean no other than Georgia.

8. Accompts of Mr. Saml. Eveleigh for necessaries bought by him for Georgia, lately arrived, were referr'd to the Committee of Accts.

9. 7 Casks of Skins arrived from Georgia were orderd to be Sold at 2 Shill. nine pence *p* hund. weight.

10. Order for paying 5.5.0 to a person in recompence for recovering a Survey of the Coast of Georgia, from the Executors of a person dead.

11. Order for paying the Revd. Mr. Cha. Wesley 25£ for officiating in Georgia, being for ½ years Sallary paid him before & now confirmed.

12. Resolv'd that the Attorney Genl. be retain'd in the cause of Watsons petition.

13. Resolv'd that on all occasions where the Trust are to be engaged in law Affairs, that the Attorny. & Sollicr. Genl. be retain'd.

14. Agreed to certain Articles for Jo. Pye to be a Clerke of the Stores at Savannah.

15. Agreed that Saml. Hurst be employ'd as Clerke of the Stores either at Savannah or Frederica, on the Same terms wth. Jo. Pye.

16. Mr. Zuberbullers proposal to carry 150 persons from Switserland to Georgia, were read, and refer'd to the Committee of correspondence.

17. A proposal from Mr. Dant McLaulan to carry over whole Clans of Scots to Georgia was read, to which I absolutly refused my consent, he being the Minister whose gown was Stript off his back for writing last year a pamphlet to prove that whoring is no Sin.

1 April. 37.

Archer, Tho.	C		Ld. Limerick	C
Bundy, Richd.	C		Oglethorpe, Ja.	C
Ayers, Robt.	C		Shaftsbury	C
Heathcote, Geo.	C		Ld. Talbot	C
Heathcote, Sr. Will.	C	P	Ld. Tirconnel	C
Holland, Rogrs.	C	Ch.	Vernon, Ja.	C
Hucks, Robt.	T		White, Jo.	T
LaRoch, Jo.	C			

A Common Council was Summond upon extraordinary business Specially to be considered. But I could not be present, being obliged to attend my Son who died this morning.

1. Upon Mr. Oglethorpes representation of Lieut. Hugh Mackay's Services in Georgia, given under his hand & specified, Thanks were orderd him & 100£ present.

2. Lieut. Govr. Broughton's letter to the Trustees dat. 7 feb. 1736/7 was read giving Acct. of the Spaniards preparations at the Havana & St. Augustine to attack Georgia, as Signified to him by Commodore Dent.

3. A letter to the Same purpose was read from Bristol dat. 26 March 1737 wrote by Mr. Will. Jeffryes to Messrs. Baker in London.

4. Orderd Copies of these letters to be Sent to the D. of Newcastle.

5. Orderd that Mr. Ayers, Mr. Hen. Archer, Mr. Tho. Towers & Mr. Holland be desired to prepare the following laws:

A law for taking Indian Evidence.

A law against the use of gold & Silver in Aparel & Furniture, and for preventing Luxury.

A law to oblige Ships clearing out of Savanna & the Allatahama Rivers to pay a pound of pistol powder *p* tun Port duty.

A law to regulate the manner of private persons giving Credit to one another, & the manner of Suing for their debts.

4 April. 38.

Egmont	C P	Oglethorpe, Ja.	C
Holland, Rogrs.	C	Shaftsbury	C
Lapotre, Hen.	C	Towers, Tho.	C
LaRoch, Jo.	C	Vernon, Ja.	C

We only did Trustee business.

1. Order'd that Mr. Ayers, Mr. Tho. Archer, Mr. Holland & Mr. Tho. Towers be a Committee to prepare the following Laws:

a. For allowing of Indian Evidence in our Courts.

b. To regulate the manner of private persons giving credit to each other in Georgia, & of Suing for debts.

c. To regulate the Watch & Settle the Militia.

d. A Sumptuary law to regulate aparel & furniture, and prevent extravagance & luxury.

e. A law to oblige Ships clearing out of Savannah and Allatahama rivers to pay a pound of pistol powder duty p Tun, according to the Tonnage for Port duty. N.B. The Gentleman appointed to prepare these laws never did any thing in them.

2. Mr. White and Mr. Paris attended to recieve further instructions in Watsons cause, and Some alterations we made to our Memorial for the Privy Council on that Subject, and orderd that the Same be Shewd to the Attorney Genl.

3. The Seal was put to our answer to Ct. Zinsendorf for Sending more Moravians over. Regularly a Trustee board could not do it, but a former Common Council, having given the Committee of Correspondence full power to make the Ct. an answer, we did it in that capacity.

4. This morning Ld. Tirconnel, Mr. Oglethorpe, Mr. LaRoch & others waited on the D. of Newcastle to communicate to him the Acct. we had recieved from Carolina of the Spaniards new design to invade Carolina & Georgia. His Grace reply'd, what ever could be done, care Should be taken to protect us.

5. A paper was prepared by us to give Sr. Robt. Walpole, expressing the impossibility of carrying on our designs, unless Some Stated allowance were made for an annual Support of our Forts & Civil Goverment, to be given into Parliament by way of Estimate, in the manner that other Governments in America are provided for. And we determin'd that as many of our Gentlemen as could be prevaild on Should wait on him Some day this week to present him our paper.

[1737] JOURNAL OF THE EARL OF EGMONT

[N.B.] 4 April 1737. This day Mr. Oglethorpe acquainted us, that his Commission of Genl. in Chief of the Forces in South Carolina & Georgia, ly's made out in the Office, but that he will not accept it until his desire be comply'd with to have a Regiment of 700 Men with the Commission of Coll. wherewith to defend the two Provinces.

He reckon'd up about 7000 Indians we may depend on for our friends, viz. 400 Chickesaws, 1500 Creeks, & 5000 Chacktaws: But that the French have 16 or 20000.

He Shew'd us the Plan of Frederica Fort, which has 4 bastions wth. a ditch and double Palisadoes, and at present contains a garison of 100 Men, but can contain 40 more, and is capable of defence unless attack'd in a regular manner with Cannon.

6 *April.* 39.

Egmont	C	Oglethorpe, Ja.	C
Heathcote, Geo.	C	Ld. Tirconnel	C
LaRoch, Jo.	C	Anderson, Adm.	T

A Common Council was Summond to consider of a letter from Inverness, and Sending a Ship to Scotland for Servants now engaging for Georgia, and other immediate business; but we were not a board.

1. Mr. Sharp Clerk of the Council came, and deliverd to us by the Ld. Presidents order a petition given by the wife of Joseph Watson to his Lordship desiring the Committee of Council would dispatch the hearing of her complaints, on Suggestion that unless Some orders are Speedily Sent by the next Ship to Bailif Causton, he will have finish'd the prison he is building, and destroy her husband by confining him therein. The petition was so absurd that we took no notice of it.

2. Mr. McLaulan (mention'd Fol. 181.17) appear'd again, & presented a proposal to carry over to Georgia 100 Scots at his own expence. Mr. Oglethorpe had appointed him to come, and was fond of the proposal because it would Strengthen the Colony: but I declared I never would consent that So vile a Wretch Should be allow'd to go & Spoil the morals of our people.

Mr. Oglethorpe reply'd, that if we discouraged the Scots from going, we Should want men to defend the Province and the reason we had for discouraging them would not be known. Wherefore he thought it prudent to call the man in, and give him the true reason for our rejecting him, to which perhapps he might give Some answer that would Satisfy us that he had been injured, & possibly he might Shew he was not the Author of that book.

Finding Mr. Oglethorpe Set upon the matter, & that I was not Supported by my Ld. Tirconnel or Mr. Anderson (who now were all the members remaining at the board and knew nothing of the affair) I acquiesced. So he was call'd in, and inform'd he had given great Scandal by a book publish'd by him *to justify Fornication* and was therefore unfit to be Sent to Georgia: However we would hear what he had to Say to it. He Said he was indeed author of that book, but had wrote it with no ill design. That Sr. ———— of Scotland having made proposals to the Goverment to raise the Rents of an Estate the D. of Arguile held from the Crown, he wrote the book to ridicule that Knight, & So the preface would Shew had it been printed with the book. That afterwards Some of his young friends advised him to print; he did So, and was Sorry for it.

I reply'd this was no Satisfactory answer; that I had read the book, and there were most Shocking passages in it, not only perverting the Scriptures, but calling God to wittness Scandalous immorality, and ending his book with a prayer to open mens Eyes.

Mr. Oglethorpe who is a man of religious principles Said this border'd on blasphemy, and was most Surprising to hear, and ask'd him whether he was not a Minister?

He reply'd he had been one, but being call'd to account by the Kirk for writing that book, he had renounc'd that Church, and had turn'd Episcopalian of the Church of England.

Mr. Oglethorpe ask'd him if [he] had publickly profest the Church of England? He answer'd no, but he had let his friends know it. Then he ask'd him if he had been to wait on the Bishop of London or any other Bishop to express repentance of his crime, and had received any censure, or made publick recantation?

He answer'd the Bishop of London had apply'd to Sr. Robt. Walpole to take him up, which when he heard he surrender'd himself, from which time he remain'd a year & half confin'd, So that he could not wait on the Bishop; but he had wrote Several times to him, with offer to make what recantation he pleased, or Suffer any punishment, So he might have his pardon & freedom. But the Bishop Sent him word the matter was now out of his hands, the Civil Power having taken notice of it. We then desired him to withdraw, and debated what to do with him. At length it was concluded to tell him, that if he could find a way to See the Bishop and make Such Submission to him as was Satisfactory, and

[1737] JOURNAL OF THE EARL OF EGMONT 257

if thereupon the Bishop would certify in his favour, we then would consider his application to go to Georgia. But till that was done, We could not be justified in Sending over a person who Stood censured both by the Civil & Ecclesiastical Power.

Upon his being told this, he answer'd that he had promises to be Speedily Set free, and then he would wait on the Bishop, and declare to him that he was ready to Submit to any punishment he Should inflict on him, and even write against his former book, if he commanded him: So we got rid of him for this time.

3. As we were rising a Packet come fresh from Georgia was brought, wherein was a letter from Mr. Jo. Bromfeild ye Register of our Province acquainting us,

a. That the Allarm of the Spaniards purpose to attack us had put the Inhabitants of Savannah on building a Fort which went on with alacrity.

b. That the People had a desire to chuse their own Bailifs.

c. That those who had not yet cultivated their lands were excusable, partly because their lands were not yet Survey'd to them, partly that Some of their Lotts were Pyne barren and half Swamp.

d. That neither had they enclosed for want of help, whereby the Cattle and Vermin had eaten up their corn.

e. In the general he gave a very indifferent account of the Colony, and desired we would not entertain So good thoughts of it as we probably did.

14 April. 40.

Ld. Carpenter	C P	Oglethorpe, Ja.	C
Egmont	C	Lapotre, Hen.	C
Heathcote, Sr. Will.	C	Ld. Tirconnel	C

A Common Council Summon'd to consider of the Terms where on Mr. Stephens was willing to Serve the Trustees as Secret. in Georgia, and to order the Arms, gunpowder & Servants by the Ship Two brothers—Capt. Thompson, going to Scotland & from thence to Georgia & other business, but we were no board.

1. Mr. Paris our Sollicitor attended to acquaint us, that he had given the Attorney Genl. our answer to Mrs. Watson's petition, which he took into the Country to peruse, and had return'd it with an endorsment, that Our answer was too general, and not Satisfactorily at all to him, but that he advised we Should make a particular answer to each particular of her complaint.

Mr. Oglethorpe Said that a general answer was all we ought to make, and this by way of Information only to the Privy Council: that otherwise, for a Set of Gentlemen in England incorporated by Charter to acknowledge the Privy Council's power as if we were Subject to their jurisdiction, and to make ourselves as in duty bound accountable to them, and obliged to obey their commands by making answer to them, would render us lyable to a Premunire, and So he had told the Ld. President. If therefore we were call'd on by the Privy Council to answer for any fault committed by us here, we are not to make answer. But if the Privy Council has power to take cognizance of any malversation in Georgia, and if they desire no more than information from us concerning Transactions in Georgia, in order to their proceeding on things done there, it would be proper to give it them, but this by way of information only, & for that a general answer was Sufficient.

Mr. Paris own'd what Mr. Oglethorpe Said was true, but he Supposed the Privy Council only Sent to us to know what proceedings in Georgia had been transmitted to us relating to Watson.

Mr. Oglethorpe reply'd, So much was proper, but Still if the Privy Council intended to determine on the complaint, they must Send to Georgia for further lights, or give us time to do it for their information: otherwise for them to proceed to judgment in the first instance without hearing Mr. Causton the person complain'd of in his defence, would be partial and unjust.

Mr. Paris reply'd the Attorney would return to town on Monday, and then he would discourse the matter with him.

2. We then desired him to present a Memorial to the Board of Trade, that we might come to a Speedy hearing on the Carolina complaint; for we thought it hard & un-usual for defendants in a cause to be denied a Speedy hearing, and harder Still to be put off So long at the desire of the Complainants. Neither was it a decent usage of a Set of Gentlemen appointed by charter. The truth is the Board of Trade were most partial against us through the whole course of this Affair, knowing how little Sr. Robert Walpole cared for us, and being prejudiced against us by the Carolina Merchants.

[N.B.] 14 April 1737. The Queen told me at Court this day, that the Georgia Trustees had been under a mistake. I reply'd I Should be glad to know where in that we might mend it. She Said the Silk of which her gown was made last year was indeed the finest She ever Saw, but She was told it came from Italy not from

Georgia. I reply'd Smiling the only ground for that report was that we had debauch'd away from Piedmont two Italians & Sent them to Georgia where I assured her the Silk was work'd. This Shews what pains was taken to injure us at Court.

18 April. 41.

Ld. Carpenter	C	Ld. Limerick	C
Egmont	C	Oglethorpe, Ja.	C
Heathcote, Sr. Will.	C	Ld. Talbot	C
Lapotre, Hen.	C	Ld. Tirconnel	C P Ch.
LaRoch, Jo.	C		

1. An answer to Lt. Govr. Broughtons letter to us (See fol. 180.3) wherein he acquainted us with the Spaniards design to attack us and the care taken by Carolina for our defence, was drawn up. I thought it not Sufficiently civil, But Mr. Oglethorpe would have it that we ought not to compliment him too much, lest advantage Should be taken by the Carolinians to think we courted them, after Sending Such a Representation against us to the King and Council. We therefore only thank'd him for his intelligence, and hoped we Should be able to make head agst. the Spaniards, not doubting but Mr. Causton would take due care therein. But no thanks were return'd him for the care that Province was taking for our Security.

2. Order'd that it be refer'd to the Committee of Correspondence to contract with the Owners of the Ship *Two Brothers* to go to Inverness in Scotland & take in 40 Servants for Georgia at 5£ *p* head. And that 20 Shillgs. *p* head be allow'd for cloathing & bedding for them. And that a reasonable allowance Should be made for as many heads as Should be wanting of that number, the Same to be Settled by a Committee to meet for that purpose. These Scots were design'd to be employ'd on Trust lands. The Capt. to be obliged to Stay 14 days at Inverness, and in case he did not receive the number within that time, he was to be at liberty to Stay or go with Such as he received.

3. Resolv'd that by the Same Ship be Sent 15 barrils of powder for Small arms, 100 Muskets & bayonets, 200 Indian arms, 300 weight of musket balls, 300 weight of Indian gun bullets, 600 weight of lead, a pair of bullet moulds of 9 holes each for musket bore & 2 Iron ladles, a quantity of nails, and 300 pair of Shoes at 4 Shillgs *p* pair.

4. The Proposals of Will. Stephens Esq. to be our Secretary

were read & agreed to, and He appointed Secretary. The conditions made with him were, that he would Serve us in that Post 6 years, and take with him his 3d Son Mr. Thomas Stephens to perform that duty in case himself Should fail. That we Should grant him and his heirs male 500 acres, pay the passage of himself & family over; pay 10 Servants to cultivate his land for one year only; give him 50£ in hand for his voyage, and 50£ more when demanded; that we would furnish his house and allow him for travelling charges when orderd to take journeys by the Board.

5. Mr. Oglethorpe read to us a letter that came to him from Mr. Eveleigh by the last packets, acquainting him, that the Spaniards had been endeavouring to buy up 400 muskets and other warlick Stores at Charlestown, and had received Some other Supplyes from another Province which past through Carolina. That the Ld. Govr. had Seized 3 gentlemen come from Augustine whom he imagined to be Spies, and than an Embargo had been laid on all the Shypping in Carolina, wch. Mr. Oglethorpe Said would be 100,000£ loss to Carolina by reason it would hinder their rice from being exported to Lisbon in the early time when the best market is to be made, and thereby oblige the Portuguese to Supply themselves from Leghorn and Barbary, after which the Carolina rice (not to Speak of the damage it Sustains by lying by) would Sell for far less: besides it might throw that trade into a new channel.

Moreover the taking Men from their farms to make Soldiers of them, on this allarm, would be another great damage to them.

This he Said might have been prevented, if the Ministry had hearken'd to the Memorials Several times presented them by the Board of Trade, Setting forth the necessity of Strengthening Carolina with Some troops.

6. I prest Mr. Oglethorpe to get all the Members he could See in the H. of Commons this day, to go jointly to Sr. Robt. Walpole to obtain of him an assurance that hence forward we Should not be obliged to ask yearly the Parliament for money, but that 6 or 7000£ Should be annually brought in by way of Estimate for Our Colony's Support, as the other Colonies are Supported, wherein the military charges Should be distinguish'd from the Civil, and the Civil Supported at a fixt rate by the Governmt. until the Province could Support itself. Otherwise that the Trustees must Surrender their Charter into the Kings hands.

7. Order'd that the Committee of Correspondence Do Settle instructions for Mr. Stephens, before he Sets out.

[1737] JOURNAL OF THE EARL OF EGMONT

20 April. 42.

Digby, Edwd.	C	Heathcote, Sr. Will.	C P
Egmont	C	Smith, Saml.	T
Ld. Tirconnel	C		

1. Mr. Paris attended, and made report that upon conversation with the Attorney Genl. he had now alterd his opinion and thought the Trustees in the right not to make themselves Parties in Watsons complaint, but to answer only by way of information, what we knew of the matter.

2. He also reported, that he had presented a Memorial to the Board of Trade for a Speedy hearing on the Carolina complaints, representing the hardship of So many & long delays, that it behoved Accusers to be ready to make out their charge, and not desire further time for Strengthening their Evidence, when the defendents were ready to joyn Issue. That the Trustees had Suffer'd in their character by the Carolinians printing their case & depositions, & dispersing it abroad before the Tryal of the cause, & the world were thereby prejudiced against us.

That Mr. Plumer, Ld. Fitzwalter & Col. Bladen were the only Members of the Board present that day. That Mr. Plummer Said nothing, Col. Bladen Said we ought immediately to have a hearing, but Ld. Fitzwilliams Said Mr. Fury Agent of Carolina had been with him that morning, to desire a forbearance of hearing until the Affidavits that were to Support their charge Should come over attested under the Colonies Seal, which he expected by the first Ship, and his Lordship thought that reasonable, otherwise they Should only hear one Side, and when the Affidavits came, there must be a hearing over again.

We desired Mr. Paris would again represent to that Board, that Since the Representation came over, Several Ships were arrived from Carolina, without bringing the affidavits expected, and that 'twas our belief they only delay'd matters till Mr. Oglethorpe and our wittnesses Should be return'd to Georgia, and we thereby be deprived of our natural defence. We also order'd our Accompt. to aprise Mr. Paris of the names of those Ships, & times of their arrival; as also of the dates of letters recd. by our board & private persons from Carolina, Since the Representation was Sent. We also desired Mr. Paris to demand of the board of Trade a dismiss of the complaint, in case Mr. Fury did not consent to proceed to a hearing.

3. Then as a Committee of Correspondence we agreed with Capt. Thompson of the Two Brothers who was to go on his own acct. to get Servants for private persons in Georgia, That he Should take on board 40 Servants on the Trust Acct. and wait a fortnight for them at Aberdeen. That he Should have 5£ p head for their freight, but if the number could not be got ready by the time, he Should Sail with as many as could, and for what were wanting of the full number Should be allow'd 2£ p head.

And as he had agreed to carry Servants for private persons in Georgia at 10£ p head, and was to Stay a month in Georgia for their payment, if the Masters did not pay him in that time, we would take them into our Service & pay him 8£ p head.

In consideration of this agreement, we further agreed that we would give him 30£ as a premium for the risk he would run of Servants dying on board, because in Such case he was to receive nothing for those who died.

27 April. 43.

Archer, Tho.	C		Holland, Rogrs.	C
Egmont	C	P	Shaftsbury	C
Heathcote, Geo.	C		Burton, Jo.	T
Heathcote, Sr. Will.	C		Smith, Saml.	T
Lapotre, Hen.	C	Ch.	White, Jo.	T
LaRoch, Jo.	C			

1. Mr. Paris attended with the draft of a fresh Memorial to the Board of Trade, for our revisal & approval. It was to reiterate our desire to have a Speedy hearing, & in it was Set forth, that Since the arrival of the Carolina Complaint, and the printing the book, 15 Ships were come from that Province, by none of which came the affidavits So long promis'd to Support the charge against us. But our Secrety. acquainting us that he heard the affidavits were come two days ago by a later Ship, we Suspended the presenting this memorial.

2. Our Accompt. acquainted us that Mr. Oglethorpe had received a letter from Mr. Eveleigh dat. in March last giving acct. that Tomachachi had repair'd to Savannah wth. 60 Indians to asist in building the Fort at Savannah; & that Col. Bull (according to the Commission left with him by Mr. Oglethorpe to command the Militia of Georgia), was march'd down to Savannah with 100 Men. That the Creek Indians had engaged to asist us with a great number in case the Spaniards attack'd us, which considerable

Service the Carolinians own is owing to Mr. Oglethorpe. (The Creeks Upper and Lower are 5000 fighting Men.) It did not appear by that letter that the Spaniards had then a design to attack us, what ever they might have intended before.

3. Mr. Burton paid in his 4th yearly gift of 10£ towards the Endowment of a Catechist in Georgia.

4. A letter was read from Mr. Millar the Botonist dat. at Jamaica, acquainting us, that at his arrival he found Some of the Ipicuana root alive, and that he would in a month Send Some of it to Georgia, where if it throve & was not neglected, it would become a valuable Commodity.

5. Mr. Holland to whom it was refer'd in concert wth. Mr. Towers to prepare the 5 new intended laws, represented to the board, that both he and Mr. Towers had So much business on their hands that they could not take the whole of that affair upon them, and therefore desired we would employ Some other Lawyer to make drafts and then they would Supervise them. Thereupon We recommended to them Counsellr. Mason, whose zeal for our Success prompted him to offer his Service, without expectation of Reward. Thus our design of new laws came to nothing, for after a time, Mr. Towers acquainted us the Counsellor had made Such bungling drafts that he could make nothing of them, and not recommending another but declaring he knew of none, no further proceeding was made in that affair.

6. Refer'd to a Committee to consider of a Device for a Town Seal for Savannah Town, which a gentleman intended to present us.

7. Seal put to the articles of Agreement made with Jo. Pye to be a Writer in the Stores.

8. Seal put to the Articles of Agreement made wth. Saml. Hurst to be a Writer in the Stores.

9. Order'd that 300 Acres be laid out at Frederica for Religious Uses there, the produce whereof when cultivated to go to the maintenance of a Minister & Cathechist there, and for other Religious Uses.

10. Resolv'd that 40 Servants be employ'd in clearing & cultivating a Farm Lot of lands reserved for the Publick, to be call'd Bouveries Farm, in discharge of Sr. Jacob Bouveries Benefaction for Sending over Servants to Georgia; which 40 Servants at 25£ p head will amount to the Expence of 1000£.

11. Order'd that an annual Acct. of the produce of Said Lands be kept distinct, and enter'd as the produce of Bouveries Farm, to be apply'd for the Benefits of the Colony.

12. Oath of Office administerd to Will. Stephens Esq. as Secy. of Georgia.

13. Additional Members appointed to the Committee for Settling Mr. Stephens Instructions. His Instructions Seal'd: & a paper Sign'd of more private instructions to him.

14. Grant past to him of 500 acres by which he is obliged to cultivate 200 acres in (blank) years, and the remaining 300 acres in 16 years.

15. Grant past to John Warwick (recommended by the Bishop of Derry) of 50 acres. Twas Said he was worth 1000£. The lot is in Savannah.

29 April. 44.

Archer, Tho.	C		Lapotre, Hen.	C
Digby, Edwd.	C		LaRoch, Jo.	C
Egmont	C		Shaftsbury	C
Heathcote, Sr. Will.	C	Ch.	Vernon, Ja.	C
Holland, Rogrs.	C		Hucks, Robt.	T

1. As a Committee for drawing up instructions to Send with Mr. Stephens, we prepared the Same to be ready next Common Council board for Setting the Seal to, altho the Committee had power given them to Set the Seal thereto, and tho this was properly the business of A board of Trustees & not of the Common Council, yet we were willing they Should be approved by as many Members as could be got.

2. One Jennings having exposed to us that the 5 guineas formerly given him, was too little for the Ms. Survey of the Coast of Georgia taken by a person by Mr. Oglethorpes direction who died in passage to England, and was redeem'd of the Ship Captain for 10 guineas: We orderd the other 5 guineas Should be paid him.

3. Read proposals from J. Mathias Kramer Secy. to Ct. Zinsendorf for translating Some part of the book call'd *Reasons for establishing the Colony of Georgia* into High Dutch at the Trustees expence.

4. Read also a proposal from the Same person for engaging more of the Moravian brethren to go to Georgia, together with the answer prepared by the Committee of Correspondents thereto.

Resolv'd that both these proposals be refer'd to the Committee of Correspondence to consider, and that they Settle instructions to the Said Kramer in case Ct. Zinzendorf Shall approve our answer, and that they contract with Messieurs Hope of Rotterdam for the passage of 60 heads of 12 years old & upwards the expence

[1737] JOURNAL OF THE EARL OF EGMONT 265

whereof the Moravians are to repay 6 weeks after their arrival in Georgia, or else be indented Trust Servants.

5. A Memorial was presented by Capt. Cha. Dempsy, Setting forth his Services (which in truth were very great, hazardous & Successful) when employ'd by Mr. Oglethorpe to conclude the Treaty with the Governr. of Augustine. The Same being read, Thanks were orderd him & a gift of 150£.

This gentleman is an Irish Papist and past his life in the French Army, yet a man of honour & a lover of England. In the prossecution of the Treatty above mention'd, he was three times cast away at Sea and ran great peril of his life, threatned to be put in prison at Augustine & chained, he had renounced an Employment at Augustine, & contracted Such Sickness as he will never recover. He was carry'd young into France by his Father who follow'd K. James's fortune, and was Sent by Monsr. Giraldini & the Ct. of Montego Ministers of Spain at our Court to be Purveyor to the Stores of the Garison at Augustine: but going over in the Same Ship with Mr. Oglethorpe was by him prevaild on to give his assistance in preventing a War, & forego his Employment.

6. Read Mr. Zuberbullers proposal for Sending 52 families from the Canton of Apenzel: but on debate we declined it, finding the execution of it would amount to 2032.10.0 besides 100£ *p* ann expence to the Trust.

7. Mr. McLaulan formerly mentioned, appeared, and produced a Certificate from the Bishop of Rochester's Chaplains, that he had made his Submission to that Bishop for writing his Scandalous pamphlet, and was reconciled to the Church, & admitted to Lay Communion. He therefore with one Cameron apply'd to us to know on what conditions & encouragmts. Scots highlanders of his procuring might be admitted to Settle in Georgia.

We refer'd him to the usual terms which Our Accompt. was directed to Shew him.

8. Order past for appropriating 1500£ out of the 20000£ granted this year by Parliament, for the payment of Sola bills issued in Georgia Since Mr. Oglethorpe left the Province, and which consequently were not endorsed by him.

It Seems these bills have Such credit, that altho not endorsed by Mr. Oglethorpe (as they ought & are directed to be) people take them for payment of the goods they Supply the Stores with: and Mr. Oglethorpe Said, that at the Havana they bear a premium of 40 *p* cent.

9. Order'd that 433£ out of moneys unappropriated in our hands be paid to Mr. Oglethorpe, to answer So many Sola bills,

and to be replaced when the Parliaments Grant of 20000£ Shall be received.

The meaning is, he was to account for this Sum, being money with which Mr. Causton charged him on account of other Sola bills not endorsed by him, which Causton disposed of in exchange for money recieved by him in Georgia.

10. Orderd payment of 150£ in 3 bills drawn by Mr. Causton on Mr. Oglethorpe, in part of 200£ advanced Said Causton to enable him to Settle his Farm.

11. A Certified Account of 112.18.11 for provision delivered in Georgia dat. 1 Dec. 1736 before the 1500£ Sola bills arrived in Georgia being presented for payment by Mr. Bland the Goldsmith. We resolv'd it Should be paid, he giving Security to prevent the Trustees paying it twice.

12. Draft made on the Bank to pay Mr. Oglethorpe 433£.
13. Imprest to Aldn. Heathcote 450£.
14. Imprest further to him 425£.

15. Order'd that Archibald Hodge be allow'd to go to Georgia, and be allow'd provision out of the Stores for one year, he paying for his passage. He has a wife & 1 child.

16. Agreed that Mr. Thomas Upton, born in England, but of Irish Parents, bred in Ireland, but of late years a dweller in Jamaica which he left through misfortunes attended, and having assured us he had made up his debts, We agreed that he Should have a grant of 150 acres, he carrying over 3 Servants. He Said he had about 300£ and would Settle at Frederica.

17. A letter from Mr. Causton lately arrived, acquainted us wth. divers inteligences of the Spaniards intention to attack Georgia, but that the advice boat he Sent out, and the Indian Partyes were return'd to Savannah and reported all was quiet, So that he doubted much if the Spaniards would meddle with us.

That under apprehension of an attack he was building a Fort in Savannah Town, at which all the people work'd chearfully, with whom he agreed to pay them 7£ currency *p* month.

That Some Indians Sent by Lieut. Govr. Broughton to the Spanish frontier, had kill'd certain Spaniards whom they found with a gun that had belong'd to one of their Nation, wch. he fear'd might produce ill blood and provoke the Spaniards. This latter was dat. 24. feby.

[N.B.] 3d May 1737. There embark'd for Georgia at the Trustees charge on board the Princess Caroline, Capt. Coe, 1 Man and 2 Women.

4 May. 45.

Egmont	C	Oglethorpe, Ja.	C P
Heathcote, Sr. Will.	C	Vernon, Ja.	C
Holland, Rogrs.	C	Bedford, Arthr.	T
Lapotre, Hen.	C	Smith, Saml.	T
LaRoch, Jo.	C		

A Common Council was Summond to finish business postponed last meeting, & then to go into a Committee of Correspondence on the letters received from Georgia, and the matters refer'd to the Committee: But we were not a Board.

1. Mr. Paris attended, to acquaint us, that the Board of Trade had fixt Thursday Sennit for hearing the Carolina Complaint.

2. Also that the Attorney Genl. approved in general our Answer to Watsons complaint, but that in our defence we Should Shew whether the expence of his confinement had been charged to him as Set forth in the complaint, or defray'd by us; and whether we had prevented his going on with his Improvments of his lands, which was another head of the complaint.

We reply'd that we ourselves had paid the charge of his confinment, as appeard by Mr. Caustons Accts. who charged the Same to us, of which we had the receipts. And as to his being hinder'd from cultivating his land, He had indeed desired land & a grant was order'd, but he never took it out, So that he has no land.

3. Mr. McLaulan attended to receive an answer to his application for encouragement to Send Highlanders to Georgia, & after Some discourse we promised to write to the chief of the Cameronian Clan. We also gave him our printed Rules, but doubted if they would acquiesce in the encouragement we were able to give them.

4. One Giles, an alehouse keeper apply'd who had a wife & 3 children & Said he was worth 140£ desired a grant of 50 acres. We Said he Should have it, & Settled at Abercorn.

[N.B.] 4 May 1737. Mr. Oglethorpe this day acquainted the Board that Mr. Horace Walpole had received an anonimous letter, Setting forth the weak condition of S. Carolina, and their apprehension of being abandon'd by the Govermt.

He also inform'd us that when he waited on the D. of Newcastle this morning, his Grace laid the blame on the Spaniards uneasiness against us, to his charge, which he resented.

It Seem'd to us that One Savy, a person of vile character, who had been a bum-Bailif in Carolina, was he who under the character of an Officer arrived at the Havana from Old Spain, and by his bragging how Carolina & Georgia might be reduced, gave occasion to the report that the Spaniards design'd to invade us.

And in this opinion we were further confirm'd by a letter recd. the 8 of June from Mr. Causton of later date than others, wherein he inform'd us, that tho the allarm continued, he could not find any preparations were made at Augustine for that End, where they were in want both of money & provision. That the new Govr. of that Town had exprest his Surprise to See our Ships hover about their harbour; that the information given by the South Sea Agent at Havana arrose from his conversation with Savy above mention'd, an empty arrogant Man, who flying from Carolina or rather being driven out, repayr'd to the Queen Dowager of Spain, who recommended him to Monsr. Patinho 1st Minister at Madrid.

Whatever the Spaniards might intend, these Allarms were a prodigious expence to us, in taking the people off from cultivating their lands, and flinging their maintenance upon the Publick Stores for another year.

7 *May.* 46.

Egmont	C	LaRoch, Jo.	C
Heathcote, Sr. Will.	C	Oglethorpe, Ja.	C
Holland, Rogrs.	C	Vernon, Ja.	C

A Common Council was Summond to Seal an answer to Watson's petition, and finish'd business postponed: But we were again no board.

1. Mr. Paris attended with the Trustees answer to Watson's petition fair drawn: but he was order'd to Suspend giving it to the attorney Genl. and therefore defer'd to Sign it, until we had his opinion in writing,

a. Whether the Privy Council can by law receive Appeals from the West Indies in Criminal matters.

b. Whether by this Answer or representation to the Privy Council, in obedience to an Order of theirs, the Trustees do Subject themselves either in this or any future complaints from Georgia, to be Parties to Such complaints.

Mr. Oglethorpe was for making Short work, & not obeying the Privy Councils Order at all, lest Such complyance Should be interpreted an obligation upon us to answer in a judicial manner before that board.

But Mr. Vernon argued very justly, that not to answer at all, would be the greatest disrespect that could be to that Board. Besides it was not design'd we Should answer judicially, or make ourselves Parties to Watsons complaint, but only to acquaint the Council board by way of Information with what we knew touching that complaint. Mr. Paris also cited a paralel case that happend Some time ago, upon a complain for redress against Some Officers of Giberaltar, which being made to the Privy Council, their Lordships order'd the Govr. to make answer thereto. But his Council urging, that his answer was not to be construed as if he was concern'd in the matter, their Lordships allowed he was no Party thereto. Besides, our answer was So carefully worded, that we could by no construction of law be judged to be made Parties thereto.

2. Then Mr. Paris acquainted us that Mr. Fury and Mr. Sharp the one Agent, the other Sollicitor for Carolina, had Since our last meeting been very urgent with the Board of Trade to defer a week longer the hearing between that Province & Us, which yet had been Settled for thursday next, on pretence their Council had not time to prepare themselves. And the Lords were very inclinable to gratify them therein.

We thought this delay not only affected, but of very great consequence to the Safety of both Provinces, and therefore order'd Mr. Paris to go again to the Lords of Trade, & insist on the cause being heard next thursday. That Some Spaniards had been murder'd by Indians at the instigation of the Carolinians, which might involve us in War. That the Spanish Agent had already complain of it, and they might revenge it not only on Carolina but Georgia.

11 May. 47.

Bundy, Ri.	C	Ch.	LaRoch, Jo.	C
Egmont	C		Oglethorpe, Ja.	C
Heathcote, Geo.	C		Shaftsbury	C
Heathcote, Sr. Will.	C		Vernon	C
Holland, Rogrs.	C		Anderson, Adm.	T
Lapotre, Hen.	C	P	Smith, Saml.	T

1. Mr. Paris attended to acquaint us, that he had again apply'd to the board of Trade to press that the hearing might come on tomorrow, As their Lordships had at first resolved, and not to be put off til tomorrow Sennit.

The Ld. Fitzwalter Said, they must do equal justice that the other Side had represented their Council was not ready to plead tomorrow, but ours were.

Mr. Paris reply'd it would not be doing equal justice if they defer'd the hearing till tomorrow Sennit, for in that case We Should lose the advantage of the Attorney Genls. pleading, who would be hinder'd by other business, but had disposed himself to plead tomorrow. On the other Side, they desired delay because the Sollicitor Genl. would then be able to plead for them, which he could not do tomorrow. That thus the loss of our best Council was an unmerited disadvantage cast on our Side who So frequently apply'd for a hearing, and to defer the hearing till they could have the best Council, was an apparent hardship on us. Besides they were the Agressors, and in the nature of the thing ought to have been the first prepared. Moreover this delay would oblige us to the expence of feeing new Council. After this he withdrew, and immediately notice was Sent him that the Board adhered to their resolution of not hearing the cause till tomorrow Sennit 10 a clock, when they would begin, and Sit de die in diem till it was over. Mr. Paris observ'd he was detain'd 3 hours before he could be admitted, and that all that time their Secretary was reading to them the printed Representation Sent over by the Carolinians.

We had just reason to complain of the Boards partiality, & determined with ourselves, that if they gave the cause against us, we would appeal to the Privy Council.

2. Mr. Paris further acquainted us, that the Attorney was not ready to give his opinion in the cause of Watson till Monday next.

3. 50£ order'd to Francis Moor Store keeper at Frederica & private Secy. to Mr. Oglethorpe for 5 quartrs. of a year's Service from October 1735 to Jany 1736–7.

4. 20£ order'd to be pd. Mrs. Watt (to be recd. out of the Rent of her house at Savannah by Mr. Causton to whom She gave a letter of Attorney) and to be repaid to the Trust.

5. 20£ Order'd to Mr. Harbin for his trouble and expences, who was directed to go to Holland to procure Servants, and afterwards countermanded.

6. 2.2.0 Orderd to Mrs. Stanley the Savannah Publick Midwife now in England, to be repaid by her husband.

7. 25£ orderd to the Revd. Mr. Cha. Wesley, being the rest of his Sallary.

8. 10£ orderd to Mr. Kramer for his long attendance to receive instructions.

9. Seal'd Instructions to the Said Mr. Kramer to bring over

[1737] JOURNAL OF THE EARL OF EGMONT 271

from Germany 60 Moravian brethren or other German Protestants to be Trust Servants.

10. Mr. Wragg's proposal was read, offering to transport to Georgia from Holland Servants at the rate of 6.6.0 p head and that none Should be paid for who died in the passage. We agreed that he Should bring over 80 heads on that foot, and that none Should be under 12 years old or above 40.

11. 202.5.9 Orderd to Ri. Wilson gun maker for muskets lately Sent over, in case his bill on examination prove right.

12. 100£ order'd to Mr. Paris in pt. of ye charges accrued & accruing on the Carolina complaint.

13. A Certified Acct. from Mr. Causton dat. 29 Dec. 1736, being the value of 218.7.5 payable to Msrs. Soloman & Minis was referd to the Committee of Accts. to take into consideration.

14. Mr. McLahlan's proposal to Send over 100 Highlanders of the Cameron Clan to go at their own expence, was read. We answer'd we would give 20 bolls or bushels of meal of the Indian kind, and a musket and bayonet to each man, once for all, but could make him no allowance for procuring these Men as he desired.

15. On Reading a Silk & Cotton Dyer in Rotterdam wrote to us a letter, desiring leave that he might go to Georgia at his own expence, & there carry on his trade. But we agreed not to allow him to go, it being our purpose not to encourage manufactures in our Colony, but only to raise materials for our Mother Country to manufacture.

16. A Memorial was read from Capt. Thompson of the Two Brothers, desiring a Grant of 50 Acres belonging to Mr. West, formerly one of our Bailifs, & then when granted he might have leave to Sell it, and convert it into money.

The Case was, that he carry'd back Mr. West to Georgia, who had no money to pay for his passage. Wherefore he having obtain'd a Grant of 500 acres, he proposed to part with his wifes 50 acre lot (the Widow Hughes) to Capt. Thompson and thereby pay the Captain, & others of his Creditors. In this Mrs. West joyned, but it was necessary to have our consent.

Our reply to the Memorial was, that We could readily consent, that Capt. Thompson Should purchasse the 50 acres, but not that he Should afterwards Sell it to whom he pleased, for by Such an example, others would expect the Same liberty, which would turn the property of Georgia into a trade of Stockjobbing, & the lands would become deserted, whereas our business was to have the

Proprietors reside and cultivate their lands. When therefore the Capt. Should have found a purchasser who had our approbation, and would reside on the Land, we would allow Mr. West to make over the lot to the Captain.

17. Imprest to Aldn. Heathcote 425£.

18. Imprest to him more 250£.

19. Order'd that James Hazlefoot be advanc'd the charge of a Servant, and he to repay the Same in Georgia.

20. Grant of 150 Acres past to Mr. Tho. Upton.

21. Grant past to George Foster (Son of a Brewer's Son in London) of 50 Acres & who designd to Set up a Brewer's business in Frederica, but is not to Sell by Retail. He was to go at his own expence, appeard a modest youth of 20 years old, and his father Said he would give him 150£.

[N.B.] This 11 May 1737 Mr. Tanner, a young gentleman of Surry & neighbour of Mr. Oglethorpe (Since an Ensign in his Regiment) dined with Some of the Trustees. Who went for his amusement in the last embarkation with Mr. Oglethorpe to Georgia, and was employ'd by him in Several Services whilst there, & particularly among the Indian Nations, where he past 4 months in driving away the Carolina Traders who pretended to traffick with the Indians within the limits of Georgia without taking lycences from Mr. Oglethorpe our Commissary for Indian Affairs.

He Said the Indians are extreamly human to those in friendship with them, perfectly just in their dealings, & know not what it is to tell a lie.

That the Old Men were much pleased that we did not trade wth. them in Rum, for it made their young people mad, and disobedient to goverment. That they like better to trade with Us than with Carolina on that Account: but the young Men with Carolina.

That Tomachachi had a house of 3 rooms built like the rest of Clay, and cover'd with plank, that he keeps his parlour lock'd wherein is the picture of the Lyon we gave him, as also Mr. Oglethorpe's picture, in whose arms he Said (when he was ill last year) he wish'd he might [die.] That when he Sees company, or calls Councils, he Sits in this room.

That when he visited him, he gave him a very good dinner of rost and boiled Pork, Bufalo beef, fowl, & pancake, and Senawky his wife made tea for him.

He Said further, that all the Indian Traders have wives among the Indians, being necessary for dressing their victuals, and carrying on their business, and he believed there were 400 children So begotten. That being left and bred up by their mothers, they Speak both Indian & English, So that there are now few Indians that do not Speak English enough to be understood: but what ever is the reason, they do not care to do it but when drunk.

[N.B.] 13 May 1737. I went alone to the Georgia Office to look over the Books, & accidentally Mr. Paris came in, who told me he had at last got the Attorney Genls. opinion, and that he Said the Trustees were parties to Watson's complaint, because we gave the Magistrates of Georgia Order to continue her husband in confinement. Nevertheless, that this was no rule we Should be deem'd Parties in future Suits, the present being a mixt case.

I Said if we were Parties, then the Council board might think fit to order us to release Watson, and thereby usurp an Authority over us, wch. Some of our Board would not relish, esteeming themselves a Society of Gentlemen incorporated by Charter, over who by law the Privy Council has no power, but that if we had done amiss, we were to be in the Kings Bench, and there only. He reply'd, Mr. Oglethorpe was So much of that opinion, that he would not be present when the Board met on this affair, beleiving that the Majority of the Trustees would acquiesce in the attorney Generals Opinion.

16 May. 48.

Ayers, Robt.	C P	Vernon, Ja.	C
Holland, Rogrs.	C		

A Common Council was Summond this day to consider of the Attorney Generals answer to our queries (See Fol. 195.1) on the Representation to the Committee of Council on Watsons petition, But they were not a Board.

1. Order'd that the Magistrate of Savannah be wrote to, to give the Trustees particular information of the State of Joseph Watson's mind, confin'd for Lunacy.

2. Approved & Seal'd a Representation to the Committee of the Privy Council in relation to Joseph Watsons case, and our proceedings therein.

[N.B.] 17 May 1737. This day Mr. Oglethorpe acquainted the Trustees, that he had very lately a conference with Sr. Robert Walpole, and Shew'd him a Memorial which we intended to present him in a body, which Memorial he read twice, and Said, there is Something in this, pray let the Trustees come together and give it me in form, that we may afterwards talk it over, for there will be a Cabinet Council upon it. I am myself well enclin'd in the affair, but there are others who want to be convinc'd. I agree with you that tis an uneasie thing for the Trustees to be annaully obliged to apply for Support to Parliament, and indeed I can well judge they are uneasie, because it gives me trouble too, and therefore the best way will be as you desire in your memorial to put the provision of 6 or 7000£ a year for the Support of the Civil Magistracy on the establishment, and give it into Parliament by way of Estimate, as the charge of other Colonies is brought in. I cant Say I think So well of the Trustees as I do of the design, for many of them dont think well of me.

Then he added his approbation of Sending a Regiment for the guard of Georgia, if a Fund could be found.

Mr. Oglethorpe reply'd he might reduce Company's in the Islands and other Colonies, the pay of which might go towards the charge of a Regiment in Georgia, and So 700 Men would not amount to more than 15000£ *p* ann.

Sr. Robert Said he Should approve it if others did, but ask'd why he would not take on his the Govermt. of Carolina?

Mr. Oglethorpe answer'd, for the reason he told him before, because he would not lose his Seat in Parliament, and it was Sufficient for the Safety of Carolina & Georgia that he accepted the chief command of the military force with a Regiment, but he would go over on no other terms.

[N.B.] 17 May 1737. Embark'd at the Trustees expence for Georgia, On board the Two Brothers, Capt. Thompson, 4 Men.

19 May. 49.

1. Order'd that a letter be immediatly wrote to Mr. Causton to inform the Trustees whether Joseph Watson be return'd to his right Senses, & in that case to give him his liberty.

[N.B.] 19 May 1737. This day I recieved in the Country a printed State of the matters in difference between Carolina and Us, the Same being drawn up and Sign'd by Mr. Murry and Mr. Charles Clarke our Council, who this day pleaded before the Board of Trade. That Board went thro hearing part of the complaint and Evidences against us, and adjourn'd the further hearing to Wednesday Sennit.

[1737]   JOURNAL OF THE EARL OF EGMONT   275

25 May. 50.

Egmont	C	P	Anderson, Adm.	T
Lapotre, Hen.	C		Smith, Saml.	T
Vernon, Ja.	C			

A Common Council was Summond to grant lands for cultivation; to raise a maintenance for the Minister at Frederica, & for other business: but we were not a Board.

1. Benefaction reported of 10.10.0 bequeath'd by Mr. Morse of Dublin to be distributed among the poor German Protestants Settled in Georgia.

2. Order'd a letter to Mr. Causton, that the Magistrates Should call to their assistance the Physicians & Surgeons of the place to enquire into the case of Watson's Lunacy, and if he now found recover'd & in his right Senses, to Set him free, he giving 200£ of his own personal Security to behave well, and not provoke the Indians within our Province.

June 6. 51.

Ld. Carpenter	C	P	Oglethorpe, Ja.	C
Egmont	C	Ch.	Shaftsbury	C
Holland, Rogers	C		Vernon, Ja.	C
Lapotre, Hen	C		Bedford, Arthr.	T
LaRoch, Jo.	C		Hucks, Robt.	T

1. Report made that Sr. Hans Sloan had paid his 20£ Subscription towards Mr. Millars Sallary, our Botanist abroad.

2. Order'd that our Members who Subscribed towards building a Church in Georgia Should be call'd on, and certified to pay their money a month after the Call.

3. We alter'd our letter to Mr. Causton relating to Watson's lunacy, and directed that if he be now in his Senses, Sentence Should be past on him according to the Verdict brought in against him.

4. Order'd that it be refer'd to a Committee to consider of a Fast to be Kept in Georgia for a blessing on the people & to avert the danger of an Invasion.

5. Read a Memorial deliver'd by Mr. Jo. Vatt of his Services in Georgia with his petition for recompence. We order'd him 46.8.7 Carolina money, being the ballance of an Acct. he gave us; also

60£ Sterlg. which with 12£ he received of Mr. Causton in Georgia was in full for his Services there, & his attendance here Since his last arrival.

6. Resolv'd that 3068 pd. weight of Skins imported from Georgia by the Two Brothers, Capt. Thompson be Sold to Mr. Simond for 415.9.2 being at the rate of 2.8½ p pound. The money to be placed in the Bank.

7. Agreed with Saml. Smallwood to be a Clerk of the Stores at Frederica for 3 years, at 40£ p ann.

8. Refer'd to a Committee to consider of a Plan for building a Church at Frederica, or Savannah. Mr. Oglethorpe was for Staying till more money came in, in order to place the Capital at Interest in Carolina at 10 p cent, and only to build with the Interest money, But we thought the delay of building would be too long.

9. A certified bill of 188.8.4 arrived from Georgia was orderd to be paid William Clay, being for Cattle deliverd at Savannah.

10. Three other certified Accounts amounting to 372.19.2½ brought to us by Mr. Robt. Ellis, were refused payment.

11. Seal'd a grant of 300 acres for Religious uses in Frederica, In Trust to Willm. Horton Esq., Tho. Hawkins, 1. Bailif, Willes Weston, & Tho. Hird.

[N.B.] 6 June 1737. This day the Board of Trade proceeded on the hearing of the Carolina complaint. Counsellor Brown pleaded on their Side, but made nothing of it (tho a very able Counsellor) Counsellor Cha. Clarke was on our Side and Spoke well.

[N.B.] The Same day Capt. Dunbar attended the Board, being lately return'd from Georgia. He told us,

1. That the Allarm of the Spaniards intention to invade Carolina & Georgia continues, and He believed they will, but the whole Province are determind to defend themselves.

2. That the Forts at Frederica & Darien are finish'd and mounted with Cannon, but the muskets and Swords we Sent over prove bad.

3. That One Butler is Secured on board Capt. Gascoign, on Suspicion of being a Spie.

4. That the Governr. of St. Augustine who made the Treaty of Peace with Mr. Oglethorpe has been put in chains, and Sent to Old Spain, & is Succeeded by an Officer from the Havana.

5. That the person's name who gave advice of the Spaniards preparations at the Havana & St. Augustine to attack us is pub-

[1737] JOURNAL OF THE EARL OF EGMONT   277

lickly known, and printed in the Carolina gazet which is very unfortunate for him, for he will certainly be cast into prison.

6. That 80 Yamasee Indians belonging to the Spaniards had been Seen about our Settlements, and at Joseph's town our Centinal had been Shot at.

7. That the Spaniards had Sent Parties out to drive all Cattel they could find to Augustine, where they had great reinforcement of Men, and their advice boats were often Seen hovering about our Coast, but always retired when our Ships made towards them.

8. That at Augustine they were laying in Stores for 3000 Men for a year, wch. must be with Some ill intention towards us.

9. That the people of Savannah in their hast to erect a Fort for their defence had cut down the fine garden wood on the East of the Town, which was an ornament and Shelter from the East Winds, and would render the Town less healthy. That Mr. Causton declared against it and would have no hand in it, apprehending the Trustees would not approve it.

10. That Mr. Causton is more condescending in his Govermt. to the people, & they begin to be better reconciled to him.

11. That Mr. Ingham who Shew'd So much zeal for converting the Indians on whom we So much depended, & who went over for that purpose, was on a Sudden motion, none Knew why, Set out for England, & that there were letters from him to the Bi. of London, and to a Fellow of Eaton.

12. That Mr. Jo. Wesley had been at Charlestown, but for what cause was likewise unknown to him.

These Methodical Gentlemen, or Methodists as they call themselves are for the general pious and zealous for advancing the cause of Religion, but what ever they deliberate on and afterwards resolve, they fancy to be a motion of the Holy Spirit.

[N.B.] 8 June 1737. The Trustees recd. a letter from Mr. Causton (mention'd Fol. 194) that the Moravians in Georgia declared they could not in conscience fight, & if expected So to do would leave the Colony. A Copy of their letter to Causton was Sent us. In a 2d letter they exprest their intention to go away. Bad Subjects for a frontier Colony.

The Number of Trustee Boards & Committees held this year were 47, and of Common Council 17. The Number of days the Gentlemen met were 51; and the times each of them attended were as follows:

Common Counsellors		Trustees	
Archer, Tho.	5	Anderson, Adam	15
Ayers, Robt.	4	Archer, Hen.	1
Bundy, Ri.	10	Bedford, Arthr.	9
Ld. Carpenter	19	Belitha, Will.	4
Cater, Robt.	5	Bouverie, Sr. Jacb.	1
Chandler, Ri.	4	Burton, Jo.	4
Digby, Edwd.	3	Coop, Ri.	0
Egmont	50	Coram, Tho.	0
Eyles, Fra.	2	Ld. Darcy	0 dead
Frederick, Tho.	0	Derby, E.	0 dead
Hales, Steven	17	Gonson, Sr. Jo.	0
Heathcote, Geo.	14	Hanbury, Will.	0
Holland, Rogrs.	17	Hucks, Robt.	18
Lapotre, Hen.	33	Moore, Robt.	1
LaRoch, Jo.	36	Page, Jo.	1
Ld. Limerick	5	Philips, Sr. Erasmus	0
Oglethorpe, Ja.	23	Rundal, Tho.	1 Bi. of
Shaftsbury	9	Smith, Saml.	20 Derry
Sloper, Will.	2	Towers, Christn.	0
Ld. Talbot	3	Tracy, Robt.	0
Ld. Tirconnel	12	Tyrer, Geo.	0
Towers, Tho.	26	White, Jo.	8
Vernon, Ja.	36	Woollaston, Will.	0
		Woollaston, Fra.	0

The Persons Sent this year at the Trustees Charge were 22 Males & 10 Females, in all 32: which with 1044 Sent in the former years, makes 1076, of whom Foreigners 302, Brittish 774.

Private Grants past this year

			Acres
4 Augst. 1736		To Mr. David Blair	500
		To Mr. Thomas Body	500
27 April 1737		To Willm. Stephens, Esq.	500
11 May		To Mr. Thomas Upton	150
			1650

Public Grant

6 June	For Religious Uses at Frederica	300
		1950
Grants past in the 4 former years		48735
Total of Publick & Private Grants past in 5 years		50685

[1737] JOURNAL OF THE EARL OF EGMONT 279

Abstract of the 5th Years Acct. of Receipts and Disbursments, endg. 9 June 1737

CHARGE

To Ballance of last years Acct. remayng unapply'd,	} 5798. 6. 9 viz.
For Establishing the Colony: Genl. uses	} 474.15.10¾
For the Use of particular persons	155. 0. 0
For the building Churches	488. 0. 4
For the Use of the Missioners	243. 9. 1½
For the Saltsburg Missioners	50. 0. 0
For the Religious Uses of the Colony in genl.	} 386.15. 4¾
For Botany and Agriculture	0. 0. 0
Appropriated to answer Sola bills	4000. 0. 0
	5798. 6. 9
Money depending to be accounted for in Georgia	6344. 7. 1
Sola bills of Exchange issued in Georgia for the Colony's Service, which were not return'd to England for payment within the time of this Accompt	} 1333. 0. 0
Recd. In America from S. Carolina on Acct. of the Rum duty, reduced into Sterlg. money	} 333.19. 6
Grant from Parliamt. includg. Fees & Offices	10000. 0. 0
Recd. private Benefactions for establishg. the Colony	} 1837.13. 9
Recd. for the use of particular persons	112. 0. 0
Recd. for building Churches	55. 5. 0
Recd. for the Use of the Missioners	239. 8. 0
Recd. for the Use of the Scots Minister at Darien	41.15. 6
Recd. for the Religious Uses of the Colony in genl.	22. 2. 0
Recd. for encouraging Botany & Agriculture	126.13. 4
Recd. for 261 barrils of Rice brought from Georgia	} 859. 1. 6
Total of Charge	27103.12. 5

DISCHARGE

Apply'd in England,
 2567. 3. 8

By Stationary Ware & printing	40.18. 2½
House Rent, necessaries & Incidents	73.17. 2
Wages to Messengers & housekeeper, Rewards to ye. Secy. & Accompt. & to Sevl. persons & extraordy. Clerkship	506. 6. 3
	621. 0. 7½
Charge of Sendg. 32 persons to Georgia	1108. 8. 9½
Do. of engagg. Servts. foreigners & others Sent to Georgia exclusive of passage, bedding &c	124.10. 0
Do. of freight of Sevl. comodities from Georgia	506. 9. 4
Do. of bills of Exchange drawn on the Trust from America, & of Sola bills Sent to be issued in Georgia instead of drawg. bills	52.11.11
Law Charges in ye. dispute with S. Carolina	129. 2. 0
A Year & ½ allowance in full of 3 years contract with the Botanist, at 10£ ⅌ ann; & for the 1. paymt. of 10£ on the 2d Contract	
	2567. 3. 8

Expended in America, 21016.14.10, as follows

By Demurrage of Ships, & carriage of passengers from Savannah to Frederica	997.10. 9¼
Provisions Supply'd the Inhabitants from 8 Feby. 1735 to 27 Jany. 1736–7	4750.10.11
Live Cattel & Swine for the use of the Colony	614. 8. 7
Stores, working Tools & other Necessaries for the Colony, besides those Sent from England	828.11.11

[1737] JOURNAL OF THE EARL OF EGMONT 281

Genl. Works in clearing ground, making Roads, Sawing timber, erecting a Beacon, Corn & Saw Mills, labour in the Trustees garden & charges of Servants deliverd in Georgia to be employ'd therein	380. 8. 4¾
Pay of garisons and Work at Fort St. George in ye N. Division	85.10. 7
Do. of Fort St. George in the S. Division	465. 4. 6
Do. of Fort St. Andrew in the S. Division	405.10. 2¼
Ordnance, Amunition, Arms, cloathing, besides those Sent from England	448. 1.11
Scout boats, pettiaguas, & other boats, & freight of goods from S. Carolina to Georgia	107.18. 6¼
Presents to Indians for purchasing land	834. 1. 2¾
Expence at Augustine to preserve peace wth. the Spaniards	343. 2. 0
Incident charges in America & from thence of persons to England on Trust Service	239. 9. 8¼
Rewards to Sevl. persons in Georgia & America	661.12. 0
Advanc'd to Sevl. persons to Set up different Callings	236.15. 9¾
Application of particular benefactions	155. 6. 0
Expended on the Missionaries & Schools for convertg. ye Indians	154. 1. 2¼
Expended on the Saltsburg Ministers & Schoolmaster to 1 Novbr. 1736	50. 0. 0
Expended for encouraging Botany and Agriculture	125. 0. 0
	11883. 6. 0½
Dependg. to be Accompted for in America Supply's to ye Store house at Savannah	3087. 9. 9½

Do. to the Store house at Frederica	1489.10. 0½		
Advanc'd to Sevl. persons in America on Acct. of further Supply of the Colony, & expended by them, particular Accts whereof are not yet return'd	4556. 8.11½		
	9133. 8. 9½		
Total disburs'd in America	21016.14.10	21016.14.10	
Total disburs'd in England & America		23583.18. 6	
Ballance remaing. carry'd to next year		3519.13.11	

Charge, 27103.12. 5

Particulars of the Ballance carry'd to next Year	
Remaining for the general Uses of the Colony	921.12. 0
for the use of particular persons	112. 0. 0
for building churches	371.19. 9
for the missionaries use	328.15.11¼
for the Saltsburg Missionaries	0. 0. 0
for the use of the Scots Ministr. at Darien	41.15. 6
for Religious Uses of the Colony in genl.	408.17. 4¾
for encouragg. Agriculture & Botany	1.13. 4
Appropriated to answer Sola Bills	1333. 0. 0
	3519.13.11

1737-1738

*Transactions of the 6th Year
From 9th June 1737 to 9th June 1738*

[N.B.] 9 June 1737. The Board of Trade gave this day a third hearing on the Carolina complaint. The time was Spend from 10 a clock till one in reading & descanting upon affidavits in favour of Georgia, concerning the Several Indian Nations claim'd by the Trustees to be within that Province; concerning the 2 channels or Streams of Savannah River divided by Hutchinsons Island & opposite to the town of Savannah; and concerning our Magistrates Staving of Rum at Savannah in execution of his Majesties law for prohibiting Spiritous liquours imported into Georgia &c. In all which the Council on the other Side (Counsellors Brown and Noel) behaved rudely, insinuating that our Evidence were bribed; nay, they objected to the boards hearing the Affidavits of persons who are now in England (but necessarily absent from London) as un-usual, tho our Council Shew'd it was frequently done & received, & that their Lordships must accept of affidavits in Such case, because there is no power in the Trustees to oblige Evidence to appear, and make out their Informations viva voce.

At length our Council & Mr. Oglethorpe insisting upon a letter being read which Mr. Jenys Speaker of the Assembly of S. Carolina wrote to Mr. Oglethorpe, the Council of the other Side opposed it: whereupon everyone was order'd to withdraw, till their Lordships resolvd whether the letter Should be read and while they were So deliberating, I came away.

15 June. 1.

Egmont	C		Anderson, Adm.	T
Lapotre, Hen.	C		Burton, Jo.	T
Shaftsbury	C	P		

A Common Council was Summond, but no board could be made.

1. Some Georgia Sola Bills were cancell'd & fyled.
2. A letter from Mr. Jo. Wesley was read, giving account of disbursments, and expostulating with us for Suspecting him of

embezling mony trusted to him, and desiring to know his accusers.

All present were Surprised at this, and we orderd Mr. Martin our Secy. to write this very night to him, that we knew of no one body had accused him of doing any thing amiss, and therefore that he Should acquaint the Trustees who he had Such intelligence from: That we were glad Mr. Causton Supported him in his labours to make piety abound in the Colony, and that Mr. Whitfeild was going over to Settle at Frederica; and that we had made a grant of 300 acres for Religious Uses there.

22 *June*. 2.

Ld. Carpenter	C	Ld. Tirconnel	C
Egmont	C	Anderson, Adm.	T
LaRoch, Jo.	C	Smith, Saml.	T
Oglethorpe, Ja.	C	Lapotre, Hen.	C P

Again a Common Council Summon'd but we were not a board.

1. We drew up a 2d application like to that made in April last, in form of a letter, to Sr. Robert Walpole, desiring that we might not be obliged to go any more to Parliamt. for Support, but that the Same may be provided for by way of estimate in the manner other Provinces are Supported, for that the Trustees found it impracticable to continue their method of petitioning the Parliament. We further Set forth that it would be necessary Such estimate Should be 7000£ *p* ann. We also desired that a Regiment of 700 Men might be order'd for defence of the Province.

Then we order'd the Accompt. Should when it was fair drawn, get as many of the Trustees and Common Council to Sign it, and go with it to Sr. Robert.

2. Directed a Memorial to the Treasury for payment of the 20000£ granted by Parliament. this Session.

3. Agreed that Several Members Should be desired to discourse with Builders, and procure from them an estimate of building a church in Georgia of brick, the Same to be 80 feet long, & 40 feet broad in the clear, with a Square tower 40 feet high, and 20 feet Square from out to out. The Walls to be 3 feet thick, 10 feet high, and 2 brick & half & half [sic] upwards, all to be render'd and white wash'd on the Inside. No windows from 10 feet high to the ground, but loop holes for muskets on occasion. A pulpit, reading desk, communion rail and table, & no pews, but benches, as at Tunbridge.

4. Mr. Paris our Sollicitor attended, to acquaint us, that the Board of Trade Sat this morning to make their report upon the hearing of the Carolina complaint, but their Secretary would not tell him their result. Only he privately learned, that they had determined to put two questions to the Attorney & Sollicitor General before they concluded their report.

We thought it extreamly unfair to put questions to the Solicitor Genl. who was of Council against the Trustees, & we resolv'd that if it were So, Mr. Paris Should desire a copy of that reference, in order to be heard against it, by Council.

This was not the only instance of the partiality of the Board of Trade against us.

[N.B.] 22 June 1737. About this time, Mr. Oglethorpe was appointed Commander in Chief of the Military Force in Georgia & Carolina.

[N.B.] 24 June 1737. The Two Brothers Capt. Thompson Saild with 50 Men & 4 Women on the Trust charge to Georgia. Whereof 40 were Trust Servants.

[N.B.] On the 28 July 1737, Mr. Boltzius Minister at Ebenezar wrote to Capt. Coram That one half of the Saltsburgers Ship'd at Dover were dead in the Colony.

29 *June.* 3.

Ld. Carpenter	C		Hales, Steph.	C
Egmont	C	P	Vernon, Ja.	C
Lapotre, Hen.	C		Anderson, Adm.	T
Oglethorpe, Ja.	C			

A Common Council was Summond to receive reports relating to the Cash in the Bank on the 9. inst., for cancelling Sola bills, and to consider of a proper Plan for building a Church at Savannah. But we were not a board.

1. Mr. Paris our Sollicitor attended to acquaint us that this morning he apply'd to the Board of Trade for a copy of their Reference to the Attorny. and Sollicitor Genl. containing two questions put to them by their Lordships to help them in making their report upon the hearing of the Cause between Carolina & Us. And that he had told them the reason why he desired a copy was, that they took advice on those questions of the Sollicitor Genl. who had been of Council against us, by which on his giving an opinion he became both judge and Party in the Same cause. Wherefore it was our intention to require a hearing before the

Attorney General and him, that the former might be truly inform'd of the matters alledged on our Side. Mr. Paris added, that their Lordships were pleased to refuse our request, tho he produced to them two instances where in paralel cases they had granted it.

Hereupon we orderd Mr. Paris to apply to the Atty. General for a copy of the Reference, which it is doubtfull he will give, tho on Mr. Paris's Speaking to him he had promis'd to allow of a hearing before him.

Mr. Paris Said further, that the Board of Trade put a great hardship on him the Sollicitor Genl. as he declared to him in thus making him both Judge and Party.

2. Benefactions received 14.14.0 for the Mission, and 20£ promised, to be employed on the best branch of the Trust.

3. We resolv'd that this mony being given to particular uses, and therefore applicable by the Trustees without the necessity of a Common Council to direct the disposal, that it Should be aply'd to the filling out Mr. Whitfeild who goes Minister to Frederica, and of a Schoolmaster by him recommended, who goes with him. Accordingly we directed a letter to be wrote to him, that his desire of cloathes, a watch &c Should be complyed with, and that the Schoolmaster Should be provided with the Same.

4. The Same Mr. Whitfeild having wrote to us concerning two persons who are desirous to go over, & to take one lot between them, we directed that he Should be inform'd, that we cannot allow of the dividing Lotts, But that one may take a Lot, & the other may work for him as a Servant, or they may each of them have a Lot, one in Frederica, the other in a vilage Lot.

N.B. The practice of dividing Lots in Savannah is not authorised by us, and has occasioned differences there. It ought to be enquired into.

5. It having been left to a Committee finally to determine upon Mr. Gordon the late Bailif of Savannah's case, who apply'd for leave to Sell his lot, and to be rewarded for his Services. We call'd for him in, and exposed to him, that he was So far from meriting any thing of us, for his Services, that he had forfeited his Grant by coming over without leave, contrary to his covenant in that Grant and to the neglect of his Trust as first Bailif. However, that in compassion to his circumstances, he Should have leave to Sell his Grant, provided it was to a person approved of by the Trustees. That it must be done by a Surrender of his Grant, and the Purchassers taking out a new One. We also order'd he Should

have a years Subsistence for him and his wife allow'd, amounting to 14£ Sterl. which during his Stay in Georgia he had not demanded. But withall We Shew'd him that he was indebted 27£ odd money to the Trustees, being Cash advanc'd him, for which he was to Accompt. He pretended he knew nothing of it, but we orderd him a copy of the Acct.

N.B. It is perhapps not So regular for the Common Council to appoint Committees finally to dispose of moneys, but our Common Council boards are So ill attended & So few, that tis impossible to carry business on, without this expedient.

6. Some Estimates for building a Church at Savannah, and at Frederica were brought to us. One amounted to 430£ Supposing the Same were to be built in England; the other to 340£. But we concluded, that all charges consider'd Each church would Stand us in 500£.

6 July. 4.

Ld. Carpenter	C	Ch.	P	Oglethorpe, Ja.	C
Egmont	C			Ld. Talbot	C
Heathcote, Sr. Will.	C			Vernon, Ja.	C
Holland, Rogrs.	C			Anderson, Adm.	T
Lapotre, Hen.	C			Bedford, Arthr.	T
LaRoch, Jo.	C			Smith, Saml.	T

1. Mr. Paris acquainted us that the Attorney Genl. had refused to give us a Copy of the questions put to him by the Board of Trade because that board had refused the Same to us. Upon which, he, Mr. Paris, drew up a Memorial in behalf of the Trustees to be presented to the Privy Council, requesting they would order the Attorney Genl. to give us a copy of them. But that Mr. Murray our Council had advised against it, because he did not See the Attorney Genls. answer to those questions could be Such as could prejudice our cause before the Privy Council, when their report Should be made, and besides it might render the Board of trade more our Enemies.

2. Report of the Committee of Accts. was recd. concerning money issued, Sola bills, &c.

3. Resolv'd that 6288.9.4¼ be apply'd out of the 20000£ given by Parliament, when received, to make good the following demands, viz.

To make good the application of Sr. Jacob de Bouveries gift of 8000£ for cultivating lands, being So much of his 1000£ apply'd by the Trustees to other occasions & to be repaid to that fund _____ 389.8.9¼

 To answer a bill drawn by Mr. Oglethorpe, dated 27 April 1736 payable to Paul Jenys Esq., not yet come to hand ____ 200. 0. 0

 For a Credit on Caleb Davies at St Augustine in Oct. 1736, not yet come to hand _____ 100. 0. 0

 For a bill drawn by Mr. Oglethorpe dat. 20 Sept. to Capt. Macpherson, payable 7 July 1737 _____ 100. 0. 0

 Mony pd. by Mr. Verelts for the Trust Since 9 July 1737 _____ 105. 3.11

 For Sola bills pd. away by Mr. Causton without Mr. Oglethorpes Endorsement for which money was appropriated by the C. Council 29 April 1737 _____ 1500. 0. 0

 For the ½ years Sallarys of the Secy. & Accompt. due Mid yr. 1737 _____ 150. 0. 0

 For ¼ years Rent of the Office _____ 7.10. –

 For Sola bills Sent for the Service of the Colony Since Lady day 1737, orderd 21 March 1736/7 _____ 1000. 0. 0

 To Answer a certified Acct _____ 997. 6. 7

 To Do. _____ 271.18.11

 To Do. _____ 234.17. 3

 To Do. _____ 578. 2. 8

 To Do. _____ 69.12. 0

 To Do. _____ 266. 1. 8

 To Do. _____ 218. 7. 5

4. Resolv'd that a Committee of Embarkation be appointed to consider what provisions & tools may be necessary to be provided for the Colony of Georgia for the year 1737.

5. A Memorial of Mr. Jo. Vatt was read Setting forth his Services in carrying over Saltsburgers to Georgia, and rejecting it, being unanimously of opinion that he had received a full and honourable compensation for his trouble considering withall that he had not whilst there corresponded with the board as he engaged to do when he went, and had been recalled by us on account of his differences with Mr. Boltzius the Saltsburg minister. He had received from the Trustees & from the Christian Knowledge Society at different times 150£.

6. Defer'd the consideration of a Memorial presented by Mr. Simonds for demurrage of his Ship in Georgia by order of Mr. Causton.

7. Resolv'd that the house of Robt. Hows Parish Clerk at Savannah burnt down, be rebuilt at the Trustees charge.

[1737] JOURNAL OF THE EARL OF EGMONT   289

8. Letter of Attorney past to Mr. Verelts to receive at the Treasury 20000£ granted us by Parliamt. and pay the Same into the Bank.

9. Committee appointed of any 5 of the Common Council to draw on the Bank for 6288.9.4¼ which Sum we expect will answer all expences in the Colony to Lady day last, & in England to midsummer last.

10. Mr. Oglethorpe reported that he had presented our Memorial of the 22 June to Sr. Robert Walpole wherein we desired to be eased for the future from petitioning the Parliamt. for money, but to be put on an establishment. He Said Sr. Robert Seem'd to approve it. But it never was his intention: For whilst he kept us to petitioning, he kept us in dependence on him, which he was the more determined to do because of the number of members of Parliament who were Trustees of Georgia.

Egmont	C	Oglethorpe, Ja.	C
Holland, Rogrs.	C	Vernon	C

The Same Evening the Gentlemen here mention'd, met as a Committee, to consider of 3 New laws for the Colony, for which a Special Committee had been appointed 4 April last (vid. fol. 183) but had been neglected by those Gentlemen. The laws taken under consideration were 1. an Act to prevent Luxury in aparel and Furniture. 2. an Act to allow of Indian Evidence. 3. An Act to prevent gaming and running in debt. For these we drew up Several heads to be laid before the Common Council.

13 July. 5.

Egmont	C		Vernon, Ja.	C
Hales, Steven	C		Anderson, Adm.	T
Holland, Rogrs.	C	P	Smith, Sam.	T
Lapotre, Hen.	C			

A Common Council was Summon'd to order the making out Sola bills to be issued in Georgia for the Charges of the Colony there this year, and to receive a Report of the charges of building a Church at Savannah: But we were not a Board.

1. As a Committee of Embarkation we agreed with Mrs. Scot a clothier of Wiltshire to furnish the Board with 30 pieces of Duffils well mill'd and cover'd with wool, each piece to contain 30 yards in length & 7 quarters in breadth at 3.5.0 *p* peice.

2. As Trustees We order'd an extract to be made from our Of-

fice books of all orders & instructions Sent over at different times to Georgia, to which no returns appear to have been made to the Trustees; And that a Copy of them be deliver'd to Mr. Willm. Stephens our Secy. that he may enquire into the reason why no returns have been made, and inform the Trustees thereof immediately after his arrival there.

3. We drew on the Bank (according to the power given by the Common Council that any 5 Common Counsellors may make drafts) for 4448.6.8, to answer the following bills & accts. of disbursments incurred for Georgia, viz.

To Aldn. Heathcote pt. whereof was paid by him, the rest on Acct.	700. 0. 0
To Saml. & Will. Baker	997. 6. 9
To Pomroy & Sons	812.19.11
To Simpson Levy	218. 7. 5
To Lawrence Williams	371.18.11
To Peter & Jo. Simond	1347.13. 8
	4448. 6. 8

4. Mr. Verelts reported that he had received the 20000£ given by Parliament and lodged it at the Bank, & that the respective Offices had forgiven their Fees.

5. Mr. Philip Von Reck wrote that he could get no Saltsburgers to Settle in Georgia. He also desired to know whether the Trustees would enable him to Subsist in Georgia without land; to which we this day order'd an answer, that it is an establish'd Rule with the Trustees to Subsist none who do not intend to cultivate lands for their own Subsistance, and that he Should inform us whether he intended to return to the Colony; because if he did not return within Six months, the Grant of land made to him 7 Oct. 1735 would be vacated.

6. Mr. Paris attended to inform the Board that the attorney Genl. persisted in his refusal to assign a day for giving his opinion on the two queries put to him & the Solicitor Genl. by the Board of Trade, and he believed the Board would not make their Report on the hearing between Carolina & us till October next. N.B.: This is a fresh proof that the Board were from the beginning determined to lay all the hardship they could upon us.

7. A Letter was read from Jo. Brownfeild Register as Savannah giving a very disadvantagous Acct. of the people, which he tells us is to Set us right in our opinions of the colony, that we might not be led into a mistake concerning the Industry & Trade of the Province by an advertisment he read in the news papers relating

to Georgia. It Seems the people have cultivated little and are much disheartn'd, the Stores being empty, and no money in Mr. Causton the 1st Bailifs hands, to pay workmen, for which reason the Fort that was begun at Savannah is left unfinish'd, no canon mounted, & in its present condition more capable of anoying us Should an enemy come, than of defending. N.B.: Mr. Verelts told me the advertisment here Spoke of was put in by Mr. Oglethorpe.

8. Mr. Verelts likewise told me that Sr. Robert Walpole had promised Mr. Oglethorpe that 7000£ p ann. for the Support of the Colony Should be Settled in Parliamt. hereafter by way of estimate. But Sr. Robt. never kept his word.

9. A letter was read from Commodore Windham to Mr. Martin our Secy. dat. 12 May, advising him that Don Manuel Joseph de justitz Govr. of St. Augustine had wrote to assure him, he had not any thoughts of invading Georgia, but it was not prudent to rely on his Sincerity.

20 July. 6.

Egmont	C	LaRoch, Jo.	C P
Holland, Rogrs.	C	Oglethorpe, Ja.	C
Lapotre, Hen	C	Vernon, Ja.	C

A Common Council was again Summond to make out new Sola bills, as also to Seal Instructions for Mr. Stephens our Secy. But we were not a Board.

1. Mr. Ingham our Missioner for converting the Indians who came over (as he Said) to take Priests orders, and arrived two days past in town, attended the Board, & made us two requests: One in behalf of the Moravian Brethren, the Other in Behalf of Mrs. Musgrove our Indian Interpreter.

The Moravians being dissatisfied that the Magistrates Should expect them to fight in defence of the colony, it being against their principle to defend themselves, addrest Mr. Causton for leave to quit the Colony, wch. they repeated in a formal Memorial Sign'd by Mr. Spangenbert their Chief; to which Mr. Causton reply'd he could not excuse them without the Trustees orders. They added in their Memorial that if it was expected of them, they desired leave to Sell their lots & Improvments that they might pay every one their due, & then quit the colony. This was the Request they desired Mr. Ingham to make us in their behalf, who gave them an extraordinary good character.

We reply'd this was an affair that required Serious consideration. That Since it was the principle of those people not to fight, the Magistrates did wrong to require it of them, and we would give immediate order not to trouble them on that Acct. So that if this was all the reason for desiring to go away, there is no doubt but they will Stay. But that there was reason to Suspect, that as Mr. Spangenberg had been lately in Pensilvanea, there has been Some negotiation between him and Govr. Pen for Settling those people under him, there being Such conformity of principels between them and the Quakers. We therefore must write to that Govr. about it. For the rest, as these Moravians are only Servants to Ct. Zinzendorf, who is Proprietor of the 500 Acres they inhabit, we could not Suffer his Servants to depart without his leave, and even if he did give leave, we could not with out great injury to the colony, let them Sell their effects & go, they having convenanted to remain three years on the land, which they forfeit, if they go before that time expires. Besides Such an example would tempt every idle Freeholder to demand the like favour, who would expect that Englishmen Should be allow'd the Same favour as Foreigners, and So the Colony might be in part deserted.

2. His next request was in behalf of Mrs. Musgrove, that She might have leave to appoint a Successor to her Lot (her children by her late husband being all dead) and to assign the Same for payment of her debts. But he was so fair as at the Same time to acquaint us, that if She obtain'd this favour, She design'd to leave the Colony, and with her new husband Mathews Settle in Carolina, which would be a great loss to Georgia, She being our best Interpreter with the Indians, & having a great Influence over them.

We Reply'd we knew Mrs. Mathews usefullness, & the consequence of disobliging her, and therefore he might write her word, that he found the Trustees well disposed to favour her in all they can do consistent with the good of the Colony. That when we were a board, we would take her request into consideration.

Mr. Oglethorpe Said he did not believe She would go to Carolina, She owing there a thousand pound.

3. A bill drawn on us of 915£ for 70 pipes of wine of Madera Sent to Frederica, came to hand, together with a letter from Mr. Jeny's Speaker of the Assembly of Carolina, professing great zeal for our Colony, and exposing the necessity of Supplying Mr. Causton with money and Stores. That for want of it, he had engaged his own credit to Mr. Ellis for that wine. This appear'd to us a prodigious article, but Mr. Oglethorpe explain'd to us, that he

had given order for a Shipload of Madera wine to be brought from the Maderas, not to fill the Stores, but to pay the labourers and Workmen in wine instead of money, which they afterwards Selling to the Spaniards might make double profit, and thereby put money in their pockets without injury to the Trust.

4. A letter from Capt. Gascoign to Mr. Oglethorpe was read acquainting him that in April last, 30 Spainards on board a launce came to Amelia, and landed 16 of their number, upon whom our garison fired. That upon this they retired on board, but afterwards pretended they were come from Havana in order to go to Augustine, and came to Amelia to get a Pilot. On wch. the Capt. observed that Amelia lay quite out of the way, to pass from Havana to Augustine, and therefore he rather believed they came to take possession of Amelia and Settle there, if they had found that Island not possest by us. He farther advised, that Some Spanish Indians had two days Successivly attempted to Surprise and Shoot our out guard at Darien.

5. A large packet of letters & Accompts of the Issues of Stores, together with a Diary of all remarkable things which have happend from Lady day 1735 to the End of April came enclosed from Mr. Causton in a letter dat. 25 April 1737.

In his Diary he Shew'd the difficulties he met with from the Constables and Inferior Officers in the execution of his duty, the unrulyness of the people &c. He also acquaints us that Jo. Brownfield Register Spoke to him disrespectully of us, as that he thought the Trustees design'd to abandon the Colony Seeing they took no care of it. That he was Sorry he built his house, that the people must Soon desert the Colony &c. To which Mr. Causton reply'd, that the Trustees would give Sufficient directions when they Should See Mr. Oglethorpe, and that if the people went away because no longer Supply'd from the Stores, it was their own fault, for they had now been 4 years a charge on it.

He also took notice of information given him by one Kent, that there are divisions at Frederica, fomented underhand by one Hird, who makes Mr. Hawkins the 1st Bailif the Catspaw in that affair; on which Acct. Mr. Horton (whom Mr. Oglethorpe appointed Military Officer there) was gone to his Lot in Jekyls Island. That this Division proceeded from an attempt to call a Court to question Mr. Hortons behaviour.

6. Mr. Oglethorpe acquainted us, that Sr. Robt. Walpole ask'd him why the Trustees declined petitioning any more for money, but insisted So Strongly to have it by way of Estimate? To which

he reply'd The way by Estimate was more Secure, for then the Governments Servants dared not Speak against it, which they threaten to do against our next petition.

27 July. 7.

Egmont	C	Smith, Saml.	T
Hales, Steven	C P		

A Common Council again Summon'd to order Sola bills, & to Seal Mr. Stephens Constitution of Secy. & instructions, but no Board.

1. Mr. Stephens's Commission & Instructions were Seal'd, he being to go next week to Georgia on board the Mary Anne, Capt. Shubrick. We conceived we had power to do this, the Common Council having before Sworn him Secretary, & left it to a Committee to prepare his instructions.

2. Benefactions reported of Several 10£ pd. by the Trustees who had Subscribed towards building churches in Georgia, and of 100£ given for the Same purpose by a person unknown.

[N.B.] 1 Augst. 1737. A letter of this days date from the Havana to Mr. Oglethorpe, assured him that the Spaniards have Still an intention to attack Georgia, and were continuing to make preparations for it.

3 Aug. 8.

Ayers, Rob.	C	Heathcote, Sr. Will.	C
Chandler, Ri.	C	Oglethorpe, Ja.	C
Egmont	C P	Vernon, Ja.	C
Hales, Stephen	C	Bedford, Arthr.	T

A Common Council was again Summon'd to make out Sola bills for this years Service, To Receive Reports from the Committees to whom business was refer'd, and to issue money for payment of several certified Accts. of provisions & necessaries deliver'd in Georgia; But no Board.

1. The Seal was put to the Appointment of the Town Courts of Savannah and Frederica to be the Courts of Law for trying Offences agst. the Rum Act.

2. Mr. Cha. Wesley acquainted us that one Mr. Morgan who is in Priests orders is desirous to go to Frederica and assist Mr. Whitfeild who is only in Deacon's orders, and that Mr. Morgan desires no Sallary, but only the provision we give to others.

We desired our thanks might be return'd, & that he might be told he Should be inform'd what that provision is, & have leave to return to England when he pleased.

3. A letter was order'd to Mr. Tho. Causton, advising him of 2 clerks Sent him for the Stores, and one to be forwarded for the Stores at Frederica. In it he was told that the Trustees approved of his care of the Stores, and Striking off Such idle people as had not cultivated their lands. He was also order'd to See that the Arms were kept clean and in good repair and to tell the Constables that we expect this from them. The Trustees hoped that the Officers in Savannah as they expected any favour from them would cooperate in their Several Stations wch. friendship and unanimity to maintain the peace of the Colony, and give good example to all the Inhabitants. He was order'd to oppose any attempt to introduce Martial law. The Moravians were not to be obliged to take arms, but only find 2 men provided they were not Servants, one for Mr. Spangenbergs lot, the other for Mr. Nitchmans, but they were to be told that they could not depart the Colony, till Ct Zinzendorf Should apply for it, which he had not yet done.

They recommend to him to See that Mr. Jones Survey the peoples lots towards the West. They direct that Robt. Hows house be rebuilt out of the Trustees money, and acquaint him with Mr. Stephens going over Secy. whom they require him to assist.

4. A letter was wrote to the Magistrates of Savannah in general to put the laws in execution, & particularly that relating to Rum.

5. A letter was orderd to Mr. Tho. Hawkins 1st Bailif of Frederica, expressing our concern for the differences that have arisen in that Town among the persons in commission there, and requiring to know how the Same began. He was enjoyn'd to Send over a regular acct. of all occurrencies by every opportunity that offer'd. It was recommended to him to press cultivation, and See that the laws are obey'd.

6. I took an opportunity to tell Mr. Oglethorpe that unless 7000£ were promised us by Sr. Robert Walpole in the way of Estimate, it would be impossible for the Trustees to proceed, but we Should be obliged to Surrender our Trust into the Kings hands. He acknowledged the truth of it, and Said unless it were done he would not go back. But it was not done, he went back, and we continued our Service.

[N.B.] 3 Aug. 1737. Mr. Oglethorpe acquainted us this day, that Giraldini of Fitzgerald the Spanish Agent had been with Sr.

Robert Walpole to renew his complaint against Georgia, which he did in an insolent manner. He told him he had a 2d Memorial to deliver him by order of his Master, the purport of which was to complain that no answer had been return'd to his first Memorial given last year on the Subject of the Settlement of Georgia by English Subjects, which Country belong'd to Spain from the Southward up northward as far as 33 degrees & 50 minutes North latitude. That England has been encroaching on the Spanish Dominions ever Since the Revolution, But his Majesty of Spain finding himself in good condition is resolved to re-anex all that formerly belong'd to the Spanish Monarchy. That he hoped there had been time enough given Since the presenting the last Memorial for the English Settled in Georgia to remove. That as his Spanish Majesty had given himself up to Gods Service, he was desirous to See his own Dominions restored to him without bloodshed, but if otherwise, it would not ly at his door. That unless the English remove by fair means, his Governours knew how to oblige them thereto by force; and if his Majesty Should Send over any troops, & particularly Mr. Oglethorpe to command them, he Should take it for a declaration of War.

He then offer'd to put the Memorial into Sr. Robert's hand, who declin'd to take it, Saying the proper person to receive it was the Duke of Newcastle. Giraldini reply'd, the Duke was out of Town, and he look'd on this refusal as a put off. Sr. Robert then bid him present it to the King himself, which the other exprest himself averse to, for reasons which (Said Mr. Oglethorpe) it is not allowable for me to tell, tho Sr. Robert informed me of them, who added, that he had never met with Such treatment from a foreign Minister in the course of his life, & he knew not how to behave under it.

Mr. Oglethorpe added, that tomorrow a Council was to be held on it, and the King would be present.

(N.B.) 7 Aug. 1737. Mr. Oglethorpe had this day very warm words with Sr. Robt. Walpole concerning the 2d Memorial of Giraldini, which So terrify'd Sr. Robert by apprehensions of the Spaniards falling out with England in case any forces Should be Sent under Oglethorpe to Georgia, as the Memorial threaten'd, that Sr. Robert proposed to him to drop the design of Sending him over with a Regiment and accept of a Regiment in England in lieu thereof. At this Mr. Oglethorpe fired, & ask'd him what man he took him to be? And whether he thought he had no conscience to be the Instrument of carrying over 3000 Souls to Georgia, and then abandoning them to be destroyed by the Spaniards for the Sake of a Regiment? He also desired to know whether Georgia was to be given up yea or nay? If So it would be just and Kind to let the Trustees Know it at once, that they might immediately write to the Inhabitants to retire, and Save themselves in time. Sr. Robert reply'd he did not See the necessity of that.

[N.B.] 9 Aug. 1737. Count Zinzendorf wrote to us from Germany, to desire We would not require his Moravians to take arms for their defence, it being their principle not to fight; or if we do insist on it, that we would permit them to withdraw.

10 August. 9.

Ayers, Robt.	C	Heathcote, Sr. Will.	C	
Bundy, Ri.	C	LaRoch, Jo.	C	
Chandler, Ri.	C	Oglethorpe, Ja.	C	Ch. P
Egmont	C	Vernon, Ja.	C	
Hales, Steven	C	Anderson, Adm.	T	
Heathcote, Geo.	C	Smith, Sam.	T	

A Common Council was Summon'd to order Sola bills; To issue money for payment of certified accompts; To receive Reports from Committees.

1. A letter was read from Mr. Paris to Mr. Verelts, informing him, that he had been with the Attorny. General again, and at length obtain'd a transient view of the two queries put to him by the Board of Trade: which to the best of his memory were,

a. Whether any Act of the Trustees of Georgia, or of any other Province, tho confirm'd by the Crown, can grant an exclusive trade to the Indians within the Province?

To which the attorney Genl. reply'd, Such Act can not: The Subjects having a right by law to trade, and any Such Act would be contrary to law here, and void. But Such an Act may regulate the trade.

b. Whether the Georgia Act for maintaining Peace with the Indians, excludes all persons resident within & without the Province from trading, except they take out lycences from Georgia?

Answer. It dos exclude all persons, unless they take out licences thereby directed, and it is a proper regulation of trade.

These opinions were entirely Satisfactory to us, For We never pretended to hinder Carolina Men or others from trading with our Indians, or insisted on an exclusive trade, but only required them to take licences in Georgia, which was the thing the people of Carolina were most averse to.

2. Report of 10£ paid in for the building Churches.

3. A very long letter containing variety of matter was wrote to Mr. Causton.

4. Upon Mr. Oglethorpes acquainting us that the Cabinet Council is to Sit tomorrow on the 2d memorial of Giraldini, lately mention'd, We immediately drew up a Memorial of our own to his Majesty, and fixt our Seal thereto, declaring our mobility to defend the Colony of Georgia from the danger with which the Spaniards threaten us, & therefore desiring his Majesty to Send Some Force over to protect his Subjects there. We desired Mr. Oglethorpe to Shew it to Sr. Robert Walpole before the Cabinet Council met, and to present it with his own hands to the King.

On this occasion Mr. Oglethorpe Said, that Sr. Robert having refused to take Giraldini's Memorial, that Minister deliver'd it to My Ld. Harrington but first had alter'd it So as to run in Smoother terms, and had dropt his Masters pretentions to Carolina insisting only on Georgia.

5. The Trustees business being over, the Common Council Order'd payment of the following certified Accts.

A bill payable to Minis & Solomon in full of a certified Acct. dat. 4 May 1737, but conditionally _____ 25. 9.11
A bill payable to Jemmet Cobley for S. Carolina Currency appearing to be due to the value of 368.5.2, at the rate of 750£ currency for 100£ Sterl. The money orderd for paymt. thereof was _____ 49. 2. 1
A bill payable to Ja. Pierce for 70 Pipes of wine from Madera at 13£ *p* pipe, 100£ being pd. before _____ 815. 5. 0
A bill certified to be due to Tho. Ware for provisions __ 180. 7. 3
A bill certified to be due to Laurence Wessel for provisions and necessaries _____ 215.18. 5

6. Order'd that Mr. Oglethorpe do issue to Fra. Moore now in England 650£ Sterl. value in Sola bills of 5£ being the residue of 3150£ Sola bills made out 4 Oct. 1736 which remain lock'd up. And that the Said Issue be dated on a day in Novbr. last, before Mr. Oglethorpe and Fra. Moore left Georgia. And that the Said bills be Sent by the Mary Anne Capt. Tho. Shubrick under assignment to Paul Jenys Esq. at Charlestown to be forwarded by him to Mr. Causton as Cash for the Supply of the Colony. And that

any 5 of the Common Council be impower'd to draw on the Bank from time to time for the payment of the Said 650£ as the Sola bills become due.

7. Order'd that Sola bills to the value of 4850£ be made out after the following manner, 1850£ at 1£; 1500£ at 5£; & 1500£ at 10£. Making in all 2300 bills. And that the plates for printing Said bills be So alter'd as that Mr. Oglethorpe may Sign them whether in England or Georgia. The Said bills being design'd to defray the Expences establish'd for Georgia to Lady Day 1738.

8. Order'd that Mr. Danl. Booth be paid 26£ for the charge of making the Silk for the Queens Suit.

9. Draft made on the Bank for 815.5.0 to pay Mr. Pierce.

10. Another draft made on the Bank imprest to Aldn. Heathcote to answer expences, it being uncertain when we Should have another Common Council board.

11. Order'd that the Magistrates of Savannah have gowns to wear in Court: the Bailifs to be edged with Fur, and the Recorders to be black tufted.

[N.B.] 10 Aug. 1737. A letter from Mr. Hugh Anderson Inspector of the Publick garden and Mulberry trees, desiring a Town lot for one of his younger Sons was wrote me from Savannah. In it he told me, that his Short residence had not allow'd him to make any observations worth communicating to me, But in general he was fully Satisfy'd that the prudent measures of the Trustees and Support of the Publick would Soon bring the Colony in a great measure to answer the expectations of the Nation.

N.B.: before two years were out he fell into the Cabal for change of Tenure and having Negroes, and in 1739 quitted the Colony & Settled at Charles Town.

With this letter he Sent a Memorial to the Trustees, giving a very particular Acct. of the publick garden, and proposing divers things to make it more usefull.

His acct. of the garden is as follows: The Publick garden at Savannah consisting of 10 Acres of cultivated ground, regularly laid out to the Eastward of the Town, ly's upon the extremity of the Bluff or rising ground that banks the River. The greater part of it declines gently towards the East, falling into a Steep descent at the Eastern extremity into a Marsh or Morass not yet drain'd or cultivated. The Soil is extream Sandy, having less mixture of clay or loamy Earth than most grounds in the Province. Being Surrounded only with pales, it is no way divided nor fenc'd with hedging of any kind. Upon the Bank towards the River on the North Side of the garden, and likewise towards the Northwest, where formerly a grove of trees much Shelter'd the garden from the violence of the Winter & N.W. winds, all now is cut down, So that the garden is equally exposed to the injuries of the weather upon all quarters, by which means the Soyl wanting influences of the Suns heat, it necessarily follows that none of the tenderer plants whose roots run near the Surface of the ground, or whose texture of parts dos require protection from the Suns extream heat, & Shelter from the cold of the Winter can here Subsist. So that excepting Mulberrys and Peaches, whose hardiness and extensive Roots in the ground Secure them from those inconveniencies, nothing else can prosper.

Another inconvenience the garden Sustains, is by all the parts being exposed to Women, children, and every person who walks therein: Fruits, grapes, and what ever else grows, is pull'd and destroyed before maturity.

Notwithstanding these inconveniencies, the garden is very proper to Serve as a Mulberry Nursery for Serving the Colony, it being much the advantage of a Planter to bring his Trees from a barren & worse Soil to a rich and better.

But if it be the Trustees design to make the garden a Nursery & Repository of other productions, Such as may be proper for the Interest of the Colony to cultivate, as Vines, Olive trees, plants, druggs &c he then proposes

a. To protect & rear up from the Stocks of those trees cut down on the North and Northwest the new groth, to furnish Shelter for the garden as Soon as may be on these quarters.

b. To raise a hedge within the pales to enclose the garden, & to divide the garden by enclosures within.

c. To drain the Marsh to the Eastward of the garden, which will furnish it with a variety of Soil.

d. To build a green house.

e. To Set up a Laboratory & furnish it with books.

f. That a Well and pump be made in the upper part of the Garden.

g. That whereas 20 Acres more of ground much of the Same nature & Soil is reserved for the use of the publick garden, that the Same be enclosed, clear'd of brush, and the person who has the care of the Cattel Should fould them there every night.

[N.B.] On the Same 10 Aug. 1737 Mr. Causton Sent over his journal, the particulars of which See fol. 235.

[1737] JOURNAL OF THE EARL OF EGMONT 301

[N.B.] 12 Augst. 1737. Establishments for Savannah and Frederica were prepared to Send by Capt. Shubrick.

[N.B.] 16 Aug. 1737. Capt. Shubrick of the Mary Anne Saild wth. 8 Males and 5 females for Georgia on the Trustees charge.

17 Augst. 10.

Egmont	C	LaRoch, Jo.	C
Heathcote, Sr. Will.	C	Vernon, Ja.	C
Lapotre, Hen.	C P		

A Common Council was Summon'd to consider of Several Petitions before the Common Council & to receive Reports from Committees but we were not a board.

1. No business done, but a letter order'd to Mr. Causton, advising him of 1000 Sola bills consigned to Paul Jenys Esq. for the use of the Colony, and directing him how to fill them up. He was also desired to Send an Acct. by the first opportunity what demands remain unsatisfied at the time he writes next that the Trustees might know the State of their Cash and provide for answering the Establishments to Lady Day 1738 by Sending Sola bills in time Sufficient for that purpose. And they again required him not to exceed those Establishments.

They also order'd that the Seal of the Town Court of Savannah Should be kept under lock & key by Two Magistrates. Together with the Books & papers of Record.

[N.B.] 17 Aug. 1737. I was well inform'd this day that Ld. Wilmington, Ld. Islay, & Sr. Joseph Jekyl were much incensed at the Insolence of Giraldini's 2d Memorial, and that the last mention'd wrote a forcible letter to the Ld. Chancellor on the occasion.

At Mr. Oglethorpe's desire I wrote him a letter concerning the Spanish Memorial, and the Trustees inability to proceed in their Trust, unless a Regiment were Sent over for defence of the Province, and provision made for Support of a Civil Government, by putting us on the Establishment for 7000£ *p* ann. It was his opinion this would farther the business.

[N.B.] 18 Aug. 1737. This day the Council consider'd of Giraldini's 2d Memorial for 2 hours and adjourn'd the further consideration to 12 aclock next day.

[N.B.] 19 Aug. 1737. This day the Council met again at 12 aclock at the D. of Newcastles Office, where they Sat till near 5. And then resolved not to regard Giraldini's Memorial. And Mr. Oglethorpe was desired to hunt with the king.

24 Augst. 11.

Ld. Carpenter	C	Lapotre, Hen.	C
Egmont	C P	LaRoch, Jo.	C
Heathcote, Sr. Will.	C	Oglethorpe, Ja.	C

A Common Council was Summoned, but no business done of any consequence.

7 Septbr. 12.

Ld. Carpenter	C	Lapotre, Hen.	C
Egmont	C	Anderson, Adm.	T
Heathcote, Sr. Will.	C	Smith, Saml.	T
Hales, Steven	C		

A Common Council was Summoned to hear the Success of our late Memorial to obtain a Regiment for the Security of the Province, and to consider what was immediately necessary to be done thereon: & for other business. But we were not a board.

We did no business.

N.B.: This Summons was issued at Mr. Oglethorpes desire to consider whether it might not be proper to present a fresh Memorial to his Majesty on the Same Subject as the former; but we were all of opinion it was improper to press the king in that manner, who possibly might take it amiss of us to be So urgent with him to make us an answer more Speedily than he Should think fitting.

[N.B.] 14 Sept. 1737. There was a Summons of a Trustee board, but I did not attend it, remaining in the Country.

[N.B.] 14 Sept. 1734 [sic]. The Board of Trade made their Report of the hearing between us and Carolina, to the Lords of Trade, which was very partial in favour of South Carolina.

21 Septbr. 13.

Ayers, Robt.	C	Oglethorpe, Ja.	C P
Egmont	C	Towers, Tho.	C
Lapotre, Hen.	C	Smith, Saml.	T

A Common Council was Summon'd to grant lands, Send Sola bills pay certify'd Accts; but we were not a board.

1. A benefaction from an unknown Clergyman was reported, being to go towards building a Church in Georgia.

2. We Imprest by draft on the bank 1000£ to Aldn. Heathcote to pay Sola bills return'd for payment.

3. We read Jo. Brownfeild the Registers Accts. of the peoples cultivation at Savannah, which gave us very little Satisfaction, there being but 400 acres cleared, not So many fenced, and Still much fewer planted. The Out Settlements, & Inhabitants of Frederica were not mentioned by him. There appear'd also a great many exchanges of Lotts made, which being done without the Trustees consent are all illegal & void.

Mr. Oglethorpe was extreamly displeased wth. Brownfeild for authorising them, and told us, that he is one of the most active in improving the discontents of the people, who indeed are represented to us as much out of humour, at their poverty, the Scarcity of provisions, and the Tenure in Tale male.

4. We wrote a letter to Ct. Sinzendorf in answer to his of the 9 Aug. (See fol. 222) That all we require is that his 2 Townships or Lotts, Should furnish each of them One Man to be paid by them for defence of the Colony, which needed not to be Moravians. That the Safety of the Colony required this, but we Should not require his Moravians to fight, liberty of conscience being allow'd to all within our Province. That if this did not please him, and he has alter'd his thoughts (for when he was in England he agreed to this) then they Shall have leave to withdraw, on his acquainting us that 'tis his desire they Should.

[N.B.] 21 Sept. 1734 [*sic*]. This day Mr. Oglethorpe acquainted me that tis at length agreed that he Shall have a Regiment of 600 Men, and name his own Officers, only Capt. Cochrane an old Officer of the Irish Establishment, and of the Queen's Court was recommended to him by Mr. Hen. Pelham whom he could not refuse. That he intends to make Capt. Hugh Mackay Major (which happend otherwise for Capt. Cook an old Officer was made Major) & Mr. Horton with Some others of Georgia, Ensigns. That the rest would be half pay Officers who had Served in Spain, of whom he had given in a list. That his Regiment is to be composed of 250 Men drafted out of the E. of Rothes Regiment on the Irish Establishment, but now at Gibraltar, and the Independant Company now at Georgia, and the remainder he is to enlist here. That Ld. Rothes Regiment is to be recruited and filled up in England, & then return'd to Ireland.

That Sr. Robert Walpole was for Sending Ld. Rothes's Regiment entire to Georgia with the present Officers, and had So persuaded his majesty, as a thing immediately necessary, to prevent

Surprise, in case the Spaniards Should attack Georgia before Mr. Oglethorpes arrival there: by which he would have obtained two Ends, One that Ld. Rothes who had voted in the Scots affair against the Court, would have been punish'd by the loss of his Regiment; The other, that the Regiment & Officers (all except the Coll. being in Georgia) Mr. Oglethorpe would be kept here to drudge for the Court in the House of Commons under the awe of losing his Regiment.

To this Mr. Oglethorpe reply'd, he would not do by others as he could not bear to be done by himself; That to take my Lords bread away in the manner proposed, would justly occasion his resentment, and a duel must ensue.

But Sr. Robert wishing him to approve this Scheme as the readiest and most expedite way to have a Regiment, and what the king had actually resolved, Mr. Oglethorpe desired he would give him leave for the future to talk with the King himself on Georgia Affairs, and particularly on this of the Regiment, for he doubted not proposing to him Some other way that he would like much better, & more proper. Sr. Robert reply'd with all his heart, for it would ease him of a great deal of trouble, & he could not do many things himself wth. ye. King.

Accordingly, Mr. Oglethorpe had an audience of the King, who had embraced Sr. Roberts Scheme, and told Mr. Oglethorpe that it was the Speedyest way could be taken for the defence of Georgia. But when Mr. Oglethorpe exposed to him the hardship of Sending Ld. Rothes Regiment with all its officers only to deliver the men up to new Ones, and then return wth. the loss of their Commissions, whereas making a new Regiment gave his Majesty an opportunity of easing the Establishment of the charge of divers half pay Officers by placing them therein, he relished the thought, & So told Mr. Oglethorpe, only he added that his breach with the Prince So took up his attention, that he could not immediatly give the necessary directions, but would advise upon it.

Two days after which was last Monday, Mr. Oglethorpe waited on Sr. Robt. and found the King had Mentioned his Scheme to him, for Sr. Robert Said his Majesty had changed his thought, and would have the Regiment raised and Officer'd in the manner above mention'd. He added, that he had order'd Mr. Arnold the Under Secy. at War to bring him a list of all the half pay Officers.

Mr. Oglethorpe farther told me, that Sr. Robert has all along been backward in this affair of the Regiment, partly from not much affecting our Colony, and partly for fear of disobliging the Spaniards, to whose Minister he had not yet given the Cabinet Councils answer to the Memorial he So long ago presented, tho drawn up & perfected, which he Supposed he defer'd to do, till the Regiment for Georgia is actually embarked. But tho Sr. Robert is So backward in our affairs, all the Scots Lords, and Mr. Hen. Pelham, as also the E. of Pembroke, who was the person that advised the King to approve of Mr. Oglethorps Scheme, and Sr. Joseph Jekyl wrote no less than 3 letters to the Lord Chancellor to Spirit him up.

As to our application for a Support of the Civil Govermt. of Georgia and to put the Same on the Establishment, Mr. Oglethorpe Said Sr. Robert Walpole had promised it, and it was his own opinion that it ought to go hand in hand with the Regiment, for there would be no occasion for the latter, if the former were not maintained.

28 Sept. 14.

Egmont	C	Oglethorpe, Ja.	C
Hales, Steven	C P	Vernon, Ja.	C
Lapotre, Hen.	C		

A Common Council was Summon'd to Seal Grants to persons who were this week to go over at their own expence; to order payment of certified accompts; and Send Sola bills; but we were not a board.

1. Mr. Ziegenhagen and another Dutch Minister introduced to us one Mr. Thiel a German Physician recommended to go to Georgia by Mr. Urlsperger of Ausburg, to take care of the Saltsburgers.

We told them we would consider what encouragement to give him; and when they were gone, agreed to propose to the next Common Council, to give Mr. Thiel his passage, to give him 3 years allowance on the Stores, Such as others have, and to keep him a Servant; this being all we are able to do in our present circumstances.

2. A Proposal being made by the Parish of St. Gyles's to give the Trustees 3£ *p* head for 50 of their Charity School children from the age of 7 to 12 to be taken off their hands & be bound to us, the boys till the age of 22 & the girls till 18, after which the boys to have 50 acres each. We thought it a matter of Serious re-

flection, and therefore order'd a Summons for a Common Council on fryday next, the Vestry being to meet the tuesday following our answer.

3. Mr. Oglethorpe acquainted us that tomorrow his commission of Coll. would be Sign'd.

4. Also that Sr. Robert Walpole had assured him we Should have 8000£ p ann. for the Civil expences of the Colony by way of Estimate.

30 Septbr. 15.

| Ld. Carpenter | C | Lapotre | C |
| Egmont | C | | |

A Common Council was Summon'd to consider of the Proposal made by the vestry of St. Gyles, mention'd above, but we were no board.

Mr. Oglethorpe was fond of the proposal, and prest it earnestly last meeting, but being a matter of money and of great consequence it could not be agreed to but in a Common Council. As for myself I did not at all like it. I could not think it justifyable to transport poor children, most of them without parents or friends, and at an age when they could not help themselves, especially at a time when the Spaniards Still propose to attack our Province, as by the last authentick accounts we are inform'd. For Mr. Nicholson a South Sea Factor just arrived from the Havana (the very place where the Spaniards are making their preparations) told Mr. Wrag, Mr. Oglethorpe & others, that they have all things ready, but only wait for an Officer who is thoroughly acquainted with fighting in the Woods.

[N.B.] Sept. 1737. The State of the Colony in this month was drawn up by Mr. John Wesley our Minister at Savannah, which tho not deliverd to us until his flight from thence and return to England many months after, yet for order of time is proper to incert here.

Savannah Stands on a high Bluff which commands the River Savannah both ways for Several miles. The Soil is a white Sand for about a mile & half in breadth South West & North West. Beyond this Eastward is a River Swamp. Northward a Small wood in which was the Old Indian Town. South westward is a large Pine barren, bounded on each Side by Swamps, on the which edge run tracts of Oak land.

Augusta distant from Savannah 150 miles, and 5 from Old Savannah (or Moors Fort) is design'd to Stand on an old Indian feild, on a bluff 30 feet above the River. Mr. Rogr. Lacy Set out for this place with 15 Men on 19 May 1737 & arrived there the 29th. 7 More Set out 28 June. Soon after his arrival he began a Fort of Wooden piles musket proof, which was about half finish'd when he came to Savannah about October last. But the Lotts even in the Town were not then run out, neither was any house built therein, nor any more land clear'd than what they found So.

Old Ebenezar ly's about 25 miles West of Savannah: the Situation is very pleasant, there being many little hills with brooks between them, but the Soil is a white Sand. Here are Some large houses, 20 hutts, and about 100 acres of rough clear'd land. The English now Settled here Say that without manuring, the land will bear nothing, and that the Saltsburgers did not receive from their Common Feild, even the corn they put into the ground.

New Ebenezar ly's 6 miles Eastward from the Old, on a high Bluff on the Savannah River. There are Some Small Tracts of fruitfull land, but the greatest part of that adjoining to the Town is Pine barren. The Hutts, 60 in number are neatly and regularly built: the little piece of ground alotted to each for a garden, is every where put to the best use, no Spot being left unplanted. Nay even one of the main Streets being no more than was as yet wanted, bore them this year a crop of corn, over and above which they have cleard & planted this year 150 acres.

About 10 Miles East from this, on a Creek 3 miles from Savannah River is the Vilage of *Abercorn*. The Creek is west of the Vilage, with a large Cyprus Swamp beyond it, which on the other Side has Oak land. Here are 6 hutts, and near 50 acres of clear'd land: But the Inhabitants are part dead, & the rest removed, So that it is now utterly desolate.

Josephs Town commonly call'd Captains Bluff, is 4 miles below the mouth of Abercorn Creek. Here are a house, a Hut, & about 80 acres of Oak land clear'd.

A Mile below at that which was *Sr. Fra. Bathurst's* Plantation about 15 acres of good land are clear'd. Here is a hut too in wch. Sr. Francis Bathurst died.

A quarter of a mile from thence is Walter Augustins Settlement, where are a Saw Mill, 3 hutts, 2 Small gardens, and about 6 acres of clear'd land. But all these are left without Inhabitant, unless now and then a few Stragling Indians.

Capt. Robt. Williams and his brothers plantation is a mile below this: They have a house here, Several hutts, and above 40 Acres of Pine land cleard.

The Cowpen where Mrs. Mathews late Musgrove, lives, is a mile hence. She has a good house, 2 hutts and near 50 acres of clear'd land, part of it Pine land, part Oak & hickory.

Captn. Watsons lot joyns to this, where are a few acres of good land clear'd, on which is an unfinish'd house Swiftly running to ruin.

A Mile from this is *Irene,* a house built for an Indian School on a Small round hill in a little piece of fruitfull ground (about 5 acres) most of which is now clear'd.

The Indian town with about 10 Acres of clear'd land is within a Furlong of it.

The Village of *Highgate* Stands 5 Miles Southwest of Savannah on a Small rise. It has Pine land on 3 Sides, and a Swamp on the 4th. Eight families out of 12 remain there, viz: 1 English, 2 Swiss & 5 French. They have 8 hutts, and 2 as good gardens as the Soil permitts, which is a barren Sand, with near 50 acres of land well cleard.

A Mile eastward ly's *Hampstead* in a more fruitfull Soil, about 40 acres of which are cleared. Here are 6 Hutts, and 5 families remaining, viz: 2 Portuguese, 1 German, & 2 Swiss.

At Thunderbolt 6 miles South East of Savanna are near 100 ac. of land cleared, 3 houses which are musket proof, and a Small Fort which was mounted with 9 guns: But part of the Walls are now fallen, which the rest will Soon follow.

Four miles South of Thunderbolt is *Skidaway,* an Island containing by estimation 6000 acres. The Vilage is at the North East point, where are a Fort, 1 house, 4 hutts, and 20 acres of Oak land clear'd. A Mile Westward are 2 families who have also a Small Fort, a hut, and 10 acres of clear Oak land. But 9 of the 10 families Settled in the Vilage are dead or gone, and the hutts and Forts are hastening to ruin.

A Small Creek divides Skidaway from Tybee Island, On the S.E. corner of which fronting the Inlet were 10 or 12 families. They began 2 hutts and a house, but finish'd neither, and clear'd about 5 acres of Pine land. After most of them had drunk themselves to death, the remainder went to other places, So that the Island is now as before a Settlement of Opossums, Racoons, & the like Inhabitants.

About 20 Miles (by water) N.W. from Skidaway, on the Side of

Vernon River, is Mr. Houstons plantation. He has a house there, and about 20 acres of land clear'd, But now lives wholly in town.

Fort St. Andrews I have not Seen.

Fort Arguile Stands 20 miles above Sterlings Bluff on a high Bluff on the River Ogeeky. Tis a Small Square wooden building musket proof, with 4 little canon. The 10 Freeholders Settled here clear'd 30 Acres of Pine land, and built 1 house, with part of another, But all of them except 2 are now gone. The Houses are rotting away: the Walls of the Fort are partly fallen already, partly waiting for the next gust of Wind, and the land lying wast, will in a few years be as it was before.

50 miles beyond Mr. Houstons plantation is Sterlings Bluff on the Ogeeky River, where are Said to be 2 good houses, and above 100 acres of land clear'd. But One of the gentlemen who Settled there is dead, and the other two have quitted their Plantation, and with all their Servants are removed to Savannah.

St. Simons Island, having on the S.E. the Gulf of Florida, and on the other Sides, branches of the Allatahama River, is (according to the Survey made 1736) 45 miles in circumference. On the W. Side of it upon a Bluff Stands *Frederica,* having Woods to the North & South, to the East partly woods, partly Savannah, & partly Marshes. The Soil is mostly a blackish Sand. There is not much Pine land on the Island, the greatest pt. of the Woods consisting of Oak & other trees, intermix'd with many Savannah's and old Spanish or Indian feilds.

Darien lies about 20 miles from Frederica, and one from the ruins of Fort St. George built 15 or 16 years Since and abandond about 3 years ago. It Stands on the Continent upon a branch of the Allatahama, on a Bluff 30 feet above the River. From hence to Savannah, (about 90 miles) one may easily ride in 2 days & ½. The Soil is a blackish Sand bearing Oak near the Town, beyond which is the Pine barren. Besides what the present Settlers have cleard, here are Sevl. feilds formerly cleard (as is Said) by those of Fort King George.

5 Oct. 16.

Bundy, Ri.	C	Lapotre, Hen.	C	
Ld. Carpenter	C	Oglethorpe, Ja.	C	
Egmont	C	Shaftsbury	C	P
Hales, Stev.	C	Vernon, Ja.	C	Ch.
Heathcote, Sr. Will.	C			

A Common Council was Summond to Seal Grants of lands to be Sent next day: To order payment of Several certified Accts. and for Several material businesses.

1. The Accompt. reported that the E. of Derby had pd. to the Trust the last 50£ which the last Earl had Subscribed towards the Support of our Bottonist Mr. Millar, but had declined continuing that Subscription.

2. Mr. Oglethorpe reported that his Majesty had given him a Regiment of 600 Men for the defence of Georgia.

3. Report from the Committee appointed to consider of Peter Gordons Memorial (late 1 Bailif of Savannah) being made, Resolv'd that he be allow'd 13.7.1 for the arrears of 1 years provisions due to him and his wife; and that he have leave to dispose of his house & land to Such person as on his appearing before the Trustees Shall be approved of by them.

4. Rejected Mr. Jo. Vatts petition for a farther consideration of his Services in Georgia.

5. Orderd that 1500£ of the 4850£ Sola bills which were made out the 10 of August last, be Sent immediatly to Georgia.

6. The Accompt. reported the State of the Trustees Cash to be on the 30 Septbr. last as follows: viz. Sola bills Orderd to be made out and yet unsent to Georgia, which will provide for an exceeding of the Establishment to Lady day 1738 as far as the Sum of 700£, and also appropriating money for all the Sola bills Sent & to be Sent, & for all particular Uses besides,
Ballance in the Bank for the Colonys use the 30

Sept. 1737	5977. 6. 0¾
And in Aldn. Heathcotes hands	1452. 6. 7¾
Total to be apply'd to ye. Colony	7429.12. 7¾

Whereof for the following demands,

The Ballance of the Accts. of Servants from Scotland unsettled, about	30. 0. 0
For 99 heads & ½ of foreign Servants Sent from Cowes, and for the Ships delivering them at Tybee	619.15. 0
For cloathing and maintaining them, & the 40 Servants from Scotland at 6.10.0 a year each head for 2 years, until their labour can defray the charge	1813.10. 0
For beef butter & Tallow from Ireland, & Flowr & beer from England, & freight & primage thereof to Georgia	1256.18. 0
For the Saw Mill & freight & primage to Georgia	331.10. 0
For 300 pair of Shoes	60. 0. 0

[1737] JOURNAL OF THE EARL OF EGMONT 311

For 6 pieces of Strowds, 40 pieces of duffils, and for dying the Strouds & packadge	185. 0. 0
For 300 Indian guns in List Cases	127.10. 0
For 500 weight of bullets, & a barril of Powder for Darien	8. 7. 6
For freight thereof, & 50 Muskets for them	1.10. 0
For freight of Mr. Tho. Stevens & 3 Men Servants to Georgia	25. 0. 0
For Working tools for 100 Men Servants at 20 Shillings each	100. 0. 0

Also the following certified Accts.

To Messrs. Crockat & Seaman	16.13. 1¼
To Mr. Simond for Stores deliver'd by Capt. Diamond	49.18. 6
To Montagu & Compy.	173.18. 5
To Capt. Dunbar	7.13. 3
To Messrs. Pitt & Tuckwell	223. 9. 8¼
To Willms. & Compy. p Ball.	96. 3. 3¼
To Robt. Perriman	132. 5. 4
	700. 1. 6¾
Office charges in England for 6 months to Lady day 1738	300. 0. 0
	5559. 2. 0¾

In cash 7429.12. 7¾
Charges 5559. 2. 0¾

Ballance 1870.10. 7 which remains to answer accidl. and unforeseen demands, out of which the expence of the Carolina & Georgia dispute must be defrayed, whereof 100£ has been paid.

7. Orderd that Pitt & Tuckwells certified Acct. for tools be paid ---- 223. 9. 8¼
Orderd that Perimans certifyd Acct. for cattel be pd. ---- 132. 5. 4
Orderd that Montaguts certified Acct. be pd. ---- 173.18. 5
Orderd that Robt. Williams certified Acct. be pd. ---- 96. 3. 3¾
Orderd that Capt. Diamonds certd. Acct. for flower be pd. ---- 49.18. 6
Orderd that Crockats certd. Acct. for Molossus be pd. ---- 16.13. 1¼

8. Resolv'd that 50£ be paid to the Revd. Mr. John Wesley for a years Sallary due Michlemass last.

9. Orderd that 50£ part of the 200£ formerly directed for a

recompence to Mr. Tho. Causton for 4 years Service be paid him.

10. Orderd that 50£ be given to Jo. Amory & his wife in provisions & necessaries, he giving proper Security to repay it.

11. Orderd that 150£ be imprest to Aldn. Heathcote on Acct.

12. Orderd that a coper Mace gift be prepared & Sent for the use of the Magistrates of Savannah.

13. Orderd that 15 barrils of Scots herrings at 15 Shillings *p* barril be Sent to the Colony.

14. Mr. Wrag desiring to be paid in hand 250£, in pt. of the agreement for carrying over the Palatin Servants, it was refused, because the Same is unusual, and because if he Should have money before hand, it would be his Interest that they Should die in the passage.

15. One Ja. Burnside petitioning that he might have lands in Georgia, (besides those he already has) to be held in the manner of Church leases in England, the consideration thereof was postponed, most of the Trustees present thinking, that altho it may be a right and advantagious thing hereafter, yet in the present infant State of the Colony it is not fit.

16. It being difficult to make Common Council Boards, and the punctual payment of Sola bills being very necessary, orderd that any 5 of the Common Council may draw on the Bank for the Same.

17. For the Same reason, Resolv'd that any 5 of the Common Council may draw on the Bank as far as 5000£ as occasion Shall require for payment of provisions from England & Scotland, for the expence of Servants from Cowes & other charges, in pursuance of the Orders of the Committee for providing necessaries for this years Service for Georgia.

18. Seal'd the Indenture with Saml. Lander who goes over to Georgia to assist Cooper the Millright.

19. Grant of 500 Acres orderd to Lieut. Ja. Cochrane.

20. Grant of 3000 Acres orderd for the Soldiers of Col. Oglethorpes Regiment, to be parcell'd out in 5 acre lots to Such of the Soldiers as Shall desire it, and to be held by them during the time of their continuance in his Majesties Service, and then to revert to the Trust, if they quit the Service or are orderd away.

Some of us objected that it was hard to deprive them of their Lotts when they had cultivated them, but Col. Oglethorpe assured us the Men would be well contented with the condition proposed.

22. Grant past to John Amory of Boston in Lincolnshire Yeoman of 150 Acres.

[1737] JOURNAL OF THE EARL OF EGMONT 313

23. Grant past of 500 Acres to Mr. Robt. Hay of Scotland.
24. Divers letters were orderd to be Sent to Mr. Causton, Mr. Willm. Bradley, Mr. William Stephens, Mr. Will. Horton, and Lieut. Moore Mackintosh, containing Several directions as to the disposal of Servants, directions concerning provisions &c.

[N.B.] 8 Oct. 1737. The 3 Sisters Capt. Hewet Saild with 160 Foreign Servants from Cows to Georgia; whereof 78 males & 82 females. They went on the Trustees charge, and arrived ye. 21 Dec. following.

[N.B.] 12 Oct. 1737. The Georgia Pink Capt. Danbur Saild with one Foreigner and 3 English Servants, all males for Georgia, but was first to call at Cork to take in a loading of provisions. He arrived in Georgia the 16 Jany. 1737/8. These 4 went on the Trustees expence.

[N.B.] 18 Oct. 1737. The Minerva Capt. Nicholson Saild for Georgia with Mr. Tho. Stevens and his Servant at the Trustees charge. He arrived in Decembr. following.

19 Octobr. 17.

Egmont	C	Vernon, Ja.	C
Lapotre, Hen.	C P	Smith, Saml.	T
Oglethorpe, Ja.	C		

A Committee was Summon'd to consider of petitions, & of proper letters to go by the King George Capt. Ayers, and to order the Sending more Sola Bills by that Ship, But we were not a board.

1. John Burtons petition for 2 Servants to assist him in Georgia, the expence of whom to be repaid by him, was rejected, 1. because we have no money left to advance on Such occasions, and have no reasonable expectation of being repaid; 2. because others would desire the Same favour, who have as great reason to desire it as he; 3. because we have occasion for the Servants we have Sent to cultivate the Trust lands, or to be placed with other persons already intended to have that favour allow'd them.

2. 109½ heads of Servants being Sent in October last from Cows to Georgia by Capt. Hewet, we order'd a letter to go by the next Ship to Causton, informing him, that those Germans are to have 6 weeks allow'd for payment of their passage by such Masters as Shall take any of them: and those only who were not taken off on Such condition were to remain Servants to the Trust.

3. Mr. Godfrey Town Clerk of Southampton, Sent us his bill

of charges for examining into the condition of those Germans, and we orderd his bill Should be paid, amounting to 15.17.3.

4. Rebecca Cheeswright (who in Dec. 1736) left the Colony, petitioned that She might have a portion of her deceased husbands effects in Georgia. It was refer'd to Mr. Verelts to examine how that affair Stands, and report what was proper to be done in it. N.B. This vile woman had received 60 lashes for barbarously cutting an Infant down the back with a knife, and then fled the Colony, but this did not occur to our minds.

5. James Burnside who marry'd the Widow Bovey, desired he might be made Secure in her Grant, wch. another person claim'd. But it appeard the person under whom that other person claim'd had forfeited, and Bovey's 1st. husband had a grant made to him, wherefore we ordered that Burnside Should be made Sensible how the affair Stands, and that his wifes Tenure is Secure.

6. Eliz. Morrice petitiond in behalf of her Son Tho. Morrice, that being near out of his time of Service, he might have a Man allow'd him, to help him in cultivating. But we refused it for the Same reason we refused John Burton.

7. Edward Jenkins complaining that thro lameness he could not cultivate his 50 acre lot, desired we would grant him 500 acres (part of an Island containing 1000 acres near Skidaway) whither he might go by water. We resolv'd it Should be first enquired whether he had cultivated his 50 acres. N.B. This man had a grant of 100 acres 17 May 1733, but was uncertain where to take it up.

8. William Cooksey, Son to an Alderman of Woster desired further time to pay the remainder of a Sum advanced him, and that we would make him a new grant of 500 acres. We made him the like answer as to Jenkins, that we must first know if his 50 acre lot was cultivated. N.B. It did not occur to our minds that his 50 acre lot in Savannah No. 9 is Swamp overflowd.

[N.B.] 22 Oct. 1737. A certain person named Jo. Savy wrote from Cadix to the Trustees, that he had run from S. Carolina for debt to Georgia, from whence in June 1735 he Ship'd himself for England, which was but a pretence, for when he came into the British Channel, he went in a French fishing boat to Diep where he landed the 19 Augst. following. That he proceeded to Paris, and being poor apply'd himself there to the Spanish Secretary, and by him wrote a letter to Don Joseph Patinto at Madrid giving an account of Georgia, who Sent him immediatly money to come to Madrid to give him a larger Acct. of those Settlements, and afterwards Sent him to the Havanah in order to go against Georgia. That in August last the Spaniards Sent 400 Men to St. Augustine, & the Vice Roy of Mexico gave order to Send 1000 more. That they had Sent Artillery, provisions, and every thing necessary to attack Georgia in May next.

That they had Sent a new Govr. to Augustine Don Antonia Redondo an Ingenier.

That himself designed for London to cast himself at the Trustees feet, and implore our pardon which he thought himself unworthy of, having offended his God, his King & his Country.

That he had Surrender'd himself to the Capt. of the Grampus, who would carry him to the Commodore at Giberaltar, from whence he would proceed to London, and as he had made the Sore, would Soon heal it. That he goes at Cadix by the name of Michael Wall, but his true name is Jo. Savy, Nephew to Jo. Lewis Paulham in Token house yard, Exchange Broker.

[N.B.] 3 Novbr. 1737. The King George Capt. Ayers Sail'd with 2 Moravian boys for Georgia.

9 Novbr. 18.

Ld. Carpenter	C	Lapotre, Hen.	C
Egmont	C P	Vernon, Ja.	C
Holland, Rogrs.	C		

A Common Council was Summon'd, to order a Grant of 500 Acres to Col. Cochran's brother; To consider of the Report of the Board of Trade upon the dispute between Carolina & Georgia; and afterwards to go into a Committee to consider of Several matters. But we were not a Board.

1. Our Accompt. gave us an estimate of the charges of the Two Brothers Capt. Thompson, who went 24 June last to Scotland, for Trustee Servants to be Sent to Georgia. And upn. casting up the Several Articles, & adding thereto half the expence of a Surgeon to go the voyage & take care of the passengers (the Owner who had many on board at his own expence, paying the other half) We found a ballance of 35£ Still due to him, over and above the money already paid him. Which 35£ we order'd Should be p. him.

2. We drew on the Bank to pay divers expences incurr'd.

3. One Mrs. Hart whose husband went to Georgia to avoid his Creditors, and is there a Servant to William Abbot appear'd, and desired her husband might have leave to return for England, She furnishing a Servant to Willm. Abbot during his absence, and

bearing all the expence of his return. Her intention was that he might take the benefit of the late Debtors Act, and that being done to return with him & her 2 children to Georgia. She Said She had an annuity of 40£ which She would Sell to make her husband a clear man with his Creditors. We thought her proposal reasonable, but doubted whether her husband could arrive time enough to receive the benefit of the Act. We desired her with Mr. Chapman her Trustee and her lawyer to meet judge Holland tomorrow at his chambers, to consider what could be done in the affair.

4. Mr. Paris our Sollicitors attended, and presented us a copy of the Board of Trades Report to the Council Board upon the dispute between Carolina & Georgia. Upon reading it, we unanimously agreed that it was a partial & untrue representation of the affair, and order'd him to prepare a Short petition for the approbation of our next Board, to be presented to the Council Board, for a hearing against the Said Report.

16 Nov. 19.

Ld. Carpenter	C	LaRoch, Jo.	C
Egmont	C	Oglethorpe, Ja.	C
Hales, Steven	C P	Vernon, Ja.	C
Lapotre, Hen.	C		

A Common Council was Summon'd to order an application to the Lds. of the Council to be heard against the Report of the Lords of Trade relating to Carolina and Georgia; To order a Grant of 500 Acres to Geo. Preston, Esq.; And then to go into a Committee of Accts. to examine the payment and Vouchers of the last years Acct. endg. ye 9 June. But were were not a board.

1. Our Accompt. acquainted us that this very day Ships are taking up by the Goverment for the Transport of 300 Soldiers, 150 Women, & 130 children for Georgia. That the King will after their arrival there maintain them for 6 months at his own expence, during which time their Subsistance Should run on, which is a great encouragement. We also purpose to allow to each Soldier 5 acres to be cultivated & enjoy'd by him whilst he remains in the Service, which is 7 years; after which, the King giving him leave to quit, the land is to go to the Recruit who Succeeds him, and the former to be allow'd in lieu thereof 20 acres to him & his heirs male for ever.

2. We examin'd all the Vouchers of the last years Acct. endg. 9 June 1737.

3. We form'd a petition to the Privy Council to be heard against the Board of Trades Report.

[N.B.] 19 Nov. 1737. The Two Brothers, Capt. Thompson, Sail'd for Georgia with 34 Males & 26 Females, all Servants at the Trustees charge, and arrived 14 Jany. 1737/8.

[N.B.] [no date] The frugality of the Admiralty at this time was admired at. For when the greatest hast was necessary to have the Regiment of Coll. Oglethorpe in Georgia, That board to Save 20 Shillgs. *p* tun hired 10 rotten transports to carry the Lieut. Col. & Stores to Giberaltar where part of the Soldiers were to be taken, which Transports after 3 weeks delay were by the Surveyor declared unservicable; whereas there were vessels enough in the River who offer'd themselves at a higher price, who had they been accepted, the Lt. Coll. would have Sail'd long Since, and by this time been on his departure from Giberaltar to Georgia.

Another Strange mistake was the Order Sent to the Ordenance board to put on board the transports only 10 barrils of powder; but the D. of Arguile Master of the Ordenance Said he was Sure it was a mistake in the Clerk who wrote the Order, and therefore command 100 barrils Should be Sent. Were the former no mistake he Said he would answer what he did. He had the order but on Satturday, & the powder was ready on monday, which Shews his affection to Georgia.

23 Novembr. 20.

Ld. Carpenter	C		Oglethorpe, Ja.	C
Egmont	C		Vernon, Ja.	C
Hales, Steven	C	Ch.	Archer, Hen.	T
Holland, Rogrs.	C		Hucks, Robt.	T
Lapotre, Hen.	C	P	Smith, Saml.	T
LaRoch, Jo.	C			

A Common Council was Summond to consider of a letter from the D. of Newcastle's Office forwarded from Madrid relating to Georgia. To order a Grant of 500 acres to Geo. Preston, Esq. To order the Encouragmt. of lands for the Soldiers of Col. Oglethorpes Regiment: And to order the payment of certified Accompts.

1. The letter of John Savy (vid. fol. 233) to the Trustees was read, with one enclosing it from Mr. Stone of the D. of Newcastles Office. We had just received another from Savy now landed at Falmouth (to the Same purpose as the former), and a prisoner in Pendennis Castle.

We order'd Copies of both these letters to be Sent the D. of Newcastle, and with them a Short Memorial that the man might be brought up to London & examin'd.

2. Whilst we were Setting, Mr. Caustons journal to the 10 August arrived, together with Several Accompts to the amount of 1379.7.4. We order'd Mr. Verelts to examine them, and if he found them truly computed & cast that they Should be paid: for which purpose

3. We drew on the Bank for the Said Sum of 1379.7.4.

4. Order'd an Instruction to the Committee for Sending over to Georgia the Sola bills orderd to be made out 10 Augst. last, that they be careful to keep So many Sola bills back as are the amount of any certified Accts. that may hereafter come to hand and be dated after the arrival of Mr. Stevens in Georgia, who Saild the middle of August last with the establish'd allowances. Of which Sola bills 1800£ part of the 4850£ have been already Sent & 3050£ remain. Orderd also that the Said Committee do consider whether the Supply of provisions & necessaries recd. in Georgia from July last to the time of Mr. Will. Stevens arrival which is or Shall be known will not be So far assisting to the Colony, as to lessen the necessity of Sending the whole Sola bills remaining, 500£ p month being the computed expences abroad one month with another.

5. John Stonier of Skidaway desiring leave to quit his Grant, And

6. Hugh Anderson desiring another 50 acre lot for his 2d Son, The Same were refer'd to a Committee to consider of.

7. Grant past to Geo. Preston junr. of Valyfeild in Perth, Esq., brother in law to Lieut. Col. Cochran, of 500 Acres, with leave to absent himself during pleasure provided he Sent 10 Servants to cultivate his land, and perform'd his Covenants.

8. Grant past to Lieut. Col. Cochran of 500 Acres.

9. Grant past to Majr. Will. Cook of 500 acres.

10. Orderd that each Soldier of Col. Oglethorpes Regiment Shall have an alottment of 5 Acres to cultivate for his own use and benefit, and Shall hold the Same during his continuance in his Majesties Service in Georgia. And for further encouragement, Resolv'd that each Soldier who Shall at the End of the 7 years Service from his inlisting in the Said Regiment be desirous to quit his Majesties Service, and Shall have his regular discharge, & Shall Settle in Georgia, Shall on his Commanding Officers certificate of his good behaviour be entitled to a grant of 20 acres, to hold to

himself and his heirs male forever. To these resolutions the Seal was put.

11. Capt. Dunbar applying for leave to change his 500 Acre Grant at Josephs town, to another to be Set out where the Regiment whereof he is a Captn. Shall be quarterd, It was refer'd to Mr. Oglethorpe to Settle that matter with him.

[N.B.] Mr. Caustons journal to the 10 Aug. 1737 mentioned on the other Side contained the following particulars:

1. That the Lt. Govr. of Carolina had recd. a letter from Capt. Davis at St. Augustine, that they Shortly expected 1000 Men there. Which confirms the Acct. John Savy wrote us.

2. That the Merchants & Shopkeepers of Carolina are very hot, angry, & full of Scurrilous language against Georgia, but the Inhabitants of the Country are the contrary: that those who are in the Interest of Georgia are brow beat and turn'd out of the Assembly.

3. That Danl. Demetree who had been at Charlestown for the Trustees Service, had a Servant taken from him there by order of 2 Justices of Peace, which Servant is the property of the Owners of the pettiagua, Inhabitants of Georgia, and was bound by Indenture at Savannah & the Same duly enrolled.

4. That the Light House on Tybee Island is in danger of falling.

5. That every thing is quiet in the Indian Nation: but there was double the number of Indian Traders, viz. 16 from Carolina, 4 from Virginia & 10 from Georgia.

6. That Mr. Bradley whom we Sent (20 Oct. 1735 & arrived feb. 1735/6) to instruct the people in agriculture, behaves himself very unseemly to the people; pretends to a Commission from the Trustees to take the care of all their lands, and that if any One possest his land without his knowledge, he would Seize on every thing he found on the Same. That under pretence of the extensiveness of his Commission, he engrosses all the Cattle, & declares he is entitled to a certain number, and will Serve himself first. That he keeps all the Trustees Cattel bought by them to his own use, whilst Several people (particularly at Highgate) have the Trustees orders for Cattel, & are in great want of them.

7. That Mr. Urlsperger had wrote to Mr. Oglethorpe, which his letter to Mr. Causton wholly contradicts.

8. That Mr. Patrick Mackay had without leave Settled on Wilmington Island, where he employ'd Negroes.

9. That Mr. Causton finds his power doubtfull not being given

him in writing, and that written orders would be necessary for him to act by.

10. That the Colony is everywhere in want of provision, which with the want of money, yeilds a melancholly prospect.

With this Journal, Mr. Causton Sent us the Copy of a letter he received from Will. Horton, Esq., Military Commander at Frederica, complaining of the turbulent disposition of many of the people, & their inclination to disperse, and also of his being try'd most unjustly for felony, he having only employ'd a boat for 2 days to Capt. Gascoign, on affairs of the Colony, and that by consent of one of the Owners of the boat. In the Same letter Mr. Horton represents Mr. Jo. Wesley in a very bad light, as that he had wrote to Some of the Freeholders of Frederica to be Steady, and abide by what they had Said of him the Said Horton, and to be Sure to prove it when call'd on. That Wesley had lately wrote to him, that he would demand justice of the Trustees against him, but he Mr. Horton despised what the formal fellow could Say or write of him: But yet he might obtain his Ends of keeping Frederica in a continued Scene of un-easiness, if his Stuff were Suffer'd to pall current among the people, many of whom were ready to mutiny.

7 Decembr. 21.

Ayers, Robt.	C	LaRoch, Jo.	C
Bundy, Ri.	C	Oglethorpe, Ja.	C
Egmont	C	Vernon, Ja.	C
Hales, Stev.	C	Anderson, Adm.	T
Heathcote, Sr. Will.	C	Hucks, Robt.	T
Holland, Rogrs.	C	Smith, Saml.	T
Lapotre, Hen.	C Ch.		

A Common Council was Summon'd to grant 500 Acres to Capt. Wood who goes over with Col. Cochran; To order payment of Several certified Accompts from Georgia in August and October last; and to consider of the letters recieved by Capt. Coe Since the last meeting.

1. Report was made from the Committee of Accts. that they had examin'd the Annual Accompts. from 9 June 1736 to 9 June 1737, and that the ballance of the Said Acct. endg. 9 June 1737 remaining unapply'd was 3519.13.11, which Sum ly's in the bank. The board agreed thereto.

2. Resolv'd that any 3 of the Common Council wait on the Ld. Chancellor & Master of the Rolls with the Said Acct.

3. Order'd that when presented, 150 copies thereof be printed.

4. Several certified Accts. being come over for paymt. they were orderd to be paid, and a draft on the bank of 1914.12.0 was made to pay them.

5. Draft made also on the Bank for 668.8.0 to pay the residue and freight of the Irish Cargo of privisions.

6. Orderd 500 whole deal boards to be bought & Sent to Savannah for building a Church.

7. Several certified Accompts being Sent over, but advice coming that Since the dates of them, 1650£ in Sola bills were arrived in Georgia (for which money is appropriated in the Bank to answer their return).

Resolved that the Said certified Accts. be returnd to Georgia for payment there, they being in themselves only bills of parcells of goods, Sold and deliver'd to be paid for in England or Georgia, as the Trustees think proper.

8. Order'd that publick notice be given in Georgia that the Trustees having Supply'd, and intending to Supply the Colony with Sola bills in order to answer the expence thereof, No bills of parcels or certified Accts. whatever for provisions or necessaries Sold and deliver'd in Georgia for the use of the Trust or money due or to grow due there, on their Acct. will be paid in England. That their Storekeepers have received orders to defray all expences & charges of the Colony by the Trustees Sola bills remitted to them, to be issued for that purpose. And that no other payments will be made by the Trustees for the charges abroad, but by the payment of the Sola bills Sent from England to defray Such charges.

N.B. This was a wise order, & it would have been well it had been given before, for the liberty of taking up goods, & making expences, & then certifying the Same for payment in England, was Strangely abused by Mr. Causton our 1 Magistrate, and plung'd the Trustees into prodigious difficulties.

9. Resolv'd that no more Sola bills be Sent to Georgia, till the Trustees are enabled by a new Supply to answer them.

10. Mr. Hugh Anderson having wrote his desire that a 50 acre lot might be granted to his Second Son who is under age, we refused it, being contrary to our Rule to grant land to Minors, neither could we grant land to others in Trust, but we were willing

to Make Mr. Anderson a Grant of a Country lot for any number of acres under 500, & then he might put his 2d Son into his grant of 50 acres now in his possession, of wch. he was to be informed. Resolv'd therefore that the Said Son of Hugh Anderson may have a 500 Acre lot if his father desires it.

N.B. We were not willing that both Father and Son Should have town lots in Savannah.

11. Grant of 500 acres in the Southern division of the Province past to Willm. Wood, formerly a Sea Capt. It was Said he is worth 3 or 4000£.

[N.B.] This 7 Decbr. 1737 was read at the board a presentment of the Gr. Jury lately arrived from Savannah against Mr. Jo. Wesley our Minister, consisting of a charge of 9 articles, the principal whereof were that he refused to bury a person because he was not of his opinion, a Methodist; refused also to christen a child without dipping, unless his Parents would declare he could not bear it without danger of his life. That he divided the publick prayers & read but half, & this at 7 a clock & not at 5. That he refused the Sacrament to Mrs. Williamson without giving a reason, & refused it likewise to others who were not of his opinion, tho they had formerly communicated. That he assumed to be Ordinary of Georgia, &c.

With this Presentment came a letter from Mr. Will. Williamson her husband, complaining heavily agst. Mr. Wesley for refusing his wife the Sacrament, and conversing with her contrary to his express command, to the disturbance of her & himself, & to the giving great Scandal, for all which he desired reparation of the Said Mr. Wesley, or he would leave the Colony. He also enclosed to us a letter wrote by Mr. Wesley to his wife, accusing her of lying, breach of faith, &c; and Sent us therewith his wifes deposition wherein She Swears that he offer'd to marry her, & on that condition to make fasting and frequent communion easie to her, and to abandon his design of preaching to the Indians, but to fix himself in Savannah.

Dr. Bundy endeavourd to excuse Mr. Wesley in Some particulars, Shewing out of the litturgy that Mr. Wesley's refusal to christen the child unless dipt, or to bury a person not of the Church of England unless Satisfy'd he had been baptized, was no more than what by law he was obliged to, and had he in the latter case comply'd, he would have lost his preferment. That possibly this might be his reason. That by the litturgy also, and law of the land, any person intending to communicate must Send his name the day before to the Minister, who if he knows of any objection to his taking it, is to admonish him of his fault, and the person must publickly declare his repentence of the Same. That by letters and papers read, it appeard Mr. Wesley had reason to take Some things ill, and it would be justice to hear what he could Say for himself before we resolv'd any thing concerning him. This we thought reasonable, and agreed that the Substance of the things charged against him Should be drawn out, & Sent to him to answer. But this came too late, for on the 2 of this Same month he fled the Colony to avoid giving Bail in the Court of Savannah to Stand a Tryall.

With the former Presentment came over a Remonstrance from the Same Grant Jury against Mr. Causton, Signd by above 40 of the principal Inhabitants of the Province.

We took notice of the principal things urged against him in order to frame a letter to Said Causton that he might answer to them. Most of the charges were trivial, & accusations of arrogance & passion, and others were matters the Trustees had before given their judgment of, and approved in Causton.

It appears there is a great Spirit of contention there, & a disposition to be under no proper Subordination of Goverment.

Mr. Oglethorpe, Mr. Vernon, Dr. Hales, judge Holland & I had Some discourse of erecting at Savannah a Sort of Council to be assistant to the Bailifs, and the Same for Frederica, but we Knew not of proper Subjects for that purpose.

14 Decbr. 22.

Ld. Carpenter	[C]	LaRoch, Jo.	[C]
Egmont	[C]	Oglethorpe, Ja.	[C]
Holland, Rogrs.	[C]	Vernon, Ja.	[C]
Lapotre, Hen.	[C]		

The Common Council were Summon'd to meet in Committee, to peruse the Brief for council prepared by Mr. Paris for the hearing at the Council board against the Report of the Lords of Trade.

1. We perused and Settled the above mentiond Brief.
2. We Imprest 500£ to Aldn. Heathcote to pay Sola bills.
3. Sundry letters were this day orderd to Mr. willm. Williamson; To Mr. Jo. Wesley: to Mr. Causton: To Mr. Stephens: To Willm. Bradley: To Mr. Hugh Anderson: & to Mr. Boltzius.

[N.B.] 14 Decbr. 1737. The Substance of the letters wrote this day, mention'd on the other Side was,

1. To Mr. Williamson, that we had Sent a copy of his letter & wifes affidavit against Mr. Jo. Wesley, to the Said Mr. Wesley to answer to, but that he had done wrong to print the presentment and affidavit agst Mr. Wesley, wch. was taking a remedy, and apealing to the World at the Same time he was applying to the Trustees to consider his case.

2. To Mr. John Wesley, that they enclosed to him Williamsons letter & his wifes affidavit to answer, and Suspended their judgment till his answer came.

3. To Mr. Causton, that tho he had Sent his Cash books from 2 Nov. 1736 to the last of June, 1737, he had omitted to Send them from the last July 1736 to the end Oct. 1736. And that he had also omitted to Send his Diary.

That Advices of and certified Accompts were come from him to the Amount of 3293.19.4 Sterl. being for provisions & necessaries Supply'd the Colony. And the Trustees having Sent him Since Capt. Diamonds arrival with 1000£ in Sola bills, the Sum of 2450 more in Sola bills & now 200£ more in like bills, These are the last Supply The Trustees can Send him until a new Grant is made by Parliament. That the last mention'd 200£ with the former Sola bills mention'd above, and the before mention'd certified Accts. Since Midsummr. last amounting in the whole to 5943.19.4, the Trustees were Satisfied he was fully Supply'd to answer the demands abroad to Lady day next, according to the establish'd allowances & orders Sent him, wch. demands he was to discharge with the Said provisions, necessaries & Sola bills without certifying any more Accts.

That he Should Supply the Ebenezar people wth. hogs & poultry, & over & above give them 30£ towards building their Ministers house. And that he Should order prayers to be made for the Prince & Princess the Duke &c the Queen being dead.

4. To Mr. Stephens, acquainting him with the Queens death, & alteration of the prayers.

5. To Willm. Bradley, that the Trustees are Surprised he took on him an authority which he was not intrusted, viz. the care of all the lands, and that he pretended to engross the cattel, as if he had a title to Serve himself first to the detriment of others who have the Trustees orders for Cattel. That the Cattel under his care are at the disposal of Mr. Causton, and that he is to communicate to him the Trustees orders wch. he is to obey. That tis

his duty to act in his proper Station, & behave orderly, and that with respect to his immediate dependance on the Trustees, they had Sent over a copy of their agreement with him.

6. To Mr. Hugh Anderson, that the Trustees think it most convenient & most for his 2d Sons advantage, that he Should have a grant of 500 acres in that Sons name, but his present lot of 50 acres must descend to his eldest Son, wherefore this last cannot have the grant of 500 acres.

7. To Mr. Boltzius, that the Trustees are Sorry to hear the Saltsburgers are in danger of losing their crops this year, but they might be assured of Such general assistance as will be granted to others on So melancholly an occasion.

That the Trustees cannot give leave to change the bad garden lots wth. better ground. That 30£ was orderd for building his house & a School, & a cock & hen to each Man, and a Sow a Turkey hen & goose to every 5 heads of the 3d Transport of Saltsburgers.

[N.B.] 20 Dec. 1737. Mr. Stephens our Secy. in Georgia wrote us a long Acct. of the difference between Mr. Causton, and Mr. Jo. Wesly, together with the flight of the latter out of the Colony. Also of Mr. Caustons difference with Will. Bradley.

He also takes notice of a Set of Malecontents, who tho ready to Support the Civil power, are like to be the occasion of great mischief, by their exclaiming agst. the Tenure of their lands, and the losses they Sustain for want of Negroes. That many had been influenced to think with them, and they design'd to make a representation of their case to the Trustees. He laments the deficiency of Magistrates, Mr. Dairne being dead before he came, and Mr. Vandeplank, 1 Constable, dead also. Coates the next Officer run away with Mr. Wesley, Mr. Tho. Jones the next, and also Surveyor Seldom in town, and Mr. Fallowfeild the 4th grown chagreen.

That the Publick garden was neglected & in a very bad condition.

That Mr. Tho. Stephens was arrived on board the Minerva, Capt. Nicholson.

He wishes there were a passage boat entertained by the Trustees to go between Savannah and Charlestown, & proposes it may be a light rowing boat with 4 or 6 Oars, the Men to be Trustee Servts. That this would be a Saving rather than an expence to the Trustees, baiting the 1 cost of the boat which may be 16£, the expence of occasional hiring boats to go to Charlestown being exorbitant.

That it might also hinder the Scandalous practice of the Carolina people's opening our letters.

That Lt. Governor Broughton of S. Carolina died the end of Novembr. last, and Col. Bull was proclaim'd Presidt. of the Council to act in his Stead, who has a good disposition towards our Colony.

That they were So healthy at Frederica, they had not buried one Man Since Col. Oglethorpe left them, and the people were orderly and industrious on their lands. That divers of them at the Darien had 20 bushels of corn on an Acre. He wish'd he could Say as much for Savannah.

That Capt. Thompson was arrived the 20th Novbr. from Scotland, and all well on board, with the loss only of 1 old Man, a woman & a little child in their voyage.

That Capt. Hewet was the day of his writing arrived with the Palatines, but had been 10 days before off our bar not daring to enter for want of a pilot, which indeed is wanting to Savannah.

21 Dec. 23.

Ld. Carpenter	C		LaRoch, Jo.	C
Egmont	C	P	Oglethorpe, Ja.	C
Heathcote, Sr. Will.	C		Smith, Saml.	T
Holland, Rogrs.	C			

A Common Council was Summond to consider of payment of more certified Accts. recd. from Georgia & for other business, but we were not a board.

1. Mr. Whitefeild our Minister design'd for Frederica attended, and desired he might not wait for Col. Oglethorpes departure but Sail next Satturday with the 3 Ships who with Lieut. Col. Cochran and other Officers of the Regiment go to Giberaltar there to take up Soldiers. He also desired that a youth recommended by him might be allow'd passage and Subsistance, being design'd for School master to the Orphan house intended to be erected by him.

We granted both his requests, not doubting but the next Common Council would yeild thereto.

2. Capt. Burrington late Govr. of North Carolina desiring the Trustees to advance him 200£ which Should be repaid us in Charlestown, the Treasury having given an order for him to receive that Sum out of the first money arrising in that Province, due to the Government. We consider'd thereof, and found Such

[1738] JOURNAL OF THE EARL OF EGMONT

difficulties attending it, that we excused our Selves from complying therewith.

3. Col. Oglethorpe acquainted us that the D. of Newcastle desired a Committee of 2 or 4 of our Members might attend him from time to time as he Should desire it, in relation to the examination & confession of John Savy, and the Spaniards design upon Georgia. That endeavours had been used for that mans escaping Since he was brought to town: that a Sallary of 1000 pistoles had been Settled on him by the Court of Spain, and great dealings past between him & Patinho ye Spanish Minister before he died: but for other Confessions he had made, the Duke desired no mention might be made of them, because they were matters that touched all Europe.

We caused the Dukes request to be enter'd in our books and appointed Mr. LaRoch, Col. Oglethorpe, Mr. Tho. Towers and Mr. Vernon to be a Committee to attend his Grace.

4. Col. Oglethorpe & Mr. LaRoch then told us, that this morning Sr. Robt. Walpole desired them with any others of the Trust to come to him, & receive his assurance, that our application for 8000£ *p* ann. for carrying on the civil affairs of the Colony to be granted by way of estimate & not by petition Shall be comply'd with.

N.B. But he broke his word Soon after.

[N.B.] 5 Jany. 1737/8. Capt. Whiting of the Whitaker Saild for Georgia with 5 Males on the Trust charge and arrived 7 May 1738.

There were also 2 men more who went by another Ship, but I know not the name or Captain. They also went on the Trust acct.

11 Jany. 24.

Egmont	C	Oglethorpe, Ja.	C
Heathcote, Sr. Will.	C	Shaftsbury	C
Lapotre, Hen.	C	Vernon, Ja.	C
LaRoch, Jo.	C	Smith, Saml.	T

A Common Council was Summond to consider of what was proper to be done on Several certified Accts. received from Georgia, whether to return them for payment there, or to pay any of them here. But we were not a Board.

1. The certified Accts. from Georgia coming So fast & in So large Sums, as not only to consume all our money, but even run us deeply in debt if not for the future prevented. We orderd our

Accomptant to write this very day to Mr. Causton that we absolutly would pay no more Such certified Accts. But had Sent him back those he had certified Since 15 July last to the 17 October amounting to 1961.17.7 to be paid out of 3650£ Sola bills that Since August to December had been Sent him.

2. We drew on the Banks 250£ to pay Several demands.

13 Jany. 25.

Egmont	C	Shaftsbury	C
Heathcote, Sr. Will.	C	Vernon, Ja.	C
Oglethorpe, Ja.	C		

A Common Council was Summond to peruse the Trustees Case on the Report from the Lords of Trade & Plantations relating to the dispute with Carolina: But we were not a Board.

1. Mr. Paris our Sollicitor presented us a draft of the State of our case above mentioned, which we found exceedingly well drawn, and orderd him to print when Sign'd by our Council, and present to the Lords of the Privy Council when the hearing or appeal from the board of Trades report Should be appointed.

18 Jany. 26.

Archer, Tho.	C	Lapotre, Hen.	C
Egmont	C		

A Common Council was Summond to consider of the Several certified Accts. lately recieved from Georgia. To order the General Accts. to the 9th of June last to be exhibited, pursuant to the Charter, & to consider who of the Trustees Should attend the Ld. Chancellor & Master of the Rolls therewith, but we were not a board.

1. Mr. Paris attended to acquaint us that the Committee of Privy Council had order'd a hearing on Wednesday next, but that Mr. Clark & Mr. Murry our Council desired our Brief might be Shorten'd, and not exprest in So Strong terms.

25 Jany. 27.

Ayers, Robt.	C		Lapotre, Hen.	C
Bundy, Ri.	C		Sloper, Will.	C
Egmont	C		Towers, Tho.	C
Heathcote, Sr. Will.	C	Ch.	Vernon, Ja.	C

[1738] JOURNAL OF THE EARL OF EGMONT 329

A Common Council was Summond to agree to the Trustees general Acct. for the year endg. 9 June last, and to order the Same to be exhibited pursuant to the Charter. And to consider of the Several certified Accts. lately received from Georgia brought for paymt.

1. The Committee of Accompts reported that they had examin'd the Annual accts. from 9 June 1736 to 9 June 1737, and that the ballance remaining unapply'd was 3519.13.11.

2. The Board agreed thereto, and orderd that any three of the Common Council might wait on the Ld. Chancellor & Master of the Rolls therewith, and afterwards that 150 copies thereof Should be printed.

3. The Accomptant reported that pursuant to the Order of Common Council of 5th Octobr. last, wherby any 5 of the Common Council were empowred to Send the residue of the 4850£ Sola bills, (directed to be made out of the 10 of Augst. last) that 500£ had been Sent, and that in the whole £2000 of the Said Sola bills had been Sent.

4. A Multitude of certified Accts. coming from Georgia to the Office, were this day read, and it appearing, that Since the dates of these certified Accts 1560£ in Sola bills were arrived in Georgia, for which money is appropriated to answer the return of them.

Resolv'd the Said certified Accts. Shall be return'd to Georgia to be paid there, they being in themselves only bills of parcells for goods Sold and deliver'd to be paid for in England or Georgia as the Trustees Shall See proper.

5. Order'd that Publick notice be given in Georgia that the Trustees having Supply'd, & intending to Supply the Colony with Sola bills in order to answer the expences thereof. No bills of parcels or certified Accts. whatsoever for provisions or necessaries Sold or deliverd in Georgia for the use of the Trust, or money due or to grow due there on their Acct. will be paid in England. That their Storekeepers have received orders to defray all expences and charges of the Colony by the Trustees Sola bills remitted to them, to be issued there for that purpose; and that no other payments will be made by the Trustees for the charges abroad, but by the payment of the Sola Bills, Sent from England to defray Such charges.

6. Resolv'd that no more Sola bills be Sent to Georgia, 'till the Trustees are enabled by a new Supply from Parliament to answer them.

[N.B.] 25 Jany. 1737/8. I and Several of the Trustees went this Evening to the Cockpit to attend the Committee of Council, being the first day of the hearing upon our Appeal from the Report made very partially by the Board of Trade in our disfavour. Our Council Mr. Clerk & Mr. Murry Spoke for 2 hours extreamly well, and then the Committee adjourn'd till Satturday Sennit to hear the Council of the other Side.

The Lords of the Council present were

Ld. Wilmington, Ld. Presidt.
Ld. Ch. Justice Lee
Ld. Fitzwalter
Ld. Cholmley
Ld. Monson, who was of the board of trade & Sign'd ye Report against us, and in decency Should not be there, being both judge and Party
Arthur Onslow, Esq., Speaker of the H. of Commons
Sr. Joseph Jekyl, Master of the Rolls
& Sr. Willm. Young, Secy. at War

1 Feby. 28.

Egmont	C	P	Vernon, Ja.	C
Hales, Steven	C		Coram, Tho.	T
Oglethorpe, Ja.	C		Smith, Saml.	T
Shaftsbury	C			

A Committee of Common Council was Summon'd to go into a Committee of Correspondence, and Settle the notice to be affix'd in Georgia relating to the certified Accts.

1. We considerd what answer to make to the Several Merchants who have apply'd to be paid the certified bills from Georgia, amounting to 1900£, and which we orderd last board day to be return'd to Georgia to be paid by Mr. Causton out of the 2650£ now in his hands in Sola bills.

Unfortunatly these bills were certified by him a fortnight before our Sola bills arrived on that Side.

The Merchants attending, we told them it was a matter that only a Common Council could consider of, which now we were not.

[N.B.] 4 feby. 1737/8. The Committee of Privy Council met for the 2d time on our Appeal, and heard the Council for the Board of Trade, Mr. Brown & Mr. Noel.

8 Feb. 29.

Archer, Tho.	C		Sloper, Will.	C
Ayers, Robt.	C	Ch.	Ld. Tirconnel	C
Egmont	C		Towers, Tho.	C
Heathcote, Sr. W.	C		Vernon, Ja.	C
Lapotre, Hen.	C		Page, Jo.	T
LaRoch, Jo.	C		Smith, Saml.	T
Oglethorp, Ja.	C			

A Common Council was Summond to consider of the Several applications of the Merchants to whom certified Accts had been Sent over for payment in England, and which were order'd to be paid in Georgia with the Sola bills Sent for the Service of the Colony to Lady day 1738.

1. After a long debate upon the certified Accts. Sent over to be paid to Several Merchants here for Stores deliverd in Georgia, which Merchants desired to be paid here, and not remanded to Georgia, at length We resolv'd, that their money Should be paid them here, And that till they were paid, that they Should be allow'd 4 p cent Interest. And that Mr. Causton Should be immediatly wrote to Send back 2000£ Sola bills, in order to pay them.

N.B. Many of us doubted whether Mr. Causton had not already employ'd the money another way, the Scene now opening of his extravagant Spending the Trustees money.

2. 500£ was imprest to Aldn. Heathcote.

3. Mr. Paris attended to recieve instruction for our Council against next Satturday, when they are to reply to the board of Trades Council. We accordingly gave him instructions after a debate of 3 hours.

[N.B.] 8 Feby. 1737/8. Mr. John Wesley who arrived last fryday from Georgia attended the Board this day and acquainted us as follows:

1. That about 100 idle persons in Georgia had within 2 months left the Colony.

2. That the Inhabitants were able last year to furnish corn of their own produce to Supply the wants of half the Colony.

3. That the Country is very healthy.

4. That the Saltsburgers had cultivated 150 Acres.

5. That Piercy the publick Gardiner had left the colony on Some distast with Mr. Causton, & the garden was under no care & half ye trees dead.

[N.B.] 11 Feby. 1737/8. I went this morning to the Committee of Council, being the last day of hearing. Mr. Clark only reply'd, Mr. Murry our other Council not attending, whether by accident or design I Know not, but it was a prejudice to us, & very ill done of him. It was intimated to me, that tho the cause is clear on our Side, yet the Lords intended to consider the affair in a more publick light than as a contention between Georgia and Carolina; which if they do, then tis manifest they intend to defeat us of the advantage that ly's on our Side with respect to the dispute, and to gratify Carolina in their desire of trading with the Indians that belong to the Province of Georgia without obliging their Traders to take out lycences in Georgia, as by our Act they are obliged to do. Mr. Oglethorpe Stood Stoutly in defence of our Act, and told the Lords that they had not power to break into the Act without the Trustees consent, which I afterwards learn'd gave great offence to divers Lords that were present.

The Committee resolv'd to take a fortnights time to form their resolution on this hearing.

13 Feby. 30.

Archer, Tho.	C	Sloper, Will.	C
Egmont	C	Ld. Tirconnel	C
Heathcote, Sr. Will.	C	Towers, Tho.	C
Holland, Rogrs.	C	Vernon, Ja.	C
Ld. Carpenter	C	Archer, Hen.	T
LaRoch, Jo.	C	Tracy, Robt.	T
Oglethorpe, Ja.	C		

A Meeting of the Common Council and Trustees was Summond this day to consider and determine the manner to move in Parliamt. for 8000£ for the ensuing years Service of the Colony.

1. Sr. Robert Walpole who had promised that the future Supply's for the Colony Should be given by way of Estimate, breaking his word, we found our Selves obliged to proceed by way of petition in the old way, And accordingly resolved to petition for 8000£.

15 Feby. 31.

A Summons of Common Council to Settle the application for money to Parliamt. for ye year 1738, as agreed on the 13 inst.;

And to hear what Mr. Jo. Wesley had to mention to the Trustees on his arrival from Georgia.

1. Accordingly a petition was drawn up, and designd this day to be presented, but Sr. Robert Walpole not being down to give the Kings consent it was deferd to another day.

[N.B.] 17 feb. 1737/8. Our Accompt. wrote to Mr. Causton the great confusion he had created by making expences before he had Sola bills to defray them; that for the future he Should certify no more Accts. to any person whatever, or contract any expences but what he was ordered to make. That he Should receive the Establishment for the year 1738 as Soon as the Trustees knew how far their Cash would enable them to form it. That to answer it he Should have Sola bills Sent him, and the Trustees would make no other payments but those for their Sola bills when return'd. That they required an Account of the remain of Stores at Lady day next both at Savannah and Frederica: an acct. of what Credit had been given by ye Stores to any, and which of the Inhabitants that have not been repaid at Lady day next; And whether any debts were due from ye Stores at that time more than the certified Accts. recieved.

N.B. The vast Sums of certified Accts. Sent to us for payment, occasioning an apprehension that the Trustees would be run deeply in debt, divers of the Common Council resolv'd with themselves to quit what they thought a falling house. Whilst affairs Seem'd in a flourishing way they were glad to partake of the honour of conducting them, but when they thought them declinging, they meanly deserted their Office, and the Service of the Publick.

22 *Feby.* 32.

Bundy, Ri.	C		Oglethorpe, Ja.	C
Hales, Stev.	C	P	Vernon, Ja.	C
Lapotre, Hen.	C		Smith, Saml.	T

A Common Council was Summon'd to hear what Mr. Jo. Wesley had to lay before the board. But there was no board. A Cold confin'd me at home.

1. Mr. Wesley gave Several papers and certificates for his justification, which tho they did not justify him of indiscretion, yet Shew'd Mr. Causton to be very blamable in the contest between them, besides which he charged him with gross misadministration in many particulars fit to be enquired into.

1 March. 33.

Ld. Carpenter	C	Towers, Tho.	C
Egmont	C	Vernon, Ja.	C
Ld. Limerick	C	Coram, Tho.	T
Lapotre, Hen.	C	Smith, Saml.	T
Shaftsbury	C P		

A Common Council was Summon'd to grant lands to Mr. Ja. Carteret, and for other business. But we were not a board.

1. Mr. Fury Agent for South Carolina having informed the Committee of the Privy Council that he had it in charge from his Province to make us Some Overtures for reconciling the differences Subsisting, We order'd our Secretary to Sound him occasionally what the proposals are he intends to make.

2. We perused the estimate or calculation of the expences of Georgia for this year on the foot of 8000£, which we Shall petition for tomorrow, and made Several alterations therein, particularly with respect to the military articles, which we thought not reasonable to charge the Trust with, but that the Govermt. Should defray them.

3. Dr. Richard Bundy Sent us a resignation of his Office of Common Counsellor, declaring he was of no use.

4. Ld. Carpenter declared to us his resolution to resign for want of time to attend the boards.

5. Aldn. Cater came when the board was up and delivered his resignation, his business hindering him to attend.

These like Seeds Sown on Stony ground had no root in themselves and So endured but for a time; afterward when affliction or persecution arose immediately they were offended & fell away.

To Say the truth, the malicious clamours & reports of the Carolina people against us, the bad State of the Colony at this time as represented by Mr. John Wesley, the low condition of our Cash, the bad but just conceptions of Mr. Causton to whom the care of the Colony was trusted, the great debts contracted by him, and little Improvment made by the Inhabitants, the unreasonable pique, which tho endeavour'd to be conceal'd was visible enough, of divers of our Members against Coll. Oglethorpe, for having accepted a Regiment, and thereupon abandon'd the Party in opposition to the Court, and Sr. Robert Walpoles breaking his word to free us of the obligation of annually petitioning, by putting our expences on an annual Estimate, together with an ungrounded apprehension that the Common Council were lyable to answer to Parliament for all the money given to the Trust from time, were circumstances that all concurr'd to cool the zeal of most of our Members, and these above mention'd were not the last who left us on one or other of these Accts. as will be Seen hereafter.

Dr. Bundy was Kings Chaplain, & Minister of St. Brides church in London & of Barnet. He was a Creature of the Bishop of London, a warm high Churchman, and angry, because we did not grant land in Georgia by way of Glebe to our Ministers there, by which they could not be turnd out at our pleasure, for which we had the Strongest reason to keep that power in our hands. It was remarkable that tho we met annually in his church, and he a Common Counsellor, he never would give us a Sermon, nor for the last years even read the Service.

Sr. Robt. Cater was a Rich Oyl Man in the City, and Sherif & Alderman. His name before was Kendal, which he changed upon an estate of 1500£ p ann. falling to him in Bedford Shire. He was a gentlemanlike fair condition'd man.

Ld. Carpenter is a man who loves his money, & his pleasure, and left us purely out of apprehension that he might one time or other be Subjected to pay his Share of debts incurr'd by the mismanagment of Mr. Causton, and because he Saw Sr. Robert Walpole at the bottom not well affectioned to the Colony.

[N.B.] 1 March 1737/8. This day wrote a letter to Sr. Robert Walpole, Sign'd by 12 Common Counsellors and 5 Trustees, expressing that the Civil provision of the Colony will require annually 8000£ until the Same be better Settled, and desiring earnestly that these expences may for the future be put into Some Estimate to be laid before the Crown before the house of Commons, Since it would be impossible for the Trustees every year to take upon them the labour of proceeding as petitioners; nor could it be thought reasonable that they Should hazard the making contracts for Men, provisions &c. which is necessary to be done the year before, upon the uncertainty of their petitions being received, or the Sum they expected being granted them.

N.B. Sr. Robert Walpole had promised this, but never granted it, because resolv'd to keep the Trustees (many of whom are members of Parliament) in dependance on him.

[N.B.] 1 March 1737/8. This day another letter was wrote to Sr. Robert Walpole Sign'd by 11 Common Counsellors and 5 Trustees, recommending Capt. James Gascoign of the Hawks Sloop to be advanced to the command of a Man of War, for his good Service in protecting our Province. But we had not Success, and Several of our Members refused to Sign, as thinking it a matter wherein we ought not to concern our Selves, and perhapps they Said truly, But Mr. Oglethorpe prest it.

N.B. These 2 articles Should have been enter'd 1 May.

8 March. 34.

Ld. Carpenter	C		Ld. Talbot	C
Egmont	C		Shaftsbury	C
Lapotre, Hen.	C	P	Ld. Tirconnel	C
Sloper, Will.	C		Smith, Saml.	T

A Common Council was Summon'd to grant lands to Mr. James Carteret, and for other business preparatory to the Anniversary meeting. But we were not a board.

1. Ld. Carpenter presented his resignation of Common Counsellor, pretending he Should be obliged to go into the Country and could not attend the duty, but Said another year if We wanted him he would come in again: He did not intend to keep his word.

2. Ld. Talbot also resign'd, pretending his business would not Suffer him to attend. What his particular reason was to leave us I know not. He is a gentleman of parts, vain of his late fathers merit, very hot, and particular in his ways. I imagine he was disgusted at Sr. Robert Walpoles obliging us to petition the Parliamt. for money and not granting it us by way of Estimate; and that he was displeased at our applying for a Ship in favour of Capt. Gascoign, to which he was much averse. Hot Men take matters too quick.

3. Alderman Heathcote Sent his resignation of a Common Counsellor, on the Score of want of health, & being obliged to remain much out of town. So now we had 5 new Common Counsellors to elect, and Scarce any time to pitch upon proper persons to Succeed them.

This occasion'd my dining with Mr. Vernon & Mr. Sloper, to consider of proper persons to Succeed them, and on the coming in of Mr. Oglethorpe & Mr. Tho. Towers we concluded on Mr. Smith, Mr. Christopher Towers brother to the other, Mr. Tracy, Mr. Hen. Archer, and Sr. Jacob Bouverie.

4. Mr. Oglethorpe acquainted us that Ct. Sinzendorf was very well Satisfied with the answer we wrote him Some months ago, that his Moravians Should remain in Georgia, and that he had Sent over two of those people (now arrived in London) to be Catechists to the Negroes at Purysburg.

[N.B.] 8 March 1737/8. This day the House in a Committee voted 8000£ for the Service of Georgia, Mr. Tracy one of our Trustees moved it, & Mr. Frederick a Common Counsellor Seconded him. No body opposed it, but there were a good many noes, which I observe annually encreases.

16 March. 35.

Ayers, Robt.	C		Vernon, Ja.	C
Egmont	C	Ch. & P.	Anderson, Adm.	T
Hales, Steven	C		Bedford, Arthr.	T
Lapotre, Hen.	C		Burton, Jo.	T
Oglethorpe, Ja.	C		Ld. Carpenter	T
Ld. Tirconnel	C		Coram, Tho.	T
Towers, Tho.	C		Smith, Saml.	T

1. This being our Anniversary day, the gentlemen here mention'd met in the Vestry of St. Brides Church were we read and approved the Accompt of Receipts and disbursments to this day, and the State of our Cash remaining.

2. We past a grant of 500 Acres to Mr. Ja. Carteret.

3. And then elected into the Common Council Mr. Robert Tracy, Mr. Hen. Archer, Mr. Christopher Towers, Mr. Saml. Smith, and Mr. Jo. Page, Sr. Jacob Bouverie declining to accept of being a Common Counsellor.

4. We also elected Sr. Hen Gough and Sr. Rogr. Burgoign Trustees.

After this, we went to Church, and Dr. Bearcroft formerly my Sons Tutor and now Preacher to the Charter house made us a very good Sermon wch. we desired him to print.

5. It was remarkable that Dr. Bundy declined not only to appear, but even his Curate (doubtless by his order) did not read the prayers, So that Dr. Burton was obliged to do it: Such was Dr. Bundy's Slight of us.

[N.B.] 18 March 1737/8. This day the Committee of Council having finally consider'd their late hearing on the dispute between us, Carolina & the Board of Trade, resolv'd not to allow of the Carolina Ordinance (agst. which we complaind) whereby that Province had tax'd themselves in 2000£ Sterl. to make amends to Such of their Traders as who for trading with the Indians of Georgia without taking Licences in our Province Should have their goods taken from them, or Suffer otherwise on that Acct. They also orderd an instruction to be Sent the Trustees of Georgia to pass a law for allowing a due number of Carolina Traders (being duly appointed by the Govermt. of Carolina) to trade in Georgia, and that the like instructions Should be Sent to Carolina to make a law for the Same purpose. But Our present Georgia law for regulating Trade with the Indians is not to be repeal'd, but only explain'd to answer the purposes above mentiond.

This abrogation of the Carolina Ordenance above mentiond, as an illegal act, and no law, is what the Board of trade did not expect, who had reported in favour of it.

22 *March*. 36.

Archer, Tho.	C		Heathcote, Sr. Will.	C
Archer, Hen.	C		Lapotre, Hen.	C
Digby, Edwd.	C	Ch.	Smith, Saml.	C
Egmont	C		Ld. Tirconnel	C
Hales, Stev.	C	P	Tracy, Robt.	C

The Trustees being Summond to Swear in the new Common Counsellors, So many Members met that we were likewise a Common Council.

1. Mr. Hen. Archer, Mr. Smith, and Mr. Tracy were Sworn into the Common Council.

2. Payment of 45.15.0 was order'd for a gilt mace for the Magistrates of Savannah.

3. Instructions were given to the Committee of correspondence to enquire how the Servants Sent to Georgia for the use of the Trust have been employ'd.

4. Also how the Silk winders have been employ'd, and what they have done, and how the directions of the Trustees from time to time relating to the cultivation of Mulberry plants and the delivering them out to the people, have been comply'd with.

5. A Grant past to Ja. Carteret Esq. of 500 acres.

23 *March*. 37.

Egmont	C	Sloper, Will.	C
Hales, Stev.	C	Towers, Tho.	C
Lapotre, Hen.	C	Vernon, Ja.	C

Some of the Trustees thinking it high time to put the affairs of our Colony on a better foot than it has been of late, to remedy abuses, to prevent un-necessary & unknown expences in Georgia by certify'd Accts. Sent us, and to reduce the establishment of the Province within the 8000£ given us this Session, met by private agreement this day as a Committee of correspondence.

1. The first thing we went on was to read over the establishment, and to Strike off all branches of expence of a military nature, the Parliamt. having given this years money for the Settling, not the defence of the Colony.

We therefore unanimously agreed to drop the Rangers, the Pettiaguas, the Garison of Fort St. George, the building a Fort at St. Andrews and all that is doing there, the Darien establishment, and the two Scout boats of Carolina & Amelia.

2. We also agreed to dismiss Mr. Causton from being Storekeeper at Savannah, and to give the employment to Mr. Tho. Stephens at a Sallary of 30£ p ann. with 1 Clerk under him at 18£ p ann.

3. To break up the Store at Frederica, the time being expired of maintaining the poor Sent over by us to Settle there.

4. We also agreed to restore the foot Messenger between Carolina & Georgia to go every fortnight, and to appoint another between Savannah & Frederica.

5. That the Millright to Ebenezar Should be paid by the day, and not by annual agreement, and the labourers under them to be taken out of the Servants Sent over on the Trust Acct.

6. That a Sea boat Should be Stationd at Tybee.

7. That Mr. Causton who remains head Bailif be directed to oversee the Millrights at Ebenezar, and be considerd for his trouble.

8. That a months time be given him after his dismission from the Office of Storekeper to make up his Accts. of the Stores, and then to deliver up the keys to young Stephens.

9. That at Frederica Mr. Auspurger the Ingenier be employ'd as Surveyor to lay out peoples lands at 3 Shillings p diem.

10. That a Sea boat be appointed for Frederica instead of a pettiagua.

11. That the Orphans and Sick be taken care of both at Savannah and Frederica by the Magistrates of both towns.

12. That the Sola bills Sent over for the Service of the Colony, be committed for the future to the care of 3 persons to be Sign'd by them or any two of them to give them currency; and that our Coper plate be alter'd for that purpose.

13. That the annual certain allowance made to Tomachachi and his Indians be Struck off: But in our Estimate to make a reserve for presents to Indians upon renewall of friendship with them, entertaining them, &c.

Some other matters were also agreed on to be regulated.

14. Then Seriously conferring upon proper methods to recover

the friendship of South Carolina, and upon means to make the Inhabitants of our Colony easie with respect to the tenure of their lands,

We thought it not unreasonable as to the former to make an explanatory law that Should allow of a certain number of Carolina Traders to be licenced by us, when recommended by the Govr. & Council of Carolina. And a doubt arising whether we Should not oblige them to give Security in Georgia as they have hitherto done, Mr. Vernon opposed it: whereupon Mr. Towers proposed the accepting those Traders bonds to comply with the terms of our Act, which the Gentlemen acquiesced in. The proportions of Traders of both Provinces to be adjusted between them and the Govr. of Carolina.

15. As to Satisfying the Inhabitants with respect to Females inheriting, I proposed that an Act Should pass, obliging our Selves and Successors to let the Parents lands fall to their female heirs or issue, conditionally that Such female marrys a man who will reside in the Province, and has no land of his own; By which means our purpose will be answerd of Securing defensible Inhabitants (which was our only reason for excluding female heirs) and the people will be Secure that the lands they have cultivated will go where they desire it Should.

To this the Gentlemen consented.

16. We gave order to prepare an advertisment in the London Gazet, and the Carolina Gazet, and to be affixt on the Town houses of Savannah & Frederica importing, that from the time of that notice, the Trustees will not allow of any agreements in Georgia for Stores &c, Or for any cargoes what ever to be bought there, or of any certified accompts; But that all things Shall be paid for in Georgia by our Sola bills only, to answer which purpose, a Sufficient quantity of them Should be Sent over, to answer all the expences we have or Shall provide for.

17. We could not but observe that Mr. Oglethorpe had been very careless of attending Summons of late, namely Since he found the Gentlemen resolv'd to reduce the Colony's expences, especially with respect to the Military articles, in which he told our Accomptant he desired to have no hand. He Sees how many Members have left us, how many of the rest are grown cool to the Work, and that there is only One Set remaining to carry it on, whom if he Should disgust, the Charter would fall for want of a Sufficient number to carry it on & Support it; and Since he is not thoroughly pleased with our economy (wch. God knows is no more than nec-

[1738]   JOURNAL OF THE EARL OF EGMONT   341

essary) he therefore chuses to be absent as often as he can with decency, and without a downright quarrel with us.

Five Common Counsellors withdrew this year as has been mention'd, Capt. Eyles Seldom attends, Mr. Frederick never, & Mr. Page came not to be Sworn, Ld. Limerick & Mr. LaRoch attend as Seldom as the rest. This is observed by the Town, and occasions a report that our affairs are desperate and under bad management. If a few more Should withdraw, we Should Scarce be able to go on with business: for tis Difficult and a great hardship that out of 24 Common Counsellors, 8 are at all times necessary to make a Common Council.

29 March. 38.

Egmont	C		Towers, Tho.	C Ch.
Heathcote, Sr. Will.	C		Towers, Christr.	C
Lapotre, Hen.	C		Tracy, Robt.	C
Smith, Sam.	C	P	Vernon, Ja.	C
Ld. Tirconnel	C		Anderson, Adm.	T

A Common Council was Summond to receive the Reports of the Committee of Accompts and Correspondence relating to the Expences of the Colony that have been or Shall be orderd, and in what manner they Shall be defrayd for the future. And relating to the Settling a regular correspondence between England & Georgia for the benefit of the Inhabitants of the Colony.

1. We read the Report of the Committee of Correspondence, & resolv'd Some articles therein Should Stand approved.

2. Read also a Report from the Committee of Accts.; and resolv'd thereupon that the following resolution be Sign'd by the Secrety. and publish'd in the London and Carolina gazets, and affixt to the doors of the Storehouses of Savannah and Frederica, viz.

The Trustees of Georgia out of a due regard to publick Credit, do hereby give notice, that they have resolv'd, that all the Expences which the Trustees have already order'd or Shall hereafter order to be made in America for the use of the Said Colony Shall be defray'd & paid for in Georgia in Sola bills of Exchange only, under the Seal of the Said Trustees. And they do further give notice, that no person whatsoever hath any authority from them or in their name or on their account, to purchasse or receive any Cargoes of provisions Stores or necessaries, or to contract any debt or create any expence whatsoever in America. And that no persons may be ignorant thereof, the Trustees have order'd that this notice Shall be affixt and remain on the door of the Storehouse of Savannah and Frederica in the Province of Georgia in America; and Shall be publish'd in the London & Carolina Gazet.

3. Refer'd to the Committee of Correspondence to consider of the Conduct of Noble Jones the Surveyor who has been grossly negligent in running out the peoples lotts.

4. After these matters were over, we adjournd to Mr. Oglethorpes house at his desire, he being confin'd by an accident, to Shew him our Plan of Expences to be made, the reductions to be thought on, and our proposal of granting new lands to the Inhabitants of Highgate, who complain'd what they possess'd was pine barren, and petitioned for better land.

5. This he Strongly objected to, as also to the putting down the Scout boats, affirming that if they were put down, the Inhabitants in general would go away. To this I reply'd, we had not money to maintain them. Then Said he, I must Save it out of Some other article.

6. As to giving new land, he Said he knew the land of Highgate was pine barren most of it, But wth. pains it might be renderd very fruitfull as other pine barren lands have been. That if these people were humour'd in this, there would not be a man in the Colony but would desire to remove to better land, who at present have no thoughts of it. That the disorder this would occasion is not to be exprest. That if these men were all owned to change their land, they would expect a new allowance of provision for a year which we are not able to give, and the Same would be expected by others. He used other arguments on the occasion which made So great impression on the gentlemen, that I Stood aloan for giving new land, tho before we were all unanimous in the point. The affair might perhapps have taken a different turn had Mr. Vernon been there, but he was obliged to attend a Committee of Counsel, being Clerk in waiting.

[N.B.] 30 March 1738. This morning I went by invitation of Col. Oglethorpe to See that part of his Regiment raised in England March through the City into Essex under the Command of Majr. Cook. They were well cloathed and young Sightly fellows. He had desired the rest of the Trustees to come, but only myself, Ld. Tirconnel, Mr. Christopher Towers & Capt. Eyles were there, which I observed was a dissappointment to him, he having prepared an elegant dinner.

[N.B.] 9 April 1738. Capt. Thompson lately arrived from Georgia gave me a tolerable Acct. of the Province: But Said the people

[1738] JOURNAL OF THE EARL OF EGMONT   343

of Savannah were in general very uneasie at their heirs female not Succeeding to their lands, and that it had made them for the most part abandon the cultivating their lands.

2. He Spoke much in commendation of Mr. Causton, and added that he took no more upon him than his Post of first Magistrate required.

3. He also commended Mr. Christie the Recorder as very Zealous for the Colony, Tho by Mr. Stevens journal it appears otherwise, for he writes that he is weary, and Suspected of taking lands in Carolina.

4. That he left the Colony healthy, but that many of the children born in Savannah die, which he imputed to the Parents drinking Spiritous liquours, and being infected with diseases.

5. That by Mr. Andersons care (the Inspector of the Publick garden) the Same is putting again into order, and that Fitzwalter formerly gardiner, who ran away to Carolina was return'd, and employ'd therein. That notwithstanding we were inform'd there were no Mulberry plants there, yet there are many.

6. That the Rancour of the Carolinians is much abated Since they heard that Mr. Oglethorpe is made General of the Forces, and Several who were violent against us, Say now that they were mislead.

7. That at Highgate from when la Fage and others wrote over Such complaints of the badness of their land bely'd it, for it will bear produce, but the lots of Some are worse than of others, and many labour under necessities that make them abandon planting, for the time of their hired Servants being expired, and their Servants having left them, they have not mony to buy new Ones. This in Some has been carelessness to lay up in Store, But most others had land that would not yeild them Sufficient to maintain themselves & Servts., cloath them, buy tools, and raise an overplus to Save money for buying new Servants.

12 April. 39.

Archer, Hen.	C		Sloper, Will.	C	
Archer, Tho.	C		Smith, Saml.	C	
Digby, Edwd.	C		Ld. Tirconnel	C	
Egmont	C		Towers, Tho.	C	
Hales, Stev.	C	Ch.	Towers, Christ.	C	
Heathcote, Sr. Will.	C	P	Tracy, Robt.	C	
Lapotre, Hen.	C		Anderson, Ad.	T	
Oglethorpe, Ja.	C		Burton, Jo.	T	

A Common Council was Summond to consider further of the Reports of the Committees of Accts. & Correspondence: And of the Accts. received from Georgia by the Ship Two Brothers Capt. Thompson just arrived. And to consider of the further necessary orders for the Service of the Colony, to be forwarded by the Ships now near upon going.

1. The following letters from Georgia were refer'd after being read to the Committee of Correspondence, viz.

2. From Mr. Hawkins, 1 Bailif of Frederica to the Trustees giving Acct. that all was peacable there, but that the Crop raised last year was all Spoilt by the bad Season and Ratts. dat. 28 Nov. 1737.

3. Mr. Hawkins to Mr. Verelts that he wanted druggs and Medicines. dat. 10 Jany. 1737/8.

4. Mr. Hird to Col. Oglethorpe from Frederica, that all was well there. dat. 5 Decembr.

5. From Mr. Causton to the Trustees that he had Sent the 40 Trustees Servants to Darien. dat. 14. Jany.

6. From Mrs. Causton to Col. Oglethorpe about Mulberry Trees and making Silk. That She has in her garden 1000 plants of 4 years growth, but by reason of want of leaves, all the worms last year were destroyed. That the Chickesaws who came to Savannah Said they had a world of Mulberry trees in their nation, and if instructed how to make Silk would bring vast quantities. dat. 16 Jany.

7. Mr. Stephens to the Trustees giving a Satisfactory Acct. of the present State of Savannah, and referring for farther particulars to his journal from the day of his leaving Charlestown for Savannah 28 Oct. to 17 Jany. dat. 20 Jany.

8. Mr. Stephens to the Trustees that Several of the Inhabitants are dissatisfied with the Trustees in Tail male. dat. 19 Jany.

9. A petition from Abraham De Lyon a jew, Setting forth his progress in planting vines, and praying encouragement, by a loan of 200£ on giving good Security to repay the Same in 6 years.

10. Agreed with the Committees Report that a Cargo of flour and other provisions Sent for to Philadelphia for the Service of Georgia, amounting to 847.5.8½ be paid for out of the money reserved for the maintenance of the Servants arrived in Georgia.

11. Orderd that a certified Acct. amounting to 504.9.11 payable to Robt. Ellis & dat. 1 feb. 1737/8 be return'd unpaid, it appearing to be for a whole Cargo taken by Mr. Causton, of which there was not 50 pounds worth of provision, and the rest not wanted by Mr. Caustons own confession in his letter.

[1738] JOURNAL OF THE EARL OF EGMONT 345

12. Orderd that 45.19.0 be paid for the Mace Sent to the Magistrates of Georgia.

13. Orderd that the druggs & medicines wrote for by Mr. Hawkins be Sent him.

14. Order'd that 90 Tun of flint Stones be Sent to Georgia for the foundations of Churches, and that 2 Tun of Swedish Iron, 2 Tun of Siberia Iron, and 200 weight of Steel be Sent for the building Churches.

15. Order'd 200£ being a farther Sum be paid Mr. Wrag on Acct. of 120 & ½ heads of Servants Sent to Georgia by the Ship Three Sisters Capt. Hewet, extraordinary charges being allow'd, for want of a Pilot.

16. Order that Mary Cooper now in England be paid 10.10.0, being the Rent of her house in Savannah inhabited by Mr. Hen. Parker one of the Bailifs, for which he is to account to the Trust.

17. Imprest to Aldn. Heathcote 1100£ on Acct.

18. Imprest 750£ more for payment of Sola bills.

19. Leave granted to Peter Gordon now in England (formerly 1st Bailif) to part with his House and Lot to Anne and Susan Cook daughters to Majr. Cook.

20. Order'd that the Secrety. write to Mr. Stephens that the Trustees will not alter the Tenure of their grants from Tail male; that he incert the clause in the printed terms Settled by the Common Council and offerd to Such persons as go at their own expence, relating to females; that the Trustees think proper to adhere to the Covenants which have been made in their Several Grants, and that they will take the forfeits of Grants of those persons who neglect to cultivate their Lotts.

N.B. Dr. Burton and I were for Mr. Martins explaining the reasons why we adhered to Tenure in Tail Male, but Col. Oglethorpe and Mr. Tho. Towers opposed it, as too great a condescencion.

[N.B.] 12 April 1738. This day we had a debate of 2 hours at the Board, whether in complyance to the desire of numbers in the Colony, we Should alter their Tenure in Tail male and admit Females to inherit.

I was for it under certain regulations, and urged the general uneasiness the people exprest for want of it, even to their abandoning cultivation. I Said our only reason for not allowing Females to inherit, was to Secure the residence of Freeholders for defending the Colony, & this was a proper caution, at first Setting out. But the case was now in a great measure alter'd by Sending over a Regiment. That the people were possest of an opinion that the Trustees might one day take to themselves the benefit of their labours (they dying without Heirs male) and threatnd that if in this point they were not gratify'd they would abandon the Colony. That great clamours have been raised against us in England for excluding females, and that tis no where done in America, where lands being as cheap as with us, Negroes and large Trusts allow'd, it was to be feard that numbers would make their words good and leave the Colony. That tis true we have favourd females on accasion, and hitherto justly adhered to a rule concerning the care of female Successions, But this was no law, and being in our own breasts to deviate from was not Satisfactory to the Inhabitants, and if our Trusteeship Should cease by resignation of our Charter to the Crown, which might possibly happen, & certainly would when ever the Parliament Should refuse their annual Supply, the Crown would not be obliged to follow our Rule. That Supposing the people were ever So much in the wrong, yet it would be wise in us to yeild to the general bent when we might Satisfy them without hurt to the Colony, and what hurt could there be by turning into a law a Rule which thought just, had hitherto follow'd, & were resolv'd always to follow?

Ld. Tirconnel and Sr. Willm. Heathcote Spoke on the Same Side. But Mr. Digby and Col. Oglethorpe opposed it, especially the latter, who pleaded that it was only a few Men desired this who had no daughters of their own, and intended when they had obtaind this point to ask for liberty to Sell their Interest and be allow'd the use of Negroes. That this was Suggested to them by the Carolinians who wanted they Should morgage or Sell their lands to them, & So make themselves Masters of all the affairs of Georgia. That the chief of these Inovaters was Patrick Mackay who fled Scotland for Felony. That it was impossible to make Such a law as would comprehend all the particular cases fit to be excepted, but it must be made general as in England, which was not the intention of any of us, and therefore would be attended by the ill consequences he mentioned, for after that, who could hinder them from morgaging or Selling, having So certain absolute & legal a property? that in length of time there would be no need of excluding females, for the Colony would be better peopled, and it Should be waited for with patience. That if any quitted the Colony because not gratify'd in this, he Knew others would take their forfeited Lotts, & give 200£ Security to perform their Covenants. That from the Southern Division of the Province Frederica, Darien &c we had not received one complaint against the Tenure in Tail Male, which Shew'd that this clamour from the Northern Division is owning to its neighborhood to Carolina.

The majority of the Gentlemen acquiesced in Col. Oglethorpes opinion.

[N.B.] 13 April 1738. Mr. Boltzius the Ebenezar Minister wrote to Mr. Verelts a very thankfull letter for the favours the Trustees had Shewn the Saltsburgers who had cultivated 200 Acres of land.

[N.B.] 14 April 1738. This day Dr. Barecroft told me, that Mr. Willm. Archer, Kt. of the Shire for the County of Berks lately told a friend of his, that he design'd to have given 500£ to the Trustees of Georgia, but Sitting in the house, and overhearing Some of the Trustees make a jest of our care for the Religious uses of the Colony, he alter'd his mind. These Trustees were undoubtedly Mr. White, Mr. Hucks &c who quitted the Common Council because we determin'd to preserve a Religious establishment in Georgia, and have Since forborn to attend us.

[N.B.] 15 April. Mr. Stephens Sent over his journal with a letter of this date, informing Mr. Verelts of Some perplexity the people of Savannah were in on the Spaniards design to invade the Province; that Some had left it for fear, but an order was issued that none Should go out of the Province.

[N.B.] 17 April 1738. Mr. Verelts acquainted me that the report of the Spaniards design to attack Georgia is true. For there was come the Capt. of one of our Ships who had been taken & carry'd into Havannah, but made his escape, and inform'd Col. Oglethorpe that there were near 4000 Men at Havannah and 2 Men of War. That he Saw 30 flat bottom boats already built there, and they were going on with more, to conceal which from the view of Ships that past by the town, they had built a blind of timber and boards 10 feet high. That they only waited the Barliavento fleet wch. usually comes to them in March, and then would joyn 3 Men of War to the other two, and invade Georgia or Carolina.

Mr. Oglethorpe acquainted Sr. Robt. Walpole with this.

19 April. 40.

Egmont	C	Towers, Christr.	C P
Lapotre, Hen.	C	Tracy, Robt.	C
Smith, Saml.	C	Anderson, Adm.	T
Towers, Tho.	C		

A Common Council was Summon'd, to grant 500 acres to Capt. Heron, and to go into Committees of Accts. & Correspondence on the Several matters before the Said Committees: but there was no board. So we acted only as a Committee of Accompts.

1. De lyon the jews petition for encouragemt. to make wine being refer'd to us, We agreed that it ought to be comply'd with, and that 200£ might be advanc'd him on bonds to repay the Same at 6 years End.

2. We took into consideration Capt. Thompsons Memorial, and agreed that the 12 Servants undisposed by him in Georgia, part of a greater number carry'd over at his own risk, might be taken into the Trust Service, and paid for by us at the rate of 8£ p head; but that we ought not to charge ourselves with the rest of the Servants he carry'd and disposed of to private Persons in the Colony, who have taken them into their Service, and therefore that Mr. Caustons certified Acct. to pay the Capt. for those Servants ought not to be allow'd. For if it were, the Trust would Stand middle Men between those private purchassers and the Captn.

N.B. This paying for other peoples Servants who cant pay for them themselves.

3. The Correspondent of Mr. Ellis was very importunate this day to be paid the certificate Accts. brought us the last meeting & then resolv'd to be return'd for payment to Georgia, having bills as we hoped there to discharge it, and but 4900£ remaining of the 8000£ given us this year by Parlt. for the whole Service of the Colony to Midsummer 1739.

4. Another demand came from Capt. Wrag for 30 days loss of time, by Capt. Hewets not putting into Savanna River for want of a Pilot from the Shoar, which obliged him to Sail to Charlestown and back again, during which time he fed our Servant passengers, which with demurrage of his Ship came as he alledged to 187£. He was by agreement to have for accidents 100£, but now he ask'd 87£ more.

We told both Mr. Ellis's friend & Capt. Wrag, that it Should be considerd when we were a board of Common Council, the Trustees not having power to order any thing therein.

[N.B.] On 21 April 1738, James Howell of Carolina Master of a Schooner made affidavid that being at Augustine 15th of Said month, the Govr. detain'd him, and would not Suffer one Englishman to Speak or write to another. That the 20th of March arrived there 37 pinaces &c well man'd & arm'd, of which 6 gallys made on purpose to go on Shoal water had 3 guns in their bows and 50 Soldiers. That in the mean time there came advice to the Govr. that the expedition against Georgia was countermanded, these preparations being made against that Province. That for 5 years he had used the trade to Augustine there never was more than 500 men in garison, but now there were 1500 disciplin'd men and 200 Florida Indians. That these Forces were to be joyn'd by others from the Havannah making together 7000 Men. Two 60 gun Ships and other Ships of War, and that 100 great guns were put on board a Spanish Man of War to Settle a Fort at Frederica, and it was reported there that 1500 french from Canada were to joyn the Spanish Forces on their Settling of Georgia. That he heard the Spanish Govr. Say, the Govermt. of England had agreed that Georgia Should be evacuated in 6 months then ensuing, and that was the reason of their keeping a launch and pinace behind, in which the Govr. was to Send an Officer in about a fortnights time then after, and demand a Surrender of Georgia. That he heard a proclamation read at St. Augustine, that all Negroes who did or Should run away from the English, Should be made free, and the Said proclamation had effect accordingly, for Several Negroes who ran away thither, and were Sold there were thereupon made free, and the Purchassers lost their money.

[N.B.] 24 April, Mr. Tho. Jenys of Charlestown confirm'd the Same Acct. by the relation of Capt. Prew just then arrived from Augustine. He also wrote the Trustees that our Forts and passes in Georgia, where he had been, were in good order and well guarded. That most of our trees in the publick garden were in very good & flourishing plight; and that he Saw our magazine of Silk worms which look'd very healthy, and he was Sure great quantities might be Soon produced and provided for.

26 April. 41.

Archer, Hen.	C Ch.	Oglethorpe, Ja.	C
Archer, Tho.	C	Smith, Saml.	C
Digby, Edwd.	C	Towers, Tho.	C
Egmont	C	Tracy, Robt.	C P
Heathcote, Sr. Will.	C	Vernon, Ja.	C
Lapotre, Hen.	C		

A Common Council was Summond to grant lands to Capt. Heron: To order a new Trust Grant for 50 acre Lotts, and then to go into a Committee of Accts. & Correspondence.

1. Grant past & Seal'd to Capt. Alexr. Heron of Coll. Oglethorpes Regiment, of 500 acres.
2. Grant, lease & Release in trust of 3000 acres, for 50 acre

Lotts to Protestants who Shall desire them within 3 years from the date thereof order'd to be prepared for the next Meetings of approbation, who are to put the Seal thereto.

3. Mr. John Wesley left at our Office his Lycence for performing Ecclesiastical offices in Georgia, which we took for a resignation, and therefore most readily revoked his commission. In truth he appear'd to us an odd mixture of a man, an Enthusiast and yet a hypocrite; wholly distastfull to the greatest part of the Inhabitants, and an Incendiary against the Magistrates.

4. Capt. Hewet of the three Sisters attended to be pd. for the maintenance of the Passengers Some days longer than he needed have done, in case he had waited at Tybee when he arrived there for the Pilot to conduct his Ship in. But having no patience, after making Signals he went to Charlestown and there took up a Pilot. This loss of Some days he would have the Trustees consider him for. But Capt. Thompson of the Two brothers who was this day with us, declaring that his boat went out from Tybee to bring him in, and thereby proving that Hewet was not under a necessity to go to Charlestown for a Pilot, We refused to make him the allowance he desired, especially as he had 100£ allow'd him before in consideration of any dissappointment he Should meet with in landing his passengers.

[N.B.] 26 April 1738. Saml. Davison a Constable at Frederica wrote to my Sons Servant Ridyard, that they had been wonderfully blest by Providence, very few had died, no one Sickly, a great encrease of children, and women bear who in Europe were thought past their time.

He also wrote to my Servant Gilbert the Same date, that he had been kept back in planting by the Spanish allarms, & had but a Small crop, but his land he clear'd was very good. That he had this year at both plantations 6 acres & 38 perches well fenc'd 6 or 7 feet high, and planted, which he hoped would afford him and his family bread: and all by his own labour, except that of a Servant, wch. for 9 months cost him the keeping 11.10.0 Sterl. That twas hard living there without a Servant, one Man being incapable to move trees and fences, wth. the other necessary labours that One must go through, before he can plant.

1 May. 42.

Archer, Tho.	C	Digby, Edwd.	C
Archer, Hen.	C	Heathcote, Sr. Will.	C Ch.

[1738] JOURNAL OF THE EARL OF EGMONT 351

Lapotre, Hen.	C	Vernon, Ja.	C
Oglethorpe, Ja.	C	Anderson, Adm.	T
Sloper, Will.	C	Ld. Carpenter	T
Smith, Saml.	C	Cates, Sr. Robt.	T
Ld. Tirconnel	C	Heathcote, Geo.	T
Towers, Tho.	C	Hucks, Robt.	T
Tracy, Robt.	C		

A Common Council was Summond to receive Reports.

1. The Committee of Accompts reported that large Credits had been given to Several persons by Mr. Causton, for which the Trustees had given no orders; and that they were of opinion he Should be call'd on to give an Acct. to the Trustees why Such credits had been given.

2. That they had also consider'd of the list of Servants transmitted by Mr. Stephens, wherein the first article consists of 40 Servants carry'd over by Capt. Thompson in November last, and order'd to the Darien for Sawing plank, under the direction of Lieut Moore Mackintosh; which being a charge on the Trust, they Submitted whether twas not necessary to appoint Some other Inspector to take care that the Servants under his care be So employ'd & an account taken of what they have done and Shall continue to do, and how the produce of this labour has been apply'd for the benefit of the Trust.

3. That 56 more Servants on board Said Captain Thompson, tho brought into the Colony at the Owners rick and 44 of them contracted for by private Inhabitants who Settled at their own expence, have been placed to the Acct. of the Trustees, and have all but 12 been distributed by him to private persons, without any authority for Such proceedings, and therefore they were of opinion that the charge of the Said 44 Servants must be answer'd by Mr. Causton.

4. That by the Ship 3 Sisters Capt. Hewet, 120 & ½ heads of foreign Servants were brought into the Colony the 24 Decbr. last; whereof 67 heads were put under the care of Mr. Bradley: And the Committee Submitted whether it is not necessary to appoint Some other Inspectors to take an Acct. how these Servants are employ'd, and how the produce of their labour Shall be accounted for to the Trust. That 9 heads & ½ more of the Said Servants were indented to Mr. Causton without any authority for So doing, wherefore the charge of them Should be answer'd for by him.

5. That they had examin'd the Sums paid in, & applicable to building Churches in Georgia, which amounting to 843.15.4 besides 65£ more Subscribed for making together 908.15.4. They Submitted whether Capt. Thomas the Ingenier on his arrival in Georgia might not be desired to make an Estimate for building a church at Savannah, and Send the Same by the first Ship. The Board agreed to all the parts of this Report.

N.B. The Committee who drew this report were only Mr. Smith, Mr. Lapotre and Mr. Vernon. They met at the Office for it, and then repai'd to Col. Oglethorpes who had invited a great many Trustees to dinner on acct. of his Speedy departure to Georgia. I Staid in the Country this day. At his house they made a board of Common Council and approved the report above mentioned.

6. 50£ Benefaction for buildg. Churches from a Lady unknown.

[N.B.] 1 May 1738. The further proceedings of the Common Council which Sat this day at Mr. Oglethorpes were

7. An order to pay for the two Sea boats purchassed by Col. Oglethorpe, to be employ'd for the pilotage of Georgia, the expence whereof amounted to 58.4.5.

8. Order'd 100£ to Mr. Verelts for his extraordinary Services not within the business of his Office as Accomptant.

9. Order'd 25£ to Jo. Brailsford for his Service in attending on the Trustees Account, to be a wittness in our dispute wth. Carolina: & that his passage back to Georgia be defrayed.

10. Several certified Accts. lately come were produced viz.

To Minis & Solomon,	dat. 23 Jan. 1737/8	98. 6. 2½
To Do.	dat. do.	434. 8. 3½
To Do.	dat. 7 March	124. 2. 8¾
To Saml. Tingley	dat. 20 March	144.16. 5½
To David Prevost	dat. 28 feby.	348. 2. 1½

All which profusion of Expence made the Gentlemen Stare.

3 May. 43.

Egmont	C Ch.&P.	Towers, Tho.	C
Lapotre, Hen.	C	Towers, Christr.	C
LaRoch, Jo.	C	Tracy, Robt.	C
Oglethorpe, Ja.	C	Anderson, Adm.	T
Shaftsbury	C	Vernon, Ja.	C
Smith, Saml.	C		

[1738] JOURNAL OF THE EARL OF EGMONT   353

1. An Act was order'd to be prepared for the better execution of the Act prohibiting Rum.

2. The Memorial to Sr. Robert Walpole for putting the expences of the Colony for the future into an estimate and thereby to excuse us from the trouble of petitioning the Parliamt. was approved & Sign'd and many absent Trustees also Sign'd the Same.

3. We also Sign'd a recommendation of Capt. Gascoign to Sr. Robt. Walpole to obtain a better Ship. Ld. Talbot and Mr. Sloper refused it as a matter that the Trustees ought not to concern themselves about, and in truth they were in the right, but we did it in complacency to Col. Oglethorpe who much desired & prest it. Both these Memorials are wrong enter'd as to time, See fol. 244. Neither of them took effect.

4. Mr. Ellis's Correspondent made a fresh application to be paid his certified Acct. But we refused to pay it on this Side as we had done before. Our Cash for the years Service being reduced very low, and we hoped Mr. Causton had Sola bills to pay it in Georgia, as he ought to have and much more unless he had Squander'd it away. We also believed that Mr. Causton had filled the Publick Store with that Ships Cargo, not that he had occasion for it, but to oblige Mr. Ellis, for which he probably received a private gratuity.

5. Robert Gilbert, a Taylor appointed 3 Bailif, in the room of Jo. Dairn deceased.

6. John Clark appointed Secy. for the Indian affairs in the room of the Revd. Mr. Cha. Wesley.

7. A Lot of 50 acres in Savannah order'd to Andrew Logie.

8. A lot of 50 acres in Frederica orderd to Hollyday Laws.

3 May. 44.

Egmont	C	Towers, Christr.	C
Oglethorpe	C	Vernon, Ja.	C
Towers, Tho.	C		

1. The Same afternoon the gentlemen here mention'd met in Committee of Correspondence and did Some business. Col. Oglethorpe finding us resolv'd to Strike off all manner of expence of labour & Credit, and to Subsist none but those we were obliged to by Contract, desired that the Common Council would write letters to that purpose, that the people might not impute So Severe an order (as he called it) to him or any advice of his.

9 May. 45.

Egmont	C	Tracy, Robt.	C
Lapotre, Hen.	C	Vernon, Ja.	C
Towers, Tho.	C		

1. We met in Committee of Correspondence, and agreed that all Reports of Such Committees Should be enter'd fair in our books, that if any parts Should be dissented to or alterd by the Board of Common Council, it might appear what was the Sense of those Gentlemen who made the Reports, that they might be justified when contrary resolutions were taken.

10 May. 46.

Archer, Hen.	C		Smith, Saml.	C
Egmont	C		Ld. Tirconnel	C
Heathcote, Sr. Will.	C		Towers, Tho.	C
Lapotre, Hen.	C	P	Tracy, Robt.	C
LaRoch, Jo.	C	Ch.	Vernon, Ja.	C
Oglethorpe, Ja.	C		Anderson, Adm.	T

1. The Report of the Committee of Accompts dat. 23 March 1737/8 was received, to the purpose following:

a. That by Accts. recd. from Georgia the expences of the Colony for 7 months from Nov. 1736 to Mid Summr. 1737 amounted to 5905.5.9½ which is 843.12.3 *p* Month. And for 9 months from Mid Summr. 1737 to Lady day 1738 (including the Sola bills Sent for defraying the Said expences to that time) they amounted to 5729.19.7¼ which is 636.13.3 *p* month.

b. That besides these Expences paid & appropriated for payment, there are demands for certified Accts. of Stores, necessaries, & pay, Still due & unpaid to the amount of 2228.15.5 which when paid out of the 8000£ granted this Session of Parliament, the Said Stores, necessaries, & Sola bills now in the Colony, will be more than Sufficient to Supply the expence thereof, on the foot of the last establish'd allowances Sent over with Mr. Stephens, until the End of July 1738. The Said Allowances not amounting to 500£ *p* month.

c. Which establish'd allowances (Sent by Mr. Stephens) being twice read over, the Committee were of opinion the following articles therein ought to be Struck off, and be no longer defray'd by the Trustees, they relating to the defence of the Colony, which the Trustees are no longer concern'd to provide for, because the money granted in this Session of Parliamt. is only towards Settling the Colony. Which Several Articles are as follows:

The expence of Capt. Macpherson & 25 Rangers at Fort Arguile *p* ann.	629.14. 4
Do. of Jo. Cuthbert & 6 Rangers	168. 0. 0
Do. of Mr. Willy & 3 Rangers	96. 0. 0
Do. of Mr. Tho. Jones & 2 Men	35. 2. 8
Do. of Capt. Mackintosh & 10 Men at Fort St. George	241. 7. 0
Do. of the Capt. Lieut. & 15 Men at Fort Augusta	324. 0. 0
Do. of the Ingenier, gunner, Master of the Pettiagua, 2 Men & 4 labourers at Frederica	143.17.10
Do. of an Ensign, Overseer of the Works, 10 Men, a Storekeeper, a Surgeon & 2 Carpenters at St. Andrews	257. 2.10
Do. of the Carolina Scout boat, consisting of a patroon, 12 Men & provisions for them	308. 2. 6
Total relatg. to ye. defence of ye. Colony	2203. 7. 2

d. That the Committee were further of opinion, that the two Men employ'd in the Store at Frederica the expence whereof is 48£ *p* ann., and the Store keeper and Cattel keeper at the Darien, the expence whereof is 26£ *p* ann. ought also to be Struck off, the time of maintenance of the Inhabitants in the Southern division expiring in Feby. last. And that for the keeping Such Stores as may be necessary hereafter for the Said division, the care thereof Should be under the direction of One Store keeper for the whole Province.

e. That the Committee afterwards took into consideration the future expences of the Colony in America, and were of opinion that they Should be limitted to the following Articles & Sums for One year to commence from Midsummer next, viz.

For the Services of the 3 Bailifs & the Recordr. of Savannah & the 3 Bailifs & Recr. at Frederica	80. 0. 0
For Do. of 6 Constables & 24 Tything Men in the Said Towns for 6 Wards in each, & a Constable & 4 Tything Men to each Ward at 5£ *p* ann. each	300. 0. 0
For the Service of a Storekeeper at 30£ *p* ann., and a Clerk under him at 10£, and 8£ in lieu of provision	48. 0. 0
For the Services of 2 more Clerks engaged by the Trust, to be employ'd as they Shall think fit, at 10£ *p* ann. each, & 8£ each in lieu of provision	36. 0. 0

To an Overseer of the Millrights, &c	10. 0. 0
To the Maintenance of the Secy. in Georgia & his Son at 10£ a year, and of his 10 Servants at 6£ a year each, and for his extraordy. charges at 40£ a year	120. 0. 0
For 4 Ministers in Georgia at 50£ *p* each	200. 0. 0
For the necessary Support of the Sick, the Widows & Orphans in the Northern division	100. 0. 0
For do. in the Southern division	50. 0. 0
To a Messenger between Frederica & Savannah	80. 0. 0
To Mr. Auspurger the Surveyor to Survey lands	54.15. 0
To an Assistant to him at 12. a day as he shall Require For the Smiths to repair Indian Arms, & do other repairs at 25£ *p* ann. each	50. 0. 0
For the charge of the Italian Silkwinders	70.12.11
To the Publick gardens at ⅛ *p* working day	23. 9. 6
To a Cowkeeper at Ebenezar	24.12. 7
And 1 Shill. *p* cow for all to one hundred, but all others to be Sent to Ebenezar	
A Sea boat at Tybee: and a Sea boat at Frederica, instead of the hive of 2 pettiaguas which charge amounted to 113.9.5	
For Contingencies, to exclude all charges of the Indians (presents excepted which are to be Sent from England) and all other accidental (except extraordinary) charges, not exceeding 5£ *p* month for the Northern Division & 5£ *p* month for ye S. division	120. 0. 0
	1367.10.10

N.B. This is exclusive of the articles which have no figures to them, Which Several expences the Committee were of opinion Should be defray'd by the Issues of Sola bills in Georgia, for that purpose to be Sent over under the Trustees Seal, and to be filled up to Will. Stephens Esq., Mr. Tho. Causton, and Mr. Hen. Parker, to each of whom an Acct. of the Expences to be defray'd Should be Sent: and that any two of them Should be empowered to issue the Said bills from time to time as occasion for those expences Should rise; and that they Should be directed to Send the Trustees an account Sign'd by both of them On every Issue, Shewing to whom, and for what Services, agreable to the expences order'd by the Trust, each respective Issue was made, with a list of the Several Issues So made.

f. To this long and material report the Common Council agreed after a considerable debate, Col. Oglethorpe labouring hard for retaining Some military expences which he Seem'd to have more concern for, than for the Civil, tho he Saw how low our Cash was reduced: but as he was now to take on him the defence of the Colony, that was most at his heart.

2. Order'd that 500£ be appropriated out of the 8000£ granted this Session of Parliament, when received, to answer the like Sum in Sola bills, to be immediatly Sent over to Georgia (being part of the 2850£ residue of the bills orderd to be made out 10 August last and Still unsent) towards defraying the above Establishment from Mid Summr. 1738.

N.B. This was intended as a Credit in Sola bills to be given Col. Oglethorpe to defray unforeseen exigences from the time of his arrival in Georgia, when all Credit is to Stop, untill our new Regulation of expences Should take place.

Order'd that when any of these Sola bills Shall return to England for payment, that any 5 of the Common Council be empowerd to draw on the bank for payment of them.

3. It appear'd to the board, that from Michlemass 1737 to March following, that wastfull Man Causton had expended 11000£ besides what other certified Accounts he may have drawn on us from that time not come to hand. We were therefore unanimous in reducing our Establishment, Col. Oglethorpe excepted, who Shew'd the greatest reluctance, and thereby did not a little displease the rest.

4. The board took under consideration a further Report of the Committee relating to the Services of Mr. Causton employ'd as Store keeper upwards of 5 years at an allowance after the rate of 40£ p ann. And that the business of the Store keeper being now much reduced, and Mr. Causton also otherwise employ'd, they were of opinion he Should have a months time after the receipt of the Trustees next letter to make out the remain of Stores, and his Several Accts. both of Cash & Stores to be forwarded to England: and that his Sallary of 40£ p ann. Should be continued from feby. last (to which time it had been paid) to the end of ye. Said month after the receipt of Such letter, and that he Should be assisted by the Clerks the Trustees Sent over, until his Said Accts. were perfected: Which when perfected and if allow'd of by the Trustees after examination) Mr. Causton Should be further gratifyed for his past Services. And that Mr. Thomas Stephens Succeed him as Storekeeper.

5. To this the Common Council agreed, only what related to Mr. Tho. Stephens, for on consideration that his father was ap-

pointed to inform us of all things that Should happen amiss, and that if his Son Should mismanage the Stores, it would be a great hardship on him to complain of him. The Common Council therefore appointed Mr. Tho. Jones (formerly High Constable of St. Gyles, to Succeed as Storekeeper of the whole Province, and take possession of the remain of Stores in Georgia, he giving 1000£ Security, and now going over with Col. Oglethorpe. And that he Should have 30£ p ann. allowance, his Clerk 10£, and 8£ more in lieu of provision for his Clerk.

6. A Petition of Majr. Will. Cook of Col. Oglethorpes Regiment was read, Setting forth that he design'd a good house at Frederica, and that his daughters Anne and Susan being joynt Proprietors of the house, garden, lot & farm lot at Savannah, lately belonging to Peter Hordon, he pray'd leave that his daughter Anne when of age might be permitted to Surrender her Interest in the lot at Savannah to her Sister, whereby his daughter Anne might be enabled to hold as her property the house garden lot and farm Lot at Frederica, which he would build & cultivate farther. The petition was granted.

7. Mr. Whitfeild on a letter dated from Giberaltar 20 Feby. desiring Some Stationary ware, and offering to be Settled in what part of Georgia we please, Since Mr. John Wesley was (as he heard) return'd to England: It was order'd that he be wrote word that he Should have liberty to exercise his Ecclesiastical function as Deacon at Savannah as well as at Frederica, until a Minister for Savannah be Sent over.

8. Orderd that Stationary ware be provided for Mr. Whitfeild.

10 May. 47.

Egmont	C	Towers, Tho.	C
Lapotre, Hen.	C	Tracy, Rob.	C
Oglethorpe, Ja.	C	Vernon, Ja.	C
Smith, Saml.	C	Anderson, Adm.	T
Ld. Tirconnel	C		

1. The Same Evening the gentlemen on the other Side mention'd met again, and Read Col. Oglethorpes Acct. of 1093.0.9½ Sterlg. Stated to be due from him the 9th of June last, with which he deliverd to us the vouchers; & the Same was refer'd to the Committee of Accounts to Settle the Same with Col. Oglethorpe after his arrival in Georgia, for we found it could not be done before, He being to Set out tomorrow.

On the ballance he agreed that he was indebted to the (amount of) 480£.

2. Read also Mr. Bradley's Acct. of Debtr. & Credr. between him and the Trust, by which he makes us Debtr. to him above 400£. But we unanimously agreed that it was unsatisfactory for want of particulars and Vouchers.

This Bradley was indented to go over and cultivate 100 Acres of Trust land, from which he was to receive out of the first proffits made of the land 100£: and he was to have 30 Trust Servants to be employ'd thereon. He also was to have 10 Servants to be employ'd thereon. He also was to have 10 Servants at the Trustees charge for his own use, and to cultivate the land granted to him. But without distinguishing his own Servants from those of the Trust (of which last he never indeed had his number) he brings us in debt to him for making use of his Servants upon other works than the cultivation of his own or the Trustees Acres, which he Says was order'd by Col. Oglethorpe.

N.B. This interposition of Col. Oglethorpes in a contract made by the Trust was very displeasing to the Trustees, and cool'd the zeal of Several, who fear'd he would involve them in expences & difficulties not to be got over by assuming more power than became him, whilst they laboured to abridge his power. Some of them also were displeased that Since he had the promise of a Regiment he quitted the Minority Side who opposed the Court measures, and behaved in Parliamt. on the opposite Side. There might be Some also Envious that he Should be the only gainer by the Establishment of our Colony, whilst the rest of the Trustees gave their Service to the publick for nothing, for they hinted that he had this point of a Regiment in view from the beginning; But I am thoroughly persuaded he never dream'd of getting a Regiment when the Charter was granted.

At parting we took leave of Col. Oglethorpe, he being to Set out tomorrow to embark.

[N.B.] 11 May 1738. Col. Oglethorpe Set out for Portsmouth, by express orders from his Majesty to embark the first fair wind.

16 May. 48.

Egmont	C	Vernon, Ja.	C
Lapotre, Hen.	C		

1. We met in a Committee of correspondence, to draw up letters to Mr. Causton and others.

2. Capt. Thomas the Ingenier attending, we gave him directions abt. building a Church in Georgia.

[N.B.] 16 May 1738. I learn'd of Mr. Verelst, that no orders are yet given by the Govermt. for embarking the Stores that are to go wth. Col. Oglethorpe, consisting of Canon, powder &c. He can do nothing agst. the Spaniards in case of an attack, and yet he was hurry'd away by a certain day, as if it was of great importance he Should be on the Spot as Soon as possible. Whether this retardment be a contrivance, or only the effect of that Spirit of dillatoriness and negligence which reigns in all our Offices & affairs, I cannot determine.

The letters prepared by the Committee, having recd. Some additions at the Common Council next day, were Sent the 19 of that month, and their Substance was as follows, viz.

To Mr. Hugh Anderson we took notice of his good care & observations relating to the Publick garden. We exprest our concern that the grove of trees which Sheltered it was cut down, and that it likewise lay exposed to every bodies coming in and destroying the fruits. That he Should Send word how many days a ditch Surrounding the garden of 4 feet deep and proportionably wide, together with a hedge on the inside of the pales would take up. Also how many days in probability the making a pump or well in the garden would take up, and how many days to make proper divisions by hedges in the garden by 2 Men. That he Should raise as many vines, Olive trees & Mulberry trees as he could, which latter are best raised from Seeds.

To Mr. Abraham DeLyon We wrote that upon a bond enterd into by Dr. Samuel Nunez, Mr. Daniel Nunez, Mr. Moses Nunez & himself of 400£ penalty, Col. Oglethorpe had direction to advance him 200£, for propagating vines.

To Tho. Hawkins Esq., First Bailif of Frederica that we were pleasd to hear the harmony the people lived in, as he wrote us in Novbr. last, That he could not be too particular in acquainting us with whatever was worth our notice, Since We can only govern our Selves by the Accts we receive from thence. That he Should constantly inform us of the Improvements in building and cultivation of land, the births and deaths of people, and their behaviour in general. We recommended Sobriety and Industry, We promised our favour to the most industrious, and acquainted him that we had order'd the druggs he wrote for.

To Mr. Geo. Whitfeild that we are pleas'd with his zeal, and permit him to perform all Religious duties as deacon of the

Church of England at Savannah as well as at Frederica, until another Minister is provided for Savannah. That We doubt not but he will lay every Spirit of dissention among the people, and that he will recommend Sobriety, and a due reverence to the Magistracy, as the most effectual means to make them quiet and happy, and qualify them for a just observance of the Worship of God. And that we had orderd him a box of Stationary ware.

To Mr. Stephens that We had recd. his letter of 19 Jany. & journal, & were well pleased his being So particular in his Accts. That we take notice of the dissatisfaction he mentions among Several people at the Tenure of their lands being confind to heirs Male, and of his observation on the advantages of their going to heirs general. That we were persuaded, this would on Second reflection appear to him impracticable, as the Colony will consist of people of So many different Countries. That to convince him that the Trustees always had and ever will have a disposition to make the people perfectly easie in this particular, and to grant the lotts when ever there is a failure of Male Issue to the daughters of any Proprietor, We enclos'd to him a Clause in the printed terms (which are always offer'd to Such persons as go at their own expence) relating to the Females, which are as follows:

When the land reverts to the Trust on the determination of Estates in Tail Male, it is to be granted again to Such persons as the Common Council of the Trustees Shall think most for the advantage of the Colony. And the Trust will have a Special regard to the daughters of those who have made Improvements on their Lotts, not already provided for by having marry'd or marrying persons in possession or entitled to lands in the Province of Georgia in possession or remainder. And the wives of Such persons, in case they Should Survive their husbands, and during their lives, entitled to the Mansion house & one half of the lands emproved by their husbands, that is to Say, enclosed with a fence 6 feet high.

We likewise inform'd Mr. Stephens that we think fit to adhere to the Covenants which were made in the peoples Several grants, and are determin'd to take the forfeit of Grants of those who neglect to cultivate their lands.

The letter to Mr. Causton is So long and contains So many particulars that it cannot be Spoke of here but in a general, and I refer to the book of letters. This Sufficient to take notice that he most egregiously mismanaged our affairs. That Servants carry'd over at the owners risk were by him taken on the Trustees Acct. and instead of being employ'd in their Service, were Sent upon credit to the Inhabitants, who afterwards hired them out to the Trustees at day labour. That he had given large credits to others. That he received large Cargoes of Ships when not wanting; that he had mounted the Expence of the Colony Since Mid Sumr. 1737 to 11684.16.7 And plunged the Trustees in debt. That he had not Sent his Accompts nor explained particular Services as required.

That therefore they had removed him from keeping the Stores & appointed Mr. Thomas Jones to Succeed him. That when the remainder of Stores Should be exhausted, the Trustees would Shut up their publick Store. We Sent him at the Same time our estimate of Expences for the year ending Midsummr. 1739; and an Invoice of goods Sent with Mr. Oglethorpe.

17 May. 49.

Archer, Hen.	C P	Smith, Saml.	C
Egmont	C	Ld. Tirconnel	C
Heathcote, Sr. Will.	C	Vernon, Ja.	C Ch.
Lapotre, Hen.	C	Anderson, Adm.	T
LaRoch, Jo.	C	Gough, Sr. Hen.	T
Shaftsbury	C		

A Common Council was Summond to receive the Report of the Committee of Accts. on the Cash Acct. of Coll. Oglethorpe, and the Several other Reports not yet made, and for what other business Shall appear necessary before the departure of the Men of War & Transports from Spithead.

1. The wife of Joseph Watson of Savannah appeard before us, and desired a copy of our order to Mr. Causton relating to her husband, and Said that if our Order was consonant to our reply to the Privy Council, then that Causton had not obey'd our order. We Show'd her the Order we Sent, and acquainted her that in pursuance thereof, her husband had been released from his confinement, and his Effects submitted to arbitration by his own consent, there being an Accompt to make up between him and others, but that the Trustees had not meddled with his effects. She Said we had Sent two orders over, which we told her was not true. She then desir'd a copy of our order, which we refused, having reason to believe She only demanded it by advice of her lawyer to give us unreasonable trouble. On this She went away complaining.

2. We prepared a letter to Mr. Hugh Anderson, in answer to his to me of the 10 August last, commending his care of the pub-

lick garden, and giving directions relating thereto, And desiring to know certain expences relating to it. This letter was Sent the 19th of this month.

3. The Committee of Accompts of 19 April 1738 reported that Abraham deLyon of Savannah might be advanc'd 200£ for advancing vines in Georgia to be repayd by him in 6 years, and that Col. Oglethorpe pay the Same to him, out of the ballance of his Acct. due from him to the Trust. The Same was agreed to.

4. The Committee of Accompts of 10 May 1738, to whom Col. Oglethorpes Acct. was refer'd, reported, that there will be due from him (after he has paid to Abraham Delyon the 200£ above mentiond), 424.2.10¾.

The Report was agreed to, and order given to acquaint Col. Oglethorpe therewith.

5. The Committee of Correspondence 26 April 1738 reported, that Mr. Hen. Parker might be allow'd 2 Trust Servants under Mr. Bradley's care, to be entertaind by the Trustees till further order, & that 20£ be Sent him in linnen &c in consideration of his Services as 2d Bailif of Savannah: and if the Said Servants have wives that they also be paid for by the Trust.

6. They reported also that in case Mr. Tho. Christie continued in his office of Recorder, he might have 2 Trust Servants now under Mr. Bradleys care to be maintaind for his use at the Trustees expence. Which reports the Board agreed to.

7. The Committee of 3 May 1738 reported their opinion that Col. Oglethorpe Should be directed to order an Acct. of the remain of Stores to be taken immediatly after his arrival, and to know of Mr. Causton what demands any person has upon the Stores, that the Trustees may be acquainted with the State of their Affairs, before they create any new expence.

8. In the Said report, the Committee gave their opinion concerning Capt. Hewets demand for the transport of 120 heads & ½ of Palatine Servants carry'd by him; upon which the board orderd that enquiry Should be made in Savannah, and an Acct. return'd us, before we would pay the whole of Capt. Wrag his Owners demand.

9. The Said Committee reported their opinion upon Capt. Dunbars demand of primage for 2 voyages of the Ship Prince of Wales 1734 & 1735, that he Should be paid 28£ in full discharge: which the Board agreed to.

10. Report from the Committee of Accts. and correspondence of 16 May 1738, that the Plan of a Church at Savannah drawn by

Mr. Flitchcroft be put into the hands of Capt. Thomas Ingenier, and that he be desired to alter the plan as he judges most likely to answer the Trustees intention, and that he make an estimate of the expence of Said Church & Send the Same to the Trustees.

This was agreed to.

11. The Board filled up Some blanks left open in the Estimate of the years establishment ending Midsummr. 1739, and added a Scout boat (for that year only) consisting of a Patroon & 10 Men & provisions for them, the expence of which is 258.15.1.

12. Order'd that Will. Stephens Esq. our Secy. take the care of our letters, and that it be refer'd to the Committee of Correspondence to draw up an advertismt. to that purpose to be fixt up in Georgia, that the Inhabitants might be aprized of a Safe correspondence with their friends in England.

13. We took into consideration the complaint made by the Inhabitants of Highgate, and orderd Mr. Stephens and Mr. Hugh Anderson to view the land wch. they alledge to be very bad. It is our intention to add Some better land to that they now hold in case their complaint be just.

14. Orderd that it be refer'd to the Committee of Accts. to determine finally the application of the Trust Servants, and make the proper disposition of them.

15. Orderd that Mr. Causton be wrote to (pursuant to the Report of the Committee of Accts. and Correspondence 23 March 1737/8) that no expences will be allow'd or defrayed, but those estimated for the Service of one year ending Mid Summr. 1739; and that notice be taken in the Same letter of the great expences incurr'd by him, for which he has given no Satisfactory Acct. Therefore that he be directed to Send over copies of all his journals or day books and ledgers from Lady day 1734, and that he continue to Send the Same every three months.

16. Orderd that Col. Oglethorpe do Set out the 3000 Acres design'd for the Soldiers of his Regiment, at 5 acres to each person.

17. Orderd that 3000 acres more be Set out for Such persons as Shall joyn the Colony, by Will. Stephens Esq., and Mr. Hugh Anderson at Savannah; and Mr. Houghton and the 1 Bailif of Frederica, & that these four be Trustees thereof.

18. Orderd that the Seal be put to all the orders made this day where requisite.

[N.B.] 20 May 1738. Mr. Verelts wrote to Mr. Hen. Parker, commending his good behaviour, and acquainting him that the Trustees had Sent him cloathing & necessaries to the value of 20£

Sterlg. as also allowd him 2 Trust Servants with their wives if married, to be maintaind by the Trustees till further order.

That they had appointed Robt. Gilbert for 3d Bailif.

That they had appointed Mr. Tho. Jones for Store keeper in Mr. Caustons room, who is a month after his arrival was to take the keys.

That the remain of Stores are in the first place to maintain the Trust Servants, who were now the only persons to maintain at the Trust expence, and Mr. Jones was to issue them pursuant to the orders he Should receive from Mr. Stephens, himself and Mr. Causton, or any two, who were likewise to defray the expences of the Estimate Sent over for the Service of the Colony for the year endg. Midsummer 1739, and Sign the Acct. of them, and Send it from time to time to the Trustees Specifying the Services for and to whom Such expences were paid. That they were to do the Same by the parcels Sent with Col. Oglethorpe, Only Col. Oglethorpe was to direct the presents Sent for the Indians, as he thought fit.

The Same 20 May 1738, Mr. Verelts wrote to Mr. William Bradley, reciting the Trustees agreement with him, and Shewing that they had done more than fulfilling it. That as to his alledging that his ten Servants had been employ'd in the Trustees Service, Mr. Tho. Jones had orders to enquire into it, by whose order they were So employ'd & for what time, who was likewise to enquire what Service the Trustees Servants under his care had done for the Trust. That he is also to examine his Acct. of demands on the Trust.

That the Trustees had order'd the following uses for Some of the Trust Servts. under his care, which he was to comply with, viz.

7 Servants for cultivating land in the Northern division of the Province, for Religious uses:

2 Men Servants to Mr. Hen. Parker and their wives if marry'd, and 2 more to Mr. Tho. Christie.

[N.B.] 25 May, Lieut. Govr. Bull wrote a Memorial to the Board of Trade Setting forth his Majesties just Title to Carolina & Georgia, and the unreasonable pretentions of the Spaniards thereto.

[N.B.] 26 May 1738. Mr. Causton wrote to the Trustees excusing exceedings of expences he had made.

Complaining that Mr. Bradley would not Stand to his Contract wth. the Trustees.

That he had given Credit to the Inhabitants, who otherwise would have deserted.

That he desired a certain Estimate of Expences & orders thereon.

That Lieut. Cochran was arrived the 6th inst. wth. his part of the Regiment.

That Mr. Whitfeild chose to Stay at Savannah, till conveniencies were made at Frederica.

That in obedience to our orders he would certify no more Accompts.

That those Sent will give an Acct. of the Colonys debts, but the whole he could not make out, till the Acct. for the year 1737 was made up, which he was about.

[N.B.] 26 May 1738, Mr. Robt. Millar wrote from Jamaica to the Trustees, that the Spaniards would not Suffer him to Search their Countries for roots plants &c So that he found himself of no further use to us as Botanist. But that the beginning of next year he would carry the Ipicuana he had collected to Georgia: in the mean time he waited our orders.

[N.B.] 27 May 1738. Mr. Stephens wrote to the Trustees, & with it Sent his journal. He acquainted that divisions Subsided, & every one followed their own business quietly.

That he Should expect a perfect reformation but for that cursed evil Rum, which in Spight of the Magistrates care was Sold in private houses. That the well being of the Colony depended on Suppressing it.

That the people (many of them) were more industrious this year than heretofore, when they were discouraged from labour by Some that had thrown up their plantations.

That the Ebenezar and Darien people will in a little time want no assistance, being an example for labour having no Rum, but the people of Savannah lived irregularly.

That the Jews are a Shame to them, for good living, and those who are of the better Sort in Savannah & would be call'd Gentlemen, and would be thought politicians, and reform the constitution of the Colony, Scarce ever go to Church.

That Mr. Whitfeild was most welcome to the Sober part.

That Mr. Delamot the Schoolmaster was going to England, who had been very diligent in instructing the children.

That the Encouragement given the Potter was well bestow'd & rightly apply'd. That Andrew Duchee the Master had built a convenient dwelling house with a large Kiln in a room annext, together with 2 Other large rooms One for a Ware house, the other a work house, all in one compact building, well contrived handsomly finish'd & well accommodated for carrying on his work. That he is a Sober diligent and Modest Man, had baked 2 kilns of handsome ware of various kinds of pots, pans, bowls, cupps & Juggs, and wants no customers. That his next aim is to do Something more curious for transportation and is making tryal of other fine clays, a Small tea cup of which he Shewd him, which when held agst. the light was almost transparent.

That the Silk manufacture will certainly come to perfection in a little more time, but this unkind March had cut off the more early Mulberry leaves, & proved no Small balk to it.

That the Assembly of Carolina had Settled a Sallary of 100£ p ann. for 7 years on a Piedmontese & his wife to teach them the manufacture in all its branches, and these were to take Several Apprentices.

[N.B.] 27 May 1738. Mr. Stephens wrote to our Accompt. that he had given publick notice to the inhabitants to Send him their letters design'd for England that they might have a Safe conveyance. but none were Sent to him, Some of the wise heads reporting that it look'd to them, that the Trustees had a mind to get all letters into their own hands. So jealous were Some folks least their dark work Should come to light.

N.B. These were Robt. Williams, Tailfer the Surgeon & other Scots who had abandon'd their plantations, and were displeased at the Tenure in Tail Male, and being deny'd the use of Negroes. But in this Suggestion they basely traduced the Trustees, who had no other design by inviting the Inhabitants to Send their letters to enclose in our Secretary's packet than to render their conveyance more Secure.

Mr. Stephens also wrote that the Servants were in general a Sad crew, that of his 10 he never had above 5 work at a time, Some whores, others theives, others Sick, So that their work paid not for their food & cloathes.

That Mr. Wanset Qur. Master of Col. Oglethorpes Regimt. who was Some years about Bordeaux and understands vinyards perfectly well, designd if a Ship on which he expected vine Slips came in before Christmass to plant a vinyard of 4000 plants: a thing of great advantage to the Colony.

30 *May.* 50.

Egmont	C	Towers, Tho.	C
Lapotre, Hen.	C		

1. We met as a Committee of Correspondence, but did no business, only read divers letters that arrived last Wednesday, together with the continuation of Mr. Stephens journal from 17

Jany to 28 feby. last, with Several lists enclosed by him. The date of the last letter was of the 1 March, which mentioned no Attempt of the Spaniards on Georgia.

2. Yesterday & to day came more certified Accts. to the amount of 707.16.7 whereby the amount come to Mr. Causton's hands Since Midsummer 1737 was encreased to 12392.13.2 and the certified Accts. unpaid, to 4542.3.11.

31 May. 51.

Egmont	C		Smith, Saml.	C
Heathcote, Sr. Will.	C		Ld. Tirconnel	C Ch.
Lapotre, Hen.	C P		Towers, Tho.	C
LaRoch, Jo.	C		Towers, Christr.	C
Shaftsbury	C		Vernon, Ja.	C

A Common Council was Summond to receive Reports from the Committee of Correspondence and Accompts. and other business.

1. Dr. John Burton pd. his annual 10£ benefaction towards maintaining a Catechist in Savannah. And Mr. Tracy pd. his 10£ Subscription to the Same use.

2. Read the Several letters lately arrived, and were greatly displeased with Mr. Caustons Sending over Such numbers of certified Accompts, and Some for whole Cargoes of goods received by him into the Stores without any necessity but only to please & Serve the owners of those Cargoes, by which it appeard he overcharged the Stores to the great diminution of our Fund, and hazard of our money, he having credited persons not upon the Stores the repayment of which was very dubious.

It was beleived by Some of the gentlemen, that Col. Oglethorpe had directed him to overstock the Stores that his Regiment at their arrival might not want provision, or the Inhabitants encouragement, and that as thereby he would exceed our estimate and the Sola bills Sent to answer it, he put him upon certifying Accts. on the credit of which he made what expences he pleasd. But this manner of certifying accounts was a manifest evasion of our orders, who when we wrote to Mr. Causton to draw no more bills upon us, mean'd that the Sola bills we Sent over Should alone answer the expences of the Colony, of which we took care to Send a Sufficient number for that purpose.

3. There were now come by Capt. Thompson two certified Accounts, one of 434.13.4 and another of 469.1.1½. The first for 56

Servants carry'd over at his own risk, yet taken by Mr. Causton on the Trust Acct.

The other was for other accounts.

We resolv'd to pay but one of them: the other we returnd to the Captain to recover of Mr. Causton. But because he had always Shew'd himself zealous for the colonies Service, and pleaded that unless his bill were paid, he Should be a great Sufferer, that money being necessary to freight his Ship anew for Georgia, we orderd that 400£ Should be advanc'd him upon his & his owners joynt bond and an assignment of his policy on his Ship out and home, that he would use all proper means to recover the Same from Causton pursuant to the instructions that Should be given him by the Trustees. And we privately intimated to him, that if he recoverd it not we would pay it. For it was the opinion of the Lawyers of our board that the Trust were obliged to pay Accts. certified by our Servant for goods actually received on our Acct.

4. Agreed to petition the Treasury for the 8000£ granted this year by Parliament.

5. Read the opinion of Mr. Strange Sollicr. Genl. on the case of our refusal to pay Mr. Ellis's bill, and resolv'd to take no notice of it, Mr. Williams his Agent having mistated the case.

6. His Majesties Order in Council was read, by which the Ordenance past in Carolina for raising 2000£ Sterlg. to indemnify the Traders of that Province who Should act contrary to the Georgia law for regulating the Indian Trade within our Province is with much expression of resentment disallow'd, and annull'd. We orderd that a copy of it Should be Sent by his nights Post to Portsmouth to Col. Oglethorpe to carry with him to Georgia.

7. Grant past to David Prevost of the Widow Hews lot in Savannah, being at the desire of John West who marry'd her, and with her consent.

8. Draft order'd on the Bank for 400£ to be advanc'd Capt. Thompson.

9. Orderd that any 5 of the Common Council may draw on the Bank for 500£ to put in Aldn. Heathcotes hands to answer expences of the Colony.

10. A Moravian lately arrived from Georgia to Settle Accts. with the Trust for moneys advanc'd them to Settle, gave us a very good Acct. of their proceedings. They are now repaying us the money we lent them.

[N.B.] 31 May 1738. Mr. Verelts, by order wrote to Col. Oglethorpe at Portsmouth that a Stop must be put to all Credit in

Georgia. That Mr. Causton had received Since Midsummer 1737, 12392.13.2, and the certified Accts. unpaid amount to 4542.3.11.

He enclosed to him a copy of the Order of Council for annulling the Carolina Ordenance for raising 2000£ Sterlg. to indemnify their traders who Should Act contrary to the Georgia law for regulating the Indian Trade in Georgia: and acquainted him that the Privy Council would give instructions to both Provinces to concert measures in the execution of the law for regulating the Indian Trade which may be for the mutual advantage & Safety of both Provinces, but the Same was not yet Settled. A day or two after they being communicated to us privately but not Sent us in form, We Sent them to Col. Oglethorpe.

1 June. 52.

Lapotre, Hen.	C	Vernon, Ja.	C
Towers, Tho.	C		

1. These Gentlemen met as a Committee of Correspondence, and prepared a letter to Mr. Oglethorpe directing him to Seize on Mr. Causton & his books as Soon as he arrived in Georgia that he may be brought to Acct. for buying whole Cargoes without orders from the Trustees, and for certifying Accts. after orders came to him not to do it. So that he had ran the Trustees out more than 5000£ of the 8000£ given this year by Parliamt. which was to Serve till Midsummr. 1739, besides 11000£ not accounted for by him.

6 June. 53.

Egmont	C	LaRoch, Jo.	C
Lapotre, Hen.	C	Vernon, Ja.	C

We met in a Committee of Correspondence.

1. A letter from Col. Oglethorpe dat. from Gosport 4th inst. was read, acknowledging the receipt of the Committees letter of 1 inst. and promising at his arrival in Georgia to Seize on Causton, which he judg'd very fit.

2. A letter from Jo. Brownfeild Register at Savannah to Mr. Tuckwell dat. 8 April last was read, containing a justification of his conduct as Foreman of the Gr. Jury, and averring his constant disposition to Support the authority of the Magistrates. He further takes notice that he could not return him money for the

goods Sold on his Acct. because Mr. Causton had refused to give him a certified bill on the Trustees.

N.B. This discovers that when Traders brought goods to Sell at Savannah, Mr. Causton either took them into the Stores and placed them to the Trust Acct. without orders, or if Sold to others who had not money to pay for them, that he gave the purchassers credit, by paying the Owners on their behalf with drafts by certified Accts. on the Trustees, whereby the Trustees were ran out of their cash, far beyond the necessary provision they made for the Colony, and were become Creditors to a number of beggerly people who will never be able to repay.

3. A letter was read from Mr. Macbane to Mr. Oglethorpe dat. 29 March last, wherein he tells him that the Virginia Traders carry away the Indian Trade from us, because no orders were given to Seize their goods or make them pay a Fyne for trading with our Indians without Licence taken in our Colony.

He added that he had been in the Cherokee nation when his (viz. Col. Oglethorpe's) house was going on.

N.B. This article was new & Strange to us.

He added that he had 27 Servants of the 56 carry'd over by Capt. Thompson.

N.B. These were carry'd at the Owners own risk, and yet the Trustees were charged with them by Mr. Causton.

4. Capt. Howells affidavit (See fol. 253) was read relating to the Spaniards design to attack Georgia.

We gave early notice of their designs in April 1736 when we apply'd to the Governmt. for a military force to be Sent over to defend our Province, wherein So much time was lost, that half Col. Oglethorpes Regiment is Scarce arrived, & the other part ly's now Windbound at Portsmouth. Had not counter Orders arrived from Spain in time, our Province had been lost.

5. An addition was made to the duplicate of the letter Sent, to Mr. Stephens, viz. that he Should go with Mr. Henry Parker to Highgate, and examine into the Settlers complaint of bad land, and want of Cattel: and that if it appear'd that any of them had not a Sufficient quantity of good land to raise Subsistence for himself, and Stock, then to order the Surveyor to Set out for him 5 acres of the best land unset, and nearest his lot, he resigning the like number of unprofitable land, & lying the least convenient to him. And that if at the time of receiving this letter they had not received the cows & calves mention'd in their representation, that Mr. Bradley be directed to deliver them.

6. Francis Piercy formerly Publick Gardiner at Savannah (who ran away with Mr. Robt. Bathurst from thence to Carolina, to avoid paying debts to the Trustees for things advanc'd his father Sr. Francis without the Trustees knowledge, by Mr. Causton) arriving last Wednesday in London, came this evening to the Committee, and complain'd agst. Mr. Causton for never giving him a receipt for work done, or making up Accounts with him. He Said there was 30 Shillings due to him.

We ask'd him why he ran away from Georgia? He reply'd he did not run away, but having lost his Father & mother in law, Sr. Fra. Bathurst & his Lady, his wife could not bear the thoughts of Staying in the Country. That indeed he came privatly away, knowing that Mr. Causton would have Stopt him. That Mr. Bathurst his brother in law came with him as far as Carolina, because Mr. Causton laid claim to all Sr. Fra. Bathurst's Effects.

We told him we could Say nothing to his complaints until they were examin'd, for which purpose he Should put them in writing, and that it was not our method to determine anything by only hearing one Side. Upon which he reply'd he was Sorry to See we receiv'd him So cooly & went away. Wch. appear'd Strange to us, but we believed him drunk.

7. We prepared a letter to Col. Oglethorpe desiring he would Send for England Mr. Causton with his books & Accompts, to answer for his misbehaviour, to be laid Before the next Common Council.

7 *June.* 54.

Archer, Hen.	C		LaRoch, Jo.	C
Egmont	C	P	Smith, Saml.	C
Holland, Rogrs.	C		Towers, Tho.	C
Lapotre, Hen.	C	Ch.	Vernon, Ja.	C

A Common Council was Summon'd to receive Reports from the Committees of Correspondence & Accompts.

1. Seal'd a duplicate of our letter to Mr. Causton dat. 19 May.

2. A letter to Col. Oglethorpe from Jo. Crosse junr. Esq. Consul at the Madera was open'd and read offering to furnish Georgia with wine at easie rates, being Vidona Canary, being cheaper and more advantageous than Madera wine. Order'd that a letter be Sent him returning our thanks, but that at present we had no

occasion. Nevertheless we would recommend it to the Merchants who trade to Georgia.

3. The board re-considered the letter to Col. Oglethorpe of yesterday, and taking the opinions of Judge Holland & Mr. Henry Archer touching our order for Sending Mr. Causton over to England, they Said it could not legally be done, and if he Should So arrive a prisoner he would Sue out a habeas Corpus and be immediatly Set free. We therefore only order'd that he Should be kept in Safe custody in Georgia, on giving Security, till his Accts. from Lady day 1734 were examined & approved, and until the Trustees gave further direction.

It appeard he has not accounted for 13832 of our money Since Midsummer 1737.

4. Orderd that a copy of Capt. Hewets affidavit concerning the Spaniards purpose to attack Georgia be enclosed in a letter to Mr. Stone Secy. to the D. of Newcastle, & that he be desired to Shew it his Grace.

5. A letter from Col. Oglethorpe dat. 6 inst. was read, expressing the highest dissatisfaction at the Privy Councils instructions to the Trustees concerning our amicably adjusting the Indian trade with the Carolinians to mutual Satisfaction, and declaring, that were he at leasure or liberty to return to town, he would come & protest against it.

We orderd an answer to him this night that We were glad he did not come on this occasion, for those instructions were only communicated to us in private by Mr. Vernon, and not yet Sent in form, So that we have no proper cognizance of them as yet, wherefore neither he nor we can take cognizance of them as yet. But that when they came, we Should think it our duty, if we find anything in them prejudicial to the Colony, to make proper representations.

6. We drew up instructions for Mr. Abercromby Attorny. Genl. of Carolina & our Standing Counsel there, concerning the receipt of letters from Georgia to England, which he promised faithfully to forward as they came to his hand.

7. Removal of Mr. Tho. Causton from being 1st Bailif of Savannah, past the Seal.

8. Appointment of Mr. Hen. Parker to be 1 Bailif in his room past the Seal.

9. Draft made on the Bank of 132.15.3 to answer certain payments.

1737 to 1738

The Number of Trustee boards held this year were 23. Of Common Council Boards 21 (Summons was issued for 24 more but they were not attended). And of Committees 10. The whole number of days the Gentlemen met were 54, And the times each attended were as follows:

Common Councellors			Trustees		
Ayers, Robt.	7		Anderson, Adam	17	
Archer, Tho.	8		Archer, Hen.	2	before el. C.C.
Archer, Hen.	6	elected 16 March 1737/8	Bedford, Arthr.	3	
Bundy, Ri.	5	resignd 1 March 1737/8	Belitha, Will.	0	
			Bundy, Ri.	0	
Ld. Carpenter	16	resignd 16 March 1737/8	Bouvery, Sr. Jacob	0	electd. 16 Mar. 1737/8
Cater, Sr. Robt.	0	resignd 1 March 1737/8	Burgoign, Sr. Rogr.	0	el. 16 Mar. 1737/8
			Burton, Jo.	3	
Chandler, Ri.	2		Ld. Carpenter	1	after he quitted C.C.
Digby, Edwd.	4				
Egmont	50		Cater, Sr. Robt.	1	after he quitted C.C.
Eyles					
Frederick, Tho.	0		Coop, Ri.	0	
Heathcote, Geo.	3	resignd 8 March 1737/8	Coram, Tho.	0	
			Gonson, Sr. Jo.	0	
Heathcote, Sr. Will.	21		Gough, Sr. Hen.	1	
Hales, Steven	17		Hanbury, Will.	0	
Holland, Rogrs.	10		Heathcote, Geo.	0	
Lapotre, Hen.	45		Hucks, Robt.	3	
LaRoch, Jo.	21		Moor, Robt.	0	
Ld. Limerick	1		Page, John	1	before elected C.C.
Oglethorpe, Ja.	30				
Page, Jo.	0	elected 16 March 1737/8	Philips, Sr. Erasmus	0	
			Rundal, Tho.	0	Bi. of Derry
E. of Shaftsbury	10		Smith, Saml.	18	before elected C.C.
Sloper, Will	7				
Smith, Saml.	12	elected 16 March 1737/8	Ld. Talbot	0	
			Tracy, Robt.	0	
Ld. Talbot	1	resign'd 8 March 1737/8	Tyrer, Geo.	0	
			White, Jo.	0	
Ld. Tirconnel	14		Woolaston, Will.	0	
Towers, Tho.	21		Woolaston, Fra.	0	
Towers, Christr.	5	elected 16 March 1737/8			
Tracy, Robt.	9	elected 16 March 1737/8			
Vernon, Ja.	39				

The persons Sent this year at the Trustees charge were 185 Males and 113 females, in all 298; which with 1076 Sent in the former years makes 1374, whereof Foreigners 465, British 709.

Private Grants past this year

			Acres
1737, Oct.	5	To Robert Hay	500
	5	To Jo. Amory	150
Nov.	25	To Lt. Col. James Cochrane	500
	25	To Majr. Will. Cook	500
	25	To Geo. Preston, Esq.	500
Dec.	21	To Capt. Will. Wood	500
March	22	To James Carteret, Esq.	500
1738, April	26	To Capt. Alexr. Heron	500
			3650

Publick Grants past this year

17 May 1738	To Col. Oglethorpes Soldiers	3000	
	For 50 acre lotts to Such Protestants as Shall take them up within 3 years	3000	
			6000
			9650
	Grants past in the 5 former years		50685
	Total of Private & publick Grants past in 6 years		60335

Abstract of the 6th years Acct. of Receipts & Disbursments ending 9 June 1738

The Ballance of last years Accts. remaining unapply'd, viz. 3519.13.11, viz.

For the General Uses of the Colony	921.12. 0
For the Use of particular persons	112. 0. 0
For the building Churches	371.19. 9
For the Use of the Missionaries	328.15.11¼
For the Saltsburg Ministers	0. 0. 0
For the use of the Scots Minister at Darien	41.15. 6

For the Religious Uses of the Colony in gneral	408.17. 4¾	
For encouraging Botany & Agriculture in Georgia	1.13. 4	
Appropriated to answer Sola Bills	1333. 0. 0	
		3519.13.11

Money depending to be Accompted for in America 9 June 1737 - 9133.8.9½ viz.

Supplys to the Store house at Savannah 1737	3087. 9. 9½	
Do. to the Storehouse at Frederica 1737	1489.10. 0½	
Advanc'd to Several persons in America on acct. of further Supplyes for ye Colony to be expended by them the particulars of which are not yet received 1737	4556. 8. 11½	
		9133. 8. 9½
Money received in America within the time of this Acct		260. 0.10

Money Recd. in England within the time of this Acct. 20649.19. 0½, viz.

The Grant from Parliamt. 1737 includg. Fees of Offices	20000. 0. 0	
Private Benefactions for establishing the Colony	30. 0. 6	
For the Use of particular persons	105. 0. 2½	
For the Building Churches	320.10. 0	
For the Use of the Missionarys	69. 7. 0	
For the Use of the Scots Minister at Darien	0. 0. 0	
For the Religious uses of the Colony in general	10. 0. 0	
For encouraging Botany & Agriculture in Georgia	106.13. 4	
Consideration money for Trust Grants	8. 8	
		20649.19. 0½
Total Of Charge		33563. 2. 7

[1738] JOURNAL OF THE EARL OF EGMONT 377

Discharge

Apply'd in England, 6466.5.11¾, viz.

Charge of Stationary ware & printing _____	68.10. 2½
Do. of House Rent, necessaries for the Office & incidl. occasions ___	114. 8. 0½
Wages to Messengers & housekeeper, Rewards to the Secrety. & Accompt. & to others, and for extraordy. Clerkship _____	493. 2.10½
Charge of Sending 298 persons to Georgia on the Charity, & of Stores, working tools, a Saw Mill, refreshmts. on board, Arms, Amunition, cloathing, bedding, freight &c _____	4135. 2. 4¾
Charge of Engaging foreign Protestants & other Servants in Georgia exclusive of bedding & passage __	203.10. 8½
Do. of dying Silk in England & making the Suit for the Queen _____	26. 0. 0
Do. of Sola bills Sent to Georgia to be issued there _____	35. 5. 1
Do. of Law in the dispute between Carolina & Georgia _____	257. 0. 0
Do. of the Botanist's 2d. Contract pd. him in full _____	13. 6. 8
Do. of Sola bills pt. of the 1333. issued in Georgia, & paid within this Accompt _____	1120. 0. 0
	6466. 5.11¾

Apply'd in America, 13473.10.1¾

Charge of Surveying lands & Setting them out _____	11. 1. 2
Do. of Provisions Supply'd the Inhabitants to 31 Dec. 1737 deliver'd in paymt. to the Garisons & employ'd in fortifying, besides Cash paid for their Services _____	7021. 2. 3¼

Do. of pettiaguas, Scout boats and

other boats, & for freight of Passengers & goods from S. Carolina to Georgia	761. 2. 4¼
Do. for poultry, Swine, live Cattel & a Cattel keeper	699.18. 8¾
Do for Stores, Working Tools, & necessaries, besides those Sent from England	1259. 6. 6¾
Do. for generl. work in clearing ground, making roads, Sawing timber, fortifying, erecting corn and Saw Mills, labour in the publick garden, & charges of Servts. employd therein	691.19. 1¾
Do. Pay and charges of the Garisons & Rangers	548.15. 4½
Do. Arms, amunition & cloathing, besides those Sent from England	675.14. 4
Do. Presents to the Indians to purchasse lands & charges on them	819.15. 4¾
Do. Charges at St. Augustine to preserve peace wth. ye Spaniards	110. 0. 0
Do. Incident Charges in America	148.19.11¾
Do. Rewards to Severl. people in Georgia & America	343.17.10¾
Do. For production of Raw Silk	149. 0. 0¾
Do. Advanc'd to Several in Georgia to enable them to produce wines, erect a pottery, & carry on other works to be repaid the Trust	233.16.11
	13473.10. 1¾

Application of particular Benefactions as directed by the Givers

Repaid Jo. Venables unapplyd his benefaction to his Son	12. 0. 0 ⎫
For Mr. Thilo Saltsburg Surgeon who went over Oct. 1737	10.10. 0 ⎬ 22.10. 0
Expended for building churches in Georgia	117.14. 9
Expended on the Missionaries & Schools	161.11. 6
Expended on the Scots Missioner at Darien	41.15. 6

[1738] JOURNAL OF THE EARL OF EGMONT 379

Expended for the Religious uses of the Colony	15.10. 0
Expended for encouraging Botany & Agriculture	61.13. 4

Depending on Sevl. persons in America

Supply'd the Storekeepers at Savannah & Frederica, for furnishing the Storehouses wth. provisions, Tools &c	6316. 3. 2½
And for Money advanc'd to Several persons in America on Acct. for the further Supply of the Colony, & expended by them, the particular Acct. of which not yet return'd	2660. 8. 1
	8976.11. 3½
Total expended in America	29337. 2. 1
Charge, 33563. 2. 7. Ballance remaining	4226. 0. 6

Particulars of the Ballance carry'd to next years Acct.

Remaining for the Genl. Uses of the Colony	913.12.11
For the Use of particular persons	100. 0. 0
For the building Churches	574.15. 0
For the Use of the Missioners	236.11.10¼
For the use of the Scots Minister at Darien	0. 0. 0
For Religious Uses in general	403. 7. 4¾
For Encouraging Bottany & Agriculture	46.13. 4
Appropriated to answer Sola bills	1951. 0. 0
	4226. 0. 6

N.B. 171.5.7 pt. of the above 913.12.11 is appropriated towards building a Church in Savannah.

Index

A collation of Egmont's yearly indices.

Abott, Will., appointed to Succeed John Brooks, 1st Constable at Frederica in case of death or mortality, 113. a wood cutter.

Abercorn, Earl of, thanks return'd him for his benefaction, 21.

Abercorn Settlement abandon'd, Mr. Jo. Wesley's Acct. of it in Septbr. 1737, 307.

Abercromby, [James], Esq., Atturney Genl. of S. Carolina, doubts whither by the late Act for allowing Rice to be exported from Carolina without calling at England, Georgia has a right to the benefit of it, 120. Standing Counsel to the Trustees; instructions given him for forwarding letters from Georgia to England, 373.

Accompts., the Yearly Accts. of the Trustees to 9 June 1733 Laid before the Ld. Chancellor & Ld. Ch. justice, 29. Acct. of Receipts and disbursments from 9 June 1733 to 21 March 1733-4 laid before the Trustees at their anniversary meeting, 47. The Yearly Accts. of Receipts and Disbursments to 9 June 1734 laid before the Trustees, 56. Abstract of the whole years Accts. of Receipts and Disbursments ending 9 June 1735, 88–92. Report made of disbursments in Georgia from 30 Jany. 1732 to 30 Jany. 1734, 118. Report made of Receipts and disbursments from 9 June 1734 to 5 May 1735, 105. Report of the Genl. Acct. of Receipts and disbursments from 9 June 1734 to 9 June 1735 approved and order'd to be laid before the Ld. Chancellor, Master of the Rolls, &c, 118. Order for printing 250 Copies, 122. Report of Receipts and disbursments from 9 June 1735 to 18 March 1735-6, 142. Abstract of the 4th years Acct. of Receipts and disbursments from 9 June 1735 to 9 June 1736, 162–66. Accompt of the years Receipts & disbursmts. endg. 9 June 1737, 279-82. Accompt of the years Receipts and Disbursments endg. 9 June 1738, 375–79.

Addison, Edwd., miller, appointed 3d Bailif of Frederica, 110.

Advertisement, order'd against a Man who made use of the Trustees name to kidnap people, 45.

Aglionby, Will., of Westminster, Grant made him of 100 acres, 157.

Allatahama River, see Frederica.

Allen, Ri., of Carolina, Shews the prejudice of the loss of the Indian Trade would be to S. Carolina, and proposes concessions to be made by Georgia for reconciling both Provinces, 159–60.

Allen, Will., baker, appointed 2d Tithing Man of Frederica, 110.

Amatis, Nics., arrived from Piedmont, 14. Order'd to write down his proposalls on what terms he will go to Georgia to introduce the making Silk, 14. He presents them to the board, 15. Order for Sending him with Jaques Camuche, his wife & 3 children, 16–17. Conditions made with him, 17. Complains of Jos. Fitzwalter, the Trustees Gardiner, 97. And of Mr. Causton, 97. Intends to quit the Colony on acct. of Mr. Causton's ill usage of him, 97. Is reconciled and made easie, 103. Proposes to come to England to inform the Trustees of the good State and prospect there is of Silk, 103. Bills drawn by him on the Trustees order'd not to be paid till Mr. Oglethorp goes over, 102, 105.

Ambrose, Jo., 2800 acres granted him in trust, 35.

Amelia Isld., near the Clothogotheo branch of the Allatahama, described, 147.

INDEX

Amory, Jo., 50£ advanc'd him on Security to repay the Trust, 312. Grant order'd him of 150 acres, 312.

Anabaptists of Saxony, desire to go to Georgia at their own expence, 39.

Anderson, Hugh, a Town Lot order'd him in Savannah, with promise that when he is disposed to part with it he Shall have a Country Grant, 157. Appointed Inspector of the Public Garden & Mulberry Plantations, 157, 189. Desires a Town lot in Savannah for a younger Son, 299. Refer'd to a Committee to be consider'd, 318. Refused, but offer'd for himself 500 acres & in that case his son shall have the Savannah lot himself now holds, 321–22.

Anniversary day, [21 March 1734], proceedings thereon, 47. [18 March 1736], 142. [17 March 1737], & what then past, 244.

Archer, Hen., Esq., elected a Trustee, 47. Elected into the Common Council, 337. Sworn, 338.

Archer, Tho., elected a Trustee, 47. Elected into the Common Council, 244.

Arguile Isld., fertile, and every way proper for a Cow pen, Tho. Gapans Acct. of it, 94. Mr. Macbanes acct. of it: That it is Situated in St. Simonds Island, on the S. Side, commands the Sea, and guards the Island. Garison'd by Capt. Delagals Independent compy. of 50 Men, & no Settlers there, 218. All the Settlers enter'd into the Rangers Troop, 237. Falling to ruin, Mr. Jo. Wesleys acct of it in Sept. 1737, 309.

Arms, order'd for the Colony, 31.

Attorney, Letter of, given to Mr. Verelts [Verelst] to receive at the Treasury the 10000£ given by Parliament, 170.

Attorney Genl., retain'd by the Trustees, in the Case of Mrs. Watson, 246, 252.

Augusta, in New Town laying out 250 miles from Savannah, 168, 183, 194.

Augusta Fort & Town, Mr. Jo. Wesleys Acct of it in Sept. 1737, 307.

Augustin, Walter, of Cat Island in S. Carolina, Grant of 500 acres made him, 109. Erects a Saw Mill, which is blown up, 237. His Settlement deserted, Mr. Jo. Wesleys Acct of it, 307.

Ayers, Robt., elected a Trustee, 47. Elected into the Common Council, 244. Sworn in, 247.

Bacon, al[ia]s Hog, intends to offer his Service to the Spaniards to overset the Colony of Georgia, 10.

Baillie, Jo., grant past to him of 400 acres, 35.

Baker, John, Esq., of S. Carolina, grant past to him of 500 Acres, 112.

Ballot, order'd for chusing all Officers & giving Commissions, 4. Agreed to ballot for new Members, and that if two Members object to the election, they Shall have a weeks time to give their reason, 45. By law proposed to that purpose, 45. Past, 47.

Baltimore, Ld., presents to Parliament the Trustees petition for Money, 137. And moves for 10000£ which is granted, 143.

Bank of England, keeps the Trustees Cash, 5.

Bank Receipts, 200 Blank forms order'd to be printed, 57.

Barnes, Jo., 2800 acres granted him in Trust, 27.

Bateman, Will., Grant past to him of 75 acres, 46.

Bathurst, Sr. Fra[ncis], Bt., Ld. Bathurst gives him 100£ to go to Georgia, 38. Grant of 200 Acres past to him, 66.

Bathurst, daughter of Sr. Francis, order for Sending her to Georgia to her father, 204.

Bathurst, Robt., 2d Son of Sr. Francis, deceased, abandons his plantation in Georgia, & steals away to S. Carolina, 372.

Bearcroft, Ri., D.D., preaches the Trustees Anniversary Sermon, & is desired to print it, 337.

Benefactions received, 34, 43, 47, 48, 69, 70, 73, 74, 84, 93, 94, 95, 105, 111, 112, 115, 116, 119, 124, 127, 144, 146, 149, 150, 153, 165, 212, 234, 247, 251, 275, 286, 294, 302, 352, 368. Persons named for receiving them, 93.

Berry, ———, Mr., his high proposal to go to Georgia to cut timber, and teach the Inhabitants to do it for the use of his Majesties Navy, 107. See Proposals.

Bienville, Monsr., see Louisiana.

Billingsley, Case, Esq., his proposal to advance the Trustees affairs, 93. Rejected, 94. See Proposals.

Bills, drawn by Tho. Causton, Bailif & Storekeeper, Some accepted, others refused, 68. A bill drawn by Jenys, the

INDEX

Bills (*continued*)
payment Suspended for want of advice, 70. Accepted by the Trustees, 98, 105, 111, 121, 127, 142, 149, 153, 156, 189, 198–99, 225, 226, 234, 235, 266, 271, 276, 298, 311, 321, 327–28, 368–69. Not accepted by the Trustees, 100, 105, 109, 127, 149, 153, 156. Certified not paid, but order'd to be return'd to Georgia, 327–28, 329, 330, 348, 353, 368, 369, 391. Publick notice order'd that the Trustees will pay no more certified Bills or Accts return'd to England for payment, 329. See Sola Bills.

Bishop, Hen., a Charity School boy, bound Apprentice to the Trust, and Sent Servant to Mr. Boltzius, one of the Saltsburg Ministers, 65.

Bishop, Philip, grant made him of 500 Acres, 25.

Blair, David, apply's for 500 acres, 175. Grant past to him, 190.

Board of Trade, see S. Carolina.

Boltzius, Jo. Martin, Saltzburg Minister at Ebenezar, writes that the people's land is bad, 121. Complains of Mr. Vat, Secy. for their affairs, 137. See Saltsburgers.

Bottanist, see Houston. See Millar.

Bouverie, Sr. Jacob, intends to present the Trustees 1000£, 222–23. Pays it, 239. Elected a Trustee, 244.

Bovey, Mrs., see Pratt.

Boyd, Tho., applys for 500 Acres, 175. His Grant past, 190.

Bradley, Will., his proposal to go over and cultivate the Trust lands, & teach the people Agriculture approved, 104–05. Seal put to the Agreement, 125. Grant made him of 500 acres, 118. He misses his passage on board the London Merchant, but goes by another Ship, 123. His insolent and abusive behaviour to the Trust, 319. Inspector order'd to enquire how he employ'd the Trustees Servants under his care, 351. Pretends the Trustees are in his debt 400£, 359. He will not stand to his contract with the Trustees, 365.

Brailsford, Jo., of Georgia, 25£ order'd him for coming over to be a wittness in the Carolina dispute, 352.

Bromfeild, Jo., Register of Georgia, commended for diligently corresponding with the Society, 171.

Brooks, John, appointed 1st Constable of Frederica, 110.

Broughton, [Thomas], Esq., Presidt. of the Council of S. Carolina. See Carolina. Lieut. Govr. of S. Carolina, his indiscretion with respect to the Spaniards, 266. Deceased, in Dec. 1737, 326.

Brown, Jo., Esq., of London, Apply's for a Grant of land to go over at his own expence, 86. Grant made him of 500 acres, 112.

Brown, Mathew, of Bristol, Order given to Send him and his Servant at the Trustees charge from Bristol, 121.

Brown, Saml., 500 acres, and an Indian Traders house mark'd out for him at Augusta, 168.

Brownfeild, Jo., appointed Register of Georgia, and to take no Fees but what the Trustees Shall order, 102. Made a Trustee for 10000 Acres granted for the County of Frederica, 102. Made Naval Officer, 104. Rewarded for his Services in drawing Mapps for the Trust, 111. His appointment of Register confirm'd, 113. Writes to the Trustees a very disadvantageous Acct. of the Colony, 290–91. Speaks very disrespectfully of the Trustees, 293. Active to improve discontents, 303. Justify's himself, 370.

Buchman, Geo., 2500 acres granted to him in Trust for the Saltsburgers, 35.

Bull, Col., Succeeds Lt. Govr. Broughton in the administration of the Province of S. Carolina, 326.

Bundy, Ri., D.D., tho of the Common Council, declines preaching the Anniversary Sermon, 124. Discountenances the Trustees tho a Member, 246. Resigns his Office of Common Counsellor as being of no use, 324. His true reason, 335. His remarkable incivility to the Trustees on the Anniversary day, 337.

Burgoign, Sr. Rogr., Bt., elected Trustee, 337.

Burnside, Ja., petitions for a grant of land in the nature of Church leases, but is refused, 312. Petitions that the Widow Bovey's land (whom he marry'd) may be made Secure to him, 314.

Burton, Jo., B.D., preaches the 1st Anniversary Sermon, 17. Order for printing it, 17. Petitions for 2 Servants to be al-

INDEX

low'd him, but is refused, and why, 313.

By Law, that upon any question proposed, a Member may have leave to give his dissent in writing, 45. Past, 47. See more in Ballot.

Calloway, Will., deceased in Georgia, order given to enquire into his Effects in favour of his Widow, 156.

Calvert, Will., a Trustee to 5000 Acres design'd for the Township of Savannah, 7.

Calwell, Jo., tallow chandler, appointed 1st Tithing Man at Frederica, 110. Appointed to Succeed Edwd. Addison as 3d Bailif in case of death or removal, 113.

Cannon, Danl., carpenter, appointed to Succeed Saml. Perkins as 2d Bailif, in case of death or removal, 113.

Carinthians, 26 Families desire to Settle in Georgia, 79.

Carolina, assistance given and intended by that Province towards the Settlement of the Colony, 28-29. An act past by them for confirmation of Grants which may affect Georgia, 29. Disapproved by the Council board in England, 29. The Govr. and Assembly of South Carolina Send over a memorial to his Majesty, complaining of the encroachments of the French at Messasippi, and Setting forth their weak condition in case of a War. That the French are labouring to debauch from the English the Creek nation, wch. if they Succeed in, their Province is undone. They thank his Majesty for establishing the Colony of Georgia which is a great protection to them, 60. The Agent of their Province apply's to the Trustees to favour a bill for enlarging their time to export Rice without calling at England, and for extending their trade to the French & Dutch settlements, which the Trustees promise, 77. The French Govr. of Mobile threatens their Province and Seeks a quarrel with it, 78. Mr. Johnson, Govr. of S. Carolina dies, and the Govermt. is offer'd to Mr. Oglethorp who refuses it, 95. Their jealousie of Georgia & pretences for the Same, 112-13, 143. Their Proceedings thereupon, 149-50. The Small prejudice the loss of trade if Georgia Should have it, Set forth by Mr. Oglethorp, 158-59. On the contrary their reasons why the loss would be considerable to them Set forth by Mr. Ri. Allen, 159. They complain the Magistrates of Savannah Stave their Rum, 150. Memorial containing their Several complaints against the Magistrates of Georgia Sent to the Board of Trade, and Copy of the Same with a letter Sent by Presidt. Broughton to the Trustees, 121. The Trustees answer thereto, 122. They attend on the Board with it, 123. They refuse to perform their promise to pay the Rangers Company in Georgia, as also the 8000£ currency formerly granted, 112.

Carpenter, Ld. [George], declares his intention to resign his office of Common Counsellor on pretence that his business will not let him attend, 334, 336. Presents his resignation, but promises to come in again next year if wanted, tho he never intended it, 336.

Carteret, Ja., Esq., grant of 500 Acres made him 22 March 1727-8, 338.

Carteret, Ld. Jo., his Grant to the Trustees of his 8th part in the property of Georgia engrost, 13. Approved by him, 14. Seal put to the Counterpart, 15.

Catechist in Georgia, Resolv'd that a competent alottment of land be made for a Catechist, 40.

Cater, Sr. Jo., Aldn., resigns his Office of Common Counsellor for want of time to attend, 334. The true reason of both their Resignations, 334-35.

Causton, Tho., appointed 3d Bailif of Savannah, 8. 3d Bailif and Storekeeper made 2d Bailif on Ri. Hodges death, 68. Appointed a Trustee of 2500 Acres granted for the new Saltsburgers, and powers granted him to Set out &c the Same, 68. Complaint that he endeavours to monopolize the Trade, and will make Strange Accompts, 83. Memorial presented by Peter Gordon, 1st Bailif, against him and the other Magistrates, 85. Complain'd against by Paul Amatis, that he converts the Servants design'd for the Trustees garden to his own use, and Says he will

Causton, Tho. (*continued*)
make up bad Accounts, 97. Elisha Dobree writes that he will undertake to Shew his Accounts neither exact nor true, 97. He complains of the 1st Bailif Peter Gordon now in England, 98. And justify's himself against the Complaints made of him, 120. Appointed Comptroller of the Rice Act, 104. Appointed an Officer to put the Rum Act in execution, 104. Made 1st Bailif in Peter Gordons room, 104. He Staves Rum brought into Savannah from Carolina, & his reasons for it, 150. A passionate Man, 108. Sends a duplicate of the moneys taken up by him and paid, 120. Orders repeated to him to draw no bills on the Trustees without giving advice, neither to draw at all (for extraordinary Services excepted) before he has communicated the reason & necessity of Such drafts, and has recieved leave from the Trustees to make Such drafts, 111–12. Instructions Sent to the Magistrates of Savannah concerning Several points contain'd in his letters, 113. Order'd to Send accounts of the Proceedings in Georgia and that he prevent as much as possible the peoples running in debt by putting them to labour, 171. Puts the Trust to a great expence for demurrage, 197. Negligent in writing, 204–05. All the complaints made against him by the Inhabitants heard by Mr. Oglethorpe, and found frivelous, 215, 219. Declares against cutting down the fine wood that Sheltered the Town of Savannah and Publick garden from the East winds, but is overborn by the Inhabitants, 277. The Inhabitants begin to be better reconciled to him, 277. His Acct. of Issues of Stores and his Diary from Lady day 1735 to 25 April 1737, 293. Strikes off from the Stores the idle who had not cultivated land, 295. Order'd to send an Acct. what demands remain unsatisfy'd at the time he writes next, that the Trustees may know the State of their Cash, & provide for answering the Establishment to Lady day 1738, 301. 50£ ordered him, being pt. of 200£ recompence for 4 years Service, 311–12. Directions given him concerning the Palatin Servants, 313. Remonstrance sent by 40 principal Inhabitants against him, 323. Order'd to certifie no more bills or Accts. for expences incurr'd by him in Georgia, 327–28, 333. Order'd to send back 2000£ Sola bills to enable the Trustees to pay his certified bills, 331. Suspected by the Trustees of extravagantly misspending their money, 331. Accused of divers misbehaviours by Mr. Jo. Wesley, 333. Commended by Capt. Will. Thompson, 343. Sends 40 Trust Servants to the Darien, 344. Takes a whole Cargo of Goods into the Stores on the Trustees Acct. tho not 50£ of it provision, and sends a certified Acct. to the Trustees to pay for them, yet distributes them to private persons, all without Orders, 348. The Trustees charge him with 49 of those Servants, 351. He makes use of the Trustees Servants without leave, 4. Expends 11000£ of the Trustees money between Michs. 1737 & March following, besides what other certify'd Accts. he may have drawn on the Trustees since that time not come to hand the 10th May 1738, 357. And from Midsumer 1737 to the 30 May 1738, 12932.13. 2£. And the certify'd Accompts, not paid amounted the said 30 May 1738 to 4542. 3. 11£, 368. He is order'd to make up his Accompts of the remain of Stores in a months time, 357. Removed from his place of Storekeeper, 357. A long letter of reproof sent him, 361–62. Order'd to send copies of all his journals, ledgers & day books from Lady day 1734, 364. He excuses his extravagance, and promises to certify no more Accts, 365–66. Order to seize his person, 370. He takes goods into the Trustees Store, and charges them to their Account, tho not belonging to them, but to Merchts. and certifies bills for the Trustees to pay for those Merchants goods, 371. Order given to send him with his books, 372. But the order revers'd & why, 373. Order given to keep him in custody upon Security not to leave the Colony, till his Accts. from Lady day 1734 are examin'd and approved: and till further direction from the Trustees, 373. It appear'd that he had not accounted for 13832£ from Midsumer 1737 to 7 June 1738,

INDEX

373. Removed from being 1st Bailif, 373.
Cheesright, Rebecca, in England (a vile Woman) petitions the Trustees for a portion of her deceased husbands effects in Georgia, and the same refer'd for examination to our Accompt, 314.
Cherokees, an Indian Nation desire the protection of the English, 158. See Indians.
Chest of medicines, order'd for Georgia, 7.
Chickesaws, an Indian Nation of 400 fighting Men & good warriours dependent on the English attack's by Monsr. Bienville, Govr. of the Louisiana, 154. And repulse him, 158. Report that they have a multitude of Mulberry trees in their Country, and if instructed to make Silk will bring great quantities, 344. See Indians.
Chocktaws, an Indian Nation of 4000 Men in the French allyance, Enemies to the Chickesaws, but no warlick people, 154.
Christie, Tho., a Trustee to 5000 Acres design'd for the Township of Savannah, 7. Appointed Recorder of Savannah, 8. Appointed a Trustee of 2500 Acres granted for the New Saltsburgers, and powers granted him to Set out &c the Same, 68. Information that he retails Rum, tho the use of it is forbid by the Trustees, 84. Justifies himself from the accusation of Selling Rum, and desires he may Sell his Town Lot and have a grant of 500 acres, 121. Order'd to Send copies of the Town Court proceedings Since Nov. 1734 wherein he has been negligent, as also an Account of what Fees have been taken, 170–71. Commended by Capt. Thompson, 343. Allow'd 2 Trust Servants to be maintain'd by the Trust, 363.
Church and Ministers house, order'd to be forthwith built, & 300 acres of Glebe laid out, 11.
Church Estimate, for building a Church in Georgia, 287. Deals bought for that purpose, 321. Flint Stones and Iron sent for that purpose, 345. Capt. Thomas order'd to give an estimate of the charge, 352. Directions given him, 360, 363–64.

385

Civil Government for Savannah, order'd to be erected, 7.
Clark, Cha., counsel for the Trustees in the Carolina dispute, 226, 328.
Clark, Isaac King, 2800 acres granted him in Trust, 35.
Clark, Jo., Appointed Secretary for the Indian affairs, in the room of Revd. Mr. Cha. Wesley, 353.
Clifton, Sr. Robert, 20.
Clothogotheo, a Branch of the Allatahama, 147.
Cochrane, Lt. Col. James, grant order'd him of 500 Acres, 312. Past the Seal, 318.
Collections, Bishop of London desired to forward them in his Diocese, 20.
Committee appointed, to impress mony as far as 3000£ for the use of the Saltsburgers going over, 31. To prepare Laws for the Colony, 5.
Committee of Accts., appointed, 13. Order that any 3 of the Common Council may compose it, 27. All the Members of the Common Council to be of it, 75. Mr. Oglethorps Accts. refer'd to them, 76. Mr. Caustons Accts. refer'd to them, 76. Mr. Chardons Accts. refer'd to them, 82.
Committee of Correspondence, empower'd to open letters and prepare drafts of answers to be laid before the Board, 42. Their first meeting appointed, 45. Order'd to prepare an answer to the Revd. Mr. Dumont at Rotterdam, who wrote in favour of heirs female Succeeding, and to Shew him the reasons why the Trustees do not admit thereof, 48. Letters from Georgia, and proceedings of the Courts of Justice there, refer'd to them, 77.
Common Council Boards, the number held this 1st year, 25. 2d year, 53. 3d year, 87. 4th year, 160–61. 5th year, 278. 6th year, 374.
Common Counsellors, appointed by Charter, 3. Their number fill'd up to 24, 16. Order that 5 of the Common Council may Sign drafts on the Bank, 23. Many Common Counsellors think of quitting on account of the debts contracted by Mr. Causton, 333.
Cook, C., Majr., grant order'd him of 500 acres, 312. Past the Seal, 318. Purchases for his 2 daughters Susan and Anne the Town Lot in Savannah be-

Cook, C., Majr. (*continued*) longing to Peter Gordon, late Bailif, 345. Petitions that his daughter Anne may be allow'd to Surrender her Interest in the lot at Savannah to her Sister Susan, & Succeed to his 500 acre lot, which the Trustees allow, 358.

Cooksey, Will., credited by Mr. Causton wth. the Trustees effects without orders, 205. Petitions for a Grant of 500 acres, and for further time to pay the remainder of a Sum advanc'd to him, 314.

Coop, Ri., Aldn. of London, elected a Trustee, 47.

Cooper, Mary, in England, advanc'd the Rent of her house in Savannah to be repaid the Trustees by Mr. Hen. Parker who rents it, 345.

Cooper, Ri., appointed Bailif of Frederica in case of death or removal of others, 110. But his appointment alter'd in favour of another, 113.

Creek Indians, see Indians.

Cumberland Island, formerly call'd St. Pedro: a Fort built there by Mr. Oglethorpe call'd St. Andrews, 143–44, 147. Divers of the Scots chuse to Settle there, 143–44.

Dairn, Jo., bailif of Savannah deceased 1 July 1737, 325.

Dalone, Monsr., his legacy for Conversion of Blacks, order for Separating that Trust from the Trusteeship of Georgia, 23–24.

Danbur, [Henry Danbuz], capt. of the Georgia Pink, see Embarkations.

Darien, al[ia]s New Inverness, a Scots Settlement (afterwards named New Inverness), where Situated, and its distance from Savannah, 147. Its distance from the mouth of the Allatahama, 156. A Fort building there, and the number of Settlers, 156. A Fort mark'd out, and a School house, Guard house and Church order'd to be built, 202. A Communication open'd from Savannah thither by land, 202. Road for that purpose making, 216. The people Surprisingly industrious, 215, 217. 45 Scots families and 30 Servants Settled there in 1736, 217. They first clear'd their land before they built their houses, which the people of Savannah Should have done, 217. They have cannon but as yet no Fort, 217. Capt. Mackintosh has the chief command, 217. On the continent, & ten miles distant from St. Simons Fort, 217. Mr. Jo. Wesleys Acct. of it in Sept. 1737, 309. Will in a little time want no assistance, 366.

Davison, Saml., a Chairman, appointed a Bailif of Frederica in case of death or Removal of others, 110. His appointment alter'd in favour of another, 113. Appointed 2d Constable of Frederica, 110. His improvements, but wants a Servant to assist him, 350.

De Farron, Lieut., goes with his Family to Georgia, 30. Deceased, his lot at Highgate order'd to be Sold, and his daughter put out Apprentice at the Trustees charge, 70.

Delamont, Cha., teaches School at Savannah gratis, 217. Prepares to return for England, 366.

De Lyon, Abrm., a jew, petitions for a loan of 200£ to cultivate vines, wth. offer to give Security to repay the money in 6 years, 344. Granted by the Trustees, 348.

Dempsy, Capt., his demand for presents paid by him at Augustin when he Settled the Treaty of Pacification, order'd to be paid, 240. Thanks order'd him & 150£ for his Services, 265.

Derby, E. of, declines continuing the late Earl, Subscription to our Botanist, 310.

Diamond, capt. of the Peter and James, arrives at Savannah with provisions from Ireland, 10. Jan. 1735–6, 124.

Dicker, capt. of the Allen, arrives from Bristol at Savannah 10 Jan. 1735–6, 124.

Dietzius, Andrew Godfrey, desires to Know on what conditions he may have lands in Georgia, 60. Grant past to him of 500 Acres, 66.

Digby, Edwd., 1st Chairman of the Common Council by Charter, 4.

Dobree, Elisha, clerk in the Stores at Savannah turn'd out by Mr. Causton, 97. Says Causton will make up Accounts neither exact nor true, and offers to be a Commissioner to examine them, 97. Desires encouragement to Set up a Salt pan, and lands for that use, 121.

Dogherty, Cornelious, Indian Trader, a

INDEX

house & 500 acres mark'd out for him at Augusta, 168.
Douglass, ——, Sollicitor, employ'd by the Trustees to enquire into the Palatin Brief money, 41. His report, 43.
Drafts on the Bank, 6. See Impress.
Drake, Will., Esq., his noble Scheme for making a Settlement of English to the West of Georgia, 180–83.
Duche, Andrew, his good Improvement of the Potters trade in Savannah, 366.
Dunbar, Geo., capt. of the Pr. of Wales, desires leave to exchange his 500 acre grant at Josephs Town for another at Frederica, which is refer'd to Col. Oglethorpe to settle, 319. His demand for Primage allow'd, 363. See Embarkations.

Edgcomb, Arthr. Ogle, 2800 acres granted to him in Trust, 35.
Elton, Sr. Abraham, 20.
Embarkation, order'd, 6. Conditions made with the people, 6. Surgeon sent with them, 8. Care taken that they defraud not their Creditors, 9. Govr. Johnson advised to defer the embarkation a year, but his letter came too late, 11. Grants past to 8 able Lawyers to go, 11. Suspected Papists not allow'd to go, 20. A Second embarkation resolv'd on of 50 able men to prepare land for the Saltsburgers against their arrival, 23. The persons appointed, 24. Necessaries for their embarkation adjusted, 24. The people Sign their Articles, 33. Muster taken on board the James, Capt. Yoakly, 27 males & 21 females, 34–35. Number of persons Sent this year, as also in the whole from the first embarkation, 54–55. Agreement made with Mr. Simons the Merchant to carry 75 persons to Georgia including the Saltsburgers, 65. Embarkment of 84 persons for Georgia 31 Oct. 1734 on board the Princess of Wales, Capt. Dunbar, 68. Committee appointed for another Embarkation, 73. Charter Party Sign's for carrying over 87 Swiss & Grisons design'd most part for Purysburg, the rest for Savannah, 75. Embarkment of 122 foreign Protestants making 100 heads 23 Jan 1734-5 on board the Two Brothers, Capt. Thompson, 75. Embarkment of 30 persons for Georgia 14 May 1735 on board the James, Capt. Yoakly, of whom 29 at the Trustees charge; 5 of them Settlers there, and 18 Trust Servants with their 6 children; of these 18 Trust Servants, 15 are Foreigners, 85–86. Seal put to the Trust Servants Indentures, 85. Report of the Muster on board Capt. Yoakly, 86. Resolved for Settling a new Town and Vilages on the Allatahama River, 94. Embarkation on board the Georgia Pink, Capt. Danbur, 15 Males and 12 females, of whom 10 Servants, 101. They Set out 6 Aug. 1735 and arrive at Savannah 27 Nov. following, 119. Charter party with the Pr. of Wales, Capt. Dunbar, to carry over 130 Highlanders to Frederica at the Trustees expence, 102. They Sail'd 20 Oct. from Scotland and arrived at Savannah 10 Jany. 1735-6, 123. Carry'd 180 persons, 114. Review of 40 families design'd to be Sent at the Trustees Expence, 104. Agreed with the London Merchant, Capt. Thomas, to carry persons over at the Trustees Expence, 107. He Saild 20 Octo. and arrived at Savannah 5 feb. 1735-6, 115. Report of the Must on board him, 136 persons, 89 men and 47 females, 115. Capt. Dunbar writes that he had on board 124 persons on the Charity Acct., 117. Mr. Verelts thinks he has but 120, 116. Charter party Sign'd with the Simons, Capt. Cornish, to carry over with Mr. Oglethorp 121 persons, 112. They Sail 14 October, 114. And arrive at Savannah, 5 feb. 1735-6, 129. Agreement with the Two Brothers, Capt. Thompson, to carry 50 Tons of Goods at 1.10. 0 p Tun to Frederica, 115. Report of the Muster on board him, 121. He Sails with 15 persons, 11 Men & 4 Women, of Whom 13 at the Trustees charge, 119. Order that no more persons be Sent this year at the Trustees expence, 121. But exception made for 4 persons if Dr. Stanley of Liverpool Should recommend them, 149.

Embarkations, 1737, June 24, Capt. Thompson of the Two Brothers embarks with 50 Men & 4 women at the Trust charge for Georgia, 285. And arrives from Scotland which he took in his way to get more Passengers on the Trust acct. & his own 20 Novbr.

Embarkations, 1737 (*continued*)
1737, 326. Augst. 16, Capt. Shubrick of the Mary Anne Sails wth. 8 Males & 4 females at the Trust charge for Georgia, 301. Octobr. 8, Capt. Hewet on the 3 Sisters Sails wth. 160 Palatin Servants, viz. 78 Males and 82 females, and arrives in Georgia 21 Decembr. following. All on the Trust acct., 313, 326. Oct. 12, Capt. Danbuz of the Georgia Pink Sailed for Georgia with 1 foreigner and 3 Servts. on the Trust Acct. all Males, but calls in his way at Cork in Ireland to take provisions for the Colony. He arrived in Georgia 16 Jany. following, 313. Oct. 18 Capt. Nicholson of the Minerva Sails wth. Mr. Thomas Stephens and a Servant at the Trust charge for Georgia, and arrives in Decembr. following, 313. Novbr. 3, Capt. Ayers of the King George Sails wth. 2 Moravians for Georgia, and arrives Jany. following, 315. Novbr. 19, Capt. Thompson of the Two Brothers Sails for Georgia with 50 Trust Servants, viz. 34 Males & 22 females, and arrives 14 Jany. 1737/8, 317. 1737/8, Jany. 5, Capt. Whiting of the Whitaker Sails with 5 Males at the Trust charge, and arrives 7 May 1738, 327. Two more went at the Trust charge 1738, but I know not by what Ship or what month, 327.

Estimate, see Parliament.

Eveleigh, Saml., abandons Georgia, because Negroes are not allow'd there, nor Females to Inherit, of which he Sets forth Some inconveniences, 106. Approves not of Capt. Pennifeathers Grant, 106.

Fallowfeild, Jo., made Collector on the Acct. for exporting Rice, 104.

Fitzwalter, Joseph, appointed 1st Constable of Savannah, 8. The Trustees Publick Gardiner, complain'd against by Paul Amatis the Silk man, 84, 96–7. Removed from being Publik Gardiner at Savannah, & Succeeded by Fra. Piercy, 217.

Flax, encouragement to be given for cultivating, intended by the Assembly of South Carolina, 154.

Fletcher, Hen., grant made him of 200 Acres, 25.

Flower, Jo., appointed to Succeed Saml. Davison as 2d Constable in case of death or Removal, 113.

Forts and Fortifications, see Georgia.

Frederica, rules upon forming for Such as go to Settle there, 93. The Common Council agree to them, 95. Order for printing them, 95. An Embarkation resolv'd on, 94. Boats order'd for the Service of that Settlement, 95. Order for Sending Halfpence over, 95. Town Court and Court of jurisdiction appointed at Frederica, 101. Ship load of provisions order'd from Cork, 102. Resolv'd that 10000 acres be vested in Trustees for erecting the County of Frederica, 102. Seal put to the Grant, 105. Seal put to the Lease and Release of the Same, 109. Resolv'd that the County Town be named Frederica, 110. Magistrates and Officers appointed, 110. Power granted to Mr. Oglethorp to administer the Oaths, 110. Magistrates appointed as also inferior Officers, to Succeed those first named, in case of death or removal, 113. The Allatahama River visited; the Middle Inlet found not safe for Ships to enter; but the mouth of the Southern Stream very Safe, having 14 feet on the Bar at dead low water, and the harbour Shelter'd; and Ships may ly either at the S. End of St. Simons Island, or 8 miles further up, 127, 141. A further Acct. of the Allatahama; the bar before the Middle Stream 7 miles broad with 11 feet at low water and 21 at high, 157. The Trustees judge it impossible to go on with the Settlement of Frederica, 144. And write to recall Mr. Oglethorp from thence, 144. The Town of Frederica and Fort laid out, and the progress made therein, 146–47. Island of St. Simons given up by Tomachachi to the English, 142. Island of St. Catherine reserved by Tomachachi to the Indians, 142. Fort St. Andrews built by Mr. Oglethorp on Cumberland Island formerly call'd St. Pedro, 143–44. The Fort finish'd Strong & compleat, 154. The Govr. of St. Augustine complains of our Settling within his Masters Territories, 141–42. Negotiations with him, 142. Advice that he intended to dislodge us by force, 142. Imprisons Mr. Horton Sent by Mr. Oglethorp to treat of

INDEX

peace, but Soon after releases him, 150, 152. Sends Plenipotentiaries to Mr. Oglethorp to agree upon a Treaty, 154. But Suspected of treachery, 153. Prevented in his design by Mr. Oglethorps artifice, 158. The Town Settled, 184–85. The people industrious, 215. Two Streets laid out and 15 or 16 houses built, 218. No Rum drunk there, 218. In what latitude Situated, 209. 60 or 80 families Settled there besides Single persons, and many come from Carolina and other parts to fix there, 217–18. The heat not so great there but white men may work in the heat of Summer as in England, 219. Depth of Water at the entrance of the Harbor, 209. Great plenty of fish, 218, 219. Plenty of fine Cedar trees and other timber, 218. And of horses and cattel, 219. The land bears hemp, flax, & barley as well as Indian corn, 219. The Fort, 210. Strong, with 4 bastions, a ditch and rampart wth. double palisadoes and 9 cannon, a Storehouse in the midst with a Platform that holds 100 Men, 218. Will contain a garison of 140 men, and cannot be taken but in a regular manner with Cannon, 255. The people are healthy, 247. But want corn to Sow, 246. They want a Minister, 247. Advantage that would arise to them by Supplying St. Augustine with provision, 223–24. Joseph Cannons Acct. of the town, 210–11. Mr. Macbanes acct. of it, 217–18. Two Forts built beyond it and garison'd, 184–85. Divisions there occasion'd by Tho. Hird, one of the Constables, 293, 320. The Town extreamly healthy, and the people industrious, 350. The Crop of corn in 1736 all spoilt by the bad Season & Ratts, 344. Great increase of children, and women bear there who in England are thought past their time, 350. The people hinder'd in their cultivation by Spanish Allarms, 350.

Frederick, Tho., Esq., reason why he quitted his attendance at the Board, 170.

French Protestants of Languedock, desire to Settle in Georgia, 79.

Forbes, Duncan, Esq., Advocat Genl. of Scotland, Seconds the Trustees petition to Parliament for money, 240.

Foster, Geo., grant of 50 acres past to him, 272.

French, defeated by the Chickesaw Indians, 172–73. Preparations made by the Govr. of Louisiana to attack the English in the Spring, 173. Their jealousie of the English making a Settlement on the Catahuchee river among the Lower Creek Indians, 182. They resolve to extirpate the Chickesaws that they may unite all their forces, and push the English into the Sea, 182–83. Are worsted a 2d time by the Chickesaws, with a relation of the action, 190–92. Had a design to invade Carolina, 224.

Fury, Mr., agent for South Carolina, obligation confer'd on him by the Trustees, 125.

Garden, Publick, see Savannah.

Gascoign, Ja., capt. of his Majesties Sloop the Hawk, Station'd at Frederica, grant made him of 500 Acres, 109.

Georgia Colony, accts of the State thereof, 44, 48. His Majesties Order for repaying the Trustees 1500£ disburst in Fortifications in Georgia, 65. 1561£ recieved on that Acct., the Offices forgiving their Fees, 67. Magistrates of Savannah allow'd each a Servant at the Trustees expence, in consideration that the duties of their Office allows them not to cultivate lands, 65–6. Six Cannon, 3 pounders, order'd for defence of Ebenezar, the Saltsburgers Settlement, 66. Powder, bullets &c order'd to be Sent, 66. Estimate order'd to be prepared for building a Church in Savannah, 70. Order for enclosing a glebe, 71. Refer'd to a Committee to consider of proper Grants for a glebe, 82. State of the Province, 71–72. 1000 Weight of Coppar farthings order'd, 83. Subsistance order'd to the Magistrates & their Servants out of the Publick Stores for 1 year longer, in consideration they could not cultivate their land, 84. 300 Weight of gunpowder Ship'd for the use of the Province, 84. Conditions minuted for further consideration, on which Several Classes of people Shall be Sent to Georgia, 87. An Insurrection in the Province discover'd and prevented, 83. Order Sent to detain the Ring-leaders in prison until a

Georgia Colony (*continued*)
Special Commission be Sent to try them, 83. The Trustees libell'd in a letter wrote from England to a person in Georgia, 113–14. They petition his Majesty not to permit the people of S. Carolina to run out lands, South of the Bounds of Georgia, 117. Their cause for petitioning, 117–18. Divers of the Trustees Subscribe towards building a church in Georgia, 118. They advertise against One Taylor, who without authority invited persons to go to Georgia with design to kidnap them, 119. Complaints against the Trustees & their Magistrates, with a Memorial Sent by Mr. Broughton, Presidt. of the Council to the Lords Commissioners of Trade, and Copies of the Same Sent by him to the Trustees, 122. The Trustees answer thereto, 122. They wait on the Lds. Commissioners of Trade with their answer, 123. They Send over an Auger to boar the Earth, 121. They encrease the Wages of their Housekeeper & Messenger, 121. They Send a Stallion & t Mares to Georgia, 124. They agree with Willm. Bradley to go over and cultivate the Trust lands and teach the people Agriculture, 125. They permit Ja. Hazlefoot to dispose of his Town Lot, and take 150 acres up in the Country; and advance him 2 Servants to be repayd, 125. A Great debate arises among the Trustees about the manner of Settling an Incom for the Minister at Savannah, and the lands for Religious Uses, 126–27, 127–31, 134–35, 136–37. Order given for Surveying 300 acres of the best land for Religious Uses, and a Plan of a Church with an Estimate of the charge of building it to be Sent them, 136–37. Seal put to the Grant of 300 acres for religious uses, 145. They resolve that a catechist be appointed, 145–46. Petition to Parliamt. for mony drawn up, 133. Seal put to it, 137. They prepare an estimate of the Supply wanting, amounting to 20000£, 133. Court Members of Parliamt. their Enemies, & why, 137. Their petition presented, 137. Obtain 10000£, 143. They judge it impossible to go on with the Southern Settlement of Frederica, 144. And write to Mr. Oglethorp to withdraw from thence, 144. But agree not to reinforce those orders, 155. They Send orders to Strike off the Stores Such as have been Subsisted thereout 2 years, 146. Great expence of keeping a Store to feed people, 157. Anniversary day kept, 142. The Trustees excuse themselves from Sending Palatines over, proposed to them by Ld. Harrington, Secy. of State, 153. They Send Strong beer & Spices to the Colony, 153. Advertisement order'd in the Newspapers of London and Charlestown that they will pay no bills drawn upon them, having Supply'd the Province with Sola bills of Exchange, 156. Order'd that any 5 of the Common Council have power to draw on the Bank for payment of Sola bills return'd from Georgia, 157. Order given to recall Mr. Vatt, Secy. for the Saltsburg affairs from Ebenezar, 155. Description of the Country, 132–33. The Advantages this Province is of to Gt. Britain Sent by a Gentleman of Jamaica to Mr. Pyne the Engraver, in London, 148. A Roadmaking 90 miles long from Savannah to Frederica, 153. Persons Sent the year 1736 at the Trustees charge, 161. Private Grants past this year 1736 at the Trustees charge, 161. Private Grants past this year, 162. The Inhabitants idle, 185. Want Ministers to reform their morals, 185. Luxury introducing among them, 205. They employ'd themselves in building houses to let and neglected cultivation, 196. The children born there mostly die, Supposed for want of milk, the pyne barren land producing So little grass that the cows run away into the Swamps, 196. Description of the Country on the banks of the Savannah for 250 miles, 192–95. Coffee planted there, and the best cotton grows there of any other place, 238. The Inhabitants will carry all the Indian trade away from Carolina, 195. Mr. Macbanes Acct. of the Province, 217–20. Capt. Jenkins Acct. of the Province, 238. Mr. Jo. Wesleys acct. of the Several Settlements in Sept. 1737, 307–09. See Frederica. Savannah.

German Families, proposal for Sending over 100 families, 37.

INDEX

Gibson, ——, and his brother, desire 50 acre lots in Savannah, but are advised to take each of them 100 acre lots, 200.

Gilbert, Robt., a taylor, appointed 3d Bailif in Jo. Dairns room, 353.

Giraldini, Monsr., the Spanish Minister at London, writes a letter to the Duke of Newcastle full of false complaints against our Colony, 202–03. And lays claim not only to Georgia but also part of Carolina, 202–03. The Duke Sends it to the Trustees to answer, 203. The Trustees reply thereto, 206–07. Offers a 2d Memorial more insolent than the first, asserting his Masters right to Georgia, & threatening to dislodge our people by force if they be not recalled, 295–96. What past between him & Sr. Robert Walpole on that occasion, 296. Sr. Robert intimidated, and his discourse thereon wth. Coll. Oglethorpe, 296. Sr. Robert refuses to take the Memorial, & Giraldini having soften'd it, delivers it to Ld. Harrington, 298. The Cabinet Council sit thereon, 298. They adjourn the further consideration to next day, and then resolve not to regard it, 301.

Gordon, Peter, appointed 1st Bailif of Savannah, 8. Upholster, arrived in England, and presents the Trustees with a Map of the Town of Savannah which is order'd to be engraved, 43–4. Order for defraying his passage back to Georgia, together with his wife & 2 Servants, 66. Appointed a Trustee of 2500 Acres granted for the New Saltsburgers, 68. Powers granted to him to Set out &c Said Acres, 68. Returns again to England, without notice or leave, 85. Presents a Memorial against the Magistrates, 85. Petitions for leave to Sell his Interest in Georgia, resolving to Settle in England, 101–02. Misbehaved himself in the Province, 101–02. Turn'd out of his Office by the Trustees, 104. Late Bailif of Savannah, reproved by the Trustees for coming to England without leave, and favouring mutineers in the Province, but obtains permission to sell his Grant, 286–87, 310, 345.

Gough, Sr. Hen., Bt., elected a Trustee of Georgia, 337.

Gough, Will., senr., grant made to him of 80 Acres, 14.

Gough, Will., junr., grant made to him of 80 Acres, 14.

Graham, Patrick, grant of 500 acres made him, 153.

Grant, [Andrew], grant past to him of 400 acres, 35.

Grant, Publick, to compose the County of Frederica, 102. Memorials of Grants order'd to be register'd in the auditor of the Plantations Office, 110, 112. Granted for Religious Uses, 145. Register Book order'd for entring all Grants past in Georgia, 100. 5000 Acres granted in Trust for the Township of Savannah, 7. Order that who ever carrys over 6 Servts. Shall have a Grant of 500 acres, 17. Number of Grants above 50 acres past this 1st year [1732–3] to particular persons, call'd Landholders, 25–6. Grants past this 2d year [1733–4], and Number of Acres granted away in the whole, 54. Number of Country Grants past this year [1734–5], 88. Total number of Acres granted in 3 years, 88. Grants past this year [1735–6] to private persons, 100, 102, 105–6, 109, 112, 113, 118, 146, 153, 154, 157, 161–2. Grants past this year [1736–7], 278. Grants of lands order & past [1737–8], 318, 322, 338, 375.

Gyles, ——, apply's with his wife & 3 children to go to Georgia, & the Trustees answer, 267.

Haines, Gregy., Indian Trader, a house & 500 acres mark'd out for him at Augusta, 168.

Hales, Steven, desired to preach the Anniversary Sermon, 41. He preaches, 47.

Hamilton, Jo., proposes to the Trustees to attempt Recovering lands given to Popish religious Uses, proceedings therein, and why declined by the Trustees, 138–40.

Hamilton, Paul, Esq., of Edistow in Carolina, grant of 500 Acres past to him, 109.

Hampsted Village, Mr. Jo. Wesley's acct. of it in Sept. 1737, 308.

Harbin, Mr., employ'd to bring from Holland 50 Men Servants for Georgia, 110. Order Sent to Stop them, 113.

Harbin, Mr. (*continued*) 20£ order'd him for going to Holland to procure Tr. Servants who were afterwards countermanded, 270.

Hawkins, Tho., Surgeon & Apothecary, appointed 1st Bailif of Frederica, 110. Appointed a Trustee for 300 acres granted for Religious uses at Frederica, 276. Order'd to write regularly to the Trustees, and acquaint them concerning the Divisions at Frederica, 295. As also of particulars of moment passing there, 360.

Hay, Robt., grant made him of 500 acres, 313.

Hazlefoot, Ja., Allow'd to dispose of his Town Lot in Savannah to Such person as he Shall recommend for a Grant thereof, and to have a Country Grant of 150 Acres, and to be furnish'd with two Trust Servants he repaying for them, 125.

Heathcote, Geo., Esq. & Ald., resigns his Office of Common Counsellor for want of health, 336.

Hemp, encouragement intended to be given the Sowing it by the Assembly of South Carolina, 154.

Herbert, Hen., B.A., goes over Minister to Georgia, 8. Minister at Savannah, dies on Shipboard in his return to England, 28.

Heron, Alexr., capt. of Col. Oglethorpes Regimt., grant made him of 500 acres, 349.

Hethrington, Robt., grant past to him of 250 acres, 29.

Hethrington, Theophilus, grant past to him of 250 acres, 29.

Hewet, Capt., of the 3 Sisters, demands allowance for being disappointed of a Pilot, at arrival at Savannah, but not granted, 349.

Highgate Village, Mr. Jo. Wesley's acct. of it in Sept. 1737, 308. Order given to enquire into the reasonableness of their complaint of having bad land, 364. Order to give them better land where found necessary, 371.

Hill, Earl Piercy, concerned in an intended insurrection at Savannah, 83.

Hodges, Archibald, allow'd to go to Georgia at his own expence, but to have provisions out of the Stores, 266.

Hodges, Ri., 2d Bailif of Savannah deceased, 30, 68.

Hollingbore, ——, Esq., 20.

Holmes, Saml., grant made to him of 500 acres, 19.

Horsey, Col. [Samuel], appointed Govr. of S. Carolina, 211, 243.

Horton, Will., Esq., grant past to him of 500 Acres, 109. Appointed a Trustee for 300 acres granted for Religious Uses at Frederica, 276. Military Officer at Frederica, an attempt to call a Court to try him for Felony, 293. He retires to his lot on Jekyl Island, 293. Is try'd for felony but acquitted; Acct. of his pretended Offence, 320.

Hough, Jo., Bishop of Woster, thanks return'd to him for his benefaction, 19.

Houston, Ja., grant past to him of 500 acres, 36.

Houston, Patrick, grant past to him of 500 acres, 31.

Houston, Will., agreed with to go Bottanist, and collect useful plants for the Colony, from Several parts of America, 5. Dies, 5–6.

Houston, ——, deserts his Plantation to live in Savannah. Mr. Jo. Wesley's acct. of it in Sept. 1737, 308–09.

Howell, Capt. Ja., makes affidavit of the Spaniards design to attack Georgia, 348–49. The Ministry hazard the loss of the Province by their negligence, 371.

Hucks, Robt., Resigns being a Common Counsellor, 244. His odd deportment on that occasion, 244.

Hughes, Joseph, a Trustee to 5000 Acres appointed for the Township of Georgia, 7. Publick Storekeeper at Savannah deceased & his books mislay'd, 39.

Hurst, Saml., Agreed wth. to be a Clerk of the Stores, 252.

Impresses, made to Geo. Heathcote, Esq., 27, 29, 38, 41, 47, 48, 57, 59, 69, 73, 77, 95, 111, 112, 116, 121, 149, 157, 168, 171, 175, 185, 189, 198–99, 225, 226, 235, 266, 272. Drafts on the Bank, 289, 290, 299, 303, 312, 315, 318, 321, 323, 328, 331, 345, 373.

Incorporate Society, for propagating the Gospel in Foreign parts, their rude Message to the Trustees, 220. Conversation thereon, 226–28. Their ill opinion of the Trustees, 228.

INDEX

Indian Town near Savannah, Mr. Jo. Wesley's Acct. of it in Sept. 1737, 308.

Indian Traders, take out Lycences in Georgia, 97. The Traders with the Cherokee Nation offer to build a town of 40 houses at their own charge 300 miles up the Savannah River, 158. All obliged to take wives among the Indians, 272–73.

Indians, treaty made with the Lower Creek Indians, 31. Arrival in England, 57. Order'd to be lodged in the Trustees Office, 57. Some Acct. of them, 57–59. Acct. of the Audience given them by the Trustees, 58. Audience given them by the King, 60. Tomachachi's Saying thereon, 60–61. Their reception by the A.B. of Canterbury, 61. They dine with the E. of Egmont, their behaviour & Speeches there, 61–62. The Trustees apply to his Majesty to Subsist them, 60. Things required by Tomachachi in behalf of his people, 63–64. His Majesty gives 1000£ for their Subsistance in England & for presents to their nations, 65. Great imposition on them in their trade with the English complain'd of by them, 66. Endeavours to Settle with them a Tariff of Trade made fruitless by the drunkenness of the Interpreter, 66. They return to Georgia, 68. Present sent by Tomachachi to the Trustees, 69. Acct. of them [1736], 131–32. An attempt to Set them against us, 140. Desire the protection of the English, 158. The Upper Creeks Side with Carolina in her dispute wth. Georgia, and pretend to recall their grant of land to the Trustees, 175. A chief Man of the Abecoe nation joyns therein, 175. The Lower Creeks to the number of 60, with Chigilly their chief, and the Chiefs of 7 towns come down to Savannah to have a talk with Mr. Oglethorpe, 172. They complain of Joseph Watson, and of our Indian Traders assisting the Cherokees against them, 175. Are friends to the Uchees, 175. Complain of the French encroachments, and depart well pleased, 175. They engage to assist us if attack'd by the Spaniards, 262. They Shew Mr. Oglethorpe the utmost Southern bounds of our Kings dominions, which extend to the River St. Juan, 174. The Chickesaws, Subjects of England, 179. Acct. of that Nation, 177–78, 190–92, 200, 214. Attack'd by the French, and defeat them, 172–73. Attack'd a 2d time, and defeat them again, 190–92. Their talk with Mr. Oglethorpe, 179–80.

Ingham, Benj., A.M., acct. of his journey from Savannah to Frederica, 132–33. Missioner to the Indians, learns their languages, 216. Suddenly abandons the Colony & returns to England, 277. Late Missioner to the Indians, makes 2 requests to the Trustees, 291.

Irene, the Indian School, Mr. Jo. Wesleys Acct. of it in Sept. 1737, 308.

Jekyl, Sr. Joseph, thanks return'd him for his & his Ladys great benefaction, 25. Presents the Trustees petition to Parliamt. for money, 21.

Jenkins, Edwd., grant past to him of 100 Acres, 22. Petitions for 500 acres on Skidaway Island, the Trustees refer it to be consider'd, 314.

Jenys, Paul, Esq., Speaker of the Assembly of South Carolina, grant past to him of 500 Acres, 112. A friend to Georgia, 292–93.

Jews, debate whether they Shall be admitted Inhabitants of Georgia, 10. Resolution against it, 12. Deputations given Jews in London to collect money recall'd, 13. Go Surreptitiously to Georgia, which gives the Trustees offence, 38. Order that the Jews who took out Commissions to collect, do return them to the Office, and recall the jews they Sent, or make Satisfaction to the Trustees, 39.

Johnson, Coll. [Robert], Governor of S. Carolina deceased, 95.

Johnson, Ri., Ensign, Appointed to Succeed Tho. Hawkins 1st Bailif of Frederica in case of death or Removal, 113.

Jones, Noble, Trustees Surveyor of land, very idle, 215–16. Grossly negligent in his duty, 342.

Jones, Tho., Formerly H. Constable of St. Gyles, made keeper of the Remains of Stores at Savannah, 358. Has orders to enquire into Mr. Bradley's management of the Trustees Servants, 365.

Josephs Town, the Scots Settled there, apply for Negroes; that they may have a Court of Record; a Civil Magistracy of their own, and be Independent of Savannah; all of which is refused them, 104. They also apply for an allowance of 2 years provision from the Stores, which is refused, 104. Order given for granting them Lots, 104. Distant 10 or 12 miles from Savannah, 192. Most of the Settlers Swept away by Sickness, 237. Mr. Jo. Wesleys Acct. of it in Sept. 1737, 307.

Kilbury, William, commander of the Trustees boats in Georgia, the most active man in Georgia deceased, 46, 96.

Kramer, Mathias, see Proposals.

Lacy, James, grant made him of 500 acres, 25.

Lacy, Rogr., proposal of Sending with him to Georgia 20 charity children to be employ'd in making Silk, but it took not effect, 23. Grant made him of 500 acres, 25. Left to him to appoint owners of 50 acre lots at Augusta, 168. Interrupts the Carolina Indian Traders who traffick with the Indians not having Licences from Georgia, with Severity, 201. Improves well at Thunderbolt, 215, 237.

Lamb, Bullfinch, grant past to him of 500 acres, 66. His Grant revoked, 156.

Lander, Saml., Indented to go over and assist the Millright in Georgia, 312.

Laws, three Laws enacted by the King in Council: 1. For maintaining Peace with the Indians of Georgia, 2. For preventing the Importation of Rum & Strong liquours in Georgia, 3. For prohibiting the use of Negroes in Georgia, 83. A Sumptuary law prohibiting the use of gold or silver in aparel or Furniture: And a law to oblige Ships clearing out of the River to pay a pound of gunpowder *p* Tun Port Duty, recommended to Mr. Towers and Mr. Holland to consider of, 83.

Laws, Hollyday, grant of 50 Acres order'd him at Frederica, 353.

Laws for Georgia proposed, 1. Agst. gaming and running in debt, 2. Agst. Luxury in Aparel, 3. For allowing of Indian Evidence, 216.

Leak, ———, bookseller of Bath, thanks return'd him for his benefaction, 12. Deputation Sent to him to collect, 15.

Letter of Attorney, past to Mr. Verelts [Verelst] to recieve the 10000£ granted by Parliament, 30.

Levally, Jo., appointed to Succeed Tithing Man at Frederica to Jo. Calwell in case of death or removal, 113.

Light house at Tybee, in danger of falling, 319.

Limerick, Ld., presents a petition to Parliamt. for a further Supply for Georgia, wch. meets with no opposition, but is refer'd to the Committee of Supply, 240. Moves for 20000£ which is not opposed, 243.

Littel, Will., junr., Samuel Mercer appointed his Guardian, 82.

Liverpool, the Chamber of the town votes 50£ towards advancing the Colony, 15. N.B. They never paid it.

Logie, Andrew, grant order'd him of 50 Acres in Savannah, 353.

Lomb, Sr. Tho., His approbation of the Trustees designs and Sense of Carolina Silk, 14. See Silk.

Louisiana, Monsr. Bienville the Governr. marches to attack the Chickesaw Indians, a nation dependent on the English, 154. Is repulst with loss, 158. Offers the Govr. of Augustine 5000 Men to assist him in case the English attack him, 144.

Lownds, Mr., offers a proposal for raising a considerable Sum of money without applying to Parliament, 59–60. His proposal agreed to, 63. He discovers his proposal to be a Lottery to be Set up in Scotland, 63. Presents a new Proposal, 74. N.B. Neither of these were relished.

Macbane, Laghlan, Indian Trader, a house & 500 acres mark'd out for him at Augusta, 168. Takes 27 Servants of those Sent over at the Trustees charge, 371.

Macbane of Darien, returns to England to procure Servants for private persons, 217. Proposes to the Trustees to advance the charge of them to be repaid by their Masters, 223. The Trus-

INDEX   395

tees decline it till further explain'd,
  223. 10.10.0£ order'd him, 234.
McGilivray, Archibald, a Town lot
  order'd him in Savannah, 98. Grant
  past to him of 50 Acres, 106.
Mackay, Hugh, Esq., settler with many
  of the Scots who went with Capt.
  Dunbar in the Prince of Wales, and
  Settled in the County of Frederica at
  a place named Barnwells Bluff, which
  they named Darien, and afterwards
  New Inverness, 123–24.
Mackay, Hugh, Lieut., grant past him
  of 500 acres, 100. Thanks order'd him
  and 100£ for his Services, 253.
Mackay, John, Esq., grant past to him
  of 500 Acres, 105.
Mackay, Patrick, Capt. of Compy. of
  Rangers, Turn'd out of the Trustees
  Service for misdemeanours, 114.
Mackay, Patrick, Esq., grant made him
  of 500 Acres, 105. Settles on Wilmington Island without leave, & employs
  Negroes there, 319.
Maclaghlan, Danl., see Proposals.
Martin, Benj., appointed Secy. to the
  Trustees, 5. His pamphlet entitled
  reasons for establishing the Colony of
  Georgia order'd to be printed, 5. Order for printing 600 copies more to
  give the members of both Houses, 15,
  20. 50£ order'd him for his Services,
  37. 100£ order'd for his Services, 156.
  50£ order'd him for his Services, 79.
  75£ order'd him for ½ years Service
  to Christmass 1736, 234.
Memorial to the Treasury, order'd for
  recieving 10000£ Granted by Parliament, 32. The money pd. to the Trustees, 32.
Messasippi, see Louisiana, 154.
Milledge, Jo., agreed that he Shall have
  his brothers house in Savannah, who
  consented thereto till he came of age,
  65.
Miller, [Robert], approved for Botanist
  at Sr. Hans Sloans recommendation to
  Succeed Mr. Houston deceased, 43.
  Agreemt. made with him, 45. Instructions given him, 45. Finds the Balsom
  Capivi & Balsom Tolu Trees, and the
  Ipicuana Root in different parts of
  America, 94. Order for paying him a
  quarters Sallary, 98. The Plants Set
  in Jamaica & grow, 111. Reason why
  he did not Send them to Georgia, 119.

Seiz'd by the Spaniards in America,
  return'd to England, & informs the
  Trustees of the dissappointment of
  the expectations in collecting plants
  &c which he left at Jamaica, 176. New
  Articles Sign'd with him, 211–12.
  Writes from Jamaica that he had
  found the Ipicuana root alive, which
  he would Send to Georgia, 263. Declines further Serving the Trustees,
  the Spaniards not Suffering him to
  Search their Province for plants &
  roots; but promises the beginning of
  next year to carry the Ipicuana root
  from Jamaica to Georgia, 366.
Missionaries, 50£ p ann. agreed to be
  their Sallary, 167–68.
Montague, D. of, thanks return'd him
  for his benefaction, 12.
Moore, Fra., appointed Recorder &
  Storekeeper at Frederica, 110. 20£
  order'd him for ½ years Sallary endg.
  Christmas 1736, 234. 1000£ Sola bills
  issued to him, 247. 5 quarters Sallary
  order'd him from Oct. 1735 to Jany.
  1736–7, 270.
Moore, Geo., grant made him of 400
  acres, 31.
Moore, Robt., Esq., resigns his Office of
  Common Counsellor, 149.
Moravians, 100 of them designing to
  come over tho unsent for, orders Sent
  to Stop them, 69. Ten of these people
  appear and desire to go to Georgia,
  and are promised that they Shall go,
  72–73. They embark, 75. 25 arrive to
  go to Georgia, 108. Order for Sending
  them over, 110. Sail with Capt. Cornish, 114. In Georgia, laborious, & the
  best Subjects in the Province, 215.
  The A.B. of Canterbury (Dr. Potter)
  pronounces them an Episcopal Apostolick Church, 236. Two of them to
  be Catechists to the Negroes at Purysburg, by Agreement wth. Ct. Zinzendorf, 237. More of these people proposed to be Sent, 240. Depute persons
  from Georgia to repay the Trustees
  the money advanced to them, 369. See
  more Savannah.
Morrice, Eliz., petitions that Thomas
  her Son who is near out of his time
  may have a Servant, but is refused,
  314.
Mount, ——, the Stationer, his proffer
  accepted to find the paper, if the

Mount, —— (continued)
Trustees will let him have the printing what they publish, 28.

Murry, ——, Counsellr. for the Trustees agst. the Bd. of Trade in the Carolina dispute, 226, 328.

Musgrove, Jo., Indian Interpreter, grant past to him of 500 acres, 109. Deceased, 109.

Musgrove, Mary, now Mathews, Indian Interpreter, desires she may have leave to appoint a Successor to her Lot, all the children by her late husband being dead, but if She obtains it, intends to quit the Colony, 292. Mr. Jo. Wesley's acct. of her Settlement in Sept. 1737, 308.

Newcastle, D. of, the Trustees Sence on a letter wrote to him by Mr. Oglethorpe, 176. He desires the Trustees to State the matter of Monsr. Giraldini's complaint against them, 203. The Trustees write to him upon it, and answer those complaints, 206-07. They write him a 2d letter thereon, 231, 234. They write to him the danger the Chickesaw nation is in from the French, & recommend them to his care, 222. They Send him a Copy of Mr. Oglethorpe's Treaty with the Govr. of Augustine, 234. They apprize him of the Spaniards design to attack Georgia, 253. His answer, 254. Lays the blame of the Spaniards falling out wth. us to Mr. Oglethorpes charge, 267. Desired by the Trustees to Send for Jo. Savy, a Traitor who had Surrendered himself, in order to be examin'd, 317-18. He desires a Committee of Trustees to be present at the examination, 327. Copy of Capt. Hewet's affidavit of the Spaniards design to invade Georgia, laid before him by the Trustees, 373.

New Ebenezer, Mr. Jo. Wesleys Acct. of it in Sept. 1737, 307. Fowl allow'd the Saltsburgers, 325. In 1736 they cultivated 150 Acres, 331. In a little time they will want no assistance, 366.

New Inverness, the Same with Darien, where Situated, 147.

Obryen, Kennedy, Indian Trader, a house & 500 acres mark'd out for him at Augusta, 168.

Ogeeky River, Good proceedings of the Settlement on this River in 1736, 237.

Oglethorp, Ja., Esq., conducts the 1st Embarkation in person, 7. Powers given him, 7. Arrives at Charlestown, 15. His proceedings, 19. Powers given him to Set out &c 2800 acres, 29, 35. Powers given him to Set out &c 2500 acres, 35. An accident befalls him, 39. He designs for England, 39. A bill of his refused acceptance for want of advice, 41. Yet other of his bills accepted tho without advice, 42. The Trustees complain to him of his negligence therein, and of his not Sending them information of his proceedings in Settling the Colony, 46. Arrived from Georgia with Indians at Cows, 56. Thanks given him for his good Services in Settling the Colony, 56. Presents the Trustees petition to Parliament for money, 78. Is offer'd the Governmt. of Carolina but refuses it, 79. Moves in Parliamt. that Savannah may be declared a Free Port, which the House allows, 83. Refuses the Govermt. of S. Carolina, 95. Appointed Commissioner for executing the Act to maintain Peace with the Indians, 104. Power granted him to Set out &c 10000 Acres granted for a new County in Georgia call'd Frederica, 105. Powers of the Militia granted him, 105. Embarks for Frederica, 14 Oct. 1735, 114. Detain'd at Portsmouth, 117. Great Hurt to the Trustees thereby, 117. Detained at Cowes, 120, 122. Arrives at Savannah 5 Feb. 1735-6, 129. Writes to the Trustees to apply for more money to Parliament & Shews the necessity thereof, 140. Sets out to view the utmost extent of the English Confederate Indians Southward of Georgia, 142. Some particulars of his expedition, 143-44. Builds Fort St. Andrews on Cumberland Island formerly call'd St. Pedro, 144. His negotiation with the Spanish Governr. of St. Augustine, 150, 152. His artifice to prevent the Governours attacking him, 158. Buys up arms at Charlestown to prevent the Governours Supplying himself therewith, 154. Draws too fast on the Trustees for money, 150. His reason for it, 158. Advises the Stopping Credit in Georgia by reason of the

INDEX

great distress it brings on the people, 158. Answers Presidt. Broughtons complaint concerning the execution of the Rum Act and the Indian Trade Act in Georgia, 158. Writes also to Mr. Jenys, Speaker of the Assembly of S. Carolina to Shew that the loss of the Indian Trade to that Province is rather an advantage than prejudice, 158–59. Mr. Ri. Allens arguments to the contrary, & proposal for reconciling the Two Provinces, 159–60. Desired to be frugal, & draw no bills on the Trust, 167. Yet draws fast on them, 196. Sola bills order'd to be made out & Sent him, 168. He orders Such Carolina Traders as have not taken out Licences in Georgia, and yet trade with the Indians belonging to Georgia, to be Seiz'd with their effects, 167. Writes to the Trustees, that if the Carolinians be Suffer'd to infringe the Georgia Act for maintaining Peace with the Indians, as they aim to do, both Carolina and Georgia will be undone, and the Indians make war on both Provinces, 185. Complains by letter to the D. of Newcastle of the opposition given by Carolina to the Laws of Georgia, & exposes the mischiefs that must attend it, 174–75. His purpose at bottom to transfer the trade for Skins from Carolina to Georgia, 194–95. He has a grant of 12000 acres near the Palachocolas Fort in Carolina, 212. The Carolinians complain that he is turn'd merchant, & bought up Skins at a dear price, more than they pay, & thereby monopolized the Trade, 212. He orders the laying out of a new Town call'd Augusta 250 miles from Savannah Town, 168. Indefatigable in the Affairs of the Colony, 216. But had yet taken no care to lay out land for religious uses, or to procure Catechists to instruct the Negroes at Purysburg, 216. He cannot comply with the Trustees desire and advice to withdraw from the Southern Division, having already Settled the town of Frederica, built two Forts and garison'd them, and engaged Rangers for a year, 184–85. Is against our Ministers going among the Indians to preach, till we have more to preach to our own people in Georgia to reform

397

their Morals, 185. Conceals from the Trustees the Governments Orders to him, 169. Sends to the D. of Newcastle a Memorial of the Kings Right to Georgia, 169. Visits the utmost Limits of the Kings possessions South of Georgia next the Spaniards, 174. Agrees with the Govr. of St. Augustine to withdraw his garison from St. George's Fort and evacuate the Islands, and to live in peace till the two Courts Should Settle the differences about bounds, 201–02. Informs the D. of Newcastle of the preparations made by the French Govr. of Louisiana to attack Carolina, & of their falling on the Chickesaws, 174. He prepares to return to England, 205. Arrives in England, 223. Thanks given him by the Trustees for his Services, 224–25. His conference with Sr. Robt. Walpole touching Georgia & its defence, 231–33. Sr. Robert agrees he Shall go over Govr. of the Troops of Carolina and Georgia, 143. His Commission made out, but he refuses it unless a Regiment be given him, 255. His Conversation with Sr. Robt. Walpole thereon, 273–74. Charged by the D. of Newcastle with provoking the Spaniards, 267–68. He puts too favourable an Acct. of Georgia into the Publick Prints, which Jo. Brownfield Register of the Province confutes by letter to the Trustees, 290–91. Orders a Ship load of Madera wine for the use of the Colony without the Trustees knowledge, & his reason for so doing, 292–93. His free answer to Sr. Robert Walpole, why the Trustees are averse to petitioning any more for money, but to have the Parliament Supply's put into an Estimate, 293–94. His warm discourse with Sr. Robert Walpole, on occasion of Mr. Giraldini the Spanish Ministers 2d Memorial, 296–97. Says he will not go back to Georgia unless the Expences of the Province are put into an Estimate, 295. Desires me to write him a letter concerning the Spanish Memorial, the necessity of sending a Military Force to defend Georgia, and putting the Trustees on an establishment for 7000£ a year, that he may shew it and make proper use of it, 301. The

Oglethorp, Ja. (*continued*)
Govermt. agree that he shall have a Regiment for the defence of Georgia, 303. His conversation with Sr. Rob. Walpole thereon, 303–05. He apply's directly to the King, who approves of a different Scheme from that Sr. Robert was for, 304–05. His commission Sign'd, 306, 310. Grant order'd of 3000 acres to be divided among his Soldiers, 312. In what manner to be divided, 316. The Grant past, 318–19. N.B. Negligence of the Ministry to provide Amunition & Transports to carry his Soldiers, 317. His having a Regiment prejudices some Trustees unreasonably against him, 334–35. He disapproves the Trustees frugality in striking out of their Estimate the Military expences of the Colony, and often absents himself from the Board on that account, 356–57. He strongly opposes granting new land to the Inhabitants of Highgate in lieu of their pine barren land, 342. He sets out for Portsmouth by his Majesties express Order, to embark for Georgia 11 May 1738, 359. N.B. Yet no Orders given for embarking the Stores that were to go with him, 360. He breaks into the agreement made by the Trustees with Willm. Bradley, which is very displeasing to them, 359. Order'd to set out the 3000 acres design'd for the Colony, 364. He is suspected by the Trustees of ordering Mr. Tho. Causton to certifie Bills or Accompts, 368. A House Building for him in the Cherokee Nation, unknown to the Trustees, 371. He is greatly offended at the Privy Council's instructions to the Trustees, for amicably adjusting the dispute wth. S. Carolina concerning the Indian Trade, and declares that if he were at leasure, he would come to town and protest against those instructions, 373.

Old Ebenezar, Mr. Jo. Wesley's acct. of it in Sept. 1737, 307.

Old Savannah, al[ia]s Fort Moore, al[ia]s New Windsor, on the Savannah River 150 miles distant from Charlestown, the great mart of Carolina for the Indian trade, 194–95.

Olive Trees, will thrive well in Georgia, 154.

Ortman, Christn., 2500 acres granted to him in Trust for the Saltsburgers, 35. Resolved that he be School master to teach the Saltsburg children the English tongue, 35. Agremt. made with him for that purpose, 35.

Osabaw Island, 40 miles from Savannah, Some Acct. of it & great plenty of Wood there, 106.

Osborn, Lady, thanks return'd her for her benefaction, 14.

Page, Jo., Esq., Elected into the Common Council, 337.

Palachocolas Fort, Situated 24 miles above Purysburg, & 60 from Savannah on the Carolina Side of the River Savannah, given up by that Province to be garison'd by Mr. Oglethorpe with Georgians, 192–93. Stands within 5 or 6 miles of the Uchee Indians, 193.

Palatin Brief money, the Trustees purpose to move the Parliamt. concerning moneys collected by Briefs in Q. Anne's reign for the relief of Palatin Refugees, which moneys they were inform'd were not yet paid into the chamber of London, 40. The Surviving Subscribers intend to petition the house, 44. Sr. Robert Meredith presents the petition & the Same referr'd to a Committee, 44–45.

Paris, ———, Employ'd as Sollicitor by the Trustees, 225. 100£ paid him on account, 271.

Parker, Hen., 2800 acres granted him in Trust, 27. Appointed 3d Bailif at Savannah, 68. Appointed a Trustee of 2500 acres granted for the New Saltsburgers, 68. Powers granted him to Set out &c the Said Acres, 68. Promoted from 3d to 2d Bailif of Savannah, 104. Allow'd 2 Trust Servants, and a present made him besides in consideration of his poverty and Services, 363. Appointed 1st Bailif in Mr. Caustons room, 373.

Parker, Robt., junr., concern'd in an intended insurrection at Savannah, 83.

Parker, Robt., Senr., late Aldn. of Lynn, appointed 1st Constable of a new intended Vilage call'd Thorpe, 35. His impertinence, 198. Fly's out of Georgia, 198. More of him, 199, 211.

Parker, Saml., appointed 2d Constable of Savannah, 8.

INDEX   399

Parliamt., petition prepared for money to carry on the Settlement of the Colony, 20. Corporation Seal put to it, 20. Presented with his Majesties consent, 21. 10000£ granted, 22. Grants 25000£ to the Trustees, 75. Received, 76. Petition to Parliament order'd to be prepared for money to carry on the Settlement of the Colony, 76. Seal put thereto, 77. Alter'd and Seal put anew, 77. Presented by Mr. Oglethorp, & refer'd to the Committee of Supply, 78. An estimate of the necessary expences drawn up by Mr. Oglethorp for the Settlement & protection of the Colony, amounting to near 26000£, 78. 26000£ voted by the Committee of Supply, 79. The Trustees considerations how to apply that Sum, 80–81. Orders given for applying to the Treasury for the money, 86. Grant of 10000£, 143. Grant recd., 175. The 20000£ granted last Session (1737) receiv'd, 290. The Trustees petition again for money, 332. 8000£ granted them for the year, 1738, 337.

Parnel, Danl., appointed to Succeed Will. Allen as 2d Tithing Man of Frederica in case of death or removal, 113.

Pavey, Joseph, Indian Trader, a house & 500 acres mark'd for him at Augusta, 168.

Pedro Island, named Cumberland, 147.

Penkerton, ——, Ensign, apply's for a Grant of 300 acres, 10–11. Grant past to him, 11. He declines it because of the Tenure in Tail male, 12.

Pen[n, William], Esq., Govr. of Pensilvanea, Thanks return'd him for his benefaction, 21.

Pennyfeather, John, Capt., grant made him of 300 acres, 13, 14.

Penrose, Jo., appointed Tything Man of Savannah, 8.

Percival, Ld. Jo., appointed 1st Presidt. of the Trustees by the Charter, and administers the Oathes of Office, 4.

Perkins, Saml., appointed a Trustee for 10000 Acres granted for the County of Frederica, 102. A Coachmaker, and appointed 2d Bailif of Frederica, 110.

Piercy, Fra., made Publick gardiner at Savannah, 217. Abandons Georgia in discontent against Mr. Causton, 331. Appears before the Trustees, excuses his coming away & behaves uncivily, 372.

Plants, collected in the Spanish Dominions to be Sent to Georgia, 94. Order'd that Sr. Hans Sloan be acquainted therewith, 98.

Polhill, Nathl., grant past to him of 150 acres, 37.

Pot Ash Compy., a bad character of them, 30.

Pot Ash people, agreed with to go over, 8, 10.

Pratt, Tho., arrives from Georgia, and desires to Sell his Lot to Mr. Bovey, 82. The Trustees forfeit his Grant for returning without Lycense, and order it to Mrs. Bovey, 82–83. Grant thereof past to her, 84.

Preston, Geo., junr. of Valyfield, grant made him of 500 acres with leave to remain in Scotland, 318.

Prevost, David, grant past to him of the Widow Hughes lot in Savannah by her and John West her new husbands consent, 369.

Proctor, Tho., appointed a Trustee for 10000 Acres granted for the County of Frederica, 102.

Proposal, that their female and collatoral branches may Succeed to lands by will of the deceased, order'd to be debated next Council day, 46. Resolv'd that any younger child, male or female, Shall on their marriage to any person who has not lands already in Georgia, and will covenant to reside there, Shall have a grant to descend to his heirs male, 48. The Unladers of coal at London complain of oppression in their wages and propose to the Trustees that if they will procure them an Act of Parliament to regulate their wages they will pay the Trust a Sum for every bushel unladed by them, which will arise to 26000£ p ann., 68. Proposal from Case Billingsley, Esq., to discover a Scheme for raising a large Sum of money for the Service of the Colony, provided the Trustees will previously agree to give him half the profits, 86. From the Canton of Apenzel to Send 2000 persons to Georgia, 238. From Geneva to Send persons, 238. From Ct. Zinzendorf to Send more Moravians, 240. From Mr. Zuberbuller to carry over 150

Proposal (*continued*)
Swiss, 252. From Mathias Kramer to carry over Moravians; from Mathias Kramer to translate the book entitled, Reasons for establishing the Colony of Georgia, wrote by our Secretary, into High Dutch, 264. 10£ order'd him for his attendance, 270. From Danl. Maclaghlan to carry over Cameronians, 253. His bad character, 253, 255. His acct. of himself, 255-57, 265. The Trustees answer to his proposals, 267, 271. From Mr. Berry renewing his former proposal to go to Georgia to cut timber for the Navy, 239. To take Parish children and Send them to Georgia, 305-06. See Lownds.

Purysburg, 200 Swiss & German Protestants intended to be Sent to Purysburg, on a loan to them from his Majesty of 1200£, which when repay'd is to go to the maintenance of an English School in Purysburg, 72. N.B., his Majesty afterward would lend but 600£ which reduced the number that went, 72, 75. On the Carolina Side of the Savannah, 14 miles from Joseph's town in Georgia, 192.

Pye, John, agreed with to be a clerk in the Stores, 252. The Agreement Seal'd, 263.

Pytt, Hen., carpenter, grant past to him of 100 acres, 154.

Pytt, Rowland, iron-monger of Gloucester, grant past to him of 500 acres with Lycense to him not to go over, but reside in Engld., 112.

Quincy, [Samuel], B.A., Recommended for to go Minister to Georgia, & order'd to attend the Incorporate Society for their approval, 10. Memorial to the Society for obtaining of them a Sallary for him, 12. A Trust Servant allow'd him, 14. Complains that 300 acres Set out for Religious Uses is all Pyne barren & good for nothing, 95. Gone again from the colony to Charleston, 96. The Trustees dissatisfy'd with his behaviour on Several Accts., 96. He writes that a Successor may be appointed him, designing to return to England, 103. Negligent of his duty, 108. Recall'd even before his desire to be recall'd was known, 108. Arrives, and gives a bad acct. of Savannah, 196. Applys to the Trustees & makes Sevl. demands, and the Trustees reply thereto, 207-08. Negligent in his duty, 244.

Ranier, ——, one of the Pot Ash Compy. declares he will not be concern'd with the others, 30. Resigns his grant, 32.

Reading, ——, a Silk & cotton Dyer Settled at Rotterdam apply's to go to Georgia and there Set up his trade, which the Trustees refuse in favour of the English Manufacture, 271.

Rice, see Savannah.

Roberts, Jo., lays claym to a Barony of 12000 Acres in Georgia, which the Trustees disallow, 72.

Rum, its pernicious effects in Georgia, 36. Order of the Trustees to prohibit the use of it, and Stave what Shall be brought into the Province, 37. Complaint made of the mischief done by Rum in Savannah, the use of which the Magistrates are not able to restrain, 366.

Rundal, Tho., D.D., elected a Trustee, 47.

Sacheveril, Joseph, 2800 acres granted him in Trust, 27. NB—He went not over.

St. Andrews Fort, Mr. Macbanes account of it, that it Stands on the Continent 50 miles S. of Darien, on the N. Side of the Allatahama river, on a high Bluff, and commands the country round; Garison'd by 30 Men who can defend it against 300; A fine Well in the middle; Mr. Cuthbert Commandant; No Settlers there, 218. See Cumberland Island; Frederica.

St. Augustine, the Garison reinforced, 197. The Govr. demands of Mr. Oglethorpe to deliver up Georgia, 201. Treaty of pacification made with him, 201-02. Makes preparations to attack Georgia, 235. The news confirm'd, 246-47, 260, 267-68, 276-77. The Govr. who made the Treaty put in chains and Sent to Old Spain, 276. Some appearance that they will not molest us, 266. The Govr. Don Manuel Joseph de justitz assures Capt. Windham that he has no thoughts of attacking Georgia, 291. Yet Sends 30 Spaniards to land on Amelia Island, who retreat on the

INDEX 401

Garrisons firing on them, 293. His Indians attempt to surprise the Outguard at the Darien, 293. His design to attack Georgia, 306. Don Antonio Redondo, an Ingeneer, Sent Govr. in Don Josephs place who continues the preparations to attack Georgia, 314–15. Confirmation of that design, 347. Further Acct. of preparations for that end, 347. Capt. James Howell's affidavit concerning it, 348–49. The Same confirm'd by the Speaker of the Assembly of S. Carolina, 349. See Frederica; Oglethorp.

St. Catherine Island, see Frederica.

St. Georges Fort, stands 60 miles South of the Limits of Georgia, 216. Yet within the Limits of S. Carolina, 218–19. Built by leave of the Indians who are mortal Enemies to the Spaniards, 219. Garrison'd very Strong by Mr. Oglethorpe, 216. Stands 50 miles South of Fort St. Andrews close to St. Juans river, which at that place is 3 leagues broad, but Some way higher up not half So much, 218–19. Capt. Mackay commands there wth. generally 200 men, a great many cannon there but no Settlers, being So near the Spaniards (to whom it gives great umbrage) as to be in Sight of their advanc'd guard on the other Side of St. Juans river. Mr. Macbanes acct. of it, 219.

St. Juans River, the bounds between the English and Spanish bounds in America, 174.

St. Julian, Mr., see Scot.

St. Simons Island, richer ground than Rhode Island, 150. Description of it, 157. Joseph Cannon's acct. of it, 210–11. Mr. Jo. Wesleys Acct. of it in Sept. 1737, 309. See Frederica.

Sale, Will., 2500 acres granted to him in Trust, 35.

Saltsburgers, agreed to Settle a number of them in Georgia, 4. Proposals considered, 11. Order past for bringing over 50 families, 11. Resolv'd to give 50 acres to every family, 18. Amount of the collection made for them in England, 20. Resolution of the Trustees with respect to a Sallary for their Minister, 23. 2500 acres granted in trust for their Township, 25. Power Sent to Ausburg to collect Saltsburgers, 33. A Minister & Catechist to be Supported by the Society for promoting Christian Knowledge, 33. Proposal concerning a Sallary to the Minister, Catechist & Schoolmaster, made by the Trustees to the Christian Knowledge Society, 37. Arrival of 40 Saltsburgers at Dover under Conduct of Monsr. Von Reck, 38. The Trustees agree with them, 38. Information that the 2d Set of Saltsburgers wrote for declined coming, 49. Acct. recd. that they go prosperously on, and had cut a road 5 miles long, 59. More to be Sent at the Expence of the Christian Knowledge Society, 59. 54 Chosen Saltsburgers Set out for Rotterdam in order to be ship'd for England, and from thence to Georgia, 65. A Further grant of 2500 acres in Trust for the use of the new Saltsburgers going over, 67. Powers granted to Set out &c the Same, 68. John Vatt, conductor of the new Saltsburgers, appointed Secretary under the direction of their Ministers, 68. The Trustees advance money to the Society for promoting Christian knowledge, for bringing Saltsburgers over to Settle in Georgia, which the Society is to repay, 98. There arrive 46, together with 11 other Germans under the leading of Mr. Philip Von Reck of Ratisborn, 108. They Sail on board the London Merchant, Capt. Thomas, 20 Oct. 1735, 114. Arrive at Savannah 2 feb. 1735–6, 129. They complain their land is bad, 121. And remove 4 miles lower, 143. The Christian Society repay the money advanc'd to them by the Trustees, 119. Mr. Boltzius complains of hardships done them, 205–06. Their complaints redrest, 236–37. Sickness among them, but few died, 237.

Sandford, Cornelius, grant made him of 500 acres, 21.

Savannah, township and Town, Civil Government, Magistrates, Court of Oyer and Terminer, judges, jurors &c order'd, 7. The Town begun to be built, 19. Order for laying out 300 acres for the Church, 8. The Town Sickly, & many die, 95, 97. Bad condition the Inhabitants are in, & the reasons, 141. Distrest by their debts, 158. Mr. Oglethorp advises to Stop credit, 158. Apprehension that the

INDEX

Savannah (*continued*)

Crop will fail, 95. 500 acres this year under corn, 98. The Inhabitants may Subsist themselves if industrious, 108. Liberty allow'd to Georgia to export Rice, 104. Officers appointed for executing the Act, 104. Seal put to their appointment, 117. Officers appointed to put the Rum Act in execution, 104. Officers appointed to put the Negro Act in execution, 104. Officers appointed for the Indian affairs, 104. The Commissioners of the Customs apply'd to, to make out Bonds and Lycenses for a Collector, Comptroller and Searcher at Savannah to be named by the Trustees, 107. State of the Publick Garden, 96–97. The Mulberry Trees in it Succeed prodigiously well, and most, if not all the Inhabitants will in 2 years be Supply'd with them, 100. By the Fall, many thousands will be ready to give the planters, 103. Silk will assuredly Succeed in Georgia, but will cost money to advance it, 97. The Silk Sent over Shewn to her Majesty, and highly extoll'd by Sr. Thomas Lomb, 102. Encouragemt. intended to be given for raising it in South Carolina, 154. Bailifs and Officers, Gratuities order'd them, 98. A Catechist for Savannah order'd, 145–46, 149. Great abuse in erecting the Light house, 143. Births, marriages & deaths in Savannah from 1 feb. 1732-33 to 13 Sept. 1735, 120–21. Mr. Quincy's Acct. thereof, 196. P. Thickness's acct. thereof, 209–10. Capt. Jenkins Acct. thereof, 238. Mrs. Stanley's Acct. thereof, 243–44. Mr. Cha. Wesleys Acct. thereof, 215. Mr. Macbanes Acct. thereof, 217. No lands for Religious Uses yet Set out, 216. Acct. of the Publick garden, 217, 219. The fine wood that Shelter'd it cut down by the Inhabitants, 277. The Inhabitants mostly idle & will never come to good; many upon Striking them off the Stores were purposing to go away, but their Creditors detain'd them, upon which Some made themselves over Servants to work out their debts, 219. Two thirds of them in debt; Mr. Oglethorpes expedient for their paying, by giving them leave to Sell their house & 5 acre lot, and wth. the remainder of their money to oblige them to Settle on their 45 acre lots, 224. Why excusable for not having cultivated their lands, 257. They get Rum notwithstanding the Magistrates care to prevent it; yet are healthy tho not So at Ebenezar, 219. They build a Fort for defence of the Town, 257, 266. But for that purpose cut down the Wood that Sheltered the town from the East Winds which will make it less healthy, 277. A great number idle, 237. Yet in 1736 raised a Sufficient quantity of Corn for their Support, 237. The Grand jury present the Carolina Memorial against the Trustees as Scandalous, unwarrantable, unjust &c, 168. And petition the Trustees against it, 229. The Constables & Tything Men refractory to do duty of Watch & Ward, and assume to chuse their own Officers, 237. The Inhabitants desire to chuse their own Bailifs, 257. The Number of Inhabitants 24 feb. 1736–7, 238. The number of children born, and brought into the world by Mrs. Stanley the Publick Midwife from the first embarkation 3 Nov. 1732 to the end of 1736, & the number of them deceased, 243. Much Sickness to the Westward of the Town, but few died, 237. The River of Savannah described for 300 miles up to Old Savannah als. Fort Moore, als. New Windsor, 192, 194, 195. An Island in the River 10 or 12 miles distant from the town where the Trustees cattel may be kept safe, 209–10. Mr. Jo. Brownfield gives acct. that the Inhabitants are discouraged, and have cultivated little; that the Stores are empty, and the 1st Bailif has no mony to employ workmen. That the Fort which was begun & now left unfinish'd, is more capable to annoy than defend the town, 290–91. Mr. John Wesleys Acct. of it in Septbr. 1737, 306. The Inhabitants mutinous, and the Constables and Inferior officers refractory to Orders, 293. Above 100 idle persons have left it in 2 months, 331. State of the peoples cultivation, 303. Which is much neglected, 325. One reason for which is their uneasiness that their heirs female are debar'd from succeeding to land, 342–3, 344. A very unruly Spirit in the people, 323. A set of malecontents exclaim against the Tenure in Tail Male, and at the not allowing the use of Negroes, and they poison the peoples minds, 325. They persuade the people not to trust the conveyance of their letters to England in Mr. Stephens hands, lest the Trustees should possess themselves of them, 367. The names of some of these Mutineers, 367. They are Such as Seldom attend Divine Service, 366. The Colony wants money and provisions everywhere, and has a melancholly aspect, 320. The Inhabitants raised corn last year sufficient to supply the wants of half the Colony, 331. Many Inhabitants more industrious this year than before, 366. The Country healthy to grown people, 331, 343. But most of the new born children die, which is imputed to the Parents diseases, and their drinking spirituous liquors, 343. The Inhabitants apprehension of the Spaniards so great that the Magistrates publish an order that none depart the Colony, to prevent their flight, 347. State of the Publick garden, 299–300. Much neglected, 325, 331. Restored to good order, 343, 349. The Light house at Tybee in danger of falling, 319. A passage boat wanting between Georgia & Carolina, 325. The land at Highgate not So bad as reported, but the Lotts of Some worse than others, and most will not yield a produce Sufficient to maintain the Owners and their Servants, and to raise money to buy new Servants, 343. The Sober part of the Inhabitants pleased with the Revd. Mr. Whitfield, 366. The Moravians Settled at Savannah apply to the Trustees that they may not be obliged to fight in defence of themselves & the Colony, being against their principle, and their request is allow'd, 291, 295. But they are required to find 2 Men, not of their persuasion, to fight in their room, 295. See Georgia.

Savy, Jo., a vile fellow, occasions an allarm that the Spaniards design to attack Georgia, 267. A Traitor to Georgia, acct. of him; writes to the Trustees that he is coming home to cast himself at their feet, 314–15. Writes again to them from Pendennis Castle where he ly's a prisoner, 317. The Trustees send copy's of his letter to the D. of Newcastle, and desire he may be Sent for to town & examin'd, 318. He arrives, & the Duke desires a Committee of the Trustees may be present from time to time at his examination, 327.

Saw Mill, Sent to Georgia, 170. 500£ insured on it, 171.

Scot, Fra., powers granted to him and Monsr. St. Julian to Set out &c 2500 acres in Mr. Oglethorps absence, 35. Like powers to him & Mr. St. Julian to Set out 2800 acres in Mr. Oglethorps absence, 35, 36.

Seeds, of the White mulberry tree & other plants, order'd to be Sent over, 12.

Servants, order past that for the future No Servt. when out of his time Shall have more than 20 acres, 17. 40 Irish Servants purchased for the Trustees use, 40. Geo. Lewis Wentz agreed with to bring over 100 German Servants, 83. The Agreement alter'd, 84. Sign'd, 85. Trust Servants Sent over, 85. Seal put to their Indentures of more Servants, 86. The number taken to 9 June 1735, 87–88. On the Trust, Seal put to their Indentures, 100. Their Scruples to go, 100. Transport of 23 Servants for the use of private persons, advanc'd by the Trust upon lands, 118. At Savannah, a Sad Crew, 367. 27 of them taken by Mr. Macbane for the use of Indian Traders tho paid for by the Trustees, 371.

Settlements in Georgia, Jany. 1733–4, & number of Souls fed by the Trustees, 39–40. Silk of Georgia, highly extoll'd by Sr. Tho. Lomb, 81. The favourable prospect of its Succeeding in Georgia, 179. The Worm thrives & multiply's, 219, 243–44. The Queen misinform'd about it, 258–59. The worms look healthy, and great quantity of Silk may be expected in a little time, 349. Plenty of Mulberry trees in Mr. Caustons garden, 344. The early leaves of the Mulberry trees cut off by the winds in March 1737/8, 366. The Chickesaw Indians offer if instructed, to bring to Savanah great quantities of Silk, having numbers of Mulberry trees in their Country, 252.

Silk Men, engaged to go over, 9. Grants past to them, 11. Order for a machine for winding Silk, 21. The Same delivered to the Trustees, 22.

Simons, Mr., the merchant, his demand for Demurrage allow'd, 124–25, 155–56.

Skea, an Indian Warriour, designedly destroyed by Joseph Watson by drinking him to death, 78. A present order'd to his relations to pacify them, 79.

Skidaway, improvments go on well there in 1736, 237. Mr. Jo. Wesleys Acct. of the condition of the Island, Vilage, & Fort in Sept. 1737, 308.

Sloop, of 8 guns, apply'd for to protect the Settlement, 10.

Smalwood, Saml., appointment to be clerk of the Stores, 276.

Smith, Saml., application to Ld. Chancellor to give him a Living, 43. Elected into the Common Council, 336. Sworn, 338.

Society Incorporated for propagating Christianity in foreign parts, apply'd to by the Trustees for a Sallary to a Minister, 9.

Sola Bills, projected to be issued in Georgia, and the Banks opinion to be had thereon, 98. The Bank made no objection thereto, 99. 4000£ in Sola Bills order'd to be made out, 99. Application made to the Treasury that 1000£ may be Sent over in Shillings & Sixpences by the Trustees to circulate their bills, 99. Seal put thereto, 100. Seal put to 4000£ Sola bills, 111. Order for appropriating 4000£ in the Bank to answer those bills, 111. Order for making out 1000£ more in Sola bills, 156. Made out, 168, 189. Send away, 199. 1500£ of them order'd to be return'd, 225. Their great credit in America, 265. Order'd to be made out, 299. Order'd to be cancell'd, 283. Sent to Georgia, 298–99, 301, 310. Order'd to be return'd from Georgia to pay certified Accts., 330.

Sollicitor Genl., order'd to be retain'd by the Trustees in the cause of Watson, 246–47.

S. Carolina, their Representation to the King and Council against the Magistrates of Savannah presented by the Gr. Jury of Savannah as Scandalous &c, 168. Proceedings of the Assembly against the Georgia Act for regulating the Indian Trade, 171–72. Mischiefs that would attend a breach into the Act, 174–75. Substance of the Assembly's Representation, 178–79. The people of this Province labour to Set the Indians against Georgia, 176–77, 177–79, 180–81, 196. Their malice to Georgia, 214–15. Appoint a Committee to Settle differences wth. Mr. Oglethorpe, 183. Their proposalls, and Mr. Oglethorpes answer, 186–88. They excite the Spaniards against Georgia, 196. And the Uchee Indians to fall on the Saltsburgers, 196. They lodge their Memorial with the Council Board, 211. Answer'd by a Counter Memorial from the Trustees, 229. The Board of Trade defer a hearing in partiality to Carolina, & the hardship thereof complain'd of by the Trustees, 230, 235. The Board of Trade fix a day for hearing, 267. Yet at the desire of Carolina go off from it, 268. The hearing proceeded on, 275. The Assembly write to Mr. Horace Walpole their weak condition, & apprehension that Gr. Britain abandons them, 267. The 3d hearing of the Board of Trade in the dispute between the Two Provinces, and the Boards great partiality to Carolina therein, 283. The Boards further partiality in putting 2 questions to the Attorney & Sollicitor Genl. before they make their Report, 285. We desire a Copy of those questions but are refused them by the Board, 285–86. We desire a copy of the Attorney Genl., 286. He refuses also, 287, 290. He at length allows a transient view of the, with his opinion which is our favour, 297–98. The Board make a most partial Report in favour of Carolina, 302. The Trustees resolve to petition the King and Council for a hearing against that Report, 316. Brief for our Counsil Settled, 323. We order our case to be printed, and given to the Committee of the Privy Council, 328. The 1st days hearing before the Committee of Council, 330. 2d Hearing, 330. 3d Hearing, 332. And final resolution, 369–70. Divided in their affections to Georgia, but her Enemies most prevalent, 319. They refuse to deliver up our Run away Servants,

319. They open our letters, 326. Their malice & Rancour Seems to abate upon hearing that Col. Oglethorpe is made Commander in chief of their Forces, 343.

Spaniards, see St. Augustine.

Speaker of the H. of Commons, thanks order'd to him for his favourable expressions of the Trustees designs in his Speech to the King on the Throne, 27.

Squire, Botham, embarks for Georgia, 12–13.

Stanley, ——, D.D., of Liverpool, recommends 5 persons to be Sent on the charity acct. to Georgia, 121.

Stanley, Mrs., publick Midwife of Savannah, her Acct. of the Town, 243–44. Advanc'd 5 guineas to be repaid in Georgia, 247. Advanc'd more 2 guineas, 270.

Stanyer, Jo., of Skidaway, desires leave to quit his grant, the same refer'd to be consider'd of, 318.

Stayley, ——, a Potter, order to be taken up, for accepting the Kings money to go to Georgia, and then withdrawing himself, 116.

Stephens, Tho., Son of Will. Stephens, Esq., Sails for Georgia, 313.

Stephens, Will., Esq., extract of his journal up the River Savannah, 192–95. Runs land out for Col. Horsey, 193. Offers his Service to the Trustees, 230. Appointed their Secrety. in Georgia, 259–60. Agreemt. made with him, 260. Instructions publick and private given to him, 264. Grant made to him of 500 acres, 264. His Commission to be Secretary of the Province Seal'd, 294. Order'd to take care of the Inhabitants letters to forward them to England, 364. But they are practiced upon not to trust him wth. them, 367.

Sterlings Bluff deserted, Mr. Jo. Wesley's Acct. of the Settlement in Sept. 1737, 309.

Stirling, Hugh, grant past to him of 500 acres, 36.

Stirling, Will., grant past to him of 500 acres, 36.

Subscriptions, letter agreed on by the Trustees for this purpose, 4.

Swiss, 50 Families come to Rotterdam proposing to go to Georgia, and recommended by Mr. Horatio Walpole & Ld. Harrington. The Trustees reply they have not mony to Send them, 70. Arrival of 80 of them to be follow'd by more, 72. Objections made by them to the conditions on which they are to go, and the Trustees reply thereto, 74. 87 of them resolve to go, 75. Of Geneva, 100 persons apply to be Sent to Georgia, but are refused, for want of money, 116.

Tailfer, Patrick, grant past to him of 500 acres, 35. Surgeon, a proud busie fellow, writes to the Trustees that Negroes may be Suffer'd in Georgia & Sets forth his reasons, 103.

Talbot, Will., Esq., elected Trustee, 47.

Talbot, Ld., elected into the Common Council, 244. Sworn in, 247. Resigns his Office of Common Council Man, pretending he wants time to attend the Service, 336. His true reason, 336.

Tanner, his Acct. of the Indians & Indian Traders, 272–73.

Taylfer, Patrick, a principal Mutineer in Savannah, 367.

Tenure in Tail male, motion made to consider the expedience of excluding heirs female from inheriting, but not Seconded, 76. Motion to alter it in favour of Female Succession, Opposed, 95–96. Arguments against it, 96. Again objected to, but Still adhered to, 229. The Inhabitants of Savannah are uneasie to have it alter'd, 325. The Trustees debate thereon, 340. Which end in not allowing of an alteration, 345–47, 364. See Proposal; Vaudois; Committee of Correspondence, 50, 53.

Terry, Will., grant past to him of 200 acres, and ground for a house in Savannah, 35.

Thomas, [William], Capt. of the Ship the 2 Brothers, agreed with to transport to Purysburg 200 Swiss & Germans at the Kings expence who lends them 1200£, 72. Sails 23 Jan. 1734-5 with but 122, the King reducing his loan of 1200 to 600£, 75. Sails for Georgia with 5 males and 1 female 18 June 1736, 170. His demands for demurrage and bringing over Mr. Oglethorpe allow'd, 240. Agreemt. with him to carry over Scots Servants, 262. Apply's for Mrs. Wests 50 acre lot that he may afterwards Sell it for a debt her husband owes him, and the Trus-

Thomas, [William] *(continued)*
tees answer, 271–72. See Embarkations.
Thorp, a new vilage design'd in Georgia, 35.
Thunderbolt Fort and Settlement, Mr. John Wesleys Acct. thereof in Septbr. 1737, 308.
Tirconnel, Ld., Seconds the Motion in Parliamt. for granting the Trustees 10000£, 143.
Tomachachi, Sends the Trustees a present of Skins, which they order to be Sold for the use of the Colony, 156. See Indians.
Towers, Christr., Esq., elected into the Common Council, 336.
Tracy, Robt., elected a Trustee, 47. Moves the Parliamt. for 8000£, and is Seconded by Mr. Frederick, which is granted, but the Noes encrease, 337. Elected into the Common Council, 336.
Trip, Tho., a Carpenter, recommended by the Trustees for a Lot of 50 acres, 37.
Trustee Boards, number of them held this 1st year, 25. 2d year, 53. 3d year, 87. 4th year, 160–61. 5th year, 278. 6th year, 374.
Trustees, appointed by the Charter, 3. New Trustees elected, 16. 1000£ granted them by Parlt., 10 May 1733, 21. Elected this 2d year, 47. Petition Parlt. for money, 46. Deliberate on Joseph Watsons confinement in Georgia for Lunacy, 241–42, 251–52. Retain the Attorney & Sollicitor General in the cause agst. Sarah Watson's petition, 246–47. Their answer to Watsons complaint not Satisfactory to the Attorney Genl. because too general, 257. They object to answer particularly & argue the case and danger of it, 257. The Attorney Genl. now of opinion they Should not make themselves Parties, but answer only by way of information, 261. Again Starts new difficulties, to which the Trustees Reply, 267. They defer making further answer to Watson's petition till the Attorney Genl. gives his opinion on two questions, and their reasons for it, 268. He now again thinks the Trustees are Parties, 269–70. They represent to the Council board the case of Watson & their proceedings therein, 273. They order Joseph Watson to be Set at liberty, if found in his Senses, 274–75. They make a Second order that if found in his Senses Sentence be past on him according to the Verdict, 275. Trustees proceedings on the Anniversary day [1737], 244–46. Persons Sent by the Trustees to Georgia, 235, 247. They order that Archibald Hodges, his wife & child who go on their own charges to have provisions out of the Stores, 266. Agreemt. made wth. Capt. Thompson to carry Scots Servants to Georgia, 259, 262. Order for contracting for 60 Moravian Servants, 264–65, 270–71. They agree with Captn. Wragg to bring over 80 foreign Servants from Holland, 271. They decline Mr. Zuberbullers proposal to carry Swiss Servants, 265. They Order 40 Trust Servants to cultivate Bouverie Farm, & that an annual Acct. of the Farm be kept distinct, 263. They Order fire arms to be Sent by Capt. Thompsons Ship, 259. They Order Mr. Causton to inform them of the State of Watsons mind, 273. They refuse to let a Silk & Cotton Dyer go to Georgia, that the Manufacture of England may not be injured, 271. They order a gratification to Capt. Dempsy for his Services, 247. Satisfaction order'd to Mr. Jo. Vatt for his Services in Georgia, 275–76. A Puncheon order'd for cancelling Sola Bills, 247. Recall 1500£, 225. They Order 433£ to Mr. Oglethorpe to answer Sola bills, which is to be repaid the Trust, & draw on the Bank for the Same, 265–66. Sola bills, Sent to Mr. Oglethorpe, 208–09. Sola bills order'd to be cancel'd, 240. Resolve to Send 1000£ in Sola bills to Georgia, 240, 247. And 3150£, 168. Seven casks of Skins from Georgia, order'd to be Sold, 252. Skins & Rice from Georgia order'd to be Sold, 225. Sold, 251. 3068 pd. Weight of Skins Sold for 419. 9. 2, at 2.8½ p pd., 276. Copies of advices received of the Spaniards design to attack Georgia, Sent to the D. of Newcastle, 253. They present to him a Memorial of the Kings Right to Georgia, 169. They are desired by the Duke to answer the Spanish Ministers complaint against us, & the Board of

Trade also desire a conference thereon, 204. The Trustees agree on a letter to the Duke in answer to the Spanish Ministers complaint, 204. They put the Seal to it, & Substance of the Same, 206, 207. They write a 2d letter to the Duke thereon, 231, 234. They recommend the Chickesaw Nation to the Dukes protection, 222. They Send the Duke a copy of Mr. Oglethorpes treaty of pacification wth. the Govr. of St. Augustine, 234. Order Arms to be Sent for the people's use, 240. Four new Laws order'd to be prepared, 253. The Trustees who were appointed to prepare them decline it, 263. Counsellor Mason appointed thereto, 263. They desire the expences of the Colony may be provided for by Parliamt. by way of Estimate, & not annually petition'd for, 254, 260. They receive from Mr. Bromfeild their Register a bad Acct. of the State of the Colony, 257. Their bad Situation on many accounts, 184. Write to Mr. Oglethorpe to draw no more bills on them, & insist on frugal management, 167. Are frighten'd at the large drafts he makes on them, 196. They order Mr. Causton to Stop as much as he can the peoples running in debt, and to put them to labour, 171. They reject German Servants brought as far as Rotterdam by Mr. Wantz for want of money, 183. They refuse to pay Capt. Dunbar for the transport of 31 Servants carry'd for the use of private persons, & why, 183–84. They comply at last, 190. They decline advancing Servants to private Settlers who went on their own account to Darien & had proposed to repay for them in Georgia, 223. They reject Mr. Berry's proposal to go to Georgia & cut timber for the Navy because he asks too much money, 239. They advertise that they will answer no bills drawn on them but only their own Sola bills, 196. The other Colonies greatly pleased therewith, 217. They refer it to a Committee to consider of appointing a Fast in Georgia, 275. They write to Mr. Oglethorpe that they cannot Support him in anything done by him beyond the Limits of the Province, 176. They refuse to pay a bill of 500£ drawn by Mr. Oglethorp for Services they Suppose done beyond the limits of the Province, 186, 189–90. Debate thereon, 189–90. But afterwds. pay it, & why, 226. They Send Mr. Oglethorpe a calculation of expences, and desire what can be Saved thereout may be apply'd to the cultivation of Lands, 167. They also Send him a computation of the charge for provisions for next years Subsistence of those who went on the poor acct., 167. They reprehend Mr. Oglethorpe for not writing to them, 212–13. They order a Memorial to the Board of Trade for a Speedy hearing of the Carolina dispute, 261, 262. The Board of Trade appoint a day, and then recede from it, 269. They prepare an Answer for Council against the Carolina Memorial, 221, 225. They represent to his Majesty & Council the injury of the Carolinians opposing the Georgia Act for maintaining peace with the Indians, 225. They produce Affidavits to Support that Representation, 229. They again represent to the Board of Trade the hardship of their delaying the Hearing on the Carolina complaint, 230, 235. They Appoint William Stephens their Secrety. in Georgia, 259–60. The Oath of Office administer'd him, 264. Private & Publick Instructions given him, & the latter Seal'd, 264. Grant past to him of 500 acres, 264. Agreement Seal'd with Jo. Pye & Saml. Smalwood to be Clerks of the Store, 263, 276. Hugh Anderson appointed Inspector of the Publick garden & Mulberry trees, 189. They Order payment of Mr. Millar the Bottonists Sallary, 189. And make a new agreement with him, 211–12. They order 300 acres in Trust for Religious uses at Frederica, 263. Seal put to the Grant thereof, 276. They agree that 50£ p annm. be the Sallary of the respective Ministers, 167–68. They are offended at a disrespectfull [resolution] Sent them by the Incorporate Society for propagating the Gospel in foreign parts, 220. And reply thereto, 223, 226. They refer it to a Committee to consider of a Plan for a church in Georgia, 276. They agree with Ct. Zinzendorf to Send two Moravians to instruct the Negroes at Purysburg, 236–37.

Trustees (*continued*)

They Grant a town Lot of 50 acres in Savannah to Jo. Warwick, 264. They pass Grants to Tho Boyd & David Blair of 500 acres each, 190. They insure 500£ on a Saw Mill Sent over, 171. They resolve that any 5 of the Common Council may draw on the Bank for a certain Sum, 171. They receive the 10000£ granted last Session, 175. They prepare a petition for a further Supply, 238. Seal put thereto, 239. Present it, 240. Move for 20000£ and obtain it, 243. Calculation of the Services for which money was wanting, 239. They renew their application to the Board of Trade for an answer & report on their Memorial for Cannon, 212. The Boards answer in a conference, 212. The Trustees reply, 213–14. They instruct Mr. Von Reck to bring over more persecuted Protestants, 223. They purchase 8 Servants of Mr. Jo. Mackay in Georgia for 120£, 235. They redress the Saltsburgers complaints, 236–37. They direct Mr. Causton to be easie with the Constables and Tything Men, till a Militia Act be past, 238. The Trustees negligent in attending, 197, 224. Thanks order'd to Mr. Oglethorpe, Capt. Windham & Capt. Gascoign for their Services in Georgia, 224–25.

Trustees of Georgia, their proceedings [1737-38] in order of time: June 1737. They cancel Sola bills, 283. They write to Sr. Robt. Walpole to desire the expences of the Colony may for the future be put into an Estimate, and they not obliged to petition the Parliament, 284. They direct a Memorial to the Treasury for obtaining the £20000 granted them by Parliament, 284. A Plan of a church for Georgia thought of, and a builder desired to give an estimate thereof, 284. An Estimate given, 287. They refuse to allow of dividing Lotts, 286. They give leave to Peter Gordon late Bailif of Savannah to Sell his Lot, 286. They appropriate money to divers Uses, 287–88.

July. They reject Mr. Vatts Memorial for further consideration of his Services, 288. They order Robt. Hows house to be rebuilt, which was burnt by accident, 288. They give a letter of Attorney to their Accompt. Mr. Verelts [Verelst] to receive the 20000£ granted by Parliamt., 289. They consider of makeing 3 New laws: 1. Against gaming & running in debt. 2. against Luxury in Aparel. 3. For allowing of Indian Evidence, 216. They Order an Extract to be made out of their books of all Orders and Instructions Sent over at different times to Georgia, to which no returns appear to have been made, 289–90. Their Answer to Mr. Von Reck, 290. They receive a bad Acct. of the State of Savannah, 290–91. They allow the Moravians request not to bear arms to defend the Colony, 291–92. Committee of Embarkation appointed, 288.

August. They seal Mr. Stephens Commission to be Secrety. of the Province, and order a Committee to prepare his Instructions, 294. They put the Seal to the appointments of the Courts of Savannah and Frederica to try Offences agst. the Rum Act, 294. They Send over 2 Clerks for the Stores at Savannah, & 1 for the Stores at Frederica, 295. They approve of Striking off all idle people from the Stores who had not cultivated land, 295. They Order the Constables to take care that the peoples arms are kept clean, and repaired, 295. They order Mr. Causton to oppose the Constables attempt to introduce Martial law, & recommend Unity, 295. They order that the Moravians be not obliged to take arms to defend the Colony, but that they find 2 Men for that purpose, 295. They recommend that Noble Jones Survey & Set out the peoples lotts to the Westward of Savannah, 295. They write to the Magistrates of Savannah to put the laws into execution, particularly that relating to Rum, 295. They order Mr. Tho. Hawkins, 1st Bailif of Savannah to give them an Acct. of the Divisions at Frederica, & to write regularly to them, 295. They present a Memorial to his Majesty, declaring their inability to defend the Province from the Spaniards, without a Military force Sent over, 298. They order Mr. Oglethorpe to issue to Fra. Moore 650£ in Sola bills for the Service of Georgia, and

INDEX

that he date them as in November 1736 before he left the Colony, 298. They order the making out 4850£ more in Sola Bills, 299. They order payment of 26£ to Mr. Daniel Booth for making the Queens Silk, 299. They order gowns for the Magistrates of Savannah, 299. They order 1000£ Sola Bills to Mr. Causton, and that he Send an Acct. of what demands remain unsatisfy'd, 301. They order the Seal of the Town Court of Savannah to be kept under lock and key by 2 Magistrates, together with the books and papers of Record, 301. They prepare Establishments for Savannah & Frederica, 301.

Septembr. They write to Ct. Zinzendorf to Satisfy him concerning the Moravians, 303. They Send a Surgeon to the Saltsburgers, 305. Proposal consider'd for sending Parish children, 305–06. My objections thereto, 306.

October. They order 1500£ in Sola bills to be Sent to Georgia, 310. Report made them of the State of their Cash on 30 Sept. 1737, and of Services to be Supply'd, 310–11. They order a Copargilt Mace for the Magistrates of Savannah, 312. They refuse to advance money to Capt. Wrag in pt. of his agreement to transport the Palatin Servants & why, 312. Grants of lands in the nature of church leases desired, but refused by the Trustees, 312. They order that any 5 of the Common Council may draw on the Bank as far as 5000£ as occasion shall require, 312. They Grant lands to Lieut. Cochran, Majr. Cook, Col. Oglethorpes Soldiers, Jo. Amory, & Robt. Hay, 312–13. They send direction to Mr. Causton, concerning the Palatin Servants, 313.

November. They resolve to petition the King & Council for a hearing against the Board of Trade's report, 316. The Petition drawn up, 316. They write to the D. of Newcastle to send for Jo. Savy a Traitor to town, to be examin'd, 317–18. Their Orders for taking care of their Cash, 318. They pass divers Grants of land, 318–19.

December. They examine and approve their annual Acct. from 9 June 1736 to 9 June 1737, 320. They order it to be presented to the Ld. Chancellor &c and that 150 copies of it be printed, 321, 329. They order 500 whole deals to be bought for building a Church at Savannah, 321. They order publick advertisements that no more certified bills or Accts. from Georgia will be paid by them, and that all future payments Shall be made in Sola bills, 321. They grant 500 acres to Capt. Wood, 322. They Settle their Counsel Brief to plead before the Privy Council, 323. They appoint a Committee to be present at Jo. Savy's examination, at the request of the D. of Newcastle, 327.

Jany. 1737/8. They send back certified bills to Mr. Causton for him to pay in Georgia, and declare to him they will pay no more of them, but he must pay these out of the Sola bills that were Sent to him, 327–28. They order a brief of their Case to be printed, and presented to the Committee of Privy Counsel against the hearing against the Board of Trades Report, 328. They Return certified Accts. to Georgia to be paid there, 329. They order publick notice in Georgia that they will pay no more certified Accts. or bills, 329. They attend the hearing before the Committee of Privy Counsel, and the names of the Lords present, 330.

February. They agree to pay certified Accts. that Should be Sent them before their orders for certifying no more arrived in Georgia, but order Mr. Causton to Send back to them 2000£ of the Sola bills supposed to be in his hands, to enable their payment of Said bills, 320. They give instructions to their Council to reply to the Council of the other side at the hearing before the Committee of Council, 337. They petition the Parliament for money, 332. Several Common Counsellors, observing the great debts contracted by Mr. Causton, and disgusted with Sr. Robt. Walpole for obliging the Trustees to petition the Parliamt. for money, contrary to his promise, think of quitting, 333.

March. They make alterations in their Estimate of 8000£ for the ensuing years expences, and Separate the Civil concerns of the Colony from the

Trustees of Georgia (*continued*)
Military, which last they think not reasonable for them to defray, 334. Several Trustees resign & give their reasons, 334–35. Others cool in their zeal, 340–41. They meet on the Anniversary day and elect into the Common Council Robert Tracy, Hen. Archer, Christopher Towers, John Page Esqr. and the Revd. Mr. Saml. Smith, as also into the Trustee Body, Sr. Hen. Gough & Sr. Roger Burgoign Barts., 336. They order an enquiry how the Trustee Servants have been disposed, 338. Order for enquiring how the Silk & Mulberry trees go on in Georgia, 338. Articles in the Estimate to be alter'd, 339. They debate how to reconcile S. Carolina to Georgia, 339, 340. They debate whether to alter the Tenure in Tail Male in favour of Females, 340. They remove Mr. Causton from being Storekeeper, 339. They agree to put down the Public Store, 340–42. Their affairs reported about town to be under bad management, and desperate, 340. The Members cool in their Zeal, 340.

April. Acct. received that the Silk worms are dead for want of leaves, 344. The Trustees Send a Cargo of flour and other provisions from Pensilvanea to Georgia, 344. They Send druggs and medicines to Frederica, 345. They order Flint Stone, Iron and Steel to Georgia towards building a church, 345. They order a payment in pt. to Capt. Wrag on Acct. of Palatin Servants transported by Capt. Hewet, 345. A long debate about altering the Tenure in Tail male, 345–47. They advance to Mary Cooper the Rent of her house in Georgia, 345. They grant leave to Peter Gordon late Bailif of Savannah to part with his house & Lot to Majr. Cooks daughters, 345. They write to Georgia that they will not alter the Tenure of lands in Tail Male, 345. They agree to Abraham De-Lyons proposal to lend him 200£ for propagating vines, upon Security to repay the Same in 6 years, 348. Their proceedings on a Memorial of Capt. Thompsons concerning Servants carry'd over by him on his own account, 348. They pass Grants to Capt. Alexr. Heron of 500 acres, & 3000 acres to Protestants who Shall joyn the Colony & take up 50 acre lotts, 349–50. They reject Capt. Hewets demand, 350.

May. They Order that Mr. Causton be call'd on to give reasons why he gave large Credits to divers persons without orders, 351, 352. They Order an Acct. to be taken of what Work the Trust Servants have done at the Darien, and how their labour has been apply'd for the benefit of the Trust, 351–52. They charge to Mr. Caustons Acct. 44 Servants carry'd over at Capt. Thompsons the Owners risk, but taken by Said Causton as Trust Servants, and by him disposed to private persons on Credit without orders, 351–52. They Order Inspectors to enquire how Will. Bradley has employ'd the Trust Servants, 351. They order an Act to be prepared for the better executing the Act against Rum, 353. They order Capt. Thomas to give them an Estimate for building a Church in Georgia, 352. They give order to pay for 2 Sea boats, 352. They appoint Robert Gilbert to be 3d Bailif in late Jo. Dairns room, 353. They appoint Jo. Clark to be Secy. of the Indian affairs, in the room of the Revd. Mr. Jo. Wesley, 353. They think of Striking off all Expence of labour & Credit, and to Subsist none but those they are obliged to by contract, 353. They agree that all Reports of Committees of Correspondence may be enter'd in a book, 354. They strike off the Military Expences of the Colony, and Settle whst expences Shall be paid for the future, 354–57. They order that any 5 of the Common Council may draw on the Bank to pay Sola bills, 351. They Order that Mr. Henry Parker, Will. Stephens, Esq. & Mr. Tho. Causton or any two of them fill up the Blanks of their Sola bills and issue them, and that they Sign the Account of the Issues of the, Shewing to whom & for what Service each issue was made, 356. They make an Establishment for the year beginning MidSummer 1738, 357–58. They order the remains of Stores at Savannah to be put under the care of Mr. Thomas Jones, 358. They give leave that Anne Cook Surrender her

INDEX

Interest in the lot at Savannah to Susan her Sister, and that She Succeed to her Father Majr. Cook's grant in Frederica, 358. They Empower the Revd. Mr. Geo. Whitfield to do Ecclesiastical Offices in Georgia as Deacon at Savannah as well as at Frederica, 358. They refer to a Committee to Settle Col. Oglethorpes Acct. of 1093. o. 9½ depending between him and the Trustees, 358–59. They are displeas'd with Col. Oglethorpe's breaking into the agreement made by the Trustees with Willm. Bradley, 359. They take leave of Col. Oglethorpe, 359. Their Answer to Joseph Watsons wife, & her complaint for imprisoning her husband, 362. Their Answer to Mr. Hugh Anderson concerning the Publick Garden, 362–63. They order Mr. Tho. Hawkins 1st Bailif of Frederica to Send them particulars of proceedings there, 360. Their answer to Abraham DeLyon the jew, 360. Their letter to Mr. Whitfield, 360–61. Their Answer to Mr. Stephens concerning the Tenure of Land in Tail Male, that they will not alter it, 361. They allow 2 Trust Servants to Mr. Henry Parker to be maintain'd for his use at the Trust charge, & send him a present of cloathing, 363. They order payment of Capt. Dunbars demand for primage, 363. They deliver a plan of a Church to Capt. Thomas, 363–64. Additions made to their Estimate of the Colonys expence for the year ending MidSumer 1739, 364. They order that Mr. Stephens take charge of letters in Georgia to forward them to England, 364. They empower Col. Oglethorpe to Set out 3000 acres for his Soldiers, 364. They empower Mr. Stephens, Mr. Hugh Anderson, Mr. Tho. Hawkins, & Mr. Horton, to Set out the Grant of 3000 acres design'd for 50 acre lotts to Such as joyn the Colony, 364. Their caution in paying a certified Acct. to Capt. Thompson, 368–69. They order a Stop to be put to all Credit on their Acct. in Georgia, 369–70. They Send to Col. Oglethorpe a Copy of the order of Council upon the hearing their appeal from the Report of the Board of Trade, 370. They petition the Treasury for the 8000£ granted by Parliament, 369. They order that any 5 of the Common Council may draw on the Bank 500£ to impress the Same to Aldn. Heathcote to answer expences, 369.

June. They direct Col. Oglethorpe at his arrival in Georgia to Seize the person of Mr. Causton, 373. They order good land where necessary to the people of Highgate, 371. They order that Mr. Causton be kept in Safe custody, or on good Security till his Accts. from Lady day 1734 be examin'd and approved, and till further order, 373. They lay before the D. of Newcastle a Copy of Capt. Howells affidavit concerning the Spaniards design agst. Georgia, 373. They Send instructions to Mr. Abercromby Attorney General of S. Carolina, touching letters from Georgia to be forwarded by him to England, 373. They remove Mr. Causton from his Post of 1st Bailif of Savannah, 373. See more in S. Carolina. See Georgia; Frederica; Savannah.

Tuckwell, Jo., ironmonger, apply's that he and two others may have lycense to furnish the colony with Iron ware, linnens & blankets &c but the Trustees demur thereon, 85. Of Wallingford, grant past to him of 50 acres, with Lycense not to go over, but to reside in England, 112.

Tybee Island, Settlers there improv'd nothing in 1736, 237. Deserted, acct. of it by Mr. Jo. Wesley in Septbr. 1737, 308.

Uchee Indians, a Town of theirs within 5 or 6 miles of Palachocola Fort, 193. That Nation excited to fall on the Saltsburgers by Capt. Green of Carolina, but refuse, 196.

Upton, Tho., acct. of him, & grant of land 150 acres order'd him, 266. Seal put thereto, 272.

Vanderplank, Jo., appointed Searcher for executing the Rice Act, 104. Appointed Naval Officer, 113. Constable of Savannah, dead, 1737, 325.

Vatt, Jo., a Swiss, appointed Conductor of the new Saltsburgers, and made Secy. under the direction of their Ministers, 68. A Town Lot in Savan-

Vatt, Jo. (*continued*)
nah order'd him, 68. Complain'd against by Mr. Boltzius, 137. Recall'd, 155. Applys for a consideration of his Services in Georgia, 230. Reward order'd him, 275–76. His Memorial for further reward of Services rejected, 288. Petitions again, and again rejected, 310.

Vaudois Protestants, Several hundreds desire to go to Georgia, 36. Mr. Poyas recommended to the Trustees for their Conductor, 38. Order given for bringing 40 over, 38. They desire Sallary for a Minister if they go, 40. Their coming countermanded for want of money, 46. But on intelligence that the new Saltsburgers do not intend to go, the resolution resumed to Send them, 49. The Society for promoting Christian Knowledge decline assisting the Trustees with money for their transport, 50. They refuse to go unless the Tenure in Tail male be alter'd, 50. And finally for want of being gratified therein none of them are Sent, 53.

Verelts [Verelst], Harmon, appointed Accompt., 5. 25£ order'd him for his Services, 10. 25£ order'd him for his Services, 37. Accompt. to the Trustees, recommended by them to the Treasy. for an Employment, 59. 50£ gratuity order'd him, 69, 79. Accompt. to the Trustees, letter of Attorney given him to receive at the Treasury the 26000£ given by the Parliamt. in 1735, 93. Order'd to make an Estimate of the Charges necessary for maintaining the Colony, 96. 50£ given him for his trouble in the last Embarkations, 115. 100£ order'd him for his Services, 156. 100£ order'd him for his extraordiny. Services, 225. Order'd him 75£ being for his ordinary Services for the ½ year ending at Christmass 1736, 234.

Virginia, their Traders trade with the Indians of Georgia without taking lycences within the Province, & thereby prejudice the Georgia Traders, 371.

Von Reck, Philip, offers himself to conduct a 2d embarkation of Saltsburgers, 59. Sets out, 60. Orders Sent to Stop his bringing over 100 Moravians for which he had no instruction, 69. Arrives with 46 Saltsburgers & 11 Germans, 108. 50£ given him for his trouble, 112. Grant past to him of 500 acres, 113. Writes the deplorable State the Saltsburgers at Ebenezar are in as also complaints agst. Mr. Vatt, 138. Order'd him 31.10. 0, 220. The Same confirm'd to him, 234. Sets out for Germany to bring more persecuted Protestants, 221–22. Instructions Sent after him, 222. Can get no more Saltsburgers for Georgia, and would be Subsisted by the Trustees in Georgia without cultivating lands; the Trustees reply his Grant will be forfeited unless he return 6 months, 290.

Wade, Edwd., grant past to him of 100 acres, 66.

Walpole, Sr. Robt., application made to him for a Parliamentary Supply, 13, 19. Why ill disposed to Georgia, 170, 233. His Conference with Mr. Oglethorpe thereon, 231–33, 273–74. He owns he likes not the Trustees, 274. The Trustees present a Memorial to him, desiring the money requisite for the future Services of the Colony may be put into an estimate, and not petitioned for, 284. He seems to approve it, 289. But never intended it & why, 289. Promises Col. Oglethorpe that 7000£ shall be given them in the manner they desire, 290, 303. Promises that 8000£ Shall be given that way for the Civil uses of the Colony a loan, 306. Renews his promise to a Committee of Trustees, 327. Breaks his word, and obliges the Trustees to go on in the old way of petitioning, 332. Is intimidated from Sending a Regiment to defend Georgia, by Giraldini the Spanish Ministers 2d Memorial, 296. Consents that Mr. Oglethorpe Shall have a Regiment, but the manner disapproved of by him, 303. Why backward to grant Mr. Oglethorpe a Regiment, 304–05.

Wanset, ———, Qur. Master to Col. Oglethorpe's Regiment, Skillful in vines, and intends to cultivate them at Frederica, 367.

Wantz, Mr. ———, acquaints the Trustees that he brought Germans to Rotter-

INDEX

dam, but the Trustees refuse to take them, 183.
Wardrope, Joseph, grant past to him of 150 acres, 40.
Warren, ——, and two Sons, deceased in Georgia, 48. His Widow, comes for England, 48.
Warren, ——, D.D., Preaches the Anniversary Sermon, 235, 245.
Warwick, Jo., grant past to him of 150 acres, 264.
Wassaw River and harbour, see Savannah.
Waterland, William, appointed 2d Bailif of Savannah, 8. Turned out, 8.
Waterland, Will., 2d Bailif of Savannah turn'd out for drunkenness, 31.
Watson, Joseph, a vile & dangerous person, order'd that his Lycense to trade wth. the Indians be revoked, and he confin'd as a Lunatick till he recover his Senses, and be tryed for killing an Indian wilfully by drink, 78. Concerned in an intended insurrection at Savannah, 83. Really out of his Senses, 215. But only at Some times, & then rather foolish than malicious, 219. Confin'd as a Lunatick, & the Trustees deliberation thereon, 241-42. Sarah his wife petitions the King and Council thereon, 246-47. The Ld. President Sends her petition to the Trustees to answer thereto, 255. The Trustees answer thereto, 257-58, 261. They represent their proceedings to the Council Board, 273. Acct. of his Settlement by Mr. Jo. Wesley in Sept. 1737, 308. The Trustees answer to his wife's complaint for imprisoning her husband, 362.
Watson, Mrs., amends order'd her for the loss of her Servant, 79.
Watt, Mrs., 20£ advanc'd her, to be repaid the Trustees in Georgia, out of the Rents of her House, 270.
Watts, ——, D.D., Preaches the Trustees Anniversary Sermon, and gives leave to print it, 142.
Weddal, Augustin, appointed Treasurer for the Indian Affairs, 104.
Wentz, Geo. Lewis, see Servants.
Wesley, Cha., B.A., brother to John, offers himself to go to Georgia, 107. Acct. of him, 107. Appointed Secrety. of the Indian affairs, 109. Return'd to England, 204. His Acct. of Georgia, 214-17. ½ year Sallary paid him, 252. Remainder of his Sallary order'd him, 270.
Wesley, Jo., A.M., Offers himself to go to Georgia to convert the Indians, 107. Appointed to Succeed Mr. Quincy in the church at Savannah, 107. Acount of him, 107. Recommended by the Trustees to the Society for propagating the Gospel in Foreign Parts for to be allow'd the Sallary they gave Mr. Quincy, 120. They agree thereto, 124. His conference with the Chickesaws on Religion, 177-78. Goes to Carolina, none knows why, 277. Thinks himself accused of embezzling the Publick money, 283-84. His Salary order'd to be paid him, 311. Bad character of him, 322. Fly's out of the Colony, 323. Arrives at London, 331. Presents the Trustees a paper of his own justification & accusing Mr. Causton, 333.
West, John, Appointed Tything Man of Savannah, 8. Made 3d Bailif, 34. Formerly Bailif of Savannah, desires leave to part with his wifes Lot in Savannah, & have a grant of 500 acres, 107-08. Granted, 110. Grant of 500 acres past to Elizabeth his wife, 113.
Westbrook Plantation of Sr. Fra. Bathurst, Mr. Jo. Wesleys Acct. of it in Sept. 1737, 307.
Weston, Willes, appointed a Trustee for the 300 acres granted for Religious Uses at Frederica, 276.
White, John, Esq., his Strange behaviour to the Trust, 128, 142-43. Resigns his Office of Common Counsellor, 151. His publick reason, 151. His private reason, 151. Withdraws from the house when our petition was presented, 151. His odd deportment on the Anniversary day, 244-45.
White, Ri., a Ministers Son, appointed to be a Bailif of Frederica, in case of death or removal of others, 110. His appointment revoked in favour of another, 113.
White, ——, his brother, Counsellr. at Law, engaged by the Trustees in the case of Watsons petition, 251. His observations on the petition, & the Trustees answer, 251-52.

Whitfield, Geo., A.B., goes Minister to Georgia, to be Settled at Frederica, 284, 286. Desires to Set out wth. Lieut. Col. Cochran to Gibraltar, 326. Power given him to exercise the function of Deacon in Savannah as well as Frederica, 360–61.

Williams, John, grant of 500 acres past to him, 21.

Williams, Robt., grant of 500 acres past to him, 21. Mr. Jo. Wesleys acct. of his Settlement in Sept. 1737, 308. A principal Mutineer in the Colony, 367.

Winants, Mr., 40£ order'd him for his trouble about the Moravians, 113.

Windham, Capt. Thanks order'd him for his Services to Georgia, 225.

Wine, very likely to Succeed in Georgia, 243.

Wollaston [Woolaston], Fra., Esq., elected Trustee, 47.

Wollaston [Woolaston], Will., Esq., elected Trustee, 47.

Wood, Will., formerly Sea Capt., grant made him of 500 acres, 322.

Woodrose, Willm., grant past to him of 50 Acres, 100.

Young, Isaac, of Gloucestershire, grant of 100 acres past to him, 157.

Zinzendorf, Count Lewis, grant past to him of 500 acres, 73. Desires that more of his Moravians may be Sent to Georgia, and for that purpose that the Trustees would lend him 500£ to be repaid in time, 79–80. The Trustees agree thereto, 80. Lands in England, 225. Agrees to Send 2 Moravian Catechists to instruct the Negroes at Purysburg, 236–37. Makes proposals to Send more Moravians to Georgia, 240. The Trustees answer, 254. Desires his Moravians in Georgia may not be obliged to fight in defence of the Colony, it being their principle not to take arms; if not granted that they may have leave to depart, 297. Is Satisfied that they remain, 336.

Zuberbuller, Mr. ——, see Proposals.

www.ingramcontent.com/pod-product-compliance
Lightning Source LLC
Chambersburg PA
CBHW011720220426
43664CB00023B/2891